Eighth Edition

Texas:
The Lone Star State

Rupert N. Richardson

Adrian Anderson

Cary D. Wintz

Ernest Wallace

Prentice
Hall

Upper Saddle River, New Jersey 07458

Library of Congress Catologing-in-Publication Data

Texas, the Lone Star State/Rupert N. Richardson; . . . [et al.]— 8th ed.
    p. cm.
  Rev. ed. of: Texas, the Lone Star State/Rupert Norval Richardson, Adrian Anderson,
Ernest Wallace. 7th ed. 1997.
    Includes bibliographical references and index.
    ISBN 0-13-028414-9
    1. Texas—History. I. Richardson, Rupert Norval, 1891- II. Richardson, Rupert Norval,
1891- Texas, the Lone Star State
F386 .T434 2000
976.4—dc21   00-037488

Editorial/production supervision: *Judith Winthrop*
Acquisitions editor: *Charlyce Jones Owens*
Manufacturing buyer: *Lynn Pearlman*
Cover Designer: *Bruce Kenselaar*
Director, Image Resource Center: *Melinda Reo*
Photo Research: *Teri Stratford*
Photo Permission Coordinator: *Debra Hewitson*

© 2001, 1997, 1993, 1988, 1970, 1958, 1943
by Prentice-Hall, Inc.
A Division of Pearson Education
Upper Saddle River, New Jersey 07458

This book was set in 10/12 Palatino by DM Cradle Associates
and was printed and bound by RR Donnelley & Sons Company
The cover was printed by Phoenix Color Corp.

Printed in the United States of America
10 9 8 7 6 5 4

ISBN 0-13-028414-9

PRENTICE-HALL (UK) LIMITED, *LONDON*
PRENTICE-HALL OF AUSTRALIA PTY. LIMITED, *SYDNEY*
PRENTICE-HALL CANADA INC., *TORONTO*
PRENTICE-HALL HISPANOAMERICANA, S.A., *MEXICO*
PRENTICE-HALL OF INDIA PRIVATE LIMITED, *NEW DELHI*
PRENTICE-HALL OF JAPAN, INC., *TOKYO*
PEARSON EDUCATION PTE. LTD., *SINGAPORE*
EDITORA PRENTICE-HALL DO BRASIL, LTDA., *RIO DE JANEIRO*

Contents

7.   *The Republic of Texas, 1836–1845*   *131*

8.   *Early Statehood, 1846–1861*   *157*

9.   *Pioneer Institutions*   *182*

Preface

Some sixty years ago, as the world was moving from depression to war, Professor Richardson completed the first edition of *Texas: The Lone Star State*, written as a comprehensive, general history of Texas and intended primarily for use in college history courses. Many years later, near the end of the 1960s, Professor Richardson, recognizing the evolutionary character of historical studies and the need to provide new insight and ideas, added two authors, Ernest Wallace and Adrian Anderson, in the preparation of the third and subsequent editions. As we move into the new millennium, a new author, Cary D. Wintz, has joined in the preparation of this, the eighth edition of *Texas: The Lone Star State*. Professor Wintz, whose suggestions influenced the preparation of the seventh edition, brings to the book his broad and comprehensive knowledge of Texas history and his long experience in the study of specialized areas, some of which were scarcely recognized at the time of the original edition.

When Professor Richardson prepared the final draft of his manuscript for the first edition of *Texas: The Lone Star State*, he wrote in his preface that his mission was to "provide, as far as the limitations of a single volume will permit, a *complete survey* of the history of Texas." His goal was to present not only the topics affording "adventure, contest, and color" but also "the more prosaic but equally important subjects." In search of balance, he sought to tell the story of "cotton pickers" and "priests and conquerors," of "filibusterers" and "farmers"–a complete story, to the extent possible.

In keeping with his purpose, Professor Richardson wrote history in narrative or "storytelling" form. Where circumstances demanded and space permitted, he analyzed and interpreted events and issues, but the essence of his work was the evolution of his story and his effort to present it in an account that was complete and fair as possible. The events of the years since the first publication of *Texas: The Long Star State* have been included in successive editions. And, the discovery of new information has sometimes led to reexamination of past events. More often, however, it is an increased awareness of the contributions and role of minorities, women, and other groups that were ignored or inadequately recognized in the past that has led to a new and, it is hoped, a more complete and meaningful story.

In reexamining the past, many of the old traditions or "myths" have been carefully scrutinized and found lacking in terms of meaning and sensitivity; others have been altered or modified. Such changes are appropriate and necessary to the preservation of a free people. But though old myths must be constantly reviewed and examined so that they will not distort our history, care must also be taken to make sure that new myths, which inevitably arise, do not likewise mislead us in our understanding of our heritage.

New materials have been added to bring the text up to date in this edition, and where new scholarship is available, some of the earlier chapters have been revised. In a few instances, the organization has been changed for the sake of clarity, and unfortunately, some material of older editions has been deleted to save space. Considerable care has been taken to add a comprehensive listing to recently published books and articles in the bibliographies at the end of each chapter.

Nothwithstanding these changes and additions, the narrative character of earlier editions is continued in the current edition of *Texas: The Lone Star State*. It was prepared with the hope that it is in keeping with Professor Richardson's purpose of providing a complete story and that the integrity of his scholarship will be maintained.

We are indebted to many people in the preparation of this eight edition. We thank the reviewers: James A. Wilson, Southwest Texas State University and Jerry Thompson, Texas A&M International. Most of all, we are indebted to the late Professor Rupert Norval Richardson for the opportunity to continue with his work. His scholarship, honor, integrity, and basic goodness as a human being and a historian will always be an inspiration. We are further indebted to the late Professor Ernest Wallace, who also contributed significantly to the success of this book. In addition, both of use owe a debt to our many colleagues and friends whose counsel and knowledge have been invaluable in the preparation of this edition as well as earlier ones. Special recognition is owed to Professor Ralph Wooster, who provided wise advice, especially concerning maps and Civil War matters. Likewise, we are grateful to the teachers, students, and general readers, whose criticism and constructive suggestions have helped greatly in the work of revision. And we are especially grateful to our wives, Sally Anderson and Celia Wintz, whose patience endured much, and whose learned and perceptive criticism was invaluable on many occasions.

Adrian Anderson

Cary Wintz

1

The Country and Its Native Peoples

The name Texas comes from *Tejas*, meaning "friends" or "allies," a name applied by Spanish explorers and missionaries to a confederacy of native people (the Hasinai) found living in this country. Although the name was given to the land very early in the era of Spanish activities and was used consistently, the boundaries of the country that it identified changed many times during succeeding centuries. At first, it was applied only to the land of the Hasinai, but borders were adjusted over the years until the present boundaries were finally established in 1850. As the size of the country grew, so did its diversity. Today it is a land of contrast, a land of forests and plains, mountains and prairies, deserts and swamps.

People have long inhabited this great land. Relics found at various points throughout the state indicate the presence of prehistoric people in Texas many thousands of years ago. In time, for one reason or another, these peoples disappeared and were replaced by the natives who inhabited the land when European and African explorers made their way to Texas. With cultures as diverse as the land they occupied, these peoples lived their lives in ways that were sometimes very similar but sometimes very different.

THE LAND

The distinctive shape that outlines Texas today evolved slowly over several centuries. The land of the Hasinai that originally was Texas included a considerable area of present-day Louisiana and only a portion of East Texas. Early in the eighteenth century, however, the borders of Texas were extended westward to include Spanish settlements that had been planted on the San Antonio River and Matagorda Bay. A definite boundary on the west

Texas contains a number of regions determined by geological makeup and the resultant physiographic forms. Grasses, timber, soils, and other natural resources have affected its history greatly. Four of the natural regions that define the lands of the North American continent are located in Texas. Three of the regions are divided into geographical sections where wildlife, vegetation, soil, and climate are more nearly identical.

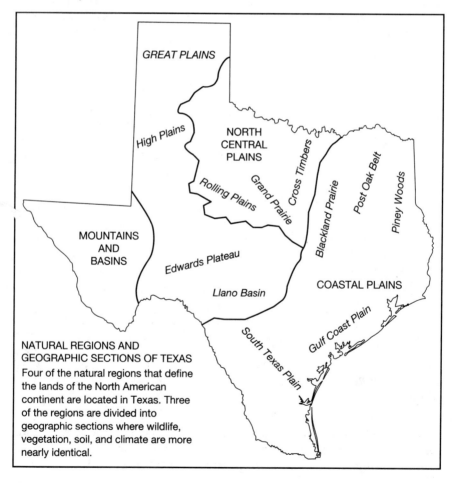

NATURAL REGIONS AND GEOGRAPHIC SECTIONS OF TEXAS

Four of the natural regions that define the lands of the North American continent are located in Texas. Three of the regions are divided into geographic sections where wildlife, vegetation, soil, and climate are more nearly identical.

was first fixed at the Medina River in 1746. A few years later this western boundary was moved farther west to the Nueces River, and in 1819 the eastern boundary was adjusted to be located in part on the Sabine River. During the time of the republic, ambitious Texans set the Rio Grande as the boundary, thus claiming portions of present-day New Mexico, Colorado, Oklahoma, Kansas, and Wyoming. As finally adjusted in 1850, a large part of the border of the state consists of natural boundaries—the Gulf of Mexico, and the Rio Grande, Sabine, and Red rivers. The remainder of the boundary consists of straight lines established by surveyors at one time or another in conformity with various treaties and agreements.

Within these boundaries are 266,807 square miles of territory, making Texas the second-largest state in the Union. One can travel 800 miles in a straight line from east to west or north to south within its borders. Variety and contrast characterize the land enclosed by these great distances. The state is made up of parts of four natural regions: the Coastal Plains, the North Central Plains, the Great Plains, and the Mountains and Basins. Within each natural region are geographic sections where wildlife, vegetation, soil, climate, and other resources are more nearly identical.

The largest natural region in Texas, the Coastal Plains begins on the eastern coast of the United States and extends into Mexico. Geographic sections within Texas in the region include the Piney Woods, the Post Oak Belt, the Gulf Coast Plain, the South Texas Plain, and the Blackland Prairie. The geographic section often called East Texas is also known as the Piney Woods or by other names that emphasize one of the most distinctive characteristics of the land—the great, tall, stately pine trees. It is a country of forests and farmlands, of rolling hills and broad valleys. Although the original timber stand has long since been cut, replanting of forests has maintained a steady and valuable timber industry that, together with petroleum and agriculture, has made the area prosperous.

Immediately to the west of the Piney Woods are two long bands of land extending from near the Red River to the vicinity of San Antonio. The first, a strip of sandy soils and post oak timber, is the geographic section known as the Post Oak Belt. Although it is primarily an agricultural area producing a variety of field crops and livestock, in recent years urban activities such as light industry, commerce, and education have supported the growth of cities such as Tyler, Bryan, and College Station and a number of smaller towns. West of the Post Oak Belt lies one of the most heavily populated geographic sections of the state, the Blackland Prairie, sometimes associated with adjacent areas and known as the Central Texas Prairies. Rich, black soils predominate, now largely cultivated except where they are too thin. Once this was the heart of cotton country, but more attention is now devoted to grain and livestock production. However, most inhabitants make their livelihood in commerce, transportation, military installations, manufacturing, health services, government, tourism, and other urban activities. Dallas and San Antonio and Austin (both located partially in other geographic sections) are the largest cities, but there are ten or so cities of lesser but substantial size.

The Gulf Coast Plain extends from the shore a little south of Corpus Christi to the Sabine River and inland for as much as 100 miles. Near the coast the land is low and marshy, and there is much heavy soil with a great variety of vegetation. There are a number of islands off the coast, generally long and narrow, the product of sand that has gradually built up from the bottom of the Gulf. Although Europeans were not quick to settle in this area, it has become one of the more populated areas of the state and now includes Houston and a host of smaller cities such as Beaumont, Galveston, Port Arthur, and Corpus Christi. A combination of petroleum production and refining, chemical manufacturing, agriculture, and transportation facilities has provided opportunities and employment.

The South Texas Plain forms roughly a triangle, bounded by a point near Corpus Christi and stretching westward by way of San Antonio to about Del Rio on the Rio Grande and southward to the Gulf. It is a land of highly eroded localities, interspersed with prairies. Petroleum production is important, but there is considerable farming and livestock raising. A portion, irrigated from wells and the water of the Rio Grande and sometimes known as the Winter Garden, produces bountiful crops of citrus fruit, vegetables, and cotton. The Spanish and Mexican heritage of Texas is particularly evident in the people and cultures of the region. San Antonio, only partially located in the South Texas Plain, is the largest city, but there are a number of others, especially along the Rio Grande.

The natural region known as the North Central Plains contains three geographic sections: the Cross Timbers, the Grand Prairie, and the Rolling Plains. Actually two narrow belts of land that are sometimes sandy and often hilly, the Cross Timbers are located generally between Fort Worth and Abilene and extend from near the Red River southward to the vicinity of the Colorado River. A variety of oaks and other hardwood trees flourished on the land in its native state. Peanuts, vegetables, dairy products, and poultry are grown today on soils that range from belts of loose, blowing sand to black loams. Like most regions, it contains some petroleum and coal deposits, and at one time was the center of a major coal mining industry.

The Cross Timbers are separated, sometimes for a distance of almost 100 miles, by the Grand Prairie. The Grand Prairie extends south from near the Red River for more than 200 miles and contains one of the state's larger cities, Fort Worth. However, the Grand Prairie is primarily an agricultural area where livestock and field crop production provide support for a relatively small population.

The Rolling Plains includes the Abilene, Vernon, and Wichita Falls country. It is bounded on the east by the Cross Timbers and separated from the High Plains to the west by the Caprock, a prominent limestone escarpment. Some of the Rolling Plains terrain is highly eroded; other areas consist of spacious prairies. There is some petroleum production, but agriculture—mainly cotton, wheat, grain sorghum, and cattle—is the foundation of the economy of most areas.

The Great Plains natural region is part of a large plain that extends from Mexico northward into Canada. The portion in Texas contains three geographic sections: the High Plains, the Edwards Plateau, and the Llano Basin. The High Plains, which extends southward to the vicinity of Midland and Odessa, was once an awesome sea of grass that was rarely broken by trees or anything else as far as the eye could see. Today, the area is frequently plowed into farmland with production largely dependent on irrigation supplied by underground water supplies. Within the area have grown the cities of Amarillo, Lubbock, and Plainview and a score of thriving towns. In more recent years, declining water supplies have become a source of concern.

The Edwards Plateau is a broken tableland, an extension of the Great Plains but eroded into rocky, hilly country. It is situated between the Rolling Plains and Cross Timbers on the north and the South Texas Plain on the south. In most places the soil is too shallow for farming, but it supports a flourishing ranching economy that produces cattle, sheep, goats, wool, and mohair. Until recent times, the area was only thinly populated, but the development of water reservoirs and the attractiveness of both land and climate have drawn a large number of people since the end of World War II. Located on the southern fringe of the region are portions of Austin and San Antonio.

The smallest geographic section of the state, the Llano Basin includes much of the area sometimes called the Hill Country. A favorite area of native peoples in earlier times, it was primarily a ranching country until recently, when tourism and recreation became major industries. A number of rivers, including the Colorado, Pedernales, Llano, and San Saba, and several lakes have turned a rugged, rocky land into a scenic, attractive land. The towns of the basin remain relatively small, but large cities such as Austin and San Antonio are nearby.

The Basin and Mountain natural region, lying mainly west of the Pecos River and sometimes called the Trans-Pecos, is the most diverse of the Texas regions but the only one not divided into geographic sections. It is a country of deserts and mountains, of cold winters and hot summers, of splendor and harshness. It is primarily livestock country, but a scattering of irrigated areas adds to the diversity and the productivity of the area. There is some petroleum production, particularly natural gas, and from time to time, a number of mines have operated. Except for the area on the Rio Grande around El Paso, which accounts for most of the population of the region, it was the last part of Texas to be settled and populated by peoples other than Indians. As is true of the South Texas Plain, the people and the cultures of the region often reflect their Spanish and Mexican heritage.

RIVERS

Although there are many streams, bayous, and creeks (altogether about 4,000) in Texas, there are only fourteen major rivers. Most of these flow from the northwest to the south and east, and all but two empty into the Gulf of Mexico or other Texas rivers. In most instances, the Spanish named the rivers and mapped their courses. The rivers, which were very important in the lives of the native peoples, have continued to play a major role in the settlement of the land and the development of towns and cities.

The rivers of Texas have influenced the land and people throughout the ages. Rivers have provided transportation but also posed problems for travelers. Rivers have guided the location of cities and affected the distribution of lands. Today three rivers form a part of the boundary of Texas; during Spanish and Mexican rule two others, the San Antonio and the Nueces, provided boundary lines.

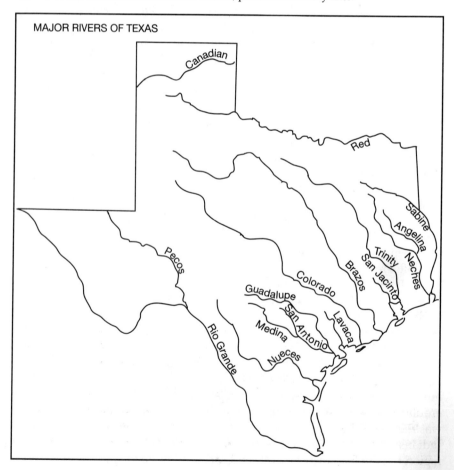

MAJOR RIVERS OF TEXAS

Three rivers make up parts of the boundary of Texas. The Sabine (named after the Spanish word for "cypress") is formed by three streams that begin in Collin and Hunt counties. A relatively large, if not very long, river, it forms a part of the eastern boundary of the state. The Red River is exceptionally long, beginning in New Mexico and traveling 1,360 miles. After flowing across Texas, it forms a portion of the boundary between Oklahoma and Texas. The Rio Grande is the other stream to form a part of the Texas border; it begins in Colorado, flows across New Mexico, and then forms the boundary between Texas and Mexico.

There are three major rivers whose location is largely confined to East Texas. The Trinity, which begins in Dallas County, travels in a relatively southern course to empty into Galveston Bay. Daring steamboat captains sometimes took their craft up the river in the nineteenth century, but only the lower reaches of the river have ordinarily been navigable for commercial purposes. The Neches is truly an East Texas river, beginning and traveling through East Texas until it empties into Sabine Lake and ultimately the Gulf of Mexico. It was near the Neches that the first Spanish settlements in East Texas were located. It was used by steamboats for a time during the nineteenth century and today forms a channel for seagoing ship traffic as far north as Beaumont. One of the shorter Texas rivers, the San Jacinto is formed by two branches that begin in Walker County and join in northwestern Harris County before entering Galveston Bay. In the story of nineteenth-century Texas, the San Jacinto is almost always associated with the battle that ended the Texas Revolution. Today, it is an important part of the water complex that forms the Houston Ship Channel to make Houston one of the major ports in the nation.

There are two major rivers that make their way from northwestern Texas southeastward through the center of the state to the Gulf of Mexico. The Brazos, which extends for 840 miles from Stonewall County near the edge of the High Plains, finally enters the Gulf of Mexico near present-day Freeport. Since much of the land on either side of the river was particularly suitable for cotton production, the Brazos River Valley attracted many settlers during the period of Mexican rule and is associated with many of the events of the Texas Revolution. The Colorado begins in canyons cut into the edge of the High Plains and travels for about 600 miles before it enters Matagorda Bay. The river and its tributaries provided many of the favorite campgrounds of the Comanches and their allies, and a number of the Indian battles fought in the nineteenth century took place on or near the Colorado.

Four rivers have their beginning in the central and west central portion of the state and flow southeastward toward the Gulf. The Nueces, which begins in Edwards County, enters the Gulf of Mexico near Corpus Christi. At one time it formed a part of the western boundary of the Spanish province of Texas, and later it was a dividing point between Coahuila and Texas during the period of Mexican rule. The Guadalupe, which is formed in Kerr

County, flows some 250 miles before emptying into the Gulf of Mexico. The first land battle of the Texas Revolution was fought on its banks. Beginning in the city of San Antonio, the San Antonio River is one of the shorter but more beautiful rivers in the state. Its attractions captured the interest of the Spanish early in their settlement of Texas, and soon thereafter the city of San Antonio was founded. Only 180 miles long, it empties into the Guadalupe River. The Lavaca River, even shorter, begins in Lavaca County and empties into Matagorda Bay. Somewhere near its banks, the explorer La Salle established the post of Fort St. Louis and claimed the land of Texas for France.

The Pecos River, more than 900 miles long, rises in western New Mexico and forms parts of the boundaries of several counties of West Texas before emptying into the Rio Grande near present-day Del Rio. Given several different names by the early Spanish explorers, the river was eventually named the Pecos, but the origin of the word is not known. In the folklore and mythology of the West, the Pecos is often pictured as the beginning of the unsettled and untamed frontier.

The Canadian, which begins in New Mexico and empties into the Arkansas River, is an unusual Texas river in that during its course across Texas it does not flow to the southeast but rather to the northeast. Flowing across the Panhandle, the Canadian is characterized by steep-sided gorges and treacherous quicksand. It was near this river that the Battle of Adobe Walls was fought in 1874, beginning the final major Indian wars fought on the High Plains of Texas.

THE CLIMATE

Although Texas generally has a mild climate, it is a land of contrast and change in matters of weather. The climate is determined in large measure by prevailing winds that affect both temperatures and rainfall and by latitude, or the distance Texas lies from the equator. Considering the size of the state, it is not surprising that climatic conditions can vary considerably from one extreme to the other in the same day.

The prevailing winds that tend to blow from the southwest to the northeast have a particularly significant effect on the rainfall of the state. Winds that blow over the waters of the Gulf of Mexico sweep up large amounts of moisture that is subsequently deposited as rainfall in East Texas. The winds from the southwest that sweep across western areas of the state have traveled over the desert areas of northern Mexico and bring little rainfall. Consequently, the rainfall pattern in Texas drops from very high—fifty or more inches per year in East Texas—to as little as eight inches per year in far West Texas.

Temperatures in Texas likewise vary significantly. Summertime in Texas is generally hot, no matter where it is, with temperatures along the Rio

Grande and in North-Central Texas sometimes exceeding 100 degrees. During the winter months, however, the temperature may vary considerably. In southern areas, the temperatures are generally mild, freezing temperatures are rare, and the growing season in some areas may exceed 300 days annually. In the northwestern areas, winters are more severe, with accumulations of ice and snow not unusual but seldom lasting for more than a few days.

PREHISTORIC PEOPLES

Discoveries during the last half-century, some in Texas, indicate that humans have been in America much longer than had been previously believed. Three stone images that may be 30,000 or more years old were found in the Trinity River gravel beds near Malakoff and Trinidad, but the evidence is too scanty to warrant certainty. The evidence of human life in Texas at least 10,000 to 12,000 years ago, however, seems convincing. As recently as 1982, archaeologists discovered intact near Leander, Texas, the remarkably well-preserved skeleton of a woman who lived perhaps 10,000 years ago.

Other sites that indicate the presence of these Paleo-Americans are those near Abilene, Midland, and Plainview, Texas, and near Clovis, New Mexico—all in the plains country, principally the High Plains, or, as it is sometimes called, the Llano Estacado. The people represented in these discoveries are sometimes designated as belonging to the Llano Culture. In this region the Paleo-Americans hunted a now extinct species of elephant. Their spear and dart points, known as Clovis fluted points, were widely distributed. Estimates, based on radioactivity measurements of artifacts, suggest that the Llano people lived some 12,000 years ago.

Somewhat later than the Llano Culture was the Folsom Culture, named after a town in northeastern New Mexico. Highly finished projectile points, apparently used in hunting huge bison, were found near Folsom. Similar points imbedded in bison skeletons have been discovered in excavations near Lubbock and Plainview. Dating with radiocarbon tests indicate that these tools and skeletons of perhaps 100 bison have been there for about 9,000 years.

About 5000 B.C., either the Paleo-American culture gave way to another, or the way of life of these people changed. Perhaps the ending of the Ice Age and the disappearance of the elephants, the great bisons, and other animals that they had hunted were contributing factors. Also, other peoples may have migrated to America during the centuries following 5000 B.C. These changes brought in the Archaic peoples. They were hunters and gatherers, but instead of a few well-made stone implements, they had a great variety of stone points and tools. They also used polished stones; pestles and mortars indicate that they relied more on seeds than did their predecessors.

In time these peoples domesticated the dog, adopted the practice of growing corn (sometime after 2500 B.C.), eventually learned the craft of pottery making, and began building more substantial abodes. In many respects their way of life did not differ significantly from that of some of the peoples living in Texas at the time of the arrival of the first Europeans.

THE NATIVE PEOPLES

Texas lies within the three areas in which Native American civilization reached its highest development in North America. These were the native civilizations of Mexico and Central America, the Pueblo of the upper Rio

In pictographs like these at Paint Rock, Indians recorded the significant events of their lives. (Courtesy of the Texas Department of Transportation)

Grande, and the Mound Builder of the Mississippi Valley. In a sense, Texas was a meeting place of these three cultures, but it appears that none of them was extensively established within its boundaries, and apparently none had a major influence on the development of Texas Indian culture. In fact, there wasn't a dominant Texas Indian culture. The ways of life of these peoples differed even more widely from region to region than do those of modern people.

Great care must be used in studying the culture of the native peoples, for our records of their lifestyles often are not clear and sometimes may be incorrect. Much of what is known was first reported by the Spanish explorers who encountered them in circumstances that were at best unusual and sometimes unpleasant. Most early Spanish explorers were ill prepared to understand and to evaluate the cultures of other peoples; the rapid decline of native populations made the task difficult, and often impossible, for later observers. Consequently, our understanding of the cultures of the native peoples may sometimes be partially or altogether incorrect.

The groups identified below were sometimes known by different names and made up only a portion of the natives of Texas. However, they represented most of the cultural patterns of their times and likely accounted for a majority of the native population. Other native groups, notably the Cherokee and the Alabama and the Coushatta, migrated into Texas in the nineteenth century.

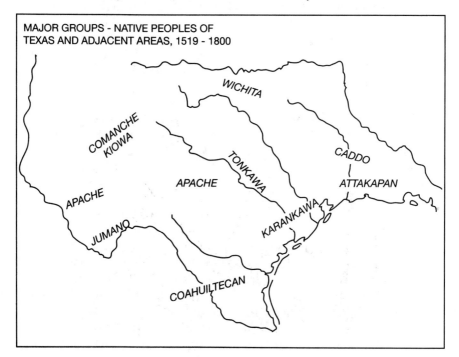

MAJOR GROUPS - NATIVE PEOPLES OF
TEXAS AND ADJACENT AREAS, 1519 - 1800

But there were certain cultural practices that were apparently common to most, if not all, native Texans. Family organization and religious beliefs in most instances were similar. Common to all was a basic belief in a supreme being or beings. Few, if any, were truly monotheistic (believing only in one supreme being), but many native groups tended to accept the ideal of a creator or being who seemingly was of more significance than other deities. In one form or another, most incorporated into their religious beliefs a reverence for nature—that is, the sun, moon, wind, rain, or other natural phenomena. Virtually all native groups believed in the supernatural power of healers called *shamans*, usually men but sometimes women, who could deal with matters of disease or injury through their ability to call upon the strength of deities.

Similarly, the family was the basic social organization. Ordinarily, the structure of the marriage was monogamous, but in most groups there were situations where it was expected that a man might have more than one wife. Marriage ceremonies were rare. Divorce was not unusual and ordinarily was arranged quickly and with little formality. Within the family there was a clear and definite division of responsibilities. In some respects, it would appear that the women were treated unfairly, inasmuch as they usually were obligated to haul the wood, cook the meals, pack the belongings and carry them on the trail, put up the housing, and do virtually all of the menial work around the camp. In a few instances, such as those of the Caddo and Wichita peoples, the men did some of the work in the fields, but this was rarely true among other nations. Ordinarily, the men spent much of their time hunting and fishing and either making war or making preparations for war. However, hunting and fishing provided an essential part of the food supply, and survival in a world where conflict with other people was frequent and required the skills of the warrior may explain in part the unequal distribution of labor.

There was some sharing of responsibility in the rearing of children. Training of children began at a very early age. Young Comanches, for example, were taught the fundamental skills of horsemanship by the age of four. Generally, young men were trained to endure danger and hardships, while young women were taught to care for the needs of the family and the camp. Punishment of children was not unknown, but it was rare. Children were expected to learn through example and apparently seldom violated family or tribal rules.

The first Europeans found many different native peoples in Texas. There were the Caddoan peoples of eastern Texas, the Karankawas along the Gulf Coast, the Wichita and Tonkawa groups in Central Texas, a number of different peoples who made up the Coahuiltecans of South Texas and northern Mexico, and the Jumanos along the Rio Grande. Later there were the Apaches and Comanches of western Texas and the Coushattas, Alabamas, and Cherokees of eastern Texas; and there were still others. In some instances, certain of these Indian peoples were called by other names; one name might refer to several different groups, each bearing in turn an additional name.

Most of the natives of East Texas belonged to the great Caddoan family and were included in two confederacies: the Caddo, located in Arkansas, Louisiana, and the part of Texas near present-day Texarkana; and the Hasinai, on the upper Angelina and Neches rivers. In the story of Texas the Hasinai confederacy is the more important of the two. It was in this confederacy that the Spaniards first established missions in the interior of Texas. Probably a dozen groups belonged to the confederacy. Each group had its own chiefs and government but owed a measure of allegiance to the head chief of the confederacy. Most powerful of all, however, was the *chenesi*, or head priest, who kept the fire temple. The fire in it was never extinguished, and from it the fires of all the confederacy were lighted. In a custom rarely found among other native peoples, women enjoyed some authority and status, sometimes holding positions of responsibility in matters of government and religion.

The Caddoes lived in domelike houses, reinforced with stakes, thatched with twigs, daubed with mud, and covered with grass. These homes were located in hamlets of seven to fifteen houses divided by woodlands and farms and situated near the bank of a river or stream. The furnishings within suggested beauty as well as comfort. In the houses were many-colored rugs, woven of reeds; beds, made of reeds resting on a framework of poles and covered with buffalo hides; reed baskets, filled with beans, acorns, and nuts; jars, filled with corn and covered over with ashes to keep out the weevils; and corn, shucked and hung where exposure to smoke would drive away the weevils. Each year these Indians kept enough seed for two years, lest one crop should be a total failure, but hunting ordinarily provided a great part of their food supplies.

Some Indians with cultures similar to that of the Caddoes did not settle in Texas until the nineteenth century. The Alabamas and the Coushattas located a small village on the Trinity River in 1807. Around 1820 in somewhat larger numbers, some members of the highly civilized Cherokee nation occupied lands to the north of Nacogdoches. And there were small numbers of immigrants from other native peoples formerly located in the southeastern part of the United States.

Immediately to the south of the Caddoes in southeastern Texas and southwestern Louisiana were the Attacapans (or Attakapans). Composed of at least four distinct groups, the Attacapans were hunters who were comfortable in the marshy wetlands, where they lived off small animals, fish, and wild fruits. In many respects their lifestyles were a mixture of the culture of the Caddo people to their north and the Karankawas, who made their home farther to the south along the Gulf Coast.

The habitat of the Karankawas extended along the Gulf Coast from about Trinity Bay on the north to Matagorda Bay on the south and inland as much as 100 miles or more. There were several different groups, but by the early eighteenth century, four bands apparently accounted for a majority of the Karankawa people. The Karankawas were strong and tall and, according to early-day European travelers, notable for their prowess as runners, hunters, and swimmers. Their diet consisted of food from the sea, small game, wild fruits and berries, and alligators. To protect themselves from the ever-present mosquitoes, they coated themselves with a mixture of shark, fish, and alligator oils, an effective insect repellent.

Although the first Europeans to encounter them were actually treated very well, the Karankawas soon gained a reputation as fierce and relentless enemies of European intruders. Adding to their fearsome reputation, there were also widely advertised reports of the practice of cannibalism. Actually, the cannibalism of the Karankawas (if it was practiced at all) was likely a ceremonial type similar to that practiced by a number of native people in Texas and elsewhere. Notwithstanding the fierce reputation of the Karankawas, the determined Spanish Catholic friars who came into their territory repeatedly attempted to convert them to Christianity and the ways of Spanish life. A few eventually were converted, or at least lived for a time in or near Spanish missions, but most had little use for the restrictions of mission life.

To the north of the Karankawas and to the west of the Caddoes in South-Central Texas lived the Tonkawa. Somewhat more advanced than the Karankawas, they were primarily hunters and traders who lived in skin houses and when possible hunted the buffalo. They were alternately at peace and at war with the Spaniards during the eighteenth century, and their relations with the Caddoes in the east, the Wichitas and Comanches in the north, and the Apaches in the west were at best uncertain. In some ways, they were more similar to the plains people who lived to their west than they were to the natives of the woodlands who lived to their east.

From the Arkansas River in Kansas southward to the vicinity of present-day Waco lived the Wichita people. Actually a confederacy of several bands with a common dialect, these Indians lived in dome-shaped grass and reed houses in permanent villages, grew a wide variety of crops, hunted the buffalo, and carried on extensive trading activities whenever possible. Of these bands, the Wichita proper (sometimes identified as the Taovayas or Tawehash) lived along the Red River and during the nineteenth century became widely known for their talented horsemanship and energetic efforts to take horses belonging to other Indians and white settlers. The Tawakoni and Waco people lived in North-Central Texas until the remnants of the groups were expelled in 1859. In some respects, the Wichita people lived much like their Caddoan kinspeople to the east; in other respects, they were like the Indians of the plains. They farmed to a limited extent and from time to time made hunting trips westward onto the plains. A proud people, they were not as warlike as some, but when involved in warfare, they were a formidable foe.

Wichita grass covered arbor and houses, Anadarko, Oklahoma. The houses of the Hasinai and Caddo in East Texas were of similar construction. (From Earl H. Elam, "The History of the Wichita Indian Confederacy to 1868," Ph.D. dissertation; Lubbock, Texas, 1971, p. 58. By permission of the author.)

The Coahuiltecans of South Texas and northern Mexico, a collection of many—perhaps eighty or more—different groups, were among the more primitive natives in Texas. Somewhat the prisoners of their environment, they followed a lifestyle adapted to living off whatever resources were available. Accordingly, their diet included lizards, seeds, rodents, snakes, mesquite beans, deer, rabbits, cactus, and even dirt—an amazingly broad collection of foods. They were nomadic, moving frequently in small bands while living in shelters made of sticks and leaves. Not especially warlike and located in the path of some of the early Spanish settlements north of the Rio

Grande, Coahuiltecans were frequently selected by priests for missionary efforts in the area around San Antonio.

Some of the most mysterious (and confusing) of Texas Indians were the Jumanos, who lived primarily along the big bend of the Rio Grande in the general vicinity of present-day Presidio. Much about the Jumanos is unknown, and much of what is known is contradictory; apparently Jumanos traveled great distances and were found in unexpected places, and other native peoples were on occasion mistakenly identified as Jumanos.

The lifestyle of the Jumanos who lived on the Rio Grande was comparatively advanced. They built their homes of sun-dried brick (adobe) with flat roofs and located them in villages. In gardens sometimes irrigated from the waters of the river, they raised crops of vegetables and lived on a diet of fish, game, corn, beans, gourds, and prickly pear. Relatively friendly with the Europeans who came among them, they were logical candidates for Spanish missionary activities, but their locations seem to have prevented or delayed most such efforts. Although the Rio Grande was the primary habitat of the Jumanos, they were indefatigable traders who traveled far enough to the east to make contact with the Caddoes of East Texas.

Some of the more powerful Indian peoples in central and western Texas were not truly native Texans but migrants who came into the land about the time of or even after the arrival of the first Europeans and Africans. These were the Apaches, Comanches, Kiowas, and some of the Wichitas. The Apaches apparently made their way to Texas from the northern plains by way of New Mexico and the Texas Panhandle shortly before the Spaniards arrived. An aggressive people, they soon dominated the western part of the state from the Panhandle to the Rio Grande. When the Spanish explorer, Francisco Coronado, traveled the High Plains in 1541, he met a tribe he named the Querechos. These were probably Apaches. Within a short period of time, the Apaches acquired Spanish horses and firearms and presented a dangerous threat to any who dared to challenge them. In every sense a plains people, the Apaches were nomads who centered their lifestyle around the buffalo hunt, lived in skin tepees, and moved frequently from place to place.

Of the several bands of Apaches who located in Texas, the Lipans, more numerous than other bands and dominating areas in or near Spanish settlements, were frequently a source of concern to the Europeans who made their way into Texas. By the eighteenth century the Lipans were located on the Edwards Plateau to the north of San Antonio, where they remained a constant threat to Spanish settlements until driven from the region by the still more powerful Comanches. Dwindling in numbers because of disease, they eventually migrated northwestward into the mountains of far west Texas, where they joined other Apache kinsmen before eventually locating in what is now New Mexico.

By the eighteenth century the Comanche peple dominated the southern Great Plains. Fearless warriors and unsurpassed in their skills on horseback, the Comanches were relentless in their warfare with other Indians and with the white man's civilization that threatened their way of life. Their life centered around the hunting of the buffalo and, after they acquired horses from the Spanish, their development of their skills in the use of the horse. Of the several different and virtually independent Comanche bands, the Penatekas, or Honey-eaters, who drove the Apaches out of the Edwards Plateau in the mid-1700s, were particularly important in the story of Texas.

The Comanches were a nomadic people who never planted crops of any kind. Although each band regarded a given region as its home and always returned to it after its wanderings, Comanches never remained for long in any one place. They would break camp on the slightest excuse or with no excuse at all. If a prominent person died, or if an epidemic caused several deaths at a certain camp, the site would be abandoned at once, and the people would never return there—a practice that, in spite of its obvious inconvenience, no doubt checked the ravages of disease.

The Kiowas were another plains people who migrated to Texas, probably about the same time as the Comanches and likely from the mountain

Comanche people of 1860. (The Institute of Texas Cultures, San Antonio, Texas)

areas of northern New Mexico. Since they arrived in Texas about the same time as the Comanches, who did not take a challenge to their territory lightly, war between the Comanche people and the Kiowas would seem to have been almost certain. However, the two groups established an alliance that remained firm until the final days of Indian freedom on the High Plains. Although the cultures of the two peoples were similar, there were differences that stood the test of time. The Comanches and Kiowas traveled together, hunted together, and fought together, but they maintained their separate identities until the end of their life of freedom on the plains.

Superb horsemen and warriors, the plains people harried the settlements of Texas and other northern Mexican provinces until the late years of the nineteenth century. Their determination to protect their territory and their way of life was a barrier to the settlement of white people until the force of numbers and superior resources at last forced them to accept life on reservations in Indian Territory.

In most instances, however, it was not warfare but disease that doomed the existence of Texas Indians. From the time of the earliest Spanish settlements, the diseases of Europeans were a threat to the lives of Indian people. Smallpox was the most serious threat, but even lesser diseases of white people sometimes brought death in large numbers. Before the end of the eighteenth century, disease had destroyed a large portion of the Caddo nation, the Karankawas, and many others. Consequently, when finally defeated in their contest for the lands of Texas, it was the remnants of a proud people who made their way to the north across the Red River to settle in Indian Territory.

The story of the native peoples is worthy of study and understanding. Their way of life, their hopes and fears, their values and traditions are a part of the heritage of Texas. They knew and understood the land and perhaps appreciated the world around them more than the people who would replace them. For more than three centuries, moreover, they were of significance in determining the fate of the people who challenged them for the land. It was, in part, the hope of finding native treasures that brought the early Spanish expeditions into Texas. A desire for trade with native peoples was a great factor in bringing other adventurers, especially the French, into the country. Of particular importance as a motive was the yearning of zealous priests who hoped to win over the natives to the Christian religion.

Indeed, Native Americans often determined the nature of frontier institutions. From them newcomers learned of crops and effective means of tillage, of the preparation and preservation of foods, and of the habits of and methods for hunting wild game. If the natives were friendly, explorers and settlers found their way in the new country with ease; if they were docile, it was easy to exploit or at least to ignore their rights. If the natives were organized in weak and fragmentary alliances, settlers quickly drove them away; but if they were powerful and warlike, they retarded the advance of the intruders for decades and even for centuries. Furthermore, native warriors largely determined the type of warfare that was carried out. The Caddo of the timber, the Comanche of the plain, and the Apache of the mountain all had different tactics, and the European and African Americans had to meet them in a fashion suited to the condition that prevailed.

Although the Spaniards, who approached from the west and south, and the Anglo-Americans and others, who came from the east, had already developed pioneering institutions before they reached Texas, these institutions proved unsatisfactory in certain important respects. For instance, the Spanish mission system, which attempted to convert native peoples to Christianity, was designed for compact pueblos or for people brought together in colonies and often already accustomed to domination by others. It failed among the Caddoes of eastern Texas, who lived in scattered hamlets and refused to move to missions and accept the restrictions of another way of life. It failed even more miserably when attempted with the freedom-loving nomads of the west. Similarly, the Anglo-Americans, who had learned to meet Indians who fought on foot, had to develop new tactics for coping with the mounted warriors of the plains who struck on horseback, fought, and retreated with the advantages of surprise and swiftness. For good reason, then, a significant part of the story of Texas for almost four centuries after the arrival of the first Spaniards is the story of the native peoples.

BIBLIOGRAPHY

All readers, whether novice or experienced, will find several bibliographies pertaining to Texas very useful. Walter L. Buenger and Robert A. Calvert (eds.), *Texas Through Time* (College Station, 1991), is a collection of thoughtful essays; and Light Townsend Cummins and Alvin R. Bailey, Jr. (eds.), *A Guide to the History of Texas* (Westport, 1988), contains several excellent essays and a description of research sources. John H. Jenkins, *Basic Texas Books* (rev. ed., Austin, 1988); Edward G. Holley and Donald D. Hendrick, *Resources of Texas Libraries* (Austin, 1968); and Chester V. Kielman, *University of Texas Archives* (Austin, 1967) are also valuable. Older works include Thomas W. Streeter, *Bibliography of Texas 1795–1845* (two vols., Cambridge, Mass., 1956); E. W. Winkler, *Check List of Texas Imprints, 1846–1876* (Austin, 1949); and E. W. Winkler and Llerena Friend, *Check List of Texas Imprints, 1861–1876* (Austin, 1963).

Readers should also be acquainted with the most comprehensive work on the history of Texas, the *Handbook of Texas* (six vols., rev. ed., Austin, 1996), published by the Texas State Historical Association. The first edition, edited by Walter Prescott Webb and H. Bailey Carroll (vols. I and II, Austin, 1952), and Eldon S. Branda (vol. III, Austin, 1977) may be more readily available and remains very useful.

The largest collection of writing in periodicals on Texas history is the *Quarterly of the Texas State Historical Association* (I-XV, Austin) from 1897 to 1912; and its successor, the *Southwestern Historical Quarterly*, beginning in July 1912. Much Texas material may be found also in the *Mississippi Valley Historical Review* (and its successor, the *Journal of American History*) from 1914; the *Journal of Southern History* from 1934; the *Southwestern Social Science Quarterly* from 1920; the *American West* from 1963; and *Texana*, published for a time after 1962. Some regional publications contain a great deal of Texas history: the *East Texas Historical Journal* from 1963; *Texas Gulf Coast Historical Publications* from 1957; the *Panhandle-Plains Historical Review* from 1927; and the *West Texas Historical Association Year Book* from 1925. The *Texas Almanac*, published biennially by the *Dallas News*, is a dependable reference.

Good basic references on Texas geography are Terry G. Jordan et al., *Texas: A Geography* (Boulder, 1984); Ray Stephens and William Holmes, *Historical Atlas of Texas* (Norman, 1989); Stanley A. Arbingast et al., *Atlas of Texas* (Austin, 1976); and William C. Pool, *A Historical Atlas of Texas* (Austin, 1975). Useful in understanding Texas in the nineteenth century and thereafter is Luke Gournay, *Texas Boundaries: Evolution of the State's Boundaries* (College Station, 1995). Reflecting recent trends in scholarship is Dan Flores, *Caprock Canyonlands: Journeys into the Heart of the Southern Plains* (Austin, 1990). An interesting combination of history and geography is Terry Jordan, "Pioneer Evaluation of Vegetation in Frontier Texas," *Southwestern Historical Quarterly*, LXXVI, 233–254. A similar study is Myron P. Gutmann and Christie G. Sample, "Land, Climate, and Settlement on the Texas Frontier," SHQ, XCIX, 137–172. Older but a classic is Roy Bedicheck, *Adventures with a Texas Naturalist* (New York, 1947).

Fundamentals of Texas archeology may be found in Dee Ann Suhm and Alex D. Krieger, *An Introductory Handbook of Archeology*, Texas Archeological Society *Bulletin*, XXV (Austin, 1954). Useful also is E. H. Sellards, *Early Man in America: A Study in Pre-History* (Austin, 1952); T. N. Campbell, "A List of Radiocarbon Dates from Archeological Sites in Texas," *Bulletin of the Texas Archeological Society*, 1959, 311–320; and Jane Holden Kelley, "Comments on the Archeology of the Llano Estacado," *Bulletin of the Texas Archeological Society*, 1964, 1–17.

Michael L. Tate (ed.), *The Indians of Texas: An Annotated Research Bibliography* (Metuchen, N. J., 1986) is a careful and reliable survey of literature on early native Texans. Containing a comprehensive bibliography and well written, W. W. Newcomb, Jr., *The Indians of Texas* (Austin, 1961, rev., 1974), provides an easily accessible survey of the Indian peoples. Rich in source material is Dorman H. Winfrey and James M. Day (eds.), *The Indian Papers of Texas and the Southwest, 1825–1916* (five vols., Austin, 1966). David La Vere, *Life Among the Texas Indians: The WPA Narratives* (College Station, 1998) contain some useful information not found elsewhere.

Among the many histories of Indian peoples are Martin Salinas, *Indians of the Rio Grande Delta* (Austin, 1990); Charles L. Sonnichsen, *The Mescalero Apaches* (Norman, 1973); Mildred P. Mayhall, *The Kiowas* (Norman, 1962); Nancy Hickerson, *The Jumanos: Hunters and Traders of the South Plains* (Austin, 1994); Kelly F. Himmel, *The Conquest of the Karankawas and the Tonkawas, 1821–1859* (College Station, 1999); Bill Wright and E. John Gesick, Jr., *The Texas Kickapoos: Keepers of Tradition* (El Paso, 1996); and Diana Everett, *The Texas Cherokees: A People Between Two Fires* (Norman, 1990). Two works, Timothy K. Pertula, *The Caddo Nation: Archaeological and Ethnohistoric Perspectives* (Austin, 1992); and Vynola Newkumet and Howard Meredith, *Hasinai: A Traditional History of the Caddo Confederacy* (College Station, 1988) provide different approaches to understanding the Indian people of the East Texas woodlands. But see also Jonathan B. Hook, *The Alabama-Coushatta Indians* (College Station, 1997). For studies on the Comanches, see Stanley Noyes, *Los Comanches: The Horse People, 1751–1845* (Albuquerque, 1993); Ernest Wallace and E. A. Hoebel, *The Comanches, Lords of the South Plains* (Norman, 1952); Rupert N. Richardson, *The Comanche Barrier to South Plains Settlement* (Glendale, Calif., 1933); and a recent study, Thomas W. Kavanagh, *Comanche Political History: An Ethnohistorical Perspective, 1706–1875* (Lincoln, 1996).

2

Exploration and Occupation 1519–1763

In October 1492, Christopher Columbus and the crew of his three small ships sighted land, an island in the Bahamas off the coast of Florida. While searching for a new way to the Far East, Columbus had opened the door to a new world, the Americas. From bases soon founded on the islands of the Caribbean Sea, other Spaniards quickly moved to the mainland of Central and North America and explored the regions bordering on the Gulf of Mexico. In 1521, Hernando Cortés defeated the Aztecs in the Central Valley of Mexico, occupied their principal city, and confiscated their rich supplies of gold and silver. Renaming the Aztec capital Mexico City, the Spanish made it the center of their new empire in the Americas, New Spain.

THE SPANISH EMPIRE

More unified than many other European nations and less involved in the religious conflicts of the sixteenth century, Spaniards moved quickly to organize their empire. Attracted by the discovery of riches but also motivated by a desire to develop other economic resources and to spread Christianity, royal officials laid claim to most of the Western Hemisphere. Expeditions with conquistadors in search of gold and glory and churchmen seeking to establish their faith in a new world made their way into areas extending from South America northward to lands far to the north of modern Mexico. Where conditions and discoveries were favorable, settlements were made, colonial governments were organized, and the establishment of a Spanish civilization proceeded as rapidly as resources and native populations would allow.

Although much of the energy of early explorations and settlements was the work of European-born Spaniards (*peninsulares*), native peoples were involved from the beginning, and the Indian population would remain a large and significant part of New Spain. However, the population of New Spain quickly became truly a multicultural mixture, made up of Spaniards (either *peninsulares* or *criollos*, who were Spaniards born in America), Native Americans, and Africans, and in time mixtures or combinations of these peoples, known as *mestizos* and mulattoes and by various other names. Together, these ethnic groups would form the people who would develop the land of New Spain or Mexico. From the earliest days, Texas was a part of Mexico, its distant corners explored within fifty years, although settlement would be delayed for more than a century.

EXPLORATION

In the same year that Cortés first met the Aztecs, 1519, a Spanish expedition commanded by Alonzo Álvarez de Pineda mapped the coast of the Gulf of Mexico from Florida to Vera Cruz. Pineda and his men undoubtedly observed the coast of Texas, but they left no report of their findings or opinions of the land. Apparently Pineda was more impressed with areas farther to the south in present Mexico.

Spaniards, however, would soon explore the coast and the interior of Texas. Alvar Núñez Cabeza de Vaca and three companions, survivors of the ill-fated Pánfilo de Narváez expedition, were destined to be the first Europeans to spend a significant amount of time in Texas. The Narváez expedition landed in Florida in 1528. After failing to find rumored riches, the 242 stranded survivors tried to reach Panuco on the eastern coast of Mexico by sailing westward along the coast. The party was shipwrecked in November, apparently on a small island near present-day Galveston, and only a few escaped from the sea. After nearly six years of servitude to natives in the area, four survivors, including Cabeza de Vaca and an African named Estevanico, who was probably the first black man to enter Texas, managed to escape into the interior. Then, after wandering many hundreds of miles through South Texas and northern Mexico, they arrived in May 1536 at the northern outpost of Culiacán, near the Gulf of California in western Mexico.

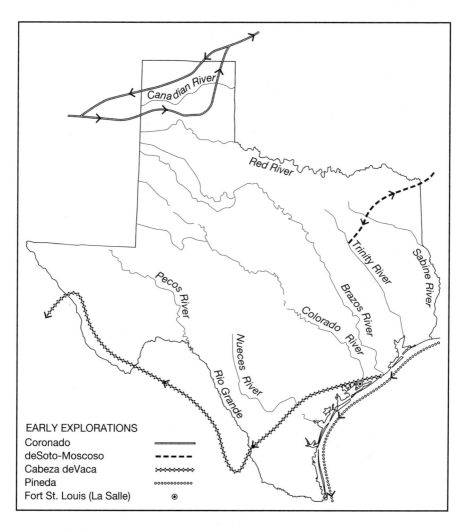

EARLY EXPLORATIONS
Coronado ·················
deSoto-Moscoso – – – – –
Cabeza deVaca ×××××××××
Pineda ooooooooooo
Fort St. Louis (La Salle) ◉

In a remarkably short time after the arrival of the first Europeans in the
Americas, European adventurers entered Texas and adjacent waters. In 1519,
Alonso Alvarez de Pineda sailed along the coast. Between 1528 and 1543, three
Spanish expedition— Alvar Nuñez Cabeza de Vaca, Francisco Vásquez
Coronado, and Hernando de Soto-Luis de Moscoso—explored widely separated
areas of Texas. More than a century later, 1684, a Frenchman, Robert Cavelier La
Salle, established Fort St. Louis on the coast.

The tales related by Cabeza de Vaca created great excitement in
Mexico City. Although he had not seen them, he had heard from the Indians met in his travels of large cities in the north, where there were gold and
silver in abundance. These, the Spaniards believed, must be the fabulous
Seven Cities of Cíbola, long promised in the tales of Spanish folklore.

Viceroy Antonio de Mendoza quickly dispatched Fray Marcos de Niza, with Estevanico, to find the fabled cities. When Fray Marcos reported that he had indeed seen from afar a great city (Estevanico had fallen to native spears and arrows), Mendoza then commissioned Francisco Vásquez de Coronado, governor of the province of Nueva Galicia, to penetrate the mysterious north country. Starting from Compostela in western Mexico in February 1540, Coronado had in his command 300 horsemen, 70 footmen, and more than 1,000 Indians.

Instead of the splendid Seven Cities of Cíbola, Coronado found, near the present Arizona–New Mexico line, only the pueblo dwellings of hostile Indians. Nor did he find anything precious at Tiguex on the Rio Grande, a few miles north of present Albuquerque, where he spent the winter of 1540–41. When spring came, he set out in search of Quivira, a "gilded land" that an Indian slave had told him lay somewhere to the east. He spent many days wandering over the treeless and level plains of Texas and probably crossed Palo Duro Canyon, located near present Amarillo. After seventy-seven days of marching across a land where he had seen "nothing but cows and the sky," he found Quivira—several Wichita Indian villages of grass houses in central Kansas. The chief wore a copper plate around his neck, but there was no gold. Thoroughly discouraged, Coronado returned by way of Tiguex to Mexico to make his report to King Charles I of Spain.

While Coronado was searching the southwestern lands of present-day United States, another Spaniard, Hernando de Soto, and about 600 men were exploring the region north of the Gulf of Mexico with no better success. After de Soto's death at the Mississippi River in May 1542, the expedition under the command of Luis de Moscoso de Alvarado entered Texas. Passing through the piney woods of the Tejas Indians in eastern Texas, it marched probably as far west as the Brazos River. Beset by a lack of food and unfriendly natives, Moscoso and his followers then returned to the Mississippi River, where they built seven crude boats, and in July 1543 they began floating downstream. Eleven weeks later, after caulking their boats with cakes of tar taken from Texas beaches, the 311 survivors reached Panuco.

Although the Coronado and de Soto-Moscoso expeditions strengthened the claim of Spain to the land that included present-day Texas, the immediate effect of their efforts was to delay Spanish activity in the area. Coronado did not consider the country he had explored of sufficient value to warrant its occupation by the Spanish. There were no precious metals, and the natives were either nomads who lived in lodges made of skin or semisedentary peoples who lived in little villages. The report of the de Soto-Moscoso survivors supported his conclusion. Therefore, for many decades thereafter, the Spaniards gave little thought to the region now known as Texas, except for an occasional venture originating from Spanish settlements in New Mexico.

Notwithstanding the report of Coronado, the Spanish continued to be interested in the lands along the Rio Grande, especially the upper reaches of the river of present-day New Mexico. In most instances, settlements in this area were in the form of missions, which were religious settlements operated by Catholic priests primarily for the purpose of teaching religion to surrounding Indians. In 1598, Juan de Oñate established a Spanish settlement on the Rio Grande a few miles north of present-day Santa Fe. In 1609, Santa Fe had its beginning, and soon several missions were scattered along the upper Rio Grande. From one of these Father Juan de Salas in 1629 accompanied some visiting Jumano Indians southeastward nearly 300 miles into Texas, perhaps to the Pecos or Concho (a tributary of the Colorado) River.

In the early 1650s, two other expeditions from New Mexico visited and traded with the Jumanos in the same area. A mission was founded on the site of modern Juarez in 1659, and early in the 1680s the Spanish established a pueblo and Mission Corpus Christi de la Isleta on the site of Ysleta (near present El Paso). This was the first permanent European settlement within the present boundaries of Texas.

From it an effort was made to establish a settlement in the Hill Country of central West Texas. Led by Father Nicolás López and Captain Dominguez de Mendoza, an expedition of thirty soldiers and two priests in 1683 located on a site probably on the San Saba River west of present-day Menard. But Apache Indians threatened the settlement, and the outpost was soon abandoned. Meanwhile, reports of a French settlement on the Gulf Coast in Texas, a flagrant violation of Spanish claims, had reached New Spain. These intruders had to be found and expelled, and toward that end the best efforts óf New Spain were directed.

THE CHALLENGE OF THE FRENCH: LA SALLE

The Frenchman whose settlement in Texas provoked Spain's ire was Robert Cavelier, Sieur de La Salle, a trader from the French colony of Quebec (Canada). In 1682, La Salle had descended the Mississippi to its mouth and claimed for his king, Louis XIV, all of the country that it drained. Returning to France, La Salle obtained a commission from Louis XIV to found a colony at the mouth of the Mississippi. On August 1, 1684, he set sail with 280 persons in four ships to carry out his plan. Missing the mouth of the Mississippi, La Salle landed at Matagorda Bay on the Texas coast in February 1685. He erected a crude stockade, Fort St. Louis, on Garcitas Creek, in the vicinity of present-day Vanderbilt, and set out to explore the country. After a six-month journey to the south and west, he returned to find that he was stranded. Not one of his four ships was left. Two were wrecked, one had been destroyed by the Spanish, and the fourth had sailed away. Furthermore, the first crop had failed, the supplies were gone, the Karankawa were making life unsafe, and only forty-five people were still alive. La Salle thus determined to find the Mississippi and go to Canada for help.

But La Salle never reached Canada. He made a fruitless journey to the east, perhaps as far as to the Sabine River, and then launched a third expedition northeastward into the piney woods. There, somewhere between present-day Navasota and Jacksonville, some of his own men assassinated him. Six survivors of the settlement who were not involved in the conspiracy finally made their way to Canada. Meanwhile, Fort St. Louis had been destroyed and its inhabitants had been slain or taken captive by local Karankawas.

Two years later the Spanish finally located the ruins of Fort St. Louis. Through captured French pirates the Spaniards had learned of La Salle's settlement soon after it was founded. Several expeditions by both land and sea, however, failed to discover the intruders. At last Governor Alonso de León of the province of Coahuila reached the ruins of Fort St. Louis on April 22, 1689. He discovered two of La Salle's men living among the Indians and from them learned the sad history of the colony. After destroying the remains of the fort, he explored the interior of the region and visited with some Caddo Indians before turning homeward.

THE FIRST MISSIONS IN EAST TEXAS

Fate (and the Karankawas) had removed the French menace from the Gulf Coast, but thoughtful Spaniards realized that Spain's claim to the region was not secure. On his return to Mexico, de León sent to the viceroy a glowing report of the country of the Caddoes. The land was fertile; the climate was desirable; and the natives were friendly. Spain should occupy the country at once. Father Damian Massanet, who had accompanied de León and had visited with a Caddo chief, was even more eager for the Spaniards to move into the region. He had promised the Caddoes that he would return. Thus, the priest and the soldier made a joint petition asking the viceroy, the Count of Galve, to authorize and support a missionary expedition to the Tejas.

With official approval in hand, Father Massanet, accompanied by three other priests, and de León, with a military escort of more than a hundred soldiers, set out from Monclova for Texas in late March 1690. The Tejas chief, with a welcoming party of his people, met them at the Trinity, and in late May, they arrived at the principal village of the Nabedache, one of the tribes of the Hasinai (Caddo) Confederacy. Fields of corn, beans, and melons and a welcoming feast gave new confidence to the Spanish. Twelve days later the

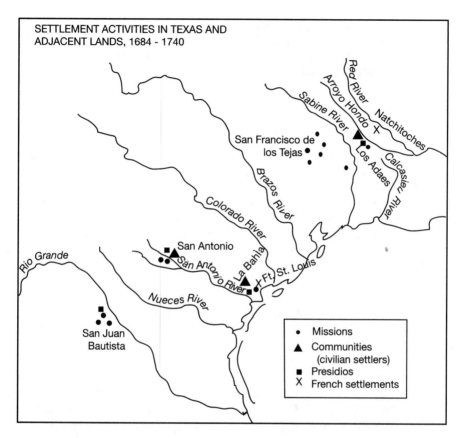

SETTLEMENT ACTIVITIES IN TEXAS AND
ADJACENT LANDS, 1684 - 1740

- Missions
▲ Communities
  (civilian settlers)
■ Presidios
X French settlements

The first mission located in Spanish Texas was San Francisco de los Tejas (1690).
Although Texas became a separate province in 1722, boundaries remained vague.

priests celebrated mass in the first mission in the land of the Tejas—San Francisco de los Tejas, near the present-day village of Weches in Houston County. On the next day de León and Father Massanet began their homeward trek, leaving behind three priests and three soldiers to man this remote post against further French intrusion.

Although a second mission was founded a few miles from San Francisco de los Tejas, the settlement in the land of the Tejas did not flourish. Before the end of 1691, an epidemic had killed many of the Indians, a priest had died, drought had destroyed the crops, and the Indians had grown first indifferent, then hostile. More supplies were sent, but by 1693 Spanish officials, including the indomitable Massanet, had concluded that East Texas should be abandoned. On October 25, 1693, even before word authorizing abandonment had been received, Spanish priests set fire to their mission and stole away.

These efforts, however, were not in vain. They had acquainted the Spaniards with the geography and the native peoples of Texas, and their failure proved that missions in that country could not succeed unless sustained by presidios (forts) and settlements.

THE RETURN OF THE SPANISH
TO EAST TEXAS

Although the administrators of New Spain had abandoned the area, the priests and the captains of the frontier did not forget the land of the Tejas. One of the priests, Father Francisco Hidalgo, spent most of his time in a settlement near the west bank of the Rio Grande, San Juan Bautista (near present Eagle Pass), hoping anxiously for an opportunity to return to Texas. The dedicated missionary had to wait many years until the threat from the French reappeared.

After a delay of more than a decade, the French had returned to the Gulf Coast, establishing a post at Biloxi in April 1699 and one at Mobile three years later. Family ties in Europe between the thrones of Spain and France led the Spanish government to accept French occupation of the Mississippi Valley (Louisiana), but the Spaniards were reluctant to open their borders to trade with the French. Nevertheless, the governor of Louisiana, Antoine de la Mothe Cadillac, was determined to find a way to trade with the Spanish. The opportunity arose when Cadillac received a strange letter from Father Hidalgo of Mission San Juan Bautista. Hidalgo suggested that the French help with the missionary work among the Indians of East Texas. Cadillac saw in the invitation a possible opportunity for the expansion of trade. Accordingly, he commissioned the Canadian-born Captain Luis Juchereau de St. Denis to go to the country of the Tejas, find Father Hidalgo, and inaugurate a trading program with the Spaniards on the northern frontier of New Spain. St. Denis, fluent in Spanish and several Indian languages, was a successful trader and commander of a military post. With goods to trade, he proceeded to a village of the Natchitoches on the Red River. In October 1713, he built a storehouse at what became the French post of Natchitoches and then traded leisurely with several native groups and inquired among the Tejas about Father Hidalgo. During the next summer he made his way with a small party across Texas to San Juan Bautista on the Rio Grande, arriving there in July 1714.

St. Denis's arrival alarmed the Spaniards. There were positive orders, without exceptions, against the introduction of foreign goods or the admission of foreigners into New Spain. Both St. Denis and Father Hidalgo were called to Mexico City for explanations, but they pled their cause well. The Frenchman had managed to win a promise of marriage from Manuela Sánchez, the granddaughter of the commander of the presidio at San Juan

Bautista, Captain Diego Rámon. When the viceroy decided to reestablish missions in East Texas, St. Denis obtained a contract to serve as a guide in the venture, and Father Hidalgo received permission to return to the Tejas.

Traveling with his new bride, St. Denis guided a sizable Spanish expedition into the country of the Tejas in June 1716. The expedition, commanded by Captain Domíngo Ramón, the son of the commander at San Juan Bautista, included twenty-five soldiers, thirty civilian men (one of whom was black) and women, nine priests, St. Denis, and two other Frenchmen. The reception by the Hasinai, like that accorded to de León and Massanet more than a quarter of a century before, was most cordial.

Before the year ended, the Spaniards had established six missions, five extending in a line from the Neches River eastward to a point almost within cannon shot of the French outpost of Natchitoches on the Red River and a sixth near present-day San Augustine, Texas. As quarters for his soldiers Ramón built Presidio Nuestra Señora de los Dolores de los Tejas on the east bank of the Neches River.

The settlements in East Texas soon led to the establishment of another on the San Antonio River between the Rio Grande and the land of the Tejas. Father Antonio de Buenaventura Olivares, who had done missionary work among some Indians along the river, had petitioned for a mission in that area. Moreover, the long distance between San Juan Bautista and East Texas made the need for a midway resting point imperative. Thus, the petition of Olivares and the need for supplies and reinforcements in East Texas resulted in the founding of present-day San Antonio. Martín Alarcón, governor of Coahuila and Texas, on May 1, 1718, founded Mission San Antonio de Valero (its chapel later to be known as the Alamo). On May 5, about one mile to the north, he established Presidio San Antonio de Béxar. The ten families that settled around the presidio constituted the Villa de Béxar, a village destined to become the most important Spanish settlement in Texas.

The halfway post was established none too soon. The Spaniards in East Texas were desperately in need of supplies, the natives were refusing to accept mission life, and France and Spain were now at war. The French in Louisiana learned of the war long before the news reached the Spaniards in Mexico. A French corporal with six soldiers from Natchitoches in June 1719 captured the mission near Natchitoches and the two residents present, a soldier and a lay brother. However, in the confusion caused by the squawking of excited chickens, the lay brother escaped and fled hurriedly to spread the word that the French were invading with a large force. Presidio commander Ramón decided that the Spaniards should again abandon East Texas, and in October the caravan of motley refugees straggled into San Antonio. The French "invasion," or "Chicken War," had revealed that the Spaniards' claim to the country of the Tejas was not yet secure.

Alarmed, angry, and somewhat embarrassed, the viceroy reacted quickly and with vigor. He appointed the Marquís de San Miguel de

Aguayo, a wealthy citizen of Coahuila who had offered to drive the French out of Texas at his own expense, to be governor and captain-general of the provinces of Coahuila and Texas. Aguayo was charged with the task of recruiting a force, driving the French from Texas, and reestablishing the missions in East Texas. In the early spring of 1721, Aguayo set out for Texas with 500 men, 5,000 horses and mules, and large herds of cattle and sheep. At San Antonio he found that some refugee priests from East Texas had dedicated a new mission, San José y San Miguel de Aguayo. Located on the San Antonio River about five miles from San Antonio de Valero, this soon became the most successful mission in Texas. Accompanied from San Antonio by the friars who had fled the area in 1719, Aguayo in mid-July reached the Tejas country, where friendly Indians welcomed the Spanish with evident delight.

Upon arrival in East Texas, Aguayo reestablished all the abandoned missions and turned them over to the churchmen with impressive ceremonies. Then, despite the protests of St. Denis (now the French commander at Natchitoches), in the autumn of 1721, he established the presidio of Nuestra Señora del Pilar at Los Adaes, and left in charge a garrison of a hundred men. Los Adaes, with its garrison, mission, and small civil settlement, became the capital of the newly created province of Texas.

In the spring of 1722, Aguayo went to the site of La Salle's Fort St. Louis and directed the construction of a mission, Nuestra Señora del Espíritu Santo Zuñiga, and a presidio, Nuestra Señora de Loreto, commonly called La Bahía. When he returned to Coahuila, Aguayo left behind 268 soldiers, quartered in presidios at San Antonio, on the Angelina, at Los Adaes, and at La Bahía. Each of the four presidios marked a mission center, and together they guarded nine missions. As a result of the Aguayo expedition, Spain's claim to Texas was never again seriously challenged by the French.

But the complete and adequate establishment left by Aguayo did not mean the end of French activity. In search of economy, the viceroy of New Spain, the Marquís de Casafuerte, in 1727 reduced the number of soldiers at Los Adaes, and the presidio on the Angelina River was abolished. In 1730, the abandonment of the presidio led to the removal of three East Texas missions—San Francisco, Concepción, and San José—and their ultimate location at San Antonio. As Spanish influence declined, French influence increased.

Nevertheless, Franco-Spanish relations on the border of Texas remained generally quiet and peaceful until 1762. Representatives of both nations accepted in practice the Arroyo Hondo, a small stream running between Los Adaes and Natchitoches, as the dividing line between the two empires. In the contest for trade, the French were more successful. By means of a trading post on the Red River near present-day Texarkana, the French controlled the trade of the Caddo people in the vicinity. Likewise, they appropriated the trade of the Wichita and Tawakoni in northern Texas and of the Tonkawa farther south.

Mission San José y San Miguel de Aguayo, founded in 1720 for the Zacatecan brotherhood in San Antonio. It was the center of Spanish mission efforts in Texas. (Courtesy of the Texas Department of Transportation)

EXPANSION

Nuevo Santander

While reducing their presence in the piney woods of East Texas, Spanish authorities undertook new ventures elsewhere, one of the most successful efforts being the settlement of Nuevo Santander. Most of Nuevo Santander was never a part of Spanish Texas, but the portion of the region that lay north of the Rio Grande would become a part of Texas in a later time. In their northward advance in New Spain, the Spaniards had bypassed the vast coastal area extending from Tampico on the Mexico coast to the La Bahía post and inland toward San Antonio, San Juan Bautista, Monterrey, and Monclova. The task of subduing the Indians and colonizing the land, which extended as much as 300 miles in some directions, was assigned in 1746 to José de Escandón, a veteran Indian fighter. The choice of Escandón was a good one. A skillful planner who avoided needless conflict, he was one of the most successful colonizers of the Spanish era. In 1749, Escandón entered the region, which had been renamed Nuevo Santander, with more than 3,000 settlers, soldiers, and priests. By 1755, he had placed almost 6,000 people in twenty-three settlements, two of which, Dolores and Laredo, were north of the Rio Grande in present-day Texas. Dolores, in present Zapata County, was soon abandoned, but Laredo's population grew quite rapidly. Meanwhile, Franciscan missionaries had founded fifteen missions. Of later significance, most of the land between the Rio Grande and the Nueces River was either granted to or appropriated by Spanish ranchers who lived south of the Rio Grande.

Modern Goliad also had its beginning with Escandón. In 1749, he had Mission La Bahía del Espíritu Santo de Zuñiga and Presidio Nuestra Señora de Loreto, originally founded by Aguayo in 1722, moved to the present site of Goliad on the San Antonio River. Although now many miles in the interior, the new establishment continued to be known simply as La Bahía. In 1754, Mission Nuestra Señora del Rosario was founded for the Karankawas, about three miles to the southwest. Around these establishments, which were under the jurisdiction of the province of Nuevo Santander until the boundary of Texas was reset at the Nueces River, grew up one of the three principal settlements in Spanish Texas—La Bahía, or Goliad.

EXPANSION

On the Coast and in the Hills

The settlement of Nuevo Santander was a part of a general program of expansion in many areas of northern New Spain. Other efforts in Texas included settlements on the coast at the mouth of the Trinity; on the San Gabriel River, northeast of San Antonio; and on the San Saba and upper Nueces rivers, northwest of San Antonio. In an effort to thwart French traders from Louisiana who traded among the Orcoquizac on the Texas coast near the Trinity River, Spanish authorities in 1756 established the presidio of San Agustín de Ahumada and a mission, Nuestra Señora de la Luz del Orcoquisac, in the general vicinity of modern Anahuac. Commonly called El Orcoquisac, the settlement never flourished and lasted only about fifteen years.

Meanwhile, 150 miles northeast of San Antonio, other Spaniards were attempting to expand the mission system. Along the San Gabriel River, called San Xavier by the Spanish, near modern Rockdale, lived the Tonkawas and a conglomeration of other natives. Harassed by both the Apaches and the Comanches, in 1745 the Tonkawas asked the Spaniards to send missionaries and soldiers to the San Gabriel. Between 1748 and 1751, the Spanish established along the San Gabriel, in the vicinity of the present towns of Rockdale and San Gabriel, three Franciscan missions and Presidio San Fran-

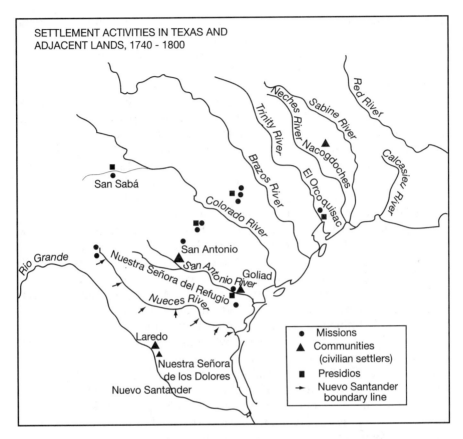

SETTLEMENT ACTIVITIES IN TEXAS AND
ADJACENT LANDS, 1740 - 1800

Legend:
- • Missions
- ▲ Communities (civilian settlers)
- ■ Presidios
- → Nuevo Santander boundary line

Influenced by the declining threat of the French (which disappeared altogether in 1763), Spanish authorities concentrated their settlement activities in Texas from 1740 on in areas west of the Brazos River. The last mission to be founded was Nuestra Señora del Refugio (1793).

cisco Xavier, all generally referred to as San Xavier. They were never free of turmoil and strife. Unfaithful natives, smallpox, measles, drought, hostile Apaches, and illegal French traders accounted for only part of the troubles. Constant friction between the military commander and the priests culminated in the murder of one of the priests. The commander was charged but never convicted. In the confusion one mission was abandoned, and in the summer of 1755 the new military commander, without authorization, moved the establishment to the upper San Marcos River. Another was temporarily relocated on the Guadalupe River, eventually to be transferred to a new mission site on the San Saba River.

Thus, the San Xavier enterprise became a part of the most ambitious and the most ill-fated mission extension program undertaken by the Spaniards in Texas—the San Sabá post for the Lipan Apaches. Lipan hostility toward the Spaniards was a matter of long standing, but in 1745 the Lipans, hard pressed by the Comanches to the north, were in San Antonio asking for a mission. After some time passed, a wealthy mine owner and philanthropist, Don Pedro Romero de Terreros, offered to finance a mission for three years for the Apaches in the area around the San Saba River, a tributary of the Colorado River and in the heart of Apache country. Terreros required that his cousin, Father Alonso de Terreros, be placed in charge, that the government bear all military expenses, that the mission's expenses be assumed by the government after three years, and that he would have a monopoly over the mining rights in the area. On May 18, 1756, the viceroy ordered the establishment of a post in accordance with these terms.

In the spring of 1757, Colonel Diego Ortiz Parilla, in command of nearly 100 soldiers, 237 Indian servants, women, and children, and 6 Franciscan priests headed by Father Terreros, founded Mission San Sabá de la Santa Cruz, Presidio San Luis de las Amarillas, and a civil settlement on the San Saba River, near present-day Menard. Troubles began almost immediately. The Apaches came but never found it convenient to stay. Comanches and their Wichita allies attacked the mission in March 1758, killing ten persons, among them Father Terreros and another priest. Another attack the next year killed nineteen persons. In retaliation, Colonel Parilla in January 1759 started out with a mixed force of 500, consisting of presidial troops and mission and Apache warriors. North of the Brazos River the expedition defeated a band of Tonkawas, and it then continued northward to the Taovayas village near the present Spanish Fort on the Red River. The Spaniards found the Comanches and Wichitas entrenched behind a stockade fortification, over which flew a French flag. Badly defeated in battle on October 7, Parilla hurriedly retreated to San Sabá, abandoning his cannon and other supplies. Spain had suffered the most humiliating defeat at the hands of native warriors in the entire history of Texas.

The mission on the San Saba was never rebuilt. Missionary activities on behalf of the Apaches were transferred to the upper Nueces River, near present-day Barksdale, where two missions were established in 1762. For a while these missions prospered, but they were never given any support by the government and were abandoned seven years later. The presidio at San Sabá was strengthened and maintained until 1769.

Thus, Spain's later efforts at expansion in Texas, except at Goliad and Laredo (in Nuevo Santander), were failures. El Orcoquisac, placed at the mouth of the Trinity, never developed into a civil settlement or even a mission center of any consequence. The mission efforts on the San Gabriel and the San Saba ended in calamity.

But the Spanish made one final effort. In 1793, Nuestra Señora del Refugio was located at the junction of the Guadalupe and San Antonio rivers. Two years later it was moved to a better site in the vicinity of Refugio, but its faithful Zacatecan padres were no more successful than their pre-

Mission and (restored) Presidio at La Bahía or Goliad. Before he withdrew from the Presidio, James Fannin buried the ancient handpoured cannon (shown below) to prevent its being taken by Mexican troops. On the prairie a few miles away, Fannin's force of some 400 men was captured; most were later shot by order of General Santa Anna. (Courtesy of the Texas Department of Transportation)

decessors had been in converting and changing the habits of the Karankawas and their neighbors.

LIFE IN SPANISH TEXAS: THE MISSIONS

In the settlement of Texas, Spaniards used three institutions: missions, presidios, and civil settlements. Of these, the mission was the most preferred method. The Spanish mission system as it was introduced in Texas was developed in the Central Valley of Mexico, where the Europeans found the natives living in relatively compact and permanent pueblos. The purpose of the mission was threefold: first, to convert the natives to Christianity (Catholicism); second, to teach them the habits and customs of Spanish life and make them acceptable and self-sustaining subjects of the king; and third, to extend the influence of Spain and to hold the territory in its vicinity against all intruders.

The mission belonged to both the church and the state. Indeed, the missionaries were employees of the king. Although they were selected by the evangelical colleges (divisions of a Catholic religious order), their stipends— generally 450 pesos a year—were paid out of the royal treasury, and their appointments had to be approved by the viceroy. The stipends were used not as salaries for the missionaries but by the college to maintain the mission. New missions could not be established without viceregal assent, and the undertaking was a function of both church and state. The government bore the initial expense of founding a mission, and the evangelical colleges maintained it. A mission was generally maintained for about ten years, after which time it was secularized; that is, its lands and property were distributed among the neophytes (religious converts) and its church taken over by the secular clergy (village priests). The time limit was not enforced, however, and in Texas the more successful missions continued in operation for many decades.

The missionaries who served in Texas belonged to the Franciscan order, nearly all sent either by the College (seminary) of Santa Cruz de Queretaro, established at Queretaro in 1683, or by the College of Nuestra Señora de Guadalupe de Zacatecas, founded at Zacatecas in 1707.

It was at San Antonio that Spanish mission activity attained its highest success. According to reports of competent authorities in 1749, 1768, and 1781, San José was the most successful. Indeed, in 1768 Father José Gaspar de Solis, inspector of the Zacatecan missions, recorded that "it is so pretty and well arranged both in a material and a spiritual way that I have no voice, words, or figures to describe its beauty."

The establishment consisted of a square, approximately 204 yards on each side, enclosed by a stone wall with towers in two opposite corners.

The Rose Window of the Mission San José y San Miguel de Aguayo is renowned as a masterpiece of art. (Courtesy of the Texas Department of Transportation)

Against the wall were eighty-four quarters built of stone, each supplied with a small kitchen and loopholes for defense. Other structures of stone and mortar inside the enclosure included the church, friary, offices, refectory, an arch granary, a workshop for spinning and weaving cotton and woolen cloth, shops for carpentry, iron work, and tailoring, and a lime kiln. The present church, started in 1768 and large enough to accommodate 2,000 persons, with its vaulted roof and its famous rose window, is reputed to be the finest mission architecture in New Spain. Outside the walls, there was a mill and an irrigation ditch so large that it "seemed to flow like a small river," which ran from the river by the houses to the fields fenced in for more than a league. There Indians grew corn, brown beans, lentils, melons, peaches (some weighing as much as a pound!), sweet and Irish potatoes, sugarcane, and cotton. So abundant were the crops that the mission, with more than 350 natives in 1768, supplied in part the presidios at San Antonio, La Bahía, San Sabá, El Orcoquisac, and Los Adaes. The Indians were described as energetic, skilled, and versatile laborers who worked even without supervision. They maintained their own guard and patrol for the defense of the establishment and had their own government with much the same officers and courts as a Spanish pueblo.

Unfortunately, not all Indians accepted mission life as well as those at San José. Reports from other missions frequently complained of Indians who ran away or who pretended to be sick to avoid work. Smallpox and other diseases were constant threats, but the priests felt sure that illness was not always the problem.

A typical day for the mission natives began with a religious service at dawn followed by thirty minutes or an hour of instruction in the catechism; breakfast; then work in the fields or the shops, or more frequently for the women, work on the looms, at the pottery wheel, or in the kitchen; and school for the children. All work and instruction were under the direction and personal supervision of the priests, or of the soldiers assigned to the mission for such purposes. In the evening all gathered in front of the church for another hour of instruction and the rosary.

Some missions enjoyed comparative prosperity, and reports indicate that in San Antonio, at least, the padres did effective work. An inspector in 1745 reported 2,441 baptisms since 1718. At the time of the report 885 natives, most of whom had been baptized, were living in the missions. They had more than 5,000 head of cattle, about half that many sheep, and large herds of goats and horses. The mission produced annually about 8,000 bushels of corn and quantities of beans, melons, watermelons, sweet potatoes, and cotton.

Life for the religious, however, was hard. Occasionally the governor or the presidial officials were hostile toward them. The most serious quarrel of this kind was with the Governor Franquis de Lugo (1736–37), who seems to have used every device within his power to annoy the missionaries and discredit them with the Indians and the populace of San Antonio. The priests appealed to the viceroy. Franquis de Lugo was reprimanded and later removed, but by the time of his leaving, many of the Indians had fled, and the whole mission field was demoralized.

Soon after Father de Solis made his inspection, the missions began a decline that continued until the close of the Spanish era. There were only nine active missionaries in 1785. Some missionary work continued at San Antonio until 1823, and Mission Refugio continued until 1830.

POLITICAL AND MILITARY AFFAIRS

The political system of Texas was similar to that of the other provinces in New Spain. It was subject directly to the viceroy, who in turn referred important matters to advisers. In important cases, before a final decision was made, a *junta*, or general council, composed of various dignitaries might be called together. All important decisions of the viceroy were subject to royal approval, and except in emergencies, policies of great consequence were not adopted until the king approved them. In 1776, in search of economy, efficiency, and more protection on the frontier, royal officials organized the Interior (northern) Provinces, or *Provincias Internas*, under a commandant general who was responsible to the king and practically independent of the viceroy.

Except for the *villa* of San Fernando de Béxar, which had self-government in some measure, the government of Texas was almost wholly military. At the head of the administration was a governor appointed by the crown. He commanded the army and the militia of the province and had the authority to grant land titles, issue licenses, hear appeals in legal matters, supervise fiscal affairs, and administer and execute laws and decrees. The terms of the governors varied in length, but the average term was about four years. Inspectors from time to time checked on the governors, and at the end of their term a *residencia* or investigation of their administration was made.

Military life in Texas, especially for the ordinary soldier, was frequently unpleasant. Discipline was harsh, sometimes cruel; the daily routine was boring; and military campaigns were dangerous. Although the buildings of the presidios at La Bahía and San Antonio were generally well maintained, elsewhere the forts often received little attention. Evidently the presidios were badly managed. The common soldiers received about 450 pesos a year, from which they had to purchase their equipment and maintain themselves and their families. They spent a great deal of time working on the private estates of the officers. The captain of a presidio served as the merchant of the post, sometimes charging the soldiers exorbitant prices for their supplies, in spite of regulations intended to prevent that abuse. In 1737, Governor Franquis de Lugo reprimanded Captain Gabriel Costales at La Bahía for failure to pay and to supply his men adequately, alleging that certain soldiers came to San Antonio from La Bahía practically naked, their arms out of order, and their horses so poor that they were a disgrace. Probably the case of Governor Martos y Navarrette (1759–67), who was charged with making $80,000 in profits on goods sold to soldiers at Los Adaes, is too extreme to be typical, but it suggests the weaknesses in the system.

LIFE IN THE CIVIL SETTLEMENTS

The first civil settlement in Texas was established in Béxar (later named San Antonio) in 1718. It consisted of 10 families under the protection of a military guard and was called Villa de Béxar. In 1731, 55 persons, most of them from the Canary Islands, were moved to the settlement at public expense. At first Béxar grew slowly. In 1770, the population was about 800, but this number may not have included persons living on ranches in the vicinity. After several years as the de facto capital, the settlement became the official seat of government of the province in 1773. In later years the population grew significantly, perhaps reaching almost 2,000 in 1820. Enjoying some rights of self-government, landowners elected an *ayuntamiento*, or council, and there was an *alcalde* who combined the responsibilities of mayor, sheriff, and justice of the peace.

The other civil settlements in Spanish Texas were Goliad, Nacogdoches, and Adaes. After the La Bahía mission and presidio moved to the site of Goliad in 1749, a settlement and important ranching interests developed in the area. The population of the community in 1782 was 512. Likewise, in the late years of the eighteenth century, Nacogdoches experienced considerable growth, including a number of French and other foreigners from nearby Louisiana. A commissary for trade with natives was established, and there was a flourishing trade with Louisiana. A census in 1790 showed a population of 480. Los Adaes, the capital of Texas from 1722 to 1773, was always a small struggling settlement.

Population records of the late 1700s report that more than half of the non-Indian population of Texas were Spaniards; in fact, the census of 1793 shows that Béxar was made up of 74 percent *españoles* (Spaniards) and 26 percent Indians and *mestizos* (mixed). Actually, only a small number of the people in Spanish Texas were *españoles* born in Europe. Most settlers came from other provinces of New Spain, primarily Coahuila and Nuevo León. A substantial number were *criollos*, and there were a few blacks. *Mestizos*, mulattoes, and other people of mixed blood made up the remainder of the population, perhaps one-third or more. The census figures more likely reflect the economic and class structure, with the majority of the population owning some land. Some, of course, did not. In most instances, Indians, some (but not all) *mestizos*, Africans, and mulattoes made up the lower economic and social group, owning little or no property and working in occupations that provided only a marginal living. However, in keeping with the character of a frontier, class structure was not as firm and inflexible as it was in some other parts of the empire.

From the early beginnings, even in the early days of exploration, Texas was never exclusively a man's world. Wives accompanied their soldier husbands on some of the first expeditions as they crossed the plains and explored the forests. Families were a part of the second effort to establish a settlement in East Texas in 1716, and more soon followed. Census figures vary somewhat, but all reports indicate that the population of Texas by 1780 was about 45 percent female and 55 percent male, with about one-fourth to one-third of it composed of children. Reflecting its stability as a community, Béxar in 1820 reported a population census showing women slightly outnumbering men. Most men and women were married, but widows and widowers accounted for about 10 percent of the population, a fact that may reflect the difficulties of life on the frontier.

The basic economy of the civilian population of Spanish Texas was based on the land. The countryside and streams contained an abundance of wild game, edible plants, and fish, and the fertile soils produced an almost unlimited supply of nutritious forage. Livestock ran unattended, with innumerable wild cattle free for the taking.

The ranching industry of Texas developed during these years and often as a commercial enterprise, even though the great *haciendas* found in other parts of the empire were not established in the province. Cattle thrived and, after markets opened in Louisiana, constituted the principal revenue. Ranchers adopted the practices of roundups, roping, branding, and driving cattle to market. By 1803, an estimated 15,000 head of cattle were annually driven to markets in Louisiana. Despite orders against it, smuggling flourished between East Texas and the French after 1716, and apparently much of the revenue derived from the sale of cattle was used to purchase goods, which were considerably cheaper than those brought overland from Vera Cruz. Spanish settlers also tried to raise sheep, but predatory animals and the wet woodlands of East Texas generally led to failure.

Despite the importance of ranching, most people were farmers, even though farming was in most instances limited to the production of goods that would be consumed on the farm or in the local area. There were very few large-scale farms that produced for commercial markets. Corn was the staple crop. Other crops included beans, chilies, sugarcane, pumpkins, melons, and gourds. Obviously, not all people were ranchers and farmers. In San Antonio in 1795, approximately one-third of the workers were servants, merchants, tailors, cobblers, teamsters, blacksmiths, and fishermen. There were no lawyers and only one physician listed on the census roll.

Religious and educational opportunities were limited and simple. The number of clergymen was never large (only nine in 1785). Yet the people remained devout adherents to their Catholic heritage. The first school, which opened in San Antonio in 1789, was short-lived. In 1803, the governor of Texas received orders to see that a school was established near each settlement or presidio, that each boy under twelve was in school, and that each parent paid monthly tuition in the amount of one-fourth peso. Schools were opened soon thereafter in San Antonio and in La Bahía, but the lieutenant governor at Nacogdoches responded that most of the boys there lived on scattered ranches and consequently it would be impossible to enroll a sufficient number for the teacher to make a living.

Illness and death were not strangers to most households. Outbreaks of the dreaded smallpox and cholera were periodic, and the major remedy was prayer. Although local officials imposed sanitary regulations, there was no pharmacist or civilian physician, and only one hospital (a military one) was established.

The behavior and social activities of the people were carefully regulated. Treason, slander of any member of the royal family, murder, arson, or major theft was punishable by death. Whipping, loss of all or half of one's property, or eight to ten years in the galleys was the penalty for robbery or the abuse of a holy person. In matters less serious, there was an abundance of rules. Travel without a passport was forbidden; men under the age of twenty-five could not marry without parental consent; a man and a woman were forbidden to ride on the same horse. Indeed, there was even a regulation against burning trash.

Yet, notwithstanding such drastic penalties and petty regulations, life was not always a matter of toil and trouble for the people of Spanish Texas. They found time for relaxation and enjoyed several kinds of entertainment. Dancing and the fandangos on the public square (although at times such dances were illegal) were popular, and horse racing—even on religious holidays, when participation might bring punishment in the form of twenty-five lashes—attracted many.

Although never large, the civilian population of Texas nevertheless played a major role in making the hold of Spain more secure. Only where there were farms and ranches and towns did the Spanish culture make itself evident and permanent.

BIBLIOGRAPHY

Although the pace of publication has slowed in recent decades, the study of Spanish activities in Texas is a matter of long standing. Readers should begin with Donald E. Chipman, *Spanish Texas, 1519–1821* (Austin, 1992), an excellent study that is comprehensive, readable, and reliable. Readers of *Spanish Texas* would also do well to turn to another volume written by Professor Chipman and Hariett Denise Joseph, *Notable Men and Women of Spanish Texas* (Austin, 1999), a fine scholarly work. Robert S. Weddle's studies dealing with particular phases of Spanish activity are thorough and balanced and often relied upon by other scholars studying the period. E. A. H. Johns, *Storms Brewed in Other Men's Worlds* (College Station, 1975) (especially valuable for information on native peoples), and David J. Weber, *New Spain's Northern Frontier: Essays on Spain in the American West, 1540–1821* (Albuquerque, 1979), are likewise perceptive in their interpretations. Other shorter accounts are O. B. Faulk, *A Successful Failure* (Austin, 1965), and *The Last Years of Spanish Texas* (The Hague, 1964); and Hodding Carter, *Doomed Road of Empire: The Spanish Trail of Conquest* (New York, 1963).

Classic histories of Texas that include sections on the Spanish period are H. H. Bancroft, *History of the North Mexican States and Texas* (two vols., San Francisco, 1884 and 1889), and Henderson Yoakum, *History of Texas* (two vols., New York, 1855). Texas and its relationship to the rest of New Spain is discussed in H. E. Bolton and Thomas M. Marshall, *The Colonization of North America, 1492–1783* (New York, 1921); and H. E. Bolton, *The Spanish Borderlands* (New Haven, 1921). The title of C. E. Castañeda's *Our Catholic Heritage in Texas 1519–1936* (seven vols., Austin, 1936–58) is misleading; it is a comprehensive study of the Spanish in Texas.

A voluminous amount of Spanish primary source material is available. The Béxar Archives, located at the University of Texas, are rich in information covering a broad range of topics. *Documents of Texas History* (Austin, 1963, rev., 1993), edited by Ernest Wallace, David Vigness, and George Ward, contain a number of excerpts from documents of this period. Older but more complete and still useful translated sources include C. W. Hackett (ed. and trans.), *Pichardo's Treatise on the Limits of Louisiana and Texas* (four vols., Austin, 1931–1947); C. W. Hackett (ed.), *Historical Documents Relating to New Mexico, Nueva Vizcaya, and Approaches Thereto to 1773* (two vols., Washington, D. C., 1923–1926); G. P. Winship, "The Coronado Expedition, 1540–1542," *Fourteenth Annual Report of the Bureau of American Ethnology, 1892–1893*, I, 329–637 (Washington, D.C., 1896; reprinted, Golden, Colorado, 1990); Juan Agustín Morfi, *History of Texas, 1673–1679* (two vols., Albuquerque, N.M., 1935); Lesley B. Simpson (ed.), *The San Sabá Papers: A Documentary Account of the Founding and Destruction of the San Sabá Mission* (San Francisco, 1959); Ralph A. Smith (ed. and trans.), "Account of the Journey of Bérnard de la Harpe: Discovery Made by Him of Several Nations Situated in the West," *Southwestern Historical Quarterly*, LXII, 75–86, 246–259, 371–385, 525–541; Margaret K. Kress (trans; introduction by M. A. Hatcher), "Diary of a Visit of Inspection of the Texas Missions Made by Fray Gaspar José de Solís in the Year 1767–68," ibid., XXXV, 28–76; and Benedict Leutenegger (trans.), "Memorial of Father Benito Fernandez Concerning the Canary Islanders, 1741," ibid., LXXII, 265–296.

There is an abundance of material on early explorers. For general studies see Robert Weddle, *Spanish Sea: The Gulf of Mexico in North American Discovery, 1500–1685* (College Station, 1985). See John Miller Morris, *El Llano Estacado: Exploration and Imagination on the High Plains of Texas and New Mexico, 1536–1860* (Austin, 1997), for material on interior areas. A detailed examination of an explorer who is mentioned often but seldom discussed carefully is the account of Donald E. Chipman, "Alonso Álvarez de Pineda and the Rio de las Palmas: Scholars and the Mislocation of a River," *Southwestern Historical Quarterly*, XCVIII, 369–385. For Cabeza de Vaca see Morris Bishop, *The Odyssey of Cabeza de Vaca* (New York, 1933); Harbert Davenport and Joseph K. Wells, "The First Europeans in Texas, 1528–1536," *Southwestern Historical Quarterly*, XXII, III, 1–42, 205–259; Donald Chipman, "In Search of Cabeza de Vaca's Route Across Texas: A Historiographical Survey," ibid., LXXXIX, 135–155, and Donald Olson et. al., "Piñon Pines and the Route of Cabeza de Vaca," ibid., CI, 175–186. The story of Coronado is told by H. E. Bolton, *Coronado, Knight of Pueblos and Plains* (New York, 1949); David Donoghue, "The Route of the Coronado Expedition in Texas," *Southwestern Historical Quarterly*, XXXII, 181–192; and W. C. Holden, "Coronado's Route across the Staked Plains," *West Texas Historical Association Year Book*, XX, 3–20. For Moscoso, see Rex W. Strickland, "Moscoso's Journey through Texas," J. W. Williams, "Moscoso's Trail in Texas," and Albert Woldert, "The Expedition of Luis de Moscoso in Texas," *Southwestern Historical Quarterly*, XLVI, 109–166.

French activities and effects are described in several works of Robert S. Weddle; see his *The French Thorn: Rival Explorers in the Spanish Sea, 1682–1762* (College Station, 1991); *Wilderness Manhunt: The Spanish Search for La Salle* (Austin, 1973); and "Spanish Search for a French Fort: A Path to Danger and Discovery," *American West*, XX, 26–34. See also Curtis Tunnell, "A Cache of Cannons: La Salle's Colony in Texas," *Southwestern Historical Quarterly*, CII, 18–43; Sandra M. Petrovich, "Robert Cavelier, Sieur de la Salle's Adventures and Texas: The Making and Breaking of French Colonial Policy," *East Texas Historical Journal*, XXXVI, 35–41; Donald E. Chipman, "Alonso De León: Pathfinder in East Texas, 1686–1690," ibid., XXXIII, 3–17; and David La Vere, "Between Kinship and Capitalism: French and Spanish Rivalry in the Colonial Louisiana-Texas Indian Trade," *Journal of Southern History*, LXIV, 197–218. Older accounts include H. E. Bolton, "The Location of La Salle's Colony on the Gulf of

Mexico," *Southwestern Historical Quarterly*, XXVII, 171–89; E. W. Cole, "La Salle in Texas," ibid., XLIX, 473–500; Kathleen Gilmore, "La Salle's Fort St. Louis in Texas," *Bulletin of the Texas Archeological Society*, LV, 61–72; and Peter Wood, "La Salle: Discovery of a Lost Explorer," *American Historical Review*, LXXXIX, 294–323. A classic not to be forgotten is Francis Parkman, *La Salle and the Discovery of the Great West* (Boston, 1893), and the story of the expedition is presented in the words of its chronicler in William C. Foster (ed.), *The La Salle Expedition to Texas: The Journal of Henri Joutel, 1684–1687* (Austin, 1999).

A detailed study on explorations during the period of mission activity that includes much material on geography, wildlife, and Indians is William C. Foster, *Spanish Expeditions into Texas, 1689– 1768* (Austin, 1995). For a description of various missions, see C. E. Castañeda, *Our Catholic Heritage*, especially vol. IV; H. E. Bolton, *Texas in the Middle Eighteenth Century*; Walter F. McCaleb, *Spanish Missions of Texas* (San Antonio, 1954); E. M. Schiwetz (historical notes by Robert S. Weddle), *Six Spanish Missions of Texas: A Portfolio of Paintings* (Austin, 1967); James Day *et. al., Six Missions of Texas* (Waco, 1965). See also Félix D. Almaráz, *The San Antonio Missions and Their System of Land Tenure* (Austin, 1989); Marion A. Habig, *The Alamo Chain of Missions* (Chicago, 1968); Billie Persons, "Secular Life in the San Antonio Missions," *Southwestern Historical Quarterly*, LXII, 45–62; Robert S. Weddle, *San Juan Bautista: Gateway to Spanish Texas* (Austin, 1968) and *The San Sabá Mission: Spanish Pivot in Texas* (Austin, 1964); Sam D. Ratcliffe, "'Escenas de Martirio': Notes on the Destruction of Mission San Sabá," *Southwestern Historical Quarterly*, XCIV, 507–554; C. L. Sonnichsen, *Pass of the North: Four Centuries on the Rio Grande* (El Paso, 1968); B. W. Aston, "Evolution of Nuevo Santander, 1746–1821" (unpublished thesis, Texas Tech University, Lubbock, 1964); William H. Oberste, *History of Refugio Mission* (Refugio, 1942); W. E. Dunn, "The Founding of Nuestra Señora del Refugio, the Last Spanish Mission in Texas," *Southwestern Historical Quarterly*, XXV, 174–184; Craig H. Roell, *Remember Goliad!* (Austin, 1994), which includes an extensive bibliography; K. S. O'Connor, *The Presidio La Bahía del Espíritu Santo Zuñiga, 1821–1846* (Austin, 1966); and Mattie Austin Hatcher (trans.), "A Description of Mission Life," in E. C. Barker (ed.), *Readings in Texas History* (Dallas, 1929).

Most works on border relations and efforts at expansion were written many years ago. Two scholarly studies by H. E. Bolton are *Texas in the Middle Eighteenth Century* (Berkeley, Calif., 1915), and *Athanase de Mézières and the Louisiana-Texas Frontier, 1768–1780* (two vols., Cleveland, 1914). Also useful are C. W. Hackett, "Policy of the Spanish Crown Regarding French Encroachments from Louisiana, 1721–1762," in *New Spain and the Anglo-American West* (Los Angeles, 1932); William E. Dunn, "Missionary Activities among the Eastern Apaches," *Quarterly of the Texas State Historical Association*, XV, 186–200; I. J. Cox, "The Louisiana-Texas Frontier," ibid., X, 1–75; XVII, 1–42, 140–187; and W. E. Dunn, "The Apache Mission on the San Sabá River," ibid., XVII, 379–414.

For Spanish political and military administration, see Gerald E. Poyo and Gilberto Hinojosa (eds.), *Tejano Origins in Eighteenth-Century San Antonio* (Austin, 1991); Félix D. Almaráz, Jr., *Tragic Cavalier: Governor Manuel Salcedo of Texas, 1808–1813* (Austin, 1971); H. E. Bolton, *Texas in the Middle Eighteenth Century*; M. A. Hatcher, "The Municipal Government of San Fernando de Béxar, 1730–1800," *Quarterly of the Texas State Historical Association*, VIII, 277–352; Sidney B. Brinckerhoff and O. B. Faulk, *Lancers for the King; A Study of the Frontier Military System of Northern New Spain, with a Translation of the Royal Regulations of 1772* (Phoenix, 1965); B. E. Bobb, *The Viceregency of Antonio María Bucareli in New Spain, 1771–1779* (Austin, 1962); Nettie Lee Benson, "Texas Failure to Send a Deputy to the Spanish Cortes, 1810–1812," *Southwestern Historical Quarterly*, LXIV, 14–35; D. M. Vigness, *The Revolutionary*

Decades (Austin, 1965); and O. B. Faulk, *The Last Years of Spanish Texas, 1778–1821* (Austin, 1965).

Many writings about Spanish Texas contain references to the economic and social life of the settlers, but the study of Oakah L. Jones, *Los Paisanos: Spanish Settlers on the Northern Frontier of New Spain* (Norman, 1979) is superior. A recent work is that of Patricia R. Lemée, "Tios and Tantes: Familial and Political Relationships of Natchitoches and the Spanish Colonial Frontier," *Southwestern Historical Quarterly*, CI, 339–358. Other accounts are O. B. Faulk, A *Successful Failure* (Austin, 1965); I. J. Cox, "Educational Efforts in San Fernando de Béxar," *Quarterly of the Texas State Historical Association*, VI, 27–63; and Sandra L. Myres, *The Ranch in Spanish Texas* (El Paso, 1969).

3

Spanish Texas 1763–1821

The last years of Spanish Texas were years of frequent change and often years of turmoil and violence. With the acquisition of Louisiana by Spain in 1762, Texas was no longer on the border of New Spain, and the maintenance of settlements in East Texas was no longer regarded as necessary or prudent. But the loss of Louisiana in 1800 and its subsequent purchase by the United States brought an immediate renewal of Spanish interest in Texas and a quarrel over the eastern boundary that almost led to war. The outbreak of the Mexican Revolution in 1810 led to violence and invasions, and there was unrest in the land until the final triumph of the revolution. Meanwhile, a trickle of immigrants from the United States entered Texas, and more significantly, the way was opened for many more.

TEXAS AFTER THE SPANISH ACQUISITION OF LOUISIANA

The Seven Years' War resulted in major changes in Spanish policy in Texas. The war, which began in 1754 between France and England, soon developed into a major world conflict. Spain, a belated ally of France, was eventually on the losing side, but before the war ended, France ceded western Louisiana to Spain. In the Treaty of Paris of 1763 ending the war, Spain was permitted to keep its recent acquisition.

Acquisition of Louisiana was not without its problems. Louisiana was a vast domain that the declining Spanish Empire did not have the resources to defend and develop. On the northeast border, the aggressive English along the Mississippi, rather than the tolerant French along the Red River, were now Spain's neighbors. Twenty years later the Republic of the United States had its beginning, and its frontier people were more restless than they had been as British subjects. In Texas and other northern provinces, Indian raids were becoming more and more destructive.

Drastic reforms and energetic measures were necessary to meet such problems. Fortunately for Spain, the king at this time was Charles III, one of the more able Spanish rulers. Among the various officials whom he sent to America to carry out his reforms was the Marqués de Rubí, appointed inspector of the northern frontier. Rubí set out in 1766 to explore the frontier from the Gulf of California to Louisiana. Entering Texas during the summer of 1767, he visited settlements throughout the province. At the end of his journey in Mexico City, Rubí confirmed what Spanish frontier officers had long been trying to impress on their superiors: the far-flung posts could not be maintained with the resources available. His very comprehensive and informative reports brought forth on September 10, 1772, a royal order, "Regulation for the Presidios," which substantially followed his recommendations.

In short, as it applied to Texas, the new regulation called for (1) the abandonment of all missions and presidios except San Antonio and La Bahía, (2) the strengthening of San Antonio de Béxar by moving to it settlers from East Texas, and (3) the inauguration of a new Indian program calling for friendly relations with the Comanches and Wichitas and a war of extermination against the Apaches. Thus, Spain had decided to abandon, except for San Antonio and La Bahía, all its establishments in Texas.

It did not take a royal order to bring about the abandonment of San Sabá and El Cañon; the Comanches forced that in 1769. Two years later the presidio at Orcoquisac was abandoned, and shortly thereafter the missionaries left their post in that vicinity. The abandonment of the East Texas settlements, however, was a different matter. These settlers were removed, not because of the problem of maintaining them, but because they were no longer needed as a barrier against French aggression and could be used to strengthen San Antonio. Baron Juan María de Ripperdá, governor of Texas, supervised the cruel removal, a task not to his liking. In the summer of 1773 the missions were abandoned, and more than 500 persons were torn away from their homes and forced to leave behind their growing crops and even their livestock.

Dissatisfied with San Antonio because of the poor land on which they were located and the Comanche raids on their livestock, the East Texans petitioned to return to Los Ais, where their leader, Antonio Gil y Barbo

(Ybarbo), had a ranch. Ripperdá endorsed their petition, but the viceroy allowed them to return no closer to Natchitoches than 100 leagues (about 260 miles). In modern Madison County, where the Nacogdoches road crossed the Trinity River, the refugees in August 1774 laid out the settlement of Bucareli. Three years later Bucareli was home to 347 people. Plagued by floods and raids by Comanche Indians, they again moved in 1779, this time without permission, to Nacogdoches. The authorities reluctantly gave their approval, and eventually some settlers scattered to their former homes.

Another part of the new regulation called for the pacification of the northern tribes and a war of "reduction or destruction" against the Apaches. Essentially following Rubí's recommendations, Spanish authorities were wise enough to rely in part on French methods and to employ Frenchmen to deal with the natives. Directing the arrangement was Athanase de Mézières, who was appointed lieutenant governor of the Natchitoches district in 1769. De Mézières—a man of unusual ability who was fluent in several Indian languages, French, Spanish, and Latin—had been seasoned by thirty years of service in Louisiana as a soldier, planter, and Indian trader. By 1771, he had made peace with the Wichitas, and in 1772 he made promising and peaceful visits with neighboring villages near present-day Waco. Hopes for peace with the Comanches, however, did not materialize. Although one band signed a treaty in 1774, others continued to harass San Antonio. For several more years de Mézières worked with Ripperdá on plans to get the northern bands to join the Spaniards in a campaign against the Apaches, but he died without achieving success.

Spain never achieved its goal of pacifying the northern Indians. A united campaign against the Apaches was never waged, although Comanche war parties occasionally joined the Spaniards on expeditions against their hated enemies. The military strength of the province was rarely sufficient to cope with the hostile warriors. With fewer than 200 troops to divide among three or four presidios or outposts, to furnish escorts for traveling parties, and to supply guards for the various missions, there were never enough soldiers.

Baron Ripperdá, who came to San Antonio as governor in 1770, sent to his superiors dramatic accounts of the plight of that place and urgent pleas for more troops. Additional troops were sent, but Ripperdá never felt secure. In 1789, his successor, Domingo Cabello, wrote Teodoro de Croix, commandant of the *Provincias Internas*: "There is not an instant by day or night when reports do not arrive from all these ranches of barbarities and disorder falling on us. Totally unprotected as we are, they will result in the absolute destruction and loss of this province." In 1792, Governor Manuel Muñoz complained that peace agreements and presents did not stop Comanche raids and that Apache depredations were chronic. The natives accepted the gifts but did not stop their marauding.

Fear of foreign intruders and pressing military needs led to several extensive explorations of Texas and New Mexico in the 1780s. The Spanish hoped to influence the Comanche and Wichitas to serve as a barrier against Anglo-American intrusion and sought out desirable travel routes linking San Antonio, Santa Fe, and Natchitoches. Pedro (Pierre) Vial, a French trader employed by the Spanish governor, in the winter of 1786–87 traveled from San Antonio by way of the Tawakoni village near Waco to Santa Fe.

Not satisfied with Vial's report, Governor Fernando de la Concha of New Mexico sent out another expedition. In the summer and fall of 1787, Corporal José Mares traveled eastward across the plains to San Antonio. On his return trip, he went near the site of present Abilene and then across the plains to Santa Fe, a journey of more than 800 miles. Subsequently, in 1788 and 1789 Vial traveled eastward from Santa Fe to Gainesville, to Natchitoches, and then to San Antonio, where he remained briefly before returning to Santa Fe.

No more explorations were made for a time, but the hope of a satisfactory route to Santa Fe from points in the province of Texas did not die easily. In 1808, Don Francisco Amangual with the aid of Comanche guides was able to go from San Antonio to Santa Fe with 200 troops. But Amangual's route, which went along the eastern side of the Caprock before turning west across the plains by way of present-day Amarillo, was no more satisfactory than were earlier ones.

In no way did these ambitious efforts meet the goals of the Spaniards. The explorers learned much about the land, and the journeys, which were filled with hardships of all kinds, amply demonstrated their courage and resourcefulness. But the natives of the north were less than impressed, and there was little to indicate that the expeditions affected either Anglo-Americans or the U.S. government. Moreover, the explorations demonstrated the impracticality of a route from San Antonio to Santa Fe and suggested that a route between Natchitoches and Santa Fe was only a marginal possibility. The inhospitality of the plains and the hostility of the Comanches were too much of a barrier.

SPAIN, TEXAS, AND THE UNITED STATES

Spanish policy in Texas changed again after 1803. Napoleon of France, hoping for a renewed French empire in America, forced Spain to return Louisiana to France in 1800. Then, after his dream of an American empire faded, in 1803 he sold Louisiana to the United States for approximately $15 million. Texas was once again on the border of New Spain, and an indefinite boundary separated it from the land-hungry Americans. To meet the new situation Spain adopted a threefold imperial policy: first, to hold the territory with its ancient boundaries in place; second, to increase its garrisons and colonize the territory with loyal Spanish subjects; and third, to keep out Anglo-American intruders.

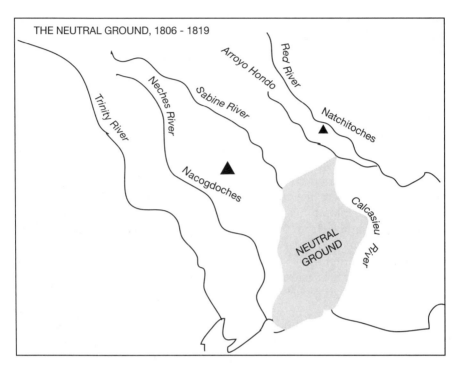

A dispute over the boundary between Spanish Texas and the territory of Louisiana in the United States led in 1806 to an arrangement known as the Neutral Ground Agreement. Opposing military commanders agreed to hold the area in dispute as neutral ground.

A controversy over the western boundary of Louisiana seemed inevitable. The purchase treaty, rather than naming specific boundaries, provided for the transfer of the territory as it had been prior to its cession to Spain in 1762. President Thomas Jefferson, on the basis of the French claim, held that the territory extended to the Rio Grande, while Spain, with more justification, contended that it did not extend west of the Red River. The Spaniards placed additional troops in Texas, including detachments at the old post El Orcoquisac at the mouth of the Trinity and at points east of the Sabine, and thwarted efforts of the United States to explore the disputed territory. The Thomas Freeman expedition, sent up the Red River in 1806, was stopped at a point near the western boundary of the present state of Arkansas, and Zebulon Pike, who succeeded in reaching the upper waters of the Rio Grande, was captured by a Spanish force.

The United States, on the other hand, sent troops into Louisiana, drove the Spanish troops from Los Adaes, and made preparations in the event of war. Strained relations between the two countries were aggravated by the report that Aaron Burr, formerly vice president of the United States, was planning to lead a filibustering expedition into Texas or some other Spanish province. Burr's force disintegrated, however, before it reached New Orleans.

Fortunately, a clash of arms was avoided. The commander of the U.S. forces in the west was General James Wilkinson, a military officer long suspected of disloyalty, perhaps treason, but one of considerable influence. In November 1806, Wilkinson made an arrangement known as the Neutral Ground Agreement with General Simon Herrera, who was in command of Spanish troops on the border. This provided that the Spaniards should remain west of the Sabine River and the Americans east of the Arroyo Hondo until their respective governments had reached a settlement. Although it was unofficial, leaders of both nations honored the understanding until the question could be resolved in a more formal way. The agreement avoided war, but the absence of law made the area between the two boundaries a haven for an assortment of outlaws and thieves. In later years there were many who believed that much of the lawlessness that sometimes occurred in East Texas had its roots in the ungoverned lands of the Neutral Ground Agreement.

The western boundary of the Louisiana purchase continued to be a diplomatic issue. Negotiations were discontinued in 1807 and were not resumed until ten years later. At last, the Adams-Onís (Florida Purchase) Treaty was signed in 1819 and became effective two years later. By that agreement the United States acquired Florida from Spain and gave up its shadowy claim to Texas. Also, the Louisiana-Texas boundary was fixed as follows: the west bank of the Sabine River from the Gulf to the thirty-second parallel, north to the Red River, along the south bank of that stream to the hundredth meridian, north to the Arkansas River, along the south or west bank of that stream to its source, north to the forty-second parallel, and along that parallel to the Pacific Ocean.

THE FIRST ANGLO-AMERICANS IN TEXAS

In the late eighteenth and early nineteenth century a few people from the United States began to make their way into Texas. Generally known and remembered as Anglo-Americans, these people most often were the descendants of long-time residents of English North America, and most were from southern states. Though an English heritage was evident in many, Anglo-Americans often could point to Irish, Scottish, and a variety of other ancestors, mixed together in ways that were complicated and often unknown. The ones who ventured into Texas were usually one of two kinds—sober, hardworking citizens who were looking for an opportunity to build a new life, or adventurers who in some way or another had political ambitions. Until almost the end of Spanish rule, official policy frowned on both types, but often the respectable citizens were accepted and even made welcome. For example, William Barr, an Irishman who had lived in the United States, formed with Peter Davenport from Philadelphia, a company that traded with the Indians and Spanish soldiers in East Texas.

A larger group of Anglo-Americans peacefully and permanently settled in northeast Texas in present-day Red River County. Because of the uncertainty of the western limits of Louisiana Territory, they settled at sites that a later boundary survey placed in Texas. The first arrivals were Indian traders, but in 1815 settlers located on the Red River, north of present-day Clarksville, at a site they named Jonesborough for a trader already there. The next year more settlers built their cabins at Pecan Point, about thirty miles downstream at the junction of Pecan Bayou and the Red River. Within two years a dozen families and several traders were there.

As Spanish rule came to an end, confusion over the location of the Jonesborough and Pecan Point settlements increased. In 1820, the newly created Territory of Arkansas claimed the area and named it Miller County, and more settlers flooded in. But in subsequent years, perhaps to take advantage of Mexico's liberal policies, many settlers applied to the government of Mexico for land titles. The settlements were without question in Spanish territory, at least after the negotiation of the Adams-Onís Treaty.

From the viewpoint of Spanish officials, the tolerant attitude displayed toward Anglo-Americans who were respectable citizens could not be extended to Anglo-American adventurers, or "filibusters," who assuredly were not working in the interest of Spain. Many of these were traders from Louisiana who appropriated much of the Indian trade and who offered a market for horses that natives stole from the Spanish posts. Some of these traders openly defied the authority of Spain. The best known was Philip Nolan, whose career is shrouded in mystery.

Nolan came to Texas as a trader as early as 1791 and with the permission of Spanish officials took horses out of the country. On one trip he drove out 1,300; on another he rounded up about 2,000 animals. The Spaniards became suspicious of his motive, and when he returned in the autumn of 1800 with a party of seventeen armed followers, they sent a force of about a hundred soldiers to arrest him. In the fight that ensued near the present-day city of Waco on March 22, 1801, Nolan was killed. His followers were imprisoned in Mexico and later cast dice to see who of the nine survivors would die to satisfy the decree of the Spanish monarch. One of the survivors was Peter Ellis Bean, who would play an important role in East Texas affairs for many years.

The true nature of Nolan's intentions will never be known. Perhaps he was merely an aggressive Anglo-American horse trader whose importance in the story of Texas has been romantically exaggerated over the years. On the other hand, some evidence indicates that Nolan was planning a more ambitious expedition against Texas. To a degree, Nolan was at the time, and has since been, judged by his association with General James Wilkinson. Nolan was a bookkeeper for, and protégé of, Wilkinson, commander of the U.S. forces in Louisiana, whose capacity for double-dealing has seldom been surpassed. Obscurity of intent, however, would not be characteristic of filibusterers to come. As revolution broke out in Mexico in 1810, more adventurers would make their way into Texas with a definite and obvious purpose in mind.

THE BEGINNING OF THE MEXICAN REVOLUTION

At the town of Dolores (about 200 miles northwest of Mexico City) on September 16, 1810, the priest Miguel Hidalgo raised the cry of revolt against the Spanish government. The examples of revolutions in the United States and in France had attracted the attention of Spanish colonials. Gradually the ideals of liberty, equality, and fraternity spread over most of the empire held by Spain in America. In Mexico, where a small group of *peninsulares* and *criollos* dominated a great mass of desperately poor people, either *mestizos* or Indians, the situation was ripe for violence and revolution. Thus, Hidalgo's *Grito de Dolores*, a cry of protest, launched a movement that would never die until independence was finally achieved. Moving from Dolores, Hidalgo with a rapidly increasing force of supporters captured and sacked Guanajuato and set up a government. Soon the city of Guadalajara fell to the revolutionaries, and the provinces of Nuevo Santander and Coahuila were added to their territory.

REVOLUTIONARY TIMES IN TEXAS

The people of Texas at first declared their loyalty to the king but soon became indifferent and critical. Then, on January 22, 1811, Juan Bautista de las Casas and a few fellow conspirators seized without a struggle Simon Herrera, commander of the troops, Governor Manuel María de Salcedo, and other officials of San Antonio. Las Casas, a resident of San Antonio and a former militia captain, then proclaimed himself governor of Texas. After his delegations, with equal ease, had taken possession of Goliad and Nacogdoches, he notified Hidalgo of his success. The season of his power was short. On March 2, the loyalists, led by Juan Manuel Zambrano, Erasmo Seguín, and Francisco Ruíz, captured Las Casas. In July they restored royal rule and shortly thereafter executed Las Casas.

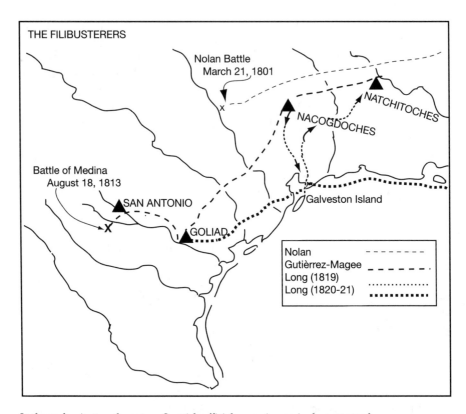

THE FILIBUSTERERS

Nolan Battle
March 21, 1801

NATCHITOCHES

NACOGDOCHES

Battle of Medina
August 18, 1813

SAN ANTONIO

Galveston Island

GOLIAD

Nolan	- - - - - - -
Gutièrrez-Magee	_ _ _ _ _ _ .
Long (1819)	....
Long (1820-21)	▪▪▪▪▪▪▪▪▪▪▪

In the early nineteenth century Spanish officials were increasingly concerned
with threats posed by adventurers from neighboring countries, sometimes
known as "filibusterers." Such threats did exist, although they were not always
of a serious character.

Although Hidalgo had already been captured and put to death (March
1811), the revolution went on under other leaders. Soon an invasion force was
making its way into Texas from the United States. Bernardo Gutiérrez de Lara,
a wealthy citizen of the city of Revilla (now Guerrero), was responsible. Gutiérrez went to the United States in 1811 as the envoy of the revolutionaries. The
U.S. government refused official recognition, but some officials and other persons encouraged him in his search for assistance. Moreover, reports from Texas
assured him that the province would revolt on the approach of an invading
army. Gutiérrez persuaded Augustus W. Magee to resign his commission in the
U.S. Army, to join him, and to recruit the nucleus of an army. Magee was an able
young officer who had made a good record on the Louisiana-Texas frontier but
who was unhappy because he had not been promoted.

Starting from Natchitoches with a conglomerate array of more than
100 Anglo-Americans, Frenchmen, Mexican revolutionaries, and Indian
allies, the Gutiérrez forces easily occupied Nacogdoches in mid-August

1812. Revolutionary propaganda pamphlets, letters, and broadsides had smoothed the way. The Spanish soldiers deserted or fled, and the people went out in a procession to greet the liberators. In November the army laid siege to La Bahía. There Magee died, perhaps from illness, although some believed he had committed suicide. Meanwhile, the offensive was stalled until February 1813, when Spanish forces withdrew to San Antonio. In March Samuel Kemper, who had succeeded Magee as military leader, renewed the advance. After defeating a Spanish army of 1,200 men commanded by Simon Herrera, the invaders occupied San Antonio on April 1, 1813. Five days later Gutiérrez issued a "Declaration of Independence of the State of Texas," a document written according to the best traditions of liberalism.

But with victory came dissension. On April 17, Gutiérrez proclaimed a constitution that provided for a centralized government, not the republican form expected by the Anglo-Americans. The constitution provided for a governor and a *junta* with dictatorial powers. Also, by declaring that the "State of Texas" formed "a part of the Mexican Republic to which it remains inviolably joined," the instrument destroyed the hopes of the Americans that Texas would become a dependency of the United States. The execution of Governor Salcedo, General Herrera, and twelve other Spanish officers, apparently with the approval of Gutiérrez, disgusted and alarmed many members of the expedition.

Although some Americans left for the United States, others replaced Gutiérrez with José Alvarez de Toledo, a revolutionary from Spain, who promised a more independent and liberal government for Texas. Gutiérrez left a few days afterward for exile in the United States, but the days of his insurrection were numbered. Torn by dissension in their ranks, the collection of 1,400 Americans, Mexicans, and Indians at San Antonio were no match for the 1,830 troops that Joaquín de Arredondo, commandant general of the Eastern Interior Provinces, brought against them. On the Medina River west of San Antonio, on August 18, 1813, the revolutionary forces were destroyed. Most of the Americans were slain; those lucky enough to escape fled to the United States. Thus, the Mexican state of Texas came to an end after a troubled career of four months.

Arredondo followed up his victory with a purge calculated to rid Texas of all Anglo-Americans and others believed to be disloyal to Spain. Rebels were shot, their property confiscated, and their wives and daughters imprisoned and forced to do labor for the loyalist army. So thoroughly did he do his work that the province was virtually depopulated save for the settlement at Béxar. Indeed, he was unable to put into effect the new liberal Spanish Constitution of 1812 because there were not enough suitable persons to fill the offices! No serious effort was again made to populate Texas until 1820, and meanwhile the officials forbade any trade with Louisiana.

But the rich lands of Texas constituted an invitation that offset the harshest decrees of the Spanish government. In 1818, the military had expelled a band of about 120 Napoleonic sympathizers who, under a French-man named Charles Lallemand, had settled on the lower Trinity River. The next year a more serious threat to Spanish sovereignty appeared under the leadership of James Long. Long, a merchant of Natchez who married a niece of General Wilkinson, was angry over the terms of the Adams-Onís Treaty. Like many Americans on the southern frontier, he believed that the terms of the treaty, which acknowledged Spain's claim to Texas, represented the "sur-render of Texas." At a meeting in Natchez, plans were formulated for driv-ing out of Texas the few royalist troops, organizing a liberal government, and attracting immigrants by the offer of generous land grants. Under Long's leadership the party set out in June 1819 for Nacogdoches, gaining recruits as it advanced, until it had 300 men, among them Bernardo Gutiérrez. Shortly after their arrival at Nacogdoches on June 23, the invaders estab-lished a civil government, adopted a declaration of independence, and invited immigrants to share with them the blessings of liberty.

To hold various outposts, Long divided his forces and left for Galve-ston Island to enlist the aid of Jean Lafitte. For several years Galveston had served as the headquarters for various adventurers or buccaneers, including Colonel Henry Perry, a survivor of the Gutiérrez expedition; Luis Aury, who held a naval commission from the Mexican revolutionists; and Lafitte. Lafitte's tenure dated from April 1817, when he set up his "republic" on the island and made it the headquarters for his privateering and lucrative slave-smuggling activities. But Lafitte refused to support Long's cause. Mean-while, the adventurer's forces scattered over East Texas and fled in the face of an advancing Spanish army. Long then made his way to New Orleans, only to return in 1820 with his family and another group of adventurers. Traveling by sea, he established his headquarters at Point Bolivar on Galve-ston Bay, where he remained for several months. Finally he made his way down the coast with about fifty men and eventually reached La Bahía on October 4, 1821, there to be warmly received as a revolutionary. Mexico, however, had already won its independence, and a few days later Long was sent to Mexico City. About six months later a Mexican soldier shot and killed him, perhaps accidentally but possibly as a way of removing a potential threat to the new nation.

Perhaps a more enduring contribution to the story of Texas was made by James Long's wife, Jane, who, accompanied only by her daughter and a young slave girl, Kiamata, survived the winter of 1821–22 on Bolivar penin-sula. During the winter she gave birth to a second daughter while enduring an endless variety of hardships and uncertainty. The experience, however, did not cause her to abandon Texas. Although she returned temporarily to her home in Louisiana, she soon came back to Texas, where she would live out her life, enjoying the admiration and respect of her neighbors, and would be known by some as the "Mother of Texas."

Jane Long. The wife of Filibuster James Long, she became one of the better-known women in nineteenth-century Texas. With only her baby, two-year-old daughter, and a young slave girl, Kiamata, she waited at Bolivar Point on Galveston Bay throughout the winter of 1821–1822 for the return of her husband who had traveled to La Bahía and eventually to Mexico City. After receiving word that he had been assassinated, she returned to Mississippi but later settled in Austin's colony. (The Institute of Texan Cultures San Antonio, Texas, Winston Farber).

A New Era: The Beginning of Foreign Immigration

Although Spanish officials had little use for filibusterers such as James Long, in these fading years of empire, Spanish policy was in the process of changing to accept, even to encourage, foreign immigration on a large scale. In September 1820, the *Cortes* (ruling council) of Spain issued a decree opening all Spanish dominions to any foreigners who would respect the constitution and laws of the monarch. News of the opportunity spread quickly, even to the western borders of the United States, and there were those who were eager to take advantage of it.

Among them was 59-year-old Moses Austin, Connecticut-born and a seasoned settler living on the Missouri frontier. On December 23, 1820, Austin appeared before Governor Antonio de Martínez in San Antonio and asked permission to establish in Texas a colony of 300 families. Austin had moved to Spanish Missouri in 1798, and he now came, he said, as a former Spanish subject who wished to renew his allegiance to the king. He also hoped for an opportunity to rebuild some of his fortune recently lost during the depression, the Panic of 1819, that had brought ruin to thousands of Americans. The role that Austin sought was that of an *empresario*. He petitioned for a contract to recruit settlers, bring them to Texas, build a settlement, and divide out the land within the terms and boundaries to be specified in the contract.

Moses Austin. In 1820, when hard times came to Potosi, Missouri, which Austin had founded in 1798, he went to Texas and obtained the governor's permission to settle the three hundred families there. (Archives Division—Texas State Library)

Perhaps it was only through chance that Austin succeeded in securing an approval of his petition. Governor Martínez was doubtful, but an old friend of Austin, the Baron de Bastrop, supported the application of the petitioner. Bastrop, a man of uncertain origins with a self-assumed title, was nonetheless an influential citizen in San Antonio. Consequently, Martínez finally endorsed the application, and on January 17, 1821, a board of superior officers, known as the provincial deputation, approved it. Somewhat surprisingly, Joaquín de Arredondo, military commandant of the area including Texas and a man who cared little for Anglo-Americans, agreed to the contract.

Moses Austin died soon after his return to Missouri, and it was left to the son to complete the task begun by the father. Although only twenty-seven years old, Stephen F. Austin was already a man of experience. He was well educated. He had served five years in the legislature of the Missouri Territory, had been appointed district judge in the territory of Arkansas, and had engaged in a variety of business undertakings. In addition, he had operated a farm in Missouri, had served as a federal territorial judge in Arkansas, and had studied law in New Orleans. He was, according to Professor Eugene C. Barker, his biographer, "patient; methodical; energetic; and fair-spoken."

Austin took a small party and went to San Antonio in the summer of 1821. There Governor Martínez received him cordially, recognized him as the heir to his father's commission, and authorized him to explore the country and to make other arrangements for his colony. News about the project had already traveled far, and on his return to Natchitoches, Louisiana, he found nearly a hundred letters from persons who were interested. Some settlers were soon on their way, but the fate of the new colony suddenly appeared to be in doubt, even before it was truly established. After years of hardship, the Mexican struggle for independence had succeeded. Spanish rule was at an end, Texas was now a part of the new nation of Mexico, and the validity of Spanish contracts such as that held by Austin was now in question.

A New Nation: Mexico

For a time after the death of Hidalgo in 1811, Spanish officials were able to control the Mexican rebellion. The upper classes—that is, the *criollos* and wealthy *mestizos*—did not support it, nor did the clergy or the merchants or the *hacendadoes*. Yet, the death of Hidalgo did not bring an end to the insurrection. For a time it continued under the leadership of José María Morelos, and after the execution of Morelos in the fall of 1815, Vicente Guerrero took up the cause. Peace was never quite restored, but open rebellion declined, almost disappearing at times. Indeed, at the end of the great European wars in 1815, it seemed that the royal government would suppress the rebels entirely. In 1819, Viceroy Juan Ruíz Apodaca reported to the king that no additional troops were necessary. Ironically, his judgment was made at the very time when events were happening that would give new life to the rebel cause. In Spain an insurrection forced King Ferdinand to restore a liberal framework of government, the Constitution of 1812. This move antagonized and threatened the privileged classes in Mexico, many of whom were already unhappy about the financial burden they were bearing in support of royal rule.

Thus, a strange mixture of privilege and poverty combined to overthrow royal rule. The key to the development of the unlikely alliance was Augustín de Iturbide, a *criollo* army officer whose loyalties were not very reliable. Iturbide persuaded the viceroy to place him in charge of a 2,500-man army to defeat the rebels, but when Iturbide marched, he did so not to fight but to negotiate an agreement with Guerrero, the liberal leader. The agreement, known as the *Plan de Iguala*, was proclaimed on February 24, 1821. The plan declared that New Spain was an independent, moderate, constitutional monarchy, guaranteed it the Catholic religion, and proclaimed racial equality. In August 1821, Juan O'Donoju, the last viceroy, recognized the independence of Mexico, and on September 27 Iturbide entered Mexico City. Thus, through an unusual combination of liberals and conservatives, the independence of Mexico was attained.

THE LEGACIES OF SPANISH RULE

In the measurements of population and settlements, Spain's three centuries of rule in Texas could hardly be termed an unqualified success. Notwithstanding all its efforts, Spain had in Texas, at the time the United States acquired Louisiana, only the settlements of San Antonio, Goliad, and Nacogdoches. San Antonio, consisting of five missions, the settlement of Béxar, and the *villa* of San Fernando, had a population of perhaps 2,500. About 1,200 persons lived in Goliad and about 500 in Nacogdoches. Faced with the threat of Anglo-American aggression, Spain renewed its efforts to populate the province. In 1805, it established the *villa* of Salcedo on the Trinity River, opposite the ruins of Bucareli, and the *villa* of San Marcos, eight miles above the site of present-day Gonzales. In 1809, there were only 16 persons living in Salcedo and 82 in San Marcos; the entire population of Texas was estimated at only 4,155 persons, more than 1,000 of whom were soldiers. The invasions and reprisals associated with the outbreak of revolution in 1810 brought more soldiers but significantly reduced the number of settlers.

The problems of Spain in Texas were partly within and partly beyond its control. Its exclusive commercial policy, which prohibited trade even among the different parts of its dominions, was certainly a retarding factor. Strict and tyrannical methods of government, strangely mixed with laxity and tolerance of graft, were also causes of failure. Certain unfavorable conditions, chief of which was the hostility of nomadic natives, were beyond its control. Yet Spain might have changed its pioneering institutions—the *villa*, the presidio, and the mission—to meet the conditions peculiar to the northern frontier in a better way.

In general it may be said that Spain suffered most because of a lack of realism in its policies and stubborn adherence to tradition in administration. For instance, it held doggedly to the notion that the pueblo type of mission was suited to Texas, although it soon proved of little value except along the Rio Grande and in the vicinity of San Antonio. It adhered rigidly to the high ideal that Indians should not have firearms and thereby left them to trade with its rivals. It never gave up the theory that since Texas was an extension of New Spain, the province should trade with New Spain only; thus it impoverished its settlements and caused people of enterprise to violate the law. Notwithstanding abundant evidence that conditions were otherwise, Spain clung to the fiction that poorly paid captains at isolated posts would be scrupulously honest, would sell supplies to their soldiers at fair prices, would keep their men employed in the public service, and would not use them for their own gain. The fact that occasional rigid inspections were made and that sometimes the guilty were punished did not ensure honesty.

Spain's achievements in Texas were considerable, however. It left upon Texas, which it held against all contenders until its empire in America collapsed, an imprint that will endure throughout the ages. Many streams and all but one major river in the state bear Spanish names, as do many other geographic points and towns. In almost every section there are land titles that go back to Spanish grants, and modern state law respecting water and its uses is a complicated combination of Spanish and English traditions. The law shows Spanish influence elsewhere, particularly that pertaining to the property rights of women and community property rights in marriage.

Our knowledge of early times in Texas is almost totally dependent upon the legacies of the Spanish. Spanish authorities, political and clerical, placed a high value on detailed and lengthy records; they relied and insisted on long and thorough reports and preserved them for future generations.

Fortunately, a few specimens of Spanish architecture still remain. In San Antonio some of the chapels of the old missions have withstood almost two centuries of assault by the elements and the occasional ravages of unfriendly hands. Their stateliness and gentle beauty command a reverent interest. They are worthy monuments to the idealism of the Spanish and fitting symbols of immortality in a transitory world.

BIBLIOGRAPHY

The general accounts mentioned in the preceding bibliography also apply to this chapter. Good sources on Texas in the years following the acquisition of Louisiana by Spain include H. E. Bolton, *Texas in the Middle Eighteenth Century* (Berkeley, Calif., 1915); Gerald E. Poyo and Gilberto M. Hinojosa, *Tejano Origins in Eighteenth-Century San Antonio*; Jack Jackson (ed.), *Imaginary Kingdom: Texas as Seen by the Rivera and Rubí Expeditions, 1727 and 1767* (Austin, 1996); H. E. Bolton, *Athanase de Mézières* (Cleveland, 1914); C. E. Castañeda, *Our Catholic Heritage in Texas, 1519–1936*, vol. IV (seven vols., Austin, 1936–58); O. B. Faulk, *A Successful Failure* (Austin, 1965); and Noel M. Loomis and A. P. Nasater, *Pedro Vial and the Roads to Santa Fé* (Norman, 1967). See also Robert S. Weddle, *Changing Tides: Twilight and Dawn in the Spanish Sea, 1763–1803* (College Station, 1995); H. E. Bolton, "The Spanish Abandonment and Reoccupation of East Texas, 1773–1779," *Quarterly of the Texas State Historical Association*, IX, 67–137; A. B. Thomas (ed. and trans.), *Teodoro de Croix and the Northern Frontier of New Spain, 1776–1783* (Norman, 1941); E. A. H. Johns, *Storms Brewed in Other Men's Worlds* (College Station, 1975); and Elizabeth Ann Harper, "The Taovayas Indians in Frontier Trade and Diplomacy, 1769–1779," *Southwestern Historical Quarterly*, LVII, 181–201 (College Station, 1975).

For the last years of Spain in Texas, among the scholarly studies are Jesús F. de la Teja, *San Antonio de Béxar: A Community on New Spain's Northern Frontier* (Albuquerque, 1995); Félix Almaráz, Jr., *Tragic Cavalier: Governor Manuel Salcedo of Texas, 1808–1813* (Austin, 1971); David B. Gracy, *Moses Austin: His Life* (San Antonio, 1987); Light Townsend Cummins, "Spanish Louisiana Land Policy: Antecedent to the Anglo-American Colonization of East Texas, 1769–1821," *East Texas Historical Journal*, XXXIII, 18–26; Virginia Taylor (ed. and trans.), *Letters of Antonio Martínez, Last Governor of Texas* (Austin, 1957); M. A. Hatcher, *The Opening of Texas to Foreign Settlement, 1801–1821* (University of Texas *Bulletin*, no. 2714; Austin, 1927); Gilbert Cruz, *Let There Be Towns: Spanish Municipal Origins in the American Southwest, 1610–1810* (College Station, 1988); O. B. Faulk, *The Last Years of Spanish Texas* (Austin, 1965); D. M.

Vigness, *The Revolutionary Decades* (Austin, 1965); N. L. Benson (ed. and trans.), "A Governor's Report on Texas in 1809," *Southwestern Historical Quarterly*, LXXI, 603–615; Félix D. Almaráz, Jr., *The Crossroad of Empire: The Church and State on the Rio Grande Frontier of Coahuila and Texas, 1700–1821* (San Antonio, 1979); Dan Flores, "Rendezvous at Spanish Bluff: Jefferson's Red River Exploration," *Red River Valley Historical Review*, IX, 4–26. L. Friend, "Old Spanish Fort," *West Texas Historical Association Year Book*, XVI, 3–27; Kathryn Garrett, "Dr. John Sibley and the Louisiana-Texas Frontier, 1803–1814," *Southwestern Historical Quarterly*, XLVIII, XLIX; Harris G. Warren, *The Sword Was Their Passport* (Baton Rouge, 1943); and Thomas M. Marshall, *A History of the Western Boundary of the Louisiana Purchase, 1819–1841* (Berkeley, Calif., 1914).

On the filibusterers, see the general references previously cited in this chapter and also K. Garrett, *Green Flag over Texas* (Austin, 1969); D. M. Vigness, *The Revolutionary Decades* (Austin, 1965); H. S. Thrall, *Pictorial History of Texas* (St. Louis, 1879); M. A. Hatcher, "Joaquin de Arredondo's Report of the Battle of the Medina," *Quarterly of the Texas State Historical Association*, XI, 220–236; K. Garrett, "The First Constitution of Texas, April 17, 1813," *Southwestern Historical Quarterly*, XL, 290–308; Lois Garver, "Benjamin Rush Milam," ibid., XXXVIII, 79–121; Henry P. Walker (ed.), "William McLane's Narrative of the Magee-Gutiérrez Expedition of 1812–1813," ibid., LXVI, 234–251, 457–479, 569–588; Ed Bradley, "Fighting for Texas: Filibuster James Long, the Adams-Onís Treaty, and the Monroe Administration," ibid., CII, 323–342; Anne Brindley, "Jane Long," ibid., LXVI, 211–238; Jack C. Ramsay, Jr., *Jean Laffite, Prince of Pirates* (Austin, 1996); James C. Milligan, "José Bernardo Gutiérrez de Lara, 1811–1841" (unpublished dissertation, Texas Tech University, Lubbock, 1975); and Ted Schwarz, *Forgotten Battlefield of the First Texas Revolution: The Battle of Medina, August 18, 1813* (Austin, 1985).

4

Texas Under Mexican Rule

For the people of Mexico in general and of Texas in particular, the end of Spanish rule was much more of a beginning than it was an end. In the new nation the uneasy alliance of conservative *ricos*, middle-class *criollos*, and liberal *pobres* soon and predictably fell apart. The knowledge and desire necessary to establish a stable and free government was not lacking, but the necessary experience and consensus were. Consequently, in their first decade of freedom the people of Mexico would change their basic framework of government twice and their leaders several times more.

Although the uncertainties of national leadership affected the events and people of Texas, the first years as part of a new nation were an exceptional period of growth and development. In East Texas the settlers of Spanish rule who had been driven from Nacogdoches during the turmoil of revolution returned to their homes, while hundreds of miles to the west, fellow Tejanos developed ranches and settlements in South Texas. Locating mostly in the area between, thousands from other nations, primarily the United States, encouraged by a generous Mexican immigration policy and sometimes bringing their African-American slaves, made their way into Texas. They cleared their lands, built roads, laid out new towns, and expanded older ones. A decree in 1830 slowed the stream of immigrants from the United States, but the more determined ones continued to make their way westward across the Sabine, and settlers from other nations added to their numbers.

THE EMPIRE OF MEXICO

Three hundred years of autocratic rule and eleven years of the war for independence combined to create a situation in which the leaders of Mexico would have a difficult time establishing a stable government. The army, conservative and fearful of popular rule, had made independence possible but remained suspicious of most civilian leaders. Conflicts erupted between monarchists and those who wanted to create a republic. There were anticlerics who wanted to break, or at least severely curtail, the power of the Catholic Church, but others defended the church and its privileges. There were liberals, there were conservatives, and there were federalists who wished to distribute political power among a pattern of states, and centralists who believed that stability and order demanded that power be exercised by a narrow elite.

Principles and ideas influenced the effort to create a strong and effective government, but other factors added to the problems. The final years of Spanish rule saw the establishment of a strong military tradition in Mexico, and within the army and various regional militias were a seemingly endless number of ambitious officers in search of power. Some were successful in winning control of portions of the country, assuming the role of military chieftains, or *caudillos,* who either attempted to control the entire nation or threatened the authority of the elected officials in their own particular region. From time to time, strong charismatic leaders emerged, but none could maintain authority over an extended period of time. Consequently, for many years, the Mexican people lived with frequent changes in government, sometimes based on principles and ideas but sometimes essentially a matter of personalities and power. Although the continuing conflicts affected all of Mexico, Texans, dependent on government immigration and slavery policies, were particularly sensitive to it.

Conservatism and monarchy won an early triumph. Appointed a temporary presiding officer, Agustín Iturbide manipulated people and events to create a monarchy patterned after that of the European nobility. With much pomp and ceremony he was named Agustín I, blessed by the Bishop of Guadalajara, and crowned emperor for life. In reality his power was based primarily on military support, and when that faded after only a few months, the empire would end.

THE OLD THREE HUNDRED

Immigration from the United States in significant numbers began during the empire of Iturbide. During the winter of 1821–22, the first settlers of Austin's colony arrived in Texas. The first was Andrew Robinson, who arrived at the Brazos in November 1821 and would eventually establish a ferry at the settlement of Washington on the Brazos. Two or three days later three more families joined the Robinsons, and soon there were others who located settlements near the site of present-day Independence. Not long afterward, Jared E. Groce, planter, lumberman, and capitalist of Alabama, arrived with his 50 wagons and 90 slaves and settled on the east side of the Brazos near the site of Hempstead. By March 1822, 50 people on the Brazos and 100 on the Colorado were building houses and planting corn.

Meanwhile, with the aid of his New Orleans partner, Joseph H. Hawkins, Austin had purchased the schooner *Lively* and had sent it to Texas with eighteen settlers and essential supplies. He returned to Texas in the fall of 1821 by way of Natchitoches and Nacogdoches in route to the mouth of the Colorado River; he expected to meet the *Lively* there, but it failed to show. Later he learned that it had mistakenly landed at the mouth of the Brazos and that most of the immigrants on board, discouraged by Austin's failure to meet them, had returned with the ship to New Orleans.

Despairing of making contact with the *Lively*, Austin went to San Antonio in March 1822 to report to the governor on his progress. There he learned of the success of the Mexican revolution. Governor Martínez, near the end of his power, informed him that the officials at Monterrey had refused to recognize Austin's authority to introduce settlers under his father's grant. The new government of the Mexican nation was considering a colonization policy for Texas and the Californias, and he was advised go to Mexico City to look after his interests. Austin, without delay, set out for Mexico City.

At the capital, where he arrived on April 29, 1822, Austin found a complex and unstable political situation and a number of Anglo-Americans seeking colonization grants. He set to work to secure the approval of his contract, but many weeks would pass before he would succeed. While Iturbide maneuvered first to acquire and then to consolidate power, Austin used his time to learn rudiments of the Spanish language and something about Mexican politics. He talked with many of Iturbide's officials about the possibility of a general colonization law that would open the way for the approval of his grant. Finally, his efforts were rewarded with the passage of the Imperial Colonization Law on January 4, 1823.

Iturbide's power began to decline, however, even as the colonization law was under consideration, and on March 19 he abdicated. But Austin's cause was not lost; the new leadership supported his petition. Congress, which Iturbide had abolished, was restored and soon approved a contract for Austin issued in accordance with the terms of the Imperial Colonization Law. The boundaries of the colony were not immediately defined, but in 1824 they were tentatively located for judicial purposes as extending from the seashore to the San Antonio-Nacogdoches Road and from the Lavaca River to the San Jacinto River. At the same time that Congress awarded Austin a contract, it also repealed the Imperial Colonization Law, thereby making Austin the only person to receive a grant under its terms.

It was not until early August 1823 that Austin, accompanied by Baron de Bastrop, the commissioner empowered to grant land titles, returned to the colony. Conditions were critical. A drought in 1822, hostile Indians in the area, and Austin's long absence had caused a number of people to return to the United States. The crisis ended, however, when Austin assured the colonists that his contract had been validated and Bastrop began issuing land titles.

The seat of government was established on the Brazos River at the Atascosito crossing and was christened San Felipe de Austin by the governor. By the close of the summer of 1824, Bastrop had issued 272 titles. Eventually there would be 297 families (including several single men who formed partnerships as "families" to secure a larger grant of land). The "Old Three Hundred," as these settlers came to be known, selected the rich plantation lands along the Brazos, Colorado, and Bernard rivers, from the vicinity of present-day Navasota, Brenham, and La Grange to the coast.

The terms of the Imperial Colonization Law were indeed generous. Each family was to receive one *labor* (177 acres) if engaged in farming, and a *sitio* (a square league or about 4,428 acres) for stock raising. Of course, most of the colonists preferred to be classed as stock raisers, and only about twenty titles called for less than a *sitio*. Special grants were made to a few men as compensation for substantial improvements such as mills. Jared E. Groce, the owner of many slaves, received ten *sitios*. Austin, as *empresario*, received about twenty-two. The law required that the land be occupied and improved within two years after the receipt of the deed, that colonists profess the Catholic religion, that for six years they be exempt from the payment of tithes and duties on imports, and that children of slaves born in the empire be freed at the age of fourteen.

THE REPUBLIC OF MEXICO

When the empire of Iturbide collapsed, there was general agreement that the new government to be created would be in the form of a republic. But there was not agreement as to the organization of the new republic. Some, primarily wealthy landowners (*hacendados*), army officers, and clergy, advocated a centralist form, while others, primarily *criollos* and *mestizos* of a liberal belief, favored a federalist form. Centralists argued that Mexico did not have the strength or experience necessary if power were to be divided between a central government and a number of states. Federalists insisted that centralism would lead to dictatorship and that only a division of power among a collection of communities and states and the national government could protect democracy.

The federalists in some respects won the argument with the writing of the Constitution of 1824. Mexico was divided into nineteen states and four

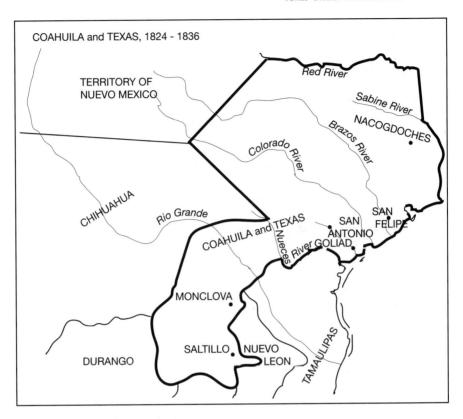

COAHUILA and TEXAS, 1824 - 1836

TERRITORY OF
NUEVO MEXICO

Red River

Sabine River

NACOGDOCHES

Brazos River

Colorado River

CHIHUAHUA

Rio Grande

COAHUILA and TEXAS

Nueces River

SAN
ANTONIO

SAN
FELIPE

GOLIAD

MONCLOVA

SALTILLO   NUEVO
LEON

DURANGO

TAMAULIPAS

Created by law to be one state, Coahuila and Texas eventually was made up of seven subareas, or departments, three of which—Béxar, Brazos, and Nacogdoches—were located in Texas. The dividing boundary between the portion of the state that was Coahuila and the portion that was Texas was never firmly established but usually was considered to be a line from a point on the Nueces River to points north and northwest and ultimately northeast to a position on the Red River near the ninety-eighth meridian. The Nueces separated the Texas portion of the state from the neighboring state of Tamaulipas.

territories. The authority of the central government was divided among three branches—the judicial, the executive, and the legislative—and in many other respects, the Constitution of 1824 resembled the Constitution of the United States. Indeed, the Constitution of 1824 promised democracy, but it also contained provisions that threatened tyranny. Particularly dangerous if abused—and it would be—was a clause giving the president extraordinary powers in the event of an emergency, authority that amounted to the power of a dictator. Liberals were also concerned about provisions in the constitution that gave special privileges to clergy and to military officials. A clause of the constitution established the Roman Catholic Church as the official church of the nation. With the election of the moderate and honest Guadalupe Victoria to be the first president, the new republic was off to a promising beginning, but before his term ended, there would be armed insurrection and turmoil.

Texans participated in the organization of the new republic and in the formation of the state governments. Erasmo Seguín was a member of the Constituent Congress that wrote the Constitution of 1824. By a federal act of May 7, 1824, the two old Spanish provinces of Coahuila and Texas were united as one state until the population of Texas should become large enough for the maintenance of a separate government. When the legislature for the state of Coahuila and Texas was organized in Saltillo on August 15, 1824, Baron de Bastrop represented Texas. Under the constitution for the state of Coahuila and Texas, Texas was allotted one of the twelve deputies that made up the legislature. This number eventually was increased to three. In 1825, Texas was made a department within the state of Coahuila and Texas, to be presided over by a political chief who was appointed by and responsible to the governor. This officer, actually a subgovernor, was to reside in Texas, maintain law and order, command the local militia, and make reports to the governor. Later, Texas was divided into three departments, with political chiefs in San Antonio, Nacogdoches, and San Felipe.

A New Colonization Program

One of the laws of Congress passed early in the life of the new republic was the National Colonization Law of August 18, 1824. By this act the government placed responsibility for colonization programs under the control of the Mexican states, with only a few reservations. The national law required that all state laws had to conform to the constitution then being framed, that, except by special approval, foreigners were not to settle within ten leagues of the coast or twenty leagues of the international boundary, and that no person should receive more than eleven *sitios*. Moreover, no alien should receive a land grant, and finally, "until after the year 1840, the general congress shall not prohibit the entrance of any foreigner, as a colonist, unless imperious circumstances should require it, with respect to individuals of a particular nation."

On March 24, 1825, the legislature of Coahuila and Texas passed the Coahuila-Texas Colonization Law. The law required immigrants to give satisfactory evidence of their Christian (Catholic) faith, morality, and good habits. Immigrants might receive titles to land individually or through an *empresario*. Each head of a family could receive, after the payment of a fee of $30, a *sitio* of land for $62.50 payable in three annual installments beginning at the end of the fourth year and had to cultivate or occupy the land within six years. For his services, an *empresario* was entitled to five *sitios* (approximately 22,140 acres) of grazing land and five *labors* (approximately 885 acres) of farming land for each 100 families, up to 800. *Empresario* contracts were to run six years and would be absolutely void if at least 100 families had not been settled before the expiration of that time. Native-born Mexicans might purchase, for small fees, as much as eleven *sitios*. There were to be no essential changes in the law for a period of six years. Colonists were exempted from general taxation for ten years and from payment of custom duties for seven years.

EXPANSION OF COLONIZATION

The adoption of the new colonization laws found many eager would-be *empresarios* prepared to apply for contracts. Moreover, Stephen Austin, who had largely fulfilled the terms of his "Old Three Hundred" contract, sought permission to bring in additional settlers. In 1825, he obtained a contract to settle an additional 500 families within the boundaries of his original grant. The "Little Colony," for which he contracted in 1827 to settle 100 families, was on the east side of the Colorado River, immediately above his original grant. Bastrop became its principal town. In 1828 Austin received permission to settle 300 additional families near the coast in the area between the Lavaca and San Jacinto rivers. Thus, by 1828 Austin had signed four contracts to settle in Texas a total of 1,200 families. By then the population of his colonies was increasing rapidly. It was 2,021 in March 1828 and 4,248 in June 1830. Tabulations after his death indicate that the *empresario* authorized a total of 1,540 grants to colonists.

In 1825, Green DeWitt, another Missourian, received a state contract to settle 400 families between the Lavaca River and a line near the Guadalupe River and south of San Antonio-Nacogdoches Road. Gonzales, the main town, was located that same year, but after an attack by Comanche Indians in July 1826, the people moved to the lower Lavaca. Their troubles did not end here, for they were within a prohibited zone and became involved in a quarrel with *Empresario* Martín de León. By the summer of 1828, they were back in Gonzales. At the expiration of his contract on April 15, 1831, 166 titles had been issued to settlers, but the greater part of DeWitt's grant was still vacant.

Martín de León, whose contract was unique, had fair success as a colonizer. A native of and a rancher in the Spanish province of Nuevo Santander, de León, soon after visiting Texas in 1805, moved his operation to the vicinity of San Patricio. In April 1824, after hearing of the Imperial Colonization Law, he obtained from authorities in San Antonio de Béxar a grant to settle an unspecified number of families near the coast and between the Lavaca and Guadalupe rivers. The settlers were predominantly Mexican. A dozen families arrived that fall, and in October de León laid out the town of Guadalupe Victoria on the banks of the Guadalupe. With the precise limits of the colony not defined, there was soon a quarrel between de León and his neighbor, Green DeWitt, in part because some of DeWitt's settlers located within de

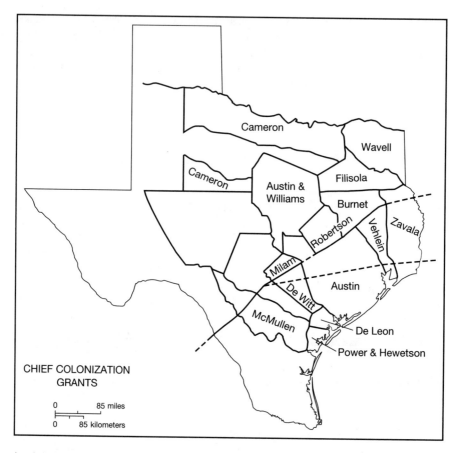

CHIEF COLONIZATION
GRANTS

0   85 miles

0   85 kilometers

Austin's contract called for 300 families under the Imperial Colonization Law of April 14, 1823. Three contracts under the state law, 1825, 1827, 1828, called for 900 additional families in the area of his first colony; and with Samuel W. Williams, he had a contract to settle 800 families north and west of his first colony. He loocated over 1,500 families.

On April 15, 1525, Green DeWitt received a contract for 400 families to be located on the Guadalupe, San Marcos, and Lavaca rivers. He issued 166 titles. The Nashville Company, known by the name of its agent, Sterling C. Robertson, as Robertson's colony, secured a contract for 800 families in 1825. After the revolution it was allowed premium lands for 379 families.

David Burnet, Lorenzo de Zavala, and Joseph Vehlein secured colonization rights in 1826 for territory on the eastern border of Texas between the twenty-ninth and thirty-third parallels. These rights were transferred to the Galveston Bay and Texas Land Company, which issued titles to over 916 leagues between September 1834 and December 1835.

On March 9, 1826, Arthur G. Wavell, an Englishman, secured a contract for 500 families to be located in northeast Texas. His associate, Benjamin R. Milam, located a number of families, but the United States contended that they were east of the boundary set by the treaty of 1819 with Spain, and the contractors never secured premium lands. Power and Hewetson granted almost 200 titles, McMullen and McGloin, granted 84. The Mexican *empresario*, de León, settled between 100 and 200 families

León's grant and in part because some of de León's settlers located within DeWitt's grant. Nevertheless, Victoria continued to prosper and grow, and by 1833 its population was over 200.

In addition to the concessions to Austin, DeWitt, and de León, the state of Coahuila and Texas made about twenty-two other contracts with *empresarios*, calling in all for about 8,000 families. The great majority of these *empresarios* located no families or only a negligible number. Others were more successful, but their colonists, almost without exception, came during a later period of colonization.

THE FREDONIAN REBELLION

One of the early *empresario* grants led to a clash between Mexican officials and certain Anglo-American colonists in Texas. The dispute had its beginning in 1825 when Haden Edwards secured an *empresario* grant that permitted him to locate colonists in a large area of eastern Texas. Within the boundaries of the grant were a number of settlers who had long been living on their lands, some for several generations. Edwards made an arbitrary ruling that all claimants must prove title or else pay him for their lands. This ruling alarmed and angered the settlers. Austin's advice to Edwards not to antagonize Mexican officials went unheeded, and Edwards's enemies took their cause to higher officials. In response, on June 3, 1826, the president of Mexico ordered that Edwards be expelled, but it was not until October 20 that state officials delivered the order canceling Haden Edwards's contract and instructing him to leave the country.

On December 16, 1826, Benjamin Edwards, the brother of Haden, rode into Nacogdoches with a small number of armed men and proclaimed the Republic of Fredonia. But Edwards could not find any support among the Anglo-Americans and Cherokee Indians in the area. Upon the approach of troops from San Antonio and militia from Austin's colony, the insurgents abandoned Nacogdoches and on January 31, 1827, crossed the Sabine into the United States. The rebellion was over, but it had a serious impact on Mexican sentiment. Mexican officials concluded that the Fredonians had intended to add Texas to the United States and became increasingly suspicious of all Anglo-Americans.

THE LAW OF APRIL 6, 1830

Suspicions aroused by the Fredonian Rebellion and the very success of the colonization movement in Texas all but destroyed it. In 1828, General Manuel Mier y Terán, soldier, scholar, and statesman, was sent to survey the eastern boundary as defined in the Adams-Onís Treaty and to investigate the need for new military posts in Texas. His report, however, went far beyond these matters, for it presented a detailed description of conditions in Texas and recommendations for policy changes. What Terán saw in Texas alarmed him. He reported that Mexican influence diminished rapidly as he proceeded eastward. In Nacogdoches, the Mexican population was poor and small in number compared with the Anglo-Americans. The Anglo-Americans included slaveholders, honest laborers, criminals, and vagabonds and were taking over the country. At Nacogdoches they maintained an English school; they were progressive but shrewd and unruly and demanding. Mexico, Terán concluded, must act "now" or Texas "is lost forever." Terán proposed that the Mexican government should (1) colonize Mexicans in Texas, (2) colonize Swiss and Germans, (3) encourage coastal trade between Texas and the rest of the republic, and (4) place more troops in Texas, among them convict-soldiers who would become permanent settlers after their sentences had expired.

Although Terán began his reports as early as June and July 1828, political upheaval in Mexico City delayed action on his recommendations for almost two years. In September 1828, Gómez Pedraza, a conservative, was elected president, but a military uprising instigated by his opponent, Vicente Guerrero, prevented him from taking office. In the spring of 1829, Guerrero, a federalist, assumed the presidency and the authority to exercise dictatorial powers that Congress had given him. Although Guerrero's rise to power was hardly in the tradition of true democracy, he remained faithful to some liberal ideals, and on September 15, 1829, issued a proclamation ending slavery throughout the nation. The decree aroused little attention elsewhere in Mexico, but Texans protested vigorously and soon were excluded from its restrictions, perhaps because of the intervention of Mexican leaders in San Antonio. Shortly thereafter, a centralist coup d'etat deposed Guerrero and replaced him with Anastacio Bustamante. Bustamante posed as a defender of constitutional rule, but in reality his administration marked the return of conservatives to power and a move in the direction of military dictatorship.

Bustamante's government took steps to check Anglo-American influence in Texas. Lucas Alamán, minister of foreign relations and a long-standing opponent of immigration from the United States, urged Congress to adopt Terán's proposals and to go beyond them with article 11 in the proposed law, a part of which read: "Citizens of foreign countries lying adjacent to the Mexican territory are prohibited from settling as colonists in the states or territories of the Republic adjoining such countries." In other words, no more immigrants from the United States could settle in Texas. The article furthermore suspended "all contracts not already completed and not in harmony with the law," and provided for the establishment of military posts by convict soldiers, for the settlement around these posts by the families of the soldiers and other Mexican colonists, and for the strict prohibition of any further introduction of slaves.

To the Mexican government, the law was a reasonal
emergency; to the colonists it seemed nothing less than a
succeeded in fending off the blow slightly, insofar as his c
DeWitt were concerned, by an ingenious interpretation tha
to complete their quota of families without respect to the la\ ___, ᴜ.ᴄ population of Austin's settlements increased from 4,248 in June 1830 to 5,665 a
year later. DeWitt's contract and one of Austin's soon expired by limitation,
however; Austin's other contracts were soon filled, and in November 1831,
Austin had to admit that immigration of Anglo-Americans was totally prohibited. He and his secretary, Samuel M. Williams, then secured a grant to
settle European and Mexican families, but in this they did not succeed.
Meanwhile, Austin and others continued to exert considerable pressure in
an effort to secure the repeal of the Law of April 6, 1830.

COLONIZATION UNDER THE LAW
OF APRIL 6, 1830

Although the Law of April 6, 1830, slowed the pace of immigration into
Texas, it did not stop it. Immigrants who were not citizens of the United
States were not barred by the law. In some instances, the law was simply disregarded or ignored; in other instances, efforts were made to evade its
restrictions. On October 16, 1830, Lorenzo de Zavala, Joseph Vehlein, and
David G. Burnet pooled their extensive grants in eastern Texas and assigned
them to the Galveston Bay and Texas Land Company, a New York City-
based organization. Although the company did not own any land and did
not have the right to sell any, it advertised in a fashion similar to that used
later by western railroad companies. It sublet huge blocks to subordinate
contractors, and it sold scrip, representing nearly 7.5 million acres at prices
of one to ten cents an acre, to prospective settlers and speculators, many of
whom evidently believed that they were buying land. The company soon
sent two groups of emigrants to Texas, but authorities would not allow them
to locate lands or to settle. Eventually, however, Mexican officials recognized
the company and allowed settlers to claim some lands. Between September
1834 and December 1835, a stream of immigrants received a total of 936 titles
to land in the area north of Galveston Bay.

Another large contract involved the lands generally known as the
Robertson Colony. This contract, first issued in 1825 through Robert Left-
wich to the Texas Association of Nashville, controlled a huge block of land
north and northwest of Austin's original grant and contained the right to
settle 800 families. For various reasons, the company agent, Sterling C.
Robertson, made very little progress toward settlement of the colony before
the passage of the Law of April 6, 1830. In 1831, the territory was granted to

ustin and his partner, Samuel M. Williams, who proposed to settle on it 800 Mexican and European families. Robertson vigorously resisted the cancellation of his contract and its transferal to Austin and Williams. A legal and political conflict began that would not be resolved for decades. The governor, after examining Robertson's claim of having settled more than 100 families before the enactment of the Law of April 6, 1830, restored the colony to the Nashville Company (Robertson's group), but Austin and Williams regained the colony in May of the following year. By the time the revolution closed the land offices, more than 600 families had located in the colony, and the towns of Nashville, Viesca, and Salado had been founded. In 1847, after Robertson's death, a Texas court ruled that his claim to the colony was valid and awarded his heirs premium land for 379 families.

Meanwhile, two Irish colonies, McMullen and McGloin and Power and Hewetson, were located in southern Texas. In August 1828, John McMullen and his son-in-law, James McGloin, both natives of Ireland but at the time merchants in Matamoros, Mexico, obtained a state contract to settle 200 Irish families in a portion of the territory east of the Nueces River and immediately above the coastal reserve. The first group to arrive, 58 in late 1829, remained for a time at the Refugio mission but in October 1831 established Hibernia, or San Patricio, the colony's principal town. The contract was voided by the Law of April 6, 1830, but in 1834 it was extended, and by the outbreak of the Texas Revolution, eighty-four land titles had been issued.

Although beset by misfortune, the other Irish colony was more successful. James Power, a native of Ireland, was engaged in business and mining in Mexico. James Hewetson, also a native of Ireland, settled in Saltillo and Monclova. In 1828, by special permission of both the national and the Coahuila-Texas governments, Power and Hewetson obtained a contract to settle 200 families from Mexico and Ireland in the area near the coast and between the Nueces and Guadalupe rivers. Power went to Ireland and in 1834 sailed for Texas with 350 immigrants, but en route they contracted cholera. The survivors were forced to abandon their ship, losing all their supplies on the coast. Refugio, on the site of the old mission by that name, became their central town, and by the time of the Texas Revolution, almost 200 land titles had been granted, many apparently to Anglo-Americans.

A third attempt to establish a colony of Europeans was a complete failure. John Charles Beales, a surgeon from England, and James Grant, a physician from Scotland, contracted in 1832 to settle 800 European families in the region between the Rio Grande and the Nueces River. The first colonists, including English, Germans, Mexicans, and Anglo-Americans, located the settlement of Dolores on Las Moras Creek near present-day Brackettville in March 1834. Another group of colonists came later, but crop failure, Indian hostility, and military campaigns of the Texas Revolution resulted in the abandonment of the colony.

One of the more unusual efforts to secure an *empresario* grant was that of Benjamin Lundy. Lundy, who spent practically all his life as an abolitionist in the struggle against slavery, believed that Texas was an ideal location for a colony of free blacks and spent much of the years between 1832 and 1835 in Mexico in search of a grant. Anglo-Americans in Texas strongly opposed the scheme, and the officials of Coahuila and Texas were inconsistent, sometimes encouraging but often not. Ultimately, Lundy secured a grant, not in Coahuila and Texas but in neighboring Tamaulipas (formerly Nuevo Santander) in the area between the Nueces and the Rio Grande. However, the grant was awarded just before the outbreak of the Texas Revolution, and Lundy, with little in the way of resources anyway, was never able to bring in any settlers. The primary consequence of these efforts, in fact, was probably the reinforcement of Lundy's critical attitudes concerning Texans and their dedication to the cause of slavery.

THE PEOPLE OF MEXICAN TEXAS

In 1834, the Mexican soldier and statesman Juan N. Almonte, after a visit to Texas, placed the population at 21,000, including slaves. Censuses taken between 1831 and 1833 suggest that the Tejano population, not including military personnel, was slightly over 4,000. Some believe that the total population may have been as much as 30,000, but if Almonte's overall estimate is correct, the population was divided thus into approximately 15,000 Anglo, 4,000 Tejano, and 2,000 slaves.

The change in the total number of Tejano people living in Texas during Mexican rule had been relatively small. However, predominantly Tejano communities had changed considerably. San Antonio declined in population, while others gained. Tejanos in the Nacogdoches area rose from slightly more than a hundred in 1823 to more than 600 in 1834. Goliad (La Bahía) and Victoria grew from about 500 to almost 2,000, and a number of Tejanos founded prosperous ranches in the area south of San Antonio.

Immigrants from the United States, however, accounted for most of the population growth during this period. The generous land policies of Mexican Texas, which attracted settlers from outside Mexico, ended legally with the closing of the land offices in November 1835. On this eve of revolution, an overwhelming majority of the immigrants were located east of the Guadalupe and south of the old road from San Antonio to Nacogdoches. Altogether, these settlers held about 3,500 land titles issued through the different *empresarios*, and there were a few who received grants directly from the Mexican government.

Who were these people? Whence had they come and what were the forces that brought them? The available evidence indicates that they were, in the main, farmers and people of some means, although many had left behind them debts they could not pay. The small amount of crime committed suggests that they were honest and law-abiding. Literacy, for that time, was high. Of more than 266 of Austin's "Old Three Hundred," only four could not write.

A surprising number of these immigrants were women. Most came in the company of their husbands and families, but some braved the dangers and hardships of the frontier alone. Austin's colonies in 1830 reported twenty widows, most of whom were responsible for the welfare of a number of children. No doubt, some of these women were widowed after their arrival in Texas, but sometimes widows and their children made their way into Texas to claim land and begin a new life.

Most Anglo-American settlers immigrated from southern states. Data kept by Austin for his colony show that the majority of his people came from Louisiana, Alabama, Arkansas, Tennessee, or Missouri, in the order named. A total of 699 registered from the trans-Appalachian states, as compared with a total of 107 from the Atlantic Seaboard. However, most adults living west of the mountains at that time had been born in the seaboard states.

Slaves made up a significant portion of the population (approximately 10 percent), despite repeated efforts in Mexican law and policy to discourage the institution. The Imperial Colonization Law recognized slavery but forbade the slave trade and declared that slaves born in the empire should be free at the age of fourteen. The Coahuila-Texas constitution of 1827 recognized existing slavery and permitted the introduction of slaves for six months after its promulgation, but no person born thereafter could be a slave. Meanwhile, the Mexican government legalized the domestic slave trade by providing that a slave might "change" his or her master "if the new master would indemnify the old," and a state law of 1828 for all practical purposes legalized slave importation by recognizing labor "contracts made in foreign countries." Afterward, upon entering Texas, most blacks were nominally servants under contract, but actually they were still slaves. After Guerrero's decree of 1829 abolishing slavery was nullified with respect to Texas, the Law of April 6, 1830 recognized existing slavery but prohibited the further introduction of slaves. An act of the state legislature in 1832 strengthened antislavery laws and limited to ten years the contracts with slaves and day laborers. Thus, by 1832, the introduction of slaves was positively barred, and peonage contracts were limited to ten years.

Although many slaves had been brought to Texas, their ratio to the free population declined in the later colonial years. In 1825, Austin's colony had 443 slaves and 1,347 free people. In 1834, Juan Almonte estimated the number of slaves in the Department of the Brazos (composed of Austin's colonies) as 1,000, out of a total population of about 10,000. No doubt, the uncertain status of the institution frequently caused anxiety and may have frightened away many prospective immigrants who were slaveholders.

These figures tell something about slavery in colonial Texas, but the description of a slave girl's trip to Texas is perhaps more meaningful. As she later told the story, on her journey from New Orleans to Texas with a group of slaves, their owners "chained us together and marched us up near La Grange. . . . That was an awful time.... If one drank out of the stream, we all drank; when one got tired or sick, the rest had to drag and carry him." All slaves were black people and most were located in the fertile valleys of the Trinity, Brazos, and Colorado rivers.

Not all black people were slaves, however. About 150 free blacks lived in Texas during the time of Mexican rule and under Mexican law enjoyed full legal and political rights. Many, such as the Ashworth family who settled in the lower valley of the Neches, were immigrants from Louisiana, and most were relatively poor farmers or laborers. However, William Goyens of Nacogdoches was an enterprising businessman with interests in a freight line, a sawmill and a gristmill, and an inn.

Slaves came to Texas because they had little choice in the matter, but the forces that brought free people were varied and complex. They came to be with relatives and friends, to escape conflicts with the law or with some individual, to drown their sorrows, to regain their health, or to satisfy their curiosity. They came because of the panic of 1819 and financial adversity. But above all, they came in search of land. Some wanted virgin soil to replace their eroded and worn-out farms, but the overwhelming majority came to get free or cheap land. Although there was an abundance of land in the public domain of the United States, a person could buy no less than 80 acres and was required to pay $1.25 per acre in cash. By comparison, in Texas the head of a family could obtain 4,428 acres of land in Austin's colony for only little more than the cost of 80 acres in the United States. The actual price varied from time to time and from place to place, but it would be fair to state that during the period of Mexican rule a *sitio* (4,428 acres) of land cost less than $150 (including fees), payable over a period of time.

GOVERNMENT IN MEXICAN TEXAS

During most of the period of Mexican rule, San Antonio, where Tejanos composed most of the leadership and were familiar with public issues and Mexican traditions, was the most influential settlement in state and national political affairs. In matters such as taxation, regulation of trade, slavery, and immigration restrictions, these leaders ordinarily defended the position of Texans. Tejanos such as José Antonio Navarro and government officials such as political chief Ramón Músquiz received sympathetic hearings when they took their causes to the state capital of Saltillo. There, the powerful brothers, José and Agustín Viesca, were effective advocates for the liberal faction in state politics and their support of economic development usually was reflected by their support for Texan interests.

Local government, however, was a peculiar mixture of Mexican institutions and Anglo-American practices. The majority of the settlers in Mexican Texas were immigrants from the United States living in a country whose government, religion, customs, and attitudes differed greatly from those they had known before. These settlers often modified Mexican institutions to conform to Anglo-American patterns, and Mexican officials seldom intervened in local affairs where Anglo-American settlers made up the majority of the population.

The most important unit of local government was the municipality, which included one or more towns and adjacent territory. It might cover thousands of square miles. The *ayuntamiento*, or governing body of the municipality, had broad duties that suggest the combined functions of a modern city commission and a county commissioner's court. At its head was an *alcalde*, the chief executive officer, whose duties were similar to those of sheriff, judge, and mayor of a city. The *regidores*, like members of our own city commissions, had certain legislative powers as well as some administrative responsibilities.

Local self-government for settlements founded by newly arrived immigrants began early when by order of the governor in November 1822,

Stephen F. Austin. He was the most successful colonizer of the state and sometimes called the "Father of Texas." (Archives—Texas State Library

Austin's first colonists elected *alcaldes*. By 1828, the municipalities of Texas included Béxar, La Bahía or Goliad, Nacogdoches, and San Felipe, and by 1834, there were a total of thirteen. Municipal taxes were light and payable largely in kind, and for a number of years, colonists were exempted from state taxes, church tithes, and national customs duties.

There were many local laws but often little enforcement, primarily because the court system was inadequate. Fortunately, there was very little crime in the colonies, and most offenders seem to have been dealt with outside the courts. Austin drove a number of undesirables from his colony; the *ayuntamientos* compelled some to leave; and occasionally the people persuaded others to move elsewhere. An act passed in 1834 provided for jury trials in both civil and criminal cases and for an appellate circuit court for Texas, but it never went into effect.

The *empresario* system was fitted into this pattern of government. The duties of the *empresario* were numerous and trying. He had to deal not only with state and national governments that were sometimes unsympathetic but also with pioneers who sometimes were prejudiced, stubborn, and disposed to find fault with those in authority. Austin's burden was much greater than that of his fellow proprietors, for his colony was seven years old before regular constitutional government was established. He was responsible

Also shown, a replica of his home near Sealy. (Courtesy of the Texas Department of Transportation)

for selecting his colonists and assuring their good character, and—although Bastrop, his land commissioner, actually issued the titles—for surveying the land and all business connected with obtaining and recording titles. At first, Austin was responsible for the government of the colony. Indeed, he was a lawgiver, for he wrote civil and criminal codes for the *alcaldes*, based on the Mexican laws but adapted to conditions in the colonies. He was commander in chief of the militia and responsible for defense and the maintenance of satisfactory relations with the Indians.

In addition, he had many informal obligations even more burdensome than those required by law. Prospective colonists expected entertainment at his home, and frequently he was called on to settle petty disputes. Many persons regarded him as a collecting agent; others expected him to make purchases and loans for them. With the establishment of constitutional government in 1828, the greater part of Austin's governmental responsibilities ceased, but there was no letup of the informal ones.

The possibility of conflict with hostile Indians added to the anxieties of settlers in many areas. The Karankawas on the coast were always a threat. In the interior the Tonkawas were generally at peace, but along the Brazos River above the San Antonio Road, the Wacos and Tawakonis were periodically dangerous and always troublesome. In eastern Texas a few hundred Cherokees and Choctaws from east of the Mississippi and some smaller bands kept the colonists on the alert.

To defend against the Indians the colonists relied mainly on their own resources. During Spanish rule, the practice of organizing what was equivalent to mounted cavalry militia was begun and used with some success. The practice continued under Mexican rule. In Austin's first colony the militia was first organized in 1822. From time to time new districts were created, until by the close of 1824, six companies had been organized. By 1830, life in Austin's colonies was safer, but Béxar, Gonzales, and Goliad did not fare as well. In 1830, DeWitt wrote the governor that unless troops were sent to his colony, his settlements would be broken up. The settlers managed to hold out, although the fifteen troops and a six-pound cannon sent the following year offered little help.

COLONIAL INSTITUTIONS

In Texas, as in other societies, religion was an important institution. By constitution and law, Roman Catholicism was the religion of Mexico, to the exclusion of any other. The Catholic faith was supposed to accompany Mexican citizenship, and heretics were subject to banishment and other punishment. At least some clergy, however, seem to have been more interested in acquiring wealth than in matters spiritual. The priest of the parish of Béxar in the 1820s, a very wealthy man, was a large land and livestock owner who was constantly involved in political intrigue and who rarely comforted the afflicted.

Although Austin informed prospective colonists of the requirement of the Catholic faith, he emphasized it less and less as his colony grew, and other proprietors apparently took much the same attitude. In fact, very few of the colonists were Catholics by faith, and not many were so even by name.

Like their Tejano neighbors, the immigrants had more cause to complain of spiritual neglect and an indifferent public than of intolerance or persecution. Repeatedly, Austin petitioned the authorities to send a priest to his colony to christen children, legalize marriage contracts, and perform various other services that were expected in a Catholic country. Finally, in 1831 Father Michael Muldoon, an Irish priest, arrived. He was good-natured, loyal, and kind, but he did not always live up to traditional standards of piety for the ministry. Most of the settlers apparently had little interest in formal religion anyway. One observer, while praising the small amount of crime in Texas, added that, when it came to abiding by the spirit of the gospel, conditions were "bad—bad! superlatively bad."

In spite of official opposition and the indifference of the colonists, the Protestants made progress in colonial Texas. As early as 1820, Joseph E. Bays, a Baptist minister, was preaching in Texas. William Stevenson, a Methodist, continued to preach despite warnings from Austin and others. Other missionaries came, and after the colonists drove out the Mexican garrisons in 1832, Protestant camp meetings became common. A few churches were organized during this period. Presbyterians taught Sunday school in San Felipe, and John and Maria Kenney and Lydia Ann McHenry worked together to establish a Methodist church at New Caney in 1834. That same year, a state law, in violation of the constitution, afforded a measure of religious tolerance. It stated that no person should be molested on account of his or her religious or political opinions, provided he or she did not disturb the public order.

Although the constitution of Coahuila and Texas required the establishment of schools in each town, there was no system of public education in colonial Texas. A public school was established in San Antonio as early as 1746, and shortly after 1813 the Spaniards erected a building there to provide for seventy pupils. But when Colonel Almonte visited in 1834, he reported that the school in San Antonio had been discontinued, although there were schools in Nacogdoches, San Augustine, and Jonesborough. A small private school in Austin's colony was taught as early as 1833; Frances Trask opened a boarding school for girls on the site of Independence in 1834, and there were schools held for brief periods elsewhere. Education on a limited scale seems to have been available for both boys and girls, although there were apparently more men teachers than women.

Most Texans were farmers, but trade and commerce was an important part of the colonial economy. In an effort to prevent smuggling, the government enacted a number of regulations, including one that attempted to make Galveston the only port. Merchants, especially those of San Antonio, protested, and the government relented. By 1832, Brazoria was perhaps the leading shipping town, but soon it shared some of its trade with the new town of Matagorda at the mouth of the Colorado. Galveston remained uninhabited during most of the colonial era. Nacogdoches, which had only thirty-six inhabitants in 1821, grew into a business center with stores well supplied with dry goods, notions, and foodstuffs.

Inadequate ports constituted a great handicap to shipping. Galveston was not convenient to the principal settlements. Even small vessels had to be partly unloaded to cross a great sandbar in order to reach Brazoria and other points on the lower Brazos. Likewise, Matagorda Bay had its perils, and small schooners had difficulty in reaching either the mouth of the Lavaca or the town of Matagorda at the mouth of the Colorado. Even after products were unloaded from shipboard, the absence of or poor condition of roads and the lack of other means of transportation made the delivery of goods difficult and slow.

The lack of money or banking facilities also hampered business and often led to an economy based on barter. The account of George B. Erath, an Austrian-American, is typical. Erath traded clothes that he had brought from Germany for cattle and hogs, and he traded a horse for corn. His partner gave an ox for a sow valued at $5, a feather bed for three cows and calves, a gun for a mare, and another gun for a cow, calf, and yearling.

Save for small quantities of salt, some horses, and occasional illicit purchases of tobacco, there seems to have been virtually no trade between Texas and the rest of Mexico. In 1821, on his first visit to Texas, Stephen F. Austin found a good trade already established between Natchitoches, Louisiana, and Goliad. Although Natchitoches continued to be a favorite trading post of Texans and most shipments into the colonies by land originated there, trade by sea with New Orleans increased throughout the period.

This pattern of trade had significant consequences. The imports supplied most colonials with necessities and a few—a very few—with luxuries. Of great political importance is the fact that these imported goods—almost wholly from the United States—kept alive the interest of the Anglo-Texans in the land of their birth.

BIBLIOGRAPHY

Materials on Texas under Mexican rule tend to emphasize Anglo-American colonization efforts and are comparatively abundant, although many accounts were written long ago. Of the older works, the best is H. Yoakum, *History of Texas* (New York, 1855). His text, along with some supplementary material, is reproduced in Dudley G. Wooten, *A Comprehensive History of Texas* (two vols., Dallas, 1897). Other general accounts are William Kennedy, *Texas* (2d ed., London, 1841; Fort Worth, 1925); H. H.

Bancroft, *History of the North Mexican States and Texas* (two vols., San Francisco, 1884 and 1889); John Henry Brown, *A History of Texas, 1685–1892* (two vols., St. Louis, 1892–1893); Louis J. Wortham, *A History of Texas* (five vols., Fort Worth, 1924); Clarence R. Wharton, *Texas under Many Flags* (five vols., Chicago and New York, 1930); and H. S. Thrall, *Pictorial History of Texas* (St. Louis, 1879).

Rich collections of source materials are E. C. Barker (ed.), *The Austin Papers* (three vols.); vols. I and II were published as *The Annual Report of the American Historical Association*, 1919 and 1922 (Washington, D.C., 1924 and 1928); vol. III (Austin, 1926); Malcolm D. McLean (ed.), *Papers Concerning Robertson's Colony in Texas* (nineteen vols., Fort Worth and Arlington, 1974–1993); E. Wallace, D. M. Vigness, and George Ward (eds.), *Documents of Texas History* (Austin, 1993); and Juan N. Almonte, "Statistical Report on Texas, 1835" (trans. C. E. Castañeda), *Southwestern Historical Quarterly*, XXVIII, 177–222.

Andrés Tijerina, *Tejanos and Texas Under the Mexican Flag, 1821–1836* (College Station, 1994), is a valuable addition to the literature on Mexican Texas, calling attention to the role of those other than Anglo-Americans. Helen Simons and Cathryn A. Hoyt, *Hispanic Texas: A Historical Guide* (Austin, 1992), lists materials dealing with this era. David J. Weber, *The Mexican Frontier, 1821–1846: The American Southwest Under Mexico* (Albuquerque, 1982), is a general study but contains much information on events in Texas.

A recently published biography of Stephen Austin written by Gregg Cantrell, *Stephen F. Austin: Empresario of Texas* (New Haven, Conn.: 1999), is a superb work and will likely remain the standard biography of the colonizer for many years. But readers may wish also to consult older scholarly studies by E. C. Barker, such as *The Life of Stephen F. Austin* (Nashville and Dallas, 1925), and *Mexico and Texas, 1821–1835* (Dallas, 1928), as well as the works of David B. Gracy, II, *Moses Austin: His Life* (San Antonio, 1987); and D. M. Vigness, *The Revolutionary Decades* (Austin, 1965).

Articles on colonies and colonists can be found in the *Quarterly of the Texas State Historical Association* (I–XV) and the *Southwestern Historical Quarterly*. Among them are "Journal of Stephen F. Austin on His First Trip to Texas, 1821," VII, 286–307; W. S. Lewis, "Adventures of the *Lively* Immigrants," III, 1–32; L. G. Bugbee, "What Became of the *Lively*?" III, 141–148; L. G. Bugbee, "The Old Three Hundred," I, 108–117; E. C. Barker, "Notes on the Colonization of Texas," XXVII, 108–119; Mary Virginia Henderson, "Minor Empresario Contracts for the Colonization of Texas, 1825–1834," XXXI, 295–324; XXXII, 1–28; Robert W. Amsler, "General Arthur G. Wavell: A Soldier of Fortune in Texas," LXIX, 1–21, 186–209; Andrew Forest Muir, "Humphrey Jackson, Alcalde of San Jacinto," LXVIII, 362–366; Charles A. Bacarisse, "The Union of Coahuila and Texas," LXI, 341–349; Henry W. Barton, "The Anglo-American Colonists under Mexican Militia Laws," LXV, 61–71; Roger N. Conger, "The Tomás de la Vega Eleven-League Grant on the Brazos," LXI, 371–382; Joseph W. McKnight, "Stephen Austin's Legalistic Concerns," LXXXIX, 239–268; John Wheat and Jesús de la Teja, "Béxar: Profile of a Tejano Community, 1820–1832," LXXXIX, 7–34; Fane Downs, "'Tryels and Trubbles': Women in Early Nineteenth-Century Texas," XC, 35–56; Nettie Lee Benson, "Texas as Viewed from Mexico, 1820–1834," XC, 219–291; Robert S. Martin, "Maps of an Empresario: Austin's Contribution to the Cartography of Texas," LXXXV, 381–400; W. H. Timmons, "The El Paso Area in the Mexican Period, 1821–1848," LXXXIX, 1–28; and Graham Davis, "Models of Migration: The Historiography of the Irish Pioneers in South Texas," C, 187-204. For the decree of April 6, 1830, see Ohland Morton, *Terán and Texas* (Austin, 1948), and Jack Jackson (ed.), *Texas by Terán: The Diary Kept by General Manuel de Mier y Terán on His 1828 Inspection of Texas* (trans. by John Wheat; Austin, 2000).

R. W. Strickland, "Miller County, Arkansas Territory, the Frontier That Men Forget," *Chronicles of Oklahoma*, XVIII, 12–34, 154–170; XIX, 37–54, is a careful study of the settlement of extreme northeast Texas. Excellent works on the colonies in southern Texas include W. H. Oberste's comprehensive *Texas Irish Empresarios and Their Colonies* (Austin, 1953); Leroy P. Graf, "Colonizing Projects in Texas South of the Nueces, 1820–1845," *Southwestern Historical Quarterly*, L, 431–448; Carl Coke Rister, *Comanche Bondage* (Glendale, Calif., 1955), about Beale's colony; and A. B .J. Hammett, *The Empresario Don Martín de León: The Richest Man in Texas* (Victoria, 1971). Margaret Henson's *Samuel May Williams: Early Texas Entrepreneur* (College Station, 1976) is a scholarly study of one of the more controversial figures of the period.

On colonial institutions, see Andrés Tijerina, *Tejanos and Texas Under the Mexican Flag, 1821–1836* (College Station, 1994), particularly with respect to matters of government. Also, see the following articles in the *Southwestern Historical Quarterly*: E. C. Barker, "The Government of Austin's Colony, 1821–1831," XXI, 223–252, supplemented by the "Minutes of the *Ayuntamiento of San Felipe de Austin*, 1828–1832," XXI, 299–326, 395–423; XXII, 78–95, 180–196, 272–278, 353–359; XXIII, 69–77, 141–151, 214–223, 302–307; XXIV, 81–83, 154–166. E. C. Barker, "The Influence of Slavery in the Colonization of Texas," *Southwestern Historical Quarterly*, XXVIII, 1–33, presents an interesting evaluation of that institution's role during the Mexican Republic. Valentine J. Belfiglio, "The Indian Policy of Stephen F. Austin," *East Texas Historical Journal*, XXXII, 15–22, is a useful summary of Austin's views and actions concerning Indians; J. H. Kuykendall, a colonist, gathered a series of valuable reminiscences of colonists; they are printed in the *Quarterly of the Texas State Historical Association* VI, 236–253, 311–330 and VII, 29–64; others, somewhat similar, are found in V, 12–18; XIII, 44–80; XIV, 24–73. Worthy of special mention are *Travel and Adventures in Texas in the 1820's: Being the Reminiscences of Mary Crownover Rabb* (Waco, 1962); and "Reminiscences of Mrs. Dilue Harris," *Quarterly of the Texas State Historical Association*, IV, 85–127, 155–189, 387, written in part from a journal kept by Mrs. Harris's father, Dr. Pleasant W. Rose. Noah Smithwick, *The Evolution of a State* (Austin, 1900, reprinted 1995), written when the author was ninety years old, is rich in detail but should be used with care. The best descriptive book of Texas written by a contemporary is Mary Austin Holley, *Texas* (Baltimore, 1833; Lexington, Ky., 1836). Mrs. Holley's text is included in M. A. Hatcher, *Letters of an Early American Traveller: Mary Austin Holley. Her Life Works, 1784–1846* (Dallas, 1933). For another biography of this remarkable observer of the Texas scene, see Rebecca Smith Lee, *Mary Austin Holley: A Biography* (Austin, 1962). Gerald E. Poyo and Gilberto M. Hinojosa (eds.), *Tejano Origins in Eighteenth-Century San Antonio* (Austin, 1991) contains some information on later years. Religion in early Texas is discussed in W. S. Red, *The Texas Colonists and Religion, 1821–1836* (Austin, 1924), and Howard Miller, "Stephen F. Austin and the Anglo-Texas Response to the Religious Establishment in Mexico, 1821–1836," *Southwestern Historical Quarterly*, XCI, 283–316.

5

The Prelude to Revolution 1826–1835

"This is the most liberal and munificent Govt. on earth to emigra[n]ts-after being here one year you will oppose a change even to Uncle Sam—." Thus wrote Stephen F. Austin in 1829 to his sister and brother-in-law. As late as 1832, to his partner and boon companion, Samuel M. Williams, he wrote: "My standing motto—'Fidelity to Mexico'—ought to be in every man's mouth and repeated. . . ." Yet three years later, Austin, the most loyal of all of Mexico's adopted sons, was leading troops in rebellion against that government. This reversal in sentiment did not take place in one week, or even in one year, but was the consequence of a long chain of developments that led from fidelity through alienation to rebellion.

EARLY TROUBLES

Although conditions for immigration to Texas remained favorable for several more years, problems appeared early in the period of Mexican rule. The Fredonian rebellion had little support among immigrants from the United States, but Mexican officials were nonetheless more suspicious after the affair. Many Mexican officials linked inseparably the Fredonian affair with the effort of the United States to acquire, by purchase or otherwise, all or part of Texas. In 1825, President John Quincy Adams, who had often asserted that the Louisiana Purchase extended to the Rio Grande, inaugurated efforts to obtain for the United States a "more suitable" boundary. Joel R. Poinsett, envoy to Mexico, was authorized to offer $1 million for the removal of the line to the Rio Grande. President Andrew Jackson raised Adams's offer to $5 million and continued the effort through Poinsett and Poinsett's successor, Anthony Butler. The only result was to aggravate Mexican suspicions concerning both the United States and the Anglo-American colonists.

In turn, a feeling of anxiety and suspicion was aroused among the colonists of Texas when on September 15, 1829, President Guerrero proclaimed the emancipation of slaves. Upon receipt of the decree, Ramón Músquiz, political chief at San Antonio, petitioned and obtained an exemption for Texas, but the colonists nevertheless were left with a feeling that the future of slavery was uncertain.

THE DISTURBANCES OF 1831 AND 1832

Greater than the Fredonian rebellion, efforts of the United States to purchase Texas, or the emancipation proclamation in promoting ill feeling was the Law of April 6, 1830. It will be recalled that this law prohibited further colonization by people from the United States and provided for the collection of customs duties and for the garrisoning of troops in Texas. Lucas Alamán, who drafted the bill, feared that when the Americans became a preponderant majority, they first would petition for changes or reforms, then create disturbances, and finally, by violence or diplomacy, take possession of the province. The law caused exactly what Alamán had hoped to prevent by it; out of it grew the chain of events that led from disturbances and petitions to rebellion and independence.

Although the provision of the Law of April 6, 1830, that halted immigration from the United States caused much anxiety and unrest, the disturbances on the coast in 1831 and 1832 were actually the product of several complex issues. Colonists, who had been exempt from most Mexican custom duties, became subject to such taxes at about the same time as the Law of April 6, 1830, went into effect. State and national authorities who depended heavily on such taxes enforced their collection diligently. On the other hand, Anglo-Americans traditionally had little use for customs taxes and fees or the people who collected them.

Another problem was the conflict between state and national authority over the question of land titles and the right to issue them. But the most serious issue concerned the matter of military authority over civilians, a question on which Anglo-American and Mexican traditions had little in common. Adding to the explosiveness of the impending crisis were a

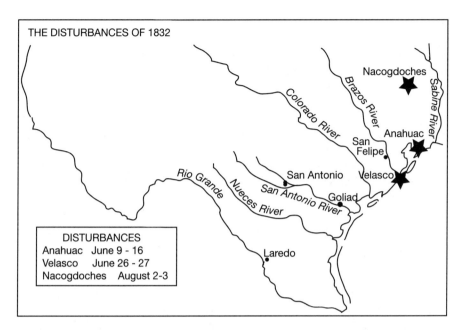

THE DISTURBANCES OF 1832

DISTURBANCES
Anahuac   June 9 - 16
Velasco   June 26 - 27
Nacogdoches   August 2-3

Traditionally termed "Disturbances," the events of the summer of 1832 were in
reality militant rebellions. A confrontation at Anahuac led to a battle at Velasco
with about forty casualties and subsequently to one at Nacogodoches, where
even more bloodshed occurred.

number of leaders on both sides who were prepared to respond to provo-
cation with intemperance.

Hostilities at Valasco and Nacogdoches led to casualties, but it was a
confrontation at Anahuac that provoked the crisis. Ironically, two of the
ranking Mexican officials involved were not Mexican-born, though both
were Mexican citizens and loyal to their adopted country. The customs collector for ports east of the Colorado River, where the conflicts would occur,
was George Fisher, a Serbian adventurer, once a citizen of the United States,
and a citizen of Mexico since 1825. The military commander assigned to
Anahuac on Trinity Bay was Colonel Juan Davis Bradburn. Bradburn, a
native of Virginia, had been a liberal revolutionary in the war for Mexican
independence but had turned more conservative and in the direction of centralism in later years. Although he knew many of the Anglo-Americans in
Texas, he stood firmly in favor of the autocratic rule of the centralist Anastacio Bustamante.

Trouble began early in 1831 between Bradburn and Francisco Madero,
general land commissioner of Texas. Defying Bradburn, who claimed that he
was violating the Law of April 6, 1830, and ordered him to desist, Madero
persisted in the issuance of land titles to settlers. Never one to back down,
Bradburn had Madero and his surveyor arrested. Eventually Madero was

released, whereupon he issued a number of land titles, formed the new town of Liberty about thirty miles above Anahuac on the Trinity, and organized the town's *ayuntamiento*. Trouble, however, was only beginning. Bradburn's commanding officer, General Mier y Terán, moved the *ayuntamiento* of Liberty to Anahuac, thus arousing great resentment, and more disputes soon developed.

Meanwhile, George Fisher, the customs collector whose loyalties were somewhat more ambiguous than those of Bradburn, added another dimension to the conflict. Fisher, acting on the orders of General Mier y Terán, decreed that all ships leaving Texas from the mouth of the Brazos and certain other ports must clear through Anahuac. Since doing this sometimes required an overland journey of about 200 miles or a dangerous sea voyage, the order provoked strong protests. In December 1831 some shippers ignored the order and ran by the guard on the lower Brazos, shots were exchanged, and one soldier was seriously wounded. A deputy collector was then placed at Brazoria, but the colonists remained unhappy.

Although the conflict over customs regulations diminished somewhat in the spring of 1832, Bradburn's relations with area colonists grew steadily worse. When a number of settlers formed a vigilante group to intimidate Mexican soldiers who allegedly had committed crimes and gone unpunished, Bradburn arrested some of the leaders and held them for a time. Moreover, a long-standing dispute between Bradburn and Anahuac settlers over the question of slavery reached a crisis stage. When Bradburn gave asylum to two runaway slaves from Louisiana in the summer of 1831, settlers had charged him with using slave labor without compensation. Matters reached a climax when the owner of the slaves employed William Barret Travis, a young attorney newly arrived in Texas from Alabama, who demanded without success the return of the slaves. Attorneys Travis and Patrick Jack began to annoy Bradburn with mysterious messages about an armed force that was coming from Louisiana to recover the runaway slaves. Bradburn arrested Travis, Jack, and eventually a number of others on charges of sedition, claiming that the offense had occurred on federal property subject to the jurisdiction of the military. Bradburn's explanation meant nothing to Anglo-Americans who had little experience with military rule over civilians, arrest without warrants, and trial without jury. To them, Bradburn's action was despotism, regardless of its legality under Mexican law.

The imprisonment of Travis and Jack led to open rebellion. William H. Jack, brother of Patrick, called on his fellow colonists in San Felipe to join him in an attack on Bradburn. In early June 1832, men began to gather in Liberty, and soon John Austin (who may have been distantly related to Stephen F. Austin) from Brazoria arrived with ninety men. By June 10, Bradburn was besieged by 160 Texans. After some skirmishing and some negotiations, the colonists withdrew a few miles to Turtle Bayou and sent John Austin to Brazoria for a cannon with which to assault the fort.

Meanwhile, far to the south in central Mexico, Antonio Lôpez de Santa Anna, claiming to support liberalism and the Constitution of 1824, was leading a rebellion against President Bustamante. While waiting for Austin to return, the Texans on Turtle Bayou, aware of the insurrection, prepared a formal statement of the causes of their own rebellion against Bradburn, a loyal supporter of Bustamante. Thus, on June 13, in "The Turtle Bayou Resolutions," they asserted their loyalty to the constitution and to Santa Anna and the liberals. The resolutions were to serve them well.

Relief for the situation at Anahuac came from Nacogdoches. As soon as he learned of the matter, Colonel José de las Piedras, commander of the garrison in Nacogdoches, rushed to the troubled scene with some of his troops. Though not particularly sympathetic to the colonists, he feared a spread of the rebellion and agreed to release the prisoners to civil authorities for trial, to replace Bradburn, to restore the *ayuntamiento* of Liberty, and to allow the settlers to petition for redress of their grievances. Bradburn soon resigned, the Texans dispersed, and most of the garrison declared for Santa Anna and sailed away.

The situation on the Brazos remained serious for a time. John Austin had returned to Brazoria, secured the cannon (also reinforcements of more than a hundred men), and started by boat for Anahuac. At Velasco at the mouth of the Brazos, Colonel Domingo de Ugartechea, commander of the fort there, tried to prevent his passage. In the ensuing battle ten Texans and five Mexicans were killed, but Ugartechea was forced to surrender the garrison and withdraw his troops to Matamoros.

The resistance spread rapidly, and the colonists determined to drive every soldier from the settlements. In August settlers defeated Piedras and his troops in a bloody battle at Nacogdoches and forced them to abandon Texas. The post of Tenoxtitlan on the upper Brazos was also abandoned, leaving the eastern part of Texas completely free of Mexican troops, and on August 30 Ramón Musquíz, the political chief in San Antonio, tardily declared for Santa Anna.

Had it not been for the developments in Santa Anna's struggle for power that favored the Texans, these events would surely have brought severe retribution. In early July in Matamoros, Colonel José Antonio Mexía was in command of the Santanista forces. Nearby was Colonel José Mariano Guerra in command of the Bustamante troops. When Mexía overhauled a ship carrying mail from Brazoria and learned of the disturbances in Texas, he proposed to Guerra that they declare a truce and pool their resources to restore constitutional and legitimate government in Texas. Guerra agreed, and soon Mexía with about 400 soldiers was off for Texas. Fortunately for the colonists, he took along Stephen F. Austin, who had come by way of Matamoros on his return from the legislature in Saltillo. It is likely that Austin spent many hours emphasizing to Mexía what he had already written to the Mexican authorities in Texas. His argument was stated thus: "There is no insurrection of the Colonists against the Constitution and Government, neither do they entertain ideas endangering even remotely the integrity of the territory."

The colonists, who expected his arrival, prepared for Mexía a most lavish reception. He was saluted at the mouth of the Brazos by a salvo of cannon, entertained in the home of John Austin, and assured by reception committees of the loyalty of the Texans. At Brazoria the general was given a dinner and ball; the crowd was "large, cheerful, and convivial," and drank many toasts to Santa Anna. Under such conditions there was little for Mexía, a loyal Santanista, to do but return to Mexico City with a report of the Texans' generous hospitality.

THE CONVENTIONS OF 1832 AND 1833

Although the insurrection of 1832 led to no reprisals, the colonists were not willing to leave matters where they stood. They wanted reforms and concessions from the Mexican government. Accordingly, on August 22, 1832, just a month after Mexía had sailed away, the *ayuntamiento* of San Felipe issued a call to the districts to send delegates to a convention to meet in San Felipe on October 1. Sixteen districts responded (not counting Goliad, whose delegation arrived too late for the proceedings) and sent fifty-eight delegates. Stephen F. Austin was elected president. Several resolutions addressed to the federal and state governments were prepared and adopted; still others related to local affairs. In lengthy memorials, the convention petitioned the national government for the repeal of that part of the Law of April 6, 1830, prohibiting Anglo-American immigration, and for the admission of Texas as a state to the Mexican confederation but separate from Coahuila. It also asked Congress to exempt the colonists from tariff duties on necessities for three years and to allow customs officers to be appointed by the *alcaldes* of the respective jurisdictions. It asked the state to issue land titles to settlers east of Austin's colony, to create additional *ayuntamientos* there, and to set aside land for school purposes. Locally, it provided for a committee, together with the *ayuntamiento* of Nacogdoches, to investigate the affairs of the Cherokees and other Indians in East Texas, and it approved a plan for organizing the militia and suggested plans for defense against the Indians. The convention adjourned on October 6 and forwarded its petitions through Ramón Músquiz, political chief in San Antonio.

The petitions were never officially presented to the Mexican officials. The governor instructed Músquiz to remind the Texans that the convention was a violation of the constitution and the laws of Mexico, and Austin believed that there was little chance of success without the support of Mexican officials in San Antonio. Moreover, Santa Anna, who had not yet assumed the presidency, frowned on the idea of unauthorized conventions.

Still determined, a Central Committee of Safety and Correspondence, organized in the Convention of 1832, issued a call for a second convention to meet in San Felipe on April 1, 1833. A larger number of discontented delegates was in attendance this time, evidenced by the selection of William H. Wharton, rather than Austin, as president of the convention. Only about one-third of the delegates had attended the first convention. But the petitions were much the same as those prepared the previous year. The convention asked for the repeal of the anti-immigration law, adopted a memorial by David G. Burnet setting forth reasons why Texas should be a state separate from Coahuila, accepted a constitution drafted for a state government by a committee chaired by Sam Houston, who had come to Texas that year, and designated three delegates to carry the petition to Mexico City. Only one delegate, Stephen F. Austin, was able to make the journey.

AUSTIN'S JOURNEY TO MEXICO CITY

When Austin arrived in Mexico City on July 18, 1833, he found a confused, even chaotic, situation reminiscent of his visit eleven years earlier. Santa Anna, elected president in January 1833, had refused to take office and had designated Valentín Gómez Farías, the vice president and a conscientious liberal, to act as president. Although Santa Anna had overthrown Bustamante and won the presidency on a platform calling for liberal reforms and the restoration of the Constitution of 1824, he was doubtful that the wealthy and powerful interests of Mexico would accept such a program. Thus, he decided to "recuperate his health at his estate" until Gómez Farías presented his reform program to Congress. If the proposed reforms proved popular, he could assume the presidency and claim the credit; if, on the contrary, they aroused strong opposition, he could assume the presidency and oppose them.

Austin conferred with Farías, who, although suspicious of the intentions of the Texans, received him cordially. The ministry submitted to the house of deputies the petition asking for a state government. Then a cholera scourge caused all business in the capital to be suspended, and Austin, impatient at the delay, on October 1 told Farías bluntly that unless the government remedied "the evils which threaten that country [Texas] with ruin," the people of Texas would organize a state government without its approval. Farías took this statement as a threat; the two men quarreled, and Austin, while still in a huff, wrote the *ayuntamiento* in San Antonio, urging it to take the initiative in a plan to organize a state government.

A little later Austin and Farías reconciled their differences, and on November 5 Austin had a conference with Santa Anna (now exercising the executive power) and his cabinet. He found Santa Anna sympathetic and friendly. The president would not approve separation from Coahuila, but he did agree to almost every other request. He promised the repeal of the prohibition on immigration; he would refer to the treasury office a request for better mail service and a modification of the tariff; and he would urge the state government to give Texas trial by jury.

Before he left the city on December 10, Austin actually witnessed the repeal of the law against immigration, to take effect six months later. On his way back to Texas he stopped on January 3, 1834, to see the commandant in Saltillo on a matter of business. There he was placed under arrest and then taken back to Mexico City. The cause was his letter of the preceding October to the *ayuntamiento* in San Antonio, written, as Austin said, "in a moment of irritation and impatience." The letter had found its way to the governor and finally back to Gómez Farías just after Austin had left Mexico City. It was the liberal federalist Farías who ordered the arrest.

For some time Austin was kept *incommunicado* in the Prison of the Inquisition. He could get no trial, for no Mexican court would accept jurisdiction of his case. Two attorneys, Peter W. Grayson and Spencer H. Jack, were sent to his aid by the people of Texas, bearing many petitions for his release, but all they accomplished was to get him out of prison on bail on Christmas Day 1834. He was finally released through an amnesty law and left Mexico City in July 1835.

SANTA ANNA AND THE POLITICS OF MEXICO (1833–35)

The central figure in these affairs, Antonio López de Santa Anna, was born in Jalapa in 1794. He became a cadet at the age of fifteen and thereafter was a professional soldier. In the various contests over the supreme authority in Mexico before 1834, he supported the constitution and popular government. Although he retired from politics for nearly two years when Bustamante came into power, in January 1832 Santa Anna prompted the garrison in Vera Cruz to start a revolt, soon became its leader, and finally forced Bustamante to capitulate. He was easily elected president for the term beginning April 1, 1833, but allowed Vice President Farías to assume the powers of the office. There then followed a strange period between April 1, 1833, and January 28, 1835, when these two men exchanged the presidency no fewer than seven times. Meanwhile, for a time the reforms to which both men were pledged were being carried out by Farías and a liberal congress. Church appointments were placed in the hands of the state; the clergy was forbid-

Antonio López de Santa Anna. The reactionary dictatorship of this opportunistic general and politician did much to provoke the Texas Revolution. His harsh treatment of the men of the Alamo and Goliad aroused fear and anger throughout Texas. Defeated and captured at San Jacinto, he nevertheless became president of Mexico twice again before his death in 1876. (Archives Division—Texas State Library)

den to discuss political matters; forced collections of tithes were suspended; and plans were inaugurated to reduce the size and influence of the army.

The army, powerful clerics, wealthy *hacendados*, and other affluent interests did not permit these reforms to proceed without challenge. Quietly they organized and found a leader in Santa Anna himself! The wily politician had permitted Farías to launch a trial balloon of liberalism, while he, in the eyes of the public, was a mere spectator. Seeing that the opposition was very powerful, he realized that, as its leader, he could make himself dictator. In April 1834, he returned to the capital and took over the supreme power from Farías. This time he repudiated liberalism, dissolved Congress, forced Farías into exile, disbanded legislatures and *ayuntamientos*, declared void the laws against the privileges of the clergy, and in various other ways imitated Napoleon Bonaparte, whom he greatly admired.

A new framework of government based on authoritarian principles soon followed. The new and subservient congress supplemented and legalized what Santa Anna had done, and in October 1835 the Constitution of 1824 and federalism were replaced by the *Siete Leyes*, a centralized system of government. The new document converted the states into departments, ruled by a governor appointed by the president, and substituted an appointive council for each state legislature. The dictatorship of Santa Anna had been legalized—but in an illegal manner.

Federalists did not abandon their cause without resistance. In many states there were protests of one sort or another, and in some, such as Zacatecas, California, Coahuila and Texas, and eventually Yucatan, there was open rebellion. Armed resistance in Zacatecas began over a decree that ordered the reduction of the number of militia and the surrender of excess arms. When the people of Zacatecas rose in rebellion, Santa Anna defeated 5,000 troops led by their governor, inflicted bloody reprisals, and permitted his soldiers to plunder the state capital.

Affairs in Coahuila and Texas (1833–35)

When Colonel Juan Almonte, an investigator for Gómez Farías, visited Texas in the spring of 1834, he was pleased with what he found. The settlements were prospering, the colonists seemed content, and there was no evidence of unrest or disloyalty. There was good reason for these conditions. During 1833 and 1834, the state government was generous with Texas. The legislature repealed the law that had prohibited any but native-born Mexicans from engaging in retail merchandising. It divided Texas into three political departments, the capitals to be Béxar, San Felipe, and Nacogdoches. Texas was allowed three deputies out of the twelve that comprised the state legislature. The English language was recognized for official purposes, and religious tolerance was granted. The court system, which had been the most constant object of complaint, was completely revised. A superior court was created for Texas, and trial by jury was established. The new court proved defective, but it, like the other concessions, was an honest attempt to satisfy the colonists.

But even as these reforms were being adopted, trouble in state government was developing. The two principal sources of strife and agitation were the quarrel between Saltillo and Monclova over the location of the state capital and the squandering of the public lands of Texas through sales to speculators. Generally, except for the disturbances of 1832 when they declared for Santa Anna as a kind of afterthought, Texans had managed to avoid entanglements in Mexican politics. Beginning with 1834, however, this was no longer true.

The quarrel over the state capital began in March 1833, when the legislature removed the seat of government from Saltillo in the southeastern corner of Coahuila to Monclova in the north. Later, a rival government was set up in Saltillo, but Santa Anna gave his nod to Monclova and the government remained there. In April 1835, the legislature challenged Santa Anna, and the dictator sent his brother-in-law, Martín Perfecto de Cós, to break up the state government. In response, Governor Agustín Viesca attempted to transfer the government to Béxar but was arrested on his way by Cós's troops. Other state officers and a swarm of land speculators fled to Béxar, but by August both the Saltillo and the Monclova factions accepted as governor Rafael Eca y Músquíz, who then moved the capital back to Saltillo.

Adding to the confusion and the chaos were the activities of land speculators whose greed seemed to know no limits. Speculation in Texas lands had been common ever since the passage of the state colonization law of 1825, which permitted a native Mexican to purchase as much as eleven *sitios* for a nominal sum. This speculation was eclipsed, however, by reckless, unwise, and perhaps dishonest, legislation in 1834 and 1835. Representatives John Durst, from Nacogdoches, and J. M. Carbajal, from San Antonio, were implicated in and profited from this business. An act of April 19, 1834, authorized the governor to dispose of as much as 400 *sitios* of land for the purpose of maintaining the militia in defense against the Indians. Another law, that of March 14, 1835, empowered the governor to dispose of 400 more *sitios*. The final act in this extravagant series was passed on April 7, 1835, authorizing the governor "to take of himself whatever measure he may think proper for securing the public tranquillity."

The operations of the partnership firm of Williams, Peebles, and Johnson are typical. In consideration for 400 *sitios* of land, they agreed to place and maintain in the field 1,000 men for the defense of the state. Without supplying a single soldier, they issued to about forty persons certificates calling for the entire 400 *sitios*. Later, the Texas convention of 1836 nullified some of these grants but validated others apparently no more meritorious.

Such activities alarmed and disgusted many Texans and also confused the issue when Santa Anna established himself as a dictator. The land speculators brought alarming reports to the effect that Santa Anna was planning to invade Texas, but most people believed that such talk was merely a cloud to screen the speculators' own bad conduct. One citizen responded to such warnings with "wolf, wolf. . . . What a pity. . . ." As late as midsummer 1835, most Texans would have endorsed the statement of George Smythe, land commissioner in Nacogdoches. He wrote in May of that year that he was confident that there would be no war and added: "Come what may I am convinced that Texas must prosper. We pay no taxes, work no public roads, get our land at cost, and perform no public duties of any kind."

Yet there was a small but active war party, people who favored war and independence, and on the other extreme, a peace party, likewise small, active, and persistent. The great majority of Texans stood between these two extreme groups, indifferent at first but finding their complacent attitude more and more untenable. Developments during the summer of 1835 favored the war party.

THE CRISIS OF 1835

The first violent action that led directly to revolution was associated with Anahuac, where the disturbances of 1832 began. Indeed, the story of Texas during the summer of 1835 reads strangely like that of 1832. In January

1835, Santa Anna sent a small detachment of soldiers to Anahuac to enforce the collection of customs there and in Galveston. The collector at Velasco on the Brazos collected certain types of duties but not all, while the officers at Galveston and Anahuac insisted on the payment of all duties. Andrew Briscoe, a merchant at Anahuac, and others complained about the inequity and declared that no more duties should be collected at that port until collections were enforced equally throughout Texas. In a subsequent quarrel, a Texan was wounded at Anahuac, and Briscoe and another citizen were imprisoned.

Meanwhile, General Cós, now military commandant of the area that included Texas, had heard of the threatening attitude of the people at Anahuac and had determined to reinforce the garrison. He wrote Captain Antonio Tenorio, its commander, to be resolute and of good cheer, that reinforcements were coming. It happened that the courier bearing Cós's letters and other communications stopped at San Felipe on June 21. There was much excitement in the community. The people knew of the breaking up of the state government and of the arrests of Governor Viesca and the citizens at Anahuac. Already concerned, the San Felipe war party seized and opened the courier's dispatches. Although there was strong opposition, the clique that favored drastic action met, elected J. B. Miller, political chief of the Department of the Brazos, chairman, and passed resolutions authorizing William B. Travis to collect a force and drive away the garrison at Anahuac. With some twenty-five or thirty men, Travis appeared before the post and demanded its surrender. Without the firing of a weapon on either side, Tenorio on the morning of June 30 surrendered with forty-four men. The prisoners were soon paroled.

A great many of the people of Texas reacted unfavorably to the action of Travis and his men. No fewer than seven communities condemned it in formal meetings. At a meeting on June 28 the people of Columbia emphatically denounced Travis's march to Anahuac as an act calculated to involve the citizens of Texas in a conflict with the central government. They pledged their loyalty to Mexico, and through a committee they asked the political chief to send to General Cós assurances of the people's loyalty. More general gatherings in San Felipe on July 14 and 15 adopted similar resolutions, and J. B. Miller, as if to atone for his alignment with the radicals a few weeks earlier, wrote an apologetic letter to Cós. Then a conference of committees from Columbia, Mina (Bastrop), and San Felipe, meeting in San Felipe from July 17 to 21, sent representatives with conciliatory letters to Cós in Matamoros.

General Cós was not in a compromising humor. He called for the arrest of Lorenzo de Zavala, a well-known political refugee and enemy of Santa Anna, who had lately arrived in Texas. Then Colonel Ugartechea, commander at Béxar, sent to Cós a list of offenders: F. W. Johnson and Samuel Williams, who had been prominent in land speculation; Robert M. Williamson, commonly called "Three Legged Willie"; and William B. Travis.

The general insisted that the colonial officials arrest these men and turn them over to the military for trial. He refused to meet with the peace commissioners (who had gone as far as San Antonio on their way to confer with him) until this was done. To the Anglo-Americans, who believed that a person should be tried only by a jury composed of his or her peers, it was unthinkable to turn their fellow citizens over to the mercies of a Mexican military tribunal. Cós, who managed to secure and read copies of the various inflammatory speeches and utterances of the Texans, particularly a Fourth of July address by "Three Legged Willie" Williamson, was adamant. Thus did the season for conciliation pass.

In the American Revolution it was the committees of correspondence that began in Massachusetts in 1772 that kept the people in touch with developments and finally made possible organized resistance. Similar organizations, some of which were originally formed for protection against Indian raids, existed during the Texas Revolution. Without them the colonists could not have been aroused to the point of resistance or have been organized with any degree of effectiveness. Mina (Bastrop) on the frontier led the communities by appointing on May 8, 1835, its Committee of Safety and Correspondence. Organizations in Gonzales and Viesca were formed a few days later. Before the end of the summer apparently every precinct had such an organization. The central committee held over from the convention of 1833 served as a guide and a clearing body for the local committees.

These committees were responsible for a decision to bring together representatives of the municipalities for a consultation. On July 4 the Committee of Safety at Mina issued an address to the *ayuntamientos* of the Department of the Brazos, urging a consultation of the representatives of the several communities. Within ten days the *ayuntamiento* of Columbia and a citizens' meeting in San Felipe likewise had called for a consultation. Actually, it was the people of Columbia who called the general meeting. At a gathering of the citizens on August 15, 1835, with William H. Wharton presiding, the Committee of Safety and Correspondence was instructed to issue a call for a consultation of all Texans. Three days later the committee framed an address in which it asked that each jurisdiction elect and send five delegates to a consultation to be held in Washington on October 15. The tenor of its message is revealed in this sentence: "The only instructions which we would recommend to be given to our representatives is to secure peace if it is to be obtained on constitutional terms, and to prepare for war—if war is inevitable."

Some three weeks later Stephen F. Austin, free at last and home again, gave the consultation his approval. He accepted the chairmanship of the Central Committee of Safety of San Felipe and by common consent became the leader of the Texan cause. The news came that Cós was on his way to Béxar with reinforcements. This destroyed the last hope of peace. On

September 19, the central committee reinforced the call for a consultation and added, "War is our only resource. There is no other remedy. We must defend our rights ourselves and our country by force of arms."

WHY REVOLUTION?

A study of the causes of the Texas Revolution reveals striking resemblances to the American Revolution. Both can be traced to the disposition of the superior government to assert its authority after the colonists had learned to expect benevolent neglect. Customs duties and customs collectors played important parts in both stories. Texans resented Mexican troops quartered among them, just as English colonials had resented the British redcoats. But though there are many similarities, there are also many differences, particularly in the nature of the underlying causes that influenced and sometimes determined the course of events. That such underlying causes existed is certain; their identification, evaluation, and measurement cannot always be done with certainty.

To many Mexican authorities and to the Mexican people, the revolution in Texas was the final drama in a conspiracy of U.S. officials and Anglo-American immigrants to foment rebellion in preparation for attaching Texas to the United States. Not without logic, the theory has survived and found acceptance in the historical writings of both countries. After all, Sam Houston, a hero of the revolution, and Andrew Jackson, president of the United States, were friends of long standing. The interest of the United States in the acquisition of Texas was clearly demonstrated by two efforts to purchase it, and many of the participants in the Texan cause were, in truth, recent arrivals from the United States; some had come after the fighting began. The problem with the theory is the term "conspiracy," which suggests planning, preparation, collusion, and secrecy. There is scant evidence of this. Nevertheless, many in the United States wanted Texas (although many did not); many Texans wanted to be a part of their former country and welcomed the opportunity presented by the outbreak of rebellion.

Of all of the underlying causes of the revolution, slavery is the most difficult to evaluate and measure. A contemporary observer and abolitionist, Benjamin Lundy, viewed the revolution as the work of pro-slavery interests who wanted not only to preserve slavery in Texas but also to add Texas to the strength of the slaveholding South. Lundy's sincere convictions rested upon a certain amount of logic. Mexican policy contained in constitutions and laws threatened slavery; many—perhaps most—Texans supported slavery and were determined to retain the institution. However, this conflict of interests was not new in 1835; it was a conflict that had long existed. To attribute the outbreak of revolution in 1835 to slavery would seem to require additional evidence showing that circumstances had changed. In this respect, Lundy offered little. Nevertheless, the importance of slavery as a cause has remained a credible theory. Indeed, a recent writer observed that "violations of the Mexican law in regard to slavery eventually led" to the revolution.

Notwithstanding the exclusiveness of that rather simplistic explanation, there is some evidence to suggest that the conflict over slavery was becoming more critical by 1835. Although the proportion of slaves to free people migrating to Texas declined for a time, in the last year or two before the outbreak of rebellion, the number of slaves brought into the colonies apparently increased. Moreover, in the tension-filled days of the summer of 1835, Stephen Austin wrote that "Texas must be a slave country. It is no longer a matter of doubt." Alarmed by the impending arrival of Mexican troops, "Three Legged Willie" Williamson warned that the troops would "compel you to liberate your slaves." And there were others who sounded the call in defense of slavery in these final days before war.

The question is not truly one of whether or not slavery was a cause. It no doubt influenced the course of events. Rather, the question is one of evaluation and comparison. Just how significant was slavery in comparison with other influences? The answer to that question is not clear and perhaps can be answered only through intuition.

Cultural and ethnic differences are another cause frequently suggested. Differences in religion, language, and government between the Mexican nation and the Anglo-American population of Texas were pronounced. Anglo-Americans were violently averse to the subordination of the civil to the military power and to any connection whatsoever of church and state. They came to Texas with a long heritage of successful experience in self-government. The first dispute at Anahuac in 1832 was a complex affair involving many different issues, but at the heart of it was a cultural conflict. Bradburn was likely correct in claiming that he acted within the law (though perhaps not always with wisdom), but Anglo-American settlers, regardless of the provisions of law and constitution, could not accept the idea of military authority over civilians.

It is possible to exaggerate the extent of cultural differences. Religious restrictions were apparently more of an inconvenience than anything else; there were instances of intermarriage between the two peoples; and there were friendships and partnerships involving peoples from both cultures. Certainly, the intensity of Anglo prejudice toward Tejanos of a later day (and a similar view of some wealthy Tejanos toward Anglos) did not prevail at the time of the revolution. But prejudice did exist. And when conflict did occur, it was generally in an area where it was not easily resolved, in matters that often provoked violence and confrontation, and in situations where ethnic bigotry prevented reconciliation. Ethnic issues perhaps had little to do with starting the conflict, but once the revolution began, ethnic differences made a peaceful resolution unlikely—indeed, virtually impossible.

A final explanation places the responsibility for revolution on the failure of Mexico to establish a stable and democratic government, a failure that led to unpredictability, tyranny, and dictatorship. These were, indeed, chaotic years in Mexico. At the heart of the confusion was Santa Anna, whose lust for power was exceeded only by his capriciousness. His turn toward centralism and despotism brought revolution in many parts of Mexico, and, unfortunately for Mexican interests, disillusioned Stephen Austin, whose loyalty to Mexico up to this point was apparently both real and meaningful. With many Texans lacking a basic faith that democratic government and tranquil prosperity were possible in the foreseeable future, the decision for rebellion, revolution, and ultimately independence was not an unexpected development.

All the influences on the coming of the revolution must be judged while keeping in mind a sometimes overlooked fact. The Texas Revolution did not occur easily or without opposition from within the Texas community. From the time of the first disturbances at Anahuac until long after the outbreak of fighting, there were substantial numbers of prominent Texans who opposed the militant stand taken against Mexican authority, albeit sometimes at a price. For their opposition to resistance in 1832, well-known Texans such as Samuel May Williams and Thomas Jefferson Chambers were hanged in effigy, and more than a score of residents in the Anahuac area were subjected to a coat of tar and feathers. When William Travis led his troops to Anahuac in the second disturbance in 1835, criticism of his action was widespread and strong. Even after the fighting was well under way, there were those who still hoped for a peaceful settlement. Generally, these opponents of insurgency were people of property, long-time residents of Texas, and sometimes tied financially to Mexican authorities. The views of these people of substance were significant and suggest that revolution in the face of their opposition was the product of exceptionally strong forces.

BIBLIOGRAPHY

Few studies of the events leading up to the Texas Revolution have been written in recent years. Therefore, Gregg Cantrell's biography of Stephen Austin listed in Chapter 4 is an especially valuable modern interpretation. The classic histories of Texas cited in Chapter 4 remain good sources for traditional accounts. See also Frank W. Johnson, *A History of Texas and Texans* (E. C. Barker and E. W. Winkler, eds., five vols., Chicago and New York, 1914). Other surveys that deal with the period include D. M. Vigness, *The Revolutionary Decades* (Austin, 1965), and William C. Binkley, *The Texas Revolution* (Baton Rouge, La., 1952).

The most comprehensive collection of source material on the Texas Revolution, compiled and edited by John H. Jenkins, is *The Papers of the Texas Revolution, 1835–1836* (ten vols., Austin, 1973). Other materials may be found in Robert E. Davis (ed.), *Diary of William Barret Travis, August 30, 1833, June 26, 1834* (Waco, 1966); E. C. Barker, *The Austin Papers* (vols. I and II, Washington, D.C., 1919 and 1922; vol. III, Austin, 1926); Malcolm McLean, *The Papers of the Robertson Colony* (Fort Worth and

Arlington, 1974–1993); C. A. Gulich, Katherine Elliott, and Harriet Smither (eds.), *The Papers of Mirabeau Bonaparte Lamar* (six vols., Austin, 1921–27); E. C. Barker, contributor of a series of important documents in the *Publications of the Southern History Association*, V, 451–76; VI, 33–40; VII, 25–31, 85–95, 200–206, 238–246; VIII, 1–22, 104–118, 343–362; IX, 87–98, 160–173, 225–233; and E. Wallace, D. M. Vigness, and George Ward (eds.), *Documents of Texas History* (Austin, 1993). Almonte's report on Texas has been translated and edited by C. E. Castañeda in the *Southwestern Historical Quarterly*, XXVIII, 177–222.

Of the more intensive studies, many are the works of E. C. Barker. See *The Life of Stephen F. Austin* (Nashville and Dallas, 1925); *Mexico and Texas, 1821–1835* (Dallas, 1928; "The Organization of the Texas Revolution," *Publications of the Southern History Association*, V, 1–26; "The Battle of Velasco," *Quarterly of the Texas State Historical Association*, VII, 326–328; "Public Opinion in Texas Preceding the Revolution," *Annual Report of the American Historical Association for 1911*, I, 217–228; "Difficulties of a Mexican Revenue Officer in Texas," *Quarterly of the Texas State Historical Association*, 190–202; and "Land Speculation as a Cause of the Texas Revolution,"ibid., X, 76–95.

See also O. Morton, "Life of General Don Manuel de Mier y Terán, As It Affected Texas-Mexican Relations," *Southwestern Historical Quarterly*, XLVI, 22–47, 239–254; XLVII, 29–47, 120–242, 256–267; XLVIII, 51–66, 193–218; Merton L. Dillon, "Benjamin Lundy in Texas," ibid., LXIII, 46–62; Llerena Friend, *Sam Houston, the Great Designer* (Austin, 1954); *The Texans* (New York, 1975); O. Morton, *Terán and Texas: A Chapter in Texas-Mexican Relations* (Austin, 1948); Margaret Swett Henson, "Tory Sentiment in Anglo-Texan Public Opinion, 1832–1836," *Southwestern Historical Quarterly*, XC, 1–34; C. Alan Hutchinson, "General José Antonio Mexía and His Texas Interests," ibid., LXXXII, 117–142; and Paul D. Lack, "Slavery and the Texas Revolution," ibid., LXXXIX, 181–202.

For a study less sympathetic to traditional interpretations, see Andreas V. Reichstein, *Rise of the Lone Star: The Making of Texas* (trans. Jeanne Willson, College Station, 1989), which argues that there was no revolution but that land speculators were responsible for whatever it was that did happen. See also David Weber (ed.), *Troubles in Texas, 1832: A Tejano Viewpoint from San Antonio* (Dallas, 1984), and Jeff Long, *Duel of Eagles: The Mexican and U.S. Fight for the Alamo* (New York, 1990).

Accounts of the disturbances of the early 1830s include Edna Rowe, "The Disturbances at Anahuac in 1832," *Quarterly of the Texas State Historical Association*, VI, 265–299; N. D. Labadie, "Narrative of the Anahuac, or Opening Campaign of the Texas Revolution," *Texas Almanac, 1859*, 30–36; Duncan W. Robinson, *Judge Robert McAlpin Williamson: Three-Legged Willie* (Austin, 1948); Forrest E. Ward, "Pre-Revolutionary Activity in Brazoria Country," *Southwestern Historical Quarterly*, LXIV, 212–231; and Boyce House, "An Incident at Velasco, 1832," ibid., 92–95. However, these traditional views of the events should be balanced with the careful study of Margaret Swett Henson, *Juan Davis Bradburn: A Reappraisal of the Mexican Commander of Anahuac* (College Station, 1982)

For Santa Anna and national affairs, see Frank C. Hanighen, *Santa Anna: The Napoleon of the West* (New York, 1934); Wilfred H. Callcott, *Santa Anna* (Norman, 1936); H. H. Bancroft, *The History of Mexico* (six vols., San Francisco, 1883–88); and Michael C. Meyer, William L. Sherman, and Susan M. Deeds, *The Course of Mexican History* (8th ed., New York, 1999).

An excellent study of a Mexican historian is Vito Alessio Robles, *Coahuila y Tejas desde la consumación de la independencia hasta el tratado de paz de Guadalupe Hidalgo* (two vols., Mexico, D. F., 1945–46).

6

The Texas Revolution 1835–1836

The Texas Revolution, which began in the fall of 1835, was similar in many respects to other revolutions of modern times. There was uncertainty in the beginning about the goal—whether the fighting was for independence or for a more democratic government of Mexico. Throughout the affair, as is typical of revolutions, there was a need to balance creation of an effective government with maintaining a successful military effort at the same time. As is so often the case in revolutions, the struggle involved civilians and brought hardship and sorrow to a sizable part of the population. There were abundant examples of heroics and bravery on both sides but regrettably, examples of cruelty and inhumanity as well.

In some respects, the Texas Revolution was unusual. It was short, lasting only about seven months in terms of military action. The battles generally involved small numbers of soldiers, and with only one or two exceptions, were astonishingly brief. Altogether, about 10,000 combatants participated in the campaigns, most of them either untrained soldiers or men with only limited military experience. Perhaps most unusual of all was the dramatic finale, a decisive victory for the Texan cause after weeks of retreat and defeat.

THE BEGINNING OF THE REVOLUTION

The Consultation of delegates from the *ayuntamientos* had been called to meet on October 15, 1835, but the events outran the plans. In September

102

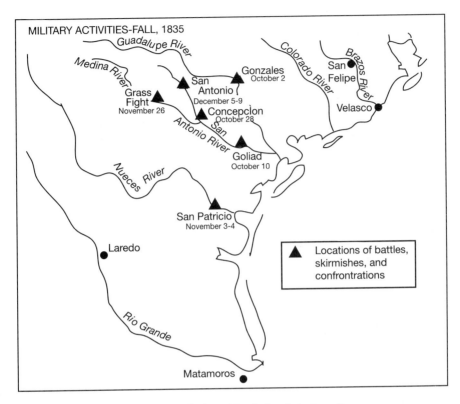

MILITARY ACTIVITIES-FALL, 1835

Gonzales
October 2

San
Antonio
December 5-9

Grass
Fight
November 26

Concepcion
October 28

Goliad
October 10

San
Felipe

Velasco

San Patricio
November 3-4

Laredo

Matamoros

▲ Locations of battles, skirmishes, and confrontrations

Military actions in the fall of 1835 took place either in San Antonio or its immediate vicinity or not more than 100 miles distant. The first, Gonzales, was primarily a skirmish; the second, Goliad, was actually a confrontation; but the last, San Antonio, was a drawn-out and bloody affair.

General Martín Cós, reacting to the opening of his official dispatches and refusal of the Texans to carry out the arrests that he had ordered, began embarking troops for Texas. Colonel Domingo de Ugartechea, commander of troops in San Antonio, sent five cavalrymen to Gonzales, 70 miles to the east, to get the six-pound cannon that had been provided to *Empresario* DeWitt about four years before for defense against the Indians. *Alcalde* Andrew Ponton hid the cannon, told the military authorities he had no authority to give it up, and sent out dispatches calling for aid. Meanwhile, some Texans were on their way to intercept General Cós, who with 400 troops had landed at Copano near Goliad. Upon receipt of the news from Ponton, they turned aside to Gonzales. Ugartechea had already sent Lieutenant Francisco Castañeda with about 100 troops to seize the cannon. On September 29 the Mexican force encamped on the west bank of the Guadalupe River, a short distance above the town. Then, on October 2, Colonel J. H. Moore and about 160 Texans with the disputed cannon loaded with chains and scrap iron and strung with a banner inscribed "Come and Take It," crossed the river and attacked the Mexican troops, killing one and forcing the others to retreat to San Antonio.

Not all the volunteers who had set out to intercept General Cós turned aside to Gonzales. One company from Matagorda under Captain George M. Collinsworth and joined by Benjamin R. Milam captured Goliad and its approximately twenty-five defenders. Cós, with most of his troops, had already left Goliad for San Antonio, but the capture of Goliad and its well-supplied stores was significant. Cós could no longer expect to obtain supplies and reinforcements by sea.

Meanwhile, more volunteers continued to arrive at Gonzales and raised the cry "On to San Antonio," but there was no organization or commander. However, upon his arrival, Austin was selected unanimously. On October 12, the ragtag army, numbering about 300, started for San Antonio, where Cós had already arrived. With Ugartechea's command, Cós had at hand 647 battle-ready troops, well entrenched in strong positions. On October 28, James Bowie and James W. Fannin, Jr., while making a reconnaissance with 90 men, skirmished near Mission Purísima Concepción de Acuña with a Mexican force of about 275. The Texans reported the loss of one man; there were at least 53 Mexican casualties, including 14 dead. Thereafter, the Texans, without heavy artillery, settled in for a siege, hoping that a lack of supplies would eventually bring the Mexican army to sur-

Benjamin Rusk (Ben) Milam. A native of Kentucky, he was a member of Dr. James Long's filibuster expedition into Texas in 1820 and an officer in the Mexican Army. Because of his opposition to Santa Anna's centralist government in Coahuila, he was captured by troops of General Martín Cós but escaped and in the fall of 1835 joined the Texas army at Goliad. On December 5, when the Texans were ready to give up the siege of General Cós at San Antonio (Béxar), Milam called for and led one group of volunteers that attacked Mexican forces. Two days later he was killed by a rifle ball, but on December 9 Cós capitulated. (Courtesy Southwest Collection, Texas Tech University, Lubbock, Texas)

render.

Time passed slowly for the Texans laying siege to San Antonio. On November 25, Stephen Austin, named to a commission to seek aid in the United States, left. The volunteers who remained voted down a proposal to storm Cós's defenses, but 400 pledged to remain and elected Edward Burleson their commander. The next day, a skirmish known as the Grass Fight occurred on the outskirts of town. When Erastus (Deaf) Smith returned to camp with word that a pack train was approaching the town, the colonists concluded that it was reinforcements and pay for the Mexican army. They set out to capture the train, only to meet a furious resistance from Mexican artillery sent out by Cós in rescue. The pack train turned out to be a foraging party sent to get grass for Mexican horses.

In some respects, the Grass Fight was a victory, for the Texan casualties amounted to 4 wounded while Mexican casualties numbered 14 wounded and 3 or more killed. But the resolve of poorly clothed and inadequately fed Texans began to weaken in the winter cold. A few days later, the staff of officers decided to abandon the siege and go into winter quarters at Goliad. Before the withdrawal began, however, Ben Milam defied the order to withdraw by calling out, "Who will go with old Ben Milam into San Antonio?" Volunteers responded, and at least 371 Texans would participate in the battle. Before daylight on the morning of December 5, the Texas volunteers led by Milam began the attack.

Met with a concentration of artillery and small arms fire for three days (Milam was killed on the third day), the Texans finally resorted to a house-to-house assault. On December 9 Cós hoisted a white flag. Under the capitulation agreement Cós gave to the Texans all the public property, money, arms, and supplies in San Antonio; in return, Cós and his men were permitted to return south of the Rio Grande after agreeing never again to oppose the restoration of the Constitution of 1824. Fewer than 400 citizen soldiers had taken a town held by more than twice their number, but many of the Mexican soldiers were newly arrived, untrained recruits of little value to their cause. The Texans' victory was not without a price. Overconfidence, stimulated by the victory, would contribute to many of their problems in the months to come.

THE CONSULTATION

While these developments were taking place in the military field, the political scene had shifted several times. Texas had formed two temporary governments and had organized a third that promised to be ineffective. Ironically, the first, which lasted only three weeks, is known as the Permanent Council. Organized on October 11, 1835, it consisted of the Committee of

Henry Smith. He was one of the first people to advocate Texas independence, and was named govenor of the Provisional State of Texas (of Mexico) by the Consultation in November 1835. (Archives Division—Texas State Library)

Public Safety in San Felipe joined by representatives from other communities. During its brief existence, the Permanent Council served well. It sent supplies and volunteers to the army in the field, commissioned privateers, established a postal system, ordered the land offices closed and surveying discontinued, authorized an agent to go to the United States and borrow money, and appealed to the citizens of the United States for men, money, and supplies. It kept the people of Texas informed about the revolution and spurred them to greater efforts.

The Consultation, the second governmental body of the revolution, was delayed because of the outbreak of hostilities and moved from Washington to San Felipe. When a quorum was finally reached on November 3, fifty-five delegates from twelve municipalities of the departments of the Brazos and Nacogdoches assembled. Branch T. Archer, a Brazoria delegate and former member of the Virginia assembly, was elected president. An early issue in the meeting concerned the question of independence. A committee, composed of a delegate from each of the twelve municipalities, could not agree on whether the colonists were fighting for independence or for their rights under the Constitution of 1824. When the issue was returned to the full assembly, there were three days of "lengthy and animated" debate before the Consultation voted on November 6 for a "provisional government, upon the principles of 1824," and then voted 33 to 15 against a declaration of independence.

The statement adopted was, however, a compromise with those who advocated immediate independence. It spoke of Santa Anna's tyranny and of the "natural rights" of the people of Texas, declared that the Texans were fighting to maintain the federal Constitution of 1824, and stated that they offered their assistance to all Mexicans who would join them in resisting military despotism. But the fifth article of the resolution suggests the possibility of more extreme action. The colonists, it stated, "hold it to be their right . . . to establish an independent government," but they would "continue faithful to the Mexican government so long as that nation is governed by the constitution and laws."

Another act of the body that constituted a definite step toward separation was the election of Branch Archer, William Wharton, and Stephen Austin as commissioners to the United States to obtain aid. The delegates must have known that their kin east of the Sabine would not send men and money to Texas merely to have a part in an internal squabble of Mexican politics. In fact, the cause of the friends of the Constitution of 1824 was already lost. Far away in Mexico City that instrument had been replaced when the Mexican Congress, under the direction of Santa Anna, had adopted the *Siete Leyes*, an authoritarian system of centralist government.

The Consultation endorsed most of the work of the Permanent Council, adopted a plan for the creation of an army, and elected Sam Houston commander in chief, but the command did not include the forces then in siege at Béxar. The delegates voted to sustain those volunteers but declared that they were not obliged to submit to its control. It drew up a plan for a provisional government made up of a governor, a lieutenant governor, and a general council to be composed of one member from each municipality. All officials were to be chosen from the members of the Consultation. The Consultation finally adjourned on November 14, agreeing to reassemble on March 1, 1836, unless called sooner by the governor and general council.

Although the Consultation performed very well in many matters, it made two serious mistakes. Despite the best of intentions, it deprived Texas of the valuable services of its two most essential men. Austin, a logical choice to head the provisional government, was sent away "in honorable exile" to the United States, and Houston was made a commander in chief without an army. Equally serious was the failure of the Consultation to delineate clearly the powers of the general council and of the governor in the new provisional government. Henry Smith, who had served as political chief of the Department of the Brazos, was elected governor, and James W. Robinson of Nacogdoches was chosen lieutenant governor. Smith sympathized with the aims of the war party; most members of the general council tended to support the aims of the more moderate peace party.

THE FAILURE OF THE PROVISIONAL GOVERNMENT

For about a month the new provisional government worked creditably. It created and filled offices and completed the framework of the political structure, provided for the organization of a post office and a navy, and gave support to the army in the field. Internal discord, however, soon made it helpless. The crises came over a matter of policy. Like the Consultation, the council favored the Constitution of 1824 and cooperation with the Mexican liberals against Santa Anna. Thus, it approved a campaign against Matamoros, believing that its seizure would encourage the people there to resist Santa Anna. Governor Smith opposed the move, and after the council had repeatedly passed measures over his veto, he determined to cow it into submission or to dismiss it. On January 10, 1836, his message, written in most intemperate language, was read to the council. Either the council should apologize for its evil ways, said the governor, and agree henceforth to cooperate with him or adjourn until the first of March. The council replied in language quite as severe, declared the office of governor vacant, and inaugurated Lieutenant Governor Robinson as acting governor. Smith refused to deliver up the archives and continued to receive much mail addressed to the executive. The council could not secure a quorum after January 17, and thereafter, until a new convention assembled on March 1, the only semblance of government was Robinson and an advisory committee. It accomplished little.

Although there were many differences between governor and council, the major controversy centered around an ill-advised and ill-fated effort to launch an invasion of Matamoros. The general council was determined to carry out the invasion, despite the opposition of the governor and General Houston. It named Frank W. Johnson to head the campaign, and Johnson in turn named James Grant, an Englishman who was a citizen of Coahuila, to be commander in chief of the expedition. What then followed was confusion that would have been comic had it not been tragic. Grant made his way to San Antonio, where he took 400 of the Texas volunteers, most of the food and medical supplies, and virtually all of the munitions, leaving the commander of the garrison in San Antonio, J. C. Neill, complaining bitterly. Then, on January 3, Frank Johnson informed the council that he had decided the Matamoros campaign would be a mistake. Four days later the general council ordered Colonel James Fannin, in command in Velasco, to raise volunteers and supplies and to invade Mexico. By then Johnson had changed his mind, and with the approval of the council, he left for Goliad to take command of the expedition.

Meanwhile, General Houston, who was trying to assemble the troops of the regular army in Goliad and Refugio and to keep Copano open, persuaded most of the volunteers with Johnson and Grant to abandon the Matamoros project. Johnson, however, informed Houston that the general council had deposed Governor Smith and commissioned Fannin and Johnson himself to raise men and supplies and to take Matamoros. Actually, his force was little more than a scouting party of a few men, and these moved into the area around San Patricio to await reinforcements. Soon thereafter (February 2), Fannin landed at Copano with about 200 men and moved inland by way of Refugio, where he learned that Mexican troops were entering Texas. He thereupon decided against the Matamoros campaign, even though he eventually assembled about 450 volunteers. These troops would most assuredly have the opportunity to fight, but not in Matamoros.

Displeased because the general council had ignored his counsel, Houston took a furlough from the army until March 1. He then went to eastern Texas to carry out a previous order to negotiate a treaty with the Cherokee Indians. In the negotiations he was aided by William Goyens, a prominent black businessman of Nacogdoches, who served as an interpreter. On February 23, he signed a treaty that assured the Cherokees title to their lands in return for remaining at peace with the Texans.

While the Texans were arguing and debating in these weeks of indecision and confusion, Mexican armies were making their way northward to the Rio Grande. On October 27, 1835, President Santa Anna concluded at a meeting with his advisers that the Anglo-American colonists in Texas were in revolt and decided that he would personally lead an expedition against them. Then, in Saltillo on January 25, 1836, he held a grand review of the army, a dazzling spectacle. Having learned of the plans of the Texans to invade Mexico, he sent Colonel José Urrea with a force of several hundred to Matamoros with orders to march from there along the coast into Texas by way of Refugio and Goliad. He then proceeded to the Rio Grande, where he joined General Joaquín Ramirez y Sesma, who commanded his left flank with about 1,500 men. Altogether, Santa Anna now had an army of about 6,000 men prepared to march into Texas.

THE ALAMO

In late December 1835, after Grant and Johnson stripped the garrison of men and supplies for the Matamoros expedition, J. C. Neill was left in command of the post at San Antonio with about a hundred poorly equipped men. The council was disposed to hold San Antonio at all costs, but on January 17, 1836, General Houston ordered James Bowie to take some men to San Antonio, destroy the fortifications, and retreat to Gonzales, taking with him the cannon and as many supplies as possible. However, the general apparently left Bowie with some discretion as to what action should be

James (Jim) Bowie. He was born in Tennessee, and at 19 moved to Louisiana and engaged in illicit slave trade with Jean Lafitte. He migrated to Texas in 1828, and in 1831 he married Ursula María de Veramendi, daughter of the vice-governor (governor 1832–1833) of Coahuila and Texas and engaged in business in Coahuila. In 1832 Bowie helped drive the Mexican troops from Texas and in 1835 he joined the Texas volunteers and commanded the volunteers in San Antonio when Willliarn B. Travis arrived with a few regular army troops. Forced by illness to relinquish command to Travis, the bedridden Bowie was killed on March 6, 1836, when Santa Anna's troops stormed the Alamo. (Courtesy Southwest Collection, Texas Tech University, Lubbock, Texas)

taken. Once there with about 25 men, Bowie decided to remain. About the same time, Governor Smith, disregarding Houston's advice, ordered Lieutenant Colonel William B. Travis, recruiting officer in San Felipe, to recruit 100 men and go to the relief of San Antonio. Travis, with only 29 men, reached San Antonio on February 3.

A few days later, Neill gave Travis command of the garrison and left for home because of illness in his family. The volunteers, however, refused to accept the arrangement and elected Bowie as their commander. Travis remained in command of the regulars. The stalemate did not last long; Bowie, already seriously ill, was compelled to leave the command to Travis.

A few other troops arrived, some already famous. James B. Bonham, a native of South Carolina, an Alabama lawyer, and the organizer of the Mobile Grays, left his company in Goliad to join his long-time friend, Travis. The most famous was David Crockett, ex-congressman from Tennessee, who with about a dozen of his "Tennessee boys" rode into San Antonio unexpectedly on February 8. The new arrivals strengthened the determination of the men to hold the garrison.

Travis and his men occupied the building and grounds generally called the Alamo. It was the old Mission San Antonio de Valero, which had later been the home of a company from Alamo de Parras in Mexico. The walls of the mission were thick and twelve feet high, there was ample room for supplies of food, and there was plenty of water. Unfortunately, the size of the grounds required far more men for defense than Travis could muster, even with the several cannon that were available, and a portion of one wall was incomplete, protected only by a makeshift arrangement of sticks and dirt. Nevertheless, as a historian of the Alamo has stated, "the place . . . seemed to cast some sort of spell over the Texas leaders." Travis wrote, "We consider death preferable to disgrace which would be the result of giving up the Post which has been so dearly won."

While Travis and his men prepared their defenses, Santa Anna's army made its way toward San Antonio. On February 16, the main army began crossing the Rio Grande at Paso de Francia (near modern Eagle Pass), and moved toward San Antonio, about 150 miles distant, in disregard of General Vicente Filisola's plea to march directly for San Felipe. Santa Anna, the self-styled "Napoleon of the West," wanted to avenge the defeat of Cós. The vanguard of the army reached San Antonio on February 23, to the surprise of Travis, who expected it but not nearly so soon.

When the Mexican army was first sighted on February 23, Travis sent two of his scouts to the *alcalde* of Gonzales with a plea for men and provisions. The men, he added, "are determined to defend the Alamo to the last." The next day, while the Mexican artillery was bombarding the Alamo, he sent out an appeal "to the People of Texas and All Americans in the World." In it he stated that "the enemy has demanded a surrender at discretion," but *"I shall never surrender or retreat . . . VICTORY OR DEATH."* During the night of February 25, Juan Seguín, a prominent San Antonian, rode through the Mexican sentries and raced for Gonzales with another urgent plea for aid.

To join the force barricaded in the Alamo required a measure of courage. Bonham twice went out and twice came back. His return through enemy fire at 11:00 A.M. on March 3, 1836, after it was evident that the Alamo was a deathtrap, should qualify him as a hero. And there were others. Albert Martin and thirty-two men from Gonzales, in response to Travis's appeal and with courier John W. Smith as guide, slipped past the Mexican lines and into the Alamo at 3:00 A.M. on March 1. The only detachment of troops that might have significantly altered the strength of the defense of the Alamo never arrived. Fannin started from Goliad for San Antonio on February 26 with most of his men, but the next day returned to his fort.

On March 3, Travis sent out his last appeal for help, this one to the convention that he knew was scheduled to be in session in Washington-on-the-Brazos. Although at least 200 shells had fallen inside the works, the Texans had not lost a person, and their spirits were still high. It was better, Travis believed, to meet the enemy "here than to suffer a war of devastation to rage in our settlements." With this and a number of other notes, John W. Smith slipped out through the south wall. Travis hoped that the convention would issue a declaration of independence, but ironically he and other defenders of the Alamo died fighting for a federalist government under the Constitution of 1824, without knowing that such action had been taken.

On March 4 and 5, the Mexican cannon were moved closer and became more effective. Then, just before dawn on March 6, with the band playing *Deguello* ("no quarter"), Santa Anna took the fortress by storm, leaving only one defender alive. On the orders of Santa Anna, the bodies of the defenders were stacked on layers of wood and burned. The number of Texans who died traditionally has been counted at 182 (183 according to a report by a Mexican official), but some recent scholarship suggests that the number was higher, perhaps as many as 250. The Mexican dead, variously estimated from 600 to 1,600, were buried in the cemetery until it was filled, and the remainder were dumped into the river.

Apparently only one Texan soldier (José Maria Guerrero, who convinced Santa Anna that he had been fighting against his will) survived, but there were several other survivors. Santa Anna ordered the release of some Mexican women and children who were in the Alamo. Mrs. Almaron Dickinson, the wife of a Texas officer killed in the battle, her daughter, and two black slaves were also allowed to leave the scene. Those who perished in the strug-

The Alamo. The Texas revolutionaries took the town of San Antonio in December 1835 and three months later about 180 men led by Travis, Bowie, and Crockett died trying to hold the Alamo against Santa Anna's forces. "Remember the Alamo" became the rallying cry of the revolutionary army. (Courtesy of the Texas Department of Transportation)

gle left a legacy of bravery and heroics. Not always recognized, but similarly worthy of admiration, were the courage and determination of the hundreds of Mexican soldiers who perished in the assault. In the face of deadly cannon and musket fire, they repeatedly attacked, while their comrades fell on all sides, until they overwhelmed the garrison and the guns fell silent.

Heroism in the Battle of the Alamo is obvious, but an evaluation of the significance of the battle is not an easy task. It was, no doubt, a battle that Santa Anna did not need to fight and one that he should not have fought. If he had bypassed the garrison, marched on into the settlements to the east, and assumed control of the more populated areas of Texas, the outpost in San Antonio would have posed no threat. Its conquest, then, was a matter of ego, a matter of revenge, and the price was high. Had he ignored the fortress, he would have saved time and supplies, not to mention the lives of hundreds of his soldiers. His march to the east was delayed for several weeks, and the stand of Travis and his men became a cause and a battle cry for the Texans. On the other hand, there is little indication that Texans used the time purchased with the blood of the Alamo to good advantage. The delay in part contributed to an opportunity for Houston to recruit and train an army, but Santa Anna's decision to ignore the Texan commander's efforts was probably more meaningful.

After his victory at the Alamo, Santa Anna devised a three-column advance eastward through the settlements. In the south, General Urrea, reinforced by a detachment of about 600 troops from San Antonio, was to march by way of Victoria and Matagorda Bay to Brazoria and perhaps as far as Anahuac. General Antonio Gaona, with 725 men, was ordered to march to Nacogdoches by way of Bastrop and the upper crossing on Trinity River. The main army, with General Joaquín Ramirez y Sesma leading the advance, would proceed eastward by way of Gonzales and San Felipe. With his troops on the move, Santa Anna and General Vicente Filisola, next in command, left San Antonio on March 31.

THE BIRTH OF THE REPUBLIC

The Texans who died at the Alamo did not know that they were fighting for independence from Mexico and for a newly created republic. On March 1, 1836, the bickering and quarreling governor, lieutenant governor, and council, were supplanted by a convention. On December 14, 1835, over Governor Smith's veto, the council had passed an act calling for the election of delegates to a convention "with ample, unlimited, or plenary powers as to the form of government to be adopted." The delegates, elected on February 1, convened on the morning of March 1 in Washington-on-the-Brazos, a new town about thirty-five miles upstream from San Felipe. It was a dismal place, a visitor from Virginia recorded; the cold rain the night before had left the one street ankle deep in mud, and the cotton cloth stretched across the openings for windows in the unfinished building in which they met only partially excluded the chilling wind.

The situation that confronted the delegates when they assembled that cold morning was anything but promising. Urrea's troops were methodically crushing Texan forces in south Texas, and Santa Anna's army was wearing down the garrison at the Alamo. Travis was pleading for aid, but there were no troops at Washington and none between Washington and San Antonio, 150 miles away. The outlook was well-nigh hopeless.

To meet this challenge, the voters of Texas had selected a group of experienced delegates. Among them were Thomas J. Rusk, James Collinsworth, and George C. Childress, who would play important roles during and after the revolution. Another distinguished and influential delegate was Lorenzo de Zavala, a former member of the Mexican Congress and a staunch opponent of Santa Anna's centralism. Sam Houston, a delegate from Refugio, was no doubt a valuable member, but he left the convention in less than a week to take command of the army. Of the fifty-nine delegates who attended the convention, fifty-two were from the United States. One was born in England, one in Ireland, one in Canada, and one in Scotland. Three were native Mexicans, two of whom—José Antonio Navarro and José Francisco Ruíz—had been born in Texas.

On the first day the convention elected as president Richard Ellis of Pecan Point, and it selected a committee to be chaired by George C. Childress to draft a declaration of independence. Childress had arrived only recently in Texas, bringing $5,000 from the citizens of Tennessee. On the next day, March 2, the convention adopted a declaration of independence, perhaps written by Childress before the convention assembled, that followed the main features of the document written by Thomas Jefferson sixty years earlier.

The convention then began preparing a constitution for the new nation. The completed document, adopted at midnight on March 16, 1836, was a composite of excerpts from the constitutions of the United States and several states. There were some unique features, however. The term for the president was to be three years (the first constitutional president to serve two years only), and he was not to succeed himself; the president was not to lead armies in the field except with the consent of Congress; ministers of the gospel were not to hold office; each head of a family in Texas was to be granted a headright of a league and a *labor* of land; and the institution of slavery was legalized, but the African slave trade was considered piracy.

The convention also constituted itself the government of Texas and took steps to meet the emergency. Dealing with the most immediate crisis, on March 4 it appointed Sam Houston to be "Commander in Chief of all the land forces of the Texan Army, both regulars, volunteers, and militia, while in actual service." On Sunday, March 6, when Travis's last message arrived, an impetuous delegate, Robert Potter, moved that the delegates adjourn and go to the relief of the Alamo, but after a long speech by Houston, who insisted that the establishment of a government should have priority, the motion was rejected. Houston then left the convention to rally a force. The last act of the convention, performed as the candles burned short on the night of March 16–17, was the selection of an *ad interim* government to direct the infant republic until the constitution could be adopted and a regular government inaugurated. The delegates elected David G. Burnet president and Lorenzo de Zavala vice president. These and other officials of the government were sworn in at 4:00 A.M.; a few hours later the convention adjourned.

THE WAR IN SOUTH TEXAS

While Santa Anna laid siege to the Alamo and delayed for about three weeks after victory, and the convention delegates at Washington on the Brazos labored to create a new republic, General José Urrea on the southern front, with no more than one-fourth of the Mexican army under his command, moved from one victory to another. Leaving Matamoros on January

David G. Burnet. He was *ad interim* president of the Republic of Texas, March 16 to October 22, 1836, and vice president, 1838–1841. A native of New Jersey, Burnet previously had commanded the launch that fired the first shot in the war for Venezuelan independence. He lived for almost two years with the Comanche Indians in West Texas while recovering from tuberculosis, and in 1826 had obtained an *empresario* grant in East Texas. In 1866 he was named to represent Texas in the U.S. Senate but was never seated. (Archives Division—Texas State Library)

18, 1836, Urrea marched rapidly along the coastal road and on February 27 at San Patricio surprised Frank Johnson, who at the time had with him about thirty-five men. All the men were killed or captured, except Johnson and four or five of his companions, who managed to escape. Twenty miles farther up the road, on March 2, Urrea destroyed James Grant and his scouting party of about thirty men and then continued toward Goliad.

At Goliad, Colonel Fannin continued to display the indecisiveness that he had shown in the past. Having failed to reinforce the Alamo, he had returned to Goliad, where on March 14 he received an order from General Houston to fall back to Victoria. He delayed to wait for the return of two detachments of troops led by Amon B. King and William Ward, but neither group returned. King and his thirty-three men had been captured near Refugio and, except for some Germans, were shot on March 16. Ward and his

The entrance of a Mexican force of 6,000 or more in February 1836 was the beginning of a series of disastrous defeats for the Texan cause. While Santa Anna lay siege to and conquered the defenders of the Alamo, Urrea in a period of four weeks between the battle at San Patricio and the Goliad Massacre won several battles and took part in a number of skirmishes.

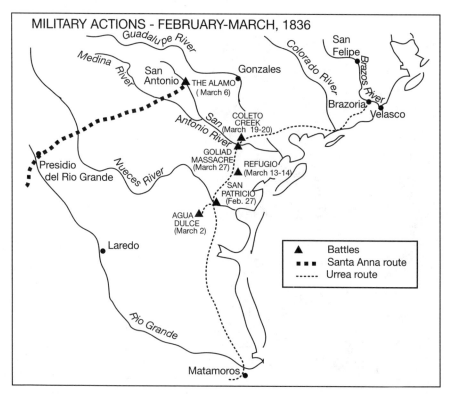

MILITARY ACTIONS - FEBRUARY-MARCH, 1836

men had escaped from Refugio but were surrounded and captured on March 22 near Victoria and were impounded with other prisoners at Goliad.

Fannin with his main force began his retreat on March 19, the day after Urrea, augmented by 600 troops from San Antonio, reached Goliad. That afternoon when a wagon loaded with ammunition broke down and the oxen needed to graze, Fannin camped on an open prairie. Another two or three miles would have brought him to timber and badly needed water at Coleto Creek. He was quickly surrounded by Urrea's cavalry. The Texans withstood the first attacks, but the next morning, when the main Mexican force arrived on the field with cannon, Fannin surrendered. Later, the survivors contended that they had surrendered as prisoners of war to be treated in accordance with international policy, but the original document in the Mexican archives shows that they capitulated "subject to the disposition of the Supreme Government." In this battle 9, possibly 10, Texans were killed, 51 wounded, and 234 captured; at least 50 of Urrea's men were killed and 140 wounded, with some sources estimating more than 200 killed. The prisoners were returned to Goliad, kept in confinement for a week, and then, on orders of Santa Anna, about 350 (including Ward and 82 of his men) were shot, despite the protest of General Urrea. Two physicians, some nurses, several needed workmen, and about 28 who somehow or another managed to avoid death were not executed. Some of the survivors owed their lives to Señora Francisca Álvarez, later remembered as the "Angel of Goliad."

RETREAT

By mid-March the settlers to the east of San Antonio were aware that Santa Anna's troops were marching in their direction and that there were few defenders to halt the advance. What hope there was depended on the efforts of General Sam Houston. From the convention in Washington-on-the-Brazos, Houston went directly to Gonzales. On his arrival on March 11 he found 374 men with less than two days' provisions, many without arms, and others without any ammunition. He immediately organized the First Regiment of Texas Volunteers with Edward Burleson in command. On March 13 he learned that General Joaquín Ramirez y Sesma with about 700 troops was marching toward Gonzales. Knowing that his small, untrained, and poorly equipped force could not defend the town, he had it burned and that night began his retreat. A rear guard shepherded the frightened settlers, who hurriedly abandoned their homes and fled eastward with the retreating army. On the afternoon of March 17, Houston arrived at Burnam's (Burnham's) Ferry on the Colorado, near La Grange. By then he had about 600 men. After getting the refugees and the troops across, he destroyed the ferry and encamped a short distance downstream at Beason's Crossing, barely ahead

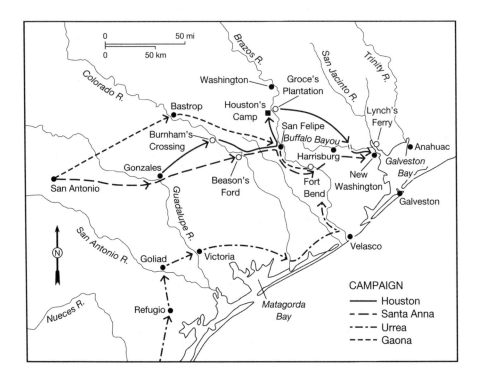

of the arrival of units of the Mexican army on the west bank of the swollen river. Hounded by his own men to let them fight, Houston considered making a stand at the Colorado, but upon the arrival of news that Fannin had capitulated, he decided to withdraw to the Brazos. He realized that a victory over Sesma would not end the war and that a defeat would mean disaster.

Ignoring the complaints of his unhappy soldiers, on March 26 Houston left for the Brazos, arriving late the next day at San Felipe, a village of five stores and twenty-five or thirty houses. Here, Captains Moseley Baker and Wiley Martin refused to retreat further. Houston thereupon assigned Baker with his company to guard the crossing at San Felipe and Martin to guard the crossing at Fort Bend, about thirty miles downstream. The remainder of the troops sloshed upstream, advancing less than twenty miles in three days, and camped on the west side of the Brazos across from the large plantation of Jared E. Groce. There, supplied with food and provisions from Groce's plantation, Houston remained for nearly two weeks, reorganizing and drilling the army.

Meanwhile, thousands of refugees fled eastward in advance of Santa Anna's soldiers. Probably as many as a thousand families lived along the Colorado and Brazos rivers along the paths of the armies. News of Houston's retreat and of the fate of the Alamo and Goliad—carried eastward into the settlements by fleeing civilians and soldiers who left with or without leave to look after their families—created widespread fear. Incessant floods, mud, and cold weather, which also caused problems for Santa Anna and his troops, added to the misery of the Texans. The frontier began to fold back upon itself in a movement that became known as the "runaway scrape." Loading their wagons, oxcarts, or sleds, or taking such simple belongings as could be carried on horseback or even on foot, the people set out in a desperate rush to keep ahead of the Mexican army. Streams were swollen, ferries became jammed, epidemics prevailed, and the misery and suffering were indescribable.

Difficult for everyone, the retreat was perhaps the most difficult for the women, who often had to assume responsibility for their families. Widow Angelina Peyton remembered that "women led donkeys packed with a few household treasures, and her more precious treasures, her children." Mary Rabb reported being driven "out of ouer houses with ouer little ones to suffer with cold and hungry." Others recalled "horrible confusion" and "pitiful and distressing" scenes of river crossings. The strong Captain Moseley Baker wept at the sad sight he witnessed as the people trudged by his camp opposite San Felipe. In her reminiscences, Dilue Rose Harris states that there were 5,000 people at Lynch's Ferry at the mouth of the San Jacinto when her family arrived there on April 10. Throughout the weeks of retreat, interrupted by delays on the banks of swollen rivers, Texas women helped to bury their dead, shared their grief, and cared for their children and those of others. Later, in describing the events of the revolution, Thomas Jefferson Rusk said "the women, with their little children around them, without means of defense or power to resist, faced danger and death with unflinching courage."

The government fled with the people. As the Mexican forces advanced, Texan headquarters were removed from Washington to Harrisburg (now within the city of Houston). Houston chastised the government for retreating, and Burnet in turn berated Houston. "The enemy are laughing you to scorn," he wrote, "you must fight them. You must retreat no farther. The country expects you to fight. The salvation of the country depends on you doing so." In commenting on his own conduct, Houston wrote Secretary of War Rusk on March 29, "I consulted none—I held no councils-of-war. If I err, the blame is mine." Meanwhile, Burnet sent Secretary of State Samuel Carson to Fort Jessup, Louisiana, to appeal for aid to General Edmund P. Gaines, who commanded a strong force of U.S. troops.

In their march eastward Santa Anna's forces, suffering in much the same manner as the Texans, moved slowly. Having left General Filisola at the Colorado with a detachment of troops to help get the artillery and supplies across the swollen river, on April 7 Santa Anna with Sesma and a part of the army reached San Felipe, which Baker had burned. With the ferry across the Brazos destroyed and his slow rafts an easy target for Baker's riflemen on the opposite shore, Santa Anna was unable to cross the river. The *ad interim* government at Harrisburg and the lower settlements were without any protection, since Houston and his army were upriver. Santa Anna therefore decided to move toward Harrisburg and to deal with Houston later. Sending orders to Filisola, Urrea, and Gaona to march their commands to Fort Bend, near present-day Richmond, he moved downstream to the settlement with an advance detachment of Sesma's troops. When all the units arrived, he would have at his command a force of about 3,400, more than three times the size of Houston's. While at Fort Bend, he received word that Burnet and the *ad interim* government were only thirty miles away in Harrisburg. Upon arrival at Harrisburg on April 15 with a only a portion of his army, he learned that the Texas officials had moved to a location on Galveston Bay. Santa Anna then set the town of Harrisburg aflame and marched toward Galveston Bay, only to find that Burnet and his cabinet had taken refuge on Galveston Island.

THE BATTLE OF SAN JACINTO

On April 12, 1836, after two weeks of drill and training on the Groce plantation, Houston made his move. With the aid of the steamboat *Yellowstone*, he ferried his command across the Brazos, where it received the famous "Twin Sisters," two cannon donated by the people of Cincinnati, that would soon help win Texas independence. Houston then marched southeastward. Not far ahead the road forked, one leading to Louisiana, the other to Harrisburg. The men, especially Moseley Baker, who had rejoined the main command, threatened to mutiny if Houston took the road toward Louisiana. Houston took the road to Harrisburg. On April 18, while he was camped near the ruins of the town, Deaf Smith, the faithful and effective scout, brought in a captured Mexican courier with dispatches that revealed more about Santa Anna's plans and movements. Houston thereupon crossed his army on rafts to the south side of Buffalo Bayou, left his baggage and sick men with a small guard hidden in the woods, and during the next night proceeded with slightly more than 900 men across the wooden bridge over Vince's Bayou to Lynch's Ferry. Taking possession of the ferry, he pitched camp soon after dawn on April 20 with the bayou at his rear, the San Jacinto on his left, and open prairie on his front and right flank.

Meanwhile, by the afternoon of April 20, Santa Anna had made camp to the south of Houston in an area lying next to marshland. The distance between the two armies was relatively small, less than a mile, mostly open country, but with a rise in the ground that prevented the two camps from direct sight of each other. At this point, the Mexican commander had made two serious mistakes; he had separated himself with a small force from the

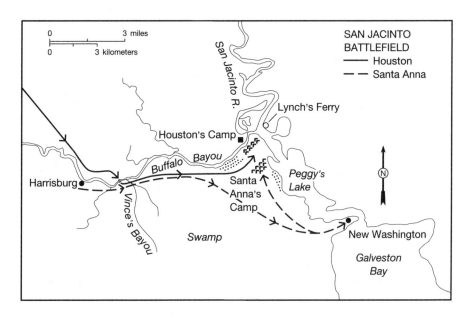

main body of his army, and he had camped in a location where organized retreat was difficult, if not impossible.

A sharp skirmish occurred during the afternoon. Upon finding the Texans in control of the ferry, the surprised Mexicans hauled a cannon to some nearby timber and began firing. During the action, Mirabeau B. Lamar, who had arrived only a few days before, performed with decision and courage, an effort that resulted in his appointment to the command of a unit of cavalry. That night, the Texans slept and the next morning, Thursday, April 21, had a good breakfast. In the early morning Santa Anna's forces received reinforcements when General Cós arrived with 542 (or perhaps more) tired and hungry troops. Santa Anna, convinced that the Texans did not intend to attack, permitted all, except for a small guard, to eat and retire to their tents for sleep and rest.

Houston prepared for battle. He sent Deaf Smith to destroy the bridge across Vince's Bayou, leaving neither army with an escape route. About noon, aware that the men were increasingly impatient, Houston told his officers to prepare for an attack. At 3:30 that afternoon, he formed his troops in a line that extended 1,000 yards along the edge of the woods. From left to right, the line order was the Second Regiment under Sidney Sherman, the First Regiment under Edward Burleson, artillery under George W. Hockley, a four-piece band, four companies of infantry under Henry Millard, and sixty-one cavalrymen under Lamar. The Texans moved quietly, hidden from view by a rise in the terrain, until they were within 200 yards of the Mexican barricades. Then the Twin Sisters fired a blast of broken horseshoes and shrapnel directly into the Mexican camp; the four-piece band began playing an inappropriate popular love song, "Will You Come to the Bow'r I Have Shaded for You"; Colonel Sherman struck the enemy to his left; and the line, center and right, charged directly into the breastworks of the camp, shouting "Remember the Alamo!" and "Remember Goliad!" Many of the surprised Mexicans fled in panic. General Manuel Fernandez Castrillon, a brave and able officer, tried to rally the confused Mexican soldiers, but, despite General Rusk's efforts to save him, other Texans riddled him with bullets. Santa Anna and some of his staff escaped into the woods, apparently hoping to reach his main army at Fort Bend.

The carnage at San Jacinto was indescribable. The battle, according to Houston's official report, lasted only eighteen minutes, but the pursuit, killing, and capture of the enemy continued much longer. The Texans, determined to exact full vengeance, could not be restrained. Arriving at the scene, where a terrible slaughter was under way, an officer who ordered the men to stop was, according to Austin's nephew, met with a cocked rifle and flat refusal. According to Houston's official report four days later, 630 of the enemy were killed, 208 were wounded, and 730 were taken prisoner, including General Cós and Santa Anna, who were captured the next day. Of the Mexican force, which numbered around 1,400 at the beginning of the battle, only a few escaped. Nine Texans were killed and thirty-four wounded, including Houston, whose right leg just above the ankle was shattered by shot in the midst of the action.

AFTER SAN JACINTO

The defeat of Santa Anna's forces saved the Texan cause for the time, but it did not immediately assure independence. There were still thousands of Mexican troops in Texas that might have to be reckoned with; Houston was helpless and soon had to take a steamer to New Orleans for the treatment of his ankle. In addition, the Texan army was almost as badly disorganized by victory as the Mexican army on the Brazos was by the reports of defeat. The Texas government faced several immediate problems: first, to restore order and establish among the people a sense of security and competence; second, to strengthen, supply, and keep control of the army; and third, to secure from Mexico the recognition of Texan independence, or at least to empty the country of Mexican troops.

Order and confidence returned gradually as the people learned of the completeness of the victory and observed that the government again was functioning. Many persons who had taken part in the runaway scrape went back to their homes at once. Government headquarters were moved from Galveston to Velasco, where better quarters could be secured. The *Telegraph and Texas Register*, whose plant at Harrisburg had been destroyed, resumed publication in Columbia in August. On July 23, President Burnet issued a proclamation calling for a general election to be held on the first Monday in September to establish a constitutional government.

The most serious problem that confronted the *ad interim* government after San Jacinto was control of the army, but the problem of the army was inseparably linked with that of deciding what to do with the prisoner Santa Anna and arriving at some understanding with the Mexican forces still in Texas. The Mexican armies to the west, however, proved not to be a problem. Shortly after he had been brought to Houston's headquarters on April 22, the Mexican president entered into an armistice. Complying with the agreement, he wrote General Vicente Filisola, second in command, to retire with his troops to Béxar and to order Urrea to fall back to Victoria "pending some negotiations . . . by which the war is to cease forever." Even as Santa Anna wrote, the Mexican forces were in retreat.

In Velasco on May 14, Burnet negotiated two treaties with Santa Anna, one public and one secret. By the terms of the public treaty an end was declared to hostilities; the Mexican army was to retire at once beyond the Rio Grande, and all Texan prisoners were to be released by the Mexicans, the Texans agreeing to release a corresponding number of Mexican prisoners. The secret treaty secured from Santa Anna a pledge to use his influence on the Mexican government to ensure the fulfillment of the public treaty. It was also intended to establish a permanent treaty whereby Mexico would acknowledge the independence of Texas, the boundary of which was not to extend beyond the Rio Grande. The Texas government in turn pledged to release Santa Anna at once, giving him an escort to Vera Cruz.

Ignoring the widespread clamor for the execution of the dictator, Burnet on June 4 placed General Santa Anna, his secretary Caro, and Colonel Almonte aboard the schooner of war *Invincible*. But a group of disgruntled military officers, led by General Thomas J. Green, a recent arrival from the United States, compelled Burnet to remove the prisoners from the vessel and place them in confinement on land. Developments during the next few weeks did not improve Santa Anna's position. Word came that the Mexican senate had annulled his treaty and had declared that the war would continue. Three Texan emissaries, sent to Matamoros under a flag of truce to determine whether all prisoners had been released and bearing passports from Filisola, were arrested and thrown into a Mexican prison. Rumors reporting the return of Mexican armies persisted. On June 17, Rusk wrote from the army that Urrea was advancing on Goliad. Urrea's threat did not materialize, nor did any other, but some time would pass before Texas leaders would feel secure. Months later President Houston finally resolved the problem of the captured dictator when he returned Santa Anna to Mexico by way of the United States.

Burnet's difficulties with insubordinate troops continued throughout the remainder of his tenure as *ad interim* president. After the Battle of San Jacinto, Thomas J. Rusk reluctantly took command of the Texan army and followed the retreating Mexican armies as far as Victoria. Word that Santa Anna was to be released provoked an army mass meeting and an insolent and threatening letter to Burnet. In an effort to improve army morale with a change of commanders, about July 1 Burnet attempted to replace Rusk with Mirabeau B. Lamar, but neither the men nor officers would accept Lamar. After a plan of the army officers to arrest and bring Rusk before the army for trial failed, Burnet attempted to divert the energies of the army by encouraging an expedition against Matamoros. Like the earlier expedition, this one never materialized, but it possibly kept the military occupied for a time. Meanwhile, the beleaguered president sent word to agents in New Orleans to send no more volunteers and left the problem of the army for his successor, Sam Houston.

AID FOR THE REVOLUTION

The expenditures of Texans in the cause of revolution were surprisingly small. Figures in the records read more like those of a retail store than of the government of a sovereign state. Virtually every device for raising money known in that day was tried. Donations amounted to about $25,000. The most substantial receipts, about $100,000, came from loans negotiated in the United States by Commissioners Austin, Archer, and Wharton. And there were other loans, either in money or supplies, amounting to a total of about $1.25 million by August 31, 1836.

In fact, the revolution was financed largely by those who advanced supplies to the infant government on faith and by the troops who served for little other compensation than the promise of land bounties. Some people pledged land, slaves, and other property to be sold for the benefit of the cause, but little money was raised in that way. Jane McManus offered to borrow money, with her land as security, to support the war effort. Other women manufactured cartridges and made clothing, donated livestock, and created more than one of the flags that flew over the ranks of the soldiers. Sometimes contributions added to the hardships of the settlers. Widow McElroy, who lost cattle and a wagon, appealed to President Burnet for compensation, for her family was in great need. Angelina Peyton, who failed to complete the proper forms, had trouble securing compensation for her oxen placed in the service of the army. Pamelia Mann, who allowed Houston to use her oxen while he traveled toward Nacogdoches, demanded their return when the general turned toward Harrisburg. Not usually intimidated, Houston apparently met his match and returned the animals.

War supplies came mainly from New Orleans. The firm of William Bryan and Company, Texan agents in that city, often used their own funds and impaired their private credit in the interests of the struggle. The Texan merchant, Thomas F. McKinney, working as a private citizen, spent large sums of his own money for shipments of flour, rifles, powder, lead, clothing, and other necessary supplies for the army.

From east of the Sabine came men as well as supplies. As early as October 26, 1835, the Permanent Council addressed the citizens of the United States with an impassioned appeal to come to the aid of "suffering Texas." From New Orleans to Cincinnati friends of the colonists held meetings, raised funds, and sent out forces of volunteers of "armed emigrants." The chief recruiting stations were Louisville, Cincinnati, and New Orleans. Some of the best-known volunteer organizations were the two companies of "New Orleans Greys," in one of which were represented five foreign countries and twelve different states; the Georgia Battalion, composed of men from Georgia and Alabama and strengthened by recruits who joined them on the way to Texas; the "Mobile Grays," originally some thirty men under Captain David N. Burk; the Alabama "Red Rovers," almost seventy men under Captain Jack Shackelford, who arrived at Matagorda early in 1836; the "Mustangs," from Kentucky and Tennessee; and some fifty Tennesseans, among them David Crockett, who arrived in Nacogdoches on January 12, 1836. For many of these the future held a tragic ending. A majority of the men who died in the Alamo had recently come from the United States, as was true of the forces of Johnson and Grant, and Fannin's men were, almost without exception, recent arrivals. The most successful work in recruiting troops abroad for Texas was done late in the war by Thomas Jefferson Chambers. By December 1836, he had sent 1,915 well-equipped volunteers. These forces arrived too late, however, to participate in the battles of the revolution.

Ironically, it was the colonists who lived in Texas before the revolution began who were some of the most effective soldiers. It was they who drove the Mexican forces out of Texas in 1835, and they made up a sizable portion of Houston's army at San Jacinto. Most were of Anglo-American heritage, but in no sense were all. Three Texans of Mexican heritage, Lorenzo de Zavala, José Francisco Ruíz, and José Antonio Navarro, signed the Declaration of Independence. Many other Tejanos fought in the armies. One authority has suggested that as many as 160 participated in the siege and battle of San Antonio in November and December 1835. Tejanos made up a portion of the garrison of the Alamo the following spring, although, according to the report of a survivor, a number took advantage of an amnesty pledge of Santa Anna and left before the battle, apparently acting on the advice of Bowie. Throughout the war, one of the most valuable military units in the war was the Tejano cavalry led by Juan Seguín. Seguín and his men took part in the battle of Concepción, participated in the siege of San Antonio, scouted the countryside and alerted the Texans to the arrival of Santa Anna's forces marching toward the Alamo, and finally insisted on the opportunity to join in the attack on San Jacinto and were in the midst of the fighting.

Many Tejanos, however, did not support the rebel cause. Some had long-standing ties with the centralists who supported Santa Anna; others were concerned about an uncertain future in a land dominated by Anglo-Americans who had little respect for their culture. In many instances loyalty was determined by a simple desire to survive the conflict and to protect their homes and families, and consequently it shifted according to circumstances. Tejano citizens of San Antonio, for instance, provided support for both sides in the fall of 1835 and spring of 1836. The Tejanos of the Goliad area were divided in their loyalties, but those who supported the forces of Santa Anna contributed significantly to the success of Mexican armies in that area.

Black Texans also made their contributions. Greenbury Logan fought at Concepción and San Antonio, where he was wounded, and Samuel McCullough suffered a wound at Goliad in the early fighting of the revolution. Hendrick Arnold saw action at San Antonio, where he was one of the more valued scouts, and at San Jacinto. In the area of diplomacy, William Goyens was a valuable participant in negotiations to keep the Cherokees from joining the Mexican cause. There were others as well.

On occasion the black people of Texas still held in bondage contributed to the cause. One of the Texans who died in the Alamo was a slave, known only as John, although two other slaves were spared by Mexican officers. Some of the information used by Houston on the eve of the Battle of Jacinto was provided by slaves who reported on the size and location of Mexican troops, and slaves James Robinson and Mark Smith took part in the battle, as did one known as Dick, the drummer. A slave named Cary saw considerable service as a courier, and others provided supplies or served in some military capacity. Not all, however, supported the Texan cause. Mexican commanders sometimes promised freedom (and occasionally carried out their promise) to slaves who would join their forces, while in other instances, slaves took advantage of the confusion of war to seek and find freedom.

THE TEXAS NAVY

Although Gonzales is generally given the credit, the first battle in the revolution occurred at sea on September 1, 1835. The Mexican war schooner *Correo* fired upon the *San Felipe* bound for Victoria with a cargo of munitions. After a two-hour fight, the *Correo* was captured and taken to New Orleans. Mexican war and transport ships continued to operate along the coast, and consequently the provisional government on November 25 provided for the purchase of four schooners and for granting a letter of marque to privateers until the navy materialized. Meanwhile, the citizens in the coastal communities had bought and equipped the schooner *William Robbins*, which subsequently took the Mexican man-of-war *Bravo* and another ship it had just taken. Sentiment in the United States, however, was so strongly against privateering that the Texans had to discontinue the practice.

The Texas navy took form when, in January 1836, the Texas commissioners purchased four naval vessels: the *William Robbins* (rechristened the *Liberty*), the *Independence*, the *Invincible*, and the *Brutus*. About the same time, in early March, President Burnet commissioned William A. Hurd to the rank of commodore and placed him in command of the fleet. The fleet patrolled the coast and convoyed shipments from New Orleans. The *Brutus* maintained a blockade along the Texas coast until it was lost in a storm in October 1837. The *Liberty* took a valuable prize, the Mexican schooner *Pelicano*, filled with munitions for the Mexican army (packed in barrels of flour and apples). The *Invincible* took prizes along the coast until it ran aground and was destroyed in Galveston harbor while engaged in a fight with two Mexican vessels. During the early months of 1836 the *Independence* captured a number of small Mexican vessels before it was eventually captured after a four-hour fight in sight of Galveston.

As the Mexican army advanced in the spring of 1836, the Texas ships centered their activity on keeping the port of Galveston open, thereby allowing the Mexican forces uncontested use of the forts at the mouth of the Brazos and Copano Bay. Anticipating that the Mexicans might send troops through these ports, General Thomas J. Rusk ordered Major Issac W. Burton with a troop of thirty mounted men to patrol the coast. Sighting a Mexican vessel in Copano Bay, the unit on June 3 managed to decoy the captain and some crew members ashore, seize them, row out in their boat, and take the ship (loaded with supplies for the Mexican army) without resistance. Two weeks later, when two other ships loaded with supplies appeared, the "Horse Marines," as Burton and his rangers became known, managed to take both without a casualty.

Thus it was the sea that was the scene of the first and final battles of the revolution.

BIBLIOGRAPHY

The Texas Revolution has long attracted historians and continues to do so. There is an abundance of writings, old and new, but readers should be familiar with two exceptionally fine books, each one comprehensive in its particular emphasis—Paul D. Lack, *The Texas Revolutionary Experience: A Political and Social History, 1835–1836* (College Station, 1992), and Stephen Hardin, *Texian Iliad: A Military History of the Texas Revolution, 1835–1386* (Austin, 1994). Other general works are those of W. C. Binkley, *The Texas Revolution* (Baton Rouge, La., 1952) and D. M. Vigness, *The Revolutionary Decades* (Austin, 1965).

Of the older general histories, all cited in chapter 4, good accounts may be found in J. H. Brown, *A History of Texas* (two vols., St Louis, 1892–1893), H. H. Bancroft, *History of the North Mexican States and Texas* (two vols., San Francisco, 1884 and 1889), W. Kennedy, *Texas* (2nd. ed., London, 1841), H. Yoakum, *History of Texas* (New

York, 1855), D. G. Wooten, *A Comprehensive History of Texas* (two vols., Dallas, 1877), reprint of Yoakum's text, C. R. Wortham, *A History of Texas* (five vols., Fort Worth, 1924), and H. S. Thrall, *Pictorial History of Texas* (St Louis, 1879). Yoakum gives much source material; Thrall has many biographical sketches; and Wortham devotes a volume to the revolution. See also Juan N. Almonte, *Noticia Estradistica Sobre Tejas* (Mexico, 1835); and Vicente Filisola, *Memoirs of the History of the War with Texas* (typescript trans. Verona Griffith, Library, Texas Tech University, Lubbock, Tex.; Mexico, 1848); Vito Allesio Robles, *Coahuila y Tejas en la Epoca Colonial* (Mexico, 1938); and A. J. Houston, *Texas Independence* (Houston, 1938).

Several biographies are extremely valuable in connection with the revolution. See Gregg Cantrell, *Stephen F. Austin: Empresario of Texas* (New Haven, Conn., 1999); E. C. Barker, *The Life of Stephen F. Austin* (Nashville and Dallas, 1925); L. Friend, *Sam Houston, the Great Designer* (Austin, 1954); Randolph Campbell, *Sam Houston* (New York, 1993); Marquis James, *The Raven: A Biography of Sam Houston* (New York, 1929); John H. Jenkins and Kenneth Kesselus, *Edward Burleson: Texas Frontier Leader* (Austin, 1990); E. Wallace, *Charles DeMorse, Pioneer Editor and Statesman* (Lubbock, 1943); Herbert P. Gambrell, *Mirabeau Bonaparte Lamar* (Dallas, 1934); Herbert P. Gambrell, *Anson Jones: The Last President of Texas* (New York, 1948); Mary Whatley Clarke, *David G. Burnet* (Austin, 1969); Herman Ehrenberg, *With Milam and Fannin* (trans. Charlotte Churchill and ed. Henry Smith; Austin, 1974); Natalie Ornish, *Ehrenberg: Goliad Survivor–Old West Explorer* (Dallas, 1997); Hobart Huson, *Captain Phillip Dimmitt's Commandancy of Goliad* (Austin, 1974); Ernest C. Shearer, *Robert Potter, Remarkable North Carolinian and Texan* (Houston, 1951); William G. Davis, *Three Roads to the Alamo: The Lives and Fortunes of David Crockett, James Bowie, and William Barrett Travis* (New York, 1998); Archie McDonald, *Travis* (Austin, 1976); W. N. Bate, *General Sidney Sherman: Texas Soldier, Statesman and Builder* (Waco, 1974); Cleburn Huston, *Deaf Smith, Incredible Spy* (Waco, 1973); Joseph Dawson, *José Antonio Navarro: Co-Creator of Texas* (Waco, 1969); J. A. Atkins, *David Crockett, The Man and the Legend* (Chapel Hill, N.C., 1956); John Henry Brown, *Life and Times of Henry Smith, the First American Governor of Texas* (Dallas, 1887); R. N. Richardson and others, *Heroes of Texas* (Waco, 1964).

The source materials for the revolution are voluminous. The most comprehensive is John H. Jenkins (ed.), *The Papers of the Texas Revolution, 1835–1836* (ten vols., Austin, 1973). Other comprehensive collections are E. C. Barker (ed.), *The Austin Papers* (vols. I and II, Washington, D.C., 1924, 1928; vol. III, Austin, 1926); Amelia W. Williams and E. C. Barker (eds.), *The Writings of Sam Houston* (eight vols., Austin, 1938–1943); C. A. Gulick, Katherine Elliott, and Harriett Smithers (eds.), *The Papers of Mirabeau Bonaparte Lamar* (six vols., Austin, 1921–27); and W. C. Binkley (ed.), *Official Correspondence of the Texan Revolution, 1835–1836* (two vols., New York and London, 1936). Useful also is C. E. Castañeda (ed. and trans.), *The Mexican Side of the Texan Revolution* (Dallas, 1928); E. Wallace, D. M. Vigness, and George Ward (eds.), *Documents of Texas History* (Austin, 1993); and John H. Jenkins (ed.), *Recollections of Early Texas; The Memoirs of John Holland Jenkins* (Austin, 1958).

Some understanding of Tejano roles in these years can be found in Jesús F. de la Teja (ed.), *A Revolution Remembered: The Memoirs of Juan N. Seguín* (Austin, 1990), and David R. McDonald and Timothy M. Matovina (eds.), *Defending Mexican Valor and Texas: José Antonio Navarro's Historical Writings, 1853–1857* (Austin, 1995). For additional materials, see Arnoldo De León,"Estudios Tejanos: A List of Historical Literature on Mexican Americans in Texas," *Southwestern Historical Quarterly*, XCVIII, 457–470.

Shorter studies dealing primarily with the early phase of the revolution include "General Austin's Order Book for the Campaign of 1835," *Quarterly of the Texas State Historical Association*, XI, 1–55; Fred H. Turner, "The Mejia Expedition," ibid., VII, 1–28; E. C. Barker, "Proceedings of the Permanent Council," ibid., IX, 287–288; E. C.

Barker (ed.), "Journal of the Permanent Council," ibid., VII, 249–278; E. C. Barker, "The Texan Declaration of Causes for Taking Up Arms Against Mexico," ibid., XV, 173–185; E. C. Barker, "The Tampico Expedition," ibid., VI, 169–186; Ralph Steen, "Analysis of the Work of the General Council of Texas, 1835–1836," ibid., XL, 309–333; XLI, 225–240; E. C. Barker, "Don Carlos Barrett," ibid., XX, 139–145; R. S. Lee, "The Publication of Austin's Louisville Address," ibid., LXX, 424–442; Raymond Estep, "Lorenzo de Zavala and the Texas Revolution," ibid., LVII, 322–335; Margaret Swett Henson, "Understanding Lorenzo de Zavala: Signer of the Texas Declaration of Independence," *Southwestern Historical Quarterly*, CII, 1–17; Miles S. Bennett, "The Battle of Gonzales, the `Lexington' of the Texas Revolution," *Quarterly of the Texas State Historical Association*, II, 313–316; E. C. Barker, "The Texas Revolutionary Army," ibid., IX, 227–261; *The Texans* (Time-Life Books, 1975); Katherine Hart and Elizabeth Kemp (eds.), "E. M. Pease's Account of the Texas Revolution," *Southwestern Historical Quarterly*, LXVIII, 79–89; and Joseph Milton Nance, "Abel Morgan and His Account of the Battle of Goliad," ibid., C, 207–233. Alwyn Barr's *Texans in Revolt: The Battle for San Antonio* (Austin, 1990) revises some long-standing interpretations on the longest battle of the war.

On the war in the field, see E. C. Barker, "The Texan Revolutionary Army," *Quarterly of the Texas State Historical Association*, IX, 227–261; E. C. Barker, "The San Jacinto Campaign," ibid., IV, 237–345; John E. Roller, "Captain John Sowers Brooks," ibid., IX, 157–209, which contains letters from a soldier with Fannin; Ruby C. Smith, "James W. Fannin, Jr., in the Texas Revolution," *Southwestern Historical Quarterly*, XXIII, 79–90, 171–203, 271–284; Harbert Davenport, "Captain Jesus Cuellar, Texas Cavalry, Otherwise Comanche," ibid., XX, 56–62; Amelia Williams, "A Critical Study of the Siege of the Alamo," ibid., XXXVI, 251–287; XXXVII, 1–44, 79–115, 157–184, 237–312; James W. Pohl and Stephen Hardin, "The Military History of the Texas Revolution: An Overview," ibid., LXXXIX, 269–308; Louis E. Brister, "The Journal of Col. Eduard Harkort, Captain of Engineers, Texas Army, February 8–July 17, 1836," ibid., CII, 344–379; Don Graham, "Remembering the Alamo: The Story of the Texas Revolution in Popular Culture," ibid., LXXXIX, 35–66; M. L. Bonham, Jr., "James Butler Bonham: A Consistent Rebel," ibid., XXXV, 124–136; Michael Costeloe, "The Mexican Press of 1836 and the Battle of the Alamo," ibid., XCI, 533–544; H. Davenport, "The Men of Goliad," ibid., XLIII, 1–41 (an interpretation of the entire Texan Revolution); H. M. Henderson, "A Critical Analysis of the San Jacinto Campaign," ibid., LIX, 344–362; Jewel D. Scarborough, "The Georgia Battalion in the Texas Revolution: A Critical Study," ibid., LXIII, 511–532; Thomas I. Miller, "Fannin's Men: Some Additions to Earlier Rosters," ibid., LXI, 522–532; James Presley, "Santa Anna in Texas: A Mexican Viewpoint," ibid., LXII, 489–512; and Thomas Miller, "Mexican-Texans at the Alamo," *Journal of Mexican American History*, II, 33–44.

Well-written and reliable longer studies of the battle of the Alamo are those of Ben Proctor, *The Battle of the Alamo* (Austin, 1991); Walter Lord, *A Time to Stand* (New York, 1961); Lon Tinkle, *Thirteen Days to Glory* (New York, 1958); and Crystal Sasse Ragsdale, *Women and Children of the Alamo* (Austin, 1994). Likewise well written but with a frequently questioned viewpoint concerning the battle and the revolution in general is the study of Jeff Long, *Duel of Eagles: The Mexican and U.S. Fight for the Alamo* (New York, 1990). Recent works with a special emphasis include Holly Beachley Brear, *Inherit the Alamo: Myth and Ritual at an American Shrine* (Austin, 1996); Timothy M. Matovina, *The Alamo Remembered: Tejano Accounts and Perspectives* (Austin, 1995); and Bill Groneman, *Eyewitness to the Alamo* (Plano, 1996). And there are many, many more.

José de la Peña, *With Santa Anna in Texas: A Personal Narrative of the Revolution*, trans. Carmen Perry (College Station, 1975), has generated a vigorous historical debate, energized by the book's reference to events at the Alamo. See Bill Groneman,

Defense of a Legend: Crockett and the De La Peña Diary (Plano, 1994), for a persuasive argument that the diary of de la Peña may not be genuine, and James E. Crisp, "The Little Book That Wasn't There," *Southwestern Historical Quarterly*, XCVIII, 261–296, for a persuasive argument that the diary is genuine.

Craig H. Roell, *Remember Goliad* (Austin, 1994), is a brief but excellent treatment of the Fannin massacre, as well as military activities leading to the event. Recently published is Clifford Hopewell, *Remember Goliad: Their Silent Tents* (Austin, 1998). For longer studies on San Jacinto, see James W. Pohl, *The Battle of San Jacinto* (Austin, 1992); and Sam H. Dixon and Louis W. Kemp, *The Heroes of San Jacinto* (Houston, 1932).

For an account of the convention of 1836, see R. N. Richardson, "Framing the Constitution of the Republic of Texas," *Southwestern Historical Quarterly*, XXXI, 191–220; J. K. Greer, "The Committee of the Texas Declaration of Independence," ibid., XXX, 239–251; XXI, 33–49, 130–149; Henderson Shuffler, "The Signing of Texas' Declaration of Independence: Myth and Reality," ibid., LXV, 310–332; and L. W. Kemp, *The Signers of the Texas Declaration of Independence* (Houston, 1944).

On developments after the Battle of San Jacinto, see Margaret Swett Henson, "Politics and the Treatment of the Mexican Prisoners after the Battle of San Jacinto," *Southwestern Historical Quarterly*, XCIV, 189–230; and W. C. Binkley, "Activities of the Texan Revolutionary Army after San Jacinto," *Journal of Southern History*, VI, 331–346. Concerning the attitude of President Jackson toward the Texan Revolution, two points of view are presented in E. C. Barker, "President Jackson and the Texas Revolution," *American Historical Review*, XII, 797–803; and R. C. Stenberg, "The Texas Schemes of Jackson and Houston, 1829–1836," *Southwestern Social Science Quarterly*, XV, 229–250. J. E. Winston has published in the *Southwestern Historical Quarterly* a series of articles on aid from the United States. See XVI, 27–62, 277–283; XXI, 36–60; XVIII, 368–385; and XVII, 262–282. See also James M. Denham, "New Orleans, Maritime Commerce, and the Texas War for Independence, 1836," ibid., XCVII, 522–534, and C. Elliott, "Alabama and the Texas Revolution," ibid., IL, 316–328.

On the Texan navy, see Alex Dienst, "The Navy of the Republic of Texas," *Quarterly of the Texas State Historical Association*, XII, 165–203, 249–275; XIII, 1–43, 85–127; Jim Dan Hill, *The Texas Navy* (Chicago, 1937); and George G. Haugh (ed.), "History of the Texas Navy," *Southwestern Historical Quarterly*, LXIII, 572–579.

7

The Republic of Texas 1836–1845

For ten years Texas existed as an independent republic. These were exciting, challenging years, often troubled with conflict and controversy but also filled with progress and accomplishment. In politics, the nation tended to align itself into factions either pro- or anti-Houston, a division that was in part a matter of politics and personalities but was also based on policy issues. Despite problems of money and Indian wars, immigrants responded to a generous land policy, and the population grew at an amazing pace.

Texans managed to achieve a degree of success in foreign affairs, although acceptance by other nations came slowly in some instances and not at all in others. Relations with Mexico were not good in the beginning and did not improve over time. A minority of Texans firmly believed that the future of Texas as an independent nation was promising, but most hoped for annexation to the United States and rejoiced when that was finally accomplished.

THE ELECTION OF 1836

Soon after the Texan victory at San Jacinto, the *ad interim* officials took steps to establish a regular government. President Burnet and his cabinet, without waiting until December as the convention had proposed, issued on

July 23, 1836, a proclamation setting the first Monday of the following September as the date for an election. Three major issues were to be decided: first, ratification of the constitution; second, the election of the officials who would take office provided the voters approved the constitution; and third, whether the next government should seek annexation to the United States.

The ratification of the constitution and a favorable vote on annexation were reasonably certain; thus the major interest in the election centered on the selection of a president. Since there were no political parties in Texas at the time, the candidates had to depend largely on their general popularity. Henry Smith, the first to announce for the presidency, sought to vindicate his policies as head of the provisional government. Austin entered the race at the solicitation of William Wharton, Branch Archer, and others, but he had lost much of his popular support. Notwithstanding his years of distinguished service to Texas, his early opposition to independence, his support of the government in saving Santa Anna from a firing squad, and a charge that he had not served Texas well while in the United States had seriously damaged his standing with the people. Austin believed that many citizens blamed him for the notoriously unpopular land speculation schemes of his friend and partner, Samuel May Williams.

It was soon evident that the third presidential candidate, Sam Houston, was the people's choice. Just eleven days before the election, he formally accepted the nomination by numerous groups throughout the nation. In the election he received 5,119 votes—almost 80 percent of the total. Smith received 743 and Austin 587. Mirabeau B. Lamar was elected vice president. The constitution was approved overwhelmingly, though voters refused to allow Congress the power to amend it. Only 93 voted against the mandate requiring the new president to seek annexation to the United States.

HOUSTON AND THE NEW NATION (1836–38)

President Houston actually took office before his term began. *Interim* President Burnet convened the First Congress in Columbia on October 3, but there was a growing demand for Houston and Lamar to take office without waiting until the second Monday in December, as provided in the constitution. On October 22 Burnet resigned, and Houston took the oath of office as the first constitutionally elected president of the Republic of Texas. In his impromptu inaugural address, Houston spoke only briefly of his program, one based on his belief that Texas would soon be a part of the United States.

Houston's cabinet, which he claimed was selected "with a total disregard to personal preference," was quickly determined. Austin was made secretary of state, and Henry Smith was appointed secretary of the treasury.

Austin died about two months after taking office and was replaced by Dr. Robert Irion, a native of Tennessee. William Wharton was sent to represent the republic in Washington, D.C. James Collinsworth was appointed chief justice, who, when acting with the four district judges, constituted the supreme court.

The First Congress likewise quickly went about its work. It created twenty-three counties, corresponding in most cases to the Mexican municipalities. Congress also defined the limits of the republic with a law of December 19, 1836, setting the boundary at the center of the Rio Grande from its mouth to its source, north to the forty-second parallel, and east and south along the Adams-Onís Treaty line to the Gulf of Mexico. In response to threats of a Mexican invasion and to fear of hostile Indians, Congress in December authorized an army of more than 3,500 soldiers and 280 mounted rangers, a chain of forts and trading houses on the frontier, the organization of militia units, and the creation of a new navy.

Houston, however, was more interested in getting rid of the army than in supporting it. The army proposed to renew hostilities with Mexico with an invasion of Matamoros. Angry when Houston named Thomas Rusk secretary of war, the army very nearly mutinied when Houston appointed Albert Sidney Johnston, a capable West Point officer, to take command. The soldiers rallied in support of their favorite, Felix Huston, a military adventurer. Huston challenged Johnston to a duel, wounded him, and retained the command. President Houston, however, solved the problem. In May 1837,

Sam Houston. Elected governor of Tenessee in 1827, Houston seemed to have a secure political future when he resigned two years later and moved to what is now Oklahoma to rejoin the Cherokee Indians who had adopted him in his youth. Houston came to Texas in 1833 and became a member of the convention that declared Texas independent of Mexico and set up a provisional government. Criticized for retreating before the Mexicans, Houston regained popular favor when he defeated Santa Anna at San Jacinto in April 1836 and was elected the first president of the republic.

he furloughed or disbanded all but 600 of the troops, offering free transportation to New Orleans or land to those who would accept a discharge. To offset the reduction in the strength of the army, Congress then provided for a corps eventually known as "Texas Rangers." Several members of this corps eventually won considerable recognition and fame.

Indian problems, which were primarily responsible for the organization of the ranger units, were indeed serious. Raids, mostly involving Comanche and Kiowas, threatened settlements on the frontier. In one of the raids, Comanches took one of their most famous captives, Cynthia Ann Parker, who subsequently married a Comanche chief. In later years her son, Quanah Parker, was one of the great war chiefs of the Comanches. Ranger patrols in 1837 did not eliminate the raids of the kind that led to the captivity of Cynthia Ann Parker, but the problem was diminished.

Relations with the Cherokees in East Texas were another threat to peace. The Cherokees, who began moving into Texas as early as 1819, settled on a vague grant given by the Spanish in the vicinity of Nacogdoches.

Quanah Parker. A great part of Texas was once Comanche country. Quanah Parker was one of the last Comanche war chiefs and the son of Chief Nocona and Cynthia Ann Parker, a captive white woman. (The Institute of Texan Cultures, San Antonio, Texas)

During the Texas Revolution, Sam Houston, by authority of the Consultation, negotiated a treaty with them providing for permanent title to their lands in exchange for their promise to remain at peace during the war.

Thereafter the Texas Senate refused to ratify the treaty, and the Cherokees threatened to make trouble. Adding to the tension and confusion were the actions of Vicente Cordova, a Mexican citizen of Nacogdoches who had some contact with the Mexican government. In the summer of 1838, he led a band of nearly 600 Mexicans and Kickapoo Indians in a rebellion near the Angelina River. The rebellion was of short duration, but Cordova and some of his Indian allies continued to pose a threat. Although the Cherokees were not involved in the affair, it increased hostility toward all Indians in the area. Houston managed to preserve the rights of the Cherokees and a fragile peace for the balance of his term, but in no way did he achieve a permanent solution.

Money was another major problem of the Houston administration. Public expenses amounted to nearly $2 million, and income was a mere fraction of this amount. A tariff produced the most revenue, and port fees, a direct property tax, poll taxes, business taxes, and land fees each added a little. The receipts were seldom paid in specie and sometimes not paid at all. At times the poverty of the government was embarrassing. For a period, Secretary of the Treasury Henry Smith could not attend to his duties because he had no stationery and no funds with which to buy any. Houston could secure supplies for the army only by pledging his personal credit. Under such conditions the government turned to the use of paper money. Acts of 1837 led to the issue of $650,000 in promissory notes that held their value very well, but a succeeding issue soon depreciated to as little as 65 cents on the dollar.

THE YOUNG REPUBLIC AND FOREIGN AFFAIRS (1836–38)

During the revolution and afterward, foreign affairs, particularly relations with the United States, were of particular concern to Texans and their leaders. The Texas government sought aid—even intervention on its behalf—diplomatic recognition, and if possible, annexation by the United States at the earliest date possible. But the United States was cautious in its commitments. James Collinsworth and Peter W. Grayson, the last representatives sent by the *ad interim* government, accomplished little except to learn that President Andrew Jackson had sent an agent, Henry M. Morfit, to secure more information about affairs in Texas.

Houston, who considered the vote of September 1836 in favor of annexation a mandate, diligently pursued both annexation and diplomatic recognition. Santa Anna, still a prisoner, suggested that he be allowed to support the transfer of Texas to the United States in an interview with President

Jackson. Despite the protests of Congress, Houston, who wanted to get his prisoner out of Texas, sent Santa Anna to Washington under escort. Jackson paid little attention to the Mexican leader and promptly sent him to Vera Cruz aboard an American naval vessel.

Houston's commissioners in Washington, William H. Wharton and Memucan Hunt, found little encouragement. Morfit, Jackson's investigator, had reported unfavorably on affairs in the new nation, and Jackson's message to the U.S. Congress in December 1836 advocated delay in recognizing Texas independence. There was doubt as to the ability of Texas to maintain its independence, a fear of offending Mexico, and a belief that recognition would be regarded as a preliminary step toward annexation. Jackson, however, told Wharton that he would approve recognition if the U.S. Congress would recommend it. Working diligently, Wharton and Hunt, with the aid of various supporters, persuaded the Congress to appropriate expenses for a diplomatic agent to Texas whenever the American president should deem it expedient. In his last official act, President Jackson appointed Alcée LaBranche chargé d'affaires to the Republic of Texas.

Recognition now attained, Texas pressed for annexation, but Hunt's formal offer made on August 4, 1837, was firmly rejected. According to John Forsythe, the United States secretary of state, treaty obligations with Mexico prevented the United States from entertaining the subject. A stream of memorials and petitions was submitted to the U.S. Congress in the fall of 1837, but opposition was very strong, particularly from antislavery forces, and no vote was ever taken. Active in encouraging the antislavery forces was Benjamin Lundy, whose experiences in Texas had convinced him of the existence of a slaveowners' conspiracy to bring Texas into the union to strengthen their cause. After a time, Anson Jones, then representing Texas in Washington and acting under Houston's order, announced the "formal and absolute withdrawal" of the offer. On January 23, 1839, the Texas Congress, along with then President Mirabeau Lamar's sanction, ratified the withdrawal. Annexation was not again an issue until 1843.

But earlier in the summer of 1837, President Houston, convinced that the United States would not consider annexation and acting with the approval of Congress, opened diplomatic negotiations with European powers. He sent Secretary of State J. Pinckney Henderson to Great Britain and France to secure recognition and negotiate commercial treaties. Lord Palmerston, British minister of foreign affairs, was disappointingly indifferent. England was opposed to slavery; British capitalists had millions invested in Mexican bonds; and England was not interested in aiding a nation that probably would soon join the United States. Henderson did, however, in 1838 secure a convention with Great Britain that provided for trade between Texas and that country.

Although there was no immediate threat, relations with Mexico were poor. The Treaty of Velasco, signed on May 14, 1836, by President Burnet and

Santa Anna, was almost immediately rejected by the Mexican Congress. At the same time, the Mexican government announced that it intended to subdue the rebellious Texans. President Houston, convinced that Mexico was too involved in internal difficulties to carry out the threat, took no steps to meet it. In large measure, he was correct. Relations with Mexico during the balance of his term were virtually nonexistent.

LAMAR'S ADMINISTRATION (1838–41)

Selecting a presidential candidate for the 1838 election proved to be difficult for Houston supporters. Houston, restricted by the constitutional provision limiting the first president to two years, was not eligible to seek reelection. His supporters turned to others but without much success. Thomas J. Rusk refused to run. Peter W. Grayson, attorney general and commissioner to Washington, agreed to run, but while on an official mission to the United States, he took his own life. The Houston party then turned to thirty-year-old James Collinsworth, a hero of the Battle of San Jacinto and chief justice of the Texas Supreme Court, but in July 1838 he drowned in Galveston Bay. A few weeks before the election, the Houston group agreed to support Robert Wilson of Harrisburg, a promoter of the town of Houston and for a time a member of the senate. By then it was clear that Vice President Lamar, a candidate but surely no Houston supporter, would be president. The vote for Lamar on November 16, 1838, was almost unanimous. David G. Burnet was elected vice president.

In his inaugural address and first message to Congress, President Lamar promised an ambitious public program in keeping with his belief that Texas should remain an independent republic. Although some of his plans did not prove successful, others were adopted and of enduring value.

A strong advocate of public education, he urged Congress to pass the necessary legislation. Accordingly, an act of January 20, 1839, provided that each county should be given three square leagues for primary schools and that fifty square leagues should be set aside for two colleges or universities. A year later a law provided additional lands for each county, and Congress also made land grants to several private institutions. Land was cheap, and many years were to pass before Texas had even the semblance of a system of public education, but these laws, in large measure the responsibility of Lamar, laid the foundations.

The location of a permanent capital for Texas, a question carried over from Houston's regime, was selected during the Lamar administration. Columbia, the first location, was a temporary one for only a few months. In December 1836, Congress voted to move the seat of government to the new town of Houston in May 1837, with the stipulation that a permanent location

Mirabeau Buonaparte Lamar. He came to Texas from Georgia to join the revolutionaries in 1835 and took part in the Battle of San Jacinto. During his term as the second President of the Republic (1838–1841), he secured foreign recognition of Texas' independence. He had hoped to make the republic self-sufficient, but his ill-advised expedition to New Mexico left Texas in financial difficulties. (Archives Division—Texas State Library)

would be designated by 1840. Prompted by Lamar, Congress in January 1839 authorized the appointment of a committee to select a site between the Colorado and Brazos rivers and north of the "Old San Antonio Road" and decided that it should be named for Stephen F. Austin. The commissioners chose a site near the small settlement of Waterloo on the Colorado River at the foot of the Balcones Escarpment. President Lamar and his cabinet proceeded to the new capital in October 1839, and within four months the town had a population of 856.

Upon assuming the presidency, Lamar immediately inaugurated a major change in Indian policy. Indians must either conform to Texas laws, leave the nation, or face extermination. Secretary of War Albert Sidney Johnston, a majority of Congress, and many others agreed with him and urged an aggressive frontier policy. Actually, relations between Texan settlers and natives were already critical. The Cherokees and associated groups in eastern Texas had been put off with promises for too long; they were uneasy and unhappy. Farther west, the Wacos, Tawakonis, and Comanches, seeing settlers penetrate their territory more deeply each season, were displaying their hostility.

The Cherokees were the first to be affected by Lamar's hostile Indian policy. Although the Cherokees remained at peace during Houston's term, other Indians in their area made sporadic raids, and some settlers continued to believe that the Cherokees were conspiring with Mexican authorities. Papers taken from a party of marauders killed in a battle near Austin in May

1839 convinced Lamar and his cabinet that the Cherokees were in treasonable correspondence with the Mexicans. Soon after the Cherokees defied Lamar's orders to leave peacefully and rejected a promise of compensation for their crops, they faced a Texan army of several hundred men. In the Battle of the Neches on July 16, near the present-day city of Tyler, the Texans defeated a Cherokee force led by Chief Bowles. Bowles, along with almost 100 of his warriors, was killed, and the remainder were driven across the Red River into Indian Territory. The Shawnees and some other groups then abandoned the area, and the peaceful Alabama and Coushatta were moved to other lands in Texas.

The war with the Comanches was longer and more bloody. Disturbed by the westward advance of the Texans, some southern Comanches in 1838 asked for peace. President Houston, however, refused their demand for a boundary, and Comanche raids on the frontier continued. When Lamar took office, Congress provided more military forces, but the early campaigns were not rewarding. Expeditions in the spring of 1839 were unsuccessful, with Texan forces accomplishing little and on one occasion narrowly escaping annihilation.

Notwithstanding their victories, early in 1840 a portion of the southern Comanches requested a peace council. The offer was accepted, provided the Comanches would bring to the council in San Antonio all their white captives. On March 19, 1840, a party of Comanches, 65 men, women, and children, arrived for the council, bringing only one captive, a badly mutilated fifteen-year-old girl. When the Texans, who had hidden troops in an adjacent room, attempted to take the Comanche warriors as hostages, a battle erupted. Thirty-five Indians were killed and 29 were taken prisoner; 7 Texans were killed and 8 were wounded. When they learned of the affair, known as the Council House Fight, other Comanches killed their prisoners. That summer a Comanche party raided Victoria and destroyed Linnville near the town of Port Lavaca. As the raiders moved homeward toward the plains, heavily loaded with booty, on August 12 they met a strong Texan force at Plum Creek near Lockhart. Led by Edward Burleson, Felix Huston, and Ben McCulloch, the Texans inflicted heavy losses. Almost 100 Comanches were killed, but others escaped with most of the plunder. War was renewed in the autumn. In October, Colonel J. H. Moore led an expedition in search of the elusive Comanches, and aided by Lipan Apaches, on October 23 surprised them and destroyed their village on the Colorado River, probably in the vicinity of present-day Ballinger. The Texans killed an estimated 130 Comanches and regained a large amount of the plunder and livestock taken on the Linnville raid. The Comanches thereupon withdrew far from the Texas frontier. By the end of 1840, Indian wars in Texas had practically ceased, but only until the end of the Republic.

The justice, humanity, and death toll of Lamar's campaigns may be questioned, but not their effectiveness. Lamar's Indian policy cost $2.5 million and the lives of quite a number of white people and a larger number of Indians. But his efforts in large measure removed Indians from the lands of eastern Texas and made the western frontier comparatively safe for several years.

Lamar's financial program was not successful. Financial affairs, not good under Houston, grew constantly worse during the Lamar administration. Tariff duties were reduced; other taxes were difficult to collect. Receipts for the three-year period were $1,083,661, and expenditures were $4,855,213. The government sought a loan of $5 million, but determined efforts over several years resulted only in one loan of $457,380 from the Bank of the United States. Lamar also proposed a gigantic Texas bank to be owned by the government. Congress refused to approve his plan, but insufficient capital made the establishment of the bank impossible anyway.

The administration resorted to the expedient of paper money—in large amounts. When Lamar assumed office, more than $800,000 in treasury notes (paper money), already valued at 80 to 85 cents on the dollar, was outstanding. In 1839, 1840, and 1841 Congress authorized more notes, known as "red backs," amounting to $3,552,800. The value of these depended upon the confidence of the people, which apparently was very little. By November 1841, the red backs were quoted at 12 to 15 cents on the dollar. Meanwhile, the public debt, approximately $2 million at the end of Houston's first term, rose to $7 million at the close of Lamar's term.

FOREIGN AFFAIRS (1838–41)

President Lamar's determination to develop a strong and secure republic was evident in the foreign policy of his administration. He actively sought recognition from European countries and enjoyed a measure of success. France, involved in a war (the Pastry War) with Mexico, was the first European power to enter into a treaty of friendship with Texas. Lamar's commissioner to France, James Hamilton, a former governor of South Carolina, signed a commercial treaty with France on September 25, 1839, but failed in his other mission, the negotiation of a much-needed loan. Hamilton remained in Europe and on September 18, 1840, he signed a treaty with the Netherlands.

Meanwhile, England, initially reluctant, had changed its position on recognition. In November 1840, Foreign Minister Palmerston and Hamilton signed a treaty of commerce and navigation, a treaty obligating England to mediate with Mexico for Texas independence (Texas to assume, if successful, $5 million of Mexico's debt to British bondholders), and a treaty giving England great liberty in suppressing the foreign slave trade. The Texas Senate, disapproving of the provisions concerning the slave trade, delayed ratification but finally accepted the treaty in 1842.

Lamar's success in Europe was not matched by similar success in Mexico. When Lamar became president in December 1838, he made clear that he considered the Mexican situation critical. In his first message to Congress, he stated: "If peace can only be obtained by the sword, let the sword do its work." However, he also sought peace with Mexico through diplomacy. To this end he sent three different agents to Mexico and solicited and secured the diplomatic aid of the United States and Great Britain. In some respects, the prospect for a diplomatic settlement seemed promising. Mexico was embroiled in a conflict with France, and Anastacio Bustamante, a weak leader but again in power, was struggling to overcome a federalist uprising in several northern Mexican states.

Lamar's first representative, Secretary of State Bernard Bee, traveled to Mexico in May 1839 with authority to offer the Mexican government as much as $5 million if it would recognize Texan independence and the Rio Grande as the boundary. Although supported by Richard Pakenham, the British minister to Mexico, Bee never got beyond Vera Cruz and accomplished nothing of consequence. The next representative sent to Mexico was James Treat, a British soldier of fortune, who claimed that he was a friend of Santa Anna and that Santa Anna, now back in power, wanted a treaty. Influenced by Bee, who was impressed with Treat and his claims, Lamar sent Treat to Mexico City in November 1839. Treat remained in Mexico City for ten months, engaged in unproductive activities that led nowhere.

After Treat failed and Congress refused to respond to a recommendation for war to compel Mexico to recognize Texas, Lamar made one more effort at diplomacy. Encouraged by the prospect of help from Great Britain contained in the treaty of 1840, Lamar early in 1841 sent Secretary of State James Webb to Mexico. Although Great Britain did pressure the Mexican government, the Texas representative was not received officially and returned home to urge war measures immediately. Lamar entered into an agreement with the Mexican state of Yucatán, then in revolt against the central government, which enlisted the services of the Texas navy in support of the revolutionaries. The alliance proved of little value. Shortly after it was made, Yucatán renewed its allegiance to Mexico.

In the final year of his administration, Lamar took a bold step that replaced unproductive diplomacy with direct action. On the east side of the upper Rio Grande were a number of settlements that made up the Spanish province and later the Mexican territory of New Mexico. As defined by the Texas Congress, these settlements were within the boundaries of Texas. Believing reports that the power of the Mexican government in this area was weak and that the people desired to be a part of Texas, President Lamar organized an expedition to go to Santa Fe, the largest and most important community. Although congress refused to authorize the venture, there were a number of merchants, soldiers, and adventurers who were eager to make the journey. Colonel Hugh McLeod commanded the military escort of 270 men;

William G. Cooke, José Antonio Navarro, and Dr. Richard F. Brenham went along as commissioners of the Texas government. The commissioners were instructed to take possession of Santa Fe and to set up a government under the authority of Texas, but to use force only if convinced that the majority of the population favored Texas.

The story of the expedition, written by George Wilkins Kendall, editor of the New Orleans *Picayune*, was a tale of woe. After leaving Austin on June 19, 1841, the group encountered heat, hunger, hostile Indians, and unfriendly Mexicans. Misfortune dogged the trail of the party as it traveled 1,300 miles by way of present-day Wichita Falls and Quitaque, across the plains, and finally to New Mexico and Santa Fe. Exhausted and at the mercy of the Mexican forces who met them, the survivors were made prisoners and marched to Mexico City and thence to Perote and other prisons. Most were released in April 1842, but José Navarro was held until 1844.

HOUSTON'S SECOND ADMINISTRATION (1841–44)

By the end of the Lamar administration, voters were divided into two distinct camps: the administration group and the opposition led by Houston. Not surprisingly, Houston, who since the end of his presidential term had served in the house of representatives, became a candidate to succeed Lamar. Administration forces supported David Burnet. There were issues such as public finances, Indian policies, and land policies, but issues were incidental. The campaign centered on gossip, scandal, and vituperation, which was of little credit to either side. The race was not even close. Houston received 7,915 votes to Burnet's 3,616. Edward Burleson, perhaps as much of an independent as one could be, was elected vice president.

As anticipated, the administration of Houston and a conservative congress was in sharp contrast to Lamar's ambitious and costly programs. The Sixth Congress carried economy to the point of parsimony. Offices were abolished; the number of clerks was reduced; and salaries were lowered below a living wage. Military expeditions after 1841 were confined to the maintenance of a few companies of rangers. Total expenditures for Houston's term of three years was only a little more than $500,000. Only $200,000 of "exchequer bills" (paper money) were issued, but even though this was the only currency to be used in the payment of taxes, the money declined in value.

The frugality of the government was well demonstrated in an effort to sell the Texas navy. When the navy continued to call for more money for needed repairs, the Congress in January 1843 solved the problem with a secret act ordering the sale of the four vessels. However, the people of Galveston were enthusiastic about the little fleet and sympathetic with its commander, Edwin W. Moore, who had refused to obey orders and had been declared a pirate and dishonorably discharged. By force certain citizens of Galveston prevented the auction of the four ships. After Texas became a part of the United States, the ships were transferred to the U.S. Navy.

Houston's pacific Indian policy, similar to that of his first administration, saved both money and lives. In September 1843, a treaty was signed at Bird's Fort with the Waco, Tawakoni, and other established groups. On October 8, 1844, near present-day Waco, President Houston and Chief Buffalo Hump for the Penateka Comanches signed the Treaty of Tehuacana Creek providing for trade and friendship. These treaties and Houston's peaceful policies reinforced Lamar's aggressive and successful military campaigns to preserve peace on the frontier.

Houston also brought peace to East Texas in the settlement of a feud between the "Regulators" and "Moderators." An old quarrel, the feud had its beginnings as far back as the time of the Neutral Ground agreement. Killings started in 1840 in Shelby County but spread to neighboring counties. The Regulators, avowedly organized to suppress crime, were opposed by the Moderators, who claimed that the Regulators burned houses, forced families to leave their homes, and committed other crimes. Soon the opposing factions numbered about 150 each. President Houston ordered 600 militia men to the scene, and partly by force and partly by persuasion, reestablished peace in the area.

HOUSTON AND MEXICO (1841–44)

Foreign affairs occupied much of the attention of Houston in his second administration. Problems with Mexico, some of which were probably caused by Lamar's policies, presented a series of crises in the early part of his term, and the quest for annexation to the United States dominated the latter part.

Partly in retaliation for the Santa Fe expedition, Santa Anna sent an army into Texas in March 1842. A Mexican force of about 500 men, commanded by General Rafael Vásquez, took San Antonio, Goliad, and Refugio but retired after a day or two, having done little damage. The most unfortunate result was a panic in central Texas, resembling the runaway scrape of 1836. President Houston declared a public emergency and ordered the archives of the government moved to Houston. Some citizens of Austin, led by Mrs. Angelina Belle Eberly, a strong-minded hotel proprietor, obtained a cannon and refused to permit their removal, thus provoking the comical but grim "archive war."

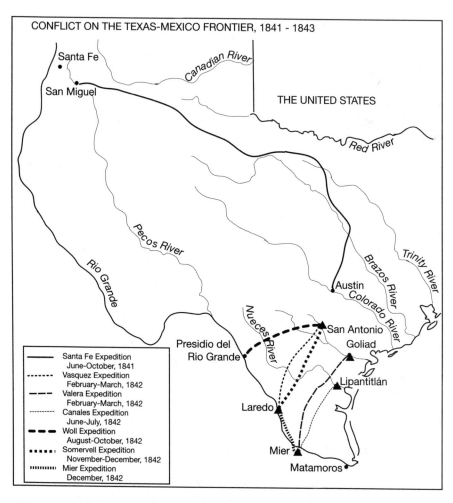

CONFLICT ON THE TEXAS-MEXICO FRONTIER, 1841 - 1843

Although the years from 1836 through 1841 on the Texas-Mexico frontier were not without incident or violence, major military crises did not occur until 1842. Probably, at least in part, in retaliation for Lamar's Santa Fe expedition, Mexican military forces entered Texas four times in 1842. Sizable expeditions commanded by Rafael Vásquez in the spring and Adrian Woll in the fall occupied San Antonio, while smaller ones led by Ramón Valera and Antonio Canales made their way to the Goliad area and lower reaches of the Nueces.

Although many Texans prepared for war, Houston adopted a cautious approach. Militia forces rushed to San Antonio, and Houston sent to the United States for men, money, and supplies for the invasion of Mexico. But he delayed the assembling of Congress until June 27, 1842, because, as he stated in confidential communications, he could not "trust their wisdom" in the crisis. When Congress met, it voted for a declaration of war and appropriated 10 million acres of land to meet the expense. Houston, obviously attempting to avoid a war if possible, pronounced this amount of support totally inadequate and vetoed the bill.

Houston's cautious policy was challenged a few months later, when a second Mexican army invaded Texas. General Adrian Woll, with about 1,400 men, held San Antonio for nine days. Again the Texas militia was called out and gathered at San Antonio, but Mexican forces defended their position vigorously. Woll's soldiers inflicted heavy losses on a militia company from Fayette County, commanded by Captain Nicholas Dawson, killing thirty-six Texans, including Dawson, and capturing fifteen. Finally forced to retreat on September 20, Woll took a number of prisoners with him on his march toward the Rio Grande, including officers, attorneys, and the jury of a district court, and some of Dawson's men.

Responding to public demand for action, Houston ordered the organization of an expedition to ensure that Mexican forces had withdrawn from Texas. About the middle of November, 750 men under General Alexander Somervell started for Laredo. After occupying Laredo on December 8, a part of the force disbanded and returned home. The remainder then marched down the Rio Grande until December 19, when Somervell ordered them to return to Gonzales. About 300 of the men refused to obey Somervell's orders, organized under Colonel W. S. Fisher, and on Christmas morning marched across the Rio Grande and occupied the Mexican village of Mier. After a desperate battle with a sizable Mexican army under General Pedro Ampudia, they surrendered the day after Christmas. Then followed their march as prisoners toward Mexico City, a break for liberty, their recapture, and a drawing for black beans to determine which one-tenth of their number would be shot. The survivors were finally imprisoned in the dank Castle Perote with the men of the Texas Santa Fe expedition and the prisoners from San Antonio who had been taken by Woll. After many months of confinement they were released, primarily because of pressure from British and U.S. diplomats, and only as Santa Anna was overthrown and pushed into exile.

While resisting the popular clamor for war with Mexico, Houston was exerting every effort to secure peace and the recognition of independence. He urged the governments of Great Britain, France, and the United States to "require of Mexico either the recognition of the Independence of Texas, or to make war upon her according to the rules established and universally recognized by civilized nations." Waddy Thompson, the U.S. minister to Mexico, urged recognition and offered the services of his government in the interest of peace. Nothing of importance came directly from these efforts, except possibly the offer of peace from Santa Anna in 1843 if Texas would recognize Mexican sovereignty. Houston had no intention of accepting the offer, but he used it as an opportunity to bargain and to buy time. He proclaimed a truce on June 14, 1843, but an armistice signed the following February lasted only four months, ending when Texas and the United States began negotiations over annexation.

HOUSTON AND THE QUEST
FOR ANNEXATION (1842–44)

If there was a positive result of the ill-fated Santa Fe and Mier expeditions, it was the rekindling of the interest of the people of the United States in Texas. At the same time, there were other influences at work to revive the subject of Texas annexation, which had been dormant since 1838. Houston reopened the issue with the United States as early as March 1842. However, it was not until October 1843 that President John Tyler, perhaps motivated by fear of growing British influence in Texas, suggested negotiations. Houston agreed to negotiations on two conditions: the United States must place its armed forces in position to prevent invasion of Texas, and the negotiations must be kept secret. A. P. Upshur, Tyler's secretary of state, refused to guarantee conditions, but his death shortly thereafter was followed by the appointment of John C. Calhoun to the office. Calhoun, fearful of aggressive British imperialism and eager to see the addition of more slaveholding territory to the United States, quickly agreed to Houston's demands. On April 12, 1844, he and Isaac Van Zandt, the Texas minister in Washington, and J. Pinckney Henderson, a special Texas envoy in the negotiations, signed a treaty. The treaty provided for the annexation of Texas to the United States as a territory and for the United States to assume its public debt. However, the U.S. Senate rejected the agreement on June 8. Antislavery forces in the United States opposed the addition of more slave territory; moreover, some senators were reluctant to make such an important decision on the eve of the national elections of 1844.

POPULATION GROWTH
IN THE REPUBLIC

Texans in the revolution had hardly returned to their homes from the army or from the runaway scrape before their kinspeople from east of the Sabine began to join them. In 1837 the *Telegraph and Texas Register* stated that "crowds of enterprising emigrants are arriving on every vessel." The following summer reports claimed that 6,000 immigrants crossed the Sabine at one ferry landing. Accounts indicate that in 1840 more immigrants arrived than had done so in any previous year and that the volume was sustained until the early part of 1842. Problems with Mexico in 1842 checked the flow sharply, but by 1844 large numbers were arriving almost daily. Trains of immigrants gathered at the ferry crossings and had to wait for hours. The white population, estimated in 1836 at 34,470, had reached 102,961 by 1847; the slave population, estimated at 5,000 in 1836, had reached 38,753. The number of free blacks slowly grew to 295, making the total population, except for Indians, 142,009.

The liberal land policy of the republic and almost universal lust for free or inexpensive virgin land was responsible for the flood of immigrants. The constitution specified that heads of families (blacks and Indians excepted) living in the republic on March 2, 1836, might receive free a First Class headright of a square league and a *labor* of land (4,605 acres) and that single men above seventeen years of age might receive one-third of a square league (1,476 acres). Congress later enacted measures that extended headright land grants to others in smaller quantities. In no instance was the amount of land given under a headright grant less than 320 acres. Altogether, the republic granted 36,876,492 acres in headright certificates to reward those who aided in the struggle for independence or to encourage immigration.

Determined to make Texas a nation of homeowners, the lawmakers went even further. They enacted a limited homestead law in 1838 (preceding similar legislation in the United States by a quarter of a century). The following year they passed the Homestead Exemption Act, exempting from seizure for debt the home, 50 acres of land, and certain improvements. The property exemption, unknown in English common law, may have been influenced by Spanish precedents. In 1845, Congress gave settlers living on vacant public lands an option to purchase (generally at 50 cents an acre) up to 320 acres. Ultimately, under the preemption and homestead laws Texas distributed 4,847,136 acres. Additional lands were granted to permanently disabled veterans, to those who had participated in the Battle of San Jacinto, and to the heirs of the men who had fallen in the Alamo and in the Matamoros and Goliad campaigns. Even the soldiers who served after the end of the fighting were given lands.

TEJANO EXPERIENCES
IN THE REPUBLIC OF TEXAS

One group of people, including some who had courageously supported the revolution, did not share equally, sometimes not at all, in the generous land policies of the republic. Tejanos successfully made a substantial number of headright claims during the republic, but many never received final title to their land. Indeed, for Tejanos these years were often filled with bitter experiences, although conditions varied from place to place. Many had served in the revolutionary cause and some were notable leaders, but prejudice and discrimination often affected their treatment. Land titles reaching far back into the past were sometimes challenged. Juan Seguín and the family of Martín de León had suffered cruel treatment from Mexican armies for supporting the revolution, and after the revolution found themselves treated as traitors by the victorious Texans.

Many of the Mexican people who had lived around Nacogdoches for generations found themselves threatened with violence, sometimes deadly. A small war developed when a leader, Vicente Córdova, emerged to form a rebel force made up of Tejanos, Indians, and blacks. Córdova's quest for aid from officials in Mexico elicited little more than promises and advice, but suspicions that Mexico was implicated in the rebellion alarmed officers of the republic. In the ensuing military action, most Mexican settlers in East Texas were driven from their lands.

Although a war similar to that of East Texas did not develop, many Mexican settlers who lived along the San Antonio and Guadalupe rivers, including perhaps as many as 200 families from San Antonio, were forced to flee, and others who lived nearer the coast or Goliad in South Texas left their holdings. According to one scholar, forty of forty-nine ranches originally belonging to Tejanos in the Goliad area were in the hands of Anglo ranchers by 1846. Meanwhile, Tejanos in the region between San Antonio and Goliad applied for and received a fairly large number of headright grants, though less than one-half of the applicants ultimately acquired a final title.

Perhaps the best conditions for Tejanos in the republic were found in San Antonio. There Anglo traditions challenged the dominant Hispanic culture of the community; the two cultures sometimes clashed and sometimes intermingled. But the culture of Tejanos endured. Maintaining the voice of their people in public affairs, four Tejanos served in the congress of the republic. On the local level, Tejanos retained much of their political power in the community, always representing a majority in the city council. In daily life, Tejanos protected their Catholic heritage, celebrated their church and national holidays, continued the use of the Spanish language, and held steadfastly to their family traditions and values.

The situation in the lands to the south and west of the San Antonio–Goliad region, the so-called Trans-Nueces between the Nueces River and the Rio Grande, was somewhat different from that in any other area of Texas. Never a part of Texas before the time of the republic and sometimes called a "no man's land," the Trans-Nueces fit this description only in that there was little security or authority in the area during the republic. Most of the land had been allocated in large grants during Spanish and Mexican rule, and more than 200 grants were awarded to claimants during the republic.

But fear of invasions, ethnic conflicts, cattle thieves, and the threat of Indian raids retarded the settlement of the area between the Nueces and the Rio Grande. Only the most hardy and adventurous, almost always Mexicans, attempted to challenge the dangers of Anglo reprisals directed against all Mexicans, cattle thieves of Anglo and Mexican heritage, and above all, the increasing frequency of Indian attacks that swept in from the north. However, in 1839 Henry L. Kinney and William Aubrey established a trading post in the vicinity of present-day Corpus Christi at the mouth of the Nueces

River. Moreover, as settlers slowly moved back into the area east of the Nueces, a sprinkling of people could be found occupying land, either newly acquired or the legacy of many generations, to the west of the river. Many miles to the west in the Rio Grande Valley but north of the river and claimed by Texas, a sizable number of people of Mexican heritage held on to grants dating back to Spanish rule, awaiting the determination of whether they would be citizens of Mexico or Texas.

THE *EMPRESARIO* SYSTEM OF THE REPUBLIC

In its eagerness for new citizens, the government of the republic turned to the use of contracts with immigrant agents, much like the *empresario* agreements under Mexican rule. Congress authorized these contracts with an act in February 1841 and a general colonization law on February 5, 1842. Most important were those made with W. S. Peters and Associates, afterward known as the Texas Emigration and Land Company; Charles F. Mercer; Henri Castro; and Fisher and Miller, afterward transferred to the German Emigration Company. Although the contracts with these companies differed in certain details, they were alike in all essentials. Within a given area designated "the colony," all unappropriated public land was closed to settlement by others until the proprietor had completed his contract or it had been declared forfeit. The contractor was allowed ten sections for each 100 families and might also secure additional compensation from his colonists. The republic retained alternate sections, and it was from the sale of these that it expected to secure revenue for the government.

In February 1841, congress approved the request of W. S. Peters and Associates, a Louisville group, for a grant. As finally amended, the contract set aside for the colony more than 16,000 square miles, bounded on the north by the Red River and extending southward to the vicinity of present Dallas. The settlers, mostly nonslaveholders from the Ohio River Valley and Missouri, began arriving in 1841. Soon, however, the company was troubled by dissatisfied colonists, Texans who held land certificates and wanted to locate in the area, and a government that had seemingly changed its mind and wanted to terminate the contract. Proceedings in 1845 to cancel the contract led to considerable legislation and litigation, but by 1848, the company had introduced 2,205 families.

Three *empresario* contracts were awarded under the general colonization law of 1842. One with Charles F. Mercer, signed just before Congress discontinued *empresario* contracts in early 1844, called for the location of families in a large area lying mainly south and east of Peters's colony and in that colony, subject to Peters's prior rights. Mercer and Associates met with difficulties similar to those that confronted Peters. A judicial decree declared the contract void in October 1848 because of Mercer's failure to meet all its requirements, but thereafter came more legislation and litigation.

Henri Castro, a Frenchman, was another and most energetic *empresario*. He advertised his colony extensively in Europe, and by March 1, 1843, about 300 colonists, mostly from the Rhine provinces of France, set out for Texas. The area assigned to him was the Indian-inhabited country between the Nueces and the Rio Grande. Castro laid out the town of Castroville located between San Antonio and the Rio Grande in September 1844, and by 1847 he had introduced 2,134 colonists.

The contract with Henry F. Fisher and Burchard Miller brought a large migration of Germans to Texas. In February 1842 and January 1844, Fisher and Miller contracted to locate colonists on a grant lying between the Llano and Colorado rivers. Before introducing any settlers, however, they sold their grant to the *Adelsverein* (Society for the Protection of German Immigrants in Texas), organized in 1842 by a group of German noblemen for the purpose of promoting German immigration to Texas. With the founding of Industry in Austin County, a German settlement had been made in Texas as early as 1838, but the *Adelsverein* developed German immigration on a large scale. Its agent, Prince Carl of Solms-Braunfels, who visited Texas in 1844, purchased for the society the Fisher and Miller lands, an extensive area north of San Antonio, and a tract on Matagorda Bay. Early in 1845, the society's first settlers established New Braunfels, named for the prince. During the next year the society founded Fredericksburg, about 80 miles north of New Braunfels but outside the Fisher and Miller grants. Indians, particularly the Penateka Comanches, threatened the settlement until 1847, when John O. Muesebach (Baron Ottfried Hans Freiherr von Muesebach, Solms-Braunfels's successor) exchanged presents for a treaty promising peace. Fredericksburg grew rapidly; by 1850 its population was 754. Other settlements, such as Sisterdale, Boerne, and Comfort, were made, but many settlers avoided the area, still fearful of the Indians and unwilling to settle that far from the coast.

One of the most interesting of the *empresario* proposals was one that was never approved. This was the plan of the Franco-Texienne Company to introduce 8,000 French families and to establish twenty forts to form a barrier between the hostile Indians in the west and the Texas frontier. Even if all other problems could have been solved, the contract would have created a semiautonomous state on the border, thus threatening the unity of Texas. A bill to authorize the contract was introduced in January 1841. It passed the house of representatives, perhaps because Congressman Sam Houston in one of his less prudent actions supported it, as did the French minister to Texas, Count Alphonse de Saligny. However, it was never considered by the senate, probably because of opposition from President Lamar and David Burnet.

Although *empresario* projects enjoyed some success, the day of the *empresario* was near its end. It was no longer expedient to exclude the general public from thousands of square miles of public lands while an *empresario* appropriated the best lands. Predictably, persons holding land certificates opposed such colonization contracts in every way possible. Early in 1844, Congress passed (over Houston's veto) a bill repealing all laws authorizing colonization contracts and requiring the president to declare forfeited all that had not been complied with strictly.

THE ADVANCE OF THE FRONTIER

The frontier of Texas, which in 1836 extended from a point south and east of San Antonio north to the Red River, moved steadily westward each year thereafter. At first the most rapid advance was from the northeast corner, where there was an abundance of timber, rich soil, good grass, and little fear of Mexican invasion. Moreover, the Red River after 1835, when a "raft" (a large logjam blocking navigation) was removed, offered an outlet to the Gulf, sometimes on steamboats, during months of high water. The advance reached the upper Trinity in 1841 when John Neely Bryan, a Tennessean, built his lonely cabin near the three forks of the Trinity in Peters's Colony. Three years later his widely advertised town of Dallas had only two families and two small cabins. Peters's Colony headquarters at nearby Farmer's Branch was the larger settlement, but Dallas grew more rapidly after 1846, when it became the county seat. Meanwhile, from settlements such as Pecan Point and Jonesborough on the Red River near Clarksville, settlers moved toward the area to the south and east of the modern cities of Dallas and Waco, seeking the rich lands where the timber and prairie country met.

Indian problems hindered the settlement of the region, especially along the valley of the Brazos. Parker's Fort, located near the Navasota River but abandoned after a major Indian attack in 1836, was reoccupied, but area settlers remained fearful. Houston's negotiation of treaties with Indians in the area in 1843 and 1844 did much to calm such concerns, however, and settlers continued to arrive. The Torrey Brothers and Associates' trading house was established in 1842 about eight miles southeast of the present city of Waco. Two years later Neal McLennan settled not far away on the South Bosque, and in 1849, George B. Erath, a surveyor for land promoter Jacob de Cordova, laid out the town of Waco. Meanwhile, settlers were likewise moving westward from the southeast along the lower Trinity, Brazos, and Colorado valleys. Indian hostilities likewise delayed settlements along the Colorado River, but a few farmers had reached the vicinity of Austin when the town was laid out in 1839.

By 1846, reflecting the westward movement of the frontier and the growing population, the number of Texas counties had grown to thirty-six. At that time, when Texas became a part of the United States and state government replaced that of the republic, location of the frontier line of settlement in a sense depended upon the ultimate location of the boundary of Texas. But, not considering the Rio Grande settlements, the frontier line extended in an uneven fashion from Corpus Christi to Castroville and San Antonio in the southwest, and northward through New Braunfels, Fredericksburg, Austin, Belton, Waco, Dallas, and Collin County to Preston on the Red River near the present city of Denison.

ANNEXATION ACHIEVED

Annexation of Texas to the United States, though delayed by the rejection of the treaty of 1844, remained a major issue in both countries (and also in Mexico and England). In 1844, Dr. Anson Jones, generally regarded as a Houston man and administration candidate, announced his candidacy for president of Texas. Jones, a physician, member of congress, and secretary of state, did not always support Houston's policies, but most people assumed that he was sympathetic to annexation. Although he denied any such connection, Vice President Edward Burleson, who ran against Jones, was considered the candidate of the Lamar party. The vote was 7,037 for Jones to 5,668 for Burleson, with Jones winning in the east and Burleson carrying the west.

In the United States the question of the annexation of Texas was vigorously debated in the presidential election of 1844. The Democratic Party nominated James K. Polk of Tennessee, an avowed expansionist who favored annexation. In the election Polk defeated Henry Clay, the Whig nominee, who opposed "immediate annexation." The terms for annexation, however, were determined before Polk took office. In December, President Tyler, who would remain in the presidency until March 4, 1845, told Congress that Polk's election was a mandate for immediate annexation and recommended that Congress take the necessary action. On February 28, 1845, Congress passed a joint resolution providing for annexation. The terms of the resolution were that (1) Texas would enter the Union as a state if the terms of the resolution were approved by its delegates in an official convention; (2) all questions concerning the international boundary were to be adjusted by the United States; (3) Texas must cede to the United States its public property, including navy, posts, fortifications, and armaments; (4) Texas would retain its public domain to be applied to its public debt; (5) as many as four additional states, by the consent of Texas, might be formed out of its territory; (6) slavery would be prohibited in any state formed out of the

"The Republic of Texas Is No More." On February 19, 1846, the last president of Texas, Anson Jones, lowered the Lone Star flag, raised the Stars and Stripes, and formally turned power over to Governor J. Pinckney Henderson. This illustration of the annexation ceremony was produced by Norman Price. (Texas State Library and Archives Commission)

territory north of parallel 36° 30′; and (7) the president, should he prefer, could withhold the joint-resolution proposal and negotiate in its stead another treaty of annexation.

Tyler signed the joint resolution on March 1 and through his agent, Andrew Jackson Donelson, promptly submitted the offer to the Texan government. Newly inaugurated President James K. Polk urged that there be no delay, but for a time it appeared that President Anson Jones of Texas might provoke one. Great Britain and France opposed annexation. Accordingly, Charles Elliot and Count de Saligny, representing Great Britain and France, respectively, persuaded President Jones on March 29 not to commit the government for ninety days. Meanwhile, Elliot would go to Mexico to secure a treaty guaranteeing Texan independence on the condition that the republic agree never to unite with the United States. On April 15 Jones called congress to meet, but not until June 16. Public sentiment for annexation, however, forced Jones to realize that he could not delay action. On May 5 he issued a call for a convention to meet in Austin on July 4. When the Texas Congress convened, he submitted to it both the proposal of annexation to the United States and the preliminary treaty with Mexico that Elliot had secured and rushed to Texas. Congress rejected the Mexican treaty, unanimously recommended the acceptance of the offer by the United States, approved President Jones's proclamation calling for the election of delegates to a convention, and adjourned. The convention met on July 4, adopted—with only one dissenting vote—an ordinance accepting the terms of annexation, and on August 27 completed a state constitution. On October 13, the voters approved annexation and ratified the constitution by a vote of 4,245 to 257 and 4,174 to 312, respectively. The U.S. Congress accepted the Texas Constitution, and on December 29, 1845, President Polk signed the act that made Texas a state of the United States.

At a special election on December 15 voters chose new state officials, and on February 19, 1846, at a ceremony in front of the Texas capitol, President Jones relinquished executive authority to Governor J. Pinckney Henderson. In concluding his address, Jones announced, "The final act in this great drama is now performed; the Republic of Texas is no more."

BIBLIOGRAPHY

There are many good accounts of the Republic of Texas; most were written many years ago and have been cited in previous chapters. These may be found in the works of H. H. Bancroft, *History of the North Mexican States and Texas:* (two vols., San Francisco, 1884 and 1889), J. H. Brown, *A History of Texas, 1685–1892* (two vols., St. Louis, 1892–1893), W. Kennedy, (*Texas* 2d ed., London, 1841), H. Yoakum, *History of Texas* (New York, 1855), H. S. Thrall, *Pictorial History of Texas* (St. Louis, 1879), L. J. Wortham, *A History of Texas* (five vols., Fort Worth, 1924), and F. W. Johnson, *A History of Texas and Texans* (E. C. Barker and E. W. Winkler, eds., five vols., Chicago and New York, 1914). A brief but useful survey is S. V. Connor, *Adventure in Glory* (Austin, 1965). Emphasizing certain phases are William R. Hogan, *The Texas Republic: A Social and Economic History* (Norman, 1946); Stanley Siegel, *Political History of the Texas Republic, 1836–1845* (Austin, 1956); Stephen B. Oates (ed.), *The Republic of Texas* (Palo Alto, Calif., 1968); John E. Weems, *Dream of Empire: A Human History of the Republic of Texas, 1836–1846* (New York, 1971); Joseph Schmitz, *Texan Statecraft, 1836–1845* (San Antonio, 1941); E. T. Miller, *A Financial History of Texas* (Austin, 1916); Edward M. Neusinger, "The Monetary History of the Republic of Texas," *Southwestern Historical Quarterly,* LVII, 82–90; Anson Jones, *Memoranda and Official Correspondence Relating to the Republic of Texas, Its History and Annexation, Including a Brief Autobiography of the Author* (Chicago, 1966); and W. P. Webb, *The Great Plains* (New York, 1931).

Good biographies of the period are those of Sam Houston; see L. Friend, *Sam Houston, The Great Designer* (Austin, 1944) Marquis James, *The Raven: A Biography of Sam Houston* (New York, 1929), and Randolph Campbell, *Sam Houston* (New York, 1993). See also A. K. Christian, "Mirabeau B. Lamar," *Southwestern Historical Quarterly,* XXIII, 153–170, 231–270; XXIV, 39–80, 87–139, 195–234, 317–324; Dorman H. Winfrey, "Mirabeau B. Lamar and Texas Nationalism," *ibid.,* LIX, 184–205; H. P. Gambrell, *Mirabeau Bonaparte Lamar* (Dallas, 1934); H. P. Gambrell, *Anson Jones* (New York, 1948); John N. Cravens, *James Harper Star: Financier of the Republic of Texas* (Austin, 1950); Charles P. Roland, *Albert Sidney Johnston: Soldier of Three Republics* (Austin, 1964); Mary A. Maverick, *Memoirs* (San Antonio, 1921); Joe B. Frantz, *Gail Borden, Dairyman to a Nation* (Norman, Okla., 1951); John H. Jenkins and Kenneth Kesselus, *Edward Burleson: Texas Frontier Leader* (Austin, 1990); and E. Wallace, *Charles DeMorse: Pioneer Editor and Statesman* (Lubbock, 1943). Also useful are John J. Linn, *Reminis-*

cences of Fifty Years in Texas (New York, 1883), and *A Biographical Directory of Texas Congresses and Conventions* (Austin, 1941).

A number of fine studies on Tejanos, their role and culture, have been published in recent years. Informative discussions of Tejano culture and life in the republic period may be found in Gerald E. Poyo (ed)., *Tejano Journey, 1770–1850* (Austin, 1996); Timothy M. Matovina, *Tejano Religion and Ethnicity: San Antonio, 1821–1860* (Austin, 1995); Arnoldo De León, *The Tejano Community, 1836–1890* (Albuquerque, 1982), and *They Called Them Greasers: Anglo Attitudes toward Mexicans in Texas, 1821–1900* (Austin, 1983); Andrés Resendez, "National Identify in a Shifting Border: Texas and New Mexico in the Age of Transition, 1821–1848," *The Journal of American History*, LXXXVI, 668–688; and David Montejano, *Anglos and Mexicans in the Making of Texas, 1836–1986* (Austin, 1987). Armando Alonzo, *Tejano Legacy: Rancheros and Settlers in South Texas, 1734–1900* (Albuquerque, 1998), deals primarily with a later period but contains some material on the republic.

On domestic affairs, the following are useful: W. P. Webb, *The Texas Rangers* (Boston, 1935); J. Schmitz, *Texas Culture in the Days of the Republic, 1836–1846* (San Antonio, 1960); Tom Henderson Wells, *Commodore Moore and the Texas Navy* (Austin, 1960); E. W. Winkler, "The Seat of Government of Texas," *Quarterly of the Texas State Historical Association*, X, 140–171, 185–245; E. W. Winkler, "The Cherokee Indians in Texas," ibid., VII, 94–165; Nancy N. Barker, *The French Legation in Texas* (Austin, 1973); D. H. Winfrey, "The Texan Archives War of 1842," *Southwestern Historical Quarterly*, LXIV, 171–184; G. F. Haugh (ed.), "History of the Texas Navy," ibid., LXIII, 572–579; Anna Muckleroy, "The Indian Policy of the Republic of Texas," ibid., XXV, 229–260; XXVI, 1–29, 128–148, 184–206; Jesse Guy Smith, *Heroes of the Saddlebags* (San Antonio, 1951); W. Eugene Hollon and Ruth L. Butler (eds.), *William Bollaert's Texas* (Norman, 1956); D. H. Winfrey (ed.), *Texas Indian Papers, 1825–1843* (Austin, 1959); D. H. Winfrey (ed.), *Texas Indian Papers, 1844–1845* (Austin, 1960); and Earl H. Elam, "The History of the Wichita Indian Confederacy to 1868" (unpublished dissertation, Texas Tech University, Lubbock, 1971). See also Katherine J. Adams and George B. Wood, "Images of the Past: Imprints from the Republic of Texas," *Southwestern Historical Quarterly*, XC, 59–78; and John Edward Weems and Jane Weems, *Dream Empire—A Human History of the Republic of Texas* (College Station, 1986).

Sources and specialized studies relating to the land policy, immigration, *empresario* contracts, and extension of settlement are numerous. On these subjects, county and regional histories are essential; H. B. Carroll, "Bibliography of Texas Counties," *Southwestern Historical Quarterly*, XLV, 74–98, 260–275, 343–361, provides information on earlier works. Two good works of a regional nature are Lucy A. Erath (ed.), "Memories of Major Bernard Erath," ibid., XXVI, 207–233, 255–280; XXVII, 27–51, 140–163; and James K. Greer, *Grand Prairie* (Dallas, 1935). The best studies on the land policy are A. S. Lang, *Financial History of the Public Lands in Texas* (Waco, 1932); Thomas L. Miller, "Texas Land Grants to Veterans," *Southwestern Historical Quarterly*, XLIV, 342–437; and Thomas L. Miller, *The Public Lands of Texas, 1519–1970* (Norman, Okla., 1972).

The best sources of information on immigration to Texas are the U.S. census returns for 1850 and the Texas census of 1847, bound with *Laws Passed by the Second Legislature* (Houston, 1848). There is much information in E. E. Braman, *Braman's Information about Texas* (Philadelphia, 1857); and Jacob DeCordova, *Texas, Her Resources and Public Men* (Philadelphia, 1858). Barnes F. Lathrop's *Migration into East Texas, 1835–1860* (Austin, 1949) is an impressive study. B. M. Jones, "Health Seekers in Early Anglo-American Texas," *Southwestern Historical Quarterly*, LXIX, 287–299, shows that many of the immigrants came to Texas because of their health.

Studies dealing with colonizers, their settlers, and their lands include Walter Struve, *Germans and Texans: Commerce, Migration, and Culture in the Days of the Lone*

Star Republic (Austin, 1996); R. L. Biesele, *The History of the German Settlements in Texas, 1831–1861* (Austin, 1930); S. V. Connor, *The Peters Colony of Texas, A History and Biographical Sketches of the Early Settlers* (Austin, 1959); Irene M. King, *John O. Meusebach, German Colonizer in Texas* (Austin, 1967); Terry G. Jordan, *German Seed in Texas Soil: Immigrant Farmers in the Nineteenth Century* (Austin and London, 1966); Suzanne Starling, *Land Is the Cry! Warren Angus Ferris, Pioneer Texas Surveyor and Founder of Dallas County* (Austin, 1998); S. V. Connor, "A Statistical Review of the Settlement of the Peters Colony, 1841–1848," *Southwestern Historical Quarterly*, LVII, 38–64; Nancy Eagleton, "The Mercer Colony in Texas, 1844–1883," ibid., XXXIX, 275–291; XL, 35–57, 114–144; Julia N. Waugh, *Castroville and Henry Castro* (San Antonio, 1934); Bobby D. Weaver, *Castro's Colony: Empresario Development in Texas, 1842–1865* (College Station, 1985); and Feris A. Bass, Jr. and B. R. Brunson, *Fragile Empires: The Texas Correspondence of Samuel and James Morgan* (Austin, 1978).

On Lamar's efforts to extend the jurisdiction of Texas over Santa Fe, see Paul N. Spellman, *Forgotten Texas Leader: Hugh McLeod and the Texas Santa Fe Expedition* (College Station, 1999); W. C. Binkley, *The Expansionist Movement in Texas* (Berkeley, Calif., 1925), and "New Mexico and the Texan Santa Fé Expedition," *Southwestern Historical Quarterly*, XXVII, 85–107; George W. Kendall, *Narrative of the Texan Santa Fé Expedition* (London, 1845); H. Bailey Carroll, *The Texan Santa Fé Trail* (Canyon, 1951); N. Loomis, *The Texan-Santa Fé Pioneers* (Norman, Okla., 1958).

On foreign relations of the Republic of Texas, the most important source material is G. P. Garrison (ed.), *Texan Diplomatic Correspondence* (three vols.), in *The Annual Report of the American Historical Association for 1907 and 1908* (two vols., Washington, D. C., 1908 and 1911); but Madge Thornall Roberts, *The Personal Correspondence of Sam Houston*, Vol. I (Denton, 1995), is also useful. A good survey is J. Schmitz, *Texan Statecraft.* Impressive studies dealing with special phases of the subject include E. D. Adams, *British Interests and Activities in Texas* (Baltimore, 1910); the comprehensive works of J. M. Nance, *After San Jacinto: The Texas-Mexican Frontier, 1836–1841* (Austin, 1963); *Attack and Counterattack: The Texas-Mexican Frontier, 1842* (Austin, 1964); and *Dare-Devils All: The Texan Mier Expedition, 1842–1844* (ed., Archie P. McDonald; Austin, 1998); and J. H. Smith, *The Annexation of Texas* (New York, 1912). Some other specialized studies of significant value are David M. Fletcher, *The Diplomacy of Annexation: Texas, Oregon, and the Mexican War* (Columbia, Mo., 1973); Milton Lindheim, *The Republic of the Rio Grande: Texas in Mexico, 1839–1840* (Waco, 1964); Thomas J. Green, *Journal of the Texan Expedition against Mier* (New York, 1845); Joseph D. McCutchan, *Mier Expedition Diary: A Texan Prisoner's Account* (ed. J. M. Nance, Austin, 1978); Sam Haynes, *Soldiers of Misfortune: The Somervell and Mier Expeditions* (Austin, 1990); Ethel Z. Rather, "Recognition of the Republic of Texas by the United States," *Quarterly of the Texas State Historical Association*, XIII, 155–256; Annie Middleton, "Donelson's Mission to Texas in Behalf of Annexation," *Southwestern Historical Quarterly*, XXIV, 247–291; E. C. Barker, "The Annexation of Texas," ibid., L, 49–74; Frederick Merk, *Slavery and the Annexation of Texas* (New York, 1972); Nancy N. Barker, "The Republic of Texas: A French View," *Southwestern Historical Quarterly*, LXXI, 181–193; L. B. Friend (ed.), "Sidelights and Supplements on the Perote Prisoners," ibid., XLVIII, 366–374, 489–496; LXIX, 88–95, 224–230, 377–385, 516–524; Ralph A. Wooster, "Texas Military Operations against Mexico, 1842–1843," ibid., LVII, 465–484; D. M. Vigness, "Relations of the Republic of Texas and the Republic of the Rio Grande," ibid., LVII, 312–321; Josefina Vásquez, "The Texas Question in Mexican Politics, 1836–1845," ibid., LXXXIX, 309–344; John H. Schroeder, "Annexation or Independence: The Texas Issue in American Politics, 1836–1845," ibid., LXXXIX, 137–164; and David E. Narrett, "A Choice of Destiny: Immigration Policy, Slavery, and the Annexation of Texas," ibid., C, 271–302.

8

Early Statehood 1846–1861

Between the time of the annexation of Texas to the United States and its secession to join the Confederacy, Texas was a part of the Union for a decade and a half. During these years, Texans took part in a war between Mexico and the United States, struggled with the national government over their western boundary, and paid off their public debt. Other problems, such as transportation, education, and Indian affairs, were not resolved. The question of slavery grew more and more serious, threatening not only the harmony of the state but also the integrity of the nation.

Despite such problems, these were years of expansion and accomplishment. A new state government was installed; Texans constructed roads and public buildings; and extensive explorations opened the way into western areas and to points beyond. Meanwhile, the population continued to increase at a rapid rate as immigrants joined with other thousands of land-hungry "old" Texans to push their settlements further westward in the state.

THE ESTABLISHMENT OF STATE GOVERNMENT

The Constitution of 1845, well designed and well written, was the work of a group of able men. Thomas Jefferson Rusk, president of the convention that wrote the document, had served the republic well in several capacities.

Many of the other delegates were men of broad experience in public affairs. José Antonio Navarro, a member of the convention of 1836, was the only native Texan.

The framers drew extensively from the Louisiana constitution, to some extent from the fundamental laws of other states, and from the Texas Constitution of 1836. The governor and lieutenant governor were to serve two-year terms but not more than four out of six years. Initially, most other state officials, except for members of the legislature, were appointed, but in 1850 amendments provided for the popular election of the attorney general, comptroller, and treasurer.

Though meeting biennially rather than annually, the legislature resembled the congress of the republic. Representatives would serve two years and be apportioned according to the number of free inhabitants. Senators were to be apportioned on the basis of the number of qualified voters and would serve for four years. Limits on legislative power prohibited debt in excess of $100,000; married women were made secure in their right to own property; and property (200 acres or less) in a homestead was exempt from foreclosure for debt.

Voters elected officers of the new state on December 15, 1845. J. Pinckney Henderson was chosen governor by an overwhelming vote, and Albert C. Horton was chosen lieutenant governor by a slender majority. President Jones called the legislature to assemble in Austin on February 16, 1846, for the purpose of organizing a state government. Three days later in a formal ceremony Jones officially transferred the government to the newly elected state officials. Completing the major structure of the government, the first legislature shortly thereafter elected Thomas J. Rusk and Sam Houston to the U.S. Senate.

THE WAR WITH MEXICO

War between the United States and Mexico began shortly after the annexation of Texas. The primary causes were the annexation of Texas, the desire of the United States to acquire part or all of California, the failure of the Mexican government to settle claims by citizens of the United States, the instability of the Mexican government, and the location of the western boundary.

On more than one occasion, after the battle of San Jacinto, the Mexican government warned that the annexation of Texas by the United States would be regarded as a step toward war. When the joint resolution establishing terms for annexation was adopted by the U.S. Congress and approved by Tyler in 1845, the Mexican minister in Washington announced that Mexico would defend its rightful territory (Texas) by every means within its power

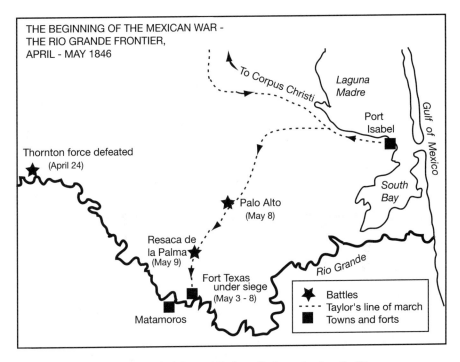

THE BEGINNING OF THE MEXICAN WAR -
THE RIO GRANDE FRONTIER,
APRIL - MAY 1846

U. S. forces under the command of General Zachary Taylor arrived on the Rio Grande in late March 1846 to confront a Mexican force in the Matamoros area. Scattered violent encounters took place earlier, but the first sizable action occurred with the defeat and capture of Captain Seth Thornton's troop on April 24. Hostilities continued in the area until after the battle of Resaca de la Palma on May 9. The opposing forces, totaling about 9,000 soldiers, suffered more than 1,000 casualties (killed, wounded, and captured).

and stated that he was returning to Mexico. Mexico's response to annexation, however, was not as simple as it appeared, primarily because the issue was mired in the entanglement of Mexican political intrigue. José Herrera, who had replaced Santa Anna as president of Mexico about the time of the joint resolution, was not particularly friendly toward the United States, but neither was he eager for war. Subsequently, the Mexican congress in mid-1845 refused to declare war, and President James K. Polk and his cabinet concluded that Herrera's government was seeking an amicable solution of the issues.

After deciding that Herrera would accept an envoy from the United States who came with full powers to settle "the question" in dispute, President Polk in November 1845 sent John Slidell of Louisiana with full power to settle "all questions," including a proposal that the United States buy California and the matter of U. S. citizen claims against Mexico. Hope for a diplomatic solution through Slidell's mission quickly faded. When

Slidell reached Mexico in December 1845, he was informed that Texas was the only question in dispute and that friendly relations could not be reestablished until Texas had been restored to Mexico. Although Polk's efforts to purchase Mexican territory angered Mexican leaders, their refusal to negotiate was also influenced by public demonstrations that threatened open rebellion if Herrera negotiated with Slidell. Early in 1846, centralists overthrew President Herrera and replaced him with a strong anti-American, Mariano Paredes. Slidell, acting on Polk's instructions, remained until March in an effort to negotiate with Paredes, but with no success.

While diplomacy failed, the two nations moved closer to a military confrontation. In the summer of 1845, U.S. troops under the command of General Zachary Taylor had established a post at the mouth of the Nueces River near present-day Corpus Christi. Mexican troops were concentrated at Matamoros but also scattered along a series of posts on the south side of the Rio Grande. For about nine months there was no significant intrusion of troops from either country into the land between the Rio Grande and Nueces River.

The question of the boundary, implicit in the stationing of troops by both nations, was in fact a complicated question within a complex group of issues. Under Spanish and Mexican rule, the Nueces was traditionally viewed as the western boundary of Texas. The legal basis for the claim for the Rio Grande as a boundary was the legislative act of the Republic of Texas designating the river as its southern and western boundaries, a position never accepted by the Mexican government. But after the end of the Texas revolution, Mexico had restricted political and military operations to areas south of the Rio Grande except for a couple of temporary military ventures. The joint resolution, which stipulated the terms for Texas becoming a part of the United States, did little to clarify the matter, stating only that "all questions of boundary that may arise with other governments" were "subject to the adjustment by this government."

The question became a confrontation in March when Polk learned that Slidell would not be received. The president ordered General Taylor to move his troops to the Rio Grande. In early April Paredes stationed several thousand additional troops at Matamoros, and on April 12, General Pedro Ampudia, newly appointed commander of Mexican forces and more aggressive than his predecessor, delivered an ultimatum to the U.S. commander. Taylor must retire with his troops beyond the Nueces within twenty-four hours, or force of arms would decide the issue. On April 23, President Paredes proclaimed a "defensive" war against the United States, and the next day Mexican troops crossed the Rio Grande and defeated a detachment of U.S. dragoons.

Meanwhile, Polk apparently had also decided on war. Writing in his diary on May 9, he confided that he had informed his cabinet that "we had ample cause of war, and that it was impossible that we could stand in *status quo*, or that I could remain silent much longer." That same day, he received news of the skirmish on the border. Before he learned of Taylor's victories on May 8 and 9 over a Mexican army at Palo Alto and Resaca de la Palma, President Polk and his cabinet decided to ask Congress for a declaration of war. Over the objections of Whigs, abolitionists, and others who questioned the necessity or desirability of war, on May 13, 1846, Congress declared war, responding to Polk's claim that Mexico had "shed American blood on American soil."

The war was unpopular with many citizens of the United States, but Texans supported it enthusiastically. Taylor immediately opened an offensive to drive the Mexican forces toward Monterrey. He asked Governor Henderson for two regiments of infantry and two of cavalry, and the legislature gave the governor a leave of absence to take command of the Texas troops who were mustered into the service of the United States. Before the end of May the Mexican troops had abandoned Matamoros to Taylor; on September 25 Taylor took possession of Monterrey; and on February 23 and 24, 1847, he met a force under Santa Anna (no longer president of Mexico but now a

John Coffee (Jack) Hays. A surveyor by profession, he became captain of a Texas Ranger company in 1840. As colonel in command of the First Regiment, Texas Mounted Volunteers, during the Mexican War, he participated with distinction in the battles of Monterrey and Mexico City. (Courtesy Southwest Collection, Texas Tech University, Lubbock, Texas)

military commander) at Buena Vista. Texans performed a key role both at Monterrey and at Buena Vista.

The United States won victory with the invasion and capture of Mexico City. Polk sent another army, commanded by General Winfield Scott, to land at Vera Cruz and fight its way to Mexico City. Scott captured Mexico City in September 1847, and Santa Anna fled the country. A number of Texans took part in the Mexico City campaign. One organization, that of John Coffee ("Jack") Hays, made up largely of rangers, lawmen, and frontier Indian fighters, had a prominent role. The unit served as efficient scouts and kept the supply lines open. At least 5,000, perhaps 7,000, Texans were in military service during the war.

In the Treaty of Guadalupe Hidalgo of February 2, 1848, which ended the war, Mexico accepted the Rio Grande as the boundary; the United States agreed to assume the claims of its citizens against that nation up to $5 million. Mexico also ceded to the United States for a payment of $15 million the provinces of New Mexico and upper California.

THE TEXAS–NEW MEXICO BOUNDARY CONTROVERSY

The Treaty of Guadalupe Hidalgo ended the boundary controversy between Mexico and the United States but opened the way for one between the state of Texas and the national government. The lands extending to the Rio Grande claimed by Texas during the republic included a vast amount of territory never a part of Texas during Spanish or Mexican rule. Within this area were most of the principal settlements of New Mexico, scattered for the most part along the eastern side of the Rio Grande and including the prosperous community of Santa Fe.

Although Texas had failed in the Santa Fe expedition of 1841 to exercise sovereignty over the New Mexico lands, Texans continued after annexation to assert their claim. The justice of the claim was certainly debatable, but denial of it by the national government was somewhat inconsistent. Congress had declared war on Mexico in response to a presidential statement that "American blood had been shed on American soil"—north of the Rio Grande but most assuredly south of the Nueces. Nevertheless, even as the war was fought, it was clear that the claim of Texas to the Rio Grande was in jeopardy. In August 1846, General Stephen Kearny, in command of the Army of the West, occupied New Mexico and established a civil government there with the approval of his superiors and without regard to the claims of Texas. On June 4, 1847, Governor Henderson reminded Secretary of State James Buchanan of the Texan claims. Buchanan replied that the question would have to be settled by Congress, but he assured the governor that

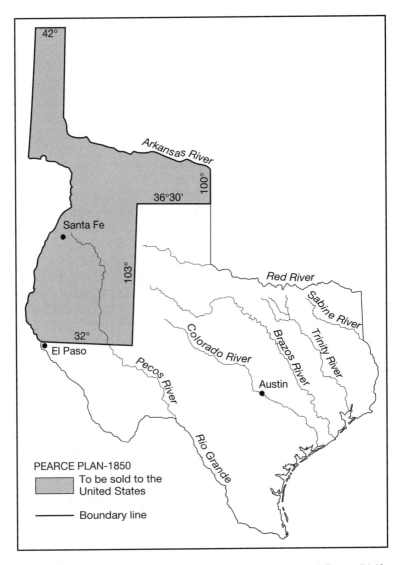

Pearce Plan 1850. (From *The Howling of the Coyotes: Reconstruction Efforts to Divide Texas*, by Ernest Wallace, published by Texas A&M Press)

the temporary civil government would not affect the claim. Their fears thus quieted, the Texans awaited the outcome of the war.

Ratification of the Treaty of Guadalupe Hidalgo on March 10, 1848, did not fulfill the expectations of Texans. In part, the obstacle to the claim of Texas to the territory east of the Rio Grande was raised by the question of slavery. During the war, antislavery interests opposed to the acquisition of any new slave territory introduced the Wilmot Proviso in Congress. If adopted, it would have prohibited slavery in any territory acquired by the United States as a result of the war with Mexico. Although the proviso was not adopted, the issue remained, and pro- and antislavery interests aligned on opposite sides with little inclination to make concessions. If the boundaries claimed by Texas were permitted to stand, slave soil thus would extend at least as far westward as the Rio Grande. Divided, Congress found itself unable to pass any laws whatever concerning New Mexico.

The inhabitants of the upper Rio Grande Valley, supported by military officials on the scene, posed the other obstacle to the claims of Texas. Their opposition to being a part of Texas, evident during the republic, was made more clear after March 1848 when Texas created Santa Fe County with boundaries including most of eastern New Mexico. Although the Texas government asked for support by the federal government and sent Spruce M. Baird to Santa Fe to organize the new county, the military and an aroused group of Santa Fe citizens opposed him. Meanwhile, in November 1848, the people of Santa Fe held a convention and adopted petitions asking that New Mexico be made a territory. When Baird arrived, the officer in command of federal troops informed him that he would sustain the government established in New Mexico by General Kearny "at every peril" until ordered to desist. Baird remained in the territory for a few months without accomplishing anything. Any hope of the Texans for an order overruling the federal officers in Santa Fe faded when Zachary Taylor assumed the presidency in March 1849. Taylor favored granting statehood to both California and New Mexico.

The situation, which became more tense with each passing month, was critical by the end of 1849. In November Governor George T. Wood, who was approaching the end of his term, suggested to the legislature that Texas assert its claim "with the whole power and resources of the state," but neither the governor nor the legislature took any decisive action. Peter Hansborough Bell, who defeated Wood's bid for reelection by pledging a more aggressive policy, shortly thereafter urged that the legislature send to New Mexico a force sufficient to maintain the authority of Texas. Meanwhile, the press and the public of Texas clamored for action.

While avoiding the use of military force, the legislature was not idle. On December 31, 1849, it designated new boundaries for Santa Fe county and created three additional counties to the south of it. Then, by authority of an act passed four days later, another commissioner, Robert S. Neighbors, was sent to organize the counties. He organized El Paso County without meeting resistance, but on arriving in New Mexico he found the majority of the people antagonistic and the military unsympathetic. Neighbors thereupon returned to Texas. His report to the governor, made public early in June 1850, caused great excitement. At mass meetings in Austin and other places there were protests, threats of secession, and proposals that the state assert its claim with arms. Governor Bell called a special session of the legislature to meet on August 12. When the legislature assembled, it heard the governor's message declaring that Texas must assert its rights "*at all hazards and to the last extremity*," and debated measures to organize the militia and send it into New Mexico.

Meanwhile, the people of New Mexico were busy organizing their own government. They adopted a constitution for their proposed state with boundaries so extended as to include most of the disputed territory and also some territory unquestionably Texan. But events in Washington nullified their actions. President Taylor, who supported their efforts, had died. Millard Fillmore, his successor, reinforced the army in New Mexico and stated flatly that he would send troops against the Texas militia if they attempted to occupy the region. Fillmore, however, favored a settlement of the controversy through compromise measures that had been debated in Congress throughout the early months of 1850.

Beginning with one introduced by Senator Thomas Hart Benton of Missouri on January 16, 1850, Congress considered three different plans to resolve the dispute but all were rejected. A fourth proposal, one of a series of five laws known as the Compromise of 1850, finally passed. This bill, written by James A. Pearce of Maryland, was accepted by the Senate and passed by the House on September 6, 1850. Supported by the Texas delegation and congressmen from both North and South, it fixed the northern and western boundaries of Texas as they now stand; Texas was to renounce all claims to territory beyond and would be paid $10 million; and the territory of New Mexico was to be organized. A desire to resolve the dispute and to ease tensions accounted for much of the support for the compromise, but there was another element involved. A group who held Texas bonds, anxious to ensure their claims, worked diligently on behalf of the bill.

There was considerable sentiment in Texas against accepting the proposition, but a majority of the voters seemed to agree with the La Grange *Monument*, which announced that it was "doubtful whether ten years' trading would give Texas a better bargain than she can now make." At a special election the voters accepted the proposition by a majority of two to one, the legislature in special session approved it, and Governor Bell signed the act of acceptance on November 25, 1850.

Settlement of the Debt of the Republic

Funds received in the boundary settlement were to be used to pay the public debt of Texas, which developed during the republic and consisted of two major types of obligations—ordinary and revenue debt. The ordinary debt was created by the claims of participants in the Texas Revolution or suppliers of the Texas army, nearly all representing at most $100 each. The revenue debt consisted of principal and interest owed to holders of Republic of Texas securities. Boundary settlement funds were divided approximately evenly for payment of each group of creditors. There were few problems involved in the payment of the ordinary debt, and the state had $3.75 million left after these claims were paid.

The federal government set aside half of the boundary settlement, $5 million, for payment of the revenue debt, retained these funds, and assumed responsibility for distributing payment. Even though this debt was considered preferred obligations, the process and amount of payment generated much controversy and ill will. Payment was delayed because some creditors neglected to file their claims, and federal officials would not pay any claims until all were in. Final settlement was made by an act of February 28, 1855. By that time, the fund, with accrued interest, amounted to $6.5 million. Congress added to this amount $1,250,000 to reimburse Texas for damages resulting from Indian depredations in Texas since 1836. Altogether, there was a fund of $7,750,000 to be distributed among the creditors. Even so, when the fund was prorated among the creditors, each one received about 77 cents on the dollar, and many of them were unhappy.

Texas used the $3.75 million that remained after the ordinary debt had been paid in ways that were generally constructive. The greater part of it, $2 million, was set aside as an endowment for the public schools and in turn loaned to railroads to aid construction. For six years, beginning in 1852, the state remitted to the counties nine-tenths of its taxes. The counties used the tax money for the construction of public buildings and various other purposes. Thus, Texas was able to endow its public schools, promote the construction of transportation facilities, construct buildings, and all the while maintain a very low tax rate.

THE POLITICS OF EARLY STATEHOOD

Although no permanent tradition was established, each of the first two governors of Texas served only one term. In fact, J. Pinckney Henderson, the first governor, only served a portion of a term. While he was absent commanding Texas troops during the Mexican War, Lieutenant Governor A. C. Horton served as governor until Henderson returned in November 1846. Henderson was succeeded on December 21, 1847, by George T. Wood, a Trinity River planter who had gained popularity as commander of volunteers in the Mexican War. The most important public issues of the Wood administration were frontier defense, the public debt, and the controversy over the Rio Grande boundary. When Wood ran for reelection in 1849, he was defeated by

Peter Hansborough Bell, a veteran of San Jacinto and the war with Mexico. Wood attributed his defeat to inadequate support by Sam Houston, but Bell's advocacy of a more aggressive policy in the boundary dispute may have influenced the outcome.

The first administration of Peter Hansborough Bell, the first governor to be reelected, was a busy one. The settlement of the boundary dispute was only one of several issues. The state took steps to explore routes across Texas and worked to secure the location of a line of military posts along the frontier. There was even a controversy over a futile effort to move the capital from Austin. When Bell ran for reelection in 1851, the growing importance of the slavery issue was evident. None of his opponents were antislavery in their sympathies, but Bell was regarded as the most pro-southern of them all and elected easily. His second term was occupied with the problems of paying of the public debt, controversies over the claims of certain emigrant agents, land claims in South Texas, and the seemingly eternal question of frontier defense. A popular governor, Bell did not complete his second term. A few weeks before it expired, he resigned to fill a vacancy in Congress.

The Pease Mansion was bought by Elisha Marshall Pease, a New England Yankee who came to Texas in 1835 and settled in Bastrop (then called Mina). An outspoken advocate of independence, Pease was a member of the Committee of Safety in Mina and took part in the convention of 1836. Under his administration as governor (1853–1857) railroads were encouraged, taxes reduced, the state debt paid off, the state university planned, and a new capitol erected. A Unionist, Pease was appointed provisional governor again in 1867 but resigned because of disagreements over Reconstruction policies. (Courtesy of the Texas Department of Transportation)

Party rivalry was evident in the race for governor in 1853. W. B. Ochiltree, a Whig politician with a large personal following, was a popular candidate. The Whigs, who were regarded as the party that had opposed the annexation of Texas and the party of the elite, ordinarily attracted only a few. But, fearing a Whig victory, some potential Democratic candidates withdrew and united to support Elisha M. Pease. Pease, a favorite in the southern and western parts of the state, was elected.

Pease was an active and able governor. His platform called for establishing a public school system, encouraging internal improvements (transportation facilities), and removing the Indians from Texas. The most important act of his administration was the school law of 1854. By its terms, the state set aside $2 million of the money received in the boundary settlement as a permanent endowment for public schools. The legislature set aside $100,000 of the boundary settlement funds for the endowment of a university, but this later disappeared into the general revenue fund and was used for other purposes. The support of Pease and others for the building of railroads was evident in a program of loans and in a number of charters granted to railroads. In efforts to resolve Indian problems, the legislature authorized and the state established three Indian reservations.

During the Pease years, conduct of political affairs along party lines became more important. Most Texans, hailing from other southern states, were supporters of the Democratic Party, although some were loyal to the opposition, the Whigs. But during the republic, party affiliation had meant almost nothing in Texas politics, and during the early years of statehood, it meant very little. Voters generally aligned themselves with the Houston or the anti-Houston leaders. Both the Whigs and the Democrats held conventions from time to time, but the attendance was small. The Democratic convention in 1855 drew delegates from only twelve counties.

A new political party appeared in Texas in 1854 to challenge the complacent and disorganized Democrats. The new political organization, the American or Know-Nothing Party, was a secret and mysterious association, founded on the Atlantic Seaboard and based on nativist (antiforeign) principles. It opposed foreigners holding office, was decidedly anti-Catholic, was opposed to secession or any move that might divide the union, and grew rapidly as the Whig party disintegrated. Support in Texas reflected a relatively strong anti-Catholic attitude and in some instances a resentment directed toward German immigrants who were sometimes Catholics, but supporters often were disgruntled Democrats whose interest in the Know-Nothings stemmed primarily from their unhappiness with Democratic leaders. The party flourished for a brief period. In a convention of June 1855, it nominated Lieutenant Governor D. C. Dickson for governor, formed a state organization, and made plans to spread the party over the state. Hopes were strengthened when Houston publicly expressed sympathy with aims of the organization.

In less than a week after the Know-Nothing convention, Democrats met in a second convention in Austin. They denounced all secret political factions and pledged support to Pease for governor. Other Democratic contestants for governor were persuaded to withdraw, and a hard-fought campaign between Dickson and Pease followed. Pease won by a substantial majority, but the Know-Nothings managed to elect about twenty representatives and five senators to the state legislature.

The Know-Nothing party did not last, however. Growing conflict over slavery led Texans to renew their loyalties to the Democrats, and many people found the secrecy and undemocratic policies of the Know-Nothings to be unacceptable. Although the disintegration of the Know-Nothing party was clearly evident by 1856, the organization left its mark on Texas politics. The Democrats were forced to improve their organization and to adopt the practice of nominating candidates by convention. When the Democrats convened to nominate candidates and select presidential electors in 1856, 91 out of 99 counties were represented.

The development of politics along party lines did not mean the disappearance of political battles between the factions of Houston and anti-Houston supporters. Since 1836, Sam Houston had twice been president of the republic and thrice U.S. senator. Popular with many, he was unpopular with others. The difference was in part a matter of personalities, but it also was a conflict over principles and policies. Houston antagonized proslavery people on a number of occasions, but it was his vote against the Kansas-Nebraska bill (the bill that opened the possibility of slavery in certain lands in the Louisiana Purchase where slavery had been prohibited) in 1854 that created the most animosity toward him. His vote was regarded as treason by many southerners, and Democrats throughout Texas condemned him. His affiliation with the Know-Nothing movement in 1855 added to his unpopularity.

Apparently believing that the legislature would not again elect him to the U.S. Senate, Houston resigned from the senate to run for governor in the election of 1857. Although his opponent was Hardin Runnels, his most determined antagonist was Louis T. Wigfall (elected a U.S. Senator in 1858), a proslavery champion of states' rights armed with extreme views and frantic energy. Whenever he could, Wigfall debated with Houston, and when Houston avoided debate, Wigfall and J. P. Henderson followed him and countered his arguments. Runnels and the Democratic ticket won a decisive victory. It was the only defeat in a major contest that Houston ever suffered.

The Runnels administration, 1857–59, coincided with the final tension-filled years on the eve of the Civil War, filled with strife as the crisis over slavery moved toward a climax. Many issues claimed the attention of the state government, but of them, only the question of frontier defense received much notice as Texans and the remainder of the nation increasingly concentrated on the growing rift between North and South.

Immigration and Extension of Settlement

Attracted by a liberal land policy, the crowds of immigrants who each year made their way to Texas during the republic increased after annexation. Indeed, the lure of cheap land in Texas was second only to that of gold in California. During 1845, newspapers in Missouri, Arkansas, and Louisiana abounded with news of settlers departing for Texas. There was a lull in 1846 and 1847 as a result of the Mexican War, but the news of the U.S. victory started the wave anew. One day in December 1848, 300 immigrants crossed the ferry at Washington-on-the-Brazos, and during November 1849 more than 5,000 on their way to Texas crossed the Arkansas River at Little Rock. A year later, the editor of the *Northern Standard* at Clarksville wrote: "For the last two weeks scarcely a day has passed that a dozen or more movers' wagons has not passed through our town." Year after year, the numbers increased. In 1858, the editor of the *Standard* claimed that no fewer than fifty wagons of immigrants were passing through Clarksville each day. The census of 1850 showed 154,034 whites, 58,161 slaves, and 397 free blacks, for a total of 212,592, or an increase of almost 50 percent since 1847. These figures increased threefold over the next decade. By 1860, the population had jumped to 604,215; of this number, 182,921 were slaves.

Almost three-fourths of the 1860 population had been born outside Texas. A majority of the immigrants had come from the states of the Old South, and Louisiana, Arkansas, and Missouri. Tennessee had contributed 42,265, more than any other state. Alabama was the next with 34,193. Foreign-born settlers, numbering 43,422, represented almost every country of Western Europe and Mexico. The Germans, numbering 20,553, made up the largest group of foreign born. German settlements were concentrated in western areas of central Texas. There they constituted a majority of the population in three counties in the San Antonio-Austin area and a substantial part in six other counties.

Immigrants from Europe, other than the Germans, included French, Czechs, Poles, Swedes, and Norwegians. La Réunion, a French colony, was established in 1855 near Dallas by followers of Victor Considerant, a socialist. The colonists, soon disenchanted with both the frontier and socialism, drifted away but generally remained somewhere in the state. The immigration of Czechs, which began during the republic, increased in the early statehood years, particularly after revolutions in Europe in 1848 brought more turmoil and tyranny into their lives. They settled in communities such as Cat Spring, New Ulm, New Bremen, Hostyn, and Fayetteville. From Poland came several hundred families in the 1850s to an area south of San Antonio, where they founded the town of Panna Maria in Karnes County. A small Norwegian settlement was planted in Henderson County in 1845, but settlers from Scandinavia did not come in numbers until nearly a half-century later.

These immigrants from other southern states and Europe, joined by other thousands of "old" Texans, advanced the frontier westward into the Western Cross Timbers. By 1849, the newly established towns of Sherman, Farmersville, Dallas, Waxahachie, Ennis, Waco, and Fredericksburg marked the western limits of white settlement. The movement of military posts more than a hundred miles farther to the west in 1851 and 1852 opened the way for more settlements in Central and West Central Texas. On the eve of the Civil War, the frontier line extended from Henrietta on the north through Belknap, Palo Pinto, Brownwood, Llano, and Kerrville, to Uvalde.

TEJANOS AND THE SETTLEMENT OF SOUTH AND WEST TEXAS

According to the census of 1860 for Texas, Mexican settlers, with 12,443, made up the second largest group of foreign-born, but some scholars believe that the number of Mexican settlers was substantially larger; some estimates place it as high as 25,000. Some people of Mexican heritage had moved south across the Rio Grande after the Mexican War, but others did not, for political turmoil and poverty continued to be common problems in northern Mexico. The return of Santa Anna to power in the early 1850s, followed by three years of violence in the War of the Reform, brought more hardships to the people of that troubled land. Moreover, some Tejanos had considerable property and land on the north side of the Rio Grande and were determined to protect them if at all possible.

It was during these years of early statehood that state authorities confronted the question of land ownership in the area between the Nueces and the Rio Grande, sometimes known as the Trans-Nueces. Under Spanish and Mexican rule, most of the region had been distributed in land grants, some of which were quite large. During the republic, a number of headright grants were issued, but otherwise, the legal questions of land ownership received little attention during those years. However, after annexation to the United States and completion of the Mexican War, owners of the grants began to take steps to protect their rights under United States and Texas law. Meanwhile, newcomers, mostly Anglos, in a variety of ways, some apparently legal and some not, attempted to acquire the properties.

Tejanos called for justice and protection of their rights, while at the same time, certain powerful interests in the region launched a movement to make the area a territory separate from Texas in hope of furthering their ambitions for the land. Responding to the situation and the request of Governor Bell, the legislature created a board, the Bourland-Miller Commission, to review the titles and rights of the claimants to Spanish and Mexican land grants, and the process of review began in 1852. The commission worked quickly and ruled that most of the claims were valid. Some that were rejected by the commission were approved by the courts, and ultimately the legislature approved still others. Of the almost 350 land grants concerned, Mexican land owners validated their claims in most instances.

The area involved contained primarily a Mexican population. Concentrated in the counties along the Rio Grande River and in South Texas where the counties of Nueces, Webb, Starr, and Cameron were created in 1848, it reflected the influence of the Mexican culture and heritage in many ways such as family values, religion, and language. In an election in Nueces County, thirty-seven of forty-four voters had Spanish surnames. Along the Rio Grande, far removed from most of the other Texas settlements, were a number of communities, including Laredo and Eagle Pass, whose populations similarly were largely Mexican. In 1850, this area and the counties of Cameron, Starr, and Webb had about 13,000 people. Higher up on the Rio Grande were several settlements, including Presidio and El Paso, with about 4,000 people and with a significant portion of the people of Mexican heritage.

While most of the attention to frontier wars during early statehood was given to hostilities in northwestern areas, the lands of South Texas and especially along the lower Rio Grande were the scene of frequent raids and violence. Lawless men on both sides of the border and from the peoples of both nations committed crimes without regard to the boundary. Adding to the troubles of the land were the bitterness and anger of a sizable portion of the population. Most of the people were of Mexican heritage, but Anglo Texans often dominated the region. Moreover, though many Mexican families had retained their lands, others had not, and even those who retained their property often complained of little protection from the law and unfair treatment.

Among the large number of outlaws and renegades in the state, attention centered on the actions of Juan Nepomuceno Cortina. Cortina claimed to be the protector of Mexican peoples, and certainly he was a hero to a large part of that population. Anglo Texans, however, generally viewed him as an outlaw who was responsible for much of the violence on both sides of the river. The owner of a ranch on the Rio Grande a few miles from Brownsville, Cortina took part in a bloody quarrel with the local sheriff, whom he accused of mistreating one of his men. Cortina at that point retreated to his ranch and issued a proclamation announcing that he was a citizen of Texas defending the rights and property of the Mexican people of Texas. In the fall of 1859, he harassed Brownsville and the entire lower Rio Grande Valley. His fame and power grew, especially after he defeated a company of Texas Rangers sent from San Antonio, but he could not hold out against the overwhelming campaign organized to meet his challenge. Two companies of state troops, under the command of John S. Ford, went to the aid of a contingent of federal troops and after a lively campaign, Cortina was forced across the border into Mexico, where he remained for some time.

THE GROWTH OF SLAVERY

The population of slaves in antebellum Texas increased at a rate even higher than that of the free population. Estimated at 5,000 in 1836, slave numbers grew at an accelerated pace after Texas became independent. A state census in 1847 counted 38,753, or approximately 27 percent of the total population, indicating a sharp rise in numbers during the republic. The number of slaves grew even more rapidly after annexation, with the 1850 count of 58,161 reflecting a slave population growth of about 50 percent in the first three years of statehood. The census of 1860 showed 182,566 slaves and 430,891 white persons, the proportion of slaves in the total population amounting to about 30 percent Since 1850, the slave population had increased 214 percent and the white population, 180 percent.

Though 64 of the 105 organized Texas counties in 1860 contained more than 1,000 slaves, the slave population tended to be concentrated in certain areas. Beginning in the early days of the Austin colony on the lower reaches of the Brazos and Colorado rivers, slaves were brought in to work on the plantations along the rivers. During the republic the number of slaves in San Augustine and surrounding counties in East Texas increased rapidly, as did the slave population in the northeastern counties. Reflecting growth during early statehood, by 1860 slaves represented a majority of the population in thirteen counties. Brazoria and neighboring counties on the coast, where sugarcane culture shared the plantation economy with cotton, maintained large slave populations, as did most East Texas counties where cotton dominated.

Notwithstanding the rapid expansion of slavery in antebellum Texas, slaveowners were a minority. In fact, the percentage of families owning slaves decreased in the 1850s. Approximately 30 percent of families in 1850 owned

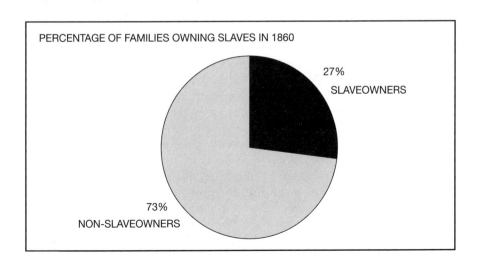

PERCENTAGE OF FAMILIES OWNING SLAVES IN 1860

27% SLAVEOWNERS

73% NON-SLAVEOWNERS

slaves, and by 1860 the percentage had declined to slightly over 27 percent, or 21,878 slaveowners, about 5.7 percent of all slaveowners in the nation. Those who profited most from slavery, the planters, made up a small minority of the population. Only 2,163 of these owned 20 or more slaves; 54 owned 100 or more. More than half of all the slaveholders owned 5 or fewer. About 10 percent of the slaveholders and less than 5 percent of all farmers operated on a scale large enough to necessitate hiring an overseer. But slaveholders, only about one-third of the state's farmers, produced 90 percent of the cotton crop.

Slaves represented a substantial proportion of Texas capital. In 1850, the average value of a slave assessed for taxes was $440, while in 1860 this amount reached $765; the aggregate value of all slaves was about 20 percent greater than the value of the farms of Texas. On the market, field hands brought from $1,200 to $2,000 and "plow boys" from $1,000 to $1,500. Rates varied widely, primarily according to age and sex, but a young male slave ordinarily could be hired out for about $200 for the year. Some enthusiasts contended that a good field hand who produced eight bales of cotton could pay for himself in a year.

OPPONENTS OF SLAVERY

Although slaveowners were a minority of the white population, there is little reason to think that most white Texans did not support and defend the institution. But there were those who did not. Certain ethnic groups were at the time and have since been viewed as opponents of slavery. Traveler Frederick Law Olmsted wrote of the antislavery attitudes of German settlers. Some German newspapers did express antislavery views and opposition to secession, and service in the Confederate cause thereafter tended to confirm the position that German Texans were generally opposed to slavery. However, recent scholarship has raised questions concerning the conventional view of Germans as opponents of slavery. Responsible and respected scholars have reached differing conclusions, and the evidence seems to be contradictory and inconclusive. Perhaps the most appropriate conclusion is that German immigrants were less likely to approve of slavery than were settlers from other southern states but that some Germans supported the institution and others did not.

Tejanos were another ethnic minority generally considered critical of slavery. Slavery was not unknown in areas of Texas where most Tejanos lived, but it was not a common practice. Certainly, very few Tejanos owned slaves, and it is likely that most did not approve of the institution. Consequently, there was fear in some Texas communities that Tejanos were aiding slaves in their efforts to run away, and there were probably occasions where such assistance was provided. However, there is little evidence to suggest that Tejanos were involved in the slave question to any significant extent, either as supporters or opponents.

Actually, determination of those who opposed slavery in antebellum Texas must be based on indirect evidence in many instances. Taking an open stand against slavery required a willingness to expose one's self not only to recrimination but also to physical danger. Abolitionists were viewed as troublemakers by a large part of the population; anyone suspected of such views could be dealt with harshly, and generally the public applauded the action. Especially in the final year before the outbreak of the Civil War, slavery supporters were alert to any public criticism of the institution or suspicious action suggesting an abolitionist plot. In September 1860, a mob in Fort Worth hanged a Methodist minister, Anthony Bewley, who was accused of involvement in an abolitionist scheme but who was probably guilty of nothing more than views opposing slavery. Such excesses were rare; public threats of extreme measures to be used against opponents of slavery were not. Only the most outspoken and determined dared to ignore or defy them.

EXPLORING WEST TEXAS

At the close of the Mexican War, Texas, west and north of a line through Denton, Dallas, Waco, Austin, Fredericksburg, San Antonio, Castroville, and Laredo, was an unknown Indian country. During the next twelve years, Texans and the U.S. Army explored and surveyed trails across the region in search of wagon, stage, and railroad routes.

Several explorations searched for practical routes between central Texas and El Paso. Texas Ranger John C. Hays, in the summer of 1848, traveled westward from San Antonio with a party of citizens and Rangers to a point beyond the Pecos River, before abandoning the venture. In March 1849, Robert S. Neighbors, under military orders, and John S. (Rip) Ford, a Texas Ranger, traveled from San Antonio to El Paso and back in search of a practical wagon road. The army carried out more explorations to evaluate the practicality of these and other routes, and eventually an "upper" route and a "lower" route between central Texas and El Paso were determined. Many emigrants, California bound, used the routes, but the lower was traveled more extensively.

Meanwhile, the military was exploring and marking wagon roads across the northern part of the state. In April 1849, Captain Randolph B. Marcy escorted a party of immigrants to Santa Fe by following the Canadian River across the Texas Panhandle. On his return, Marcy traveled from near the present town of Pecos northeastward to a point on the Red River near present-day Sherman. This trail of Marcy's, with some variations, later served as the basis for a railroad proposed in the 1850s, and subsequently it was partially followed by the Southern Overland Mail Service, which began operations in 1858.

In an attempt to solve transportation and supply problems in the arid regions of the west, the army experimented with camels. Secretary of War Jefferson Davis in 1856 and 1857 introduced seventy-five camels into Texas and headquartered them near present-day Kerrville. Camels were used as far west as California but were abandoned as a system of transportation before the Civil War and eventually vanished.

THE INDIAN FRONTIER

Those Texans who believed that annexation to the United States would put an end to Indian hostilities were soon disillusioned. The United States Army added its strength to the services of state troops and the efforts of frontier citizens, but Indian wars would continue for more than thirty years. Conflicts, in fact, actually increased in the years immediately following annexation. Although the primary responsibility for defense properly rested with the federal government and the army, the outbreak of the Mexican War left Texas to defend its own frontiers. A treaty with the Penateka Comanches in 1846 did little to preserve peace, and defense was soon needed. Before the end of the war, the state placed nine companies of Texas Rangers in service on the frontier.

When the United States began withdrawing its troops from Mexico, it stationed seven companies of regulars in Texas to replace the state troops and constructed a line of eight military posts, beginning with Fort Duncan near the Rio Grande in the south and extending northeast to Fort Worth on the Brazos. Beginning in 1851, another line of seven forts was placed generally along an irregular line about a hundred miles to the west. A third chain of forts, located along or near the Rio Grande, was built to protect the boundary lands where marauders of various types from both Mexico and the United States committed depredations on both sides of the border.

Although the effectiveness of military forces was often questioned and criticized, there is little doubt but that the army reduced the number of Indian raids. During 1853, for instance, there were 3,265 soldiers in Texas, the greatest at any time before the Civil War. The frontier was comparatively tranquil. During the following year, after many troops had been withdrawn and the country between the Colorado and the Red rivers was defended by only four small companies of infantry and two of dragoons, conditions became so bad that the army called on Governor Pease for state troops.

While relying on the army and force, the federal government also turned to the use of Indian agents and reservations to bring peace to the frontier. Two reservations were established in Texas in 1855. The state contributed the land located at the junction of the Brazos and Clear Fork rivers

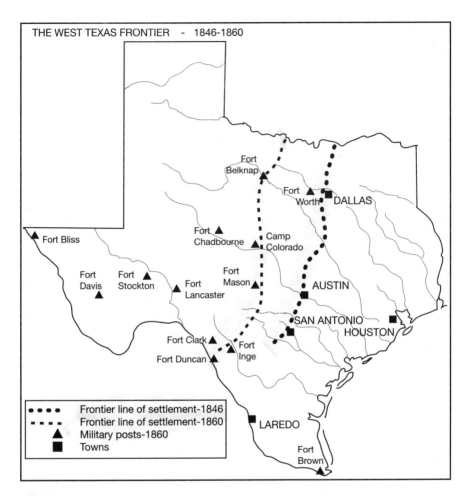

THE WEST TEXAS FRONTIER   -   1846-1860

Fort Belknap
Fort Worth
DALLAS
Fort Bliss
Fort Chadbourne
Camp Colorado
Fort Davis
Fort Stockton
Fort Lancaster
Fort Mason
AUSTIN
Fort Clark
Fort Inge
Fort Duncan
SAN ANTONIO
HOUSTON
LAREDO
Fort Brown

● ● ●   Frontier line of settlement-1846
■ ■ ■   Frontier line of settlement-1860
▲   Military posts-1860
■   Towns

The frontier line of settlement edged westward during early statehood, but not as rapidly as the rate of immigration suggested. Indian resistance remained strong and frontier defense was often a major issue in state politics, even though federal troops and military posts were primarily responsible for protection of the frontier.

near present-day Graham for about a thousand survivors of the Caddo and Wichita people. A second reservation on the Clear Fork in Throckmorton County was set aside for the Penateka band of the Comanches. Only about half of the Penatekas could be persuaded to move onto the reservation, and hostilities continued. Neither reservation could be termed a success in a permanent sense, but conditions on the frontier may have been improved temporarily. If so, much of the credit was due to the faithful Indian agents who worked under great handicaps to persuade Indians to move to the reservations and to protect them once this was accomplished. Of these, the most effective was Robert S. Neighbors, who had served the Republic of Texas as an Indian agent and afterward continued in the service of the federal government for most of the years of early Texas statehood.

Conditions near the Indian country improved temporarily in 1856. In part the change seems to have been caused by the reservations, but the work of army troops and other forces deserve some of the credit, perhaps most of it. Hostilities increased, however, by 1858, and both state and federal troops increased their activities. Campaigns in the spring and autumn led to battles and Comanche defeats in Indian Territory (present-day Oklahoma) and even as far north as Kansas.

Meanwhile, the reservation system of North-Central Texas came to an end. Swarms of nearby settlers claimed that reservation Indians were raiding their homes and repeatedly threatened the lives of the reservation people. Only the presence of federal troops prevented a massacre. In the late summer of 1859, the Indians of both reservations were moved across the Red River into the valley of the Washita River in Indian Territory. A much smaller reservation established in 1854 in Polk County by the state for the Alabama and Coushatta tribes was allowed to remain in existence.

The removal of the reservation Indians did not bring peace to the frontier. The northern Comanches and the Kiowas, aroused by the attacks from Texas, retaliated in the fall of 1859 with devastating raids. Although slavery dominated politics throughout the nation in 1859, the critical situation on the frontier was a major factor in the gubernatorial election that year. Houston, though not usually in favor of aggressive warfare against Indians, won over Hardin Runnels with a promise of strong measures. It was a time when neither the settlers nor the Indians were in a mood for treaties.

After he took office, Houston acted promptly and decisively. Before the end of March 1860, he sent to the frontier seven ranger companies. These, combined with almost two dozen county militia companies, made up a state force of more than 1,000 men on active duty to reinforce the 2,651 federal troops in Texas. Faced with such numbers, the Indian forces temporarily moved back from the frontier, and for a brief period, there was relative peace.

Vigorous efforts in South Texas and on the northwestern frontier in 1859 and 1860 thus brought a measure of peace to the troubled frontier of Texas. However, Texas was on the eve of secession. Soon there was to be no peace, on the frontier or elsewhere. Indeed, the crisis on the frontier would soon return, and resolution of the problem of Indian wars would require many more years.

BIBLIOGRAPHY

For a good bibliography on early statehood, see Ralph A. Wooster, "Early Texas Statehood: A Survey of Historical Writings," *Southwestern Historical Quarterly*, LXXVI, 121–141.

General accounts of the period are S. V. Connor, *Adventure in Glory*; E. Wallace, *Texas in Turmoil* (Austin, 1965); O. M. Roberts, "A Political, Legislative, and Judicial History of Texas, 1845–1895," in D. G. Wooten (ed.), *A Comprehensive History of Texas, 1685–1897* (two vols., Dallas, 1898); and previously cited, older works by H. H. Bancroft, *History of the North American States and Texas* (two vols., San Francisco, 1884 and 1889), J. H. Brown, *A History of Texas, 1865–1892* (two vols., St. Louis, 1892–1893), H. S. Thrall, *Pictorial History of Texas* (St. Louis, 1879), F. W. Johnson, *A History of Texas and Texans* (E.C. Barker and E.W. Winkler, eds., five vols., Chicago and New York, 1914), and L. J. Wortham, *A History of Texas* (five vols., Fort Worth, 1924). For source material, see Amelia W. Williams and E.C. Barker (eds.), *The Writings of Sam Houston* (eight vols, Austin, 1938–1943). and E. Wallace, D. M. Vigness, and George Ward (eds.), *Documents of Texas History* (Austin, 1993).

Biographies that are essential for an understanding of the period include L. Friend, *Sam Houston, The Great Designer* (Austin, 1954); Randolph Campbell, *Sam Houston* (New York, 1993); Marquis James, *The Raven: A Biography of Sam Houston* (New York, 1929); William Seale, *Sam Houston's Wife; A Biography of Margaret Lea Houston* (Norman, 1970); H. P. Gambrell, *Anson Jones* (New York, 1948); Claude Elliott, *Leathercoat: The Life of James W. Throckmorton* (San Antonio, 1938); Thomas W. Cutrer, *Ben McCulloch and the Frontier Military Tradition* (Chapel Hill, 1993); John H. Jenkins and Kenneth Kesselus, *Edward Burleson: Texas Frontier Leader* (Austin, 1990); W. J. Hughes, *Rebellious Ranger: Rip Ford and the Old Southwest* (Norman, 1964); E. Wallace, *Charles DeMorse: Pioneer Editor and Statesman*; (Lubbock, 1943) J. K. Greer, *Colonel Jack Hays* (New York, 1952); Ben H. Procter, *Not without Honor: The Life of John H. Reagan* (Austin, 1962); A. L. King, *Louis T. Wigfall: Southern Fire-eater* (Baton Rouge, 1970); and Elizabeth Silverhorne, *Ashbel Smith of Texas: Pioneer, Patriot, Statesman, 1805–1886* (College Station, 1982).

Much has been written about the Mexican War, and the following is by no means a complete listing. For a background study, see Charles H. Harris, III, *Mexico Views Manifest Destiny, 1821–1846* (Albuquerque, N.M., 1976). Justin H. Smith, *The War with Mexico* (two vols., New York, 1919) is the classic study and still useful, but Jack K. Bauer, *The Mexican War, 1846–1848* (New York, 1974), is balanced, reliable, and often viewed as the standard account in recent years. Richard Bruce Winders, *Mr. Polk's Army: The American Military Experience in the Mexican War* (College Station, 1997), is an excellent analysis of the organization and practices of the United States military. Also dealing with military matters and offering a limited amount of information on the Mexican War is Thomas T. Smith, *The U. S. Army and the Texas Frontier Economy, 1845–1900* (College Station, 1999). Other works include S. V. Connor and O. B. Faulk, *North America Divided: The Mexican War, 1846–1848* (New York, 1971); W. P. Webb, *The Texas Rangers* (New York, 1935); John E. Weems, *To Conquer a Peace: The War between the United States and Mexico* (New York, 1974); N. W. Stephenson, *Texas and the Mexican War* (New Haven, Conn., 1921); Otis A. Singletary, *The Mexican War* (Chicago, 1960); Edward H. Moseley and Paul C. Clark, Jr., *Historical Dictionary of the United States-Mexican War* (Lanham, Md., 1997); Charles M. Haecker and Jeffrey G. Mauck, *On the Prairie of Palo Alto: Historical Archaeology of the U.S.-Mexican War Battlefield* (College Station, 1997); J. K. Greer, *Colonel Jack Hays*; Ernest C. Shearer, "The Carvajal Disturbances," *Southwestern Historical Quarterly*, LV, 201–230; H. W. Barton, "Five Texas Frontier Companies during the Mexican War," ibid., LXVI, 17–30; Douglas W. Richmond, *Essays on the Mexican War* (College Station, 1986); and Tom Reilly, "Jane McManus Storms: Letters from the Mexican War, 1846–1848," *Southwestern Historical Quarterly*, LXXXV, 21–44. One of the more interesting participants in the war (who had little influence on its outcome) is presented in Samuel Chamberlain (William H. Goetzmann, annotation and introduction), *My Confession: Recollections of a Rogue* (Austin, 1996), and William H. Goetzmann, *Sam Chamberlain's Mexican War:*

The San Jacinto Museum of History Paintings (Austin, 1993). A modern interpretation from the viewpoint of Mexico may be found in Josefina Zoraida Vásquez, *La Intervención Norteamericana, 1846–1848* (Mexico City, 1997).

The controversy over the Texas-New Mexico boundary and the settlement of the debt of the Republic of Texas are dealt with in W. C. Binkley, *The Expansionist Movement in Texas* (Berkeley, Calif., 1925); E. T. Miller, *A Financial History of Texas* (Austin, 1916); Mark J. Stegner, *Texas, New Mexico & the Compromise of 1850: Boundary Dispute and Sectional Crisis* (Kent, Ohio, 1996); Holman Hamilton, *Prologue to Conflict: The Crisis and Compromise of 1850* (Lexington, Ky., 1964); Holman Hamilton, "Texas Bonds and Northern Profits: A Study in Compromise, Investment, and Lobby Influence," *Mississippi Valley Historical Review*, XLIII, 579–594; Kenneth F. Neighbours, "The Taylor-Neighbors Struggle over the Upper Rio Grande Region of Texas in 1850," *Southwestern Historical Quarterly*, LXI, 431–463; C. A. Bridges, "Texas and the Crisis of 1850" (unpublished manuscript, University of Texas Library, Austin); and S. V. Connor, *Adventure in Glory* (Austin, 1965).

On the politics of the era, besides the biographies and the general works mentioned above, see the work of Ralph A. Wooster: "Membership in Early Texas Legislatures, 1850–1860," *Southwestern Historical Quarterly*, LXIX, 163–173; "An Analysis of the Texas Know-Nothings," ibid., LXX, 414–423; "Early Texas Politics: The Henderson Administration," ibid., LXXIII, 176–192; "Early Texas Politics: The Wood Administration," *Texana*, VIII, 183–199; "Democracy on the Frontier: Statehouse and Courthouse in Ante-Bellum Texas," *East Texas Historical Journal*, X, 83–97; and "Ben H. Epperson: East Texas Lawyer, Legislator, and Civil Leader," ibid. V, 29–42. See also F. B. Sexton, "J. Pinckney Henderson," *Quarterly of the Texas State Historical Association*, I, 187–203; Louis F. Blount, "A Brief Study of Thomas J. Rusk," *Southwestern Historical Quarterly*, XXXIV, 181–202, 271–292; S. H. Sherman, "Governor George Thomas Wood," ibid., XX, 260–268; Roy Sylvan Dunn, "The Knights of the KGC in Texas, 1860–1861," ibid., LXX, 543–573; G. L. Crockett, *Two Centuries in East Texas*; E. W. Winkler (ed.), *Platforms of Political Parties in Texas* (Austin, 1916), indispensable to a study of Texas politics; Kenneth E. Hendrickson, Jr., *The Chief Executives of Austin: From Stephen F. Austin to John B. Connally, Jr.* (College Station, 1995); Francis R. Lubbock (C. W. Raines, ed.), *Six Decades in Texas* (Austin, 1900); Norman G. Kittrell, *Governors Who Have Been, and Other Public Men of Texas* (Houston, 1921); and James T. DeShields, *They Sat in High Places: The Presidents and Governors of Texas* (San Antonio, 1940). On the constitution of 1845, see a study by F. L. Paxson in *Southwestern Historical Quarterly*, XVIII, 386–398; and another by A. Middleton, ibid., XXV, 26–62; also see *Debates of the Convention of 1845* (Houston, 1846). With special reference to education, see J. J. Lane, *History of Education in Texas* (Washington, D.C., 1903); Frederick Eby, *The Development of Education in Texas* (New York, 1925); and J. C. Jeffries, "Sketches of Old Baylor," *Southwestern Historical Quarterly*, LVI, 498–506.

For accounts of exploration, see Grant Foreman, *Marcy and the Gold Seekers* (Norman, 1936) and "Marcy's Report on His Return from Santa Fé," *West Texas Historical Association Year Book*, I, 30–54; M. L. Crimmins, "Captain John Pope's Route to the Pacific," *Military Engineer* (March–April, 1931); W. J. Hughes, *Rebellious Ranger: Rip Ford and the Old Southwest* (Norman, 1964); W. Turrentine Jackson, *Wagon Roads West* (Berkeley, Calif., 1952); A. B. Bender, "Opening Routes across West Texas, 1848–1856," *Southwestern Historical Quarterly*, XXXVII, 116–135; W. H. Goetzman, "The United States-Mexican Boundary Survey, 1848–1853," ibid., LXII, 164–190; T. L. Connelly, "The American Camel Experiment: A Reappraisal," ibid., LXIX, 442–462; E. B. Lammons, "Operation Camel: An Experiment in Animal Transportation in Texas, 1857–1860," ibid., XLI, 20–49; W. H. Goetzman, *Army Exploration in the American West* (New Haven, Conn., 1959); Chris Emmett, *Texas Camel Tales* (Austin, 1969); and Eva Jolene Boyd, *Noble Brutes: Camels on the American Frontier* (Plano, 1994).

For land policy, immigration, population growth, and the extension of settlements, most of the sources and studies cited under these subjects in the preceding chapter are also valuable for the period of early statehood. The expansion of slavery was a major development of the period and is well described in Randolph B. Campbell, *An Empire for Slavery: The Peculiar Institution in Texas, 1821–1865* (Baton Rouge, 1989). For other developments, see W. C. Holden, *Alkali Trails* (Dallas, 1930); W. J. Hammond and Margaret F. Hammond, *La Réunion, a French Settlement in Texas* (Dallas, 1958); Bobby D. Weaver, *Castro's Colony: Empresario Development in Texas, 1842–1865* (College Station, 1985); Ermance V. Rejebain, "La Réunion: The French Colony in Dallas County," *Southwestern Historical Quarterly*, XLIII, 472–478; H. R. Marsh, "The Czechs in Texas," ibid., L, 236–240; Rondel V. Davidson, "Victor Considerant and the Failure of La Réunion," ibid., LXXVI, 275–296; R. N. Richardson, *The Frontier of Northwest Texas, 1846–1876: Advance and Defense by the Pioneer Settlers of the Cross Timbers and Prairies* (Glendale, Calif., 1963); James Day, *Jacob de Cordova: Land Merchant of Texas* (Waco, 1962); B. P. Gallaway, "The Physical Barrier to Settlement in the Western Cross Timbers Frontier," *West Texas Historical Association Year Book*, XLII, 51–58; Mrs. William L. Cazneau (Cora Montgomery), *Eagle Pass or Life on the Border* (Austin, 1966); and W. H. Timmons, "American El Paso: The Formative Years, 1848–1854," *Southwestern Historical Quarterly*, LXXXVII, 1–36.

Writings concerning the Trans-Nueces frontier and Tejano life may be found in works listed in the bibliography of the previous chapter, but also see Galen D. Greaser and Jesús de la Teja, "Quieting Title to Spanish and Mexican Land Grants in the Trans-Nueces: The Bourland and Miller Commission, 1850–1852," *Southwestern Historical Quarterly*, XCV, 445–464. A comprehensive study with respect to time and subject is Jerry Thompson, *A Wild and Vivid Land: An Illustrated History of the South Texas Border* (Austin, 1997). Materials relating to a Mexican leader who affected Texas affairs for three decades can be found in Jerry D. Thompson, *Juan Cortina and the Texas-Mexico Frontier* (El Paso, 1994).

Of the large body of material dealing with the frontier and the Indians, the following are among the most useful: R. N. Richardson, *The Comanche Barrier* (Glendale, Calif., 1933); W. P. Webb, *The Texas Rangers* (New York, 1935); C. C. Rister, *The Southwestern Frontier* (Cleveland, 1928); D. H. Winfrey, *Texas Indian Papers, 1846–1859* (Austin, 1960); E. Wallace and E. A. Hoebel, *The Comanches* (Norman, 1952); W. C. Holden, "Frontier Defense, 1846–1860," *West Texas Historical Association Year Book*, VI, 35–64; Kenneth S. Neighbours, "Indian Exodus out of Texas in 1859," ibid., XXXVI, 80–97; George Klos, " 'Our People Could Not Distinguish One Tribe From Another': The 1859 Expulsion of the Reserve Indians From Texas," *Southwestern Historical Quarterly*, XCVII, 599–619; A. B. Bender, "The Texas Frontier," ibid., XXXVIII, 135–148; M. L. Crimmins (ed.), "Colonel J. K. F. Mansfield's Report on the Inspection of the Department of Texas in 1856," ibid., LXII, 122–148, 215–257, 351–387; "W. G. Freeman's Report on the Eighth Military Department," ibid., LII, 227–233; Thomas T. Smith, "Fort Inge and Texas Frontier Military Operations," ibid., XCVI, 1–25; Lena Clara Koch, "The Federal Indian Policy in Texas, 1845–1860," ibid., XXXVIII, 223–234, 259–286; XXIX, 19–35, 98–127; W. J. Hughes, " 'Rip' Ford's Indian Fight on the Canadian," *Panhandle-Plains Historical Review*, XXX, 1–26; J. K. Greer (ed.), *A Texas Ranger and Frontiersman: The Days of Buck Barry in Texas, 1845–1906* (Dallas, 1932); T. R. Havins, *Beyond the Cimarron: Major Earl Van Dorn in Comanche Land* (Brownwood, 1968); Kenneth F. Neighbours, *Robert Simpson Neighbors and the Texas Frontier* (Waco, 1975); Kenneth Neighbours, *Indian Exodus: Texas Indian Affairs* (Quanah, 1973); E. H. Elam, "The History of the Wichita Indian Confederacy to 1868"; and Roger N. Conger and others, *Frontier Forts of Texas* (Waco, 1966).

9

Pioneer Institutions

By 1861, when the Civil War divided the nation, the pattern of Texan civilization had been formed, and the state's cultural institutions had been established. In many respects they were like those of the Old South, from which a majority of the population had come, but there were many variations and a few distinct differences. Texas, in fact, belonged to both the Old South and the New West. Basic to the state's economy were the slaves and cotton of the South, but whereas in the older states, the frontier was a thing of the past, in Texas it still affected the people either directly or indirectly. As was typical of the frontier, men outnumbered women, and in contrast to the Old South, the number of immigrants from Mexico and Europe was comparatively high.

Although most Texans were small subsistence farmers, owning few or no slaves, plantation owners and townspeople contributed much to the values and cultural institutions of the time. Of particular concern was the improvement of the primitive frontier transportation system. Otherwise, Texans worried about epidemics and disease and amused themselves in rather conventional fashion. Although they acquired a reputation for lawlessness, they also made positive and long-lasting achievements in such areas as education, literature and the arts, and religion.

THE PEOPLE

The customs and values of the Old South dominated pioneer institutions in some areas of the state, but the broad and diverse culture of ante-

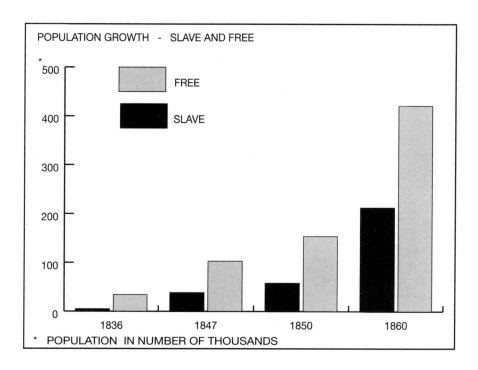

POPULATION GROWTH - SLAVE AND FREE

* POPULATION IN NUMBER OF THOUSANDS

bellum Texas reflected the influence of people from many other parts of the world. Most made their homes on farms, but in 1860 foreigners constituted more than one-third of the free population in five of the six largest towns. Whether on farms or in the cities, Europeans, Mexicans, and African Americans all made their contributions.

German immigrants concentrated their numbers on farms and ranches in the hill country of Central Texas, but by 1860 one-fifth of the population of Houston, Galveston, and San Antonio were Germans. The townspeople were usually merchants or craftsmen, but some were known nationally for their achievements in science, medicine, and the arts. Immigrants from Poland, the Scandinavian nations, and other Western European countries added to the cultural mixture.

According to the census of 1860, the second largest group of foreign-born people living in Texas was the Mexican-Americans. Concentrated in south Texas and along the Rio Grande Valley, most of them lived off the land on farms and ranches, but some were attracted to the towns. Regardless of where they lived, most held proudly and with determination to the more essential parts of their cultural heritage—their religion, language, and customs and traditions. Most were poor and lived simply in humble homes, but some were prominent and influential public figures. Santos Benavides, a mayor of Laredo, rose to the rank of general in the Civil War; José Navarro, a hero of the revolution, participated in the writing of the Constitution of 1845 and thereafter served in the Texas legislature.

Although most of the black people who made up one-third of the population of Texas in 1860 were slaves, some were free. A small number of free blacks lived in Texas under Spanish rule, though not without some restrictions. More came under Mexican rule when they were accorded equality under the law, and some won their freedom for their service in the revolution. In 1850, the census numbered 397 free blacks, but in 1860 the number decreased to 355. No doubt the restrictions placed on free blacks in Texas discouraged growth in their numbers. The Constitution of 1836 prohibited free blacks from living in the republic unless permitted to do so by a special act of congress. A law of 1840 required all free blacks to leave the republic within two years, though subsequently a number were granted permission to remain. However, free blacks could not vote or in most instances own property and were in many respects subjected to the rigorous laws applied to slaves. After statehood additional restrictions were imposed, especially with respect to punishments assessed for the conviction of crimes.

Most free blacks were farmers or farm laborers and were quite poor, but a few were relatively well-to-do landowners, either with or without special legislative sanction. The most famous of them was William Goyens of Nacogdoches, although the Ashworth family of Jefferson County may have been more wealthy. Both owned slaves, as did two other black families.

OCCUPATIONS

Occupations of antebellum Texans included both the ordinary and the unusual. Merchants increased rapidly during the fifties, numbering 2,223 by 1860, while 3,541 persons found employment as domestic servants. Four Texans described themselves as "catchers of wild horses," a conventional occupation of the times. Less expected were 4 toymen, 6 daguerreotypists, 3 actors, 45 artists, 5 clockmakers, and 6 dancing masters.

The professions were represented surprisingly well. In 1850 the town of Marshall, serving a wide area but with a relatively small population of 1,189, had 28 lawyers and 11 doctors. Certainly, there was no shortage of lawyers; the 428 located in Texas in 1850 doubled in number by 1860. Physicians, though often poorly trained, were likewise plentiful, their number increasing to 1,471 by 1860. But at the same time Texas had only 65 dentists, most of whom traveled from town to town to carry out their practice. There were 758 clergymen, but, as one might expect in a frontier society, only 8 architects.

Manufacturing and the crafts provided a living for some. The census of 1860 reported 3,449 persons employed in 983 manufacturing establishments.

More than 400 worked in grist and saw mills, and an equal number of wheel-wrights suggests the manufacture of wagons, carriages, and other vehicles. A plant in Houston manufactured hats; a factory in Harrison County produced textiles. In the crafts the 1,361 carpenters of 1850 doubled in number by 1860, and there were many brick and stone masons, blacksmiths, and saddle and harness makers.

By far the most common occupation was farming. In 1850, approximately 25,000 of the 43,000 persons who listed occupations called themselves farmers, and no doubt many others were similarly engaged. Farmers and farm laborers accounted for more than half of the 105,491 occupations of 1860. Appropriately, improved land in farms increased from 639,111 acres in 1850 to 2,650,781 acres ten years later, and during the same period the value of farms increased more than fivefold, reaching a total of about $88 million.

For the marketplace, the most important crop was cotton. Except for occasional years when pests ravaged the crops, the output increased each year. It reached 58,072 bales in 1849–1850 and 431,463 bales a decade later. During the period of the republic, cotton farming had been confined to the river valleys of the Coastal Plain and to eastern Texas from the upper Neches River northward. By 1860, these regions still produced the great part of the crop, but cotton farming was being extended into Central Texas, even though the notion still prevailed that it was a bottomland crop not suited to the black prairies.

Although cotton was the money crop, in early Texas corn was indispensable. To a very large extent it sustained both the people and their animals. Reports claimed that an average yield in early years was 40 to 80 bushels to the acre and that as much as 110 bushels had been grown without the application of manure.

Other food crops included sweet potatoes, wheat, and sugarcane. Next to corn in importance were sweet potatoes, grown not only by the small subsistence farmer but also on the large plantations. Less abundant was wheat, not grown at all in southern Texas and a secondary crop elsewhere. During the period of low prices for cotton that followed the Panic of 1837, the planters near the coast turned to raising sugarcane. The industry grew until 1852, but because of occasional droughts and freezes it declined thereafter.

During this period there was some organized effort to improve farming. Agriculture societies were formed as early as 1843, but apparently their efforts were not long sustained. The first exposition known actually to have been held was the Corpus Christi fair of 1852. At Dallas in 1858 the first recorded state fair in Texas was held. Formally chartered in 1886, it has become one of the leading annual exhibitions of the nation. Thomas Affleck, long active in the improvement of agriculture in the South, in 1858 established Glenblythe near Brenham as a model for Texas plantations.

Efforts to improve livestock breeds began at an early date. Purebred livestock was introduced during the Mexican regime; English-bred hogs, sheep, horses, and cattle were imported in 1840. In a land of horses, many were highly bred, some of racing stock. But cattle accounted for most of the value of Texas livestock, placed at $42,825,447 in 1860.

SLAVERY AND THE PLANTATION SYSTEM

Descriptions of slave life in Texas suggest that slaves could expect at best a life with basic necessities but few comforts and, at worst, a life of drudgery and brutality. Slave quarters on the plantation generally consisted of a one-room or a two-room cabin for each family, located along a street or around an empty square and near the overseer's house. The food of the slaves was much like that of the poorer whites; bacon and corn bread were the basis of the diet. Some, however, raised gardens and kept poultry. On the best plantations food was served from a common kitchen, especially during the planting and harvesting season. Clothing generally consisted of two suits each year, seldom made of homespun, for the planter considered ready-made articles more economical. Medical attention in most cases was perhaps as good as that available to sick white people. Religion was important in the life of many slaves. Some owners encouraged their slaves to attend and participate in services, and many were apparently eager to do so. However,

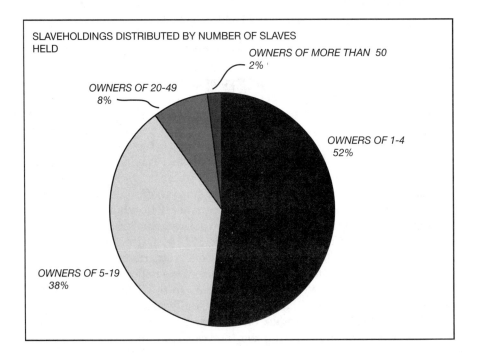

SLAVEHOLDINGS DISTRIBUTED BY NUMBER OF SLAVES HELD

OWNERS OF MORE THAN 50
2%

OWNERS OF 20-49
8%

OWNERS OF 1-4
52%

OWNERS OF 5-19
38%

some owners either discouraged or prevented involvement in religious activities.

For most slaves work was hard, monotonous, and never-ending drudgery. Working conditions on farms and plantations varied from owner to owner and depended on the season of the year, but there are reports of slaves working from four in the morning to nine at night. Sometimes there was little or no work on Sunday or perhaps even on Saturday, but at harvest time or in other busy seasons, the slaves might be in the fields every day of the week. The brutality of slave life was apparent in many ways, but the most common form was whipping. Owners were authorized by law to punish their slaves and seem to have usually done so through whipping. Slaves convicted of crimes were often whipped. For example, a slave in Hunt County charged with larceny in 1856 received seventy-six lashes at the instruction of the court. Owners accused of excessive cruelty could be charged in court, but instances where such charges were brought were rare and convictions even more rare.

Slavery was indeed a legal institution, with a sizable number of laws— in effect, a slave code— regulating its operation. Laws guaranteed the right to own slaves and protected the ownership of slaves as a property right. Laws prohibited the stealing of slaves, enticing of slaves to run away, inciting rebellion, trading with slaves, or even the sale of liquor to slaves. A complex body of law proscribed the punishment to be meted out, either by the courts or by their owners, to slaves who committed a crime or otherwise misbehaved. Another group of laws concerned runaways. Citizens were charged with the responsibility of returning runaway slaves to their masters and were in some instances entitled to cash rewards. A law of 1846 provided for a system of slave patrols to search for and capture runaways.

One aspect of slavery not regulated by the numerous laws was family life. In fact, marriage and family life of slaves was not a legal matter in Texas. Nevertheless, slave families did exist in many situations, probably in most, and their creation and maintenance were encouraged by many, probably most, owners. Sometimes there was an elaborate wedding ceremony; sometimes the couple just "jumped over a broomstick"; sometimes there was no wedding at all. Families ordinarily were large, with many children, and the family relationship was a source of strength that enabled the members to bear the burdens and trials of slavery. The family relationship, however, was a potential source of pain and anguish. Punishment, often by brutal whipping of a family member, brought suffering to all. Even more devastating was the breakup of slave families that occurred when one or more members were sold to another owner. Some owners made an effort to keep families together; others did not.

In Texas as elsewhere, those in bondage longed for freedom. Slaves frequently ran away. Some returned voluntarily, but others were arrested and returned, while still others made their way to Mexico or to Indian Territory.

It is estimated that more than 4,000 escaped to Mexico. During the decade preceding the Civil War, there was growing uneasiness about slaves who might escape or rebel. More vigilance committees were organized, and slaves charged with disobedience were punished more severely.

Rapidly expanding agriculture created a demand for slaves that was never satisfied. Apparently most of the slaves were brought in by immigrants, and most sales were private transactions involving neighbors only. Yet dealers in Galveston and Houston kept on hand slaves of all ages and held regular auctions; in most communities there were sale or auction days. During the late 1850s, there was considerable demand for the reopening of the African slave trade, a move supported by a number of prominent Texans and even by some church groups. The illicit African slave trade, meanwhile, brought in hundreds, perhaps thousands, through Galveston and other coastal points. Free blacks were sometimes enslaved, either through kidnapping or legal subterfuge.

Towns in antebellum Texas were few and small, but urban slavery expanded as Texas towns grew. By 1860, Houston and San Antonio each contained more than 1,000 slaves, and smaller towns numbered slaves in the hundreds. Many of the urban slaves were household servants, but others worked in flour mills, sawmills, or other factories, while some were carpenters, blacksmiths, or skilled in other crafts. In fact, there were instances where free workers protested the competition offered by slave workers.

But most slaves lived on the land, more than 90 percent, and a majority lived on plantations holding ten or more slaves. In fact, almost half of the slave population in 1860 was owned by planters holding twenty or more slaves. In proportion to the total population, the number of such slaveowners was relatively small, but their influence was far out of proportion to their number. Nearly all were leaders in their communities, and many exercised statewide influence. More than any other group they stamped upon early Texas society its distinguishing features.

A study of those planters with more than a hundred slaves revealed wide variations in wealth but several relatively consistent characteristics. Property holds of forty-seven great planters ranged from $60,000 to more than $600,000, cotton production from less than 250 bales to more than 800, and livestock holdings from $1,400 to more than $53,000. Although all but three were cotton planters, their agricultural practices were surprisingly diversified. Practically all owned cattle and hogs, about half of the group raised sheep, every planter grew corn, more than three-fourths grew sweet potatoes, and a somewhat smaller proportion planted other food crops. The Texas plantation was far from self-sufficient, but it was likewise far from complete dependency on outside sources for many staple products.

The wealthier planters lived better than any other people of their day. They had food in great abundance and variety, and elaborate meals were frequently assembled from garden, woods, and stream, with hot breads, cakes, jellies, preserves, and rare delicacies from New Orleans. As they acquired more property, the planters replaced their log cabins with larger and better constructed buildings of cedar, walnut, or pine, and occasionally of brick. Many of these houses were built during the decade preceding the Civil War. Tastes varied from time to time, but a desire for luxuries remained constant. In 1831, cottonades and candle molds were in special demand; sideboards, tables, and jewelry were bought in quantity during the 1840s and 1850s.

LIFE ON THE FARMS

For most rural Texans the plantation system was something only to be observed and perhaps envied. For them their existence depended upon their own labor, their houses were simple, and their luxuries were few.

The houses built by country people were only slightly better than those of colonial times. Here and there was to be found a frame dwelling, well designed and carefully built, but the prevailing type in the middle of the century was still the log cabin. The double log cabin, or dog-run house, was the most popular. It consisted of two rooms under a continuous, gabled, roof, separated by an open space or dog run. Commonly, a porch extended across the entire front. In addition to serving as a sleeping place for the dogs (and for overflow guests) and providing a space for family and friends to sit during warm weather, the dog run and the porch served as catchalls for saddles, bridles, harnesses, chests, boxes, guns, and a dozen other things. The logs were hand-hewn and dovetailed at the corners. As the family grew, a lean-to might be added to the back of one or both rooms. A kitchen and perhaps a smokehouse might also be built, but they were separate from the main house. Spaces between the logs were chinked with boards and daubed with clay or mortar. The roofs were of clapboards held securely in place by weight poles. Chimneys were commonly made of sticks, covered with mud. Floors, if any, were puncheon (timber). While traveling in eastern Texas in 1855, Frederick Law Olmsted wrote of stopping for the night at a comparatively comfortable house, but he could "look out, as usual, at the stars between the logs." Traveler Rutherford B. Hayes, the future president of the United States, described a house he saw in Texas whose walls you "could throw a cat through at random." Olmsted frequently made note of houses having glass windows, but he mentioned them in such a way as to indicate that they were the exception rather than the rule. There was much building during the 1850s, and houses made of lumber became more common. Often such houses were flimsy, boxlike affairs, not as good as the sturdy log cabins they displaced. In the southwestern area of the state, many Mexican-American families lived in *jacales*, small houses built of vertical mesquite posts, covered with a mixture of grass and adobe mud. In the hill country, German families frequently used the native stone in building their homes.

For a country that might have produced fruits, vegetables, cereals, and honey in bountiful quantities, and where cattle were abundant, the diet of most early Texans was strangely monotonous. Even by 1860, many farm families lived as the earliest Texans did, almost wholly on salt pork, corn bread, and syrup. The most common vegetable was the sweet potato. Many people tasted fresh meat only occasionally, and a large percentage of them did not have milk and butter. Except in the northern counties, wheat bread was almost unknown in the poorer homes. Water was obtained from a nearby spring or stream or occasionally from a well or cistern.

Much of the burden of pioneer life was carried by the women of the family. To them fell the tiresome tasks of washing and making clothes, making soap, taking care of the children, preparing and preserving food, taking care of the sick, and often looking after the livestock. In busy seasons and sometimes other times, many worked in the fields, chopping or picking cotton or doing whatever needed to be done. Education and cultural activities of the family, if any, were usually the responsibility of the women of the household. But, notwithstanding the heavy burden of everyday life, pioneer Texas women were active in community affairs, promoting the establishment of schools, starting Sunday schools, and encouraging the formation of churches.

The farm was substantially, though not totally, self-sufficient. Candles or lard-burning lamps supplied light. Ash hoppers and pork fat supplied materials for soap; corn was ground in steel hand mills; and cotton was carded, spun, and woven into cloth. Within less than five years one Texan recorded in his diary that he made a wheel, a coffin, a reel, a churn, a cradle, a bucket, a pump auger, an ox yoke, and a pair of shoes, in addition to working at the loom, hewing puncheons, and graining deerskins. Isaac Van Zandt, a man of distinction, made in emergencies a saddle, a pair of shoes, candles, and a baby's cradle. Toward the end of the period, however, imported manufactured cloth and ready-made clothing were rapidly supplanting homemade materials.

THE TOWNS

A person coming into Texas, direct from the Northern States might, perhaps, be surprised upon seeing many places called towns in Texas. He would, probably, as has been frequently the case, inquire, "where is the town?"

Thus did Melinda Rankin, a missionary from New England, comment on Texas municipalities in 1850. In truth, the state had no towns to spare.

The Texas capitol building in Austin, 1853. It was destroyed by fire in November 1881. (Courtesy Southwest Collection, Texas Tech University, Lubbock, Texas)

Galveston, with 4,177 inhabitants, was the largest. San Antonio, Houston, New Braunfels, and Marshall followed in the order named. No other towns had populations of as many as a thousand. Austin, long buffeted by hostile Indians and the threat of Mexican invasion, was the home of only 639 persons. Through trade with Mexico and growth as an army center, San Antonio forged ahead, and by 1860 showed a total of 8,236. Galveston moved to second place, Houston was third, and Austin fourth. Sixteen other towns, making twenty in all, are shown in the eighth census of 1860 to have had a population of 1,000 or more each.

Civic improvement came but slowly. Observers found Houston streets filled with "bottomless" mud and San Antonio streets almost impassable in bad weather. In 1857, however, Galveston paved its most traveled street with shells, and San Antonio spent $1,200 on street improvements and also built some bridges. About the same time San Antonio organized a "fire association" and in 1860 installed gas lights.

The best buildings in a town generally were the hotels. Dr. Ferdinand Roemer found the hotel in Houston "a rather pretentious two-story building," but the interior was so neglected as to remind him that he had reached the "borders of civilization." Service was poor and one was expected to occupy a room with several strangers. The pride of San Antonio was the Menger Hotel on Alamo Plaza, which opened in 1859. The building of fine cut stone, two and one-half stories high, together with its carpets, decorations, and beautiful furniture, cost $16,000. Only wealthy people and professional travelers patronized hotels; the rank and file put up at the wagon yards.

By 1860, one could purchase in the larger Texas towns almost any article to be had in the stores and warehouses in the East. Advertisements indicate that merchants kept in stock all kinds of farm machinery, carriages, wagons, building supplies, furniture, kitchen supplies, many kinds of cloth and clothing, jewelry, gold and silver plate, a large assortment of processed foods, ice, quantities of drugs and cosmetics, and liquors—indeed, an almost endless list of items. There were jobbers and wholesalers in Texas, but many merchants made their purchases in New Orleans or in other cities.

The scarcity of money and lack of banking facilities constituted a handicap for business during the period of the republic and early statehood, just as it had in colonial times. This condition was aggravated by the provision in the Constitution of 1845 prohibiting the chartering of banks. Although various firms carried out certain banking functions, only one bank was incorporated in Texas before the Civil War. This was opened in Galveston in 1847 under an old charter of the state of Coahuila and Texas.

During the early years of the republic quantities of depreciated bank notes from the United States circulated in Texas, and the paper money issued by the Texan government was even less dependable. Promissory notes were sometimes used as money, with the most common hard money consisting of hammered Spanish dollars (old Spanish dollars with the royal effigy defaced) and Mexican dollars. Later the quality of bank notes brought in from the East improved.

TRANSPORTATION

"No one walks in Texas if the distance is more than a mile," said Dr. Ferdinand Roemer, who visited the country in 1846. Nevertheless, Texans found inadequate transportation facilities in the vast land to be one of their more difficult problems, one that for a long time retarded development in the state. Travelers and merchants depended on coastal and river traffic, roads, stage lines, and freight contractors. Railroad construction began in the 1850s.

Invaluable for foreign and interstate traffic were the coastal outlets. The most serviceable ports were Galveston and Matagorda. Houston did considerable business through Buffalo Bayou; and Indianola, founded by Prince Carl of Solms-Braunfels in 1844, near the present-day Port Lavaca, came to be the principal port of West Texas. It was destroyed by a storm in 1875, rebuilt, and destroyed again in 1886.

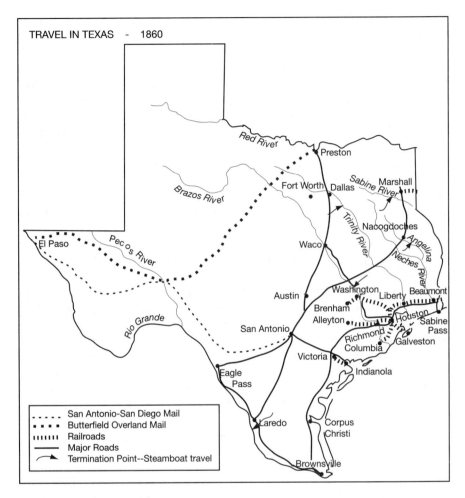

Railroad construction, especially in the Houston area, was under way in 1860 and steamboats were invaluable on the rivers of East Texas, but travel was nevertheless primarily dependent upon roads. About thirty-five stagecoach lines were in operation, including two interstate lines.

Some areas relied on the rivers. The Brazos was navigable as far as Brazoria, and occasionally boats went even higher up the river. Red River was navigable to Shreveport and under favorable conditions to Pecan Point and Jonesborough. Through Big Cypress Bayou, Caddo Lake, the Red River, and the Mississippi, Jefferson had water connection with New Orleans. In seasons of abundant rain, small boats ascended the Sabine to Sabinetown near San Augustine; the lower Trinity would carry boats of shallow draft; and some cotton was shipped down the San Jacinto. Buffalo Bayou afforded good navigation to Houston. Because of a raft that closed its channel near the Gulf, the Colorado was useless for navigation.

The great majority of Texans depended on such roads as existed. The chief roads, or routes of travel that were called roads, were the old military road, from Red River through Dallas, Waco, and Austin; the old San Antonio-Nacogdoches Road, passing through Bastrop and Crockett; the road from Indianola to San Antonio; and a road from Dallas and vicinity southward to Houston. The roads, which were bad even under favorable conditions, became impassable quagmires in wet weather. Olmsted, who entered Texas from the east, pronounced the road in Leon County "little better than a cowtrack." Yet all roads were not so nearly impassable. Rutherford B. Hayes, in the winter of 1848–49, recorded in his diary, "Rode 14 miles on good dry roads on the banks of the Brazos [near Columbia]."

Freight contractors and stage lines provided public transportation. Using strong, heavy wagons of bois d'arc, "shaped like boats," with iron axles, wheels five and a half feet high, and tires six inches wide, freighters hauled loads averaging 7,000 pounds. These huge wagons, pulled by teams of ten to twenty mules or horses or from twenty to thirty oxen, sometimes moved in long trains. Freight rates varied with the weather and season, averaging about one cent per mile for each 100 pounds but more in bad weather. For many years Mexican-American teamsters driving carts hauled large quantities of freight between San Antonio and other points, mostly on the coast. However, in 1857 gangs, probably hired by Anglo-American teamsters, attacked the cart operators, killing seventy-five or more.

Of the many vehicles used for public conveyances, the stagecoach was the most popular. The quality of the coaches, at least on certain lines, was greatly improved during the 1850s, but travel was nevertheless uncomfortable, sometimes dangerous, and usually expensive. Mud, high water, cold weather, Indian attacks, and robberies combined at times to make travel hazardous. The usual charge for a passenger was 10 cents a mile, but some contractors doubled the charges in wet weather.

Interstate stage traffic was fast and dependable. In August 1857, a semi-monthly mail and passenger service was opened between San Antonio and San Diego, California. The scheduled thirty-day trip cost $200; during the first year there was not a single failure to complete the journey. Still better service was that inaugurated in 1858 by the Southern Overland or Butterfield Mail Lines, which skirted the settlements of North Texas on its route from St. Louis and Memphis on the east to San Francisco on the west. Stages ran each way twice weekly and completed the journey of about 2,700 miles in twenty-five days or less.

Federal mail subsidies were largely responsible for the long stage lines. Mail contracts supplied the large expenditures necessary for stage stands, coaches, road repairs, and labor. Mail service otherwise was substantially improved by 1861, though it did not even approximate present-day standards. Wet mail and late mail were common causes of complaint, and post offices were scarce. Not until 1850, for instance, did San Antonio have one.

During the 1850s the railroads began both to compete with and to feed the stage and freight lines. Late in 1852, construction on the first railroad line in Texas was begun in Harrisburg, nine miles south of Houston. It was the Buffalo Bayou, Brazos, and Colorado, commonly called the Harrisburg Railroad and later a part of the Southern Pacific system. Several other lines were built in the Houston area, and by 1860 there were railroads linking Victoria to Port Lavaca and Shreveport to Marshall. With a combination of rail and steamship service, passengers could travel between New Orleans and Galveston in twenty-two and a half hours.

With all its inconveniences, railroad travel was far superior to travel by other conveyances. Reflecting the contrast of the old and the new, the Harrisburg Railroad advertised in 1860, "The River Bottom and Wet Prairies are *NOW BRIDGED*, and what was (and is now on some routes) a journey of days is now performed in the same number of hours." Charges were five cents per mile for passengers and about one cent per mile for each 100 pounds of freight.

HEALTH

Early-day Texans claimed that their state was the most healthful in America, yet it seems to have been a place where people were often in need of care. Most citizens relied upon their own resources in times of illness. Women, in particular, took care of the sick, some developing community-wide recognition for their skills. Childbirth usually occurred at home, sometimes with the assistance of a physician, but more often it was a community midwife who assisted in the delivery.

From time to time epidemics took a heavy toll. In the spring of 1833, cholera took eighty lives at Brazoria and nearly depopulated Velasco. The dreaded scourge returned in 1834, ravaging Nacogdoches and taking ninety-one lives in Goliad. Later cholera epidemics in 1849, 1850, and 1852 particularly endangered the slave population. In 1846 an epidemic, which may have been typhus, killed scores of people in New Braunfels and Fredericksburg and also many German immigrants in Indianola on their way to the settlements. Yellow fever appeared from time to time and, next to cholera, was the most dreaded disease. The people suffered from many other ailments—chills and fever, inflammation of the eyes, summer complaints, rheumatism, biliousness, measles, whooping cough, and smallpox.

Although informed people did associate cholera with filth, claims for nostrums and cures were far more extravagant than in our own day, and stores were filled with patent medicines ranging from cancer cures to cough remedies. Warning of an impending cholera epidemic, the San Antonio Board of Health in 1834 prescribed a cleanup campaign and also recommended that a copper amulet be hung around the neck. Another prescription (almost 100 percent effective, it was claimed!) consisted of water from the boiled peyote cactus, a little lime, and a few drops of laudanum. Later "cures" were little, if any, more specific than those of earlier years. Brandy, cayenne pepper, and mustard were favorite remedies.

There was, however, some progress in medical science. Although it did not hold a second meeting for sixteen years, the state medical association was organized in 1853, with Ashbel Smith and J. W. Throckmorton among its more prominent members. In 1854 the distinguished surgeon, Ferdinand Charles von Herff of San Antonio, performed a major operation using chloroform.

AMUSEMENTS

The people of Texas brought to their new homes the traditional amusements of frontier times. Athletic contests in which trained teams participated were almost unknown, but there were house raisings, log rollings, shooting matches, bear hunts, wolf hunts, quilting bees, and a dozen other activities in which work, sport, and play were mixed. Dancing was popular in the country and in town, but the most active church people objected to it. Traveler Rutherford B. Hayes described a dance that began at two o'clock in the afternoon and lasted until half-past four the next morning. Men and women came on horseback ten or fifteen miles through mud and rain.

Balls and formal dinners frequently were given in honor of some distinguished visitor or on some other special occasion. Apparently everybody joined in the patriotic celebrations on July 4 (Independence Day of the United States), March 2 (Texas Independence Day), and April 21 (the anniversary of the Battle of San Jacinto). Barbecues, patriotic songs, processions, and fervid oratory were the favorite forms of entertainment. Organizations, such as the Sunday School Union or the Sons of Temperance, sponsored and directed the programs on these occasions. Christmas and New Year's were times for dances, torchlight processions, and other amusements. Thanksgiving was celebrated on various dates, according to the proclamation of the president of the United States. The most popular sport was horse racing, and every community had its racetrack. The track at Velasco was famous in Texas and well known in New Orleans. Different ethnic groups, such as Tejanos and Germans, often remembered the holidays of their former lands with celebrations, sometimes in recognition of special religious days. However, weddings and other special family events were more often the occasion for festivities.

Interest in cultural entertainment was creditable. Most towns had amateur theatrical organizations. As early as 1838 San Augustine had its "Thespian Corps." The distinguished lawyer, W. B. Ochiltree, was a member, and John Salmon ("Rip") Ford, famous as an editor, soldier, and statesman, wrote a play for it. Houston and Galveston each had an active lyceum during the 1850s. San Antonio, with its large German population, was a center for artists. The German Casino Association owned a fine building there that was used for theatrical performances, concerts, lectures, exhibits, and dramatic readings. In almost every community, literary societies sponsored debates on ponderous subjects; there were many lectures, both pay and free; vocal and band concerts could be heard; and professional troupes appeared in all of the larger towns.

LAW AND ORDER

Early Texas society, like that of our own day, presented many facets to observers. It could be clean and wholesome, violent and immoral, or somewhere between these two extremes, depending on the point of view of the person describing it.

Colonel John S. "Rip" Ford. South Carolinian by birth, he came to Texas in 1836. In the course of a long career he practiced medicine in San Augustine, edited the *Texas Democrat* and later the *State Times* in Austin, and served in both the Congress of the Republic of Texas and the State Senate. He attained renown as a ranger, defeating the Indians in two notable engagements, and as an officer in the Confederate army, commanding the troops that won the Battle of Palmito Ranch, the last land engagement of the war. His nickname "Rip" came from his practice during the war with Mexico of introducing death notices in his newspaper with "Rest in peace," which in the stress of battle became "R. I. P." (Archives Division—Texas State Library)

At an early date Texas acquired a reputation for crime and lawlessness, which was not altogether undeserved. The *Houston Telegraph* of January 19, 1842, lists several homicides, and the editor states that they are so frequent as to "foster opprobrium upon the national character." Dueling continued, although the provision against it in the Constitution of 1845 reduced its frequency.

As late as the republic (1836–45), the criminal code was harsh, and several offenses were punishable by death. One rather notorious woman was sentenced to death for forgery, but President Lamar pardoned her. Whipping and branding were not infrequent. There was no penitentiary until 1849. Jails were small and crowded, and jail breaks were common. Law enforcement was lax, a condition that vigilance committees used to justify their own violent disregard of the law. In 1852, one such group hanged twelve or more persons in the vicinity of San Antonio.

More common were lesser vices; for example, gambling was quite prevalent. Gamblers were held in low esteem, but public disapproval apparently was not strong enough to stop their operations. In 1842 the Harris County grand jury brought seventy-seven indictments for "playing at cards." The number found by grand juries after 1848 was decidedly smaller, but the decline was probably due more to greater laxity on the part of the officers than to any change in the habits of the people. Betting on horse races was very common, and occasionally men of some means lost all their property in a single day at the tracks. Drinking was widespread and drunkenness common. In some communities, at least, it was customary for candidates to set before voters an open barrel of whiskey. "Profaneness, gaming, and intemperance are prevailing vices against which we have to contend," wrote Martin Ruter, the Methodist missionary of Texas, in 1838.

Beyond a doubt, the temperance movement, which entered from the East shortly after annexation and enlisted the services of prominent churchmen, brought some change. The Sons of Temperance, a national organization opposing the use of alcohol, was organized in Texas in 1848 and in a little more than a year claimed 3,000 members. During the following year it was stated that a majority of the members of the legislature belonged to it. Sam Houston, whose excessive drinking had often been a matter of public comment, had mended his ways and now worked in behalf of the organization. In 1851, a traveler found local organizations of the Sons in nearly every town and in many rural communities.

Meanwhile, there was some legislation on the subject of alcoholic drink. The republic had found it a troublesome subject and enacted laws requiring the licensing of dealers and a bond guaranteeing that they would keep orderly, reputable houses and prevent gambling and quarreling on their premises. A law in 1854 went much further. It permitted the electors of a county, by majority vote, to forbid the licensing of the sale of liquor in quantities of less than a quart, a provision aimed at the saloon. Of the forty-one counties in which the issue was submitted to the voters, restriction of sale was adopted in thirty-five. The law was declared unconstitutional, however, and never went into effect.

EDUCATION

By 1850, there was strong sentiment for a public school system. People generally were taking a greater interest in education; the slavery question was a divisive issue; and many Texans were reluctant to send their children to schools in the North. Pressure for state support increased, even though many parents expected to pay a portion of the cost. After 1854, some monies were available from the $2 million permanent school fund, but distribution of the meager amounts presented problems. An initial effort to divide counties into school districts proved impractical, and thereafter, any group of people were allowed to set up a school, employ a teacher, and draw from the state fund each child's money. The share for each child was pitifully small; it amounted to only 62 cents in 1854 and $1.50 the following year. Under the terms of the law it was not even necessary that the people of a community organize and start a public school to receive state funds, and only a few were established.

It was the private schools, often under the control of one or two men or women, that were the most important institutions of learning in Texas before the Civil War. Frances Trask founded a boarding school in 1834; Lydia McHenry established one the next year; and there were others. Still others were community enterprises, and some were under the control of lodges or religious denominations. The Constitution of 1836 did not prohibit private or denominational schools from receiving public aid, and several of these early schools were given land grants by the republic. There was no classification or uniformity of standards. Although with two or three exceptions, their work was confined to elementary and secondary levels, they were called, indiscriminately, institutes, academies, colleges, and universities.

The churches regarded Christian education as an important church function, and they began to establish schools at a very early date. Schools not under church control generally maintained religious environments. Most of the teachers were preachers. For instance, of the fourteen Presbyterian ministers who came to Texas as missionaries during the republic, nine engaged in teaching. As late as 1866, of the thirty-five teachers who attended the Texas teachers' state convention, eighteen were ministers.

The first Protestant denominational school was Rutersville College (named for Martin Ruter), which was established by the Methodists near La Grange. Chartered by the republic, it opened in January 1840. For a few years, the community was the leading school center in Texas, but in about 1850 the school began to decline rapidly. The University of San Augustine opened in 1842 with a grammar school, a female department, and a college, and for a few years was widely known. Perhaps the most prosperous and best-known school in its day was McKenzie College, founded near Clarksville in 1841. For a period it had as many as 300 boarding students.

Baylor University, a Baptist school chartered in Independence by the republic in 1845, attained a position of leadership at an early date. It granted sixteen degrees in 1858 and twenty-two in 1859, more than all other schools in Texas combined. Waco University was founded in 1861. The two schools were consolidated as Baylor University and were located in Waco in 1886. The female department of Baylor University became Baylor Female College in 1866 and was moved to Belton in 1886.

From annexation to the beginning of the Civil War, the legislature granted charters to 117 schools and incorporated, in addition, nine educational associations. Of these, only three have survived with anything like a continuous history: Austin College, founded in 1849 in Huntsville through the influence of Dr. Daniel Baker and moved to Sherman in 1879; Ursuline Academy of San Antonio; and Ursuline Academy of Galveston.

Through their emphasis on discipline, as well as on the knowledge they dispensed, these old schools were great civilizing agencies. "Course of study full, instruction thorough and discipline strict," ran a typical advertisement of the 1850s. "A strict discipline rigidly enforced," stated another. The curricula emphasized ancient and modern languages and philosophy. Even the simplest subjects were described in awe-inspiring terms. Surely parents would be impressed and children terrified on reading that the city schools of Houston in 1841 were teaching "English, French, Spanish, and Latin, grammatically and etymologically, on the most approved and expeditious principles." Apparently, some of the teachers taught everything they had studied, and some, like the Reverend Marcus A. Montrose, graduate of Edinburgh, had liberal training. At San Augustine University he taught mathematics, Latin, Greek, history, navigation, astronomy, rhetoric, logic, political economy, natural philosophy, chemistry, botany, and geology. In fact, for a period, he alone made up the faculty of the university.

Evidently a large majority of early-day Texas youths received their training either in their homes or in "old field schools," unknown beyond the confines of a single community. Such training must have been effective, for by 1860, illiteracy had decreased to less than 4 percent among the men and slightly more than 5 percent among the women.

Unlike some southern states, Texas did not have a law prohibiting the education of slaves. Few, however, were educated, and at the end of the Civil War, more than 95 percent were illiterate.

NEWSPAPERS, LITERATURE, AND ART

Newspapers in surprising numbers served the people of antebellum Texas. By 1840, no fewer than thirteen newspapers were being published, one or two of which were semiweeklies. The federal census of 1860 reports three daily, three triweekly, and sixty-five weekly newspapers (claiming a circulation of 90,615), and three monthly publications, numbers sufficiently large to have reached practically every person in the state.

The most venerable publication was the *Telegraph*, revived in Columbia after the Texan Revolution and moved to Houston in 1837. A neighbor of the *Telegraph*, the *Daily News* of Galveston, started in 1842 as a "puny four-page sheet... born in a one-room, unpainted shack on the Strand" but lived to become the oldest business institution in Texas. Both the *Dallas Morning News* and the *Galveston News* of our own day trace their lineage to this paper. The *State Gazette* of Austin, established in 1849, was noted for its opposition to Sam Houston. Beginning in 1842, Charles DeMorse, soldier, statesman, and editor, published the *Northern Standard* in Clarksville. Its files, unbroken until 1861 and renewed in 1865, constitute the richest source of information available on early civilization in northeast Texas.

The newspapers of early Texas do not meet the standards of our own day. Apparently little or no use was made of such news-gathering agencies as the Associated Press, which was organized in 1848. Also, not until the late 1850s was there sufficient telegraph mileage to distribute the news well. News from the outside generally came through New Orleans. Many social activities were ignored. It was not deemed good taste to print the names of women in newspapers, except under very unusual conditions. Yet, more clearly and fully than any other source, these papers describe for us the way of life of that era.

Texans who wanted to read beyond the offerings of newspapers could turn to other writings. Travel accounts were popular. Mary Austin Holley, a cousin of Stephen F. Austin, wrote down in vivid style her impressions of the new land. Her second work, more complete than the first, was published in 1836 as *Texas*. Matilda C. F. Houston, an English woman who visited about 1843, wrote *Texas and the Gulf of Mexico*, an informative account of the Galveston-Houston region. In 1849, a German scientist, Dr. Ferdinand Roemer, published *Texas*, a perceptive description of the frontier as it was at that time. A few years later came Frederick Law Olmsted, a landscape artist and engineer with broad interests. His *Journey through Texas* described the state as he saw it through critical eyes.

Other writers turned to history. George Wilkins Kendall, founder and associate editor of the New Orleans *Picayune*, who accompanied the Texan Santa Fe expedition of 1841, recorded in his history of the journey experiences that represented practically every element of adventure and peril that could have befallen people on the Southwestern frontier. William Kennedy, an Englishman, published his *Texas* in 1841. Fourteen years later, Henderson Yoakum brought forth *A History of Texas*, a truly remarkable study that received wide circulation.

The number of books and magazines increased rapidly during the 1850s. In the census returns for 1850, 12 libraries were listed; the returns for 1860 showed 132. The bookstore of Francis D. Allen of Galveston advertised books: "Standard, Classical, Scientific, Mechanical, School, Historical Law, Medical, Theological, Agricultural, Poetical, Biographical, Voyages, Novels, etc." Richardson and Company sold 10,000 copies of the *Texas Almanac* for 1857, increased the output of the 1858 issue, and published 30,000 copies of the 1859 issue.

Artists who recorded the scenes and people of antebellum Texas numbered literally in the dozens. José Sanchez, a Mexican army officer who visited Texas in 1828, did sketches of some of its scenes and people. James Strange painted creditable portraits of the captives Santa Anna and Juan Almonte. Some of the Germans who located in Texas in the 1850s were artists of truly superior talent. Among these were Herman Lungkwitz and Richard Petri. Lungkwitz was known more for his landscape scenes, Petri for his Indians. Carl G. von Iwonski did portraits and groups of people. In San Antonio, Louisa Heuser Wueste was another popular artist who specialized in portraits.

A contemporary of the German artists, Frenchman Theodore Gentilz of Castro's colony, painted the Indian peoples. Another French artist, Eugenie Lavender, won acclaim at the French court before she came to Texas in 1851. Best known of her work was "Saint Patrick," in the cathedral in Corpus Christi.

RELIGION

Of all the forces affecting early Texas society, none had a greater influence than the churches. Catholic clergy were involved from the time of the earliest of Spanish activities; itinerant Protestant preachers began their work during the period of Mexican rule, but it was not until after Texas had its independence that a well-organized Protestant missionary program was launched. "Dear brethren, we ask you again," called the fervent Texans, "come over into Macedonia and help us!" Methodists and Baptists led the way, but Presbyterians were active.

When news of the defeat of Santa Anna reached the general conference of the Methodist Episcopal Church in session in Cincinnati, Ohio, in May 1836, church leaders were quick to realize that it meant the opening of a mission field rich with opportunities. Martin Ruter and two other Methodist missionaries responded to the call, working feverishly to build churches, form circuits, and organize classes. In 1840, the Texas Conference was organized with 1,878 members and 25 local preachers. With 30,661 members and 224 traveling preachers, the Methodist Church in 1860 was, by far, the strongest in Texas.

Since Baptists relied on the authority of the local congregation in church matters, it was easy for them to establish churches under frontier conditions. The first church in Texas was the Pilgrim Church, brought intact in 1834 by immigrants from Illinois under Daniel Parker. Another church was organized in Washington early in 1837, and at once it sent an appeal to organized Baptists in the United States to send missionaries. Churches and associations were organized rapidly, and a state convention was formed in 1848. By 1860, there were approximately 500 Baptist churches in Texas. The denomination had 280 church buildings, as compared with 410 for the Methodists. Baptists, however, led all denominations in number of church publications.

Presbyterian mission work was begun in 1837 under the special patronage of the Synod of Mississippi. Joining the earlier missionaries in 1840 came Daniel Baker, destined to be a major figure in both religious and educational matters. Already, Presbyterian churches had been established near Independence, and in Houston, Austin, and Galveston. In 1857, the Presbyterians had 2,261 members in Texas, and by 1860, had seventy-two church buildings.

Other churches were active. The Episcopal Church sent R. M. Chapman of New York as a missionary to Texas in 1838, and by 1860, there were nineteen Episcopal church houses in Texas. The Christian church grew rapidly during the decade before the Civil War. In 1850, it owned only five buildings; ten years later it had thirty-nine. The Catholics maintained churches in Nacogdoches, San Augustine, and probably in other Texas communities continuously from colonial times. A Catholic church was established in Houston shortly after the Texas Revolution, and by 1860, there were thirty-three Catholic church buildings in the state, with membership concentrated among German and Mexican people.

The church people brought with them to Texas practices that had been developed in the United States and tried for a century—protracted meetings, basket meetings, and camp meetings. Sermons were usually long and fervent. Church women gave suppers, "refreshment parties," "fairs," and bazaars to raise money for the church. Sunday schools were maintained by the more active churches of all Protestant denominations. Belinda McNair Fullinwider and her husband taught a Sunday school in San Felipe as early as 1834. In time, the larger Sunday schools had libraries. The union school in Brownsville had 1,000 volumes and another in Austin had 1,300.

Protestant leaders advocated a strict observance of Sunday as a day of worship but were less than successful in their efforts. Melinda Rankin complained that the day was ignored by many people, and in Crockett, Olmsted found all the stores open on Sunday and was told that it was the merchants' best day. Nevertheless, the churches were effective civilizing agencies. They brought the people together, clean and in their best apparel. At church the men exchanged greetings and talked on subjects ranging from the weather and crops to the political issues of the day. Here chatted farmers' wives and daughters, tired of drudgery and starved for companionship. The churches, moreover, set the moral standards for many of the people. They attacked immorality of every type; their leaders praised or condemned almost all conduct and every institution.

Closely associated with the churches and next to them the most influential social agencies were the lodges. Freemasonry had barely been planted before the Texas Revolution uprooted it, but the Masons reestablished their order within less than a year. The order was supported by many distinguished Texans, including Anson Jones and Sam Houston; by 1860, 252 lodges had been organized—one for practically every community—and the lodge maintained or sponsored a score or more schools. The Independent Order of Odd Fellows was introduced into Texas from Louisiana in 1838, chiefly through the efforts of Jacob De Cordova, publisher and land agent, and by 1860 there were seventy-four active lodges.

BIBLIOGRAPHY

A good introduction to life in antebellum Texas is Llerena B. Friend, "The Texan of 1860," *Southwestern Historical Quarterly*, LXII, 1–17, but a look through the eyes of the people of the day will be most helpful. For contemporary accounts, see Marilyn McAdams Sibley, *Travelers in Texas, 1761–1860* (Austin, 1967); and "Bishop Morris in Texas, 1841–1842," *East Texas Historical Journal*, III, 149–168; Gilbert J. Jordan, "W. Steinerts' View of Texas in 1849," *Southwestern Historical Quarterly*, LXXX, 57–78, 177–200, 283–301, 399–416; LXXXI, 45–72; Levi Lamoni Wight, *The Reminiscences and Civil War Letters of Levi Lamoni Wight: Life in a Mormon Splinter Colony on the Texas Frontier* (Davis Bitton, ed., Salt Lake City, 1970); Adolphus Sterne, *Hurrah for Texas! The Diary of Adolphus Sterne, 1838–1851* (Archie P. McDonald, ed., Waco, 1969); A. F. Muir (ed.), *Texas in 1837: An Anonymous Contemporary Narrative* (Austin, 1958); Mary Austin Holley, *The Texas Diary, 1835–1838* (J. P. Bryan, ed., Austin, 1967); R. S. Lee, *Mary Austin Holley: A Biography* (Austin, 1962); Fredrick L. Olmsted, *A Journal through Texas* (1857; James Howard, ed., Austin, 1962); F. R. Lubbock, *Six Decades in Texas*; Charles Michael Gruener, "Rutherford B. Hayes' Horseback Ride through Texas,"

Southwestern Historical Quarterly, LXVIII, 352–360; and Melinda Rankin, *Texas in 1850* (Boston, 1950).

Some studies of life and institutions are W. R. Hogan, *The Texas Republic* (Norman, 1946); and his "Pamelia Mann, Texas Frontierswoman," *Southwest Review*, XX, 360–370; Kent Keeth, "Sankt Antonius: Germans in the Alamo City in the 1850s," *Southwestern Historical Quarterly*, LXXVI, 183–202; Susan Jackson, "Movin' on: Mobility through Houston in the 1850's," ibid., LXXXI, 251–282; J. B. Frantz, *Gail Borden*; W. P. Webb, "Christmas and New Year in Texas," *Southwestern Historical Quarterly*, XLIV, 357–379; Elizabeth Silverthorne, *Christmas in Texas* (College Station, 1987); J. W. Schmitz, *Texas Culture in the Days of the Republic, 1836–1846* (San Antonio, 1960); Dorothy Kendall Bracken and Maurine Whorton Redway, *Early Texas Homes* (Dallas, 1956); Kenneth W. Wheeler, *To Wear a City's Crown: The Beginnings of Urban Growth in Texas, 1836–1865* (Cambridge, Mass., 1968); Joe Tom Davis, *Historic Towns of Texas: Columbus, Gonzales, Jefferson* (Austin, 1996); Roy B. Broussard, *San Antonio during the Texas Republic: A City in Transition* (El Paso, 1968); A. F. Muir, "Intellectual Climate of Houston during the Period of the Republic," *Southwestern Historical Quarterly*, LXII, 312–321; William Seale, *Texas Riverman* (Austin, 1966); and D. H. Winfrey, *Julian S. Devereux and Monte Verdi Plantation* (Waco, 1962).

Scholarly analysis of population characteristics may be found in three articles by R. A. Wooster: "Notes on Texas' Largest Slaveholders, 1860," *Southwestern Historical Quarterly*, LXV, 72–79; "Foreigners in the Principal Towns of Ante-Bellum Texas," ibid., LXVI, 208–220; and "Wealthy Texans, 1860," ibid., LXI, 163–180. See also Randolph B. Campbell and Richard G. Lowe, *Wealth and Power in Antebellum Texas* (College Station, 1977); "Slave Property and the Distribution of Wealth in Texas, 1860," *Journal of American History*, LXIII, 316–324; and "Wealthholding and Political Power in Antebellum Texas," *Southwestern Historical Quarterly*, LXXIX, 21–30.

For economic developments, see Robert L. Jones, "The First Iron Furnace in Texas," *Southwestern Historical Quarterly*, LXIII, 279–289; Charles H. Dillon, "The Arrival of the Telegraph in Texas," ibid., LXIV, 200–211; and Randolph Campbell and Richard Lowe, "Some Economic Aspects of Antebellum Texas Agriculture," ibid., LXXXII, 351–378. Also see Jorge A. Hernandez, "Trading Across the Border: National Customs Guards in Nuevo León," ibid., C, 433-450, and David G. Surdam, "The Antebellum Texas Cattle Trade Across the Gulf of Mexico," ibid., C, 477-492. William Seale emphasizes architecture in "San Augustine, in the Texas Republic," ibid., LXXII, 347–358. A. L. Carlson tells the history of Texas banking in the *Texas Monthly*, IV, 481–499, 615–641; V, 74–102. See also Mary Rena Green, *Sam Maverick, Texan, 1803–1870* (San Antonio, 1952).

Transportation in early Texas has received considerable study. See Ralph Moody, *Stagecoach West* (New York, 1967), for a general treatment; also J. W. Williams, "The Butterfield Overland Mail Road across Texas," *Southwestern Historical Quarterly*, LXI, 1–19; Emmie Giddings Mahon and Chester V. Kielman, "George H. Giddings and the San Antonio-San Diego Mail Line," ibid., XLI, 220–239. River travel is examined in Keith Guthrie, *Texas Forgotten Ports* (three vols., Austin, 1989, 1991, and 1995); Pamela Puryear and Nath Winfield, Jr., *Sandbars and Sternwheelers: Steam Navigation on the Brazos* (College Station, 1976), and Pat Kelley, *River of Lost Dreams: Navigation on the Rio Grande* (Lincoln, Neb.,1986).

Another approach to water transportation is described in Allan D. Meyers, "Brazos Canal: Early Intracoastal Navigation in Texas," *Southwestern Historical Quarterly*, CIII, 175-189. For railroads, good studies are C. S. Potts, *Railroad Transportation in Texas* (University of Texas Bulletin, no. 119; Austin, 1909); and S. G. Reed, *A History of Texas Railroads* (Houston, 1941). See also P. Briscoe, "The First Texas Railroad," *Quarterly of the Texas State Historical Association*, VII, 279–285; A. F. Muir, "Railroads

Come to Houston, 1857–1861," *Southwestern Historical Quarterly*, LXIV, 42–63, and his "The Destiny of Buffalo Bayou," ibid., LXVII, 19–22; and Eugene O. Porter, "Railroad Enterprise in the Republic of Texas," ibid., LIX, 363–371.

For an understanding of slavery, readers should turn to Randolph Campbell, *An Empire for Slavery: The Peculiar Institution in Texas, 1821–1865* (Baton Rouge, 1989), a comprehensive, thoughtful study that considers virtually all aspects of the institution. Other works of Campbell include "Human Property: The Negro Slave in Harrison County, 1850–1860," *Southwestern Historical Quarterly*, LXXVI, 384–396; "Slaveholdings in Harrison County, 1850–1860: A Statistical Profile," *East Texas Historical Journal*, XI, 18–27; "Intermittent Slave Ownership: Texas as a Test Case," *Journal of Southern History*, LI, 15–30; "Slave Hiring in Texas," *American Historical Review*, LXXXIII, 107–114; and *A Southern Community in Crisis, Harrison County, Texas, 1850–1880* (Austin, 1983). See also Richard Lowe and Randolph Campbell, *Planters and Plain Folk: Agriculture in Antebellum Texas* (Dallas, 1987), and Elizabeth Silverhorne, *Plantation Life in Texas* (College Station, 1986). A view more sympathetic to the institution is found in Abigail Curlee, "The History of a Texas Slave Plantation, 1831–1863," *Southwestern Historical Quarterly*, XXVI, 79–127, and "A Glimpse of Life on Antebellum Slave Plantations in Texas," ibid., LXXVI, 361–383. Other studies include Alwyn Barr, *Black Texans: A History of Negroes in Texas, 1528–1971* (Austin, 1973; 2d ed., Norman, 1996); Ruthe Winegarten, "Texas Slave Families," *Texas Humanist*, VII, 29–33; Billy D. Ledbetter, "White over Black: Racial Attitudes in the Ante-Bellum Period," *Phylon*, XXXIV, 406–418; Karl E. Ashburn, "Slavery and Cotton Production in Texas," *Southwestern Social Science Quarterly*, XIV, 257–271; and E. Fornell, "Agitation in Texas for Reopening the Slave Trade," ibid., LX, 245–259. See also Paul D. Lack, "Slavery and Vigilantism in Austin, Texas, 1840–1860," *Southwestern Historical Quarterly*, LXXXV, 1–20; William T. Kerrigan, "Race, Expansion, and Slavery in Eagle Pass, Texas, 1852," ibid., CI, 275-301; Michael Phillips, "White Violence, Hegemony, and Slave Rebellion in Dallas, Texas, before the Civil War," *East Texas Historical Journal*, XXXVII, 25-35; Ronnie C. Tyler, "Fugitive Slaves in Mexico," *Journal of Negro History*, LVII, 1–12; and Rosalie Schwartz, *Across the Rio Grande to Freedom: United States Negroes in Mexico* (El Paso, 1975). M. L. Dillon ably presents the activities of an early abolitionist in Texas in *Benjamin Lundy and the Struggle for Negro Freedom* (Urbana, Ill., 1966). Later effects of the slavery issue are discussed in Wesley Norton, "The Methodist Episcopal Church and the Civil Disturbances in North Texas in 1859 and 1860," *Southwestern Historical Quarterly*, LXVIII, 317–341. Legal aspects are considered in A. E. Keier Nash, "The Texas Supreme Court and Trial Rights of Blacks, 1845–1860," *Journal of American History*, LVIII, 623–642. Also see Ronnie C. Tyler and Lawrence R. Murphy (eds.), *The Slave Narratives of Texas* (Austin, 1974; republished 1997); and T. Lindsay Baker and Julie P. Baker, ed., *Till Freedom Cried Out: Memories of Texas Slave Life* (College Station, 1997).

The story of Tejanos is told well in a number of recently published outstanding works listed in the bibliographies of earlier chapters. See previous listings on publications by David Montejano, Arnoldo De León, Timothy M. Matovina, Armando Alonzo, Jesús de la Teja, Gerald Poyo, and others. Gerald E. Poyo (ed.), *Tejano Journey, 1770-1850* (Austin, 1996), contains a number of essays describing Tejano life in the two or three decades before the Civil War. Also see Caroline Remy, "Hispanic-Mexican San Antonio, 1836–1861," *Southwestern Historical Quarterly*, LXXI, 564–570.

Most studies of nineteenth-century women in Texas focus on frontier life in a later period, but see the Fane Downs, "Tryels and Trubbles': Women in Early Nineteenth Century Texas," *Southwestern Historical Quarterly*, XC, 35–56, for an excellent discussion; Jane Dysart, "Mexican Women in San Antonio, 1830–1860: The Assimilation Process," *Western Historical Quarterly*, VII, 365–373; Bessie Melvina Pearce,

"Texas Through Women's Eyes, 1823–1860" (unpublished dissertation, University of Texas, Austin, 1965); and Paula Mitchell Marks, *Hands to the Spindle: Texas Women and Home Textile Production, 1822-1880* (College Station, 1998). Ruthe Winegarten, *Black Texas Women: A Sourcebook* (Austin, 1996), and Sylvia Ann Grider and Lou Halsell Rodenberger (eds.), *Texas Women Writers: A Tradition of Their Own* (College Station, 1997), contain some materials on antebellum Texas women.

Pioneer medicine is dealt with in George Plunkett Red, *The Medicine Man in Texas* (Houston, 1930); J. V. Haggard, "Epidemic Cholera in Texas, 1833–1834," *Southwestern Historical Quarterly*, XL, 216–230; P. I. Nixon, *A Century of Medicine in San Antonio* (San Antonio, 1936), *The Medical Story of Early Texas* (San Antonio, 1953), and *A History of the Texas Medical Association, 1853–1953* (Austin, 1954). See also Ashbel Smith, *Yellow Fever in Galveston* (Austin, 1951); B. M. Jones, *Health Seekers in the Southwest, 1817–1900* (Norman, 1967); and Paul J. Scheips, "Albert James Myer, An Army Doctor in Texas, 1854–1857," *Southwestern Historical Quarterly*, LXXXII, 1–24.

F. Eby, *The Development of Education in Texas* (New York, 1925), remains a useful history of education in Texas; but see also C. E. Evans, *The Story of Texas Schools* (Austin, 1955); Mrs. Jonnie L. Wallis (ed.), *Sixty Years on the Brazos* (Los Angeles, 1930), an account of a schoolboy in old Washington; William M. Baker, *The Life and Labours of the Reverend Daniel Baker* (Philadelphia, 1859); F. B. Baillio, *A History of the Texas Press Association* (Dallas, 1916); Murl L. Webb, "Religious and Educational Efforts among Texas Indians in the 1850s," *Southwestern Historical Quarterly*, LXIX, 22–37; H. B. Carroll, *Masonic Influence on Education in the Republic of Texas* (Waco, 1960); James David Carter, *Masonry in Texas: Background, History, and Influence to 1846* (Waco, 1958); John C. English, "Wesleyan College of San Augustine," *East Texas Historical Journal*, III, 141–148; and James A. Tinsley, "Genesis of Higher Education in Texas," *Proceedings of the Philosophical Society of Texas* (1968). A glimpse of early schools may be had in Emily Jones Shelton, "Lizzie E. Johnson: A Cattle Queen of Texas," *Southwestern Historical Quarterly*, L, 349–366. See also Jefferson Davis Bragg, "Baylor University, 1851–1861," ibid., XLIX, 37–65, and "Waco University," ibid., LI, 213–224.

For studies on the arts see Pauline A. Pinckney, *Texas Artists of the Nineteenth Century* (Austin, 1967); William W. Newcomb, Jr., *German Artist on the Texas Frontier: Friedrich Richard Petri* (Austin, 1978), and "German Artist on the Pedernales," *Southwestern Historical Quarterly*, LXXXII, 149–172; and James McGuire, *Hermann Lungkwitz: Romantic Landscapist on the Texas Frontier* (Austin, 1983).

Valuable for information on newspapers are Marilyn McAdams Sibley, *Lone Star and State Gazettes: Texas Newspapers Before the Civil War* (College Station, 1983), and Wesley Norton, "Religious Newspapers in Antebellum Texas," *Southwestern Historical Quarterly*, LXXIX, 145–165. Lorna Geer Sheppard, *An Editor's View of Early Texas: In the Days of the Republic as Depicted in the Northern Standard* (Austin, 1998), describes the work of one of the most influential newspapers of the period.

On religion and the churches, see C. E. Castañeda, *Our Catholic Heritage in Texas 1519–1936* (seven vols., Austin, 1936–58); and *The Historical Magazine of the Protestant Episcopal Church*, September, 1941; Macum Phelan, *A History of Early Methodism in Texas, 1817–1866* (Nashville, 1924); W. S. Red, *A History of the Presbyterian Church in Texas* (Austin, 1936); J. M. Carroll, *A History of Texas Baptists* (Dallas, 1923); L. R. Elliott (ed.), *Centennial Story of Texas Baptists* (Dallas, 1936); Mary Angela Fitzmorris, *Four Decades of Catholicism in Texas, 1820–1860* (Washington, D.C., 1926); G. L. Crockett, *Two Centuries in East Texas*; Stephen Daniel Eckstein, *History of the Churches of Christ in Texas, 1824–1950* (Austin, 1963); George H. Paschal, Jr. and Judith A. Benner, *A Hundred Years of Challenge and Change: A History of the Synod of Texas of the United Presbyterian Church in the U.S.A.* (San Antonio, 1968); R. Douglas

Brackenridge, *Voice in the Wilderness: A History of the Cumberland Presbyterian Church in Texas* (San Antonio, 1968); Carter E. Boren, *Religion on the Texas Frontier* (San Antonio, 1968); and Ronald C. Ellison, *Texas and Baptist Sunday Schools* (Austin, 1997).

Good general references on Texas pioneers are J. D. De Cordova, *Texas: Her Resources and Public Men: The Texas Almanac* (Galveston) from 1857 through 1862; C. C. Rister, *Southern Plainsmen* (Norman, 1938); W. Gard, *Rawhide Texas* (Norman, 1965); Earl Fornell, *The Galveston Era* (Austin, 1961); and R. N. Richardson, *The Frontier of Northwest Texas, 1846–1876* (Glendale, 1963).

10

Secession and War
1860–1865

While Texans of the 1850s opened new lands, built new towns, and struggled to overcome the dangers of the frontier, the nation divided more and more into two well-defined camps. Citizens and leaders of North and South quarreled over many issues—states' rights, distribution of western lands, the tariff—but it was the rancorous controversy over slavery that dominated public affairs. By 1856, proslavery Southern extremists were threatening secession from the Union if an antislavery Republican were to be elected president. The population of Texas consisted mostly of immigrants from Southern states who were sympathetic to slavery; thus, Texans generally supported the Southern position. Although concerned about other matters, particularly frontier defense, they took part more and more in the conflict over slavery as the controversy intensified in the late 1850s.

When Southern states began to secede from the Union after Republican Abraham Lincoln won the presidential election of 1860, Texas joined the secession movement. Secession led to war, and for four years Texas supported the Confederate cause. Few battles were fought within the state, but these were difficult years. Thousands of Texans served in the armies, while at home conflicts between Confederate and Union sympathizers generated distrust and sometimes violence. Indian raids threatened the frontier, and life for those who remained at home was at best filled with toil and anxiety and sometimes with genuine hardship.

PRELUDE TO SECESSION

Most white Texans supported slavery, but some were unwilling to risk destruction of the Union. Consequently, the growing crisis in the 1850s over slavery brought dissension in Texas public affairs. Other issues demanded attention, however, and it was not until 1857 that the electorate became aligned in conservative and radical or Unionist and states' rights groups. In that year the states' rights faction gained control of the Democratic Party. The Whig Party was no more; gone also was the Know-Nothing organization, which had been basically Unionist. Henceforth the friends of the Union had no organization.

During the next two years Texas Democrats moved more and more toward the position of proslavery extremists east of the Mississippi. The legislature authorized the governor to send delegates to a Southern convention if it should be deemed expedient. John Marshall, chairman of the state Democratic committee, vigorously advocated the reopening of the African slave trade. The party convention of 1859 refused to endorse a proposal so extreme, but it applauded the decision of the Supreme Court in the *Dred Scott* case (which included an opinion that slavery could not be prohibited in territories), and it nominated Hardin Runnels, a strong advocate of slavery, for reelection.

Against this organization, Houston, running as an independent on a platform endorsing the U.S. Constitution and promising allegiance to the Union, entered the contest for governor. Ex-Governor Pease supported him, as did J. W. Throckmorton, B. H. Epperson, and other old-time Whigs. Touring the state in a buggy, wearing an old linen duster, on hot days sometimes appearing without a shirt, the old warrior made a mighty appeal to the people. In this, his last political battle, he defeated Runnels by nearly 8,000 votes, 35,257 to 27,500. By a much narrower margin, Edward Clark, running with Houston as an independent, managed to defeat Francis Lubbock for lieutenant governor. No doubt various factors affected the results of the election. Houston's personal popularity weighed heavily, as did the dissatisfaction of the people on the frontier, who charged Runnels with neglecting their protection. It is possible, however, that the states' rights leaders had moved too rapidly for the majority of the voters.

Events thereafter strengthened the hands of the proslavery faction. Abolitionist John Brown's raid on Harper's Ferry, Virginia, in October 1859 antagonized and alarmed people. At the Democratic state convention at Galveston in early April 1860, the states' rights leaders gained complete control and abandoned all restraint. Texas as a sovereign state had the right, they stated, "to withdraw from the confederacy, and resume her place among the powers of the earth as a sovereign and independent nation." The platform deplored "the unnatural efforts of a sectional party at the North to carry on an 'irrepressible conflict' against the institution of slavery" and implied that the election of a Republican president would bring about a dissolution of the Union.

The strong proslavery views of the state Democratic Party were evident in the actions of the national Democratic convention of 1860. The state party sent to the national convention, which met in April in Charleston, a delegation of staunch champions of the slavery cause. At that convention, when Stephen A. Douglas and the Northern Democrats insisted on a platform endorsing the theory of popular sovereignty in the territories, a moderate position, and denouncing the *Dred Scott* decision, the delegates from Texas and seven other Southern states withdrew.

Divided over the slavery issue, the Democrats held two more conventions and nominated two presidential candidates. The Charleston convention adjourned to meet in Baltimore on June 18. In Baltimore, the Northern Democrats nominated Douglas for president. The Southern Democrats then met in Richmond, chose as their candidate John C. Breckinridge of Kentucky, and adopted a platform that supported the *Dred Scott* decision.

The Republican Party encountered fewer problems. At its national convention, which met in Chicago on May 18, the party adopted a resolution that slavery could not legally exist in a territory and selected Abraham Lincoln and Hannibal Hamlin as its nominees.

Since none of these tickets was to their liking, a group of pro-Union Southerners, including some of the large slaveholders, organized the Constitutional Unionist Party. Believing that secession would be ruinous to the South, organizers argued that the only hope lay in fighting for Southern rights in the Union. In a convention held in Baltimore, Sam Houston received 57 votes as against 68.5 for John Bell of Tennessee for the party's presidential nomination on the first ballot, but Bell was nominated on the second. Houston permitted his name to go before the country as "the People's candidate," but on August 18 he withdrew formally.

While politicians battled over nominations, public excitement in Texas verged on hysteria. Severe fires, of incendiary origin, it was alleged, broke out in Dallas, Denton, Waxahachie, Kaufman, and various other points in North Texas. The fires were charged to abolitionists and linked with stories of slave uprisings, poisonings, and assassinations—generally exaggerated if not wholly unfounded. Vigilance committees sprang into action. In Dallas three blacks were hanged in the presence of a large crowd; three white men, supposedly abolitionists, were hanged in Fort Worth because they had been "tampering" with slaves. By 1860, a growing spirit of intolerance pervaded the entire state.

A secret order known as the Knights of the Golden Circle was introduced into Texas in 1860 and soon had established a number of local lodges, or "castles." The plans of the organization seem to have been to make slavery more secure in the South, particularly by incorporating into the Union additional slave states carved out of territory belonging to Mexico. Two poorly organized filibuster movements against Mexico in 1860 never got beyond the borders of Texas, but the Knights did supply organized forces that took an active part in the secession movement.

Thus, in the midst of conflict and fear, the people made their decision at the polls. Nationally, the voters chose Abraham Lincoln, but the pro-Southern position won an overwhelming victory in Texas. In Texas the Lincoln ticket was not placed on the ballot, and Douglas received only 410 votes; 15,463 Texans voted for Bell and 47,548 for Breckinridge.

SECESSION

Abraham Lincoln's election alarmed many Texans who wanted to preserve the Union. The Unionists had no organization, but among them were able men: Sam Houston, David G. Burnet, E. M. Pease, J. W. Throckmorton, E. J. Davis, and A. J. Hamilton. The election of Lincoln, they argued, was unfortunate but did not warrant secession. The South could better protect its interests in the Union than out of it. Houston wrote: "Mr. Lincoln has been constitutionally elected, and, much as I deprecate his success, no alternative is left me but to yield to the Constitution."

But each day the conservatives lost ground, and the radicals grew stronger. Some Southern leaders had warned that Lincoln's election would mean the dissolution of the Union; to yield at this late date would, they argued, constitute a surrender of their rights. Rhetoric was often extreme and inflammatory. The editor of the *Navarro Express* wrote: "The North has gone overwhelmingly for Negro Equality and Southern Vassalage! Southern men, will you submit to the degradation?"

By early December Texans were moving toward secession. Various petitions, editorials, and letters directed at Governor Houston urged him to convene the legislature or call a convention. He refused to do either, whereupon the radicals took matters into their own hands. In Austin on December 3, a group of leaders, including George M. Flournoy, O. M. Roberts of the Texas Supreme Court, Guy M. Bryan, W. S. Oldham, and John Marshall, drew up an address to the people of Texas. They called on the voters of each representative district to select, at an election to be held on January 8, two delegates to a state convention. Similar resolutions were adopted in several other meetings throughout the state. The elections were held, and the convention met as called on January 28, 1861. Meanwhile, on December 17, 1860, Houston had issued a call for the legislature to convene on January 21, 1861, in a special session. The legislature ignored Houston's claim that the recent election was illegal and authorized the convention to act for the people, subject only to the condition that the question of secession be submitted to the voters.

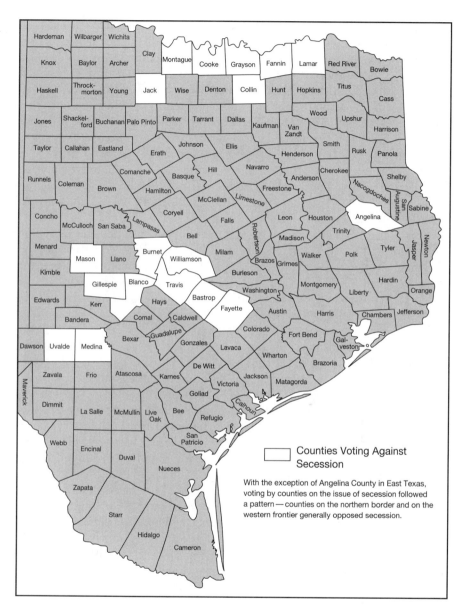

Counties Voting Against Secession

With the exception of Angelina County in East Texas, voting by counties on the issue of secession followed a pattern — counties on the northern border and on the western frontier generally opposed secession.

By a vote of approximately 3 to 1, voters of Texas on February 23, 1861, indicated their approval of secession. The size of the vote was similar to that of the vote in the previous election for governor.

The convention acted quickly. On the second day, with O. M. Roberts as president, it approved, by a vote of 152 to 6, a resolution stating: "It is the deliberate sense of this Convention that the State of Texas should separately secede from the Federal Union." A committee on federal relations then drew up an ordinance of secession that declared that the ordinance of 1845 by which Texas had accepted annexation "is hereby repealed and annulled." The proposed ordinance was to be submitted to the voters on February 23, and, unless rejected by a majority of the votes cast, was to take effect on March 2, exactly 25 years after independence had been declared. The vote on the ordinance was taken at noon on February 1 in the presence of packed galleries. The scene had its drama. As the roll of delegates was called, only very infrequently was the response "No." Among those who voted thus was J. W. Throckmorton, who, while voting, violated the no-discussion rule. A hiss, and applause followed, to which he made the memorable retort: "Mr. President, when the rabble hiss, well may patriots tremble." The final vote was 166 to 8.

In South Carolina and certain other Southern states the secession movement had moved more rapidly than it had in Texas. In Charleston on December 20, 1860, a special state convention had formally dissolved the union between South Carolina and the federal government. Soon Mississippi, Florida, Alabama, Georgia, and Louisiana followed; representatives of these commonwealths were about to form a government in Montgomery, Alabama. Technically, Texas could not join a new government until the voters had spoken at the polls, but the convention nevertheless sent seven delegates to the meeting in Montgomery.

Shortly thereafter, on February 5, 1861, the Texas convention adjourned to meet again on March 2, after the election. During the interim, it left in session a powerful select group called the Committee on Public Safety. The legislature adjourned also, to convene again on March 18.

In the brief period available, many of the delegates took part in the campaign for the public vote on the ordinance of secession. Judge Roberts issued an appeal to the voters to support secession, and 20,000 copies of a "Declaration of Causes" explaining the reasons for secession were distributed. In support of secession, states' rights journals of long standing, such as the *Telegraph* (Houston), the *Galveston News*, *State Gazette* (Austin), and *Texas Republican* (Marshall) were soon joined by more conservative papers such as the *Dallas Herald*. Outnumbered, the Unionist. nevertheless held their position. Twenty-four opponents of secession, from the convention and the legislature, issued an address to the people of Texas urging that they oppose secession, at least until efforts to reach a compromise were made. The speakers against secession, including Houston, Throckmorton, John Hancock, and others, had the editorial support of several newspapers, including the *Southern Intelligencer* (Austin), the *Bastrop Advertiser*, the *La Grange True Issue*, and the *Weekly Alamo Express*.

The secessionists amassed a vote of 46,153, their opponents, 14,747. Ten counties in the vicinity of Austin showed antisecession majorities, a fact to be attributed to the large German population, frontier defense issues, several

Unionist newspapers, and the efforts of such leaders as Sam Houston, A. J. Hamilton, and John Hancock. Throckmorton and a few associates managed to carry several counties in northern Texas, where there was a large immigrant population from the northern and border states. Angelina County in east Texas voted against secession for reasons that are not easily explained. With only a few exceptions, the heavy slaveholding counties yielded huge majorities for secession.

By their vote on February 23, the electors approved secession, but they had taken no action on joining the Confederate States of America. In the minds of most people, however, the two steps seem to have been inseparably linked. The convention reassembled on March 2. Three days later it "approved, ratified, and accepted" the provisional government of the Confederate States of America by a vote of 109 to 2 and directed the Texas delegates in Montgomery to apply for admission to that government. The application was not necessary; already the Confederate Congress had passed an act to admit Texas.

Shortly thereafter Houston was removed from office. When the convention called on him, along with other state officers, to take the oath of allegiance to the Confederacy, Houston refused. Thereupon, the convention on March 16, 1861, declared the office of governor vacant and made Lieutenant Governor Edward Clark governor. President Lincoln offered to aid Houston if he would oppose the convention with force, but the governor, unwilling to bring on civil war, rejected the proposal. The convention ratified the constitution of the Confederacy on March 23 and three days later adjourned.

While the convention was directing the course of secession, it also acted on military matters. Distributed along the frontier at twenty-one widely separated posts were about 2,700 federal troops under the command of Major General D. E. Twiggs. Twiggs, a Georgian in sympathy with the South, in anticipation of the crisis asked his superiors for instructions but received no orders. He submitted his resignation, but before he turned his command over to his successor, he was confronted with a crisis. The Committee on Public Safety, acting under authority of the secession convention, demanded that he surrender to its representatives all public arms and munitions of war under his command. When Ben McCulloch, military commander representing the convention, led an armed force into San Antonio, Twiggs agreed to evacuate the 160 troops in San Antonio and surrender to representatives of the committee all federal property. On February 18, Twiggs agreed to the evacuation of all other forts in Texas under similar terms. Henry E. McCulloch received for the Texans the surrender of the northern posts, and John S. Ford took over the posts in the southern part of the state. Thus did the convention without the firing of a shot put out of action more than 10 percent of the regular army of the United States and acquire military supplies and other property valued at $3 million.

Elsewhere the course of secession was not as peaceful. At Fort Sumter, South Carolina, where federal forces refused to evacuate their post, guns were fired on April 12, 1861. For the next four years troops of the Confederacy and of the Union would meet on the battlefields of the Civil War.

AT THE BATTLEFRONT

Texas was a border state in the Confederacy, exposed to attack from the north, west, and south. In May 1861, the immediate threat of invasion from the north was removed when W. C. Young, a former sheriff and a resident of Cooke County, led a volunteer regiment of Texas cavalry across the Red River and took Forts Arbuckle, Cobb, and Washita without firing a shot, thereby making an invasion from the north unlikely.

The problem of protection from the Indian raids that had troubled Texas for a century and a half was not solved so easily. The Confederacy assigned a Texas regiment under John S. Ford the task of guarding the Rio Grande frontier from Fort Brown, near the Gulf Coast, to Fort Bliss, near the site of El Paso. During 1861, however, companies of minutemen bore the brunt of Indian warfare. Early in 1862, they were replaced by the Frontier Regiment, a state organization that for a time used a combination of outposts and regular patrols along a line from the Red River to the Rio Grande but ultimately sent out scouting expeditions in hope of surprising the Indians. In December 1863 the Frontier Regiment was transferred to Confederate service, but a part of it was assigned to defend the frontier along the Red River. To offset the loss, the state organized militia companies, enrolling more than 4,000 men by early 1864, and most of the burden for frontier defense fell on these troops. But the raids continued. In October 1864, about 200 Comanches and Kiowas attacked settlements near Fort Belknap in Young County, killing 16 persons and capturing 7 others. Shortly thereafter, Governor Pendleton Murrah placed James W. Throckmorton in command of the northern district, where the situation was the most critical,

Hostilities on the frontier were never completely controlled. Because the troops and militia were unable to provide protection, groups of people along the frontier moved into stockades—"forting up" they called it. About 125 people northeast of present-day Albany joined together at "Fort Davis," one of the largest such places. During the last two years of the war, deserters added to the threat of hostile Indians by creating confusion on the frontier.

Poor judgment of Texan leaders in failing to identify and count a group of Indians resulted in the bloodiest battle with the Indians during the Civil War. In January 1865, at Dove Creek a few miles southwest of the present San Angelo, state militia joined Confederate troops of the Frontier Regiment, altogether a force of 380 men, in an attack on about 600 to 1,000 Kickapoos.

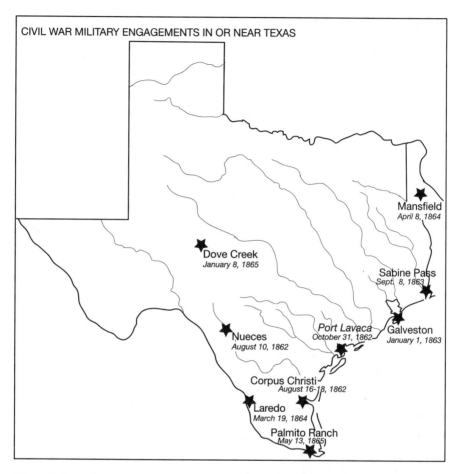

CIVIL WAR MILITARY ENGAGEMENTS IN OR NEAR TEXAS

Mansfield
April 8, 1864

Dove Creek
January 8, 1865

Sabine Pass
Sept. 8, 1863

Port Lavaca
October 31, 1862

Galveston
January 1, 1863

Nueces
August 10, 1862

Corpus Christi
August 16-18, 1862

Laredo
March 19, 1864

Palmito Ranch
May 13, 1865)

Relatively few military engagements, most of which were on the coast or borders
of the state, occurred in or near Texas. The largest battle occurred at Mansfield,
Louisiana, when Union forces attempted to invade East Texas. In the interior, a
tragic error led to a battle between Kickapoo Indians and Texan forces at Dove
Creek near present-day San Angelo, and German settlers resisted conscription
efforts in the Battle of Nueces.

The Kickapoos, who were migrating from Indian Territory to Mexico,
inflicted heavy losses on their attackers and thereafter maintained a hostile
attitude toward Texans.

The most aggressive campaign in which Texans participated was an
effort to occupy New Mexico. John R. Baylor, commander of a detachment of
Texas troops, marched into New Mexico Territory and on August 1, 1861,
issued a proclamation establishing the territory of Arizona, which was to
comprise that part of New Mexico lying south of the thirty-fourth parallel.
Later, with Baylor as governor, a constitutional government was established,

and for a short while Confederate troops occupied the country as far west as Tucson. In early 1862, General H. H. Sibley, with three regiments of Texans, sought to drive the Federals out of New Mexico. He defeated a force of over 3,800 at Val Verde on February 2, 1862, and took Albuquerque and Santa Fe. On March 28, however, at Glorieta Pass the Federals checked his advance and destroyed his supply train. As a result of this and other disasters, Sibley was obliged to retire from the territory. When he returned to San Antonio in the summer of 1862 with the shattered remnant of his troops, the territorial government retreated with him. Thus ended the attempt to extend the Confederacy to win control of a port on the Gulf of California and to control the gold and silver mines of the West.

Defense of the Texas coast was far more successful. In July 1861, Union forces extended their blockade to include Texas. Before a formidable enemy force, state and Confederate troops evacuated Galveston in October 1862. But John B. Magruder, fresh from campaigns east of the Mississippi and now in command of the Department of Texas, determined to recover the town. With two riverboats armored with cotton bales and 300 veterans of Sibley's New Mexico campaign serving as marines, he moved against it by sea. A land force was concentrated at Virginia Point, opposite Galveston. On January 1, 1863, the combined forces took Galveston with a loss of twenty-six killed and 117 wounded. The Federals suffered the loss of two warships and 414 men killed or captured. Four federal gunboats made their escape.

Fighting also took place around Sabine Pass, the outlet for both the Sabine and the Neches rivers. In September 1862, a federal blockade patrol forced the Confederates to abandon it. After retaking Galveston, the Confederates on January 21 reoccupied and fortified the post at Sabine Pass, Fort Griffin, as well as their limited means would permit. However, Union leaders Admiral David G. Farragut and General N. P. Banks planned for a major campaign against Texas that would begin with the retaking of Sabine Pass. Four gunboats and twenty-three transports, bearing about 5,000 troops for the initial landing, approached the outlet guarded by Fort Griffin on September 8, 1863. To meet the formidable force, Lieutenant Dick Dowling had a small gunboat and a garrison of forty-six men! Yet he disabled and captured two enemy craft, took about 350 prisoners, and turned back the entire expedition. His victory was a blow to the morale of the North and augmented doubts about the efficiency of the federal navy.

Banks's next thrust was more successful. With a combined naval and land force of about 7,000 men, he moved against the lower Rio Grande, where the Confederate garrisons were weak. Beginning by taking the island of Brazos de Santiago off the mouth of the Rio Grande on November 1, 1863, seizures were extended to include Brownsville, Corpus Christi, Aransas Pass, Indianola, and other points. Ultimately, Galveston, Port Lavaca, and Sabine Pass were the only ports left to the Confederates.

In the spring of 1864, Banks made his last campaign against Texas. From Alexandria, Louisiana, 25,000 well-equipped veterans, sustained by a powerful flotilla of gunboats, moved up the Red River. Banks planned to unite this army with 13,000 men under General Frederick Steele, who was moving southward from Little Rock. It was expected that the combined forces would crush all opposition and extend their operations over all of northern Louisiana, southern Arkansas, and eastern Texas. The Confederate shops at Marshall and Henderson and the rich East Texas farm country constituted choice prizes. While the main force of Banks moved toward Texas, Confederate General E. Kirby Smith, in command of the Trans-Mississippi Department, worked desperately to form an army to meet him. Magruder in Texas sent every man he could spare; and as the regiments hastened eastward, old men and young boys were enlisted to offset losses by death, disease, and desertion. On April 8, Richard Taylor, in immediate command of the army that faced Banks, with 11,000 effective troops, attacked and defeated Banks's army at Mansfield, Louisiana, fifty miles below Shreveport, taking 2,500 prisoners. The Confederates were repulsed on the following day at Pleasant Hill, but Banks retreated back down the Mississippi. Meanwhile, the attack from Little Rock halted when Confederate Sterling Price, with 8,000 troops, including Walker's Texas division, stopped Steele at Camden, Arkansas.

In the summer of 1864, the Confederate forces under John S. Ford recaptured Fort Brown and held control of the mainland of South Texas, where Federals had already withdrawn most of their troops. The last battle of the Civil War was fought in the valley in the spring of 1865 after Lee had surrendered at Appomattox and Confederate troop units were beginning to melt away. On May 13, at Palmito Ranch near Brownsville, Ford and a force of 300 or more met two federal regiments and a company of unmounted Texas (Union) cavalry, taking 113 prisoners and inflicting twenty-five to thirty casualties. Ford and other Confederate leaders in the area, however, soon concluded that continuation of their war was futile.

SUPPLYING MEN

Texans responded quickly to the call for volunteers when the fighting began, and as early as September 30, 1861, ten regiments of Texas troops had already been organized. It was thought at first that Texans would not be needed east of the Mississippi. Early in 1862, however, Governor Lubbock received a call for fifteen regiments of infantry, and volunteers, he stated in his memoirs, supplied these "in a few months." He thought Texas had about 20,000 men in military service before conscription went into effect.

Soldiers served either in state military units or as Confederate troops, or sometimes in both types of services. Many were volunteers, but some became soldiers only because of the conscription laws. The first Confederate conscription act was passed on April 16, 1862, applying to men from eighteen to thirty-five years of age. In September of that year the age limit was raised to forty-five, and a later act extended the limits from seventeen to fifty. On December 25, 1861, the state provided for the enrollment and organization of the militia; an act of March 7, 1863, provided that the militia might be transferred into Confederate service for a period of not more than a year. A state act of May 28, 1864, provided for the transfer, with some exceptions, of state troops to Confederate service.

Liberal exemptions allowed many to avoid military service. Officeholders, owners of large numbers of slaves, persons supposedly indispensable to the professions, agriculture, and industry, and certain Texans involved in frontier defense were exempt. The law furthermore permitted the hiring of substitutes. Beyond a doubt the exemption policy and the provision permitting a man to hire a substitute had a bad effect on the morale of the troops and the people behind the lines.

Texas contributed significantly to the Confederate military effort. It furnished two full generals (Albert Sidney Johnston and John Bell Hood), two major generals (Thomas L. Rosser and John A. Wharton), thirty-three brigadier generals, and ninety-seven colonels. Although as many as 75 or 80 percent of those white men of eligible age may have served—an astonishing number—it is impossible to determine the number of men who saw military service either as state or Confederate troops during the war. Even Governor Lubbock, who should be a dependable authority for the period when he was chief executive, gives figures that are difficult to reconcile. In February 1863, he stated that Texas had in actual service 68,500 men, including 6,500 state troops. In November 1863, he reported 90,000 Texans in military service. His figures evidently included a number of duplications, particularly among those who volunteered for state duty and afterward entered Confederate service. According to the census of 1860, white males in Texas between the ages of eighteen and forty-five numbered 92,145. Some 58,533 men were recruited in the cavalry alone. Probably two-thirds of those who served remained west of the Mississippi.

Texans fought on every battlefront. For mobility and daring, the cavalry regiment named after B. F. (Frank) Terry was unsurpassed; Ross's Texas Brigade fought well on both sides of the Mississippi; Hood's Texas Brigade, a part of the first division of Longstreet's famous corps, broke the federal lines at Gaines' Mill, Virginia, and in the Second Battle of Manassas. Hiram Granbury's Brigade and Mathew Ector's Brigade fought with the Army of Tennessee in the Atlanta campaign and in Hood's 1864 Tennessee campaign. The Second Texas Infantry Regiment, commanded first by John Moore and later by William P. Rogers and Ashbel Smith, played a significant role in the Shiloh, Vicksburg, and Corinth campaigns. Walker's Division, the largest Texas military unit in the war, fought with distinction in Louisiana and

Arkansas. Indeed, throughout much of the war, large numbers of Texans, at times as many as 20,000 or more, took part in the seemingly endless campaigns in Arkansas.

Although the exact number of Texans killed and wounded in the Civil War is not known, war took a heavy toll. In March 1862, Ben McCulloch, veteran of the Texas Revolution and the Mexican War, was killed while leading an unsuccessful attack against Pea Ridge, Arkansas. The next month Albert Sidney Johnston, the highest-ranking Confederate field general, was killed at Shiloh. Another popular Texas general, Tom Green, was killed in the Red River campaign. And there were many, many more.

THE STATE AND THE CONFEDERACY

Party political activity did not cease, but it declined during the war. Unionists were obliged to keep their counsel in most areas, for secessionists were usually in control. No party nominations were made in 1861. In the race for governor, Francis Richard Lubbock, who had served as lieutenant governor during Runnels's administration, defeated Edward Clark, the incumbent, by only 124 votes. In the same election, congressmen were chosen to represent the state in Richmond. Louis T. Wigfall and W. S. Oldham were elected to the Confederate Senate, and John H. Reagan accepted an appointment as postmaster general in President Jefferson Davis's cabinet.

State efforts during Lubbock's administration were centered on winning the war. A military board consisting of the governor, comptroller, and treasurer was authorized to dispose of the bonds of the United States held by Texas or to use other means in purchasing military supplies. Legislative action suspended all laws for the collection of debts, validated bonds issued for military purposes, authorized special county taxes for war purposes, appropriated money for equipping troops, and authorized the receipt of Confederate notes and treasury warrants for taxes. Confederate reverses, Lincoln's Emancipation Proclamation, and "signs of a latent dissatisfaction at the existing state of things if not a positive disloyalty to the Confederacy" caused Lubbock to call an extra session of the legislature for February 2, 1863. The special session doubled taxes and appropriated $600,000 for the use of needy families of soldiers and $200,000 as a hospital fund for sick and wounded Texans in the Confederate armies.

In late 1863, Lubbock entered the Confederate service and did not stand for reelection. The race soon became a contest between T. J. Chambers (candidate for the fourth time) and Pendleton Murrah, a Harrison County lawyer. Murrah, more emphatic than Chambers in his promise to support the Confederate cause, defeated Chambers by a vote of 17,511 to

John H. Reagan. He served Texas, the
United States, and the Confederate
States of America with distinction. He
resigned as U. S. Senator to accept the
chairmanship of the first railroad
commission of Texas in 1891. (Archives
Division—Texas State Library)

12,455. The total vote was only a little more than half that cast in the preceding election, primarily because many able-bodied potential voters were
away at war.

Every war governor proclaimed his loyalty to the Confederacy and his
determination to work with it harmoniously, but there were occasional problems. The Texas Supreme Court upheld the constitutionality of the Confederate conscription law. However, Brigadier General P. O. Hebert, a West
Point valedictorian and former governor of Louisiana, who succeeded Earl
Van Dorn as commander of the Department of Texas, created considerable
resentment when he proclaimed martial law for the entire state in order to
enforce the conscription law. Moreover, many Texans believed that he
unnecessarily allowed the Federals to occupy Galveston. He was replaced in
November 1862 by Brigadier General John B. Magruder. Magruder had
some problems with state officials, particularly with Governor Murrah, but
fared better in his relations with the Texans.

The most serious clash of authority grew out of a Texas law of 1863,
which provided for organizing into companies for defense all men of military age in frontier counties and for exempting them from conscription

under the Confederate laws. The proposed exemption was in conflict with the Confederate constitution, but Governor Murrah insisted on its enforcement. When General E. Kirby Smith, desperately in need of troops to repel Banks in Louisiana in the spring of 1864, called on Murrah through Magruder to send more men, the governor quibbled until it was too late for the state troops to be of service. It is likely that Murrah's hesitation to transfer men from state control to the Confederate authorities was influenced by the fact that the Trans-Mississippi states were increasingly dependent more and more on their own resources.

As the war proceeded, complaints of neglect of the West by the Confederate government became more emphatic. The governor of Arkansas stated in June 1862 that if the western states were not to be protected, the sooner they knew it the better. In response to the unrest, western leaders held two conferences. At the request of President Davis, Governor Lubbock and Confederate Missouri Governor Claiborne F. Jackson met in Marshall, Texas, in July 1862. Their request to the Richmond government for a commanding general for the Trans-Mississippi West, for money, and for arms and ammunition led to the appointment of a commanding general and the creation of an agency to provide money and supplies.

E. Kirby Smith, commander of the Trans-Mississippi Department, called another conference of western state representatives in Marshall for August 15, 1863. The conference, presided over by Governor Lubbock, favored more friendly relations with the French (who were in control in Mexico), agreed on a plan of exchanging cotton for supplies in Mexico, suggested that Confederate notes be reissued for meeting military expenses, and recommended that in his department General Smith "assume at once and exercise the powers and prerogatives of the President of the Confederate States."

The sale of cotton, a matter considered by the second Marshall conference, was responsible for another conflict between state and Confederate authorities. Under the agreement reached at the conference, the Confederacy agreed to purchase (on credit) half of the cotton held by growers, leaving the other half in the hands of the owners. State officials, who had adopted a state plan for the purchase of cotton, were unhappy with the arrangement. After considerable bickering took place, the Confederate Congress, through an act of February 6, 1864, took control of the situation and prohibited the exportation of cotton, tobacco, and certain other commodities, except under regulations made by the president. At a conference in July 1864, Governor Murrah and General E. Kirby Smith arrived at an understanding, and thereafter Murrah cooperated more fully.

The financial condition of the state during the war is difficult to describe accurately. Most of the transactions were made in depreciated Confederate currency and equally depreciated state treasury warrants. Net expenditures actually paid by the treasurer from August 31, 1861, to June 8,

1865, amounted to almost $5 million, more than three-fourths of which was attributable to war expenses. Total net receipts for the same period were slightly over $8 million, about 40 percent derived from a wide variety of taxes and about 38 percent from profits on the penitentiary. On August 1, 1865, the treasury contained $3,368,510 (most of which was in the form of worthless money), and there was a debt of about $8 million. In its desperation the state government had used special trust monies, such as the school fund and the university fund, to the amount of almost $1,500,000. A commentary both on the confusion of the times and the poverty of the state is the fact that when looters raided the state treasury on the night of June 11, 1865, all they found of value was $5,000 in specie. Far greater than the burden of state taxes were Confederate taxes, which during the four years from 1861 through 1864 amounted in Texas to $37,486,854.

CRITICS OF THE CONFEDERACY

Although the overwhelming white majority of Texans were loyal to the Confederacy, Union sentiment in Texas was very strong in some areas. The rank and file of Union sympathizers may be classified into three groups: (1) those who despite their Union sympathies accepted the decision of the state electorate as binding upon them and supported the Confederate cause, (2) those who tried to remain neutral, and (3) those who left the state or tried to do so. J. W. Throckmorton, who became a general in command of state troops, is perhaps the most widely known representative of the first class. Of those who remained neutral, the best known were Sam Houston, David G. Burnet, and E. M. Pease. Also in this class belong many Germans in the settlements along the lower Brazos River and north of San Antonio and many Tejanos in South Texas. A third group, headed by A. J. Hamilton, John Hancock, John L. Haynes, James P. Newcomb, and Edmund J. Davis, energetically served the Union.

Unionist sentiment was strongest along the lower Rio Grande, among the German settlements, and in certain counties in the north. The lower Rio Grande area, where escape to Mexico was easy and where sometimes the Mexican population refused to support the Confederacy, became a site for many Unionist refugees and for the recruitment of volunteers for the U.S. Army. Numbers of Unionists managed to leave Texas early in the war and many others made their way to Matamoros, where they were rescued by federal ships. But some remained in Texas and supported the Union. Almost 1,000 Mexican-Americans served in Union forces, mostly in the Second Texas Cavalry, a Union unit operating in South Texas.

However, sizable numbers of Tejanos and Germans served the Confederacy. More than 2,500 Tejanos joined Confederate military units; Colonel

Santos Benavides was one of the more effective commanders along the Rio Grande. Germans made up a majority of several Confederate cavalry companies that participated in some of the major battles, and the Third Texas Infantry counted many Germans and Tejanos among its ranks.

Conscription, for Germans, Tejanos, and others who opposed secession or who had no desire to serve in the military, was the issue that provoked the most bitter controversy. Efforts to enforce the conscription laws among the Tejano population were for the most part failures, and for all practical purposes were abandoned long before the end of the war. Efforts to enforce conscription among Germans were apparently more determined and provoked more violence. For protection against Indians and for avoiding conscription, German settlers in 1861 organized the militant Union Loyal League (500 members in Gillespie, Kerr, and Kendall counties) but later were forced to disband. A few Germans left the state, and one group of sixty-five on its way to Mexico in August 1862 had thirty-four killed by the Texas militia. Another group of fifty was hanged, and others were killed before German resistance in the western area was broken. In Colorado, Austin, and Fayette counties, Germans and some Anglo-Americans organized to resist the draft, but General Magruder declared martial law over the areas, arrested the leaders, and quelled open resistance.

Antiwar sentiment in the northern part of the state was also troublesome. There in 1862, a secret organization, popularly referred to as the Peace Party, was organized. The aims of its members were to avoid the draft, to provide a spy system for the Northern army, to desert during battle, if drafted, and to prepare the way for an invasion of North Texas by federal troops. Spies visited its meetings, and soon the excited people were repeating in whispers reports that its leaders were planning arson, murder, and a general reign of terror. The Confederate military forces joined civilians in a grim campaign to destroy the movement. About 150 men were arrested and tried in Gainesville by "people's courts," which were neither military nor constitutional nor "courts" in a true sense. Some confessed; forty were hanged, most of them on no other charge, it seems, than membership in the organization. The Wise County people's courts were more deliberate; only five men were hanged there. In Grayson County forty men were arrested, but J. W. Throckmorton interceded with a plea for justice; a court of investigation reviewed their cases, and all but one were released.

Adding to problems over conscription was the number of desertions that increased as the war continued. By February 1863, the problem had become so serious that General Magruder was urging Governor Lubbock to aid him in suppressing it. Eight months later, Henry E. McCulloch, in command of the northern submilitary district, estimated that there were a thousand deserters in his territory and declared that he did not have sufficient troops to arrest them. He offered them special inducements to join the army and succeeded thus in enlisting 300, but he found that these "bush soldiers" had a weakness for returning to the brush! Soon deserters were so numerous in Wise, Denton, and neighboring counties that they intimidated loyal citizens. Sterner measures apparently brought about improvement in 1864, but during the last few weeks of the war conditions grew distinctly worse.

Many outspoken critics of the war were arrested, in most cases by the military under laws that had suspended the writ of habeas corpus. Of such cases the best known is that of Dr. Richard R. Peebles, from near Hempstead, and four other prominent citizens who were arrested in October 1863 on charges of plotting treason against the Confederate government. Peebles and two associates were exiled to Mexico.

SLAVES AND SLAVERY DURING THE CIVIL WAR

Slaves, another group that might have threatened the Confederate war effort, seldom did so. Slaves were carefully supervised; instances of sabotage were isolated; there were no rebellions, and the number of runaways increased little. The ordinary work of the day went on very much as usual. In fact, in some instances slaves were assigned and assumed additional responsibilities. In a few areas along the coast, such as Galveston, slaves were evacuated in anticipation of Union occupation, but these moves were usually temporary.

More disruptive to both slaves and owners were the repeated efforts of Confederate authorities to impress slaves for purposes of the war. Officials initially attempted to persuade owners to volunteer the services of their slaves to build fortifications, to serve as teamsters, and work on other types of defenses. When pleas for volunteers went unanswered, General Magruder from 1863 forward made several efforts to impress slaves to perform these duties. Slaveowners, however, were less than cooperative, and Magruder's superior, General Kirby Smith, refused to support Magruder's order. Nevertheless, Magruder continued to seek slave labor until near the end of the war but without a great deal of success. Slaveowners were reluctant to risk their property, and slaves realized that work on military projects would likely be more difficult and dangerous than their regular plantation duties.

Although some in isolated areas apparently knew little about the war, slaves generally knew something about the issues it involved and the prospect of freedom if the North won. It is unlikely that many supported a Confederate victory, but the absence of Union occupation denied black Texans the opportunity to join the Union cause. Only 47 black soldiers out of about 100,000 in the Union Army came from Texas.

Even as prospects for a Confederate victory faded, slaves continued to be valuable—worth several hundred dollars in money or property— and they were bought and sold as late as the early months of 1865. As a matter of fact, the number of slaves in Texas increased significantly in the last two years of the war. Exact numbers cannot be determined, but it seems probable that more than 30,000 slaves were brought into Texas from neighboring states as Union forces moved into those areas.

LIFE AT HOME DURING THE WAR

The war forced radical readjustments in farming. The demand for cotton declined and that for food crops increased. Newspapers urged the planting of more corn. There was some agitation for laws to compel changes in acreage to meet the emergency, but no such legislation was enacted. From time to time there was a shortage of farm labor, and the families of poor soldiers frequently found it difficult to work their farms. However, crops were good during the years of the war, and for the most part, no one suffered from lack of food.

But people did confront shortages of other kinds. The war brought thousands of refugees into the state, mostly from Louisiana and Arkansas, and housing was scarce, often practically unavailable. By 1863, many newspapers were forced to suspend publication for want of paper. There were never enough medicines and hospital supplies. In 1864, a serious effort was made by the military authorities to encourage the growing of poppies for opium, and the press frequently called the attention of the public to shrubs and plants of medicinal value. As people dealt with shortages, they soon learned to make various substitutions. The ashes of burnt corncobs served as baking soda; parched sweet potatoes, rye, and okra were substitutes for coffee. Substitutes were found for glue, ink, shoe black, and even for pins and needles. But some items had no substitutes. Salt, an absolute necessity for livestock and the preservation of meat, became so scarce that a soldier's salary for a month would not buy a sack. Texas had salt in abundance—the Grand Saline in Van Zandt County, the Brooks salines, Ledbetter's Salt Works near the site of Albany, the salt flats along the upper Brazos, and the salt lakes in the vicinity of El Paso. But procedures for mining and distribution were not in place.

Although people took great pride in their self-sufficiency, there was obvious concern for those who might be in need. Relief committees received donations and distributed funds and goods for the benefit of the wives and children of soldiers. In 1863, it was said that the citizens of Houston were contributing nearly $3,000 a week to this purpose. But the state still found it necessary to appropriate funds to purchase food and other necessities for needy families of soldiers off at war. County governments took the funds, purchased the food, and distributed it to the families.

Imported consumer goods were in great demand, but there never was enough to go around. After the arrival of a shipment, stores were more crowded than present-day bargain counters on the morning of a special sale. Mrs. Maverick of San Antonio related that she "went and stood wedged up and swaying about till near 12," when, at last, she managed to get "one bolt of domestic cloth, one pr. shoes and 1 doz. candles for $180.00." Although that particular merchant's stock had cost $60,000 in specie, she expected it would be exhausted within a week. As the value of the currency declined and prices soared, there was much complaint about "unfair and unjust speculators." Efforts were made to rely on homemade items to thwart the greed of speculators and to conserve valuable products for the war effort. Governor Lubbock was inaugurated in a homespun suit, and the "homespun dress that Southern ladies wear" became a theme of song and story.

Indeed, the contribution of Texas women to the war effort went far beyond the wearing of homespun clothing. Through ladies' aid associations women did their best to supply bandages and other equipment for the wounded; much clothing was also contributed. Women learned to make hats and fans out of shucks and straw; and the spinning wheel again came into use. While supporting the war effort, they also had to assume the role formerly filled by their men, who were off at war. Some administered large plantations, where supervision of slaves was a major part of their responsibilities. Large slaveowners were exempt from military duty, but most served in the army, leaving their slaves in the care of others, very often their wives. Available evidence suggests that those left in charge encountered few problems of a disciplinary nature and were able to carry out their duties without fear or harm. Far more women were responsible for small, essentially subsistence, operations where they actually did the daily work of farm life— planting and harvesting and caring for the livestock. But whether the farms were small or large, the efforts of Texas women provided desperately needed supplies for the armies, supported the families who remained at home, and maintained the production of the land.

Though most remained on the land, some women entered other professions. Some were teachers and others cared for the sick and wounded. At least a few were found in unusual places; one served as a spy providing information on the activities of Union troops. Another found herself working as a teamster and a horse trader, and eventually as a gunrunner.

Gunrunners were important in the Confederate cause, for the Union blockade made the flow of imports and exports to and from the South uncertain and at times an intermittent trickle. Cotton, the chief export commodity, was hauled to the Rio Grande over different routes and in such quantities that one observer declared that "the chaparral would be almost white in places from the lint detached from passing bales." In spite of the costs and hazards of the trade, men would undertake it, for cotton in 1862 at the Rio Grande brought from 20 to 72 cents per pound, and in 1864 the price in New York ranged from 72 cents to $1.90 per pound. On their return the cotton wagons brought sugar, coffee, cloth, nails, and sometimes medicines and military supplies.

Despite blockade running (most ships were successful in evading capture) and trade through Mexico, there remained a shortage of manufactured goods. To meet the need, the state chartered many corporations organized for the purpose of manufacturing. Most of them never reached production, but some factories were established. An arsenal, which turned out a few cannon, and a cap and cartridge factory began operations in Austin. The largest cloth factory was at the penitentiary in Huntsville. Iron foundries were opened near Jefferson and Rusk, and the tanning industry increased rapidly. Likewise, the output of wagons, ambulances, harnesses, and saddles increased sharply.

Morale was perhaps nearly as important as the materials of war, and as the war progressed with reports of Confederate reverses and tragic news of sons and husbands, maintenance of morale presented a difficult challenge to those at home. Accounts suggest that determined and deliberate efforts were made to carry on in some manner appropriate but as near to normal as possible. There are accounts of Christmas celebrations as in ordinary times, of parties and receptions for returned soldiers, and of "war meetings" with stirring speeches and "dinner on the grounds." Education suffered as the war continued, but churches took on more responsibilities. Much of the social life of Texas communities had traditionally been found in the churches, and this continued to be true. But churches often collected funds for the war effort and families of soldiers; many sermons were devoted to a defense of the Confederate cause.

THE FINAL DAYS

Although most news in the final months of the war consisted of reports of Confederate defeat, and morale continued to decline, the news of Lee's surrender in Virginia found many Texans determined to continue the struggle. Even after Joseph E. Johnston had surrendered the last major Confederate army on April 18, 1865, Governor Murrah, General E. Kirby Smith, and other leaders insisted that the war be continued in the West. But the reports of surrenders convinced large numbers of soldiers and civilians that the war was over. Military units began to disintegrate as men left for their homes to protect their families against a swelling tide of violence, for bands of thieves and renegades threatened the countryside. Confronted with the reality of an army that was melting away, Magruder and Smith had little choice but to accept defeat and await the arrival of Union officials with the terms of surrender.

With Magruder at his side, on June 2, General Kirby Smith signed articles on a federal ship in Galveston harbor, making the military surrender of the Trans-Mississippi official. Magruder and Smith then joined a party of Confederate leaders, including Governor Murrah, making their way toward the Rio Grande and Mexico. Those who remained behind faced the immediate challenge of living in a violent land where established government and law and order had virtually disappeared and looked beyond the immediate future to one filled with uncertainty, even fear.

BIBLIOGRAPHY

Writings on Texas during the Civil War are abundant, and only a partial listing is possible. For additional sources, see the comprehensive bibliography found in Ralph Wooster, *Texas and Texans in the Civil War* (Austin, 1996), and the historiographic essay of Alwyn Barr contained in B. P. Gallaway (ed.), *Texas: The Dark Corner of the Confederacy: Contemporary Accounts of the Lone Star State in the Civil War* (3d ed., Lincoln, Neb., 1994).

The most recent scholarly studies of the period are the works of Ralph Wooster. *Texas and Texans in the Civil War* is a comprehensive history of the war. Balanced, thoughtful, and reliable, it will surely be the standard account for many years to come. *Civil War Texas* (Austin, 1999) is a brief (82 pages including index) but remarkably complete history; *Lone Star Blue and Gray: Essays on Texas in the Civil War* (Austin, 1995) is a collection of essays taken from various journals; and *Lone Star Generals in Gray* (Austin, 2000) presents, analyzes, and judges the records of the thirty-seven men of Texas who held the rank of general.

A good book is Carl Moneyhon and Bobby Roberts, *Portraits of Conflict: A Photographic History of Texas in the Civil War* (Fayetteville, Ark., 1998); much more than a picture book, it is well-written history. Other useful accounts are Allan C. Ashcraft, *Texas in the Civil War: A Resume History* (Austin, 1962), and Robert L. Kerby, *Kirby Smith's Confederacy: The Trans-Mississippi South, 1863–1865* (New York, 1972). O. M. Roberts, "Texas," *Confederate Military History*, XI (Atlanta, 1899), contains information not readily available elsewhere. The works of D. G. Wooten, *A Comprehensive History of Texas* (two vols., Dallas, 1897), F. W. Johnson, *A History of Texas and Texans* (E. C. Barker and E. W. Winkler, eds., five vols., Chicago and New York, 1914), J. H. Brown, *A History of Texas, 1685–1892* (two vols., St. Louis, 1892–1893), and H. H. Bancroft, *History of the North Mexican States and Texas* (two vols., San Francisco, 1884 and 1889), all previously cited, are also valuable. Accounts of some merit by participants are F. R. Lubbock, *Six Decades in Texas* (Austin, 1900); and E. L. Dohoney, *An Average American* (Paris, Tex., 1907).

The list of publications on secession is long. The chief sources are E. W. Winkler (ed.), *Journal of the Secession Convention of Texas, 1861* (Austin, 1912); and *War of the Rebellion, Official Records, Union and Confederate Armies* (130 vols., Washington, D.C., 1880–1900). Good studies are Walter L. Buenger, *Slavery and the Union in Texas* (Austin, 1984); "Secession and the Texas German Community: Editor Lindheimer vs. Editor Flake," *Southwestern Historical Quarterly*, LXXXII, 377–402; and "Texas and the Riddle of Secession," ibid., LXXXVII, 151–182; Ralph Wooster, "Analysis of the Membership of the Texas Secession Convention," *Southwestern Historical Quarterly*, LXII, 322–335; Anna Irene Sandbo, "Beginnings of the Secession Movement in Texas," ibid., XVIII, 41–73; and "The First Session of the Secession Convention of Texas," ibid., 162–194; Joe T. Timmons, "The Referendum in Texas on the Ordinance of Secession, February 23, 1861: The Vote," *East Texas Historical Journal*, XI, 12–28; James Alex Baggett, "The Constitutional Union Party in Texas," *Southwestern Historical Quarterly*, LXXXII, 233–264; Donald E. Reynolds, "Reluctant Martyr: Anthony Bewley and the Texas Slave Insurrection Panic of 1860," ibid., XCVI, 345–361; and Harold C. Westwood, "President Lincoln's Overture to Sam Houston," ibid., LXXXVIII, 125–144; J. J. Bowden, *The Exodus of Federal Forces from Texas, 1861* (Austin, 1986); and Laura W. Roper, "Frederick Law Olmsted and the Western Texas Free Soil Movement," *American Historical Review*, LIV, 58–65. Older but still helpful are the works of C. W. Ramsdell, *Reconstruction in Texas* (New York, 1910); "The Frontier and Secession," reprinted from *Studies in Southern History and Politics* (New York, 1914); and *Behind the Lines in the Southern Confederacy* (Baton Rouge, 1944).

Many biographies and memoirs are available. See Paul Casdorph, *Prince John Magruder: His Life and Campaigns* (New York, 1996); Richard M. McMurray, *John Bell Hood and the War for Southern Independence* (Lexington, 1993); John P. Dyer, *The Gallant Hood* (New York, 1950); A. L. King, *Louis T. Wigfall: Southern Fire-Eater* (Baton Rouge, 1970); C. Elliott, *Leathercoat: the Life of James W. Throckmorton* (San Antonio, 1938); C. P. Roland, *Albert Sidney Johnston: Soldier of Three Republics* (Austin, 1964); O. B. Faulk, *General Tom Green: Fightin' Texan* (Waco, 1963); Tom Cutrer, *Ben McCulloch and the Frontier Military Tradition* (Chapel Hill, N.C., 1963); Ernest Wallace, *Charles DeMorse: Pioneer Editor and Statesman* (Lubbock, 1943); Victor M. Rose, *The Life and Services of General Ben McCulloch* (Philadelphia, 1888); Walter P. Lane, *The Adventures and Recollections of General Walter P. Lane* (Marshall, 1887); Theophilus Noel, *Autobiography and Reminiscences* (Chicago, 1904); W. J. Hughes, *Rebellious Ranger: Rip Ford and the Old Southwest* (Norman, 1964).

Accounts of Texas troops in the war often focus on a particular military unit or campaign. See Harold Simpson, *Hood's Texas Brigade* (four vols., Waco, 1968–1977), and *Touched with Valor: Civil War Papers and Casualty Reports of Hood's Texas Brigade* (Hillsboro, 1964); J. P. Blessington, *Campaigns of Walker's Texas Division* (1875, Reprint, Austin, 1994); J. K. P. Blackburn, L. B. Giles, and E. S. Dodd, *Terry Texas Ranger Trilogy: Terry's Texas Rangers: Reminiscences of the Terry Rangers and the Diary of Ephraim Shelby Dodd* (Austin, 1996); C. C. Jeffries, "The Character of Terry's Texas Rangers," *Southwestern Historical Quarterly*, LXIV, 454–462; Anne J. Bailey, *Between the Enemy and Texas: Parson's Texas Cavalry in the Civil War* (Fort Worth, 1985); B. F. Galloway (ed.), *The Dark Corner of the Confederacy* and *The Ragged Rebel: A Common Soldier in W. H. Parsons' Texas Cavalry, 1861–1865* (Austin, 1988); Stanley S. McGowen, *Horse Sweat and Powder Smoke: The First Texas Cavalry in the Civil War* (College Station, 1999); J. Douglas Hale, *The Third Texas Cavalry in the Civil War* (Norman, 1993); Victor M. Rose, *Ross' Texas Brigade* (Louisville, 1881); Xavier Blanchard DeBray, *A Sketch of the History of DeBray's (26th) Regiment of Texas Cavalry* (Waco, 1961); and Jane M. Johansson, *Peculiar Honor: A History of the 28ᵗʰ Texas Cavalry, 1862–1865* (Fayetteville, 1998).

Several studies have been written on the New Mexico campaign in recent years. There is Thomas S. Edrington and John Taylor, *The Battle of Glorieta Pass: A Gettysburg of the West, March 26-28, 1862* (Albuquerque, 1998); Don E. Alberts, *The Battle of Glorieta Pass: Union Victory in the West* (College Station, 1998); Terry G. Jordan-Bychkov, et al., "The Boesel Letters: Two Texas Germans in Sibley's Brigade," *Southwestern Historical Quarterly*, CII, 456–485; and Donald Frazier, *Blood & Treasure: Confederate Empire in the Southwest* (College Station, 1995). Also, see Robert Lee Kerby, *The Confederate Invasion of New Mexico and Arizona, 1861–1862* (Los Angeles, 1958)),

South Texas military operations are discussed in Jerry Don Thompson, *Vaqueros in Blue and Gray* (Austin, 1977), *Mexican Texans in the Union Army* (El Paso, 1986), and *A Wild and Vivid Land: An Illustrated History of the South Texas Border* (Austin,

1997). See also Bruce S. Cheeseman, "'Let us have 500 good determined Texans': Richard King's Account of the Union Invasion of South Texas, November 12, 1863, to January 20, 1864," *Southwestern Historical Quarterly*, CI, 77–95; and Don Alberts (ed.), *Rebels on the Rio Grande: The Civil War Journal of A. B. Peticolas* (Albuquerque, 1984).

Military actions in other coastal areas are discussed in Edward T. Cotham, Jr., *Battle on the Bay: The Civil War Struggle for Galveston* (Austin, 1998); Alwyn Barr, "Texas Coastal Defense, 1861–1865," *Southwestern Historical Quarterly*, LXV, 1–31; "The Battle of Calcasieu Pass," ibid., LXVI, 59–67; and "The 'Queen City of the Gulf' Held Hostage: The Impact of War on Confederate Galveston," *Military History*, 27, 119–138; Charles C. Cumberland, "The Confederate Loss and Recapture of Galveston, 1862–1863," *Southwestern Historical Quarterly*, LI, 109–130; and Donald S. Frazier, "Sibley's Texans and the Battle of Galveston," ibid., XCIX, 175–198. Paul A. Levengood, "In the Absence of Scarcity: The Civil War Prosperity of Houston, Texas," ibid., CI, 401–426, suggests that fear of invasion did not cause problems to the extent that might have been expected.

For studies on frontier defense, see David Paul Smith, *Frontier Defense in the Civil War: Texas Rangers and Rebels* (College Station, 1992); W. C. Holden, "Frontier Defense in Texas during the Civil War," *West Texas Historical Association Year Book*, IV, 16–31; and R. N. Richardson, *The Frontier of Northwest Texas* (Glendale, 1963).

For other works on military affairs, see Harold Simpson (ed.), *Texas in the Civil War* (Hillsboro, 1965); Ludwell Johnson, *The Red River Campaign: Politics and Cotton in the Civil War* (Baltimore, 1958); Stephen B. Oates, *Confederate Cavalry West of the Mississippi River* (Austin, 1961); James L. Nichols, *The Confederate Quartermaster in the Trans-Mississippi* (Austin, 1964); J. B. Hood, *Advance and Retreat* (New Orleans, 1880); W. H. Watford, "Confederate Western Ambitions," *Southwestern Historical Quarterly*, XLIV, 161–187; S. B. Oates, "Recruiting Confederate Cavalry in Texas," ibid., LXIV, 463–477; Ralph A. Wooster, "With the Confederate Cavalry in the West: The Civil War Experiences of Isaac Dunbar Affleck," ibid., LXXXIII, 1–28; Ralph A. Wooster and Robert Wooster," 'Rarin for a Fight': Texans in the Confederate Army," ibid., LXXXIV, 387–426; Allen W. Jones, "Military Events in Texas during the Civil War, 1861–1865," ibid., LXIV, 64–70; E. C. Barker and Frank Vandiver, "Letters from the Confederate Medical Service in Texas, 1863–1865," ibid., LV, 378–401, 459–474; Harry M. Henderson, *Texas in the Confederacy* (San Antonio, 1955); and Richard Taylor, *Destruction and Reconstruction* (Richard B. Harwell, ed., New York, 1955).

Studies on Texans in Union military service include F. H. Smyrl, "Texans in the Union Army 1861–1865," *Southwestern Historical Quarterly*, LXV, 234–250; and Jerry Don Thompson, *Vaqueros in Blue and Gray; Mexican Texans in the Union Army* (El Paso, 1986) and *A Wild and Vivid Land: An Illustrated History of the South Texas Border* (Austin, 1997), all cited previously. Scholarly accounts of two prominent Texans who served as officers in the Union Army are Ronald N. Gray, "Edmund J. Davis: Radical Republican and Reconstruction Governor of Texas" (unpublished dissertation, Texas Tech University, Lubbock, 1976), and John L. Waller, *Colossal Hamilton of Texas: A Biography of Andrew Jackson Hamilton* (El Paso, 1968). An older account is August Santleben, *A Texas Pioneer*, (New York, 1910).

Phases of home life and public affairs during the Civil War are dealt with in Mrs. E. M. Loughery, *War and Reconstruction in Texas* (Austin, 1914); Thomas North, *Five Years in Texas* (Cincinnati, 1871); Grover C. Ramsey (comp.), *Confederate Postmasters in Texas, 1861–1865* (Waco, 1963); Alma D. King, "The Political Career of William Simpson Oldham," *Southwestern Historical Quarterly*, XXXIII, 112–133; James Marten, "Slaves and Rebels: The Peculiar Institution in Texas, 1861–1865," ibid., XXVIII, 29–36; David C. Humphrey, "A 'Very Muddy and Conflicting' View: The Civil War as Seen from Austin, Texas," ibid., XCIV, 369–414; Jolene Maddox Snider, "Sarah Devereaux: A Study in Southern Femininity," ibid., XCVII, 479–508; C. W. Ramsdell, "The

Texas State Military Board, 1862–1865," ibid., XXVII, 253–275; Carland Elaine Crook, "Benjamin Theron and French Designs in Texas during the Civil War," ibid., XLVIII, 432–454; Thomas L. Miller, "Texas Land Grants to Confederate Veterans and Widows," ibid., LXIX, 59–65; and Nancy Head Bowen, "A Political Labyrinth: Texas in the Civil War," *East Texas Historical Journal*, XI, 3–11. Randolph Campbell, *An Empire for Slavery* (Baton Rouge, 1989), cited previously, contains an extensive discussion of slaves and slavery during the war.

Unionism on the eve and during the Civil War may be studied in the following: Dale Baum, *The Shattering of Texas Unionism: Politics in the Lone Star State During the Civil War Era* (Fayetteville, Ark., 1998); C. A. Bridges, "The Knights of the Golden Circle," *Southwestern Historical Quarterly*, XLIV 287–302; Sylvan Dunn, "The KGC in Texas, 1860–1861," ibid., LXX, 543–573; C. Elliott, "Union Sentiment in Texas, 1861–1865," ibid., L, 449–477; Frank H. Smyrl, "Unionism in Texas, 1856–1861," ibid., LXVIII, 172–195; Walter D. Kamphoefner, "New Perspectives on Texas Germans and the Confederacy," ibid., CII, 441–455; David R. Hoffman, "A German-American Pioneer Remembers: August Hoffman's Memoir," ibid., CII, 486–509; Floyd F. Ewing, "Origins of Union Sentiment on the West Texas Frontier," *West Texas Historical Association Year Book*, XXXII, 21–29; and "Unionist Sentiment on the Northwest Texas Frontier," ibid., XXXIII, 58–70; Walter Buenger, "Unionism on the Texas Frontier," *Arizona and the West*, XXII, 237–254; and James A. Marten, *Texas Divided: Loyalty and Dissent in the Lone Star State* (Lexington, 1990).

For violence directed at unionists during the war, see J. Richard McCaslin, *Tainted Breeze* (Baton Rouge, 1994); David Pickering and Judy Falls, *Brush Men and Vigilantes: Civil War Dissent in Texas* (College Station, 2000); Stanley S. McGowen, James Smallwood, "Disaffection in Confederate Texas," *Southwestern Historical Quarterly*, XXII, 349–360; Richard B. McCaslin, "Wheat Growers in the Cotton Confederacy: The Suppression of Dissent in Collin County, Texas, During the Civil War," ibid., XCVI, 527–539; Robert W. Shook, "The Battle of the Nueces, August 10, 1862," ibid., LXVI, 31–42; Sam Acheson and Julie Ann Hudson O'Connell (eds.), "George Washington Diamond's Account of the Great Hanging at Gainesville, 1862," ibid., LXVI, 331–414; and Thomas Barrett, *The Great Hanging at Gainesville* (Austin, 1961).

For biographies of the governors of Texas, see Ralph Wooster, "Texas," in W. Buck Yearns, *The Confederate Governors* (Athens, Ga., 1985); Fredericka Ann Meiners, "The Texas Governorship, 1861–1865: Biography of an Office" (Ph.D. dissertation, Rice University, 1974); and J. T. DeShields (San Antonio, 1940), *They Sat in High Places; The Presidents and Governors of Texas*.

Scores of county histories deal with certain phases of the war, and many excellent unpublished studies are available in the university libraries in Texas.

11

Reconstruction 1865–1874

The decade following the end of the Civil War, generally called Reconstruction, was difficult for both the victors and the vanquished. The victorious North endeavored to assure the permanency of its major objectives in the war—the preservation of the Union, the abolition of slavery, and the establishment of government by and for all of the people. The war had preserved the Union, but restoration of the Southern states to a constitutional system of local and state government presented a host of difficult problems. Slavery was ended, but the political, economic, and social future of the former slaves had not been defined. The war had promoted the cause of democracy, but restoration of order and civil government in the South sometimes involved military government, martial law, and voter disfranchisement. Four years of war left a heritage of violence and hatred that combined with racial prejudice to bring strife and trouble to the postwar years.

In addition to these challenges, Texas faced a few unique problems, particularly because of its isolation on the southwestern frontier. By 1865, thousands of refugees, white and black, had entered Texas, and some contributed to the turbulence that followed the war. Furthermore, as the war ended, civil government collapsed, and for a time, anarchy prevailed. On the frontier, Indian raids repeatedly threatened the lives and property of the settlers. And, though the end of slavery was proclaimed upon the arrival of federal troops in Galveston, little was done to assure the welfare of the newly freed population.

As Texans struggled to contend with these problems, Reconstruction presented them with three underlying questions. First, under what terms would the conquered former Confederate states be restored politically to the Union? Second, what steps must be taken to assure that the rebellion and secession truly were crushed and would not rise again? Third, what political, social, and economic role would African Americans play in the post-Civil War South? The answers to these questions not only would define the era of Reconstruction but would, for better or worse, leave their mark on the state for the next century.

RECONSTRUCTION: FIRST STEPS

From the time Union armies first conquered segments of the Confederacy, northern leaders were divided over how reconstruction should be accomplished. President Lincoln held that secession was illegal and that reconstruction was thus the responsibility of the executive branch of the government. But some Republicans, termed "radicals," maintained that the Confederate states, by secession, had forfeited their statehood, and since Congress alone had the power to admit new states, it also had the power to reconstruct. Radical Republicans generally favored a program that was much more strict than Lincoln's, one that would promote the welfare of the newly freed population and exclude former Confederate leaders from exercising political power. Not incidentally, this radical program would also promote the interests of the Republican Party.

Lincoln acted first. On December 8, 1863, he set forth his plan of reconstruction. Basically, the plan provided that when 10 percent of the those who had voted in 1860 took an oath of allegiance to the United States and accepted all official acts regarding slavery, they could establish a state government. In conformity with this plan, Lincoln restored civil government in Tennessee, Louisiana, and Arkansas. Congress, concerned that Lincoln's plan would not safeguard the Union victory or assure the loyalty of the South, responded with the Wade-Davis Bill. Congress required 50 percent of the electorate to affirm their loyalty and then restricted political participation to those Southerners who could take an "ironclad" oath of past loyalty. The deadlock between Congress and the president lasted for the rest of Lincoln's presidency.

After Lincoln's death, President Andrew Johnson on May 29, 1865, attempted to use executive authority to implement a process of reconstruction for the former Confederate states that was essentially the same as Lincoln's. On June 17, as federal troops prepared to occupy Texas, Johnson named Andrew Jackson Hamilton, a staunch Unionist and former congressman, provisional governor, and instructed him to establish civil government among loyal Texans.

Meanwhile, on June 2, the same day that General E. Kirby Smith formally surrendered, General Philip H. Sheridan assumed command of the Military Division of the Southwest, which included Texas, and established his headquarters in New Orleans. As soon as ships were available, he sent troops to Texas. On June 19, 1865, General Gordon Granger, with 1,800 troops, occupied Galveston, and in the name of the president of the United States issued a proclamation that declared that the slaves were free, that all acts of the Texas government since secession were illegal, and that officers and men of the late Confederate army should lay down their weapons and consider themselves on parole.

EMANCIPATION

Granger's proclamation ending slavery directly affected the status of more than 30 percent of the population of Texas. Estimates of the slave population in June 1865 vary considerably, but though an accurate number cannot be determined, a figure somewhere near 250,000 seems likely. Many of these were recent arrivals, brought from other Southern states during the war, and in time many of these newcomers would leave Texas.

The practical implementation of Granger's proclamation took time, and in some instances, quite a bit of time. Some masters immediately read the announcement of freedom to their slaves, other slaves found out from the former slaves of neighboring plantations, and still others learned about their emancipation only when officials forced the owners to obey the decree. By the end of the year, virtually all African Americans in Texas were aware of their freedom, but there were still reports of owners from isolated regions of the state who had refused to free their slaves.

Even though emancipation brought uncertainty and confusion about their future, slaves reacted joyfully to the news of their freedom. The reaction of both whites and blacks to the new circumstances varied from place to place and from person to person. Some whites bitterly ordered their former slaves off of their land. Others attempted to hire them as wage laborers. Some blacks left the plantation as quickly as they could, others stayed on to work, at least for a time, for their former owners. For many former slaves freedom meant the freedom to travel, and many took to the road, looking for work, looking for protection from Union authorities, and most of all looking for relatives from whom they had been separated. All, though, faced the reality of having to find work. Approximately half of the former slaves worked for their former masters for a year or more, usually by working for wages, sometimes paid as a portion of the crop. A few owners provided their former slaves with livestock, food, or even land, but such treatment was the exception rather than the rule. For most of the newly freed people, survival and progress would depend upon their success in obtaining work and fair pay for their work.

THE FREEDMEN'S BUREAU

A federal agency, the Bureau of Refugees, Freedmen, and Abandoned Lands, offered some protection for blacks in their transition from slavery to freedom. Congress created the Freedmen's Bureau (as the agency was commonly known) on March 3, 1865, and empowered it to take control of all affairs relating to freed slaves, refugees, and abandoned lands in the conquered states. In September 1865 General E. M. Gregory arrived to direct the Texas branch of the bureau. Idealistic and enthusiastic, Gregory set to work to protect the freedom of the black population. Gregory focused much of his efforts on solving problems related to the employment of blacks. He required that labor contracts be registered with the bureau in an effort to ensure fairness, and to protect blacks from unscrupulous employers. The bureau also did some relief work among blacks and provided night schools for several thousand. Another activity, which generated some controversy, was its intervention in the courts in cases in which blacks were involved. Above all, it labored to make real the promise of freedom.

Many obstacles confronted the bureau. White Texans generally were hostile and uncooperative—sometimes to the point of violence. The program was never adequately funded or adequately staffed. It relied heavily on the army (about 40 percent of the agents were soldiers and a succession of military officers directed the bureau in Texas), but the army had too many other responsibilities to devote much attention to the bureau. It was expected to provide protection for agents, but such protection was limited and sometimes nonexistent. To a large degree the effectiveness of the bureau varied from community to community, depending on the ability and commitment of the local agent in charge. Some agents were committed, courageous, and energetic; others were not. Bureau leadership changed frequently and left much to be desired in its effectiveness. The program lasted only about forty months, from the fall of 1865 until January, 1869.

Not withstanding these handicaps, the bureau enjoyed some success. Though only for a limited period of time and probably only for a minority of the black population, agents protected the interests of black workers who entered into labor contracts. Though the bureau courts were offensive to many Texans, they did ensure that African Americans received the justice they would be unlikely to find in the county courts. The most enduring and beneficial activity of the bureau was its operation of a system of schools for blacks. In January 1866, it had 16 schools attended by 1,041 students, and in June the numbers had increased to 100 schools and 4,447 students; by 1870 there were 6,499 students enrolled. In many communities Freedmen's Bureau schools would form the nucleus of the public school system.

President Johnson's Plan for Reconstruction

President Johnson's proclamation of June 17 began the presidential phase of Reconstruction in Texas. Johnson's goal was to establish a provisional government backed by military authority that would establish the sovereignty of the federal government, restore law and order, administer loyalty oaths, and oversee the creation of a new constitution and the reestablishment of civil government in Texas. By the end of 1865 there were an estimated 50,000 federal troops in Texas. Some were sent into the interior, but a larger number were concentrated along the Rio Grande to protect the border from the French who had occupied Mexico in 1864. In the interior, the troops were supposed to restore the authority of the United States and preserve order. They met with no organized resistance; in fact, a few commanders, including the colorful George A. Custer, who reached Austin with a detachment of troops in November 1865, became quite popular among the townsfolk. In other instances, soldiers encountered sullen and hostile citizens and occasionally angry defiance. There were never a sufficient number of troops in Texas to adequately police the state. As a result the lawlessness that followed the collapse of the Confederate government continued in Texas for a number of months and delayed the institution of civil government.

The beginnings of provisional civilian government occurred when Governor Hamilton arrived in Galveston on July 21 and proceeded slowly to Austin. On August 9 he began establishing a new state government, appointing Union men to the office of attorney general and secretary of state. As rapidly as practicable Johnson appointed former Unionists to the district, county, and precinct offices throughout the state. In keeping with President Johnson's plan of Reconstruction, the governor set an election, on January 8, 1866, to select delegates for a constitutional convention to convene on February 7. Four conditions had to be met before Johnson would accept the work of the convention: the abolition of slavery, the definition of the status of newly freed blacks (though he did not require that blacks be given the right to vote), the repudiation of the ordinance of secession, and the repudiation of public debts incurred in behalf of the war.

When the convention assembled, two old factions, Unionists and secessionists, faced each other under new conditions. John Hancock, I. A. Paschal, and Edward Degener were sitting opposite such confirmed rebels as H. R. Runnels and O. M. Roberts. Between them was a group, larger than either,

Andrew Jackson Hamilton. A native of Alabama, he moved to Texas in 1846, became a Unionist in the Civil War, and was appointed provisional governor of Texas in 1865. (Archives Division—Texas State Library)

inclined to avoid party labels and to avoid any permanent alignment with the opposing factions. J. W. Throckmorton, a moderate who had been a Unionist before the war but served the Confederacy as a brigadier general, was chosen president of the convention.

The convention spent much time trying to decide what disposition to make of the ordinance of secession. Obviously, it was no longer in effect, but was it null and void from the date it was enacted, or did it become null and void as a result of the war? The question was never answered. By a vote of 55 to 21 the convention finally simply acknowledged the supremacy of the Constitution of the United States and declared the ordinance of secession void without reference to time.

The most important subject with which the convention dealt was the status of blacks. The questions of slavery and civil rights were combined in a single ordinance. The convention agreed that slavery no longer existed and that it could not be reestablished in Texas. However, it formally refused to approve the Thirteenth Amendment to the Constitution of the United States, which prohibited slavery. The convention also refused to grant blacks equality before the law. After a sharp debate, it provided for their security in person and property, but it abridged their right to testify in court in cases in which blacks were not involved. Furthermore, it denied them the right to vote and to hold office. The new constitution thus resisted efforts to establish civil and political rights for blacks.

The convention was expected to repudiate the war debt; otherwise, it would be tantamount to recognition that secession and the war were legitimate. It went further and canceled all the state debts incurred during the war. This measure brought much criticism from the conservative press, for the state had incurred obligations in no way connected with carrying on the war. In defense of nullification it was pointed out that the debt had been acquired in violation of the Constitution of 1845 and that nearly all warrants were in the hands of speculators. Unionists, secessionists, and moderates united in support of repudiation.

Before it adjourned, the convention approved all laws and all acts of officers of the Confederate state government not in violation of the Constitution of 1845 and without any direct relation to the war. The new constitution was actually prepared as a series of amendments to the Constitution of 1845. Among the changes proposed was a plan to lengthen to four years the terms of most officers and to provide for a possible division of the state.

An election to approve the constitution and officers of the new government was held on June 25. Unionists supported E. M. Pease for governor, and their opponents supported J. W. Throckmorton. A major issue dividing the two candidates was their position on African American political rights. Throckmorton opposed black suffrage in any form, while the more moderate Pease favored granting the right to vote to black males who could read and write. Throckmorton received 49,277 votes to Pease's 12,168. By a comparatively close vote the new constitution was ratified.

Within a few weeks the newly elected government assumed office. The Eleventh Legislature convened on August 6, 1866. Three days later Governor Throckmorton was inaugurated, and on August 20, President Johnson proclaimed the insurrection in Texas at an end.

The character of the new legislature was immediately evident. Though party labels were avoided, the men in control were for the most part Democrats, in many instances those who had led the state through secession and war. By a decisive vote, it elected to the U.S. Senate David G. Burnet, a Unionist in 1861 who had come out of retirement to denounce many of his former Unionist allies, and Oran M. Roberts, who had been the president of the secession convention. When Burnet , Roberts, and the three men elected to the House arrived in Washington, Congress refused to seat them because they could not take the ironclad oath affirming that they had never borne arms against the United States or supported the Confederacy. Congress did not trust the new government in Texas (or in the other Southern states).

Congress was further irritated when, following the suggestion of Governor Throckmorton, the Texas legislature refused to ratify the Thirteenth Amendment to the Constitution of the United States. In addition the legislature enacted a number of measures designed to restrict the freedom of blacks. The legislature took the position that the freedmen were a subordinate caste occupying a position somewhere between slavery and freedom. In taking this position they ignored the advice of John H. Reagan, former postmaster general of the Confederacy, who warned that the Radical Republicans were gaining control of the government and would demand racial equality in the South. Instead they passed a series of laws that would reduce most blacks to a state of peonage and deny them their civil and political rights.

The labor laws were particularly onerous. Though black workers could freely choose their employers, once a labor contract was signed, their rights were severely limited. They could not leave employment without the permission of their employer, they were required to be obedient and respectful, they could not have visitors during working hours, and they could not leave home without permission. Employers could make deductions from their wages for time lost, poor or sloppy work, and damaged tools. In addition, an apprentice law allowed employers to easily indenture black children until they reached adulthood, and a vagrancy law provided for arresting and sentencing to public labor without pay the unemployed and blacks accused of being truant from their contracted employer. The effect of these laws was to create a labor system that perpetuated many of the features of slavery.

The legislature supplemented this labor legislation with a series of restrictive acts known collectively as "black codes." Texas was not unique in doing this. Throughout the South, states adopted similar laws that differed only in detail from state to state. Some states were more repressive than others, but the determination of all was to place black people in a restricted and subordinate status. The black codes of Texas reflected such determination. In addition to restricting the freedom of laborers, the Texas black codes outlawed interracial marriage and prohibited blacks from voting, holding public office, or serving on juries. Blacks could present testimony only in court cases involving other blacks. They were segregated on public transportation and denied the opportunity to obtain free land under the state's homestead law.

Governor Throckmorton's efforts to reestablish the supremacy of civil over military authority were undermined by the growing conflict in Washington between President Johnson and the Radical Republicans in Congress. The president's authority diminished day by day, and the strength of the Radical Republicans increased. Outraged by the black codes and the return of former Confederate leaders to political power in Texas and the other Southern states, Congress took decisive action in the spring of 1866. First they approved, over the President's veto, a bill that extended the authority of the Freedmen's Bureau, particularly in policing labor contracts and in establishing Freedmen's Bureau courts to protect the legal rights of the freedmen. Then, again overcoming a presidential veto, Congress passed the Civil Rights Act of 1866. This law declared that all persons born in the United States were citizens and declared that all citizens, regardless of race, enjoyed equal rights, including the right to own property, and were guaranteed equal protection under the law. Finally in June 1866 Congress passed the Fourteenth Amendment and sent it to the states for ratification. The Fourteenth Amendment extended civil rights to African Americans, penalized Southern states for refusing to allow blacks the right to vote, and denied political rights to a large number of white Southerners who had served the Confederate military or government. Finally, in the congressional elections of November 1866 the voters repudiated the leadership of President Johnson and elected a Congress controlled by the Radical Republicans.

Meanwhile, Governor Throckmorton attempted to establish civil authority over military authority in Texas. Throckmorton had three major objectives for his administration. First, he hoped to restore order to the state, enforce all laws, and suppress the lawlessness and terrorism that had followed the collapse of Confederate authority. Second, he hoped the accomplishment of the first goal would eliminate the need for military and Freedmen's Bureau courts and restore full authority to state and county courts. Finally, he hoped to arrange the transfer of all federal troops in Texas from police duty in the populated areas of the state to the frontier, where they could protect settlements from Indian attack.

Throckmorton's failure to achieve his first objective prevented him from achieving the other two. Throughout 1866, violence and lawlessness continued to plague much of the state. Indeed, the situation worsened as a growing number of clashes occurred between citizens and federal troops, and as more and more freedmen and Unionists encountered terrorism. Many Texans blamed the lawlessness on federal authorities. For example, there was widespread outrage when a unit of drunken soldiers looted and burned several buildings in Brenham in September 1866, and when Bosque County agents of the Freedmen's Bureau ordered the release of a black man charged with rape. In Victoria, which was occupied by a company of black troops, citizens complained that the soldiers released black prisoners from the county jail and lynched a white man accused of murdering a black. On the other hand, General Sheridan noted that freedmen and Unionists were frequent victims of violence in Texas. Whatever the cause, continued examples of lawlessness, and particularly of racial and political violence, prevented Throckmorton from eliminating military and Freedmen's Bureau courts and dashed his hopes of transferring federal troops to the frontier. As General Sheridan observed in January 1867, there were "more casualties occurring from outrages perpetuated upon Union men and freedmen in the interior of the state than occur from Indian depredations on the frontier."

In an age filled with racial tensions and resentment provoked by war and military occupation, violence could be expected. Between January and June 1867, the Freedmen Bureau agents reported thirty to forty crimes each month, ordinarily instances of white attacks upon blacks. Gangs of whites in Hoffman County raided black homes to collect any arms that might be found. Outlaws, such as John Wesley Hardin, added to their reputation as "badmen" by killing blacks. Another member of an outlaw gang shot to death a young black who refused to stand at attention when he rode by. Indeed, a committee of the Constitutional Convention of 1868 reported that 509 whites and 468 blacks had been murdered since the end of the war.

RADICAL RECONSTRUCTION

When the new Congress convened following the Radical Republican victory in November 1866, it was not pleased with developments in the South. President Johnson's Reconstruction program was turning the state governments of the former Confederacy back into the hands of the former slaveholders and placing freedmen and Unionists at the mercy of ex-rebels. Not incidentally, it would also give the Democratic Party control of eleven states. Recalcitrant, and unwilling to accept the reality of a new era, Southerners had honored prominent leaders of the Confederacy with high office. State legislatures had passed black codes calculated to reduce blacks to serfdom. Southerners had failed to prevent occasional race riots and many acts of lawlessness or punish those responsible, and, with the exception of Tennessee, Southern states had refused to ratify the Fourteenth Amendment.

A delegation of Texas Unionists, led by A. J. Hamilton and E. M. Pease, went to Washington and lobbied for congressional intervention in Texas. In particular they urged Congress to depose the conservative government in Texas and the rest of the South, replace them with loyal Unionist governments, and pass a new constitutional amendment guaranteeing black suffrage. Many of these demands were incorporated in the Reconstruction Act of 1867. This act, passed over the president's veto on March 2, 1867, declared inadequate and illegal the existing governments in the Southern states (except for Tennessee), divided the South into five military districts, and granted the commanding generals authority superior to that of state laws and civil officials. The act required that new constitutional conventions be convened, with the delegates elected by voters of both races, exclusive of those disqualified as former rebels. It required that the conventions frame and the qualified voters ratify new constitutions that granted black males the right to vote, and it required that the legislatures elected under the new constitutions ratify the Fourteenth Amendment. General Philip H. Sheridan, then stationed in New Orleans as commander of the Military Division of the

Southwest, was given charge of the Fifth District made up of Louisiana and Texas, and under him General Charles Griffin was made commander of the subdistrict of Texas.

Hamilton, Pease and their associates returned to Texas, not as Unionists but as Republicans. They set out to accomplish a difficult task—to build a Republican Party in Texas that united the interests of both white Republicans and freedmen. To do so they had to overcome the racial prejudice of whites, who were reluctant to extend suffrage to blacks, much less to share power with them.

Meanwhile, Throckmorton pledged his cooperation to Sheridan and Griffin, but conflict developed within a short time. Basic to the quarrel were two fundamental issues: Throckmorton's determination not to subordinate civil government to military intervention and the belief of Sheridan and Griffin that Throckmorton was determined to keep ex-Confederate leaders in power, and that he would not protect the rights of African Americans. On July 30 Sheridan declared Throckmorton "an impediment to reconstruction," removed him from office, and appointed E. M. Pease as provisional governor of Texas. Over the next several months Griffin and his successor, General J. J. Reynolds, dismissed many other state and local officials.

The appointment of Pease was a wise and prudent move. Long a resident of the state, Pease had served four years as governor before the war. As a founder of the Texas Republican Party, he generally enjoyed the confidence of military authorities and Congress. He was concerned about the welfare of black citizens and prepared to protect their rights, especially their right to vote; yet he enjoyed the respect of much of the white population and was regarded as fair and honest.

Griffin moved quickly to bring the civil government under his control and to prepare for the election of the constitutional convention. Key to this was voter registration—registering black voters and disfranchising white voters who could not meet the test of past loyalty contained in the Fourteenth Amendment and the Reconstruction Act of 1867. Sheridan applied this restriction rigidly. According to his instructions, even persons who had held minor offices, such as school trustees, and had later taken part in the rebellion should be disfranchised. The actual application of the rule varied considerably from place to place and from time to time, especially when the more moderate W. S. Hancock succeeded Sheridan as commander of the fifth military district in November 1867.

When the registration of voters had been completed, the rolls showed about 59,633 white and 49,479 black voters. It was estimated that the number of men disfranchised was not more than 7,500 to 10,000. The Republicans, organized through the Union League and the Grand Army of the Republic, solicited the votes of the freedmen and white Unionists. The Ku Klux Klan, which operated in Texas under various names, used threats, intimidation, and violence in an effort to prevent blacks and Unionists from voting. In the five-day election, held in February 1868, the vote was 44,689 (7,757 white and 36,932 black) for the convention and 11,400 (10,622 white and 818 black) against it.

THE CONSTITUTION OF 1869

The constitutional convention assembled in Austin on June 1, 1868. Of its ninety-four members (including four replacements as a result of deaths and resignations), two had served in the constitutional convention in 1845, six in that of 1866, and one in the German National Assembly in Frankfurt. Ten were blacks, including George T. Ruby, the well-educated political organizer from Galveston. No more than twelve of the original ninety delegates were conservatives, including eight to ten Democrats, and seventy-eight were Republicans. The Republicans were irrevocably divided on the major issues. A. J. Hamilton, the leader of the moderate Republicans, had the support of all the Democrats. The Radical Republicans were led by Edmund Jackson (E. J.) Davis of Corpus Christi, a former judge and the president of the convention, who had organized in South Texas a regiment of Union cavalry and attained the rank of brigadier general. Other prominent radicals included Morgan Hamilton, the wealthy brother of A. J. Hamilton; James P. Newcomb, an antisecessionist newspaper owner and editor, who had left San Antonio for California at the outbreak of the war; and George T. Ruby, president of the Union Leagues of Texas, the principal African American political organization.

The convention had to resolve three major issues before it could go to work on writing the constitution. The first was the issue of *ab initio*. Supporters of *ab initio* argued that laws passed by the state during the period of the Confederacy had no legal basis. Though the debate was framed in constitutional terms, it actually concerned issues of economic self-interest. Radicals supported *ab initio*, and moderates opposed it. Ultimately moderates prevailed, largely because voiding every contract, court case, and legal action for four years would have resulted in chaos.

Having failed with *ab initio*, radicals next attempted to divide Texas into three separate states. Their reasons were purely political. Radicals in East Texas and West Texas hoped to separate their sections from Central Texas, the region that had dominated the state politically and economically before the war. Politically the radicals hoped that they could maintain Republican control in the strongly Unionist West Texas and perhaps even in East Texas with its large African American population. Moderates opposed the division, arguing that it would increase the tax burden and interfere with efforts to offer education and other public services. Moderates also prevailed on this issue.

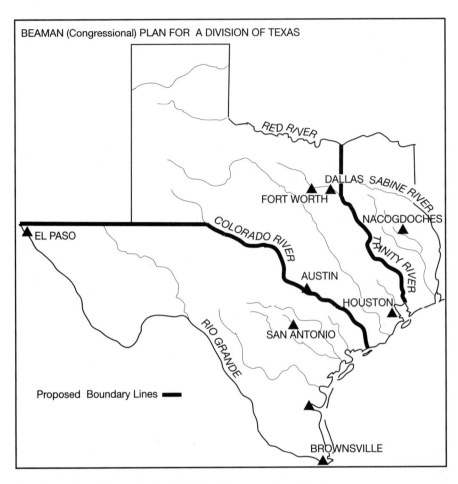

BEAMAN (Congressional) PLAN FOR A DIVISION OF TEXAS

RED RIVER

DALLAS
FORT WORTH
SABINE RIVER
NACOGDOCHES

EL PASO

COLORADO RIVER

TRINITY RIVER

AUSTIN

HOUSTON

SAN ANTONIO

RIO GRANDE

Proposed Boundary Lines ━━

BROWNSVILLE

One of a number of proposals for division of Texas considered during
Reconstruction, the Beaman plan was considered in Congress in 1868, was
sometimes known as the "Congressional Plan," but was the basis for some of the
proposals considered in the Convention of 1868.

The third issue involved civil rights. Radicals, led by Ruby and the
black delegates, wanted to include a strong civil rights provision, outlaw discrimination in public accommodations, and provide for a well-funded, integrated system of public education. Their purpose was to give blacks a means
to escape the life of economic peonage that seemed to lie before them. Moderates, on the other hand, expected that blacks would continue to provide
Texas with agricultural labor, and consequently saw no need to provide education or to expand civil rights beyond what Congress had already enacted
in the Civil Rights Act and the Fourteenth Amendment. The convention
compromised on these issues, establishing a desegregated school system but

refusing to specify civil rights beyond a simple guarantee of the equality of all persons before the law.

While these issues were being debated, convention committees examined a number of other issues, including chartering railroads, gathering evidence of lawlessness in East Texas, and debating proposals for the sale of a portion of the state to the United States. With the constitution almost completed, the delegates decided to delay its completion until after the presidential election. Since the funds of the convention had been depleted, the delegates provided for the collection of a special tax to finance another session, and then, on August 31, recessed until the first Monday in December. During the recess, Ulysses S. Grant, the Republican nominee for president, won an overwhelming victory.

By the time the convention recessed, political divisions in Texas had deepened and political and racial violence was increasing. Republicans blamed the violence on the reorganized Democratic Party, which used racial fears and racist propaganda in their campaign. Democrats accused the Radical Republicans of trying to impose black rule on the state and argued that when this happened, blacks would disfranchise whites, enforce racial intermarriage, and promote miscegenation. These tactics were designed to strengthen the party's hold on the white vote, but they also resulted in the emergence of a number of organizations committed to the use of terror to preserve white supremacy. By the late spring of 1868 the Ku Klux Klan and similar groups launched a full-scale attack on Republican and black political organizations in Texas. Arsonists targeted Freedmen's Bureau offices and schools and Republican newspapers, while black and white Republican leaders were kidnaped and terrorized. In Bastrop, for example, a masked band lynched two delegates to the state convention of the Union League, in Burleson County A. R. Wilson, a prominent black politician, was assassinated, and in other parts of the state black leaders simply vanished. The worst outbreak of racial violence occurred in Brazos County in July 1868, when a Klan mob lynched Miles E. Brooks, the head of the local Union League. When a black posse attempted to arrest Klan leaders, a race war erupted. Before federal troops arrived to restore order, the battle raged for four days and about 100 blacks were killed.

This racial violence disrupted black and Republican political organizations and discredited Governor Pease, who was blamed for not maintaining order. It also accelerated the split in the Republican Party between the radicals, now relying almost entirely on the black vote, and the moderates, who, seeking conservative white support, dropped their support for denying former Confederates the right to vote.

When the convention reconvened in December, the radicals, convinced that they would have support from Washington, resumed their struggle to divide Texas into three states. The convention in January 1869 voted to divide the state and to send a delegation to Washington to lobby for approval of the

Edmund Jackson ("E. J.") Davis. A native of Florida, he moved to Texas in 1838, became a brigadier-general in the Union forces, and returned to Texas after the war to become a radical Republican leader. After serving one term as governor, he was defeated in his bid for reelection, but he remained active in politics until his death in 1883. (Archives Division—Texas State Library)

division. Radicals then attempted unsuccessfully to adjourn the convention without completing the constitution. Instead, on February 3, 1869, a coalition of moderates gained control of the convention, turned over the nearly completed constitution to the military authorities, and then adjourned. General Reynolds appointed a three-man committee to complete the constitution. The document was ultimately signed by forty-six of the ninety delegates.

Despite the fact that it was criticized by both Conservative Democrats and Radical Republicans, the Constitution of 1869 contained a number of positive features. It centralized political power in the hands of a governor elected for a term of four years. The governor appointed the other major executive officers and the judges of the state courts. The constitution guaranteed that no citizen would be denied the right to vote on the basis of "race, color, or former condition," and disfranchised only those not permitted to vote by the United States Constitution. It did not, however, extend the suffrage to women. In a major concession to blacks, the constitution provided generous funding for public education and declared that educational funds would be used for the education of all children, regardless of race or color.

When the radicals failed to convince Congress and President Grant to reject the constitution and divide Texas, they abruptly withdrew their opposition, endorsed the work of the convention, and nominated E. J. Davis as their candidate for governor. In opposition, the moderate Republicans and the Democrats supported A. J. Hamilton as their candidate. Governor Pease resigned on September 20 to protest General Reynolds' interference in Texas politics, and the general, as military commander of the state, assumed the responsibilities of the governor and ordered the registration of voters. Registration boards enrolled 81,960 white voters and 53,593 black voters.

The campaign centered on the issue of race. Although the radicals endorsed the Fourteenth and the Fifteenth Amendments in their platform, Davis avoided discussing civil rights in order to downplay his radical image and appeal to white voters. Ruby cooperated with this strategy by keeping black candidates out of several key legislative races and using the Union Leagues to deliver the black vote. Nevertheless, Hamilton accused Davis and the radicals of trying to create a "Negro Party." Though Hamilton supported black suffrage and invited blacks to support his candidacy, he directed his campaign principally at white conservatives and Democrats.

Voting took place on Tuesday, November 30, and the three days following. Fearing violence, Reynolds stationed 600 federal troops at polling places around the state. Approximately 53 percent of the eligible whites and 63 percent of the eligible blacks voted. The turnout was also good among German-Americans and Mexican Americans. The vote for governor was exceptionally close, and military authorities impounded the ballots. Each side accused the other of voter irregularities, and these charges were probably accurate. Nevertheless, on January 8, 1870, General Reynolds declared Davis the winner by a 771-vote margin, 39,831 to 39,060. The constitution was adopted by a huge majority—72,466 as against 4,928. The Republicans elected three of the four congressmen and controlled both houses of the legislature.

Reynolds fulfilled the responsibilities of governor until January 8, 1870, when he instructed the successful candidates to take office. In a special session beginning on February 8, the legislature ratified the Fourteenth and Fifteenth Amendments and elected two radicals, Morgan Hamilton and J. W. Flanagan, to the U.S. Senate. On March 30, 1870, President Grant signed the act of Congress admitting Texas senators and representatives; the executive officers of Texas dropped the qualifying title "provisional"; and on April 16, 1870, General Reynolds formally brought military rule to an end.

Texas had been restored to the Union, but for many Texans it was not until four years later, when a government was established under the control of Democrats, that Reconstruction came to an end.

E. J. DAVIS AND RADICAL RULE IN TEXAS

Pursuant to Governor Davis's call, the Twelfth Legislature met in special session in April 1870. Sixteen of the thirty senators, including two blacks, and fifty of the ninety members of the house, including nine blacks, were

Davis supporters. Thus, the governor had most of his program enacted into law. In his first message to the lawmakers, Governor Davis stated that the army was not adequately protecting the northern and western frontiers against Indian raids and stressed the need for a ranger force for frontier defense. The legislature immediately approved his recommendation for a force of twenty companies, totaling 1,220 men, but because of insufficient funds and War Department disapproval, the organization never materialized. The legislature then authorized the establishment of companies of minutemen for frontier defense, but they were never very effective.

The most controversial measures proposed by Davis consisted of five acts that the Democrats called the "obnoxious acts," a characterization that was essentially political in nature. The first two of these measures dealt with law and order and involved the organization of a state militia and the creation of a state police force. Both of these measures were passed, over Democratic opposition, in the summer of 1870. Critics argued that both measures potentially gave the governor power that could be used against his political enemies. In reality both were effective tools against the violence and lawlessness that had infected Texas since the collapse of the Confederacy.

The other three controversial acts of the 1870 legislature were unrelated to the issue of law and order. The Enabling Act authorized the governor to fill state, district, county, and city offices made vacant by the act readmitting Texas into the Union. One critic estimated that under this law Davis appointed 8,538 government employees. Though this estimate was likely an exaggeration, the governor was able to appoint a large number of officials. The second of these acts provided for a state printer, an official state journal, and the printing of public notices and other official matters in a newspaper in each judicial district. Critics claimed, with some truth, that this act provided Davis with support from a subsidized press, but the practice was one that Democratic administrations had used for years. The final act postponed the regular election for governor and state officials until November 1872 so it would correspond with congressional elections. The logic of this move is clear; it was criticized because it extended the term of office for the radicals elected in 1869 by one year.

Of all actions associated with the E. J. Davis administration, those that generated the most controversy pertained to the activities of the state police and the imposition of martial law. Much of the conflict simply reflected the struggle for political power between the conservatives and Radical Republicans. But there were allegations that some members of the state police had criminal records, as well as charges of police brutality and abuse of police power by poorly trained and poorly supervised lawmen. In some instances these allegations were fueled by the fact that 40 percent of the 258-man force consisted of African Americans. A final blow to the reputation of the state police came in 1872 when its commander, Adjutant General James Davidson, absconded with $32,000 in state funds. In spite of these problems, many critics, including some of the most outspoken conservatives, acknowledged that the state police were conducting an effective campaign against crime and lawlessness.

Governor Davis's use of the state militia and martial law was equally controversial. The Militia Bill gave the governor the authority to declare martial law and use the militia in counties experiencing serious civil unrest. In spite of complaints by conservatives that placing control over the militia in the hands of the governor created a dangerous concentration of power, Davis actually used this authority judiciously. In 1870 the militia suppressed mobs in Madison and Grimes counties that threatened the lives of blacks and white radicals. Similar uprisings in Hill and Walker counties in early 1871, and in Freestone and Limestone counties later that year again prompted the governor to place these areas under martial law and utilize the militia to restore order. Though conservatives questioned the seriousness of these incidents and the necessity of such drastic action, black leaders praised Governor Davis for his willingness to use force to protect their lives and property. As with the state police, a significant number of blacks served in the militia.

The radicals also addressed several significant social and economic issues. They sought to provide a public road system and levied taxes for that purpose. They enacted a homestead law and established a bureau of immigration to attract European settlers to the state. They were generous in appropriations to provide state troops to supplement the inadequate frontier defense provided by the federal forces. Theirs was the first administration to envision a genuinely public, free school system. In making attendance compulsory and levying taxes adequate for the maintenance of the schools, they were a half-century ahead of their time.

More controversial was the action taken by the Twelfth Legislature to promote railroad construction, but in this case the Democrats were at least as much to blame as the Republicans. The state was in great need of a modern railroad system, especially with the rapid population growth that followed the Civil War. The Constitution of 1869 prohibited land grants to subsidize railroad construction, but supporters of the railroads used city or state bonds for the purpose. Generally the support for these measures came from Democrats and moderate Republicans, while a majority of Radical Republicans were opposed. Davis opposed the practice of subsidizing railroad construction and vetoed several bills, including one providing subsidies to the Southern Pacific. In 1873 the constitution was amended to authorize the use of land grants for railroad subsidies, and in later years Democratic legislatures voted subsidies of some 32,000,000 acres.

In spite of the success of many of their programs, the radicals had little chance of continuing this success over time. Davis and the radicals had gained control of the state by a slender margin, and their victory was due to the demoralized state of the Democratic opposition. Their power rested mainly on black suffrage, but blacks never constituted a majority of the voters in Texas. The deep divisions within the Republican Party, especially the conflict between moderates and radicals over the role of blacks in the party, also did not bode well for the future. Finally, even though much of the radical legislative program was meritorious, it was not popular with a majority of the voters.

Democrats and conservative Republicans united in attacking the radicals. In September 1871, the representatives of ninety-four counties met in Austin at a taxpayers' convention to condemn the extravagance of the administration. Such men as A. J. Hamilton, Morgan Hamilton, and E. M. Pease united with ex-Confederates to argue that the Davis administration was flagrantly violating the constitution and laws and was bankrupting the state. At a special election in October 1871, the Democrats took control of all four congressional seats. In 1872, Horace Greeley, the Democratic (and Liberal Republican) nominee for president, outpolled President Grant in Texas by almost 20,000 votes, and the Democrats again won all the seats in Congress and gained control of the legislature.

When it assembled in Austin on January 14, 1873, the Thirteenth Legislature proceeded to repeal the basic laws of the radical program. It began by enacting a new printing law that withdrew official patronage from radical newspapers. It repealed—over the governor's veto—the state police act, limited the power of the governor to declare martial law, and reduced drastically the appointive powers of the governor. It simplified requirements for the registration of voters and provided for precinct voting and one-day elections. The centralized school system of the radicals was reshaped by a law abolishing the board of education and school supervisors and reducing the power of the state superintendent. Before it adjourned, the legislature provided for a general election of state officers on the first Tuesday in December 1873.

The election was the final test of the strength of the radicals. Davis headed the Republican ticket, running against Richard Coke, the Democratic nominee. By 1873 the national Republican leadership had abandoned the radical program and the party's commitment to civil rights. Many accepted as inevitable the restoration of Democratic control of the Southern states; some even believed the conservative Democrats would improve business opportunities in the South. Davis and the radicals, with no prospect of outside support, once again allied themselves with Ruby and the black political leadership in Texas. In an election characterized by racial intimidation and voter fraud, Coke and the Democrats won by a landslide, 85,549 votes to 42,663.

Though Davis did not challenge the election results on the grounds of fraud, he did question the validity of the Election Law of 1872 that established a one-day voting period. The state supreme court, which had been appointed by Davis, agreed with his argument. The court's ruling was ignored by the general public, and Coke was inaugurated late at night on January 15, 1874. Davis appealed to Ulysses Grant, but the president advised that it would "be prudent as well as right" to accept the verdict of the voters. Davis still refused to recognize the new administration, and for several days it seemed that bloodshed was inevitable. Davis was supported by some of his state police and black militia, while a local militia company, the Travis Rifles, took the side of the new governor. At last, after he had received another message from the attorney general of the United States, stating positively that President Grant would not sustain him against Coke, Davis retired under protest.

EFFECTS OF RECONSTRUCTION

Although Texas did not suffer to the extent of other Southern states, the years that followed the collapse of the Confederacy proved destructive to the fortunes of many wealthy plantation owners and difficult for smaller landowners and farmers. The war itself had bankrupted many, while those who held on to their estates through the war found themselves land-poor, sometimes without sufficient livestock and without slaves to provide labor. Of all the problems, that of securing labor was the greatest. A new system of labor and land management acceptable to both black and white people had to evolve. In the meantime, thousands of acres lay idle. Land values fell to 20 percent of 1860 prices. Cotton, practically the only money crop, declined in value from 31 cents per pound in 1866 to 17 cents in 1870, and to 13 cents in 1875. The total production of cotton declined from 431,000 bales in 1859 to an average of 343,000 bales for the years from 1866 to 1870.

In the later years of Reconstruction conditions improved significantly. Work for wages gave way to leasing or renting, when black labor was involved, and by 1870 the sharecropping system was becoming common. Under this practice, landowners supplied the laborers with all houses and farming equipment and took as their share from one-half to two-thirds of the crop. Improvement in the agricultural situation is reflected in the production of cotton, which by 1873 was exceeding 500,000 bales per year. Following the discovery that cotton would thrive on the rich uplands of North Texas, the increase in acreage was rapid. Immigration stimulated the production of all farm commodities. During this period southern and western Texas became comparatively prosperous from the pouches of gold brought back by drovers who each year took hundreds of thousands of cattle to northern markets. The industrial development of the country is reflected in the railroad mileage, which increased from 395 in 1865 to 1,650 in 1874.

Public indebtedness and taxation increased during Reconstruction. Money appropriated for law and order, expanded judicial processes, the public school programs, frontier defense, and the expenses of long legislative sessions amounted to millions. In 1871 and the three years following, state taxes increased by nearly $4 million. Besides the increase in state taxes, there were large increases in local taxes. In 1871, these combined rates amounted in some instances to as much as $2.17 on $100.00 of valuation, an increase of 1,450 percent over 1866. Meanwhile, the state government had to resort to borrowing to balance its books, and the public debt increased by more than $2 million. Some of the funds had been spent unwisely, small amounts had been lost through fraud and embezzlement, and the debt would be a burden to future generations. But the need for public expenditures during these troubled times had been real, and most of the money had been spent for good purposes.

Economic losses through the war and Reconstruction were soon overcome, but the effect on political and social institutions was more enduring. Many white voters did not forget their antagonism toward the Republican Party. The Republican Party did not disappear. It took part in elections, occasionally with success, and its members claimed federal jobs in significant numbers. But as a truly effective part of the state political system, the Republican Party offered little. Whether justified or not, memories of Reconstruction rendered Texas a one-party state controlled by the Democrats for the next century.

For the black people of Texas, Reconstruction was a mixture of success and failure. Blacks achieved some gains—the beginnings of an educational system, land ownership for a few, a degree of civil equality, and some political influence for a time—and they bore the responsibility of freedom in a manner worthy of respect and admiration. But the tide of racial prejudice would have been strong under the best of circumstances, and Reconstruction policies and programs stopped far short of solving the problems of prejudice and discrimination. In the decades to come, segregation, political and economic discrimination, and eventually disfranchisement would become a way of life for African Americans in Texas. And, for most black Texans, the peonage that replaced slavery as the agricultural labor system provided little hope for the future.

BIBLIOGRAPHY

There is no definitive work on Reconstruction in Texas. In many respects, the adversarial character of the Civil War carried over into the Reconstruction period and has often been reflected in subsequent literature. Readers who wish to be familiar with the interpretations of Reconstruction that dominated early in the twentieth century should read Charles W. Ramsdell, *Reconstruction in Texas* (New York, 1910); William C. Nunn, *Texas under the Carpetbaggers* (Austin, 1962); *Escape from Reconstruction* (Fort Worth, 1956); and Ernest Wallace, *Texas in Turmoil*. For more recent interpretations see Carl H. Moneyhon, *Republicanism in Reconstruction Texas* (Austin, 1980), and Randolph B. Campbell's *Grass-Roots Reconstruction in Texas, 1865–1880* (Baton Rouge, 1997).

Biographical studies of participants in the Civil War and Reconstruction include Ben. H. Procter, *Not without Honor: The Life of John H. Reagan*; C. Elliot, *Leathercoat: The*

Life of James W. Throckmorton; W. J. Hughes, *Rebellious Ranger: Rip Ford and the Old Southwest*; Ernest. Wallace, *Charles DeMorse: Pioneer Editor and Statesman*; John L. Waller, *Colossal Hamilton of Texas: A Biography of Andrew Jackson Hamilton* (El Paso, 1968); Ernest Wallace, *The Howling of the Coyotes: Reconstruction Efforts to Divide Texas* (College Station, 1979); R. N. Gray, "Edmund J. Davis: Radical Republican and Reconstruction Governor of Texas" (unpublished dissertation, Texas Tech University, Lubbock, 1976); and Betty J. Sandlin, "The Texas Reconstruction Constitutional Convention of 1868–1869" (unpublished dissertation, Texas Tech University, Lubbock, 1970).

For the writings of participants, see Oran M. Roberts, "The Experiences of an Unrecognized Senator," *Quarterly of the Texas State Historical Association*, XII, 87–147; John H. Reagan, *Memoirs, with Special Reference to Secession and the Civil War* (W. F. McCaleb, ed., New York, 1906); and A. W. Terrell, *From Texas to Mexico in 1865* (Dallas, 1933).

Special studies include Dale A. Somers, "James P. Newcomb: The Making of a Radical," *Southwestern Historical Quarterly*, LXXII, 435–448; W. A. Russ, Jr., "Radical Disfranchisement in Texas," ibid., XXXVIII, 40–52; Louise Horton (ed.), "Samuel Bell Maxey on the Coke-Davis Controversy," ibid., LXXII, 519–525; George Shelley, "The Semicolon Court of Texas," ibid., XLVIII, 449–468; Lance A. Cooper, "'A Slobbering Lame Thing'? The Semicolon Case Reconsidered," *Southwestern Historical Quarterly*, 320–338. O. A. Singletary, "The Texas Militia during Reconstruction," ibid., LX, 23–35; J. R. Norvell, "The Reconstruction Courts of Texas," ibid., LXII, 141–163; J. E. Ericson, "Delegates to the Texas Constitutional Convention of 1875: A Reappraisal," ibid., LXVII, 22–27; and Carl Moneyhon, "Edmund J. Davis in the Coke-Davis Election Dispute of 1874: A Reassessment of Character," *Southwestern Historical Quarterly*, C, 131–151.

For an analysis of the often violent struggle for racial justice in post-Civil War Texas see Barry A. Crouch and L. J. Schultz, "Crisis in Color: Racial Separation in Texas during Reconstruction," *Civil War History*, XVI, 37–49; Barry A. Crouch and Donaly E. Brice, *Cullen Montgomery Baker: Reconstruction Desperado* (Baton Rouge, 1997); Edgar P. Sneed, "A Historiography of Reconstruction in Texas: Some Myths and Problems," *Southwestern Historical Quarterly*, LXXII, 435–448; Barry Crouch, "'Unmanacling' Texas Reconstruction: A Twenty-Year Perspective," ibid., XCIII, 275–302, and "'All the Vile Passions': The Texas Black Code of 1866," XCVII, 13–34; Ann Patton Baenziger, "The Texas State Police during Reconstruction: A Reexamination," ibid., LXXII, 470–491; Gregg Cantrell, "Racial Violence and Reconstruction Politics in Texas, 1867–1868," ibid., XCIII, 333–355; Dale Baum, "Chicanery and Intimidation in the 1869 Texas Gubernatorial Race," ibid., XCVII, 37–54; Carl Moneyhon, "Public Education and Texas Reconstruction Politics, 1871–1874," ibid., LXXXIX, 393–416; Philip J. Avillo, Jr., "Phantom Radicals: Texas Republicans in Congress, 1870–1873," ibid., LXXVII, 431–444; John M. Brockman, "Railroads, Radicals, and the Militia Bill: A New Interpretation of the Quorum-Breaking Incident of 1870," ibid., LXXXIII, 105–122; James Smallwood, "Perpetuation of Caste: Black Agricultural Workers in Reconstruction Texas," *Mid-America*, LXI, 5–23; Ricky Floyd Dobbs, "Defying Davis: The Walker County Rebellion," ibid., XXXII, 34–47; Billy D. Ledbetter, "White Texans' Attitudes Toward the Political Equality of Negroes, 1865–1870," *Phylon*, XL, 253–263; Barry Crouch, "A Spirit of Lawlessness: White Violence, Texas Blacks, 1865–1868," *Journal of Social History* (Winter 1984), 217–232; Randolph B. Campbell, "The End of Slavery in Texas: A Research Note," *Southwestern Historical Quarterly*, LXXXVIII, 71–80; "Carpetbagger Rule in Reconstruction Texas," ibid., XCVII, 587–596; and "The District Judges of Texas in 1866–1867," ibid., XCIII, 357–377.

Excellent studies on the Freedmen's Bureau have appeared in recent years. See William L. Richter, *Overreached on All Sides: The Freedmen's Bureau Administrators in*

Texas, 1865–1868 (College Station, 1991); and " 'The Revolver Rules the Day!': (College Station, 1991); and " 'The Revolver Rules the Day': Colonel DeWitt C. Brown and the Freedmen's Bureau in Paris, Texas," *Southwestern Historical Quarterly*, XCIII, 303–332; James Smallwood, "Black Education in Reconstruction Texas: The Contribution of the Freedmen's Bureau and Benevolent Societies," *East Texas Historical Journal*, XIX, 17–40; Barry A. Crouch, *The Freedmen's Bureau and Black Texans* (Austin, 1992); and Alton Hornsby, Jr., "The Freedmen's Bureau Schools in Texas, 1864–1870," *Southwestern Historical Quarterly*, LXXVI, 397–417. An older and more critical view of the agency is C. Elliott, "The Freedmen's Bureau in Texas," ibid., LVI, 1–24.

Studies that focus on the African American experience during Reconstruction include James M. Smallwood, *Time of Hope, Time of Despair: Black Texans during Reconstruction* (Port Washington, N.Y., 1981); Billy Bob Lightfoot, "The Negro Exodus from Comanche County, Texas," *Southwestern Historical Quarterly*, LVI, 405–416; Charles A. Israel, "From Biracial to Segregated Churches: Black and White Protestants in Houston, Texas, 1840–1870," *Southwestern Historical Quarterly*, CI , 429–458. Alwyn Barr's survey *Black Texans: A History of African Americans in Texas, 1528–1995*, (2d ed., Norman, Okla, 1996) contains material about blacks during Reconstruction.

The role of the U.S. Army in Texas is discussed in the thorough and balanced works of Robert W. Shook and William L. Richter. See Robert W. Shook, "Federal Occupation and Administration of Texas, 1865–1870" (unpublished dissertation, North Texas University, Denton, 1970), and William L. Richter, *The Army in Texas during Reconstruction, 1865–1870* (College Station, 1987); "Texas Politics and the United States Army, 1866–1867," *Military History of Texas and the Southwest*, X, 159–186; and " 'We Must Rub Out and Begin Anew'; The Army and the Republican Party in Texas Reconstruction," *Civil War History*, XIX, 334–352.

The most essential documents may be found in W. L. Fleming (ed.), *Documentary History of Reconstruction* (two vols., Cleveland, 1906–1907); H. P. N. Gammel, *The Laws of Texas*; and Ernest Wallace, David M. Vigness, and George B. Ward (eds.), *Documents of Texas History* (Austin, 1994).

There are many other studies pertinent to the period. Useful dissertations include John P. Carrier, "A Political History of Texas during the Reconstruction, 1867–1874" (unpublished dissertation, Vanderbilt University, 1971), an excellent study; James A. Baggett, "The Rise and Fall of the Texas Radical, 1867–1883" (unpublished dissertation, North Texas State University, Denton, 1972); and John C. McGraw, "The Texas Constitution of 1866" (unpublished dissertation, Texas Technological College, Lubbock, 1959). Publications containing sections dealing with Reconstruction include Paul D. Casdorph, *A History of the Republican Party in Texas, 1865–1965* (Austin, 1965), and Allen W. Trelease, *White Terror: The Ku Klux Klan Conspiracy and Southern Reconstruction* (New York, 1971). The *Texas Almanac* for the years of the Reconstruction period contains a voluminous amount of statistical, factual, and even descriptive information. W. P. Webb has a chapter on the state police in *The Texas Rangers*. Sam Acheson, *35,000 Days in Texas* (New York, 1938), a history of the *Dallas News*, brings out the flavor of the Reconstruction era. For an account of E. J. Davis's appeal to the courts, see J. H. Davenport, *The History of the Supreme Court of the State of Texas* (Austin, 1917). Good sketches may be read in S. S. McKay, *Seven Decades of the Texas Constitution of 1876* (Lubbock, 1942); Louis J. Wortham, *A History of Texas* (Austin, 1924); F. W. Johnson, *Texas and Texans*; and Oran M. Roberts, "A Political, Legislative, and Judicial History of Texas for Its Fifty Years of Statehood, 1845–1895" in Dudley G. Wooten, *Comprehensive History of Texas, 1689-1897* (Dallas, 1898). Short biographical sketches of the governors of the Reconstruction era are in Kenneth E. Hendrickson, Jr., *The Chief Executives of Austin: From Stephen F. Austin to John B. Connally, Jr.* (College Station, 1995), and James. T. DeShields, *They Sat in High Places*. (San Antonio, 1940).

12

From Reconstruction to Reform, 1874–1890

With the election of the Democratic legislature of 1872 and of Governor Coke in 1873, political power came into the secure grasp of those committed to redeeming the state from radical rule. Only the judiciary remained, temporarily, a Republican stronghold. Legislative maneuvering soon removed several district judges, who were replaced with Democrats; a constitutional amendment created a new supreme court with five positions; and within a month after his inauguration, Coke named five Democrats to fill the vacancies.

The triumph of the redeemers initiated more than a decade of conservative government. Reflecting the attitudes shared by most white Texans, these conservative Democrats sought to wipe out the last vestiges of radical rule, the most obvious being the Republican-written Constitution of 1869. Suffering under the economic miseries of the Panic of 1873, they promoted public economy and retrenchment, sometimes to the point of parsimony, but simultaneously they encouraged the distribution of the public lands and the construction of railroads. Initially preoccupied with the legacies of war and Reconstruction, such as crime and public indebtedness, they soon found another perplexing challenge. Agrarian unrest, provoked by the extended agricultural depression and characterized by falling prices, tight credit, and strangling freight rates, would be a persistent problem.

Although the conservative Democrats failed to cope successfully with the problems of unhappy farmers, and although their policies were sometimes shortsighted, the period was not without significant progress. Certainly, old enmities were being forgotten. When U. S. Grant and Philip Sheridan visited Texas in 1880, they were received cordially, and Sheridan apologized for having once said that if he owned Texas and hell he would "rent out Texas and live in hell." Crime was reduced, personal and property rights were made comparatively secure, railroads were built, industry and agriculture expanded, as did the population of the state, and finally, the low prices and the business stagnation that followed the Panic of 1873 gave way in the early 1880s to a period of economic growth and prosperity.

A New Constitution

After winning control of the legislature in 1872, the Democrats agreed with near unanimity that there must be a new constitution. Critics found the Republican origins of the Constitution of 1869 a sufficient cause to discard it, but they offered more substantial reasons. Deeply distrustful of government in general, and especially of the powers that Governor Davis had wielded, they wanted judges elected rather than appointed, fewer courts, and shorter terms for senators, the governor, and other executive officers. They advocated the repeal of "oppressive" features of government, including the road tax, the maintenance of roads by personal service, and the process of voter registration that had been used to disfranchise ex-Confederates. They advocated a biennial legislature with severely limited powers, especially concerning taxation and indebtedness, and a governor with substantially reduced authority.

After failing to remodel the constitution in 1874 through a legislative commission, the legislature, on the advice of Governor Coke, submitted the question of a constitutional convention to the people. On the first Monday in August 1875, the voters approved the convention and elected three delegates from each of the state's thirty senatorial districts.

The San Antonio *Herald* provided a fairly accurate assessment of the convention delegates who assembled in Austin on September 6, 1875. "We know," observed the newspaper, "that the convention has relatively but a few able men in its composition, but those we deem very able, with sound clear judgment." Certainly the roll of delegates bears impressive testimony that the old Texans were again in the ascendancy. Seventy-five were Democrats, and only fifteen, including five blacks, were Republicans. Forty-one were farmers, and twenty-nine were lawyers. Eight had participated in the secession convention of 1861; nineteen had served in the Texas legislature, two in the Congress of the United States, one in the Confederate Congress, and one in the cabinet of Jefferson Davis. More than a score had held high rank in the Confederate army, and three had been officers in the U.S. Army. One had served in the constitutional convention of 1845 and another in the convention of 1866, but, significantly, none had sat in the convention of 1869.

Particularly influential in the convention proceedings was a contingent of forty or more delegates who were members of the Patrons of Husbandry. This powerful farmers' organization, better known as the Grange, had entered Texas in 1873. Spurred by the Panic of 1873, membership climbed rapidly, until by 1876 the order claimed 45,000 members. In the convention, Grange initiatives included reducing taxes and expenditures, undermining the public school system, prohibiting the state from chartering banks, and restricting corporate and railroad practices.

From the moment it convened this convention focused its efforts on economy and retrenchment. In keeping with the frugal principles to be incorporated into the fundamental law, the delegates voted themselves only $5 per day—although members of the legislature had been receiving $8— refused to have the proceedings of the convention printed because of the expense, and even refused to employ a stenographer when they could not secure one for less than $10 a day. Surely, few would quarrel with a delegate's remark that "if future State Governments prove burdensome and onerous, it ought not to be the fault of the Convention."

THE CONSTITUTION OF 1876

In keeping with a trend in the making of state constitutions, the Constitution of 1876 is longer than the fundamental laws that preceded it, and it contains many provisions that the framers of the earlier instruments left to the discretion of the legislatures. It changed the framework of government in several important respects. The legislature was to be composed of two houses, the Senate to consist of 31 members and the House of Representatives never to exceed 150. The term of senators was reduced from six to four years. Returning to a long-standing tradition, the framers called for biennial sessions and meager pay for the legislators. Like the Constitution of 1845, the new instrument severely limited the powers of the legislature. It was forbidden to incur indebtedness to an amount greater than $200,000, and the maximum tax rate, except for the payment of debt, was set at a low level. All property was to be taxed in proportion to its value. The duration of all offices created by the legislature was two years. As a reaction against conditions of the war and reconstruction periods, the constitution affirmed that the writ of habeas corpus was a "writ of right" that would never be suspended.

The article describing the executive department provided for seven officers: a governor, lieutenant governor, secretary of state, comptroller, treasurer, commissioner of the land office, and attorney general. All but the secretary of state were to be elected by the voters. Terms of the executive officers were fixed at two years, with no prohibition against reelection.

The governor's powers and duties were set forth in considerable detail. He might convene the legislature in special session, call out the militia and declare martial law to suppress insurrection, and fill various vacancies by appointment, subject to approval of the senate by a two-thirds vote. He was given power to veto laws and items in appropriation bills, but his veto could be overridden by a two-thirds vote of both houses. The constitution declared that the governor, as the chief executive of the state, should cause the laws to be "faithfully executed," but it did not grant him powers equal to such great responsibility. He was given no control over local officers or other elected state executive officers.

The judicial article reflected a reaction against the appointed courts of the Reconstruction era. The new constitution provided that all judges would be elected by popular vote. The number of district courts was reduced to twenty-six. The convention established a dual system of appellate courts, a supreme court with power to review only civil cases, and a court of appeals with appellate jurisdiction over all criminal cases and certain classes of civil cases.

Following the leadership of some northern states, the convention forbade consolidation of competing railroads and authorized laws to prevent unjust discrimination and to establish maximum freight and passenger rates, but it made no provision for a commission to regulate the railroads. To promote the construction of new tracks, the legislature could grant public land to railroads up to an amount not more than sixteen sections for each mile of road constructed. It was forbidden, however, to grant state funds or bonds to railroads. The convention also provided for homestead grants of 160 acres to heads of families and half that amount to single men over eighteen years of age.

Although there was never a move to formally deny black men the legal right to vote, suffrage was an intensely debated issue. The most divisive contest was over the proposal, supported largely by the East Texas delegates, to make payment of a poll tax a prerequisite for voting, the chief purpose obviously being the indirect disfranchisement of blacks. At the forefront of the opposition to this measure were the black delegates. Together with all but one of the Republicans and a majority of the powerful Grange faction, they defeated the move. Women's suffrage, on the other hand, produced little discussion and received little support in the convention.

The provisions regarding public education were especially controversial. Texas had never had a satisfactory public school system, measured even by the standards that prevailed in the nineteenth century. At the time of the convention some contended that education was a private duty and that no person should be taxed to educate another's child. Many whites especially resented the use of their tax dollars to pay for the education of blacks. Supporters of public education overruled these arguments, but provisions for education were meager compared with those under the Constitution of 1869. The new constitution limited the funding of public schools at both the state and local level, abolished the office of state superintendent and decentralized control of education, eliminated compulsory attendance, and ordered that schools be segregated. Apparently the delegates saw no inconsistency between these provisions and their declaration that the legislature should "establish and make suitable provisions for the support and maintenance of an efficient system of public free schools." An aroused *Galveston News* observed that the convention, after "decreeing universal suffrage, had now also decreed universal ignorance."

The convention was more generous with school endowments. It set aside as a perpetual fund all monies, lands, and other property previously granted to the schools and a large portion of the public lands. All told, the land grant amounted to about 42.5 million acres, and the permanent school fund invested in securities at that time was $3,256,970. Largely as a result of the sale of land, oil royalties, and leases, this endowment had grown to almost $19.6 billion by May 1999.

To the University of Texas, yet unborn, the convention gave with one hand and took away with the other. By a law of 1858, the school would have been entitled to about 3.2 million acres, a part of which had already been located and surveyed within the rich domain of North Central Texas. The delegates repealed this provision and gave the university a million acres of land to be selected from the public domain unappropriated at that time, an exchange very disadvantageous as to both the quantity and the quality of the land. Only additional grants by the legislature and the fortuitous discovery of oil on some of the West Texas lands kept the university from suffering severely.

RATIFICATION OF THE CONSTITUTION

Ratification of the Constitution of 1876 was accomplished without effective opposition but without much enthusiasm. Only one delegate expressed hearty approval, declaring that the constitution was "the noblest instrument ever submitted to the verdict of a free people." The six Republicans remaining in the convention joined five Democrats in a vote against adoption, and many delegates were opposed to portions of the document. Nevertheless, by a vote of fifty-three to eleven, the convention adopted the constitution on November 24, 1875, and submitted it to the voters for their approval.

Anticipating criticism, the convention issued a statement praising its handiwork and explaining that its economies would save the state $1.5 million annually. Significantly, the delegates felt obliged to defend at length the measures on public education, the part of the constitution that had been attacked by the press more severely than any other. Their statement noted the extravagance of the former school system and the poverty of the state, and emphasized the generous permanent school fund that the new Constitution provided.

Some opposition to ratification did develop. By a vote of 674 to 176, the state Democratic convention evaded endorsement, while the Republican convention denounced the document in a unanimous vote. More progressive opponents claimed that the constitution crippled education; hard-core Democrats argued that the failure to enact a poll tax would surrender a large number of counties to black rule. However, Governor Coke and much of the state press, together with the powerful Grange, backed ratification. Given their mood for change, the voters probably would have approved a much poorer instrument. The vote for adoption in a remarkably quiet election was 136,606 to 56,652.

All in all, the constitution reflected public opinion quite accurately. Biennial sessions of the legislature, low salaries, no registration requirement for voters, precinct voting, abolition of the road tax, a homestead exemption clause, guarantees of a low tax rate, a more economical school system with schools under local control, a less expensive court system, and popular election of officers—all these were popular measures with Texans in 1876.

The constitution was a logical product of its era and a fairly adequate pattern for government for the period in which it was made. It was also an enduring fundamental law with many unfortunate features. One of the most notable features of the constitution was the deep distrust of government that it reflected. The resulting limitations that it placed on the powers of the legislature have necessitated many amendments to the original instrument, most of them giving the legislators additional power. The amendment process requires a two-thirds vote of each branch of the legislature at a regular session and approval by a majority vote of the electorate—effectively taking power from the hands of elected officials and placing it in the hands of the people. Although during the first half-century of the instrument few amendments were added, adoptions have come in an ever-increasing pace in recent times. Of 90 submitted up to September 1928, only 43 were adopted. Through 1999, however, 566 have been submitted, and of this number, 389 have been approved by the voters, an average of more than 3 per year since 1876.

Efforts over the years to completely revise or replace the constitution of 1876 have accomplished little. No provision was made in the document for calling another constitutional convention, and legal authorities have generally agreed that this can be done only by the approval of the voters after the question has been submitted to them by a vote of two-thirds of the members of both houses. At different times there has been considerable agitation for a new constitution, but when the question was submitted to the voters in 1919, only 9 percent of them were sufficiently interested to express an opinion, and in 1975 voters turned down an extensive revision prepared by the legislature.

THE POLITICS OF CONSERVATISM, 1874–90

For nearly a decade and a half following the adoption of the Constitution of 1876, politics were characterized by the same tone of conservatism that prevailed in the convention. Democrats, who won state and local elections with monotonous regularity, differed on various particulars, but most generally agreed that economic retrenchment was more necessary than aggressive reform. Political conflicts focused on the problems of the farmer, and elected officials concentrated on such matters as law enforcement, debt retirement, and disposal of public lands.

Although the composition of the state legislatures varied and the number of black representatives declined steadily as the years passed, the legislature elected in 1878 was fairly typical of this period. Business and professional men, mostly attorneys, accounted for sixty-four members, and forty-four were farmers or were involved in activities related to farming. More than 90 percent were native-born southerners, eleven were born in Texas, and at least half had served in the Confederate army. Blacks in the delegation numbered ten. Nine of the legislators were members of the Grange, and ten formerly had endorsed Whig policies. An overwhelming majority were Democrats, but there were nine Republicans and seven independents or members of the Greenback Party.

Throughout the period, the Republican Party, torn by factional quarrels even when in power, continued to decline and ceased to seriously challenge the Democrats. The party elected various local officials, a few state legislators, and occasionally even a congressman, but by and large it found little success at the ballot box. Republican politicians were most successful when they allied their party with agrarian reform groups, but usually they concentrated on establishing their power within the party to assure their control over federal patronage in Texas. Central to the conflict within the Republican Party was the intense disagreement over the role of blacks. African American voters comprised the core of popular support for the party, and consequently blacks expected a significant role in the party's leadership. White Republicans found black leadership and control unpalatable, if not totally unacceptable. Furthermore, since blacks never constituted a majority in Texas, Republicans needed to attract significant white support if they expected to win elections. This was unlikely if the party was perceived to be controlled by African Americans. Nevertheless, after the death of E. J. Davis in the mid-1880s, the most powerful figure in the party was Norris Wright Cuney, the black customs collector in Galveston and one of the most perspicacious politicians of his time.

Cuney's influence reflected the continued activities of blacks in politics. After regaining power, white Democrats avoided disfranchising blacks, feeling that the black vote could be controlled or outnumbered. But in fourteen counties located along the Gulf Coast and in East Texas, blacks constituted a majority of the population, and in thirteen others they amounted to nearly one-half. Thus, for a time black voters controlled several counties. Beginning with Harrison County in 1878 and followed subsequently by others, notably Fort Bend County in 1888, white Democrats used organization, intimidation, and other means, sometimes extralegal, to eliminate these local pockets of black power. But extensive curtailment of black suffrage through legislation was an early-twentieth-century phenomenon. Meanwhile, blacks participated in politics, often without effective strength but sometimes holding office. Primarily, they operated in the Republican Party, but they also formed a significant portion of the strength of the Greenback Party.

The Greenback Party, a threat more serious to Democratic suzerainty than the Republicans, was a voice of agrarian discontent calling for extensive reforms. It was particularly powerful in West Texas, settled recently by poor farmers who had remained poor and deeply in debt. Unlike the Grange, which usually operated within the Democratic Party, the Greenbackers formed their own party. Organized originally in the Midwest in 1874 to protest restoration of the gold standard, the Greenback Party wanted "more money and cheaper money." They supported an inflationary monetary system, based on paper money (greenbacks), that would cause farm prices to rise and make it easier to pay off debts. In Texas, Greenbackers also advocated an income tax, a better

Norris Wright Cuney. A native of Texas, he was educated in the north but returned to Texas where he became a federal official in Galveston and an able leader in the Republican party after the Civil War. (The Institute of Texas Cultures, San Antonio, Texas)

school system, reduction of the salaries of state officers, the elimination of waste in government, the regulation of railroads, and various other reforms.

Introduced into Texas in 1877, the party entered politics the following year, electing two senators and ten representatives to the legislature and indirectly assisting the election of a number of Republicans. Its strength declined somewhat in the election of 1880, but the Greenbackers gained new hope in 1882. In that year they joined Republicans in backing an independent candidate for governor and gave the Democrats their biggest fright of the decade. Efforts to perpetuate the independent coalition through the election of 1884 were only partially successful, and thereafter both the coalition and the Greenback Party faded from Texas politics.

Between 1875 and 1890 major state offices were controlled by a parade of conservative Democrats. Sam Bell Maxey, an "ultra-simon-pure-secession-anti-reconstruction Democrat," was elected to the U.S. Senate in 1874 and remained there until 1887. The Grange favorite, Governor Coke, was reelected in 1876, only to resign in December of that year to accept the other seat in the U.S. Senate, where he remained until 1895. When Lieutenant Governor Richard H. Hubbard, who succeeded Coke as governor, sought reelection on his own in 1878, he found a crowded field. Critics impugned Hubbard's integrity and wisdom, while James W. Throckmorton, who had served as governor in the early days of Reconstruction, and W. W. Lang, master of the state Grange, also vied for the nomination. A deadlocked convention brought about the selection of Texas Supreme Court Chief Justice Oran M. Roberts, an elderly ex-Confederate colonel known affectionately as the "Old Alcalde." Frugal and legalistic but strong-willed and aggressive, Roberts easily defeated W. H. Hamman, his Greenback opponent, an accomplishment he repeated in 1880, defeating both Hamman and E. J. Davis, the Republican nominee.

In 1882 Roberts refused suggestions that he accept a third term. The Democrats instead nominated Judge John Ireland. A native of Kentucky, ex-member of the Know-Nothing Party, and ex-Confederate colonel, Ireland was an intense and intelligent man of integrity, often called "Ox-Cart John" in tribute to his opposition to railroad land grants. His opponent, George W. ("Wash") Jones of Bastrop, was a delightful addition to Texas politics. Jones had been a Unionist but had served as a Confederate colonel during the war, and as Throckmorton's lieutenant governor in 1866–1867. In 1878 he was elected to Congress as an independent, and in 1880 he won reelection as a Greenbacker; on both occasions he had welcomed Republican support. In 1882 he ran for governor as an independent. If party regularity was not one of Jones's virtues, he was nonetheless widely respected for his honesty and engaging oratorical talent. He was awkward but kind, earnest but humorous, and shrewd but forthright. The rather colorless Ireland, who wisely declined to speak against him on the same platform after suffering through an early debate, won the gubernatorial election, but the contest was the closest of the decade. Ireland received 150,891 votes to Jones's 102,501. In a rematch in 1884, however, Jones's votes declined and Ireland's increased substantially.

Oran M. Roberts. He was a judge, secessionist leader, governor, and professor of law at the University of Texas where he was awarded the title "The Old Alcalde." (Archives Division—Texas State Library)

The practice of electing conservative governors continued through the end of the decade. With his campaign directed by railroad attorney George Clark, a shrewd and successful conservative political manager, Lawrence Sullivan Ross gained the nomination from a field of five candidates and easily won election in 1886. Agrarian discontent had increased significantly by 1888, but Ross, not a reactionary but certainly no reformer, again won by a margin of almost three to one, this time over Marion Martin, the candidate of an incipient farmers' protest movement.

A number of factors explain the ease with which conservative Democratic elements maintained their political domination. Challenge from outside the party was limited by the lingering memories of Reconstruction and Radical Republican government. To put it simply, most whites, rich or poor, were unwilling to vote for the "party of Reconstruction." Republican factionalism and the visible role of blacks in the party of Lincoln, as well as the ability of Democrats to tap into agrarian discontent by supporting some of the more moderate agrarian reform programs, reinforced Democratic domination. Radical insurgence within the Democratic Party was controlled by the nominating process. Candidates generally were chosen by conventions, where the entrenched political establishment easily controlled the outcome.

Primary elections did not become widespread until near the end of the century. Finally, conservative policies, such as promotion of railroads, frugal expenditures, and low taxes, were attractive to most Texans, even those who wanted more extensive reforms, such as railroad regulation and augmented state services.

PUBLIC POVERTY, PUBLIC DEBT

Poverty-stricken public finances constantly plagued the government of Texas during the decade following the adoption of the Constitution of 1876. When Coke entered office in January 1874, the state debt was $3,167,335. The

Four Texas Governors. The four nineteenth century Texas Governors, Francis Richard Lubbock (1861–1863), Oran Milo Roberts (1879–1883), Lawrence Sullivan Ross (1887–1891), and James Stephen Hogg (1891–1895) were posed for this photograph either during or immediately following Hogg's second term of office. (Texas State Library & Archives Commission).

receipts for that year did not cover half of the state's expenditures. Industry and commerce, not yet recovered from the Civil War and Reconstruction, were prostrated by the Panic of 1873. Taxes already seemed too burdensome. No new sources of revenue were available, and it seemed that the only way to balance the budget was to reduce government spending.

With the cooperation of the legislatures, Governors Coke and Hubbard struggled to reduce expenditures, but their efforts were offset by increased demands on the treasury—funds for buildings for the new agricultural and mechanical college, pensions for veterans of the Texan Revolution, frontier defense, and interest charges. The treasury did not operate on a cash basis until the spring of 1879, by which time the state's indebtedness had increased to approximately $5.5 million.

When he took office in 1879, Governor O. M. Roberts insisted that the legislature balance the state's budget at any cost, and he outlined a plan for achieving this. He proposed to refinance state bonds at lower interest rates, reduce the outlay for veterans' pensions, make the penitentiaries self-supporting, and, most extreme of all, lower the appropriation for public schools. To increase income he suggested a better system of tax assessment and collection, and to hasten the payment of the public debt, he favored sale of the unappropriated public lands to any person in any quantity desired. For his own part, he discontinued the payment of rewards for the arrest of criminals and followed a liberal policy for reprieves and pardons to relieve prison overcrowding.

The legislature responded to many of Governor Roberts's suggestions. It adopted a law offering for sale in any quantity the public domain at 50 cents an acre, one-half the receipts to go to the permanent school fund and the remainder to be applied to the public debt. It passed laws to improve the collection of taxes, to provide fees for government services, and to broaden and increase occupation taxes. To reduce expenditures, it substantially lowered the appropriation for the maintenance of the state frontier force. The legislators exceeded the governor's wishes by discontinuing pensions altogether and substituting instead the grant of one section of land to each indigent veteran.

To complete his program of economy, Governor Roberts resorted to the veto. When lawmakers failed to lower the appropriations for the public schools from one-fourth to one-fifth of the general revenue as he had recommended, the governor vetoed the school item. Sharp criticism was hurled at him, but he stood firm. At a special session in June 1879, the legislature reenacted the measure fixing the school appropriation at one-sixth of the general revenue. In 1881, during Roberts's second term, it raised the school appropriation to one-fourth of the general revenue but lowered the tax rate.

At the end of his administration, the Old Alcalde could report with pride that the public debt had been reduced by more than $1 million, that annual interest expenditures had been cut by one-third, and that there was a liberal operating surplus in the treasury. Probably he found the greatest satisfaction of all in the fact that the ad valorem tax rate had been reduced by 40 percent. The achievement was made at considerable cost. Public lands were disappearing into the hands of speculators, and state services, particularly education, were operating at a minimal level.

John Ireland, who took the oath of office as governor in January 1883, differed from his predecessor in several important matters. He opposed the rapid sale of public lands and favored reserving them to meet the needs of settlers in future years. He opposed the state's purchasing its own bonds at high prices to hasten the retirement of the debt, he urged stricter enforcement of the criminal laws, and he promised to follow a less liberal pardoning policy. In the matter of economy, however, he supported the Roberts program. The voters themselves in 1883 broke the spell of public parsimony by approving a constitutional amendment authorizing special state and local school taxes, but the legislature continued to provide funds only with great reluctance. For example, in 1883 and in 1885, it denied appropriations for the maintenance of the University of Texas.

State finances improved substantially during the 1880s, due in part to rigorous and frugal public policies and in part to the improving national and state economy. The prosperity that began in the mid 1870s led to an increase in wealth and economic expansion. Texas wealth increased 200 percent between 1875 and 1890. This growth had a positive impact on tax receipts.

Notwithstanding the frugality of the times, slow but visible improvement was made in the physical plant of the state's institutions. The first hospital for the insane had been built in Austin in 1856, and a sister institution was completed in Terrell in 1885. In 1887, the state established an orphan's home in Corsicana and founded a school for deaf and blind black children in Austin. The crowning achievement of the building program was the capitol in Austin, authorized in 1879 and completed in 1888. For this imposing structure of Texas granite, the state exchanged the 3,050,000 acres of land located in the Panhandle that became the famous XIT ranch.

LAW AND ORDER

The greatest accomplishment of state government during this period was the victory for law and order. Except in the extreme western part of the state, Indian depredations did not constitute a serious problem after 1875, but there were many other problems. Mexico was in a state of war and confusion, and border troubles were plentiful. Juan Cortina, a folk hero in the eyes of some people but a ruthless murderer in the eyes of others, continued to cause unrest along the lower Rio Grande. The criminal and lawless elements had become so powerful that they did not yield

The Texas state capitol in Austin, constructed between 1883 and 1888 of native granite and financed by an appropriation of 3,050,000 acres of public domain land. It is an example of classic architectural style. (Archives Division—Texas State Library)

readily to the authority of the new government, especially along the western frontier.

Often the spirit of rowdyism and the yearning to establish a reputation as a "tough" turned young men into criminals. Thus, certain frontier characters would occasionally "take a town" just to see its inhabitants "hunt cover." More desperate and generally more dangerous was the professional criminal. During the 1870s and 1880s, the far-flung ranch headquarters and isolated cow camps afforded concealment and a measure of protection for numbers of renegades and desperadoes. In 1876, the adjutant general compiled a list of 3,000 fugitives from justice and noted that additional names were arriving in every mail. In his message to the legislature in 1879 Governor Roberts stated that there was "an amount and character of crime and civil wrong entirely unprecedented in this country."

Horse theft, cattle rustling, and stage robbery were the most common crimes. The editor of the Jacksboro *Frontier Echo* estimated that there had been 100,000 horses stolen in the state during the three years preceding March 8, 1878, that 750 men were regularly engaged in the business, and that not more than 1 in 10 was ever caught and brought to justice. The Northwest Texas Stock Association (which later became the Texas and Southwestern Cattle Raisers' Association), organized in Graham in 1877, worked diligently to suppress crime, but for several years the results were discouraging. Men of wealth and influence were doing a considerable part of the stealing. Stage robbery also became epidemic between 1876 and 1883.

Feuds presented defenders of law and order with one of their most perplexing problems. For instance, in the spring of 1874 feudists in DeWitt County defied local officers and made it impossible to convict their friends in court. A bitter feud took place in Mason County in 1875 between the Germans and the Anglo-Americans. Meanwhile, the Horrell and Higgins feud of nearby Lampasas County, which had begun in 1873, grew in intensity. During the chronic quarrel, each side committed murders, and the clans were so powerful that local peace officers and even the local courts were helpless to deal with them.

To cope with lawlessness, vigilantes, more or less formally organized, were found in almost every community. Such a group at Denison seems to have been quite active; the Hill County vigilantes warned thieves in open letters; and during one week at Fort Griffin in 1878 vigilantes were credited with shooting one man in his jail cell, hanging another, and being responsible for the disappearance of a third.

During this period the Texas Rangers were the most effective state law enforcement agency in the war on crime. From the Gulf to the Panhandle they terrified evildoers and brought a sense of security to those who obeyed the law. Captain L. H. McNelly and his Rangers at least made it possible to hold court in the DeWitt County feuds. Major John B. Jones restored order in the Mason County dispute, though he could not remove the cause of the trouble. In Lampasas County he arrested the leaders of that feud and persuaded them to enter into a peace covenant that temporarily preserved law and order. When Kimble County became notorious as "the worst section of the country there is for men to work in and a better hiding place for rascals than any other part of Texas," the Rangers entered the county and arrested forty-one men. In 1879, Captain George W. Arrington, a Ranger, was sent with a force to the Panhandle, where, working with another great foe of cattle thieves, Charles Goodnight, he played a leading part in bringing first order and then law to the High Plains.

The Rangers were indeed effective, but not everyone held them in high esteem. In South Texas some of the Rangers who rode with great skill and dedication were Mexican-Americans, but many other Mexican-Americans complained about instances where the organization abused and mistreated their people.

Improvement in law enforcement was not left altogether to the peace officers. Court procedure was also made more effective. A law of 1876 made it more difficult for the defense in criminal cases to stack the jury with men who were incompetent, venal, or biased. The number of district attorneys was substantially increased in 1879. When cases continued to stack up in the appellate courts, the legislature in 1879 provided for appointed commissioners of appeals to assist the supreme court and court of appeals by deciding certain civil cases in order to clear the way for criminal matters. This plan was continued until 1892, when a system of courts of civil appeals was devised. In many respects, the courts represented the end of a frontier society and the transition to civilized communities where the violence of an earlier day was not tolerated.

THE PUBLIC LANDS

If the establishment of law and order was the state government's greatest accomplishment during this period, the formulation of a public land policy may very well have been one of its least satisfactory achievements. In 1876, the state still retained a public domain of 61,258,461 acres. Distribution of these lands brought conflict and confusion, provoked charges of fraud and favoritism, and promoted speculation. In 1881, state officials discovered that railroad land grant commitments exceeded land available for that purpose by 8 million acres. Meanwhile, state policies on the sale of school and otherwise unappropriated lands produced a political, if not necessarily an economic, crisis.

Governor Roberts bore primary responsibility for the crisis. To help defray the cost of public education and to pay the state debts, he persuaded the legislature to pass the so-called Fifty-Cent Law, whereby unappropriated lands could be purchased in any quantity by anyone for 50 cents an acre. Separate laws provided for sale of school lands at prices of $1 and $2 per acre in amounts of up to seven sections per purchaser.

Critics of these land laws declared that they were an open invitation to speculation and fraud and that the heritage of the people was being wasted for an absurdly small return. Corporations and syndicates, they warned, would soon own most of the western area of the state. The control of vast tracts of land by investors and speculators would retard the settlement of the west. In response to these charges, the Ireland administration enacted legislation in 1883 that established a land board to investigate frauds and terminated the sale of large blocks of land. The law provided for sale by auction with minimum prices set at $2 and $3 per acre, and it offered liberal credit terms to bona fide settlers.

Supporters of Roberts's land policy argued that the sale of land was in the best interest of the state. Roberts himself maintained that it was far better to place land in private hands, where it would be put to productive use and generate taxes, than to have it remain under the control of the government. Actually, the damage done by the notorious Fifty-Cent Law was largely indirect. Less than 2 million acres of land actually was sold under its provisions. On the other hand, the law depressed land prices to almost giveaway levels, sometimes as little as 15 cents per acre, and produced less than $1 million in revenue.

Modification of the Roberts administration's land policies did not eliminate problems with the public domain. Fence cutting and the leasing of public lands caused trouble throughout the decade. The state land board was abolished in 1887, and the entire responsibility of administering the public lands was placed on the commissioner of the General Land Office. In an effort to prevent speculation, each purchaser of agricultural land was required to swear that he desired to "purchase the land for a home" and reside on the land at least six months each year for a period of three years before the state would pass title to him. These provisions, according to the 1908 statement of the commissioner of the General Land Office, engendered "untold perjury." In western counties the number of sales greatly exceeded the number of settlers. The greater part of the land went into the ownership of the ranchers, whose use of the land necessarily slowed down population growth.

If, in a frontier society, acquisition of a population is of highest priority, and if, in depressed circumstances, reasonable revenue from the disposal of the public domain is a logical objective, Texas public land policy between 1876 and 1890 failed to measure up on either count. The failure is particularly strange, considering the preoccupation of the government with fiscal prudence and the dominance of farmers in the population.

BUILDING THE RAILROADS

Railroad development in Texas began before the Civil War. There was considerable activity in the years immediately after the war, but interest in railroad construction reached new heights and intensity in the 1870s and 1880s. To Texans of the late nineteenth century, the railroads symbolized progress and prosperity. Farmers and townspeople alike recognized the necessity of a cheap, fast, and dependable means of transportation so that they could market their products. The railroads provided this transportation. Without the market afforded by the rails, there would have been little point in mining coal at Thurber or in raising cotton at Sweetwater. Wagon freight rates averaged $1 per 100 pounds per 100 miles. With cotton bringing about $35 a bale in 1876, wagon freight from North Central Texas to Galveston would have absorbed more than half the value of the crop. After 1879, rail freight rates, though often discriminatory, were never more than 50 cents per 100 pounds per 100 miles and declined more or less consistently from that figure.

Thus, Texans understandably courted the builders of the roads. Citizens of Brenham, for example, were agreeable to a railroad's demand for a right of way through the county and $150,000 in cash. For a time Fort Worth granted bonuses to all railroads building into the city. For the communities already built, the railroad meant population and profit. When the railroad bypassed a community, the town in almost all cases was doomed to a certain and often swift death.

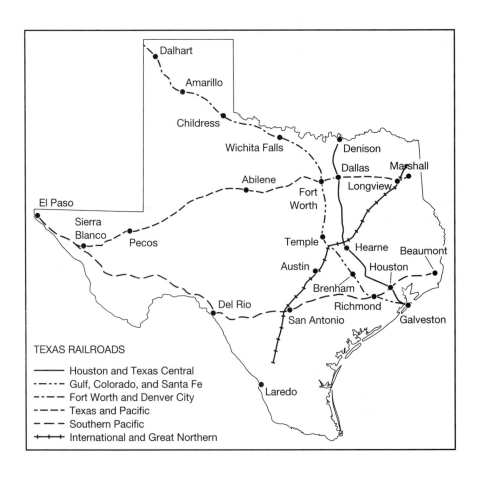

TEXAS RAILROADS

——————— Houston and Texas Central
· — · · · — Gulf, Colorado, and Santa Fe
· — · — Fort Worth and Denver City
· — — — Texas and Pacific
— — — Southern Pacific
+—+—+ International and Great Northern

In addition to the enticements offered by local communities on their own authority, a number of state laws made local and state support available for railroad construction. Under the terms of an 1871 state law cities and counties used public resources amounting to more than $2 million to subsidize the cost of railroad building. In 1856, a state law authorized lending school funds to railroads in amounts up to $6,000 per mile; under this law nearly $2 million was lent to the railroads. During Reconstruction, from 1869 through 1871, the legislature voted bonds to support railroad construction, but most of these obligations were later paid in land. In fact, by far the greatest bounty to the railroads came from the public lands. From 1854 until 1882, except for the period from 1869 to 1873, when it was prohibited by the Constitution of 1869, Texas maintained a policy of liberal land grants. In most cases the state provided sixteen sections of land for each mile of track constructed. About forty-one railroad companies received state land before the repeal of the land-grant act in 1882. The greatest single beneficiary was the Texas and Pacific, which was given 5,167,360 acres. Approximately 32,150,000 acres, an area as large as the state of Alabama, was granted to the railroads.

The wisdom of such generous land grants was questionable. Critics contended that the aid was more generous than necessary, that it caused the building of some lines that were not needed, and that in many instances the land grants actually retarded the development of the country. On the other hand, most of the railroads never received any real benefits from their lands. In many instances the lands could not easily be converted into cash, the companies were forced into receivership, and the land was sold at a few cents an acre. Furthermore, the railroads, with all that land, were the major colonizers of the West.

Construction of the bulk of the state's railroads was accomplished in the span of two decades. Only eleven short railroad lines, with less than 500 miles, existed in Texas before the Civil War. Most of these lines radiated from Houston. The debacle of Civil War brought an end to railroad building, and only one line, the Houston and Texas Central, made any progress before the state was readmitted to the Union in 1870. The pace of construction varied in the next two decades, depending primarily on the general prosperity of the state and the availability of subsidies, but by the close of 1890 the state had 8,710 miles of railroads.

Railroads transformed the state. The Gulf Coast was connected to northern markets, as the Houston and Texas Central built northward through Dallas, while the Missouri, Kansas, and Texas (the Katy) built southward through Indian Territory. Citizens of Dallas hailed the coming of the rails with a buffalo meat barbecue, and a few months later the two roads met in 1872 in a cornfield, where Denison now stands. By the early 1880s the International and Great Northern Railway provided service from Longview in East Texas, through Austin and San Antonio, and to Laredo on the Rio Grande, where connections were made with Mexican lines. About the same time, leaders of Galveston, frustrated by yellow fever quarantines imposed almost annually by Houston, built around their neighbor to the north, going by way of Richmond toward Fort Worth. By the mid-1880s this railroad was a part of the Atchison, Topeka, and Santa Fe, with connections going in a number of directions.

Two transcontinental roads of particular importance to West Texas were constructed in the 1880s. The Galveston, Harrisburg, and San Antonio reached San Antonio in 1877, and six years later connected with the Southern Pacific, which was being built eastward from El Paso. These railroads merged and with others formed the Southern Pacific system. The Texas and Pacific Railway, organized in 1872 with construction beginning at Longview, reached Fort Worth in 1876. Westward construction resumed in 1880, and two years later the westbound Texas and Pacific met the eastbound Southern Pacific at Sierra Blanca. Here C. P. Huntington of the Southern Pacific and Jay Gould of the Texas and Pacific negotiated their famous agreement. The two roads publicly agreed to share the lines from Sierra Blanca to El Paso. Secretly they agreed to distribution of traffic and pool of receipts between designated lines of the two systems and promised that neither company would build lines to compete with the other.

Railroad service for northwest Texas and the Panhandle came with the building of the Fort Worth and Denver City line. Built to Wichita Falls in 1882, the road was extended through Amarillo to Texline in 1888. In 1893 it became a part of the Burlington system.

ECONOMIC DEVELOPMENT

In several respects, the economy of Texas changed significantly in the years after the end of the Civil War. In part, the change was a matter of growth, made possible by the building of railroads, population expansion, and new technology. In some respects, however, the changes represented fundamental alterations in the ways the people of Texas earned their living and lived their lives. Agriculture became more of a business enterprise, industry developed, and workers began to organize to protect their interests.

The change in the nature of agriculture in Texas was significant, even revolutionary. In earlier times, a large part of the population was made up of subsistence farmers who lived off the products of their land, sold little at market, and relied only to a limited extent on a cash economy. By the 1870s, there was an apparent trend away from such self-sufficiency toward commercialization, wherein the farmer produced for the marketplace and in turn purchased many of his necessities. Although Texans produced a variety of crops for market, cotton dominated the emerging commercial agricultural economy. In the late nineteenth century, the average male Texan was more familiar with the cotton sack and hoe than with the lariat rope and branding iron—he was a farmer, not a rancher. By 1880, farmers on slightly less than 2.5 million acres produced a cotton crop valued at about $57 million.

Cotton production expanded in the face of innumerable problems and persistent opposition. The vagaries of nature—worms, boll weevils, Johnson grass, root rot, dry weather, wet weather—were enough to try the patience and test the will of the most determined farmer. Moreover, critics repeatedly questioned the farmer's intelligence. Farm organizations, editors, agricultural colleagues, and self-appointed advisers persistently condemned specialization in general and cotton farming in particular. Diversification—in essence a return to the self-sustaining farm—would ease the burden of the farmer. The cotton farmer paid them no heed.

Although some critics argued that ignorance accounted for the cotton farmer's stubborn refusal to restrict his acreage, the reasons were actually more complex and convincing. Prices declined steadily between the 1870s and 1890s, but cotton almost always returned more income per acre than other crops suited to the farmer's labor, land, and machinery resources. Cotton was the most dependable of the southern crops, and contrary to popular opinion, it did not exhaust the soil as quickly as many other crops. Furthermore, the machinery for marketing cotton was more advanced than that for other commodities.

Few farmers, whether they raised cotton or other products, found the marketplace and commercial farming an avenue to substantial wealth. Returns fluctuated unpredictably from one year to the next, and prices, costs, mortgages, and weather frequently combined to leave the farmer looking anxiously to the "next year" rather than rejoicing in the present one. Theoretically an avenue to a higher standard of living, commercial agriculture often led to a relentless cycle of debt and worry.

While Texas farmers turned from subsistence farming to commercial farming, other Texans turned to industry. Although Texas possessed vast natural resources, industry in 1870 was still confined primarily to small shops that seldom supplied a market beyond the immediate community. Industrial workers made up less than 1 percent of the population. During the next several decades, however, the pace of industrialization quickened, mostly in the areas of manufacturing related to agriculture and exploitation of basic natural resources.

Processing agricultural products was one of the major businesses in the late nineteenth century. Into the 1880s, flour milling was the leading industry, ranking ahead of lumbering. Meanwhile, the manufacture of products from cottonseed steadily increased in importance, ranking second in the state's industrial economy in 1900. Meat packing, which began at Victoria in 1868, was soon extended to other communities, and a number of small plants added to the output. The first small packing plant was built in Fort Worth in 1884. Six years later, the Fort Worth stockyards were opened, and the packing business in that city expanded rapidly. Textile manufacturing began before the Civil War when a frontier businessman set up a cotton mill in New Braunfels. A plant manufacturing cotton goods was operated in the penitentiary for a number of years during and after the Civil War. Later, plants were established in Dallas, Sherman, and Post, but they remained comparatively unimportant. In Sealy a manufacturer used locally grown cotton to produce mattresses.

One of the early Texas industries was the production of lumber. With more than 20 million acres of timberland to supply them, pioneers soon started their sawmills turning. Peter Ellis Bean had a sawmill near Nacogdoches in 1829, and there were several in Texas by 1834. With the coming of the railroads after the Civil War, the lumber business attained huge proportions and by the end of the century was the largest industry in the state. By 1900, Orange and Beaumont had become important sawmill centers. The production from Texas mills passed the billion-board-foot total in 1899, and in 1900 the mills of Orange alone were cutting 700,000 feet of lumber a day.

After 1880, mining operations contributed to the industrial economy. Coal deposits existed in many regions of the state, but commercial mining was concentrated in Palo Pinto and Erath counties. Oil, the key to the Texas industrial economy in the twentieth century, was not of great significance until after 1900. In 1865 near the town of Saratoga, Edward von Hartin drilled for oil, only to drill the first dry hole in Texas, not the first oil well. A year later Lyne T. Barret completed the first Texas oil well at Oil Springs, a few miles east of Nacogdoches. By 1890 Oil Springs had forty shallow wells, a crude refinery, and a pipeline, but another decade would pass before Texas would truly enter the oil age.

Although industrialization proceeded relatively slowly in Texas during these years, some workers in Texas began to look to unity as a means of protecting and advancing their interests. Sometimes organizations such as the Screwman's Benevolent Association of Galveston, formed originally as a workers' insurance group, evolved into labor unions seeking shorter hours, higher wages, and more control of the working conditions. Often these early "workingmen's associations" focused their efforts on protecting the interests and jobs of their members from competition by unskilled, often African American workers. By the 1870s, railroad brotherhoods in the state were organizing, and there were scattered militant groups found in a few other industries. Until the mid-1870s general public sentiment toward labor unions was either neutral or perhaps even sympathetic. However, confronted with inconvenient and sometimes violent railroad strikes during the 1870s, public opinion turned antilabor.

In the 1880s, the Knights of Labor, a national organization, became an industrial and a political force of consequence. Claiming 300 locals and 30,000 members in the state, the Knights opened their membership to farmers and allowed blacks to join, usually in segregated locals. The Knights probably organized the highest percentage of nonfarm laborers ever brought into unions in Texas, perhaps at its peak amounting to 50 percent of the nonfarm workers.

Although officially opposing the use of the strike, the Knights resorted to it on several occasions in Texas. When a shop foreman on Jay Gould's Texas and Pacific Railway was fired, the Knights called a strike and about 9,000 men walked off the job. In what was soon known as the Great Southwest Strike of 1886, the conflict between Gould and the Knights developed into open violence. After a bloody clash in Fort Worth over the movement of a freight train, Governor Ireland ordered the state militia and rangers to the area and suppressed the disturbance. Meanwhile, Gould's control over the Texas and Pacific had passed into the hands of a federal receiver, and the strike was ruled in contempt of court. Failure of the Great Southwest strike, violence elsewhere in the nation, and poor management brought a rapid decline in the Knights of Labor in the late 1880s. New organizations would take its place, but labor unions would not again play a significant role in Texas until after the turn of the century.

BIBLIOGRAPHY

For a reliable and comprehensive study of politics of this period, see Alwyn Barr, *Reconstruction to Reform: Texas Politics, 1876–1906* (Austin, 1971). See also Ernest W. Winkler, *Platforms of Political Parties in Texas* (Austin, 1916); Francis R. Lubbock, *Six Decades over Texas* (Austin, 1900); Ernest Wallace, *Charles DeMorse* (Lubbock, 1943); Paul Casdorph, *A History of the Republican Party in Texas, 1865–1965* (Austin, 1985); Ben H. Procter, *Not without Honor, the Life of John H. Reagan* (Austin, 1982); Billy Mac Jones, *The Search for Maturity* (Austin, 1965); Louise Horton, *Samuel Bell Maxey: A Biography* (Austin, 1974); and Judith Ann Benner, *Sul Ross: Soldier, Statesman, Educator* (College Station, 1983).

Seth Shepard McKay published several early works on the Constitution of 1876. He wrote *Making the Constitution of 1876* (Philadelphia, 1924); he brought together and edited newspaper accounts of the convention as *Debates of the Texas Constitutional Convention of 1875* (Austin, 1930); and he wrote *Seven Decades of the Texas Constitution* (Lubbock, 1943). See also his "Some Attitudes of West Texas Delegates in the Constitutional Convention of 1875," *West Texas Historical Association Year Book*, V, 100–106. For other studies, see Ernest Wallace, *Texas in Turmoil* (Austin, 1965); S. D. Myers, Jr., "Mysticism, Realism, and the Texas Constitution of 1876," *Southwestern Political and Social Science Quarterly*, IX, 166–184; Ralph Smith, "The Grange Movement in Texas, 1873–1900," *Southwestern Historical Quarterly*, XLII, 297–315; J. E. Ericson, "Delegates to the Texas Constitutional Convention of 1875: A Reappraisal," ibid., LXVII, 20–27; and Oscar Walter Roberts, "Richard Coke on Constitution-Making," ibid., LXVIII, 69–75. The constitution with amendments is published and indexed biennially in the *Texas Almanac*.

There are a number of studies that deal with the role of blacks in politics. See the comprehensive work of Lawrence D. Rice, *The Negro in Texas, 1874–1900* (Baton Rouge, 1971). See also Paul Casdorph, "Norris Wright Cuney and Texas Republican Politics, 1883–1896," *Southwestern Historical Quarterly*, LXVII, 455–464; Fred Arthur Bailey, "Free Speech and the 'Lost Cause' in Texas: A Study of Social Control in the

New South," ibid., 453–477; Merlin Pitre, *Through Many Dangers, Toils and Snares: The Black Leadership of Texas, 1868–1900* (Austin, 1985); Barry Crouch, "Hesitant Recognition: Texas Black Politicians, 1865–1900," *East Texas Historical Journal*, XXXI, 41–58; Donald Nieman, "Black Political Power and Criminal Justice: Washington County as a Case Study, 1868–1884," *Journal of Southern History*, LV, 321–420; Randall Woods, "George T. Ruby: A Black Militant in the White Business Community," *Red River Historical Review*, I, 269–280; and Maud Hare, *Norris Wright Cuney: A Tribune of the Black People* (New York, 1913; reprint, Austin, 1968).

Several recent studies have focused on Mexican-Americans in late-nineteenth-century Texas. These include Armando C. Alonzo, *Tejano Legacy: Rancheros and Settlers in South Texas, 1734-1900* (Albuquerque, 1998), and Kenneth L. Stewart and Arnoldo De León, *Not Room Enough: Mexicans, Anglos, and Socioeconomic Change in Texas, 1850–1900* (Albuquerque, 1993). Other studies include Mario T. Garcia, *Desert Immigrants: The Mexicans of El Paso, 1880–1920* (New Haven, 1981); David Montejano, *Anglos and Mexicans in the Making of Texas* (Austin, 1987); Arnoldo De León, *They Called Them Greasers: Anglo Attitudes Toward Mexicans in Texas, 1821–1900*, (Austin, 1983); and Arnoldo De León, *The Tejano Community, 1836–1900* (Albuquerque, 1982), and *In Re Ricardo Rodrìquez: An Attempt at Chicano Disfranchisment in San Antonio, 1896–1897* (San Antonio, 1979). Also see Mary Romero, "The El Paso Salt War: Mob Action or Political Struggle?" *Aztlán*, XVI, 119–143, and the excellent work of Evan Anders, *Boss Rule in South Texas: The Progressive Era* (Austin, 1982), which contains some material on this era.

On state finances, the best sources are E. T. Miller, *Financial History of Texas*; Aldon S. Lang, *Financial History of the Public Lands in Texas* (New York, 1979); Reuben McKitrick, *The Public Land System of Texas, 1823–1910* (Madison, WI, 1918); and "Memories of a Land Commissioner, W. C. Walsh," *Southwestern Historical Quarterly*, XLIV, 481–497. Also see Thomas L. Miller, *The Public Lands of Texas, 1519–1970* (Norman, Okla., 1972).

Much literature deals with lawlessness in Texas. Some examples are W. C. Holden, "Law and Lawlessness on the Texas Frontier, 1875 and 1890," *Southwestern Historical Quarterly*, XLIV, 188–203; W. Gard, *Frontier Justice* (Norman, Okla., 1949); C. L. Sonnichsen, *I'll Die Before I'll Run* (New York, 1961); and Jack Martin, *Border Boss: Captain John R. Hughes* (San Antonio, 1942).

For a general study of economic affairs in Texas between 1875 and 1900, see John Stricklin Spratt, *The Road to Spindletop: Economic Change in Texas, 1875–1901* (Austin,1955). Other general works of value are Ralph Steen, *Twentieth Century Texas: An Economic and Social History* (Austin, 1942), and Billy Mac Jones, *The Search for Maturity* (Austin, 1965). Also see Ralph A. Wooster, "Wealthy Texans, 1870," *Southwestern Historical Quarterly*, LXXIV, 24–35. The *Texas Almanac* is rich in economic information.

The two standard studies on railroads are S. G. Reed, *A History of Texas Railroads* (Houston, 1941); and Charles S. Potts, *Railroad Transportation in Texas* (Austin, 1909). See also Ira G. Clark, *Then Came the Railroads* (Norman, 1958); Vera L. Dugas, "A Duel with Railroads: Houston vs. Galveston, 1866–1881," *East Texas Historical Journal*, II, 118–127; William S. Osborn, "A History of the Cane Belt Branch of the Gulf, Colorado & Santa Fe Railway Company," *Southwestern Historical Quarterly*, 302–319; Donald Everett, "San Antonio Welcomes the 'Sunset'—1877," *Southwestern Historical Quarterly*, LXV, 47–60; and Ralph Traxler, Jr., "The Texas and Pacific Railroad Land Grants," ibid., 357–370; Maury Klein, *The Life and Legend of Jay Gould* (Baltimore, 1986); and Keith Bryant, *History of the Atcheson, Topeka, and Santa Fe Railway* (New York, 1974). A recent study of the link between urbanization and railroad development is Earle B. Young, *Tracks to the Sea: Galveston and Western Railroad Development, 1866–1900* (College Station, 1999). A valuable description of the political intrigue on behalf of railroad construction on the eve of the period is John M. Brockman, "Railroads, Radicals, and the Militia Bill: A New Interpretation of the Quorum–Breaking Incident of 1870," previously cited. Also see William D. Angel, Jr., "Vantage on the Bay: Galveston and the Railroads," *East Texas Historical Journal*, XXII, 3–18, for a good summary of early railroad building.

The evolution of a commercial economy in agriculture and industry is emphasized in J. Spratt, *The Road to Spindletop*, cited above. An original approach to the commercialization of cotton production and the impact of this development on the agricultural labor force can be found in Neil Foley's *The White Scourge: Mexicans, Blacks and Poor Whites in Texas Cotton Culture* (Berkeley, 1997). Other works include B. P. Gallaway, "Population Trends in the Western Cross Timbers of Texas, 1890–1960: Economic Change and Social Balance," *Southwestern Historical Quarterly*, LXVII, 376–396; L. Tuffly Ellis, "The Revolutionizing of the Texas Cotton Trade, 1865–1885," ibid., LXXIII, 478–508; Robert A. Calvert, "Nineteenth Century Farmers, Cotton and Prosperity," ibid., LXXIII, 509–521; and Henry C. Dethloff, "Rice Revolution in the Southwest, 1880–1910," *Arkansas Historical Quarterly*, XXIX, 66–75.

For additional information on industry, see Vera Lee Dugas, "Texas Industry, 1860–1880," *Southwestern Historical Quarterly*, LIX, 151–183; Edwin L. Caldwell, "Highlights of the Development of Manufacturing in Texas, 1900–1960," ibid., LXVIII, 405–431; Dwight F. Henderson, "The Texas Coal Mining Industry," ibid., LXVIII, 207–219; Robert S. Maxwell, "The Pines of Texas: A Study in Lumbering and Public Policy, 1880–1930," *East Texas Historical Journal*, II, 77–86; William R. Johnson, *A Short History of the Sugar Industry in Texas* (Houston, 1961); Mary Lasswell, *John Henry Kirby: Prince of the Pines* (Austin, 1967); Robert S. Maxwell, "The First Bag Mill: The Beginnings of Commercial Lumbering in Texas," *Southwestern Historical Quarterly*, LXXXVI, 1–30; and John S. Spratt, Jr., *Thurber, Texas: The Life and Death of a Company Coal Town* (Austin, 1986).

Published materials on organized labor are scarce but are becoming more available. Pioneering studies were made by Ruth A. Allen, who published *Chapters in the History of Organized Labor in Texas* (Austin, 1941); *The Great Southwest Strike* (Austin, 1942); and *East Texas Lumbering Workers, An Economic and Social Picture, 1870–1950* (Austin, 1961). Dealing primarily with an earlier period but useful for later years is James V. Reese, "The Early History of Labor Organization in Texas, 1838–1876," *Southwestern Historical Quarterly*, LXXII, 1–20; more appropriate to this era is his "The Evolution of an Early Texas Union: The Screwmen's Benevolent Association of Galveston, 1866–1891," ibid., LXXV, 158–185. Recent studies include those of Marilyn D. Rhinehart, *A Way of Work and A Way of Life: Coal Mining in Thurber, Texas, 1888–1926* (College Station, 1992); Roberto R. Calderón, *Mexican Coal Mining Labor in Texas and Coahuila, 1880–1930* (College Station, 2000); " 'Underground Patriots': Thurber Coal Miners and the Struggle for Individual Freedom, 1888–1903," *Southwestern Historical Quarterly*, XCII, 509–542; and Majory Harper, "Emigrant Strikebreakers: Scottish Granite Cutters and the Texas Capitol Boycott," ibid., XCV, 465–486.

13

The Conquest and Settlement of the Frontier

In 1860 the frontier, except for some settlements along the Rio Grande near Presidio and El Paso, extended along a line from Henrietta southward through Brownwood, Kerrville, and Uvalde to Brackettville. During the Civil War there was no further advance. Indeed, in many areas Indian raids pushed the line many miles back to the east. By 1890, however, there was no true frontier line. At the end of the century, western Texas was the home of 500,000 people, and by the middle of the twentieth century, it contained about one-third of the population of the state.

Stages in the westward movement included the conquest and removal of the Indians, the expansion of the open-range cattle industry, the conversion of the open ranges into big pastures, the advance of the subsistence farmers, the development of commercial farming, and the growth of industry. The latter two, dependent upon transportation, had to await the building of transportation systems to get their products to distant markets. Meanwhile, the stubborn contest between Texans and the Indians for possession of the land and the short interlude before the arrival of the railroads, when cattlemen dominated the newly won empire of grass, constitute a colorful and significant segment in the history of Texas and the American West.

THE DEFEAT OF THE INDIANS

For several months after the collapse of the Confederacy, settlers in West Texas were without protection. The Indians, aware of the opportunity, took full advantage and pushed the line of settlements eastward. The country west of a line drawn from Gainesville to Fredericksburg was abandoned by all but a few of the most daring settlers, who moved into stockades. The worst raids were made on moonlit nights, and the soft summer moon became a harbinger of death. Charred rock chimneys stood guard like weird sentries, symbolizing the blasted hopes of pioneers and often marking their nearby graves. A Waco newspaper in April 1866 claimed that not more than one-fifth of the ranches in its vicinity were still occupied. Later that year a large group of citizens in a mass meeting in Denton resolved to abandon their homes unless help arrived before November. Incomplete reports from county judges covering the period from May 1865 to July 1867 showed that 163 persons had been killed by Indians, forty-three carried away into captivity, and twenty-four wounded. These figures did not include Wise and Young counties, whose combined population declined from 3,752 in 1860 to 1,585 in 1870.

Reconstruction military authorities in the fall of 1866 rejected efforts to organize a ranger force to protect the settlers, but a portion of the 4,000 federal troops in Texas were stationed on the frontier. In September a cavalry detachment was sent to Fredericksburg, and by the end of the year federal troops had reoccupied Fort Mason, Fort Duncan, Fort Inge, Fort Clark, and Camp Verde to provide protection against Apaches and other bands from Mexico. Within another year the line of frontier forts ran from Fort Richardson (in Jacksboro) to Fort Duncan (in Eagle Pass). The extreme western line was marked by Fort Stockton, Fort Davis, and Fort Bliss (near El Paso).

The protection afforded by this military action was inadequate. The troops in these frontier posts were poorly disciplined and too few in number, and many of their officers were unfamiliar with Indian warfare. The strategy employed was strictly defensive—to keep the Indians out of the settlements by scouting maneuvers instead of by attacking their villages. Furthermore, the distance between the posts was too great for the soldiers to prevent the Indians from crossing the defense line.

The official policy of the government further limited the military. Washington officials believed that peace on the frontier could be obtained through treaties and the appointment of Quakers as Indian agents. Congress authorized a commission to negotiate a permanent peace among all the Plains Indians. In October 1867 at Medicine Lodge Creek, Kansas, the commissioners met with the Cheyennes, Arapahoes, Kiowas, Kiowa-Apaches, and Comanches in what was one of the most colorful councils between Indians and whites ever held in the American West. Satanta, the principal leader of Kiowa raiding parties into Texas, insisted that western Texas belonged to the Kiowas and Comanches and refused to part with any of it. Ten Bears, a Comanche chief who realized that the Indians must accept the terms offered by the commissioners or be destroyed, pleaded that his people should be allowed to continue their nomadic way of life. They argued in vain. Accord-

Established in 1867, Fort Griffin was an important link in the chain of
military posts along the frontier. Troops from this fort were called on to
escort government mail, surveying parties, and cattle drives, and to
protect nearby settlers from Indian raids. The town that grew up around
the fort attained fame as a headquarters for buffalo hunters, cowboys,
and frontier adventurers, but it declined rapidly after the fort was
abandoned in 1881. (Courtesy of the Texas Department of Transportation)

ing to the Treaty of Medicine Lodge Creek, the Indians present agreed to
accept reservations in the Indian Territory and to cease their depredations.
But raids continued. Some of the Kiowas and about half the Comanches
refused to move onto the reservation. In fact, the Kwahadi Comanche band
was not even represented at the Medicine Lodge Creek council and did not
recognize the treaty. Later that year a government agent who visited them at
present-day Quitaque reported that the band had about 15,000 horses, 300 or
400 mules, and innumerable stolen cattle, and that eighteen parties were at
the time raiding the Texas frontier.

Nevertheless, President Grant, who assumed office in 1869, endorsed
the peace policy. He appointed as Indian agents Quakers who believed that
kindness and reason would be more effective than force in dealing with the
Indians. One of these was Quaker Lawrie Tatum, a strong devotee of the
peace policy. As the new agent at the Kiowa-Comanche reservation, he soon
found that his wards would not remain at peace unless compelled by armed

force. In the absence of a military presence, the reservation became a sanctuary for warriors who regularly slipped away to plunder in Texas.

The most audacious of these raids was the Salt Creek massacre of May 1871. A band of Kiowas attacked a wagon train between Jacksboro and Fort Griffin, killed or wounded most of the twelve teamsters, and stole the mules. For the Indians the timing of the attack proved unfortunate. General of the Army William Tecumseh Sherman, escorted by Inspector General of the Army Randolph B. Marcy, had passed the site only a few hours before the attack. The two generals were in Texas on an inspection tour to see for themselves whether conditions on the frontier were as bad as had been reported. Marcy thought they were. He noted in his journal that the Indian raiders, unless controlled, would soon have the country between Belknap and Jacksboro completely depopulated. The tragedy at Salt Creek also convinced Sherman that the Indian menace on the Texas frontier had not been exaggerated. Sherman recommended military action.

As a result of the Salt Creek massacre, the War Department unleashed its troops against Indians who left the reservation. To lead the offensive, General Sherman transferred to the Texas frontier Colonel Ranald Slidell Mackenzie, regarded by U. S. Grant as the most promising young officer in the army at the end of the Civil War. With his tough Fourth Cavalry regiment, in the autumn of 1871 Mackenzie led an expedition northwest from old Camp Cooper on the Clear Fork of the Brazos to Blanco Canyon, where he harassed the Kwahadi Comanches under Quanah Parker. In April of the following year at Howard's Well, Indians attacked and killed sixteen members of a wagon train party. In July, Mackenzie renewed his campaign. On September 29, on the North Fork of the Red River he decisively defeated a camp of Comanches who had participated in the attack at Howard's Well. As a result of this defeat and the imprisonment of their captured people, the Comanches and Kiowas remained peaceful for more than a year.

With the Comanches and Kiowas seemingly at peace, General Sherman ordered Mackenzie and his Fourth Cavalry to the Rio Grande border to suppress raiding in the area between San Antonio and the Rio Grande by Kickapoo and Apache Indians living in Mexico. By 1873 these Indians had killed a number of citizens and inflicted almost $50 million in damages. The troops quickly destroyed three of their villages, captured some of the Indians, and established an effective border patrol. By the end of the year, Indian raids along the Rio Grande had ceased, and Mackenzie moved his regiment back to northwestern Texas.

In the spring of 1874, the Indians of the southern plains, led by Quanah Parker, renewed their attacks on the Texas frontier. The new war erupted on June 27 when several hundred Comanche and Cheyenne warriors and perhaps a few Kiowas attacked a buffalo hunters' stockade, known as Adobe Walls, near present-day Borger. Marksmen among the twenty-eight buffalo hunters in the stockade, armed with their "big fifty" buffalo guns, were more than a match for the Indians. Although repulsed with heavy losses in their initial attack, the Indians were determined to keep Texans off their favorite hunting grounds. They again began hitting the isolated settlers along the Texas frontier. In response, on July 26, 1874, President Grant terminated the Quaker peace policy and placed the military completely in charge of restoring peace on the frontier. In August the army moved against all Indians who had refused to return to the reservations. The majority of the determined natives took refuge in the wild canyons and breaks along the eastern edge of the Llano Estacado. There they were pursued relentlessly by well-mounted, well-armed, and thoroughly seasoned troops, guided by Indian scouts, and led for the most part by officers who were now experienced in Indian warfare. Altogether, forty-six companies, about 3,000 men, marching in five commands, converged on the headstreams of the Red River in the eastern Panhandle of Texas and inflicted serious defeats on the Indians encamped there.

Colonel Mackenzie, however, delivered the most effective and dramatic blow to the Indians of the southern plains. After establishing his base on the upper Brazos River, Mackenzie with about 500 men, including a detachment of Indian scouts, headed northward along the edge of the Caprock for the headstreams of the Red River. After beating off an attack by Comanches at Tule Canyon, and following an all-night march, on September 28, in a daring move, Mackenzie led his men down a narrow path to the bottom of Palo Duro Canyon. Here he defeated five villages of Comanches, Kiowas, and Cheyennes, burned their lodges and the supplies they needed for survival during the ensuing winter, and captured 1,424 horses and mules.

Flushed from hideouts that they believed could not be found by the blue-coated troopers, many of the Indians sought safety at the water holes on the Llano Estacado. Mackenzie, however, did not intend that they should find safety anywhere except on the reservation. Early in November he surprised and defeated a band of Comanches near the present town of Tahoka. Most of the Indians, however, had already gone or were on their way to the reservation. The Red River War was almost over. By June 1875, the remainder, including a large band of Kwahadies led by Quanah Parker, had straggled to Fort Sill and surrendered. Relatively few Indians had been killed or taken captive in this struggle, but left without lodges and supplies or horses, they could no longer continue their nomadic existence.

On the southwestern frontier, from the vicinity of Laredo to the outskirts of El Paso, another five years would elapse before the Indian issue was settled. In the eastern portion of that area, the Apaches and Kickapoos from Mexico renewed their destructive forays after Mackenzie and his Fourth Cavalry had returned north. To stop the marauding by Indians based in Mexico, Sherman sent Mackenzie to Fort Clark early in 1878. Mackenzie quickly reactivated his system of border patrols, and in June led an expedition across the Rio Grande in search of the renegade Indians. Mexican officials cooperated in the efforts to bring peace to the border region, and before the end of the year, affairs were "most satisfactory."

Farther west, the frontier enjoyed comparative peace in 1875, in part because of a successful scouting expedition led by Lieutenant Colonel William R. Shafter, but the next year Victorio, commanding a band of Apaches from New Mexico, began raiding in Texas. In 1879 Victorio again left the reservation and from his hideouts on both sides of the Rio Grande made life and property insecure for all who entered the Trans-Pecos country. For a time the efforts of federal troops and the Texas Frontier Battalion were ineffective. But Benjamin H. Grierson, in command of U.S. troops, and George W. Baylor, with a contingent of Texas Rangers, cooperated with the commander of a Mexican military force and relentlessly pursued hostile Apaches on both sides of the international border. At the Battle of Rattlesnake Springs in August 1880, U.S. troops, including African American "buffalo soldiers," defeated Victorio and drove him south into Mexico. There, in October 1880, Mexican troops cornered and killed the Apache leader, thereby eliminating the last Indian barrier to the settlement of western Texas.

As during the pre-Civil War years, the federal government's efforts to pacify the frontier were supplemented by the state. After a militia plan authorized in 1871 failed, the state created in 1874 two organizations of rangers destined to attain renown. The first, the Special Force of Rangers under the command of L. H. McNelly, marched into the lower Rio Grande, where violence was frequent.

The violence on the South Texas frontier involved not only Indians but also clashes between Anglos and Mexican-Americans. Much of this conflict centered around the activities of Juan Nepomucino Cortina and his men. While the Mexican-Americans and Mexicans of the Rio Grande viewed Cortina as a popular hero and a protector of their rights, Anglo-Americans considered him an outlaw. Actually there was truth in both viewpoints. Cortina, a ranch owner in South Texas, became a fugitive in 1859 after killing a deputy sheriff who was brutalizing one of his ranch hands. Although the extent of his activities cannot be determined, Cortina was accused of many crimes and almost daily raids on Mexican and Texas ranches. In 1875 Captain McNelly moved vigorously in pursuit of Cortina. He soon reported that his men had slain an entire party of twelve cattle thieves, near Brownsville, but Cortina was not among them. Later, McNelly crossed the Rio Grande with thirty men, moved against Las Cuevas Ranch, where several hundred bandits and soldiers were established, and recovered some stolen cattle. Shortly thereafter the Mexican Army arrested Cortina and removed him from the Rio Grande Valley.

McNelly's aggressive action and the removal of Cortina by Mexican authorities brought a measure of security to several South Texas counties. Thereafter forces of both nations patrolled the border and reduced the lawlessness on both sides of the river. Nevertheless, peace did not come easily. Mexicans and Mexican-Americans continued to remember the Ranger forces with bitterness, contending that the Rangers abused and persecuted their people.

Juan Nepomucino Cortina. Juan Cortina became a fugitive in 1859 after killing a deputy sheriff who was brutalizing one of his ranch hands. For the next sixteen years he and his followers eluded capture and operated in the South Texas–Northern Mexico borderlands. Depending on your perspective, he was either a Robin Hood who defended the poor Mexicans of the region, or a brutal outlaw. His activities reflect the lawlessness and violence that characterized the border region in the mid- to late nineteenth century. (Texas State Library and Archives Commission)

The other famous fighting unit was the Frontier Battalion, commanded by Major John B. Jones, an unassuming but highly efficient officer. Although, like the Special Force of Rangers, it had been created principally to deal with lawless white men, the Frontier Battalion took the field in time to have an important part in bringing to an end the Comanche and Kiowa raids in Texas. Jones placed his six companies in camps along the frontier in positions calculated to offer maximum protection. From these camps, scouts and patrols were kept constantly on the move to intercept any Indian raiding party that might try to make its way into the settlements. During the first six months of its existence the Frontier Battalion had fifteen engagements with Indians. When the Indian campaigns were over, the Frontier Battalion concentrated its efforts very effectively against lawless white men.

THE BUFFALO SLAUGHTER

Closely associated with the problem of Indian removal and the advance of the Texas frontier was the extermination of the buffalo, or bison. This large, shaggy animal, which roamed the grassy plains in millions, provided the Plains Indians with what they needed for their very existence. In addition to food, clothing, and shelter, buffalo robes provided an important trade commodity. Although 199,870 buffalo robes reached New Orleans in 1828, the peak year, the number of buffalo killed before the end of the Civil War made no apparent reduction in the size of the immense herds, nor did it give the Indians cause for alarm. Beginning in 1870, however, when experiments showed that buffalo hides could be made into good leather, the demand for hides increased sharply. Buyers gathered at convenient points near the buffalo range and offered good prices for all hides. Hunters who were superb marksmen penetrated the plains, beginning near the railroad lines in Kansas, and wreaked havoc with the Indians' "cattle."

After slaughtering most of the buffalo in Kansas, in 1873 the buffalo hunters moved from Dodge City to the Panhandle of Texas, where they found a massive herd. The attack on their supply post at Adobe Walls in June 1874 checked their operation only for that season. By the end of the year several hunters had taken a long, circuitous route around the Indian country and had entered the range from the east by way of Fort Griffin. Before the end of 1875, J. Wright Mooar and his brother John, Joe S. McCombs, and others were hunting in the vicinity of the present towns of Sweetwater, Colorado City, and Haskell. During the 1875–76 season an estimated 1,500 hunters were engaged in their bloody work.

Life for the buffalo hunters was always unpleasant, often dangerous, but usually profitable. They lived for months at a time in danger from hostile Indians and rarely had as much as a tent to protect them from the wind and the rain. They were an adventurous group, and the nature of their lifestyle is evident in their names. The inhabitants of one camp included "Shoot-em-up Mike," "Prairie Dog Dave," "Light-fingered Jack," and "Dirty-face Jones." Whatever their character, they engaged in a significant business operation that involved substantial amounts of money. In one day in 1877, hunters shopping at F. E. Conrad's general mercantile store in Fort Griffin bought guns and ammunition in the amount of $2,500. Another supply base, Rath City, or Reynolds City, in Stonewall County, had a hide business that year that was valued at $100,000. Other bases and camps evolved into towns such as Buffalo Gap, Hide Town (Snyder), and Mobeetie. During the two months at the peak of their kill—December 1877 and January 1878—the hunters took at least 100,000 hides from the Texas range. During the following season, however, only a few small herds could be found, and by 1880 the buffalo were gone.

THE PRICE OF CONQUEST

Frontierspeople long engaged in lively arguments over the comparative effectiveness of the three factors that helped to remove the Indians from the plains: the U.S. Army, the Texas Rangers, and the buffalo hunters. Each made some contribution. The army broke up large-scale resistance, the

Buffalo Hunters. A camp of buffalo hunters in Taylor County in 1874 at the peak of the buffalo hunt. This photograph was one of a series taken by George Robertson as he toured the Texas hunting camps. (Texas State Library and Archives Commission)

rangers made raiding too hazardous for even the most reckless warrior, and the buffalo hunters destroyed the Indians' larder and opened the way for the herds of the cattle ranchers.

But the question of who was responsible for victory is actually not the most meaningful question. Far more significant is an understanding of the basic nature of the conflict. For the settlers who awaited the opportunity to move west, the defeat of the Indians of West Texas and their removal to reservations was a great and glorious accomplishment. The exploits of the heroic settlers, Texas Rangers, and even of the blue-coated troopers became a part of Texas tradition and folklore. As generally told, it is a story of sacrifice and victory, and often it is told as a story of good versus evil, with the eventual triumph of the good.

The conflict between the Indians and the advancing tide of white civilization was indeed filled with heroic exploits and sacrifices, as well as cruelty and suffering. But it was not necessarily a battle between good and evil. It was a story of conquest, of one civilization using force to acquire and control a land held by another civilization. Considering the circumstances and the times, the course of events was predictable, if not inevitable, but it was a victory with a price. The Indian peoples, removed from their heritage, were destined to suffer even more in the years to come. In effect, one civilization perished in order that another might prosper.

THE CATTLE KINGDOM

Before the farmers could establish themselves on the prairies vacated by the retreating Indians, new inventions and discoveries were necessary. While they impatiently waited for the necessary adaptations, for a relatively short interval of less than three decades, the cattle kingdom rose, flourished, and declined on the free or cheap but nutritious grass that covered the plains. Originating in Spanish times, the cattle kingdom eventually spread from Brownsville to Montana. Besides furnishing a large part of the nation's beef supply, Texas cattle stocked the middle and northern plains. The techniques, the lingo, and other aspects of the culture of the cattle kingdom contributed significantly to the history of the West.

When the first Spanish soldiers and priests came north from Mexico, they brought along cattle. The Spanish cattle were the progenitors of the wild cattle that in later years were to be found in various parts of the state, and also of the famous longhorns, a type that evolved in southern Texas and came to be known throughout the West. Apparently, cattle brought in from the Old South in the early nineteenth century materially affected the strain of animals on the range. But whether they were the lanky longhorns of South Texas or the better-built, round-barreled "Texas cattle," they were hardy and able to protect themselves. They made fairly good beef when fat and furnished their own transportation to market. Except for roundups at branding time, they were given no attention and needed none.

The open-range cattle industry had its beginnings in South Texas between San Antonio and Brownsville and between Matagorda Bay and Laredo. In climate this region is unsurpassed for free-range cattle. Large herds already grazed these lands during the Spanish era. In 1774 at Goliad, Mission La Bahía Espiritu Santo claimed 15,000 and Mission Rosario 10,000 head. Also during the Spanish period ranchers developed many of the practices used in raising cattle on the open range. Riders mounted on horseback, or *vaqueros*, tended the herds. The *vaqueros* wore leather coverings or "chaps" to protect their legs from the thorny brush that sometimes covered the land. Their skills as horsemen were highly developed, and they were proficient in their use of ropes or, *reatas*, to catch cattle whenever necessary. Periodically the *vaqueros* gathered the cattle together in a "roundup," sometimes collecting them in pens or corrals. The cattle were branded with hot irons to indicate ownership. Spanish brands were large designs that sometimes covered one side of the cow.

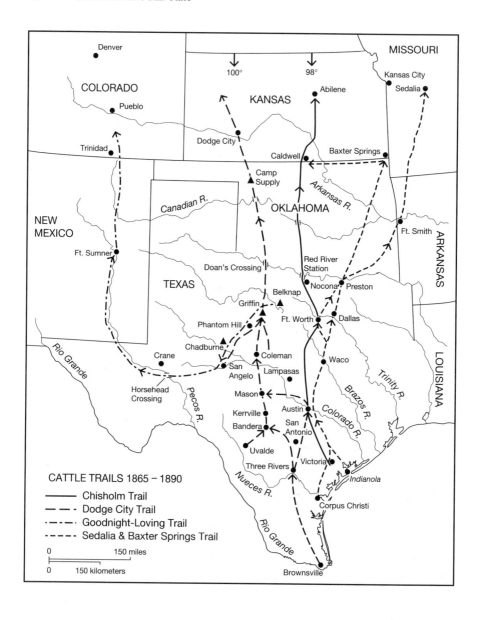

Anglo-Americans who moved into Texas prior to the Civil War and expanded the cattle industry were already familiar with such practices. In fact, ranchers in southern states from the Carolinas to Louisiana had used most of these procedures for generations. Roundups and branding were practices of long standing, although their brands were much smaller than those used by the Spanish, and Anglo drovers sometimes trailed their herds to market. Anglo-Americans had not relied much on horses, developed roping skills, worn chaps, or ridden with saddles equipped with horns, but otherwise they were already prepared for work on the Texas range.

The ranching industry established during Spanish days expanded during Mexican rule, the Republic, and early statehood. After the retreat of the Mexican army following Santa Anna's defeat at San Jacinto, many Mexicans withdrew from the country between the Nueces and the Rio Grande. However, other Mexican *rancheros* continued to operate large ranches and control much of the land in the region. Anglo-Americans gradually entered the area. H. L. Kinney, an adventurous Irish-American from Illinois, who established a trading post at the site of Corpus Christi in 1839, soon engaged in ranching. Kinney hired a retinue of followers both to work and to fight. The war with Mexico brought other Anglo-Americans to this area, among them Captain Mifflin Kenedy and Captain Richard King, who enlarged his initial Santa Gertrudis tract of 75,000 acres into the famous King Ranch of more than a million acres. Many gold seekers on their way to California passed through Corpus Christi and created a limited market for the cattle. The number of cattle increased rapidly, and a few cattlemen prospered, but marauding Indian bands and bandits, and above all, the lack of a good market, limited the growth of the industry. Nevertheless, in 1860 there were an estimated 3,786,433 cattle in Texas, six times as many cattle as people.

Texas cattle were much easier to raise than to sell. During the Spanish era they were worth very little and could scarcely be disposed of at any price. Occasionally a herd was driven to Louisiana, notwithstanding the fact that trade with that province was forbidden, and at times dried beef was carried by pack trains to cities in Coahuila. After the Texas Revolution herds were sometimes driven to the East, and ranchers shipped cattle in considerable numbers to New Orleans. But cattle were of so little value that many thousands were slain for their hides and tallow.

After the war with Mexico, the range cattle industry spread into the vast prairie region of North Texas where Dallas-Fort Worth area is today. John Chisum, later the best-known cattleman in New Mexico, owned a herd in Denton County during this period. By 1861, the cattlemen had extended their domain westward, appropriating the best ranges in the Western Cross Timbers. The Civil War halted their westward march, but in 1867, with the reestablishment of a line of military posts, the rangemen began appropriating the Rolling Plains. By 1876, they had reached or passed the 100th meridian, from Kimble County in the Edwards Plateau to Childress County in the eastern Panhandle.

Meanwhile, the industry had swung around the High Plains and was well established along the slopes of the Rocky Mountains and the valleys farther west. The career of Charles Goodnight illustrates this movement. Goodnight went to Palo Pinto County in the Cross Timbers of West Texas in 1857. A few years of trail driving, scouting, and ranger service made him one of America's finished plainsmen. With Oliver Loving he drove a herd by the

Concho and Pecos rivers to New Mexico in 1866, opening the Pecos (or Goodnight-Loving) Trail. He soon drove herds by this route into Colorado and in 1869 established his home near Pueblo. After business reverses had brought losses and the range had become crowded, Goodnight turned again to Texas. He moved his herd southeastward to the Texas Panhandle. He entered the Palo Duro Canyon in 1876 and in partnership with John Adair, an Irish capitalist, established the JA Ranch.

Goodnight's selection of Palo Duro Canyon was in part an effort to solve one of the most serious problems of ranching—the necessity for a reliable supply of water. Indeed, the plentiful grass was useless without the control of water. Surface water was impounded in tanks where there were creeks and draws, but for several years after the Indians had been removed, ranchers doubted that the millions of acres of fine grass on the High Plains could ever be grazed because of the lack of water. Underneath most of the area lay an ample supply, but before it could be used, it was necessary to locate this supply and devise methods for making it available. Wells were drilled as early as 1855, and by the 1880s wells with windmills were providing adequate water supplies and opening lands where there were no creeks or rivers to supply the thirsty cattle.

While solving problems of production, ranchers also developed a solution for marketing problems. Trail driving, used occasionally before the Civil War, began in larger volume and in a somewhat different manner after the war. Before the Civil War a few drovers had proved that trail driving to the railhead in Missouri was practical. Left at the end of the war with very little money and an overabundance of cheap cattle, Texans in great numbers renewed their efforts to reach the markets of the North by means of the long drives. In 1866, an estimated 260,000 cattle were started on the trail for Sedalia and other railroad stations in Missouri from which they could be shipped to eastern markets.

But these pioneering trail drives met with unanticipated obstacles. In southern Missouri and eastern Kansas bands of farmers turned them back or broke up their herds, contending that the Texas cattle destroyed their crops and transmitted to their herds the dreaded Texas fever. By following a circuitous route west of the farmers' frontier, some of the herdsmen managed to reach St. Joseph and from there shipped their cattle to Chicago. By midsummer of the next year, however, the Kansas Pacific Railroad had extended its line beyond the farmers' frontier. The trail drives could reach rail lines at Abilene, Kansas, without interference.

Each year for the next two decades, thousands of Texas cattle were driven to railroad stations in Kansas and then shipped to eastern markets. During the first few years of the drives, fortunes varied, but 1874 and the decade following constituted a prosperous era for the cattle owners. A combination of factors created a strong market. Only a part of the cattle driven out of Texas went directly to the slaughter pens. Cattlemen soon discovered that the rich grasses of the northern plains would sustain and fatten cattle, and in the cow towns of Kansas, purchasers of stock cattle competed with those who bought for beef. Also, the process of refrigeration, introduced in 1875, made it possible to ship dressed beef across the ocean. By 1882, good steers brought $5^1/2$ cents a pound on the Chicago market, at that time the highest price ever paid in the United States. The boom lasted until 1885, when a severe winter, followed by a drought, forced many owners to sell their animals on a weak market. Cattlemen lost a fortune and the open-range cattle industry collapsed. Within a few years, the trail drives had almost disappeared. Even without the blizzards of 1885, new quarantine regulations, the expansion of barbed wire fences, and the westward advance of the farmers made the drives more difficult and more costly each year.

The perils of the trail loom large in the literature of the cattle kingdom. The monotonous fare on the trail, the lonely night guards, the storms with their wind, hail, and lightning, the stampedes when the roar of the 10,000 charging hoofs and the clatter of half as many sharp-pointed horns reminded the rider that his life depended on his surefooted horse, cold wind that chilled men to the marrow and blistering sun that scorched the earth, the swirling water of swollen streams, and the hazards of marauding Indians were experiences that caused many a trail driver to swear that he would quit for good at Abilene, Ellsworth, or Dodge City. Yet when it next came time for the drive, he was usually ready to go again.

Trail driving was economical. Eight, ten, or a dozen men with few supplies and a small amount of equipment could deliver a herd of 2,000 or more animals from Texas to the railhead in Kansas at a cost that was a small fraction of the charge for shipping by rail. Thus, during the later years many herds were driven past Texas railroad stations and on to Kansas to get them as near as possible to eastern markets before loading them on rail cars.

There were several major cattle trails to the North. The first was the Sedalia Trail, which started near Matagorda Bay and passed through or near Austin and Fort Worth to Sedalia or, in later years, to more western railheads. The Chisholm Trail, which was opened in 1867 by Jesse Chisholm, a Cherokee Indian trader, and named for him began in South Texas, ran by Austin, passed between Fort Worth and Weatherford, crossed the Red River near present-day Nocona, and crossed Indian Territory to Abilene and Wichita, Kansas, and to other points. The Dodge City or Great Western Trail, formed at Mason, led northward to the Red River near Doan's Store north of Vernon, and then continued in an almost straight line to Dodge City, Kansas. An extension of the trail was used for driving many cattle from Dodge City to stock the vast northern ranges of western Nebraska, Wyoming, and even Montana. The Goodnight-Loving (or Pecos) Trail went westward up the Middle Concho to the Pecos River at Horsehead

Crossing, and up the Pecos into New Mexico. Later it was extended into Wyoming and Montana.

THE BIG PASTURE COUNTRY

The open-range cattle industry spread with marvelous rapidity; its decline was even more rapid. The crowded ranges, the westward advance of farmers and railroads, the introduction of barbed wire, and the utilization of drilled wells and windmills for economically obtaining water transformed the open range into a country of big pastures. In brief, the open range ceased to exist about 1890 when most ranchers enclosed their land with fences.

The very success of the open-range cattle industry contributed to its destruction. Reports of huge profits attracted eastern and European capitalists as well as many small investors. A number of syndicates, such as the

Work camps, chuck wagons, and other ranching practices established in the nineteenth century continued to be a familiar sight in certain areas of West Texas where large ranches operate. (Courtesy of The Southwest Collection, Lubbock, Texas)

Matador Land and Cattle Company, invested millions in the business. These concerns had the money to buy their lands and to fence them. Furthermore, the ranges soon became overcrowded with cattle. Protracted droughts interspersed with severe blizzards from 1885 through 1887 either decimated many herds or forced owners to sell thousands of gaunt animals, thereby bringing about a disastrous collapse in the cattle market. Quarantine laws of northern states against Texas cattle further undermined open range production. Fencing seemed to be the logical solution for these problems. Even before the use of barbed wire, which offered a cheap and effective fencing material, cattlemen in South Texas were enclosing their better grasslands with smooth wire or with boards.

Fencing was hastened by at least three factors: the extension of railroads into West Texas, the invention and sale of barbed wire, and the development of an adequate groundwater supply. The network of railroads available in most areas by the 1880s not only shipped cattle out but also allowed the importation of fencing material. Within another decade the best range lands had been fenced with barbed wire. J. F. Glidden, a farmer of De Kalb, Illinois, and later a Panhandle rancher, invented barbed wire in 1873. Henry B. Sanborn, Glidden's partner in the ranching venture and the founder of Amarillo, was responsible for popularizing barbed wire and marketing it in Texas. At first Sanborn and his product met resistance in Texas, but by 1880 there were a few barbed wire fences in a number of counties. Three years later practically all the cattle country of South and Central Texas had been enclosed, and fencing was well under way in the Panhandle and North Texas.

Opposition to fencing swelled with its spread. The first lands to be fenced were those with a supply of surface water. It soon became evident if the fencing movement was not stopped, those who did not fence would be ruined. The commissioners court of San Saba County asked the legislature to prohibit by law the building of barbed wire fences. In 1888, the stockmen's association of Nolan and Fisher counties approved a resolution that the land west of the one hundredth meridian was "fit only for grazing" and that fences should not be allowed. Some cattlemen expressed their opposition to fencing more directly by cutting fences, and public opinion generally supported the fence cutters. In many cases large proprietors fenced in land that did not belong to them and closed public roads. Fences also cost many cowboys their jobs. "Nesters" and small farmers who pushed ahead into the cattle country might find themselves entirely surrounded by a fence without an outlet, or they might have their own fences cut by those who resented their intrusion into the ranching areas. The public opposed fencing because it believed that eastern and foreign capitalists used fencing to dominate the cattle industry. One newspaper editor linked the emergence of large ranches, fencing, and the state's land policy. He believed fencing was responsible for "creating principalities, pashalics, and baronates among a few capitalists and arousing a spirit of agrarianism among the poorer classes."

During 1883, fence cutting occurred in more than half the 171 organized counties of the state. It was especially serious along the agricultural frontier. In some areas sentiment was so evenly divided that the local officers and the Texas Rangers were helpless to resolve the dispute.

To deal with the fencing crisis, Governor John Ireland called a special session of the legislature in 1884. It enacted legislation that made fence cutting a felony but also made it unlawful to enclose land not owned or leased. Although fence cutting continued in some localities for several more years, the new law, the energetic efforts of a few sheriffs and the Texas Rangers to enforce the law, and growing public sentiment for law and order combined by the close of the decade to put an end to fence cutting.

Fencing was not the only problem that surfaced during the transition from the open range to big pastures. In the conversion, some of the cattle companies confronted the problem of consolidating their holdings. A few had managed to secure compact tracts of lands, but many of the large concerns had fenced in land they did not own. They bought a large part of their land from the railroad companies, paying from 25 cents to $1 an acre for it. Interspersed with the sections of railroad were alternate sections of school land, which the ranchmen might lease but could not purchase except in small quantities. State law limited the amount of school land that one person could buy from the state. The ranchers bought as much school land as possible, but still there was generally land open to settlers in every large pasture. Immigrants in time sought out and purchased or squatted on these lands. The ranchmen ultimately bought out or forced out the nesters, and a number of big, consolidated ranches emerged.

The King Ranch of South Texas was the first and the most famous of these large ranches. Nearby, Mifflin Kenedy, a former partner of Richard King, established a ranch that encompassed most of Kenedy County. In northwest Texas the JA Ranch under Goodnight's direction had 40,000 cattle and 700,000 acres of land under its control by 1887. Thomas Sherman Bugbee, who began grazing cattle in the Texas Panhandle in 1876, eventually expanded his Shoe Bar Ranch to 450,000 acres. Within another decade several other very large ranches were operating in the area. The Matador, a Scottish syndicate, at its peak owned 861,000 acres in Texas; the Spur, a British company adjoining the south side of the Matador, obtained a total of 439,972 acres; and the XIT, a Chicago-based syndicate and the largest of the Texas ranches, held 3,050,000 acres it received for building the state capitol in the Panhandle along the border of New Mexico from Hockley County in the south to the Oklahoma line in the north. J. W. Williams, an authority on the subject, listed nineteen ranches in 1954 with a range of more than 150,000 acres each. The list included the King and Kenedy ranches, the W. T. Waggoner Estate, the West Cattle Company, and the Burnett ranches, all with ranges in excess of 400,000 acres.

Once ranchers enclosed their pastures, select breeding of animals, impossible under the open-range system, came into practice. Durham,

Angus, and Hereford cattle replaced the Spanish longhorns, with the Herefords emerging as the favorite. In time the ranchmen also began experimenting with crops to supplant their pastures of grass. At first they planted sorghum, then grain sorghum, and eventually wheat on larger and larger acreage. In 1999, cattle in Texas numbered 14 million, about one-seventh of the total for the entire United States, and the cash receipts from this one commodity were over 40 percent of Texas's total revenue derived from agriculture.

OTHER LIVESTOCK: HORSES, SHEEP, AND GOATS

Cattle was not the only important product of the ranching industry. For many years in the middle of the nineteenth century, horses were also valuable items for market. "Mustangers" captured and trained wild horses, or mustangs, and sold them in various locations over the West. In most instances, the mustangers were Mexican *mesteñeros*, who developed considerable skill in this difficult and dangerous work.

Before the Civil War there was a constant demand for horses of all kinds, and mustangs, hardy and spirited animals, were especially prized. Consequently, *mesteñeros* captured large numbers, tamed them, and sold them either to the army or to ranchers. Mustanging remained an important part of the ranching industry until the 1870s, when cattle ranching reduced the number of wild horses to the point that few could be found and little profit could be made.

A more permanent part of the ranching industry was the raising of sheep and goats. Sheep, like cattle, were brought to Texas during the early Spanish era and were first raised on a large scale in Texas in the country south of San Antonio. In fact, the sheep industry was confined principally to that region until the 1870s, when sheep raising spread to the rangelands between Del Rio and San Angelo, north and west of San Antonio. Between 1870 and 1880 the number of sheep raised in Texas increased rapidly.

Mexican-Americans were especially important in the raising of sheep and goats. The shepherds who tended the flocks were usually Mexican-American *pastores*. Practically all of the shearers who cut the wool off the sheep were *tasinques* of Mexican heritage, and many of them were from Mexico. Mexican-Americans owned many of the sheep ranches, some of which contained herds that numbered in the tens of thousands.

Almost without exception, the sheepmen appeared in an area after the cattlemen had established their ranches. This fact, as well as the belief that sheep would ruin the range by eating the grass so short that a cow could not subsist on it, precipitated clashes between the sheep herders and cattlemen

Cattle were introduced into Texas by the Spanish explorers and counted on for the principal wealth of the missions. Herds increased during the Civil War when they were neither tended nor thinned. Barbed wire, first available to Texans in quantity in 1879, revolutionized land values and made it possible to fence the open range and to establish homesteads in frontier plains areas. (Courtesy of The Southwest Collection, Lubbock, Texas)

that sometimes resulted in bloodshed. On the other hand, there were instances of ranchers who ran both sheep and cattle.

The rapid growth of the sheep industry is reflected by the fact that between 1870 and 1880 the number of sheep grazed in Texas increased from 1,223,000 to over 6,000,000. The number of sheep then declined to less than 2 million in the early twentieth century, before it rebounded to nearly 11 million during World War II, making Texas at that time the leading sheep-producing state. Since then, however, the number has declined steadily, especially in the late 1990s. In 1999, there were only 1,400,000, and they produced only $5.6 million in revenue from wool, about half of what was produced in 1997.

Angora goats that produce quality mohair were brought to America and to Texas from Turkey in 1849. Goat raising became concentrated chiefly on the Edwards Plateau. In 1994, Texas had 1,960,000 goats; by 1999 the number had dropped to 1.4 million. Still, Texas produced nearly half of the world's mohair and 92 percent of the U.S. production.

THE PEOPLE OF THE RANGE

Although most ranchers and cowboys were Anglo-Americans who moved west from eastern areas of Texas, people of many cultures met and mingled on the ranges of South and West Texas. Anglo-Americans, Mexican-Americans, African Americans, Germans, and people of other heritages shared the hardships of the trail drive and the daily routine of the range. In the hill country, Germans established prosperous ranches, and Scottish, English, and Irish investors invested millions in ranches on the plains of northwestern Texas.

African Americans participated in the ranching industry in various ways. Cattle drives often included black cowboys. Some worked as cooks or horse wranglers; others earned their way as foremen or, in a few instances, owners of their own ranches. Daniel Webster ("80 John") Wallace began life as a slave, worked as a trail boss on the drives north, and eventually owned a ranch near Colorado City. For skilled African American cowboys, ranching provided relatively well-paying jobs with less discrimination than was found in other industries in the late nineteenth century.

Most Mexican-American *vaqueros* were found on the ranches of South Texas, but north of that area, about one out of every ten cowboys was a Tejano. There were also a number of Tejano-owned ranches, particularly between the Rio Grande and Nueces rivers. In 1900 Tejanos accounted for about 60 percent of the landowners in Cameron, Star, and Zapata counties. Some of these ranches were quite large; Hipolito García's Randado Ranch in Zapata County ran a herd of 25,000.

Women also shared the life of the ranching frontier. Doña Maria Hinojosa and Doña Maria del Carmen Calvillo were pioneering ranch owners in South Texas during the Spanish period, and Margarita Villareal was one of several Mexican-American women who ran ranches in that region following the Civil War. Perhaps the best-known woman rancher was Lizzie Johnson, who personally took her cattle on the trail to Kansas to ensure that she received the best price. Another, Margaret Bouland, drove her herd from Victoria to Kansas. In Palo Duro Canyon, Mollie Goodnight lived in a dirt-floored dugout while she worked with her husband in the establishment of the JA Ranch. After the death of her husband, Henrietta King directed the great King Ranch for more than forty years.

THE ADVANCE OF THE FARMERS

In 1870, the extreme western line of the farmers' frontier extended from the common border of Montague and Cook counties irregularly to the vicinity of Bandera and thence to the coast a few miles below Corpus Christi, comparatively close to the cattlemen's frontier. But within another decade the cattlemen's frontier had left the farmers' frontier hundreds of miles behind. The cattlemen appropriated the choice watering places and best grasslands but generally did not constitute a large enough population to form communities or establish local governments. The lawmakers created counties (54 by one act in 1876), and geographers marked them on maps in checkerboard fashion, but the herdsmen generally had to wait for the coming of at least a few farmers before they could secure the 150 signatures required to organize a county government. For land records and judicial purposes most of these western counties were attached to older counties to the east until a few farmers arrived to augment the adult male population.

Although they advanced more slowly, the farmers came in far greater numbers than did the cattlemen, and their movement gained momentum as the Indians were confined to reservations. Many of the thousands of immigrants who entered Texas in 1876 went directly to the frontier. The increase in population each year was phenomenal. Jack County, which had only 694 inhabitants in 1870, had 6,626 in 1880. Taylor County was populated only by a handful of Indians until about 1874, but by 1880 it was the home of 1,736 settlers. While some of the frontier settlers during the 1870s came from older communities in Texas, the vast majority were immigrants who moved into the state from other regions. As a result, the population of Texas surged during the three decades following the Civil War from 604,215 in 1860 to 2,235,521 in 1890. Over 90 percent of these residents lived in rural areas, and many settled in the developing frontier areas.

Though most of the frontier settlers moved west as families or individuals, some came as members of colonies. During the late 1870s and early 1880s several colonies of farmers moved to western Texas, some locating far in advance of the other settlements. The best known included a group of 400 Germans from the vicinity of Indianapolis, who settled in 1878 in Baylor County; Lewis Henry Carhart's Christian Colony, which located in 1879 in the vicinity of the town of Clarendon; a colony of Quakers from Ohio and Indiana, who, under the leadership of Paris Cox, in 1879 established a settlement on the High Plains in Lubbock and Crosby counties; and a colony of German Catholics from Anderson County, who were induced by the Texas and Pacific Railroad to locate in 1881 at the present-day town of Stanton. Unacquainted with the agricultural techniques needed to successfully farm the arid plains, most of these pioneer farmers did not succeed, but their efforts paved the way for others who came later and profited by their experience.

With the development of railroads in the 1880s, the farmers' frontier abruptly ceased its comparatively orderly and solid advancement. No matter where the rails ran, farmers soon followed, and fingers of settlement followed the tracks across West Texas. The Texas and Pacific Railroad in 1880 overtook the line of settlements in Taylor County. Within a year Abilene, Sweetwater, Colorado City, and Big Spring were flourishing

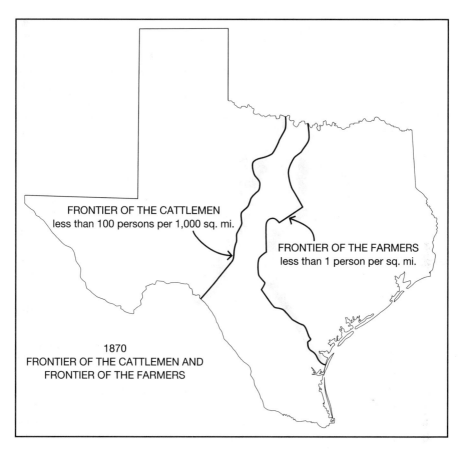

FRONTIER OF THE CATTLEMEN
less than 100 persons per 1,000 sq. mi.

FRONTIER OF THE FARMERS
less than 1 person per sq. mi.

1870
FRONTIER OF THE CATTLEMEN AND
FRONTIER OF THE FARMERS

As late as 1870 only a few farmers had ventured into the western one-half of the state. Cattlemen, however, had carved out ranches as far west as the edge of the High Plains and Mountains and Basins regions.

towns, and the better lands in their vicinity were soon occupied by farmers. A terrible drought in the mid-1880s temporarily halted the farmers' advance. When the drought broke in 1887, the tillers of the soil arrived in greater numbers than ever. The mainstream of this new wave of settlers followed the Fort Worth and Denver Railroad along the upper Red River valley and across the Texas Panhandle. Railroad towns like Quanah, Childress, Memphis, Clarendon, and Amarillo became commercial centers for farmers.

By 1890, the farmers had settled in large numbers throughout the region east of the hundredth meridian and along the railroads to the west. A decade then passed before any significant additional westward advance occurred. Legislation in 1897 and 1901 reduced land prices and precipitated land rushes and conflicts between cattlemen and farmers before the 1906 legislature created a more orderly system of land sales requiring competitive sealed bids, a procedure that brought prices as high as $22 an acre.

Actually, the land rushes around the turn of the century marked the end of the old conflict between the cattlemen and the farmers. As long as there was free grass or land in quantity to lease, the cattlemen opposed the advance of the farmers. But once they had acquired legal possession of their lands, the ranchmen had no reason to oppose the coming of the farmers or of anybody else who would develop the country and increase the value of all land.

Of all the factors that promoted the settlement of West Texas, the railroads were the most important. They had agents who distributed promotional materials advertising the advantages of western Texas to prospective settlers. Some railroads ran exhibition trains to bring prospective settlers west, and even erected immigrant depots to house people while they selected their lands. Some railroads also established demonstration farms to teach the agricultural techniques needed to farm the arid lands, and all provided special transportation rates for the settlers. Finally, the railroads had land to sell—land that they had been given by the state and that they now sold at a reasonable price.

The rush of immigrant farmers into West Texas continued after the turn of the century. Farmers settled around San Angelo and along the Pecos River around 1900, and then began settling the High Plains. They quickly exhausted the supply of the best school and railroad lands, and by 1908, the land rush shifted to the western counties of the South Plains. By 1920 the State had disposed of virtually all the lands held for the support of asylums, and practically all surveyed school tracts. Ranchers also began dividing their pastures and selling off land in small tracts.

While some farmers were establishing themselves on the High Plains, others were moving into the ranchlands of South Texas. They practiced both dry farming and irrigation, but irrigation drew in the greater number, especially in the lower Rio Grande valley. The growth of this region began with the construction of the St. Louis, Brownsville, and Mexico Railroad in 1904. Commercial production of fruits and vegetables by irrigation began to transform the region. By 1910, a few commercial citrus fruit orchards had been set, and in 1914 producers discovered that grafting grapefruit and oranges on the native orange stock would produce a tree adapted to the Rio Grande soil and climate. An amendment to the Texas constitution and subsequent legislation encouraged the organization of irrigation and drainage districts.

The agricultural development of South Texas differed from that of West Texas. The cost of land and irrigation made it difficult for small farmers to compete with wealthy landowners and corporate farms. The railroads again promoted land sales. From North Texas cities agents ran excursion trains of Pullman cars and diners only, frequently making the passengers their guests, without charge for transportation or meals. At times, land sales on a single excursion of this kind aggregated more than $1 million. Between 1920 and 1930 the population of the lower Rio Grande valley more than doubled.

Typical of the agricultural transformation of South Texas was the Taft Ranch. Founded in 1879 as a cattle ranch, it began shifting to cotton production in the 1890s. Also at that time it began to rely on Mexican-Americans and African Americans for labor. By the early twentieth century the Taft Ranch had become a model of industrial farming, relying on low-paid wage workers for labor and containing its own cotton gins, stores, and worker housing.

In no other area of Texas was the disparity between wealthy landowner and abysmally poor laborer as apparent as in the valley. Discrimination, long a part of the life of many Tejanos, but tempered in earlier years by tradition and a relatively static social and political order, intensified as people unsympathetic with Tejano customs and traditions moved into the region from other states and other parts of Texas and assumed positions of power.

BIBLIOGRAPHY

The great volume of literature on the frontier allows only a limited listing of available studies. Traditional works include Rupert N. Richardson, *The Comanche Barrier* (Glendale, 1933); and W. S. Nye, *Carbine and Lance, The Story of Old Fort Sill* (Norman, Okla., 1937). More recent works include T. Lindsay Baker and Billy R. Harrison, *Adobe Walls: The History and Archeology of the 1874 Trading Post* (College Station, 1986); W. H. Leckie, *Military Conquest of the Southern Plains* (Norman, Okla., 1963); Robert Wooster, *Soldiers, Sutlers, and Settlers: Garrison Life on the Texas Frontier* (College Station, 1987); *The Military and United States Indian Policy, 1865–1903* (New Haven and London, 1988); and "The Army and the Politics of Expansion: Texas and the Southwestern Borderlands, 1870–1886," *Southwestern Historical Quarterly*, XCIII, 151–167; Arlan L. Fowler, *The Black Infantrymen in the West, 1869–1891* (Westport, Conn., 1971); Robert Wooster, *History of Fort Davis, Texas* (Santa Fe, 1990); and H. Allen Anderson, *Fort Phantom Hill: Outpost on the Clear Fort of the Brazos* (Lubbock, 1976). A general survey of frontier defense may be found in C. C. Rister, *The Southwestern Frontier*; Rupert. N. Richardson and C. C. Rister, *The Greater Southwest* (Glendale, Calif., 1934); and Ernest Wallace, *Texas in Turmoil* (Austin, 1965). See also Thomas T. Smith, *The Old Army in Texas: A Research Guide to the U.S. Army in Nineteenth-Century Texas* (Austin, 1999).

For studies of major military leaders in the conquest and removal of the plains Indians, see Ernest Wallace, *Ranald S. Mackenzie on the Texas Frontier* (Lubbock, 1964); R. G. Carter, *On the Border with Mackenzie* (New York, 1961); Michael D. Pierce, *The Most Promising Young Officer* (Norman, 1993); and Charles M. Robinson, *Bad Hand: A Biography of General Ranald S. Mackenzie* (Austin, 1993). Paul H. Carlson, *"Pecos Bill," A Military Biography of William R. Shafter* (College Station, 1989), and Robert Wooster, *Nelson A. Miles and the Twilight of the Frontier Army* (Lincoln, 1993), tell the story of two other prominent frontier commanders. For a firsthand account of the one individual's experiences on the Texas frontier, see George Wythe Baylor, *Into the Far, Wild Country: True Tales of the Old Southwest*, ed. Jerry D. Thompson (El Paso, 1996).

Valuable studies of Native Americans include Ernest Wallace and E. Adamson Hoebel, *The Comanches* (Norman, 1952); M. P. Mayhall, *The Kiowas* (Norman, 1962); A. M. Gibson, *The Kickapoos: Lords of the Middle Border* (Norman, 1963); William T. Hagan, *United States-Comanche Relations: The Reservation Years* (New Haven, 1976); and Charles M. Robinson, III, *Satanta: The Life and Death of a War Chief* (Austin, 1998).

The Indian side of the story is presented by Thomas C. Battey, *The Life and Adventures of a Quaker among the Indians* (Boston, 1875), and W. S. Nye, *Bad Medicine and Good: Tales of the Kiowa* (Norman, Okla., 1962).

Considerable source material dealing with the Indian wars is published in J. M. Day and D. H. Winfrey, *Texas Indian Papers, 1860–1916* (Austin, 1961); Ernest Wallace, *Ranald S. Mackenzie's Official Correspondence Relating to Texas, 1871–1873* (Lubbock, 1967); and Ernest Wallace, *Ranald S. Mackenzie's Official Correspondence Relating to Texas, 1873–1879* (Lubbock, 1968).

Among the many articles dealing with specific battles or campaigns are G. Derek West, "The Battle of Adobe Walls (1874)," *Panhandle-Plains Historical Review*, XXXVI, 1–36; Adrian N. Anderson, "The Last Phase of Colonel Ranald S. Mackenzie's 1874 Campaign against the Comanches," *West Texas Historical Association Year Book*, XL, 71–82; Ernest Wallace and Adrian. N. Anderson, "R. S. Mackenzie and the Kickapoos: The Raid into Mexico in 1873," *Arizona and the West*, VII, 105–126; Paul Carlson, "'Pecos Bill' Shafter: Scouting the Llano Estacado," *Military History of Texas and the Southwest*, XVI, 33–53; "William R. Shafter, Black Troops, and The Opening of the Llano Estacado, 1870–1875," *Panhandle-Plains Historical Review*, XXXXVII, 1–18; and Frank Temple, "Colonel B. H. Grierson's Victorio Campaign," *West Texas Historical Association Year Book*, XXXV, 99–111. For more on the experiences of black soldiers, see Bruce J. Dinges, "The Court Martial of Lieutenant Henry O. Flipper," *American West*, IX, 12–17, 59–61; Theodore D. Harris, ed., *Black Frontiersman: The Memoirs of Henry O. Flipper* (Fort Worth, 1997); and William Dobak, "Black Regulars Speak," *Panhandle-Plains Historical Review*, XXXXVII, 19–27. For a description of military posts where troops were quartered, see Eugener Graham, "Federal Fort Architecture in Texas during the Nineteenth Century," *Southwestern Historical Quarterly*, LXXX, 165–188. For military life from a woman's perspective see Sandra L. Myres, ed., *Cavalry Wife: The Diary of Eveline M. Alexander, 1866–1867* (College Station, 1977).

The story of the shortest-lived frontier industry is told by M. Sandoz, *The Buffalo Hunters* (New York, 1954); W. Gard, *The Great Buffalo Hunt* (New York, 1959); and Charles L. Kenner, *A History of New Mexican-Plains Indian Relations* (Norman, 1969).

Reading on the ranching industry in Texas should begin with Terry G. Jordan, *Trails to Texas: Southern Roots of Western Cattle Ranching* (Lincoln, 1981), and *North American Cattle Ranching Frontiers* (Albuquerque, 1993), for a thoughtful discussion of the origins of the ranching industry. But also see Jack Jackson, *Los Mesteñeros: Spanish Ranching in Texas, 1721–1821* (College Station, 1986), and Joe S. Graham, *El Rancho in South Texas: Continuity and Change from 1750* (Denton, 1994), for views that emphasize Spanish origins of ranching.

Otherwise, historical literature of the range cattle industry is voluminous. General studies are Ernest S. Osgood, *The Day of the Cattleman* (Minneapolis, 1954); E. E. Dale, *The Range Cattle Industry* (Norman, Okla., 1930), and *Cow Country* (Norman, Okla., 1942); and James Cox, *The Cattle Industry of Texas and Adjacent Country* (St. Louis, 1895). Bearing especially on Texas is William Curry Holden, *Alkali Trails* (Dallas, 1930); Coleman McCampbell, *The Saga of a Frontier Seaport* (Dallas, 1934); Billy M. Jones, *The Search for Maturity* (Austin, 1965); Robert M. Utley, "The Range Cattle Industry in the Big Bend of Texas," *Southwestern Historical Quarterly*, LXIX, 419–441; and Lewis Nordyke, *Cattle Empire* (New York, 1949).

There are several historians of the cattle trails: W. Gard, *The Chisholm Trail* (Norman, Okla., 1954); J. Marvin Hunter and George W. Saunders (eds.), *The Trail Drivers of Texas* (Dallas, 1925); Harry Drago, *Great American Cattle Trails* (New York, 1965); Andy Adams, *The Log of a Cowboy* (Boston, 1931); Emerson Hough, *The Story of the Cowboy* (New York, 1923); Jimmy M. Skaggs, "The Route of the Great Western (Dodge City) Cattle Trail," *West Texas Historical Association Year Book*, XLI, 131–143; and *The Cattle Trailing Industry: Between Supply and Demand, 1868–1890* (Lawrence,

1973); Chandler A. Robinson (comp. and ed.), *J. Evetts Haley and the Passing of the Old West* (Austin, 1978).

Ranches and ranchers have been popular subjects for writers. Among the best are Lewis Atherton, *The Cattle Kings* (Bloomington, Ind., 1962); Tom Lea, *The King Ranch* (two vols., Boston, 1957); William M. Pearce, *The Matador Land and Cattle Company* (Norman, Okla., 1964); J. E. Haley, *The XIT Ranch of Texas* (Chicago, 1929; Norman, Okla., 1953); Cordia Sloan Duke and Joe B. Frantz, *6000 Miles of Fence: Life on the XIT Ranch of Texas* (Austin, 1961); William Timmons, *Twilight on the Range: Recollections of a Latter Cowboy* (Austin, 1962); David J. Murrah, *C. C. Slaughter: Rancher, Banker, Baptist* (Austin, 1981), and *The Pitchfork Land and Cattle Company* (Lubbock, 1983); Ron Tyler and Bank Langmore, *The Cowboy* (New York, 1975); William W. Savage, Jr. (ed.), *Cowboy Life: Reconstructing an American Myth* (Norman, Okla., 1975); Willie N. Lewis, *Tapadero: The Making of a Cowboy* (Austin, 1972); William Curry Holden, *The Espuela Land and Cattle Company: A Study of a Foreign-Owned Ranch in Texas* (Austin, 1970); J. E. Haley and W. C. Holden, *The Flamboyant Judge: A Biography* (Canyon, 1972); J. E. Haley, *Charles Goodnight, Cowman and Plainsman* (Boston and New York, 1936); A. Ray Stephens, *The Taft Ranch* (Austin, 1964); Charles Kenner, "John Hittson: Cattle King of West Texas," *West Texas Historical Association Year Book*, XXXVII, 70–81; David B. Gracy, II, "George Washington Littlefield, Portrait of a Cattleman," ibid., LXVIII, 237–258. For cowboy life and lore, see Ramon Adams, *The Cowman Says It Salty* (Tucson, 1971). For a glimpse of the life of the African American cowboy see Sara R. Massey, ed., *Black Cowboys of Texas* (College Station, 2000).

In recent years, a number of studies either written by or telling the story of women in the West have been published. For representative works, see Elizabeth Maret, *Women of the Range: Women's Roles in the Texas Beef Cattle Industry* (College Station, 1993); Jacqueline S. Reinier, "Concepts of Domesticity on the Southern Plains Agricultural Frontier, 1870–1920," in *At Home on the Range: Essays on the History of Western Social and Domestic Life*, ed. John R. Wunder (Westport, Conn., 1985); Frances Mayhugh Holden, *Lambshead Before Interwoven: A Texas Range Chronicle, 1848–1978* (College Station, 1982); Sallie Reynolds Matthews, *Interwoven: A Pioneer Chronicle* (College Station, 1982, reprint of 1936 edition); Ottilie Fuchs Goeth, *Memoirs of a Texas Pioneer Grandmother* (Austin, 1982); Jo Ella Powell Exley (ed.), *Texas Tears and Texas Sunshine: Voices of Frontier Women* (College Station, 1985); Sandra Myres, *Westering Women and the Frontier Experience, 1800–1915* (Albuquerque, 1982); and Susan Armitage and Elizabeth Jameson (eds.), *The Women's West* (Norman, 1987).

Several other phases of the cattle industry have attracted authors. Some excellent studies in this miscellany are W. P. Webb, *The Great Plains*; Frank S. Hastings, *A Ranchman's Recollections* (Chicago, 1921); R. D. Holt, "The Introduction of Barbed Wire into Texas and the Fence Cutting War," *West Texas Historical Association Year Book*, VI, 65–79; Henry D. McCallum, "Barbed Wire in Texas," *Southwestern Historical Quarterly*, LXI, 207–219; T. R. Havins, "The Passing of the Longhorns," *Southwestern Historical Quarterly*, LVI, 51–58, and "Texas Fever," *Southwestern Historical Quarterly*, LVII, 147–162; David L. Wheeler, "The Blizzard of 1886 and Its Effect on the Range Cattle Industry in the Southern Plains," *Southwestern Historical Quarterly*, XCIV, 415–432; J. Fred Rippy, "British Investments in Texas Lands and Livestock," *Southwestern Historical Quarterly*, LVIII, 331–341; W. Gard, "The Impact of the Cattle Trails," *Southwestern Historical Quarterly*, LXXI, 1–6; Lowell H. Harrison, "British Interest in the Panhandle-Plains Area, 1878–1885," *Panhandle Plains Historical Review*, XXXVIII, 1–44; Gene M. Gressley, *Bankers and Cattlemen* (New York, 1966); J. B. Frantz and Julian Ernest Choate, *The American Cowboy: The Myth and the Reality* (Norman, Okla., 1955); and John I. White, *Git Along Little Dogies: Songs and Songwriters of the American West* (Urbana, Ill., 1975).

A number of works have been published on the sheep industry. Paul Carlson's studies include *Texas Woollybacks: The Range Sheep and Goat Industry* (College Station, 1982); "Bankers and Sheepherders in West Texas," *West Texas Historical Association Year Book*, LXI, 5–14; and "Sheepherders and Cowboys: A Comparison of Life-styles in West Texas," ibid., LVIII, 19–28. Other works are those of Edward Norris Wentworth, *America's Sheep Trails* (Ames, Ia., 1948); Harold M. Gober, "The Sheep Industry in Sterling County," *West Texas Historical Association Year Book*, XXVII, 32–57; and Douglas Barnett, "Angora Goats in Texas: Agricultural Innovation on the Edwards Plateau, 1858–1900," *Southwestern Historical Quarterly*, XC, 347–372. For the correspondence of George W. Kendall, Texas's leading sheep rancher, see H. J. Brown, *Letters from a Texas Sheep Ranch* (Urbana, 1959).

Preeminent among the accounts of the settlement of West Texas are William Curry Holden, *Alkali Trails* (Dallas, 1930); Rupert N. Richardson, *The Frontier of Northwest Texas, 1846 to 1876* (Glendale, CA, 1963); Billy Mac Jones, *The Search for Maturity*; Austin, 1965); and Frederick W. Rathjen, *The Texas Panhandle Frontier* (Austin, 1975). An interesting economic perspective on the development of the West Texas frontier can be found in Paul H. Carlson, *Empire Builder in the Texas Panhandle: William Henry Bush* (College Station, 1996), and in Thomas T. Smith, *The U.S. Army and the Texas Frontier Economy, 1845–1900* (College Station, 1999). Other writings dealing with various phases of the subject are Mrs. S. C. Miller, *Sixty Years in the Nueces Valley, 1870–1930* (San Antonio, 1930); Walter B. Stephens, *Through Texas* (reprint of a series of letters published in the *St. Louis Globe Democrat*, 1892); Willie N. Lewis, *Between Sun and Sod: An Informal History of the Texas Panhandle* (College Station, 1977); David B. Gracy, *Littlefield Lands: Colonization of the Texas Plains, 1912–1920* (Austin, 1968); Vernon G. Spence, *Judge Legett of Abilene: A Texas Frontier Profile* (College Station, 1977); Kathryn Duff, *Abilene on the Catclaw* (Abilene, 1970); Clayton W. Williams, *Texas' Last Frontier: Fort Stockton and the Trans-Pecos, 1861–1895* (College Station, 1982); and Wayne R. Austerman, *Sharps Rifles and Spanish Mules: The San Antonio-El Paso Mail, 1851–1881* (College Station, 1985). For South Texas, see J. Lee Stambaugh, *The Lower Rio Grande Valley of Texas* (San Antonio, 1954); Julian Samora et al., *Gunpowder Justice: A Reassessment of the Texas Rangers* (Notre Dame, 1979); Charles Goldfinch, *Juan N. Cortina: Two Interpretations* (New York, 1974); Jerry D. Thompson (ed.), *Juan Cortina and the Texas-Mexico Frontier, 1859–1877* (El Paso, 1994); and Arnoldo De León, *The Tejano Community, 1836–1900* (Albuquerque, 1982). On the public land system, see Aldon S. Lang, *Financial History of the Public Lands in Texas* (New York, 1979); and R. D. Holt, "School Land Rushes in West Texas," *West Texas Historical Association Year Book*, X, 42–57. An account of the transition from ranch to farm is found in David B. Gracy, II, *Littlefield Lands: Colonization on the Texas Plains, 1912–1920* (Austin, 1968). The effects of drought are portrayed in Richard King, *Wagons East: The Drought of 1886* (Austin, 1965).

14

The Populists and Progressives 1890–1910

The conservative and frugal policies of the years immediately after Reconstruction were not acceptable to many Texans. Often desperately poor and convinced that their plight was both unfair and unjustified, they began as early as the 1870s to seek, without much success, government intervention to improve their circumstances. Economic conditions improved somewhat in the 1880s, but the level of dissatisfaction seemed to increase.

By 1890, the demands for reform in political and economic affairs could no longer be ignored or rejected. Texans in the next two decades adopted laws regulating business, expanding education, reforming the electoral system, and making other changes designed to meet the needs of the emerging modern society. In the 1890s, the primary impetus for reform was the unhappy farmer. Seeking the elimination of economic inequities and the expansion of political democracy, the more militant agrarian radicals organized a third party, the People's or Populist Party, while other reformers sought similar goals within the Democratic Party.

With the decline of agrarian protest, sentiment for reform subsided temporarily, only to be revived after 1900 with the spirit of the progressive movement. The progressivism of the new century was not merely a renewal of agrarian protest. The base of the movement was broader, with more emphasis on the role of businessmen, teachers, and professional people, and on new organizations such as the State Federation of Labor and the Texas Local Option Association. The goals were more complex. Business regulation continued to be a primary objective, but progressives also stressed humanitarian reforms, reorganization of municipal government, expansion of education, and other changes affecting not only the rural but also the urban population. In many ways, it was as much an attitude as it was a program. In short, progressivism reflected the growing importance of industrialization and urbanization. Nevertheless, early twentieth-century Texas progressivism preserved a strong rural influence. Many of the goals and some of the leadership of former years were the same. Reflecting this, a new agrarian organization, the Farmers' Union, was one of the more effective reform groups.

Reform, however, was not the only element determining the course of politics during these years. Except for the Populist challenge, most political conflicts took place within the Democratic Party. In the one-party structure, personal and factional rivalry sometimes disregarded ideology for the sake of political expediency and formed coalitions not particularly related to the matter of progressive change.

THE GROWTH OF POLITICAL DISCONTENT

During the first two decades following the Civil War, the prevailing attitude in Texas toward big business was friendly. The Constitution of 1876, though framed by a convention controlled by farmers, contained no provisions hostile to organized wealth. The Grange and the Greenback Party repeatedly criticized the Democratic administration, contending that it was too generous toward corporations, but the dominant party continued to encourage business development with a minimum of regulatory measures. The demand for regulation increased, however, and during the later 1880s the number of malcontents grew rapidly.

As in former years, the center of dissatisfaction was among the farmers, who still constituted a majority of the people. Since the Civil War the farmer had faced many serious problems. The price of cotton, the great money crop of Texas, declined from 31 cents a pound in 1865 to less than 5 cents in 1898. With declining prices it seemed that the harder the farmers worked, the more cotton they grew, the less money they earned. The supply of money in circulation, limited anyway, seemed unreasonably diminished when the "Crime of 1873" eliminated coinage of silver into money. The resulting deflation contributed to the decline of the prices of farm products and made it nearly impossible for the farmer to pay his debts. Meanwhile, taxes and interest charges on mortgages seldom diminished, and the cost of many other articles the farmer had to buy increased from year to year. It was easy for him to believe that the corporation that held a mortgage on his farm charged him exorbitant interest, that the railroads were overcharging him for hauling his crops, and that the middlemen were appropriating too much for their services.

Amid the collapse of the first farmers' movements, the Grange and the Greenback Party, arose a new one, the Farmers' Alliance. The Farmers' Alliance was founded in Lampasas, Texas in 1875, primarily to protect farmers from unscrupulous land dealers. It was reorganized in 1879 as a secret, nonpolitical, self-help organization. In the mid-1880s it restructured itself again, becoming an avidly political organization championing the causes of both farmers and labor. At its state meeting in Cleburne in 1886, the Alliance set forth its political agenda. First it denounced "the shameful abuses that the industrial classes are now suffering at the hands of arrogant capitalists and powerful corporations," then it listed its political demands. These included the removal of fences from illegally enclosed land, the sale of school land to settlers only, higher taxes on land owned by speculators, the regulation of railroads, the free coinage of gold and silver to expand the supply of currency, raise farm prices, and ease the burden of debt, and the creation of a national bureau of labor statistics. Two years later the Alliance added a call for an antitrust law and reiterated its demand for effective regulation of railroad rates. In 1887, it became a national organization, and soon its strength was estimated to be between 1 million and 3 million members.

The Alliance and, to a lesser extent, the Knights of Labor pushed the Democratic Party toward a more reform-minded agenda. The party's 1886 platform called for the sale of land "in tracts of reasonable size" to settlers only, favored laws correcting abuses practiced by the railroads, and—most extreme of all—contained a plank that made stockholders of a corporation liable, within limits, for the debts of the corporation. In 1888, the Democratic convention adopted a stronger plank on railway regulation and called for an antitrust law. Two years later the Democratic candidate for governor ran on a platform calling for the abolishment of the national banking system, free coinage of silver, and a state railway commission. This platform contained the heart of the Alliance program, and the candidate received the endorsement of the Alliance. The agrarian reformers had triumphed; they felt that they had captured the Democratic Party.

Meanwhile, other Texans worked hard for reforms at the national level. In Congress, Roger Q. Mills, chairman of the Committee on Ways and Means, proposed a tariff reform measure that was passed in the House of Representatives in 1888 and became the Democratic manifesto in the national campaign of that year. John H. Reagan was even more successful as a national reformer. In 1887 the veteran Senator coauthored the Interstate Commerce Act, which marked the beginning of federal regulation of the railroads.

Prohibition was the most controversial and politically explosive reform movement in late-nineteenth century Texas. As Governor Oran Roberts recalled, the controversy over Prohibition generated the most exciting political conflict that Texas had seen in years, as it "stirred up society to its very foundations with a greater manifestation of universal feeling and interest than had ever occurred before in Texas." Prohibition was a moral issue that inflamed passions and defied compromise. Its advocates sincerely believed that alcohol was at the root of all social evils, from crime to poverty to corruption. Opponents believed just as strongly that Prohibition was an attack on individual liberty and freedom of choice.

The first step in the Prohibition campaign came in 1875 when E. L. Dohoney managed to insert a local option provision in the Constitution of 1876. When few counties took advantage of this opportunity to prohibit the sale of alcoholic beverages, Dohoney and others launched a campaign to implement statewide Prohibition through a constitutional amendment. Dohoney picked up support from the Grange in 1880 and the Greenback Party in 1882. Also in 1882, the Women's Christian Temperance Union opened a chapter in Texas. The W.C.T.U. recruited the wives of a number of prominent Texans, including Senator Samuel Bell Maxey, and became the most effective voice for Prohibition in the state.

Fearing that Prohibition would divide their party and threaten their control of the state government, the leaders of the Democratic Party resisted taking action on this issue. Finally, succumbing to growing pressure, the 1887 legislature sent a constitutional amendment to the voters that would replace the local option with statewide Prohibition.

With both the Prohibitionists and their opponents organized, the campaign was heated and bitter. Leaders of the Prohibition campaign included Baptist and Methodist ministers, the head of the Texas Grange, and prominent Democrats like Senator Maxey and Congressman John H. Reagan. Anti-Prohibitionists included Governor Ross and former governors Roberts, Throckmorton, and Coke. They made a successful appeal for the black vote, reminding blacks that they had not been allowed to purchase alcohol during slavery, and they linked prohibition to anti-German and anti-Catholic prejudice. Their campaign culminated with a huge rally in Fort Worth, where State Treasurer F. R. Lubbock, addressing a crowd of 40,000, read an anti-Prohibition letter from former Confederate President Jefferson Davis.

On August 5, 1887, the voters of Texas defeated the Prohibition amendment 220,627 to 129,270. Democratic leaders hoped that the election would end prohibition agitation and reunify the party. Instead, frustrated prohibitionists, convinced of the morality of their cause, found defeat hard to accept. They blamed their loss on the opposition organized by the conservative Democratic leadership and remained alienated from the party. This was particularly true in those counties that already were suffering from agricultural distress.

Related to some extent to the Prohibition issue was another reform—women's suffrage. After meeting with little success in the writing of the constitutions of 1869 and 1876, supporters of women's suffrage were largely inactive for more than a decade. However, in 1887, following their defeat in the Prohibition election, the W.C.T.U. endorsed women's suffrage. In 1893 Rebecca Henry Hayes, already a vice president of the National American Women's Suffrage Association, founded the Texas Equal Rights Association to spearhead the suffrage fight in Texas. An effort to secure endorsement of women's suffrage by the Democratic and Republican parties failed in 1894, as did an effort the following year to lobby the legislature for a suffrage amendment to the state constitution. These failures and internal dissension led to declining interest, and by 1896 the movement was again virtually inactive. Women, however, were very active in the Prohibition campaign, and they played an important role in the reform movements of the 1890s and early 1900s.

James Stephen Hogg and Reform Democrats

For more than a decade, James Stephen Hogg was instrumental in determining the tone of Texas government. First elected to state office in 1886 as attorney general in the administration of Lawrence Sullivan Ross, Hogg stood in striking contrast to the conservative governors who preceded him. The son of a Texas statesman and Confederate brigadier, and left an orphan at age twelve, Hogg had grown to manhood in his native East Texas during the Reconstruction era. He had not finished the intermediate grades when he left school in Tyler in 1866. Unaided, he made his way at such jobs as he could secure. Years as a typesetter and printer furnished the background for his sympathetic understanding of the problems of the common people. Eventually Hogg began studying law and he was admitted to the bar. After serving as prosecuting attorney and spending a few years in private law practice, in 1886 Hogg was elected attorney general. He realized that the dominant question facing Texas was the regulation of corporations. On that issue he soon appropriated the center of the political stage, and he was elected governor in 1890 on a platform promising to correct the abuses of big business.

People who knew him were never indifferent to Jim Hogg. As a campaigner he had few equals. He knew the mind of the common man and how to appeal to it with fluent speech and expressive vernacular. Newspapers of the opposition charged that his frequent "by gatlings" and the earthy epithets he hurled at his enemies "were offensive to the ladies who honored him with their presence," but the ladies and all others continued to go to hear him. In the scant shade of a picnic arbor he could hold crowds for hours, while he berated the railroads and denounced discrimination against

James S. Hogg. He earned a reputation as champion of the people's rights when he served as attorney general and governor of Texas during the last quarter of the nineteenth century. This was a period when efforts were made to regulate practices of big business that were not in the public interest. (Archives Division—Texas State Library)

farmers. When the heat became unbearable, he would doff his coat, fling off his suspenders, and periodically gulp water from a pitcher or a bucket.

His public record was punctuated with incidents that made good news and kept him ever in the public eye. When the Southern Pacific Railroad in 1894 deliberately stranded 700 marchers of Coxey's Army at a West Texas desert station, a Hogg ultimatum forced the railroad to convey the men across the state.

Corporation lawyers soon learned that he was a dangerous antagonist. After he became attorney general in 1887, Hogg first directed his efforts against insurance companies that were operating in unlawful fashion. He drove about forty of these from the state and compelled others to pay taxes and to obey the laws.

Hogg also contributed to the passage of antitrust legislation. Many Texans believed that monopolies, or "trusts," were conspiring to fix prices and to eliminate competition. Agitation on the subject in Congress, moreover, inspired legislation on the state level. Hogg assisted in framing the Texas antitrust law. Enacted on March 30, 1889, it was the second such law in the nation. The law levied heavy penalties against combinations of any kind that restricted trade, fixed prices, or limited production. The law was extended in 1895 to apply to insurance companies, and subsequent changes added to the effectiveness of antitrust regulation.

Hogg's greatest efforts were directed toward regulation of the railroads. The Constitution of 1876 authorized the legislature to pass laws to "correct abuses, to prevent unjust discrimination and extortion" in railroad rates and fares. This provision had not resulted in effective railroad regulation before Hogg's administration as attorney general. Using existing laws, he forced the dissolution of the Texas Traffic Association, a pool through which nine railroads with headquarters outside the state dominated Texas rail traffic.

In spite of this victory, Hogg realized that existing laws were insufficient to secure meaningful railroad regulation. Consequently he worked to secure the enactment of a railroad commission law. In 1889 the legislature sent a constitutional amendment authorizing such a commission to the voters for approval.

The commission amendment became the leading political issue in the 1890 gubernatorial election. An organization of businessmen known as the State Freight Rate Convention endorsed it, and the Farmers' Alliance favored it. In his campaign for governor, Hogg championed it with the zeal of a crusader. He noted that with unregulated rail rates it cost less to ship East Texas lumber to Nebraska than to Dallas. Hogg easily won the Democratic nomination, and in November the voters elected him governor and ratified the amendment. The legislature in April 1891 set up the Texas Railroad Commission with the power to set railroad rates and fares. As originally established, the commission consisted of three members appointed by the governor. John H. Reagan resigned his seat in the U.S. Senate to accept the chairmanship of the commission. A second constitutional amendment, which became effective in 1894, made the commissioners elective.

The Texas Railroad Commission enjoyed a measure of success. It secured the reduction of freight rates and claimed credit for the resulting increase of milling and manufacturing in the state. The railroads brought suits in 1892 to restrain the commission from enforcing its orders, and for nearly two years the commission could not function. The long fight in the courts ended in victory for the state, and in July 1894 the body again took up the work of rate regulation. While litigation over rate regulation was under way, the commission acquired additional authority. At Hogg's behest, the legislature passed a law in 1893 regulating the amount of stock that a railroad might issue, limiting it to an amount reasonably equal to the value of the railroad.

While railroads and the state battled in the courts, a bitter political controversy raged over the railroad commission. In the gubernatorial campaign in 1892, the railroads and most leading newspapers supported George Clark of Waco, a railroad attorney. Clark had opposed the commission amendment in 1890 as "wrong in principle, undemocratic and unrepublican"; its only function, he said, was to harass the railroads. Now he accepted the commission as an established fact but insisted that it should be conservative, completely democratic, and elective, and that the law should be liberalized to permit the railroads to appeal to the courts. Hogg defended the commission and eloquently and vigorously attacked his opponent. At the famous "Street Car Barn Convention" in Houston in August 1892, the Democrats divided, one group nominating Hogg, the other Clark; and in the autumn the warring factions continued their campaign before the voters. Although one wing of the Republican Party supported Clark, Hogg was reelected by a substantial majority.

Other reforms of the Hogg administration—or "Hogg laws," as they were often termed—addressed a variety of issues. In response to Governor Hogg's urgent plea, the legislature passed several laws limiting the right of aliens and corporations to own land in Texas. Otherwise, Hogg promoted prison reform, the establishment of a board of pardon advisers, extension of the school term from four to six months, and additional funding for the University of Texas. Hogg's record on race relations was mixed. On the one hand, he did not oppose a law authorizing railroads to segregate facilities for blacks and whites; on the other hand, he organized "Negro Hogg Clubs" to attract the black vote, he campaigned actively against racial violence, and, following a brutal lynching in Paris, Texas, in 1893, he urged the legislature to pass an antilynching law.

After retiring from politics in 1895, Hogg spent the final decade of his life amassing a fortune, though he never abandoned his interest in public affairs. Ironically, the wealth he accrued in his later years came in large measure from the interests he had sought as a reformer to control. Though his zeal as a reformer diminished somewhat, he remained alert to the dangers of corrupt business practices. Hogg had made reform respectable, and, notwithstanding his acquiescence to segregation, he has remained a symbol of the Texas reform tradition.

THE POPULISTS

Reforms either promised or accomplished by Governor Hogg and the Democrats temporarily quieted criticism from the Farmers' Alliance, but the Democrats did not go far enough to suit the more militant of the agrarian radicals. The latter's support for government ownership of railroads and similar proposals found little sympathy among Democratic leaders. Governor Hogg even refused to name a leader of the Farmers' Alliance to the railroad commission. Moreover, Hogg and his followers in the Democratic Party refused to endorse the favorite program of the Texas Alliance, the subtreasury—a plan whereby the federal government would make loans to farmers directly, at a nominal rate of interest, with farm produce as collateral. In fact, in 1891 the Democratic leaders purged from the party those Alliance men who supported the subtreasury plan.

The Farmers' Alliance, disenchanted with Hogg and snubbed by the Democrats, evolved into a third party before the election of 1892. The People's Party (or Populist Party) organized not only in Texas but across the United States. The new party grew rapidly. When the 1892 Democratic national convention chose Grover Cleveland, the conservative, sound-money advocate, as its standard bearer, many of the Democratic faithful were alienated. The memory of their "betrayal" in the Prohibition struggle, reinforced by the economic hard times of the early 1890s, fed their discontent, and thousands of small farmers enlisted in the Populist cause. With this grassroots support, the Populists contested each election in Texas for several years. Their rivalry with the Democrats was at times comparable in bitterness to the politics of the Reconstruction era.

The list of reforms that the Populists supported was lengthy and comprehensive. Some were borrowed from earlier reform movements, some from the Democrats themselves, while others were Populist innovations. They demanded government regulation of business, public ownership of railroads, free coinage of silver, abolition of the national banking system, and establishment of the subtreasury system. The Populists also supported laws to improve the status of the laborer and to implement a graduated income tax. To further democracy, they advocated direct election of U.S. senators and the president and vice president, limiting all officeholders to two terms, and the use of referendum and recall. But Texas Populists, fearing the divisive nature of these issues, avoided taking a position on Prohibition and women's suffrage.

Populism, however, was more than the platform of an organization; it was also an attitude, a crusade to use the machinery of government to ameliorate the miseries of those who felt economically or politically oppressed. The Populists, with their vision of a class-conscious politics, sometimes oversimplified problems and their solutions, but the problems they saw were real and the solutions they proposed had merit. It was a rural movement, strongest among the poorer farmers of East and West Central Texas. Though it had support among some laboring groups, Populism had little attraction for most business and professional men. Its greatest appeal was to the alienated, to those who felt that they could no longer depend on traditional institutions to protect their interests and advance their cause.

Basing their program on doctrines of economic and political equality, the Populists launched a campaign against various abuses of the prevailing order. Seventy-five weekly newspapers, among them the *Southern Mercury*, printed in Dallas, carried the gospel of Populism to every part of the state. A corps of stump speakers, led by a few men of superior ability, including Thomas L. Nugent, Jerome Kearby, T. P. Gore (who later represented Oklahoma in the U.S. Senate), and James H. "Cyclone" Davis, served as ardent evangelists of the new gospel. Many of their leaders were Protestant preachers, who not only appropriated the camp meeting, the hymns, and the religious fervor of the rural churches, but took from the Bible many of their utterances and arguments.

As the campaigns became more and more acrimonious, Populists and Democrats resorted to various political strategies and political tricks. The People's Party made a strong bid for the black voters, many of whom were naturally attracted by the Populist demand for economic justice. Though they did not endorse racial equality, the Populists promised blacks equal protection under the law and affirmed their support for black suffrage. In their scramble for the black vote, both parties, but especially the Democrats, employed "'fluence men," white and black politicians who could deliver the black vote. The Democrats also used similar practices to control the Mexican American vote in South Texas.

Although the Populists never gained control of state government, they had some success at the ballot box. The party's maximum strength in the legislature came following the election of 1894, when it held 22 of the 128 seats in the lower house and two in the senate. In the gubernatorial campaign of 1894, Populist Thomas Nugent received nearly one-third of the vote in his campaign against Hogg's successor, Charles A. Culberson.

The real test between the Populists and the Democrats came in the election of 1896. The gubernatorial campaign was the closest in years and one of the most heated. Both sides again used "'fluence men" in an effort to control the minority vote. Democrats accused the Populists of spreading socialism and of reviving black Republicanism by courting the African American vote. In the election the Populist candidate, Jerome Kearby, aided by the Republicans, threatened Democratic supremacy more seriously than had any candidate since Reconstruction. Kearby polled 238,692 votes to 298,528 for Governor Culberson. Again the Populists elected large numbers of county and precinct officers.

After 1896 the Populist Party faded quickly from Texas and national politics. With William Jennings Bryan as their standard bearer, the Democrats on the national level had sealed the doom of the third party by appropriating its chief plank, free coinage of silver, and a number of other reform proposals. The Populist Party then surrendered its identity by endorsing Bryan and the Democrats. "Fusion"—merging with the Democrats—and Bryan's subsequent defeat left the Populists in shambles. Moreover, the wave of prosperity that appeared in Texas following the election silenced the more strident voices of discontent.

While successfully meeting the challenge of populism, the Democratic political leadership moved cautiously to extend the reform programs of Governor Hogg. Governor Charles Culberson's record as a reformer was decidedly mixed. Between 1895 and 1899 he signed laws regulating primary elections, strengthening antitrust regulations, adding to the authority of the railroad commission, improving the judicial system, and setting aside school lands for a black university. This latter act, which was intended to fund a full-scale black university equivalent to the University of Texas, was invalidated by the Texas Supreme Court, and the projected institution was not established. Culberson's overall record on the regulation of big business also was mixed, and he vetoed a number of reform measures. He was neither an enthusiastic supporter nor an opponent of reform, and his administration represented a transition from the preceding reform-minded regime of Governor Hogg to the relatively conservative era that followed.

THE CONSERVATIVE RESURGENCE

Although the reform impulse did not entirely disappear, the years between 1898 and 1906 represented a return to conservatism. With the Populists fading and the Republicans quarreling, Democratic rule was virtually unchallenged. In the Democratic Party much of the tumult usually associated with gubernatorial politics was eliminated by the shrewd and efficient manipulations of Colonel Edward M. House, a well-to-do Houston planter and railroad builder who made politics his avocation and surpassed the professionals in it. House first became involved in the campaign to reelect Hogg in 1892 and then directed Culberson's campaigns in 1894 and 1896. House followed this success by managing the campaigns of Culberson's successors, governors Joseph Sayers (1899–1903) and Samuel Willis Tucker Lanham (1903–7). Unknown to most Texans, House was not a leader of a political machine in the usual sense. Instead, he relied on careful, thorough organization and the assistance of a few intimate and powerful friends to exert a degree of influence without parallel in Texas politics. In 1912 he moved to the national level, helping elect Woodrow Wilson and then serving his administration.

Both Governors Sayers and Lanham contributed to the resurgence of conservatism. Both were genteel, high-minded men; both were ex-Confederates, the last to serve as chief executive of the state; and both had rendered their previous public service mainly in Congress. Both brought to the office mature judgment but little imagination. By temperament and training, neither was a zealous crusader for change.

Other forces also contributed to the decline of reform fervor. The emotionalism and political agitation of the Hogg years and the Populist uprising had run its course, and the Spanish-American War diverted the attention of many Texans. Moreover, an attitude more favorable toward business prevailed. Oil discoveries, including the fabulous Spindletop, excited the hopes of Texans and enticed a welcome flow of capital to the state. Other industries, such as the East Texas lumber business, bolstered the state's economy. Reflecting the shift of economic power in the state, the proportion of farmer members of the legislature declined from about one-half in the early 1890s to about one-third after 1900. Political leaders, such as Colonel House, though surely not subservient to corporate interests, were not as suspicious of them as were the agrarian radicals of the 1890s. Texas remained a rural land, but the industrial age was fast approaching.

Despite the conservative temper of the times, some worthwhile reforms were accomplished. The legislature adopted several laws protecting labor. An 1899 statute exempted organized labor from antitrust regulations, and in 1901, the legislature outlawed the use of blacklists to control union organization and the use of company script that could be spent only at company stores. In 1903, the legislature limited the hours of railroad employees and required specified safety measures on street railways. The same year it enacted the first Texas law regulating child labor. Unfortunately, the enforcement of labor laws was often weak and erratic.

A state banking system, prohibited for many years by the Constitution of 1876, was established during the Lanham administration. In 1904, the voters ratified a constitutional amendment permitting the state to charter banks, and the legislature of the following year established a commission of insurance and banking. Directed by Thomas M. Love, a progressive Dallas politician, the commission supervised the chartering of more than 500 banks during the next five years.

Tax reform, sought unsuccessfully during the Sayers administration, was partially accomplished in the second Lanham term. The general property tax provided the greater part of the state's revenue, but property valuations had not kept pace with the increasing demands. Railroad properties in particular were undervalued. In response to Governor Lanham's request, the legislature in 1905 raised taxes on assets of the railroads and certain other industries. Laws providing for taxes and levies on express companies, sleeping-car companies, pipelines, and other businesses were also adopted.

Guided by a peculiar mixture of progressive and reactionary goals, the legislature also reorganized the state's election system. Before 1903, party candidates in some counties were nominated by primaries and in others by conventions. In either case, abuses and fraud were widespread. Although the constitution empowered the legislature to police the voting process, little had been done to eliminate such practices as the purchase of votes, extravagant campaign expenditures, and dishonest election returns. In 1895, the legislature passed a law that regulated primary elections in those counties where they were held, but it was inadequate. The law was changed in 1897 and again two years later, but it did little to prevent abuses. Registration of voters was finally assured when a constitutional amendment adopted in 1902 made a poll tax receipt or exemption certificate mandatory for voting.

During the Lanham years the legislature addressed the problem in earnest. Two laws, named after their author, Judge Alexander W. Terrell, affected both primaries and general elections. The first became effective in 1903, and the second, repealing the first and passed in 1905, constitutes the foundation of Texas election laws to this day. The law of 1905 described who would be permitted to vote in both primary and general elections and required that primary elections be held for all political parties that had received at least 100,000 or more votes in the previous general election. The effect of these laws and subsequent legislation that refined the process was that the primary election would be the process by which candidates were nominated for public office. Party conventions would be used for selecting party leadership and determining party platforms.

Although the electoral reforms made at the turn of the century eliminated many abuses, the changes also undermined political democracy. The poll tax discouraged all poor people from voting, but blacks generally fared worse than others. Inspired by a long-standing fear of black suffrage, which was reinforced by the success Populists had in attracting the black vote and the threat they mounted to the power of the Democrats, and by the rising tide of racial antagonism and racial violence prevalent near the end of the century, white politicians deliberately sought to eliminate the black voter from politics. The result was an undemocratic but effective device known as a "white primary." By the early 1900s most Democratic primaries, which were almost always tantamount to election, were open only to white voters. For the next several decades, blacks would be denied an effective voice in the politics of the state. Not until the Supreme Court of the United States in 1944 ruled white primaries unconstitutional was the black voter assured of his or her place at the polls. Progressive electoral reform—indeed, progressive reforms in general—did little to improve the lives of black people.

Another electoral issue, women's suffrage, briefly surfaced again during the Sayers-Lanham years. In 1903 Annette Finnegan, her sisters, and others organized the Texas Woman Suffrage Association in Houston and attempted to form chapters in other cities, but with little success. The Finnegan sisters left the state in 1905, and for several years thereafter the only organized suffrage effort was a local group in Austin. Though they failed in their efforts to achieve the vote, women won another battle during the Lanham administration. In 1903 Helen Stoddard, president of the Texas W.C.T.U., achieved victory in her ten-year campaign to enhance educational opportunities for women when the legislature established Texas Women's University.

The one area where reform spirit remained dominant during the Sayers-Lanham era was the state's strong antitrust activity. More stringent antitrust acts were passed in 1899 and 1903, and state attorneys successfully prosecuted a number of violators. In fact, the Texas antitrust policy was more effective than that of the federal government. Of the 110 prosecutions brought under the Texas statutes up to 1915, 84 were settled by compromise, with penalties totaling $3,324,766 exacted in 74 cases. In comparison, federal antitrust laws during about the same period of time brought 187 prosecutions with fines or penalties totaling $548,881 in only 33 cases.

The most famous Texas antitrust case of this era involved the Waters-Pierce Oil Company, a Missouri corporation with Standard Oil affiliations. In 1897, the attorney general brought suit for violations of the Texas antitrust act. A verdict revoking the firm's permit to do business in the state was upheld by the U.S. Supreme Court in 1900. Then, claiming that it had reorganized and had severed all ties with the Standard Oil combine, the company secured a new Texas license, over the objections of some Texans such as Jim Hogg. Subsequently, a suit brought by the state of Missouri in 1905 revealed that a majority of the stock of the "new" company actually belonged to the Standard Oil Company. Acting quickly, the state of Texas sought and obtained a judgment for ouster and penalties of $1,623,900. When the decision was upheld on appeal, the corporation paid a fine amounting to $1,808,483.30, the largest ever collected by the state, and the properties of the firm were sold at auction.

Meanwhile, the case had provoked an even greater controversy—Baileyism. While a candidate for the U.S. Senate in 1900, Congressman Joseph Weldon Bailey, ignoring the possible conflict of interest, urged Governor Sayers and the state attorney general to allow Waters-Pierce to return to the state. Though he did not receive a fee for this service, he was employed by Henry Clay Pierce in other matters. Furthermore, he had borrowed $5,000 from Pierce, who, unknown to Bailey, had placed the note on company records.

Almost immediately some questioned the propriety of Bailey's intervention, but not until new investigations in 1905 and 1906 (after he had been elected to the senate) publicly disclosed the relationship between the senator and the oilman did the state divide into angry camps of pro- and anti-Bailey men. Though Bailey was unopposed for reelection in the Democratic primary of 1906, critics argued that the legislature should ignore the primary and refuse to return him to the Senate. Bailey, in response, contended that the whole affair was a conspiracy to deprive the nation of his great services.

By a vote of 108 to 39, the legislature reelected the senator, but meanwhile, a legislative investigating committee was studying the ethics of the colorful figure. The Texas Senate quickly exonerated him, but the house committee was divided in its report. Not satisfied with this victory, Senator Bailey announced that he would make the selection of the Texas delegation to the Democratic National Convention in 1908 a test of his strength; he insisted that none but Bailey men would go to the convention. Both the Bailey and the anti-Bailey forces waged a contest with heat and rancor that has rarely been equaled in the annals of Texas politics. By an overwhelming vote Bailey and his slate of delegates won. Nevertheless, differences still rankled, and no doubt the controversy would have flared up again if Bailey had not voluntarily retired to private life in 1913. For nearly a decade Baileyism had divided the Democratic Party into Bailey and anti-Bailey factions.

THOMAS M. CAMPBELL
AND PROGRESSIVE REFORM

A definite swing away from conservatism was apparent in the gubernatorial contest of 1906. For the first time in more than a decade, Colonel House did not take an active role in the contest, and none of the candidates had a decided advantage. Each of the four major contenders favored a war on the trusts, an antilobby law, tax reform, and generous support for the state's institutions. Thomas M. Campbell, a lawyer from Palestine, emerged as the victor from a rather evenly divided race. Generally regarded as the most progressive of the candidates, Campbell had the endorsement of ex-Governor Hogg, who repeatedly had voiced his dissatisfaction with the attitude of the Sayers and Lanham administration toward big business, and the last-minute support of Senator Bailey. Armed with the support of farmers, labor, and various others, Campbell energetically promoted tax reform, insurance regulation, improvements in education, additional laws protecting labor, and a number of other changes. Though sentiment for reform declined in his second term and progressivism did not extend beyond his own administration, nonetheless he joins Hogg as one of Texas's true progressive governors.

Powerful and well-organized interest groups committed to reform contributed to Campbell's election. The State Federation of Labor, which met for the first time in 1898, claimed 158 unions and more than 9,000 members by 1906. The Farmers' Union, organized in 1902, claimed 100,000 members by 1906. Sometimes working together, these organizations lobbied for laws protecting workers, compulsory school attendance, free textbooks, and laws against child and convict labor. The Texas Federation of Women's Clubs, with 5,000 members, worked hard on behalf of better schools, pure food and drug laws, conservation of natural resources, improved legal rights for Texas women, and more libraries.

One of the first targets of the Campbell administration was tax reform. In 1907 the legislature enacted the "full-rendition law," requiring that property be rendered for taxation at its "reasonable cash market value." The full-rendition law very nearly doubled the value of property on the tax rolls, but it also provoked anguished protests, not only from corporate interests but also from landowning farmers.

Other aspects of Campbell's fiscal program were similarly controversial. The governor's plea for an income tax had little success; he did obtain a light inheritance tax, but it produced more complaints than revenue. In the interest of economy he vetoed $1.7 million worth of appropriations, some of which were for badly needed improvements. At the end of his administration, officials lowered the tax rate to an unrealistic level, leaving a deficit of nearly $1 million for the next governor. In spite of the tax reform efforts of both the Lanham and Campbell administrations, the general property tax continued to produce the greater part of the state's operating revenue, and real estate continued to bear approximately two-thirds of the tax burden placed on property.

Campbell was more successful promoting reform in the insurance industry. Under his guidance the legislature adopted comprehensive codes for life, health, accident, home, and fire insurance. Furthermore, the Robertson Insurance Law, enacted in 1907, required life insurance companies to invest at least 75 percent of their reserves in Texas securities. When they failed to defeat the bill, twenty-one insurance companies withdrew from the state, contending that its requirements were harsh and unreasonable. As a matter of fact, other states had similar requirements. Furthermore, of the $40 million in reserves held by the companies, less than $1 million had been invested in Texas. Some of the companies returned, but others continued with great persistence to work for the repeal or modification of the law. It was not repealed until 1963.

In a related area, in 1909 the state established an insurance program protecting funds deposited in state banks. Bank failures during the panic of 1907 had centered public attention on the need of greater protection for small depositors. For a number of years the plan worked quite successfully, but numerous failures in the early 1920s put a heavy strain on the system, and it was abolished in 1927. The Texas effort anticipated the Federal Deposit Insurance Corporation enacted during the New Deal.

Reforms in municipal government, a prominent feature of progressive change elsewhere, were most noticeable during the Campbell administration. The commission system of government, first used in Galveston in 1901, was encouraged by the governor, who approved thirteen city charters containing the plan. Other cities adopted the city manager system or received new state charters providing them with greater regulatory power. In addition practically every city charter issued under Campbell provided for more direct democracy through the use of the initiative, referendum, and recall. However, these efforts to extend direct democracy were not implemented at the state level.

A number of other progressive measures were adopted. Campbell, who had consistently advocated greater regulation of corporations, signed a law in 1907 strengthening antitrust restrictions. Several laws improving conditions for labor were passed, and the legislature created the state medical board and the state board of health. Significant improvements, particularly in the area of financing, were made in education. Campbell also approved laws restricting free passes by railroads, promoting pure food, and prohibiting nepotism in state administration, as well as laws against lobbying and several acts for the improvement of roads.

The Campbell administration devoted much of its reform effort to prison reform. Texas prisons had long been a problem, in many respects a disgrace. In 1871, Texas adopted the prison-lease system, under which the state leased the penitentiary to private individuals. The lessees were to employ the convicts in any way they wished, subject only to the mandates of state inspectors, who were supposed to see that the prisoners were not abused and that the prison property was not damaged. This was perhaps the worst system practiced in modern times. The death rate of convicts doubled, and the number of escapes per year more than tripled.

In 1883, the state completed a new prison at Rusk and adopted a new plan for administering the penal system, the contract-lease system. Under the new arrangement the state retained control of the prison and prisoners but leased to private operators the shops within the penitentiary walls and also hired out gangs of convicts to railroad construction foremen, planters, and others. Though this was better than the old lease plan, it was still unsatisfactory. The industries established at Huntsville and Rusk to employ prison labor failed. In response, the Texas prison system began operating its own farms, but without plan or design, prison farming presented its own set of problems. Complaints about prison conditions continued to surface, but no significant action was taken for many years.

Spurred by a series of newspaper articles in 1908 and 1909 that exposed prison abuses and charges made in the gubernatorial campaign of 1910, Campbell called a special session of the legislature in 1911. An investigating committee of state senators and representatives uncovered serious problems. Convicts had been shot or whipped to death for trivial offenses, women prisoners had been abused, and the sanitation was abominable. Furthermore, the financial affairs of the system were in such confusion that it was impossible to audit the books.

Acting on the recommendation of the committee, the legislature abolished the contract-lease system. Management of the prison system was placed under the direction of three commissioners appointed by the governor. Under the new regulations sanitation and medical service improved, and each convict received 10 cents a day for his or her labor.

With the close of the Campbell administration the progressive movement in Texas was, in many respects, nearing an end. Prohibition, absorbing much of the energy of Texas reformers after 1908, would dominate the election of 1910 and political affairs for sometime thereafter. Women's suffrage also resurfaced as a major issue, and the plight of tenant farmers would have a dramatic effect on Texas politics, but for the most part Campbell's successors would back away from reform. By this time the progressives in countless ways had already turned the services of government to the benefit of the many rather than the few. In Texas, as elsewhere, they had not succeeded in every instance in their quest for reform. Indeed, in some areas, such as the political rights of African Americans, their success had actually been a major step backward. Despite the laws calling for corporate regulation, giant corporations continued to grow larger and more powerful. Nevertheless, some of the more obvious abuses had been eliminated, and some of the most pressing needs had been addressed.

BIBLIOGRAPHY

General studies dealing with these years are Alwyn Barr, *Reconstruction to Reform: Texas Politics, 1876–1906*; S. Acheson, *35,000 Days in Texas*; B. M. Jones, *Search for Maturity*; and S. S. McKay and O. B. Faulk, *Texas after Spindletop*.

Very useful are the biographies of figures active in the era. For James S. Hogg, see Robert C. Cotner (ed.), *Addresses and State Papers of James Stephen Hogg* (Austin, 1951), and *James Stephen Hogg, A Biography* (Austin, 1959); and H. P. Gambrell, "James Stephen Hogg; Statesman or Demagogue?" *Southwest Review*, XIII, 338–366. See also Ben H. Procter, *Not without Honor: The Life of John H. Reagan* (Austin, 1962); Wayne Alvord, "T. L. Nugent, Texas Populist," *Southwestern Historical Quarterly*, LVII, 65–81; S. Acheson, *Joe Bailey: The Last Democrat* (New York, 1932); Rupert N. Richardson, *Colonel Edward M. House: The Texas Years, 1858–1912* (Abilene, 1964); Charles E. Neu, "In Search of Colonel Edward M. House: The Texas Years, 1858–1912," *Southwestern Historical Quarterly*, XCIII, 25–44; Evan Anders, "Thomas Watt Gregory and the Survival of His Progressive Faith," *Southwestern Historical Quarterly*, XCIII, 1–24; Janet Schmelzer, "Thomas M. Campbell: Progressive Governor of Texas," *Red River Valley Historical Review*, III, 52–64; and Pollyana B. Hughes and Elizabeth B. Harrison, "Charles A. Culberson: Not a Shadow of Hogg," *East Texas Historical Journal*, XI, 41–52. There is also a biographical essay on Edward M. House in Kenneth Hendrickson, Jr. and Michael L. Collins (eds.), *Profiles in Power: Twentieth Century Texans in Washington* (Arlington Heights, Ill., 1995).

Concerning reforms, on railroad regulation, see M. M. Crane, "Recollections of the Establishment of the Texas Railroad Commission," *Southwestern Historical Quarterly*, L, 478–486; Robert L. Peterson, "Jay Gould and the Railroad Commission of Texas," ibid., LVIII, 422–432; and J. R. Norvell, "The Railroad Commission of Texas: Its Origin and History," ibid., LXVIII, 465–480. See also O. D. Weeks, "The Texas Direct Primary System," *Southwestern Social Science Quarterly*, XIII, 95–120. Difficult to classify but a reminder that Texans were concerned about things other than politics and economics is Charles Carver, *Brann the Iconoclast* (Austin, 1957). For reforms in local government, see Bradley R. Rice, "The Galveston Plan of City Government by Commission: The Birth of a Progressive Idea," *Southwestern Historical Quarterly*, LXVIII, 365–408; Patricia E. Hill, "Women's Groups and the Extension of City Services in Early Twentieth-Century Dallas," *East Texas Historical Journal*, XXX, 3–10; and Paul E. Isaac, "Municipal Reform in Beaumont, Texas 1902–1909," *Southwestern Historical Quarterly*, LXVIII, 409–430. Texas penitentiaries are considered by Donald Walker in *Penology for Profit: A History of the Texas Prison System, 1867–1912* (College Station, 1988). See also C. S. Potts, "The Convict Labor System in Texas," *Annals of the American Academy of Political and Social Science*, XXI.

On politics and political parties, see Roscoe C. Martin, *The People's Party in Texas* (Austin, 1933); Ralph Smith, "The Farmers Alliance in Texas," *Southwestern His-*

torical Quarterly, XLVIII, 346–369; Ernest W. Winkler, *Platforms of Political Parties in Texas* (Austin, 1916); and Seth S. McKay, *Texas Politics, 1906–1944* (Lubbock, 1952).

Several recent studies have focused on the role of women in Texas political reform movements. See James D. Ivy, "'The Lone Star State Surrenders to a Lone Woman': Frances Willard's Forgotten 1882 Texas Temperance Tour," *Southwestern Historical Quarterly*, CII, 44–61; Elizabeth Hayes Turner, *Women, Culture and Community: Religion and Reform in Galveston, 1880–1920* (New York, 1997); Marion K. Barthelme (ed.), *Women in the Texas Populist Movement: Letters to the* Southern Mercury (College Station, 1997); and Judith N. McArthur, *Creating the New Woman: The Rise of Southern Women's Progressive Culture in Texas, 1893–1918* (Urbana, Ill., 1998).

A number of studies in recent years have examined the role of farmers' organizations on politics. See Lawrence Goodwyn, *Democratic Promise: The Populist Movement in America* (New York, 1976); Robert C. McMath, Jr., *Populist Vanguard: A History of the Southern Farmers Alliance* (Chapel Hill, N.C., 1975); James R. Green, *Grass-roots Socialism: Radical Movements in the Southwest, 1895–1943* (Baton Rouge, 1978), and "Tenant Farmer Discontent and Socialist Protest in Texas, 1901–1917," *Southwestern Historical Quarterly*, LXXXI, 133–154; Charles W. Macune, Jr., "The Wellspring of a Populist: Dr. C. W. McCune before 1885," *Southwestern Historical Quarterly*, XC, 139–158; E. Dale Baum and Robert A. Calvert, "The Texas Grangers: A Statistical Analysis," *Agricultural History*, LXIII, 36–55; Gregg Cantrell, "John B. Rayner: A Study in Black Populist Leadership," *Southern Studies*, XXIV, 432–443; Gregg Cantrell and D. Scott Barton, "Texas Populists and the Failure of Biracial Politics," *Journal of Southern History*, LV, 659–692; Worth Robert Miller, "Building a Progressive Coalition in Texas: The Populist-Reform Democrat Reapprochement, 1900–1907," *Journal of Southern History*, LII, 163–182; Donna K. Barnes, *Farmers in Rebellion: The Rise and Fall of the Southern Farmers' Alliance and the People's Party in Texas* (Austin, 1984); Graham Adams, Jr., "Agrarian Discontent in Progressive Texas," *East Texas Historical Journal*, VIII, 24–28; Robert Saunders, "Southern Populists and the Negro, 1893–1895," *Journal of Negro History*, LIV, 240–261; Evan Anders, *Boss Rule in South Texas: The Progressive Era* (Austin, 1982); "Boss Rule and Constituent Interests: South Texas Politics During the Progressive Era," *Southwestern Historical Quarterly*, LXXXIV, 269–292; and "The Origins of the Parr Machine in Duval County, Texas," *Southwestern Historical Quarterly*, LXXXV, 119–138.

15

Life at the Turn of the Century

As the twentieth century opened, Texans could point with pride to the growth and progress their state had made in the nineteenth century. More than 3 million people made their home in Texas in 1900. The number had increased fivefold since the Civil War. An added indication of the growth of the state was the fact that slightly more than one-fourth of the population had been born in other states, and almost 200,000 were foreign-born. Racial and ethnic minorities included African Americans, Mexican Americans, Germans, a variety of European immigrants, and a small number of Asians.

Lifestyles reflected not only the diverse cultural backgrounds but also rapidly changing patterns of living. For decades Texans had depended primarily on the land for their living, and most still did in 1900. Cities were growing, however, and the effects of industrialization were noticeable, particularly in the cities, but in rural Texas as well. On the other hand, Texas literature and art tended to reflect the past, especially the heroic and romantic past.

THE GALVESTON STORM OF 1900

Life in the twentieth century began with tragedy for Texas. A massive hurricane swept inland over Galveston Island on September 8, 1900. The magnitude of the storm and the destruction it brought almost defied description. The storm raged for more than twelve hours, with winds of

Galveston, September 9, 1900. Looking south toward the beach from the corner of Twelfth and I Streets on the day following the great storm of 1900 captures a sense of the destruction wrought by this disaster. The survivors of the storm faced a monumental task of rebuilding and protecting their city from future storms. (Texas State Library and Archives Commission)

more than 120 miles per hour and tidal waves that completely covered the land. No completely accurate count of the fatalities was ever made, but estimates of 6,000 were commonly heard, and many placed the count much higher. When the waters receded, the city was in ruins, with thousands of people left homeless.

Galvestonians were determined to rebuild. The Red Cross provided first aid and emergency care for the survivors. From throughout Texas and the nation people sent food and supplies; the state government allowed the city to retain taxes for use in rebuilding, and it organized committees to raise money for supplies. But it was the determination of the people of Galveston that was most important in rebuilding the city. Within a short time they had reorganized their city government, within five years they had built a sea wall on the Gulf side of the island, and in an amazing feat of engineering they jacked up the buildings, pumped in soil dredged from off shore, and raised the elevation of the city by an average of eight feet. The sea wall, seventeen feet high and more than seven miles long, and the increased elevation successfully protected the city from storms that struck in 1909, 1915, 1961, and 1983.

LIVING AND WORKING IN TEXAS

Approximately 80 percent of the population lived in rural areas in 1900, with about six out of every ten workers directly involved in agriculture. Horses and mules still provided most of the power; the age of the tractor would not come until the 1920s. But here and there were seen huge steam tractors, and threshing machines, reapers, and new types of plows and riding cultivators were commonplace.

Work patterns on farms had changed little from pioneer days. The farm family was a relatively tight, cohesive unit, and all shared in the work. Daylight to dark was the schedule, with some planting, plowing, and cultivating, while others chopped weeds and tended the livestock. Harvest season demanded the efforts of everyone. Many youngsters could not attend school until the cotton crop was at the gin.

In the towns, work schedules were not usually as demanding. Family income in urban areas generally was provided by a business or by the employment of the father, though employment of women, especially among African Americans, was becoming more and more common. In smaller communities where opportunities were available, young people living in towns found summer jobs on nearby farms.

Living conveniences were a mixture of old and new. Farm homes were usually small, warmed by fireplaces, iron heaters with coal, or wood cookstoves and had kerosene lamps for light. City homes ranged from the simple to the elegant but often offered little more in the way of conveniences than did the farm homes. Although gas and electricity were available in the larger cities before 1900, many homes had neither, and the revolution in living conditions that electricity produced would not be widespread until the 1920s.

Nevertheless, before the turn of the century the services and conveniences associated with urban life were available in Texas cities. By 1900 all cities had telephone exchanges, and practically all were linked by telegraph systems. The electric light and power industry was not quite as advanced. Galveston had a power plant in the early 1880s and other cities soon had electric service, but the power these plants generated was insignificant in comparison with the output of our own day. The production of power was a local industry until about 1913, when the Texas Power and Light Company constructed a transmission line from Waco to Fort Worth and Dallas. Soon various small concerns were consolidated, and outlying communities were supplied by high-voltage transmission lines radiating from huge plants.

Travel was slow and difficult for both rural and urban Texans at the turn of the century, though the period was one of transition and transportation methods were improving. Long-distance travel by railroad was relatively comfortable, fast, and safe. For day-to-day travel over short distances wagons and buggies typically were the only choice. There were no paved roads and few bridges, and the dirt roads were poorly kept, dusty in dry weather and muddy in wet. A twenty-mile wagon journey required the better part of a day.

In the cities, street construction and maintenance were major problems. Large cities by the end of the century had begun paving their main thoroughfares; Houston, for example, had paved twenty-six miles. Streetcars and trolleys powered by electricity appeared by 1890 and were available in the larger cities by 1900.

Two new inventions in transportation hailed the opening years of the twentieth century. The first automobiles were seen in Texas about 1900, and the success of these machines was apparent within a short time. Houston was the home of eighty automobiles by 1905 and had already experienced a fatal automobile accident. The state recognized the automobile in 1907 with the adoption of an eighteen-mile-per-hour speed limit. Airplanes had attracted attention by 1910, but mostly as a curiosity. In 1912 a race was staged along the beach at Galveston between an airplane and an automobile. Unfortunately, the record does not show which won. Airplanes remained rare in Texas skies until World War I introduced military aviation to the state.

URBAN TEXAS

Although most Texans still lived in rural areas at the turn of the century, city life was becoming more common. In 1870, only 6.7 percent of the people lived in incorporated urban areas with a population of 2,500 or more. By 1900, cities and towns contained 17.1 percent of the population. The appearance of urban centers is even more impressive when the growth of individual cities is considered. In 1870, only two towns, Galveston with a population of 13,818 and San Antonio with 12,256, contained more than 10,000 people. Houston counted slightly more than 9,000, Dallas had an estimated 3,000; and Fort Worth was a village of about 500. By 1900, eleven towns claimed more than 10,000 people. San Antonio was the largest city with 53,321, followed by Houston, Dallas, Galveston, and Fort Worth. Urban growth would continue to accelerate in the new century.

Two factors contributed to urban growth. First, the development of modern transportation systems allowed strategically positioned communities to become leading market centers. Houston, Dallas, and Fort Worth exploited their strategic locations in the railroad network to accomplish this. Second, industrial development, especially that related to the discovery of oil, fueled city growth. Beaumont, a sleepy lumber town of 9,000 people, grew to more than 50,000 within a few months after the discovery of oil at Spindletop a few miles to the south. Often such population growth was only temporary, with the people housed in tent cities and troubled by lawlessness and disease, but oil and related industries promised a more permanent impact on the lives of twentieth-century Texans.

OIL AND INDUSTRIALIZATION

Until 1901 oil did not play a major role in the Texas economy or lifestyle. Commercial oil production and exploration began to have an impact on the state's economy in the 1890s, with Corsicana in Navarro

County as the site of most of the activity. By 1898, there were more than 300 wells in the Corsicana field and an operating refinery, but the wells were small and the project attracted little national interest.

The discovery of oil on January 10, 1901, on Spindletop Hill south of Beaumont, was a different matter. The well, drilled by Captain Anthony F. Lucas, began spewing oil more than 100 feet in the air. Before it was finally capped, the gusher roared out with nearly one-half million barrels of oil, and a new age in Texas was at hand. At least two giant oil companies and many smaller ones were born out of the Spindletop boom. Oilmen began to search for discoveries in other parts of the state, and refining and marketing operations were soon providing jobs and profits for Texans.

More discoveries came quickly. By 1903, there were fields opened at Sour Lake, Saratoga, and Batson. The following year oilmen discovered a large field north of Houston in the community of Humble. Meanwhile, the first fields were opened near Wichita Falls in North Texas, and by 1912 the search for oil had moved into north central Texas.

Oil Derricks outside Beaumont, 1903. As this image of "Boiler Avenue" near Beaumont on April 23, 1903, indicates, the discovery of oil in 1901 at Spindletop transformed not only the Texas economy but also the landscape. The oil boom re-created the excesses associated with the California Gold Rush and other similar economic phenomenon. (Spindletop/Gladys City Boomtown Museum)

Closely associated with oil production was that of natural gas. Corsicana and Marshall were the first towns to secure natural gas distribution systems. In 1910, a pipeline was completed to supply Fort Worth and Dallas. Various other towns and cities secured this service during the next fifteen years, though the gas companies encountered many difficulties, chief of which was securing a dependable supply of gas.

Also allied with oil production were the refining and manufacturing of various petroleum products. The first refineries were small, crude units built in the 1890s, but major companies began constructing large operations soon after the discovery of Spindletop. By 1919, there were forty-three refineries in the state.

In the oil industry, as well as in other Texas industries, the trend toward consolidation was evident by the turn of the century. Initially the quantity of new oil put on the market by the Texas oil boom broke the near-monopoly that John D. Rockefeller's Standard Oil Company held at the turn of the century. But out of the Texas oil discoveries came new gigantic companies such as Gulf, Texaco, Humble (which became Exxon), and Mobil. Business consolidation in Texas was not just limited to big oil companies. In the last decades of the nineteenth century, the number of flour mills declined by about 50 percent, but production increased about sixfold. Like the grasslands of West Texas, the timberlands of East Texas came to be owned by comparatively few people. After 1879 timberlands (which had been set aside for the schools) could be bought in small quantities at $5 an acre. Soon capitalists of vision, among them, H. J. Lutcher, G. B. Moore, and John H. Kirby, made heavy investments that later brought them large fortunes. The Kirby Lumber Company, chartered in 1901 as the first multimillion-dollar industrial corporation in the state, dominated the lumber business.

LEISURE ACTIVITIES

From the earliest days of settlement Texans found opportunities for amusement and entertainment. These opportunities became more frequent as Texas entered the twentieth century. Visiting with neighbors remained an important social activity, especially on Sunday afternoons. Church socials, the general store, cotton gin offices, sewing circles, and community parties provided many occasions for people to meet and relax together. Children were often a part of these affairs, taking advantage of them to participate in marbles, various ball games, and other activities. Dancing, one of the most important social diversions throughout the nineteenth century, declined somewhat, primarily because many church groups strongly opposed it.

Holidays were important, especially the Fourth of July and Christmas. Texans often celebrated the Fourth with community picnics and parties, but

Christmas was more of an occasion for family gatherings. Among African Americans, June 19 was a day for celebrating their emancipation from slavery, and Mexican Americans celebrated the two national holidays of Mexico, Cinco de Mayo and Diez y Seis de Septiembre. Less often celebrated, but not entirely ignored, were Thanksgiving and Easter.

Sports, though not nearly as important to the culture as they would become later in the twentieth century, were popular. Horse racing, the most popular sport throughout the nineteenth century, continued to attract large crowds. In 1887, the Texas League of Professional Baseball Clubs was organized, and in the 1890s Texas schoolboys began to play football. A Galveston dock hand, Jack Johnson, became the first African American boxing heavyweight champion of the world in 1908 and held the title until 1915.

Music, theater, and shows provided diversions for many. Sometimes local talent put on the plays or shows, but there were many traveling groups, some with national reputations. At one time or another there appeared on Texas billboards the name of almost every distinguished actor or actress who played in the United States during the late nineteenth and early twentieth centuries. Among these were Joseph Jefferson, noted for his portrayal of Rip Van Winkle; Edwin Booth, renowned Shakespearean actor; and Sarah Bernhardt, the greatest actress of her generation. Larger towns and many of the smaller ones built theaters for the performing arts in which operas, plays, concerts, and minstrel shows were performed on a more or less regular basis. An opera house was opened in Galveston in 1871, one in Dallas two years after, and others in the following years. Many communities organized bands, some had singing societies, and Mexican American communities often had string orchestras. The traveling circus was a popular show of the time. In Texas the Mollie Bailey Circus, replete with tigers, elephants, acrobats, and clowns, began its tour of Texas about 1880 and continued for nearly 30 years. Shortly after the turn of the century, motion pictures were shown in Texas for the first time. The event attracted statewide attention and interest, but Texans would not attend the movies in large numbers on a regular basis until the 1920s.

PUBLIC HEALTH

Disease was a dreaded and frequent occurrence in Texas homes at the turn of the century. Cholera, typhoid, diphtheria, and occasionally smallpox epidemics swept the state from time to time. Malaria was common along the coast, and yellow fever epidemics regularly struck Houston and Galveston from 1839 until the last one in 1867. Children's diseases, such as measles, whooping cough, mumps, and chicken pox, afflicted most families sooner or later.

Professional medical care was limited and often not particularly good. There were few physicians, and only large towns had hospitals. For a time the state suffered from an abundance of "quack" medical schools that offered quick but poor training. The Medical Association of Texas, organized in 1853, became more active near the end of the century and made the establishment of standards for the training of physicians one of its primary goals. Toward the end of the century, medical care improved somewhat. By 1900, there were several competent medical schools, the best known of which was the University of Texas Medical Department, which opened in Galveston in 1891.

Texas nurses also became professionalized around the turn of the century. Nurses were important health care providers, especially in times or places when trained physicians were unavailable. For example, Mary Coffee-Jones educated herself by studying her son-in-law's medical books and then began serving as a midwife and providing general health care, first in Mount Pleasant and then in San Saba. Kezia de Pelchin served as a voluntary health care provider during yellow fever outbreaks in Houston and in other southern cities. By 1883 she had become head nurse at Houston's city hospital. A more formal approach to the education of nurses was taken with the opening of the state's first nursing school in 1890 at Galveston's John Sealy Hospital. In 1896 the nursing school became a component of the University of Texas Medical Department in Galveston. The drive for professionalism culminated with the founding of the Texas Graduate Nurses Association in 1907, and the enactment by the legislature in 1909 of the Nurse Practice Act. This act regulated nursing education and established licensing exams for registered nurses.

Medical education for African Americans lagged behind that for whites. Black physicians had to leave the state for training until the desegregation of higher education in the 1950s. The first nursing school for blacks, the Wright Cuney Memorial Nurse Training School, opened in Dallas about 1912. Eight years later the first class of registered nurses graduated from Prairie View, and a year later a class graduated from the "colored hospital" in Galveston that was part of the University of Texas Medical Department.

Given the shortage of professional medical care, Texans often relied on their own resources when disease struck. Neighborhood women, in particular, acted as midwives and sometimes treated the sick. Midwives provided obstetrical services in Texas, especially among the minorities and the poor and especially in rural areas. It is estimated that as late as 1935 over half the African American births were attended by midwives, and over 4,000 midwives, mostly older black women, practiced in the state. Mexican Americans often turned to a *curandero* when confronted with illness. *Curanderos*, who used herbs and folk medicine in their treatments, were generally given high respect in their communities, and some attracted patients from distant parts of the country. Native American women also based their healing practices in the use of herbs and other folk remedies and occasionally shared these practices with frontier women. Margaret Hallett, the founder of Hallettsville, learned herbal cures from Tonkawa women. Home remedies remained the preferred approach to medicine for many families well into the twentieth century. In the spring, a mixture of sassafras tea, sulfur, and molasses paved the way for a healthy year. Castor oil, quinine, and calomel were also frequently used as home medicines.

RELIGION

By the turn of the century, religion in Texas had changed somewhat from what it was at midcentury. At the time of the Civil War, the Methodist Church, with more than 400 churches and more than 30,000 members, was easily the largest denomination in the state. The Baptists, who claimed more than 500 congregations but fewer members than the Methodists, were second, and the Presbyterians, Disciples of Christ, Episcopalians, and Catholics were all considerably smaller in number. By 1906, Baptists, with about 33 percent of the state's churchgoing public, had surpassed the Methodists, who now accounted for about 27 percent. Catholics, consisting of large numbers of German, Polish, Czechoslovakian, and Mexican immigrants, were not far behind, while the Disciples of Christ, Presbyterians, Lutherans, Episcopalians, and a number of smaller denominations accounted for the remainder. The state's Jewish community, which dated back to the Spanish period, had increased to about 15,000 by 1900 and 30,000 by 1930.

African Americans provided for much of the growth of the Baptists. Although there was some debate among white Baptists over whether to accept blacks as members of predominantly white churches, black Baptists for the most part ignored the controversy and proceeded to organize their own churches. After the first black Baptist church was organized in Galveston in 1865; others quickly followed. By 1890 there were 111,138 black Baptists, while black Methodists numbered only 42,214.

Whether black or white, Baptist or Methodist, or in some instances other denominations, Texas churches were activly involved with many social and political issues at the turn of century. The Prohibition movement, long present but growing in intensity, was a major concern. In 1900 one prominent churchman expressed the views of many Texans when he proclaimed that the tavern was the "greatest curse" of the nation. The success of the Prohibitionists in the next two decades would be due largely to the efforts of Baptists, Methodists, and other denominations. Horse racing and, to some extent, dancing also came under church scrutiny, and in communities where sentiment was strong, they either disappeared altogether or were severely curtailed.

Not all religious groups held such views. In parts of the state where German, Czech, Polish, and Mexican heritage was strong, sentiment for Prohibition was almost nonexistent, and dancing and horse racing encountered little criticism. Often these groups were Catholic in their religious affiliation, but there were other denominations that held similar views. Since issues like Prohibition, horse racing, and dancing generally were defined in moral terms, the conflict over them involved religious controversy as well as secular arguments. In one way or another religion affected most aspects of life. The role of religion in Texas culture at the turn of the century was strong, perhaps stronger than it had ever been.

EDUCATION

As Texans entered the final quarter of the nineteenth century, they organized their first public high school, but the state still did not have a public school system worthy of the name. Land was set aside for support of public education during the Republic and again during early statehood, but no system was created. During Reconstruction the Republican government created a system, potentially well supported, but most of this effort was undone by the Constitution of 1876. At the same time, the legislature in 1876 adopted a "community school system" that had no boundaries, no means of acquiring and controlling property, and no assurance that it would be continued from one year to the next. It was, in fact, no system at all. Governor O. M. Roberts's veto of the school appropriation bill in 1879 reduced the meager expenditures authorized by the constitution even more.

African American children suffered even more than white children from inadequate educational facilities. In spite of the fact that black legislators were among the most ardent supporters of public education, the school system authorized by the Constitution of 1876 was to be segregated. Although black schools were supposed to receive the same resources as white schools, this did not happen. By the 1920s black schools received a third less funding than white schools, and black teachers received about three-quarters of the salary of white teachers.

Though public sentiment in the 1880s supported the dual school system, it did demand that Texas schools receive an adequate share of public revenues. However, efforts to support education primarily through the sale of public lands failed to provide schools with a secure financial base. As the crises grew, a number of prominent Texans championed the cause of public education. Among the most outspoken were O. N. Hollingsworth, secretary of the state board of education; Dr. Ashbel Smith, a friend of education since the days of Mirabeau B. Lamar; R. C. Burleson, president of Waco University; and William Carey Crane, president of Baylor University. Their efforts resulted in an 1883 constitutional amendment that provided for a 20-cent state ad valorem school tax and allowed district voters to supplement this with local taxes.

The following year witnessed the complete rewriting of the school law and a major step toward the development of a true public school system. The law of 1884 provided for an elective state superintendent of instruction and placed schools under the immediate supervision of county judges. It required most counties to be divided into school districts with the authority to assess local taxes. It provided schooling for children from age eight to sixteen, it required that teachers hold certificates, and it required local districts to file regular reports with the state.

Progress under the new system was slow. Immigration and a high birth rate caused the scholastic population to increase more rapidly than available resources. The law of 1884 placed a significant part of the responsibility for supporting public schools on local taxes, but local voters frequently were reluctant to approve local school taxes. Some progress was made during the reform administrations in the 1890s and early 1900s. Governor Hogg signed a law extending the school term from four to six months. The legislature in 1901 authorized the state board of education to use the permanent school fund to support bonds for the construction of school buildings. Many communities organized independent school districts (free of county control), and by 1904 about 90 percent had begun to collect local taxes for school purposes.

Unfortunately, country schools, most of which were organized as common school districts under county control, lagged far behind urban programs. Primarily because of conditions in rural schools, as the new century began, Texas ranked near the bottom among the states of the nation in terms of the adequacy of its school system. In 1900, towns and cities spent $8.35 per student for education, while the country schools spent only $4.97; students in cities and towns averaged 162 days per year in the classroom, while their rural counterparts averaged only 98 days. A strange and unreasonable restriction in the constitution limited the taxing authority of country districts to less than one-half that of independent school districts. Adding to the unfairness of the situation was the fact that these inadequate rural schools served more than three-fourths of the school-age population.

Progressive reformers during the Campbell administration directed much of their energy to improving public education. The Conference for Education in Texas, organized in 1907, struggled to awaken people to the needs of the schools. It found allies for its campaign in the state's department of education, the Congress of Mothers, and parent-teacher associations. In 1908, the campaign achieved significant results. The greatest change provided increased funding for schools by liberalizing the use of local tax revenue to support educational programs. As a result of these reforms between 1905 and 1910, local school taxes increased by 153 percent. Although Texas continued to lag behind many other states in the availability of educational opportunities, by the end of the first decade of the new century, the educational foundations of the state were firmly in place.

While establishing a system of public schools, Texans also created a system of higher education in the last quarter of the nineteenth century. The first institution of higher learning supported by public funds was the Agricultural and Mechanical College of Texas, which opened its doors near Bryan in October 1876. It was a land-grant college and owed its origin to the Morrill Act passed by Congress in 1862. This act provided Texas 180,000 acres of federal land to establish a college for the study of agricultural and mechanical arts. Texas accepted the offer in 1866, but the school did not admit its first students until 1876. The legislature in 1876 also authorized the creation of an "Agricultural and Mechanical College for the Benefit of Colored Youth" under the administration of the white Agricultural and Mechanical College. The black school, established on the old Alta Vista plantation near Hempstead, admitted its first students in March 1878. When the 1879 legislature authorized the creation of two "normal" schools, one white and one black, for the training of teachers, the A&M regents renamed the Hempstead school Prairie View Normal Institute and added teacher education programs to its offerings in agriculture and mechanics. It was not until 1901, when Prairie View received authorization to begin offering college level courses in the arts and sciences, that black youth in Texas had a state-supported college to attend. The second normal school established in 1879 was Sam Houston Normal Institute at Huntsville, which opened when the state matched a donation of $6,000 and the citizens of Huntsville made available the former campus of Austin College.

Although there was considerable interest in the matter from the earliest days of the Texas Republic, it took almost fifty years for the University of Texas to become a reality. During the days of the Republic, fifty leagues (about 220,000 acres) of land were set aside for the endowment of two universities. Twenty years later, in 1858, the state legislature passed a bill establishing the University of Texas, but the Civil War and subsequent problems delayed the project for another twenty years. The Constitution of 1876 granted a million acres of land to the university and its branches but contained no provisions to compel the actual organization of the school. In 1880 the State Teachers' Association took the lead in the campaign to create the university. It presented Governor O. M. Roberts with a plan for organizing the school. The governor forwarded the report to the legislature, which approved an act on March 30, 1881, providing for the establishment of the school. In an election the voters selected Austin as the site for the main university and Galveston for the medical department. The main university was opened in 1883 and its medical branch in 1891.

WOMEN AT THE TURN OF THE CENTURY

In 1900 slightly less than half—about 48 percent—of the population of Texas were women. Reflecting the change from a frontier society to that of a more civilized one, the population of women was increasing at a rate more rapid than that of men, but women would not outnumber men in the state for several years.

Although the women of Texas enjoyed more rights than those of many other states, Texas women were less than equal in terms of their legal rights. Not only were women denied the right to vote, but they also were limited in their right to conduct business. Because of the heritage of Spanish civil law, a woman could own and convey property, make contracts, and sue or be sued. However, a married woman's property was subject to the management of her husband, even if the property was hers before marriage. She could not dispose of property without her husband's consent, but her husband could do so, unless the property involved was the family homestead. A husband was required by law to support his wife and was liable for any debts she might incur, while under some circumstances wives were not responsible for their own debts. Single women generally retained more rights than married women, inasmuch as they were legally responsible for their own acts and could legally manage their own property.

Educational opportunities for Texas women of the late nineteenth century were available but limited. By 1890 female students outnumbered males, but few females attended college. The Texas Women's Council, however, stressed improvement in vocational education for girls, and there were other organizations working to improve educational opportunities for women. Business colleges and trade schools appeared, and many of these institutions encouraged the enrollment of women, claiming that many jobs in business were available for them. More traditional forms of women's education persisted, however. Some colleges, such as Baylor University, began to offer courses equal in difficulty to those offered to men, but often courses for women beyond basics in reading and writing were taught at a lower level or consisted of learning the social graces or studying the arts. The University of Texas was coeducational from the time it opened, and Texas Women's University opened in 1903.

At the turn of the century most Texas women devoted their lives to the role of wife, mother, and homemaker. The percentage of women who married outnumbered that of men. Women tended to marry earlier in life, often to older men, and frequently were widowed at a young age. Divorce was rare. In 1890, slightly more than 2 percent of the female population was divorced.

In 1890, approximately 8 percent (86,015) of the women of Texas were involved in occupations outside the home. Almost half this number were in occupations related to agriculture, holding jobs as laborers, farmers, planters, or ranchers. The next largest number, 37,210, worked as domestic or personal servants. The remainder of the female work force was scattered among a wide variety of occupations. Among approximately 6,000 women employed in the professions, about 75 percent were teachers. In addition, there were writers and journalists, librarians and ministers, lawyers and physicians, merchants and clerks, seamstresses and copyists, and even gamblers and outlaws. No women held jobs as sailors in 1890, but two claimed to be locomotive engineers.

Organizations to improve conditions for women and for society in general were numerous at the turn of the century. Suffrage and temperance were the most common goals, accounting for a large number of the organizations and for most of the membership. But there were many other women's groups. Literary clubs were organized in small towns and large, with one reported in Clarendon in 1885 and one in Houston the same year. By the 1890s, Houston women had organized the City Federation of Women's Clubs, and in 1897 Waco was the scene of the organization of the Texas Federation of Women's Clubs.

Women's clubs were frequently dismissed as merely social organizations. In reality, in the period before suffrage they were the principal vehicle for the political activism of Texas women. This activism took a variety of forms. In 1898 at the first statewide meeting of the Texas Federation of Women's Clubs the organization passed a resolution endorsing the creation of public libraries. This launched a statewide campaign that resulted in the establishment of libraries in most Texas communities. In 1906 the Texas Federation of Women's Clubs turned its attention to prison reform. Though the group did not enjoy the same success that it did with libraries, it accomplished some of its goals during Governor Dan Moody's administration in the mid-1920s.

As women's clubs increased their political activism, their reform vision expanded. By 1907 the Texas Federation of Women's Clubs could claim credit for laws that established the juvenile court system, regulated the practice of adoption, and required blood tests for marriage licenses. In 1908 the *Dallas Clubwoman* outlined a political agenda for women reformers. This agenda included the improvement of parks, public health, and sanitation; pure-food legislation; civil service reform; laws controlling child labor and improving the status of women workers; and improvements in public education. Women also turned their attention to national and international issues. Under the leadership of Anna Pennybacker, who served as president of the Texas Federation of Women's Clubs before assuming the leadership of the national body (the General Federation of Women's Clubs), the Texas organization endorsed world peace and supported U.S. involvement in the League of Nations.

Minority and immigrant women also organized to influence political and social reform. African American women in a number of communities established women's clubs during the first quarter of the new century that were committed to self-improvement and community service. Since the Texas Federation of Women's Clubs was segregated, in 1905 M.E.Y. Moore of Gainsville organized the Texas Association of Colored Women. Six years later Jovita Idár of Laredo established La Liga Femenil Mexicanista (The League of Mexican Women). She used this organization to protest lynching and advocate both racial and gender equality. The first major project of La Liga was the establishment of free schools for poor Mexican American children. When fighting in the Mexican Revolution spread to the border area, Idár joined with Leonór Villegas de Magnón to establish La Cruz Blanca (the White Cross) to provide nursing care for wounded soldiers. In 1917 Idár moved to San Antonio, where she opened a free kindergarten and continued her work in the Mexican-American community.

Anna Hertzberg of San Antonio was one of the most prominent club-women in Texas's Jewish community. As president of the San Antonio Council of Jewish Women, she established the city's first night school and convinced the school board to take over the project. Jewish women in other Texas cities followed Hertzberg's example. In Dallas, for example, the Council of Jewish Women established a free milk fund and provided "penny lunches" for poor school children. Hertzberg's influence spread beyond the Jewish community. In 1911 she became president of the Texas Federation of Women's Clubs and successfully lobbied the legislature to enact a law protecting the property rights of married women. She also served as president of the Texas Kindergarten Association, and in 1915, before women had gained the right to vote, she was elected to serve on the San Antonio School Board.

RACE AND ETHNICITY

Blacks and Mexican Americans, with about 25 percent of the population, accounted for the majority of the non-Anglo cultures in Texas at the turn of the century. But there was a constant flow of immigrants, especially from Europe, and cultural diversity was one of the most notable features of the state.

Blacks in Texas numbered 620,722 in 1900, or approximately 20 percent of the total population. The ratio of blacks to the general population had declined from about one (black) to two (whites) at the beginning of the Civil War, but the actual number of blacks inTexas totaled more than three times what it was in 1860. Most, about 80 percent, lived on farms and about 90 percent lived in the eastern parts of the state. Houston contained the largest number of urban blacks, with Austin, Dallas, Waco, and Galveston also containing substantial numbers.

Although some were ranchers and cowboys, most blacks who lived on the land were cotton farmers. About 25 percent of the black farmers owned their own land, but the remainder were tenants, mostly sharecroppers, and usually very poor. Even when the black farmer owned his own land, his situation was often insecure. In 1910, the average value of a black farmer's holdings was about one-fifth the value of a white farmer's.

Urban blacks accounted for about 25 percent of the nonfarm workforce at the turn of the century. The greater number held jobs as laborers, and a significant number were employed as domestic or personal servants. Together, these occupations accounted for 80 percent of the black urban workers. Fewer than 5 percent entered the professions, and an even smaller number were craftsmen. Most black professionals were either teachers or ministers, but Texas in 1900 claimed the largest number of black physicians in the nation, 136. The percent of African Americans who were skilled laborers, however, was smaller in Texas than in other states.

Wages for black workers were low. Wages paid in 1910 ranged from a low 30 cents a day for hotel workers to a maximum of $10 per day for certain jobs in mills, but the average pay was about $2 daily. Apparently, black and white workers who performed the same job were generally paid at the same rate; discrimination occurred in the assignment of the jobs. Black women received substantially lower wages than did the black men. In fact, women, whether black or white, generally were paid lower wages, even when the tasks performed were the same as those of men.

Black workers assumed contradictory roles in the development of labor unions in Texas. In the lumber, railroad, and shipping industries, in which labor unions were most often formed, there were large numbers of black workers, and many were involved in the organization of unions. On the other hand, many unions refused to admit black workers or discriminated against them in pay or access to higher-paying jobs. Management, in turn, frequently used black workers as strikebreakers in labor disputes. One exception to this pattern was on the docks of Houston and Galveston, where black longshoremen, organized in their own unions, shared equally in the available work.

Businesses owned by blacks were few in number and generally quite small. Often operated by the entire family, the business was usually a grocery store, restaurant, tavern, blacksmith shop, or some other type of service agency, and was often, but not always, confined to providing for the needs of the black community. However, there were several black insurance companies, most of them connected with black fraternal groups, and there were at least eight black banks in business in the early twentieth century.

Provisions for education of blacks, segregated in their schools by the Constitution of 1876, were especially inadequate. Black education in Texas for a time compared favorably with that of other southern states, and illiteracy declined from more than 75 percent in 1880 to less than 40 percent in 1900. By 1900, however, Texas ranked fifth among southern states in the enrollment of black students and daily attendance and third in the number of black teachers. Inequality in funding, facilities, and faculty undermined the promise of "separate but equal" in educational opportunity. Secondary education suffered most of all. As late as 1900 there were only nineteen black high schools in the state. A black student in Texas seeking an education during these years could likely learn the rudiments of reading and writing, but he or she probably would find little opportunity beyond those humble beginnings.

All in all, the situation of black Texans at the turn of the century suggests a mixture of regression and progress. Economically, black Texans were at a disadvantage when compared with their white neighbors. Poverty was common among white Texans, but black people were even poorer. Education for blacks was not equal to that offered whites, and black access to political power declined in the decade before the end of the century and would decline further in the early twentieth century. Mortality rates for black people were much higher than those for whites, probably as a result of inadequate diet and limited access to medical care. Segregation and violence, long a part of life in the black community, continued. In a twenty-one-year period ending in 1903, 199 blacks were lynched; 171 were lynched during the next twenty-four years. A disturbance involving soldiers and civilians in Brownsville in August 1906 led to the death of one civilian and the wounding of a policeman. In a questionable decision, President Theodore Roosevelt responded to the Brownsville incident by ordering the summary discharge "without honor" (and without a hearing) of three black infantry companies, totaling 167 soldiers.

But despite the problems and inequities, there was also substantial evidence of progress. In 1900, black Texans were only thirty-five years removed from slavery. During those years a number of capable black leaders had emerged, illiteracy had been reduced, and some blacks had acquired sufficient capital to buy land or establish businesses. Perhaps of most significance to the future was the formation of literally dozens, possibly hundreds, of black organizations of all types. Some were religious; others were political. A large number were fraternal, and there were many primarily concerned with social affairs. Perhaps most important of these organizations were the chapters of the National Association for the Advancement of Colored People (NAACP), the first of which formed in Houston in 1912. But all of these organizations were ultimately concerned with the improvement of the black community; from them would come the black leadership of the twentieth century.

Much smaller than the black population but comprising a major ethnic minority were the Mexican Americans. At the turn of the century, natives of Mexico living in Texas numbered at least 70,000 and were the largest group of foreign-born. The number of people of Mexican heritage was many times larger, with some families able to trace their origins back to the days of the Spanish. Well into the twentieth century, 60 percent of the landowners in Cameron, Starr, and Zapata counties were descendants of the original land-grant recipients. Other Mexican Americans were recent arrivals, for increasing agricultural production in South Texas as well as railroad construction and maintenance attracted workers from Mexico beginning in the 1890s. In 1910, Mexican Americans made up slightly less than 6 percent of the population, but revolution and subsequent political upheaval in Mexico increased immigration in the 1910s and 1920s.

At the turn of the century most Mexican Americans still lived in South Texas and along the Rio Grande. San Antonio was the largest urban center for Mexican Americans, and there were many in El Paso and other towns along the Rio Grande; but other cities, particularly Houston, would prove attractive to the immigrants who moved northward after 1910.

Mexican Americans, whether descendants of old settlers or recent immigrants, often found life in Texas difficult. Prejudice, poverty, and discrimination were common problems. Sometimes signs declaring "No Mexicans Allowed" prevented Mexican Americans from receiving service in restaurants and other public businesses. In some towns they could live only in certain areas, and generally only low-paying and physically exhausting jobs were available to the Mexican American worker. Language was also a barrier. Since schools normally allowed only English to be spoken, Mexican American students who spoke only Spanish often dropped out at an early age. In spite of the lack of formal education, most Mexican Americans were not illiterate. By the 1890s several newspapers were being published on a more or less regular basis for the benefit of Spanish-speaking Texans. The number of these newspapers would grow as the Mexican population increased.

Poverty was a problem almost always present. Although some Mexican Americans entered professions such as law, medicine, or teaching, and others owned ranches or businesses, most were laborers in the towns, on the roads or railroads, or, more frequently, on the land. Often they were *vaqueros* who took care of cattle or sheep or workers in the cotton and vegetable fields of South Texas. Some owned the land on which they worked, but most did not and received meager pay for their efforts.

To cope with their poverty, Mexican Americans used imagination and ingenuity. They frequently depended on inexpensive and readily available materials provided by nature. Where it was appropriate, they built their homes out of sun-dried brick or adobe. Where this was not feasible, they built *jacales*, sturdy and simple houses made from straw, mesquite, and other available materials that cost little or perhaps nothing. Their clothing was simple and colorful but practical for their way of life, as was their food, which was simple and inexpensive but tasty.

For help in times of adversity, Mexican Americans formed *mutualistas* (mutual aid societies), organizations that provided financial assistance in times of death or sickness or other crisis. The *mutualistas*, active in most of the communities of South Texas, also raised funds to help Mexican Americans preserve their heritage and to meet the general needs of their community. As the community grew, some of these *mutualistas* evolved into political, labor, or civil rights organizations, like the League of United Latin American Citizens (LULAC), which was founded in Corpus Christi in 1929.

In the late nineteenth century, Mexican Americans exercised only limited influence on state politics, but often they assumed a major role in local politics in those areas where the population was large. On the state level only three Mexican Americans were elected to the legislature in the period between 1865 and 1900. One of these was Santos Benavides, mayor of Laredo, a brigadier general in the Civil War and three times a member of the Texas legislature. In some instances economic pressure or open coercion was used to prevent Mexican American voters from going to the polls. But frequently voting was allowed, and the vote was controlled to the advantage of local political bosses. Some of the political bosses were Anglos, but others were Mexican Americans. Manuel Guerra of Rio Grande City was the most powerful politician in Starr County for many years. Although most of the political leadership, whether Anglo or Mexican American, was quite conservative, sometimes Mexican American leaders were successful in efforts to correct abuses. When San Pedro Park in San Antonio was closed to Mexican Americans in the 1880s, protests forced its reopening. In later years protests against economic discrimination led to the organization of a number of labor unions made up primarily of Mexican American workers. These unions achieved victories in a streetcar strike in 1901, a coal mining strike in 1903, and a railroad strike in 1906.

Somewhat smaller in number but generally more prosperous were the Germans, Czechs, Poles, and Scandinavians. In 1900, almost 50,000 Texans had been born in Germany, and people of German heritage made up the majority of the population of several counties. Large German communities also existed in Houston, Galveston, and San Antonio. More German immigrants arrived in Texas in the late nineteenth century than in the years before the Civil War. In most instances the newcomers settled in communities established by Germans before the war, with Austin, Fayette, Lee, and Washington counties receiving large numbers. Attracted primarily by the lure of cotton-growing lands, German settlers were scattered in isolated communities, known as "folk islands," over Central and West Texas in the late nineteenth and early twentieth centuries. German settlers tended to retain their cultural heritage. Often German was spoken in the daily routine, in church services, and occasionally in the schools. There were a number of German newspapers. Foods, holidays, architecture, and other customs made the distinctly German culture quite visible.

Immigrants from Czechoslovakia, then Bohemia and Moravia, made their way to inland areas. Fayette County was a favorite destination, but some chose other locations, usually in communities where the German population was large. Polish settlements founded before the Civil War similarly grew with the new immigration, until by the early 1900s there were some 17,000 people of Polish heritage in Texas. Smaller numbers of Swedes joined the tide of settlers, mostly locating near Austin in Travis and Williamson counties.

The Jewish population of Texas stood at approximately 15,000 in 1900 but increased to over 30,000 by 1920. Part of this increase was due to increased immigration from Russia and eastern Europe in the late nineteenth

Jewish Immigrants Arriving in Galveston. In the early twentieth century there was an effort to make Galveston a major port of entry for Jewish immigrants from Eastern Europe. This group of immigrants awaiting processing in Galveston represented a small fraction of that effort. Though the attempt to shift Jewish immigration from the East Coast to Galveston failed, the program did significantly increase the size of the Jewish community in Texas. (Texas State Library and Archives Commission)

and early twentieth century in response to the rise of anti-Semitism in Russia. Rabbi Henry Cohen of Galveston worked with Jewish leaders in New York and Europe to channel a portion of these immigrants through Galveston into the American heartland, in part to reduce the potential for increased anti-Semitism in the United States by dispersing the Jewish population. Although this dispersion plan failed, between 1907 and 1914 approximately 10,000 Jewish immigrants entered the United States through the port of Galveston.

Unlike German and Czech immigrants, who generally settled in rural communities and small towns, Jewish immigrants concentrated in Texas cities and larger towns. Houston, Dallas, Fort Worth, and San Antonio witnessed a rapid growth in their Jewish population in the early years of the new century, and an accompanying increase in Jewish religious, social-service, and educational organizations. The first Jewish newspaper, *The Jewish Herald Voice*, began publication in Houston in 1906, and San Antonio and Dallas newspapers followed. Economically, most Jewish immigrants were fairly successful. Most chose trade rather than agriculture for their occupation, and some who began as peddlers and then settled down as shopkeepers watched their businesses grow into large mercantile establishments.

Texas attracted settlers from other areas as well. Nederland in Jefferson County was founded by immigrants from the Netherlands. Galveston became the home of a colony of Yugoslavians who made their living by fishing; San Antonio was selected to be the home of a group of Lebanese; and there were sizable numbers of English, Irish, and Italians who settled in the towns and cities. Smaller number of immigrants came from Belgium, Denmark, France, Hungary, Norway, Russia, Scotland, Switzerland, and Wales. By 1900, almost a thousand Chinese lived in Texas, and a small number of Japanese rice farmers had settled along the Texas Gulf coast.

LITERATURE AND THE ARTS

The last third of the nineteenth century witnessed a substantial increase in the quantity of Texas writings as well as some improvements in quality. These achievements carried over into the early twentieth century. Many of the most popular books of this period were adventure stories, many of which were reminiscences of the Texas Revolution and early statehood period and were of genuine historical value. Dozens of books of this genre were written. Perhaps the best known is *The Adventures of Big Foot Wallace*, a biography of a famous Ranger who had come to Texas in 1836 to avenge the death of his brother, killed in Goliad. Closely related were books that focused on the conquest of the frontier in the late nineteenth century. Many of these, too, were firsthand accounts, such as the work of Charles A. Siringo, a real cowboy whose tales fascinated readers. In 1886 he published *Texas Cowboy or Fifteen Years on the Hurricane Deck of a Spanish Pony*, a paperback thriller that sold many thousands of copies and established a market for scores of similar books. Also popular were late-nineteenth-century versions of "true crime" stories featuring notorious outlaws such as Sam Bass or John Wesley Harding.

Poetry was not a strength among Texas writers. In the nineteenth century some of the best poetry was incorporated in the cowboy ballads and borderland *corridos*, which were a version of folk song that celebrated the adventures of local heroes. The best known of these cowboy poems was William Lawrence (Larry) Chittenden's "Cowboy Christmas Ball." The only other poet of note during this period—John P. Sjolander, a Swedish American—has been called the "Dean of Texas Poets" for the magazine verse he published while working as a farmer and shipbuilder on Cedar Bayou.

The late nineteenth century was also characterized by many works of fiction. Although few of these had any enduring value, there were some notable exceptions. Mrs. Molley E. Moore Davis, the wife of a New Orleans editor, began her writing in Texas, and her best work had a Texas setting. *Under the Man-Fig*, probably her best-known novel, dealt with the destructive effects of gossip in a small town. William Sidney Porter, who wrote under the name O. Henry, came to Texas from his native North Carolina in 1882. Two years on a ranch in La Salle County and a decade in Austin and Houston, where he held and lost various jobs, supplied much of the experience and setting for the literary work that made him one of the greatest short story writers of all time. His collection of stories *Heart of the West*, published during the first decade of the twentieth century, is based almost wholly on Texas scenes.

Historical writing in Texas took a major step forward in 1897 with the organization of the Texas State Historical Association. The association began the publication of the *Quarterly of the Texas State Historical Association*, which in 1912 became *The Southwestern Historical Quarterly*. George Pierce Garrison and Herbert E. Bolton contributed much to the success of this publication, and, under the editorship of Eugene C. Barker, it earned a reputation as an important historical journal.

Garrison and Bolton were at the vanguard of a group of outstanding Texas historians who were active in the early decades of the twentieth century. In his *Texas, a Contest of Civilizations*, Garrison brought to bear on the subject years of research and historical training. Bolton, a noted scholar of the Spanish Southwest, published some studies pertaining to Texas, among them *Texas in the Middle-Eighteenth Century* and *Athanase de Mézières and the Louisiana-Texas Frontier*. A contemporary, Charles W. Ramsdell, earned a place among the authorities on the Old South and the Civil War. Barker's studies on the Austins remained the standard work for almost seventy-five years, and his scholarly articles filled several volumes.

Among the well-known artists of the period was H. A. McArdle, whose pictures "Battle of San Jacinto" and "Dawn of the Alamo" attracted

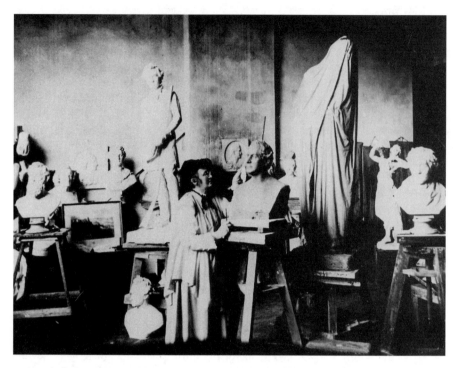

Elizabeth Ney—beautiful, talented, and willful—learned sculpture in Munich and Berlin where she cast busts of such famous men as Schopenhauer, Garibaldi, and King William I of Prussia. She moved to the United States with her British husband in 1870 and settled in Texas two years later. Unhappy on a remote plantation, she received commissions from the state for busts of Stephen Austin and Sam Houston that enabled her to move to a studio in Austin. One of her best works, a statue of General Albert Sidney Johnston, is now in the state cemetery. It was her last work, a statue of Lady Macbeth, that won her the fame she enjoyed. Here she is shown at work on a bust of William Jennings Bryan. (Archives Division—Texas State Library)

much attention when they were hung in the state capitol. A contemporary of McArdle was William H. Huddle, whose "Surrender of Santa Anna" also hangs in the state capitol. Robert Jenkins Onderdonk left some superior portraits and paintings of scenes in the vicinity of Dallas and San Antonio. His son, Julian, who died in 1922 at the age of forty, was probably Texas's most distinguished painter. Of particular note were his landscape scenes, especially "Dawn on the Hills." In sculpture one name stood supreme—Elisabeth Ney. Ney came to the state in 1870, with her husband, Dr. Edmund Montgomery, from her native Bavaria, where she had already attained fame. Best known to Texans were her statues of Stephen F. Austin, Sam Houston, and Albert Sidney Johnston. Of higher quality, however, were her imaginative works: for example, the group that she called *Sursum,* now in the Chicago Art Institute, and her statue of Lady Macbeth, now in the National Gallery in Washington, D.C. After Miss Ney's death, her studio in Austin became a museum and a shrine for Texas artists and art lovers.

In the early decades of the twentieth century, Texas musicians contributed to the cultural development of the state. Much of Texas music was based on the traditions of European classical music. Carl Vent, born in Germany and trained in Europe and already a noted musician when he moved to Texas in 1909, contributed much to the musical growth of the state. Texas's most significant and creative musician of this period was Scott Joplin. Joplin, who was one of the creators of ragtime, wrote an opera and a number of popular songs. The state's noted early jazz and blues musicians included Blind Lemon Jefferson and Hudie ("Leadbelly") Ledbetter. Texas's cultural diversity influenced the music of this period. Many of the familiar ballads and folk songs reflected the culture of the Mexican Americans or African Americans. Folklorist John Limax collected the songs of the frontier as well as the music of Texas's many cultures. His first published collection of Texas folk songs, *Cowboy Songs and Other Frontier Ballads*, appeared in 1910.

BIBLIOGRAPHY

There are a number of autobiographical studies that tell much about life at the turn of the century. See Edward Everett Dale, *The Cross Timbers* (Austin, 1966); Bertha McKee Dobie, *Growing Up in Texas* (Austin, 1972); Drury B. Alexander, *Texas Homes of the Nineteenth Century* (Austin, 1966); Adah Robertson Hadlock, *My Life in the Southwest*, ed. Kenneth A. Goldblatt (El Paso, 1969); C. C. White and Ada Moreland Holland, *No Quittin' Sense* (Austin, 1969); and Robert W. Richmond, (ed.), "Letter from Wise County, Texas," *The American West*, IX, 42–47. See also Catherine Ikard Carrow, "Amusements of Men and Women in Texas in the 1880s," *West Texas Historical Association Year Book*, XXXV, 77–96; Calvin Dickerson, "Collegiate Life in Nineteenth Century Texas," *Texana*, VII, 313–321; Jim Tom Barton, *Eighter from Decatur: Growing Up in North Texas* (College Station, 1980). A readable and comprehensive discussion of the Galveston flood is available in Herbert M. Mason, Jr., *Death from the Sea: Our Greatest Natural Disaster, The Galveston Hurricane of 1900* (New York, 1972). Eric Larsen, *Isaac's Storm: A Man, a Time, and the Deadliest Hurricane in History* (New York, 1999) is a new interpretation of the Galveston disaster.

For information on medical care, see Pat I. Nixon, *A History of the Texas Medical Association* (Austin, 1953); and Billy M. Jones, *Health Seekers in the Southwest, 1817–1900* (Norman, 1967). See also Chester R. Burns, "The Development of Galveston's Hospitals During the Nineteenth Century," *Southwestern Historical Quarterly*, XCVII, 239–257, and Elizabeth Silverthorne and Geneva Fulgham, *Women Pioneers in Texas Medicine* (College Station; 1997).

Increased interest in urban studies is evident in the availability of city histories. *Houston: A History and Guide* (Houston, 1942), compiled by the Federal Writers' Program of the Works Projects Administration in the state of Texas, is useful, but for a more specialized aspect of the city, see also Marilyn Sibley, *The Port of Houston* (Austin, 1968). For twentieth-century developments, see James Howard, *Big D Is for Dallas* (Dallas, 1957). A superior study is Lawrence Graves (ed.), *History of Lubbock* (Lubbock, 1962). Also see Dan E. Kilgore, "Corpus Christi: A Quarter Century of

Development, 1900–1925," *Southwestern Historical Quarterly*, LXXV, 435–443; Roger N. Conger, "Waco: Cotton and Culture on the Brazos," *Southwestern Historical Quarterly.*, LXXV, 54–60; and Keith L. Bryant, Jr., "Arthur E. Stilwell and the Founding of Port Arthur: A Case of Entrepreneurial Error," *Southwestern Historical Quarterly*, LXXV, 19–40. Among the longer studies are Robert L. Martin, *The City Moves West: Economic and Industrial Growth in Central West Texas* (Austin, 1969); David G. McComb, *Houston: The Bayou City* (Austin, 1969, rev. ed., 1981), and *Galveston* (Austin, 1986); Donald E. Everett, *San Antonio: The Flavor of Its Past* (San Antonio, 1975); A. C. Greene, *A Place Called Dallas: The Pioneering Years of a Continuing Metropolis* (Dallas, 1975); Katherine Hart and others, *Austin and Travis County: A Pictorial History, 1839–1939* (Austin, 1975); Leonard Sanders, *How Fort Worth Became the Texasmost City, 1849–1920* (College Station, 1986); and John S. Garner, "The Saga of a Railroad Town: Calvert, Texas, 1868–1918," *Southwestern Historical Quarterly*, LXXXV, 139–160.

In recent years a number of new community studies has added to our understanding of Texas cities and Texas urbanization. See Elizabeth York Enstam, *Women and the Creation of Urban Life: Dallas, Texas, 1843-1920* (College Station, 1998); Patricia Evridge Hill, *Dallas: The Making of a Modern City* (Austin, 1996); David G. McComb, "Galveston as a Tourist City," *Southwestern Historical Quarterly*, C, 331-360; Alan Lessoff, "A Texas City and the Texas Myth: Urban Historical Identity in Corpus Christi" *Southwestern Historical Quarterly*, C, 305- 329; David C. Humphrey, *Austin: A History of the Capitol City* (Austin, 1997); Michael V. Hazel, *Dallas: A History of 'Big D'"* (Austin, 1997); and C. David Pomeroy, Jr., *Pasadena: The Early Years* (Pasadena, 1993).

Considering the importance of the industry, the large number of studies on oil is to be expected. C. C. Rister's *Oil! Titan of the Southwest* (Norman, 1949) is the standard general work, and a colorful account of the first important discovery in Texas is William A. Owens, "Gusher at Spindletop," *American Heritage*, IX, 34ff. Those seeking additional sources should consult Walter Rundell, Jr., "Texas Petroleum History: A Selective Annotated Bibliography," *Southwestern Historical Quarterly*, LXVII, 267–278, which lists and describes more than sixty studies. See also Walter Rundell, Jr., *Early Texas Oil Photographic History, 1866–1936* (College Station, 1977), and John O. King, *Joseph Stephen Cullinan: A Study of Leadership in the Texas Petroleum Industry, 1897–1937* (Nashville, 1970). Considering economic matters generally is J. S. Spratt, *The Road to Spindletop* (Dallas, 1955), while Ray Miles, *King of the Wildcatters: The Life and Times of Tom Slick, 1883-1930* (College Station, 1996), presents a personal view of the industry.

Sources on the story of women in Texas are listed in Ruthe Winegarten (ed)., *Texas Women's History Project Bibliography* (Austin, 1980). A wide variety of studies are available: some examples are Winegarten, *Texas Women: A Pictoral History, From Indians to Astronauts* (Austin, 1986); Lawrence W. Neff, *The Legal Status of Women in Texas* (Dallas, 1895); Kathleen Lazarou, "Concealed under Petticoats: Married Women's Property and the Law in Texas, 1840–1913" (unpublished dissertation, Rice University, Houston, 1980); James M. Day et al., *Women of Texas* (Waco, 1972); Emily Jones Shelton, "Lizzie E. Johnson: A Cattle Queen of Texas," *Southwestern Historical Quarterly*, LVIII, 315–348; Evelyn M. Carrington. (ed.), *Women in Early Texas* (Austin, 1975); Elizabeth York Enstam, "The Frontier Woman as City Worker: Women's Occupations in Dallas, Texas, 1856–1880," *East Texas Historical Journal*, XVIII, 12–28; Ann Fears Crawford and Crystal Sasse Ragsdale, *Women in Texas: Their Lives, Their Experiences, Their Accomplishments* (Burnet, 1982); Mary S. Cunningham, *The Women's Club of El Paso: Its First Thirty Years* (El Paso, 1978); Megan Seaholm, "From Self-Culture to Civic Responsibility: Women's Clubs in Texas, 1880–1920" (unpublished dissertation, Rice University, Houston, 1988); Francis Edward Abernethy (ed.), *Legendary Ladies of Texas* (Dallas, 1981); Ada Morehead Holland, *Brush Country Woman* (College Station, 1988); and Jayne A. Sokolow and Mary Ann Lamanna, "Women and Utopia:

The Woman's Commonwealth of Belton, Texas," *Southwestern Historical Quarterly*, LXXXVII, 371–392.

There is a growing body of work on the history of African Americans in Texas. The life of black Texans at the turn of the century is described thoroughly in Lawrence Rice, *The Negro in Texas, 1874–1900* (Baton Rouge, 1971), and in Alwyn Barr, *Black Texans* 2nd. (Norman, 1996). There is an abundance of literature dealing with specialized topics: John D. Weaver, *The Brownsville Raid* (College Station, 1992) and *The Senator and the Sharecropper's Sons: Exoneration of the Brownsville Soldiers* (College Station, 1997); and Garna L. Christian, "The Brownsville Raid's 168th Man: The Court-Martial of Corporal Knowles," *Southwestern Historical Quarterly*, XCIII, 45–59, examine the racial incident at Brownsville and the long struggle for justice that followed; Garna L. Christian, *Black Soldiers in Jim Crow Texas, 1899-1917* (College Station, 1995), expands this topic in a study of other racial incidents involving black troops in the early twentieth century Texas. Other works include Alwyn Barr, "Occupational and Geographic Mobility in San Antonio, 1870–1900," *Social Science Quarterly*, LI, 396–403; and Mason Brewer, *Negro Legislators of Texas and Their Descendants* (Austin, 1970). Also invaluable is Bruce Glasrud, "Black Texans, 1900–1930: A History," Ph.D. dissertation, Texas Tech University, 1969; and that of William J. Brophy, "The Black Texan, 1900–1950: A Quantitative History," in the library of Vanderbilt University. Additional studies are Alwyn Barr and Robert A. Calvert (eds.), *Black Leaders: Texans for Their Times* (Austin, 1981); Paul Wright, "Residential Segregation in Two Early West Texas Towns," *Southwestern Historical Quarterly*, CII, 294-320; Bruce Glasrud, "Enforcing White Supremacy in Texas, 1900–1910," *Red River Valley Historical Review*, IV, 65–74; James M. Sorelle, "The `Waco Horror': The Lynching of Jesse Washington," *Southwestern Historical Quarterly*, LXXXVI, 517–536; Randy Roberts, "Galveston's Jack Johnson: Flourishing in the Dark," *Southwestern Historical Quarterly*, LXXXVII, 37–56; Judith W. Linsley, "Main House, Carriage House: African-American Domestic Employees at the McFaddin-Ward House in Beaumont, Texas, 1900-1950," *Southwestern Historical Quarterly*, CIII, 17-51; and Michael Gillette, "The Rise of the NAACP in Texas," *Southwestern Historical Quarterly*, LXXXI, 393–416. For material on African American women see Ruthe Winegarten, *Black Texas Women: 150 Years of Triumph* (Austin, 1995), and *Black Texas Women: A Sourcebook* (Austin, 1996); and Annie Mae Hunt and Ruthe Winegarten, *I Am Annie Mae: An Extraordinary Black Texas Woman in Her Own Words* (Austin, 1996). For material on African American religion see Clyde McQueen, *Black Churches in Texas: A Guide to Historic Congregations* (College Station, 2000).

Useful as a starting point for additional study on Mexican American history is Juan Gómez-Quiñones and Luis Leobardo Arrayo, "On the State of Chicano History: Observations on Its Development, Interpretations, and Theory," *Western Historical Quarterly*, VII, 155–185. Also see Kenneth L. Stewart and Arnoldo de León, *Tejanos and the Numbers Game: A Socio-Historical Interpretation from the Federal Censuses, 1850–1900* (Albuquerque, 1989), and *Not Room Enough: Mexican, Anglos, and Socioeconomic Change in Texas, 1850–1900* (Albuquerque, 1993); Paul S. Taylor, *An American-Mexican Frontier: Nueces County, Texas* (Chapel Hill, N.C., 1934); Pauline R. Kibbe, *Latin Americans in Texas* (Albuquerque, 1946); William Madsen, *The Mexican Americans of South Texas* (New York, 1964); Arnulfo D. Trejo, *The Chicanos As We See Ourselves* (Tucson, 1979); Clifford Alan Perkins, *Border Patrol: With the U. S. Immigration Service on the Mexican Boundary, 1910–1954*, ed. C. L. Sonnichsen, (El Paso, 1978); Lawrence A. Cardoso, "Labor Emigration to the Southwest, 1916 to 1920; Mexican Attitudes and Policy," *Southwestern Historical Quarterly*, LXXIX, 400–416; Mario T. García, *Desert Immigrants: The Mexicans of El Paso, 1880–1920* (New Haven, 1981), and "Porfirian Diplomacy and the Administration of Justice in Texas, 1877–1900," *Aztlán*, XVI, 1–25; Rodolfo O. de la Garza, et al. (eds.), *The Mexican-American Experience: An Interdisciplinary Anthology* (Austin, 1985); Robert J. Rosenbaum, *Mexicano Resistance in the*

Southwest: The Sacred Right of Self Preservation (Austin, 1981); Elliott Young, "Red Men, Princess Pocahontas, and George Washington: Harmonizing Race Relations in Laredo at the Turn of the Century," *The Western Historical Quarterly,* XXIX, 46-85.

For information on other ethnic groups, see Terry G. Jordan, "The German Settlement of Texas after 1865," *Southwestern Historical Quarterly,* LXXIII, 193–212; Edward J. M. Rhoads, "The Chinese in Texas," *Southwestern Historical Quarterly,* LXXXI, 1–36; T. Lindsey Baker, *The First Polish Americans: Silesian Settlements in Texas* (College Station, 1979), and Hollace Ava Weiner, *Jewish Stars in Texas: Rabbis and their Work* (College Station, 1999). The Institute of Texan Cultures has published a number of studies on individual ethnic groups that are useful introductory materials.

On the history of education, see Frederick Eby, *The Development of Education in Texas* (New York, 1925); and Cecil E. Evans, *The Story of Texas Schools* (Austin,1955). For an understanding of daily life in the schools, see Thad Sitton and Milam Rowold, *Ringing the Children In: Texas Country Schools* (College Station, 1988); Dorothy Robinson, *The Bell Rings at Four: A Black Teacher's Chronicle of Change* (Austin, 1978); Lel Purcell Hawkins, *A Texas Pioneer Teacher: Mrs. R. K. Red.* (Quanah, 1996); and Luther Bryan Clegg, (ed.), *The Empty Schoolhouse: Memories of One-Room Texas Schools* (College Station, 1997).

For colleges and universities, there is George Sessions Perry, *The Story of Texas A&M* (New York, 1951); William Hooper, Jr., "Governor Edmund J. Davis, Ezra Cornell and the A&M College of Texas," *Southwestern Historical Quarterly,* LXXVIII, 307–312; W. J. Battle, "A Concise History of the University of Texas, 1883–1950," *Southwestern Historical Quarterly,* LIV, 391–411; George P. Garrison, "The First Twenty-five Years of the University of Texas," *Southwestern Historical Quarterly,* LX, 106–117; E. Bruce Thompson, "William Carey Crane and Texas Education," *Southwestern Historical Quarterly,* LVIII, 405–421; Roger A. Griffin, "To Establish a University of the First Class," *Southwestern Historical Quarterly,* LXXXVI, 135–160; and Michael R. Heintze, *Private Black Colleges in Texas, 1865–1954* (College Station, 1985).

The most valuable sources for the literature of this period are Martin Shockley (ed.), *Southwest Writers' Anthology* (Austin, 1967); Mabel Major et al., *Southwest Heritage: A Literary History* (Albuquerque, 1948); and J. Frank Dobie, *Life and Literature of the Southwest* (rev. ed., Dallas, 1973); David Stuart, *O. Henry: A Biography of William Sydney Porter* (Chelsea, 1990); "The Southwest, a Cultural Inventory," *Saturday Review of Literature,* May 16, 1942; and Sylvia Ann Grider and Lou Halsell Rodenberger, (eds.), *Texas Women Writers: A Tradition of Their Own* (College Station, 1997).

For a comprehensive overview of the visual arts in Texas see Paula L. Grauer and Michael R. Grauer, *Dictionary of Texas Artists, 1800-1945* (College Station, 1999). Other works include Pauline Pinckney, *Texas Artists of the Nineteenth Century* (Austin, 1967); Lota M. Spell, *Music in Texas* (Austin, 1938); Susan Curtis, *Dancing to a Black Man's Tune: A Life of Scott Joplin* (Columbia, Mo., 1994); Emily Cutrer, *The Art of Woman: The Life and Work of Elisabet Ney* (Lincoln, 1988); and Cecilia Steinfeldt, *The Onderdonks: A Family of Texas Painters* (San Antonio, 1976).

16

Crusades and Complacency
1910–1930

Crusades and complacency characterized Texas politics in the score of years between the Progressive Era and the Great Depression. Many Texans enthusiastically joined the crusade for Prohibition, practically all supported the great crusade of the First World War, and far too many endorsed the reactionary crusading of the Ku Klux Klan. It was, moreover, an age of social, technological, and economic change. Yet in some respects it was an era of complacency. Particularly in the 1920s, politics was largely the story of governors who sought reforms, reforms that were mainly moderate and generally needed but that indifferent legislators and a still more indifferent electorate would not accept. Prohibition, a world war, the impeachment of a governor, and the rise of a hooded tyranny contributed to a sense of political and social turmoil. But the public response to these issues as well as to the rapid pace of industrialization and urbanization and a corresponding decline in the role of agriculture was a conservative and sometimes reactionary resistance to change.

Oscar Branch Colquitt,
1911–1915

In 1910 Oscar Branch Colquitt captured 40 percent of the vote in the Democratic gubernatorial primary, and won the nomination, and subsequently the general election. A former Hogg man, an opponent of Prohibition, and railroad commissioner, Colquitt was generally regarded as the most conservative man in the race. Most assuredly he was not a crusader, and he received the support of some corporate interests. Once he was in office, his record, in part, fulfilled conservative expectations. He attempted to block some labor legislation, curbed appropriations for higher education, and opposed free textbooks for the public schools. Yet the Colquitt years were not without progressive achievements. There were laws regulating child labor, promoting factory safety, and limiting the hours of women workers. Most significant was the creation of a state workers' compensation system.

An old vexing problem returned during the Colquitt administration. Provoked by the Mexican revolution of 1910 and the turmoil that followed, violence erupted along the Rio Grande, and there were rumors of a Mexican insurrection in the United States. Ill will and confusion persisted on the border until long after the First World War. Governor Colquitt twice sent state troops to the Rio Grande; they were soon supplanted by federal soldiers. A thousand Texas Rangers stationed along the border afforded a measure of protection, but violence did not cease until several months after the close of the war. A number of Anglo-Americans and a much larger number of Mexicans and Mexican Americans were killed in the violence, in some instances the victims of those who were charged with enforcing the law. Following a sweeping legislative investigation in which it was charged that the Rangers had abused peaceful Mexican American citizens of the United States, a law of March 31, 1919, reduced the force to four regular companies of seventeen men each.

Less dramatic than rumored insurrection but certainly serious were the state's financial problems during the Colquitt years. When the outgoing administration set tax rates too low, Governor Colquitt inherited a deficit of nearly $1 million. A rising cost of living, various calamities, and the growing cost of the state prisons added to the burden. During his second administration, Colquitt vetoed some appropriations, but even then it was necessary to raise the state tax rate. State expenditures, in fact, more than doubled between 1903 and 1914.

PROHIBITION: THE TRIUMPH OF A MORAL CRUSADE

Although discouraged temporarily by their severe defeat in 1887, Prohibitionists soon renewed their fight to ban the sale of alcoholic beverages, directing their efforts mainly toward local option. Their strategy was to use the existing constitutional provision for local option to establish Prohibition from county to county until the whole state was dry. The Texas Local Option Association was organized in Dallas in 1903 for this purpose, and in 1907 the

Anti-Saloon League entered the state. To meet this challenge, the powerful Texas Brewers' Association assessed its membership more than $2 million between 1902 and 1911 for the liquor campaign. In 1907 the Retail Liquor Dealers' Association was organized to stop the march of prohibition. Nevertheless, through the extension of local option, the Prohibitionists gained ground steadily. During the 1890s, they drove the saloons out of most of North and West Texas, and in the following decade they began to make inroads into South and Southeast Texas. Encouraged by their victories but frustrated that some areas resisted their efforts, Prohibitionists again turned their aims toward a statewide ban.

Prohibition became such an all-absorbing political contest because both sides viewed it primarily in moral terms. Each side was convinced that it held the moral high ground and that its opponents were immoral and corrupt. As in the 1880s, the struggle pitted advocates of freedom of choice (the anti-Prohibitionists) against those who believed that alcohol use and abuse were the greatest moral, social, and public health threat confronting society. There was no easy way to engineer a compromise between these views.

By 1908 Prohibition dominated state politics. In fact, from the primary campaign of 1908 when the question of statewide prohibition was again submitted to the voter until the First World War, there were in effect two Democratic parties in Texas—one Prohibitionist, the other anti-Prohibitionist. True, there was no formal division; there was only one set of party committees, and there was only one Democratic primary. But the factions were so pronounced that every prominent leader was forced to join one side or the other, and the rank and file of voters took their places in the respective camps.

The forces were evenly matched. In the primary election of 1908 the Prohibitionists won by a slender margin, but the brewery interests were able to defeat the submission of a constitutional amendment by the legislature. When the entire question was fought out again in the primary election of 1910, the Prohibitionists again committed the party to submitting a Prohibition amendment to the voters. In the nomination of candidates, however, they were not so successful. The anti-Prohibitionists centered their votes on Colquitt, who was elected by a large plurality over three opponents, two of them ardent Prohibitionists who split the votes. Thus, in its primary the Democratic Party called for a Prohibition amendment and at the same time made sure of the election of an anti-Prohibitionist governor.

The legislature submitted the Prohibition amendment to the voters on July 22, 1911. The two factions aligned themselves for another desperate contest. With great fervor, politicians, lay leaders, and ministers campaigned for the cause, while Governor Colquitt joined others in opposition. By a close vote, 231,096 for to 237,393 against, statewide Prohibition again failed.

Although they kept up the fight, the Prohibitionists in Texas made little headway for some time. However, suits filed by Attorney General B. F. Looney in 1915 revealed that brewers had violated the state's antitrust laws and had illegally used funds in elections. Then came the impeachment of Governor James Ferguson in 1917 and evidence indicating that the brewers had helped finance his political career. Moreover, Prohibition became a patriotic issue, a measure with which to win World War I. Women, long a strong voice in the movement, renewed their efforts with the formation of the Texas Woman's Anti-Vice Committee, and focused their attention on providing a wholesome environment for servicemen. A law that became effective on April 15, 1918, forbade the sale of liquor within ten miles of any place where troops were quartered. Shortly thereafter, a state law closed all saloons. Then, on January 16, 1920, the Eighteenth Amendment to the U.S. Constitution made prohibition national policy. Meanwhile, the legislature of Texas had ratified the Eighteenth Amendment, and on May 24, 1919, the voters of Texas had adopted a Prohibition amendment to the state constitution. Traces of the rift caused by the issue would linger nearly as long as the experiment. But other national and state issues had already diverted the interest of both voter and politician alike.

THE BIRTH OF FERGUSONISM, 1915–17

In 1914, a man appeared in Texas politics who was destined to stir the emotions of the people for a generation. Rising from poverty and a meager formal education, James E. Ferguson became a successful banker, lawyer, and businessman, but he was a virtual unknown in state politics. Yet Ferguson, who was often referred to as "Farmer Jim," was twice elected governor, serving from January 1915 to September 1917. Through his wife, Governor Miriam A. ("Ma") Ferguson, he guided policies of the state when she served as governor from 1925 to 1927 and again from 1933 to 1935. In addition to his successful campaigns, he was an unsuccessful candidate for governor in 1918, for president of the United States in 1920, and for the U.S. Senate in 1922. In addition to the years in which she was elected, Miriam Ferguson ran for governor in 1926, 1930, and 1940. Meaning different things to different people, "Fergusonism" became a dominant force in Texas politics for two decades. Critics angrily denounced the Fergusons as unprincipled demagogues, but to their loyal supporters they were undaunted crusaders seeking justice for the oppressed.

Believing that the majority of Texans were tired of the Prohibition controversy, Ferguson announced as a candidate for governor in the primary of 1914 with the declaration that he would remain aloof from Prohibition and direct his campaign to other, more important issues. Although he posed as a businessman's candidate, the principal plank in his platform appealed to tenant farmers. For many decades tenantry in Texas had been increasing. In

1880, 37 percent of all farms were operated by tenants, in 1900 the percentage had increased to 59 percent, and in 1910 it was 62.6 percent. Though their number had increased, the lot of tenants was growing harder and the outlook for them more discouraging. The time-honored custom of the landlord's taking a rental of one-fourth of the cotton and one-third of most other crops was not being followed uniformly in Texas. Ferguson proposed to fix farm rentals at one-third and one-fourth by law and to make higher rates illegal. He opened his campaign in Blum, Hill County, a tenant community. Of the 155 speeches that he delivered before the primary election, only 10 were made in towns and cities. In the primary he defeated Thomas H. Ball of Houston, who was supported by the Prohibition wing of the party. In November he was elected governor with little opposition.

Ferguson's first administration was characterized by harmony and an imposing list of constructive laws. Of the 160 general laws enacted during the regular session of the Thirty-fourth Legislature in 1915, the governor vetoed only 5. Ferguson was easily reelected in 1916, and the first five months of his second administration witnessed the continuation of a constructive legislative program. The governor's rental plank was enacted into law in 1915. Never strictly enforced, the law was declared unconstitutional in 1921. Interesting and indicative of a new era was a law setting automobile speed limits at 15 miles an hour in towns and 18 miles an hour in the country. More significant and, in view of subsequent developments, more incongruous, were a number of laws substantially improving educational services.

Governor Ferguson's popularity declined during his second administration, but he still had a large following both in the legislature and among the rank and file of voters. In March 1917, the Texas House of Representatives investigated charges of irregular conduct on the part of the governor and discovered some questionable financial transactions; the committee nevertheless recommended that the charges be dropped. The regular session of the legislature completed its work and adjourned, but developments soon occurred that prevented the governor from completing his second term.

Although charges of corruption and incompetence were leveled at Ferguson, both friend and foe have usually agreed that he would not have been impeached if he had not antagonized the alumni of the University of Texas. The governor's quarrel with the university began as early as 1915 when he attempted to dictate to acting president W. J. Battle the interpretation of the appropriation law for the school. In the following year he apparently became piqued because he was not consulted by the regents in their selection of a president for the university. Later, he demanded that the regents dismiss President Robert E. Vinson and several other faculty members, threatening to veto the entire university appropriation if they did not. The regents, supported by the powerful alumni association, refused to yield. The governor was not bluffing; in June 1917, just after the legislature had adjourned, he vetoed the university appropriation. Although the attorney general declared the veto void on a technicality, the fight between Ferguson and the university was then eclipsed by a movement to impeach the governor.

Another Ferguson foe appeared as impeachment proceedings began. The Texas Equal Suffrage Association looked upon the governor as a man of questionable morality and an obvious opponent of women's suffrage. Led by Minnie Fisher Cunningham, the association's president, the suffragists enthusiastically urged that impeachment be pursued.

Responding to rising sentiment for impeachment proceedings, on July 23, 1917, the Speaker of the House issued a call for a special legislative session. He had no constitutional authority for such an act, but Governor Ferguson made the session legal by issuing a call after it became evident that the legislature was going to meet anyway. When the legislature convened, the House impeached the governor on twenty-one articles. On September 24, the Senate convicted Ferguson on ten charges. The most serious counts held that he had appropriated for his own use certain state funds, that he was guilty of irregularities in connection with deposits of public funds in the Temple State Bank, of which he was a stockholder, and that during his campaign in 1916 he had secured currency in the amount of $156,500 from unknown sources. It was discovered later that most of this money had been borrowed from the brewing interests and apparently had never been repaid. The court of impeachment removed Governor Ferguson and prohibited him from holding a state office in Texas again, a restriction that would yield strange developments in later years.

Despite the ban on holding office, Ferguson returned to the political wars the following year, contesting William P. Hobby, the lieutenant governor who had taken his position after his impeachment, for the Democratic gubernatorial nomination. Ferguson campaigned with enthusiasm, venting his ire on the University of Texas in particular. One professor of the school, he declared, had devoted two years to an attempt to grow wool on the back of an armadillo. Faculty members were "educated fools," "butterfly chasers," and "two-bit thieves"; crooks and grafters controlled the school's administration. Governor Hobby was a "political accident." Hobby won the nomination with a comfortable margin of almost 70 percent of the vote. But the state had not heard the last of "Farmer Jim" Ferguson.

TEXAS IN THE FIRST WORLD WAR

The impeachment of a governor in Texas took place in the midst of a war in Europe that was shaking the foundations of civilization. When German submarines took the lives of U.S. citizens, Texans, along with other Americans, became aroused. When Congress declared war on Germany on April 6, 1917, sentiment in Texas in support of the measure was overwhelming.

Politics determined that Texans would play a prominent role in the world conflict that dominated the second term of President Woodrow Wilson. It was the Texas delegation in the Democratic National Convention in Baltimore in 1912 that voted for Wilson first and last and possibly assured his nomination. Later Wilson appointed Thomas Watt Gregory, of Austin, as attorney general and David F. Houston, a former Texan, as secretary of agriculture. Albert Sidney Burleson, of Austin, served as postmaster general and during the war directed government operation of the nation's telephone and telegraph systems. Colonel E. M. House was for some time the president's most trusted and important private counselor and personal representative. He spearheaded Wilson's unsuccessful efforts to achieve a negotiated end to the European war and served as the president's liaison to the Allies once the U.S. entered the war. Thomas Love of Dallas served as assistant secretary of the Treasury, and many other Texans held positions of responsibility.

Within the state the military demands of war were quite apparent. Thousands of soldiers trained in four large camps, and a number of aviation schools scattered over the state provided many citizens with their first view of an airplane. Through the Selective Service law and voluntary enlistment, 197,389 Texans, representing a number of different cultures, served in the army, navy, and marine corps. About 25 percent of these soldiers were African Americans. Some Mexicans living in Texas were not citizens and therefore not required to serve, but many thousands volunteered. Several combat infantry regiments in France contained a large number of Mexican Americans, and a number were decorated for bravery. Women made their contribution to the services, providing 449 nurses. Of those Texans in the armed services, more than 5,000 lost their lives.

At home, the war effort represented more of an inconvenience than a hardship. To conserve food so that more might be available for the armed forces and allies in Europe, Texans ate no pork on Thursdays and Saturdays; on Tuesdays they ate no meat at all. Since wheat was especially scarce, food made from wheat was not eaten on Mondays and Wednesdays. In fact, corn bread for breakfast, lunch, and dinner was the menu in many homes, no matter what the day of the week. Otherwise, to support the war effort people took part in the Liberty Loan campaigns, buying Liberty Bonds, Victory Bonds, and War Savings Stamps.

Industry expanded during the war. Shipbuilding yards and factories producing goods for the war effort were located in various cities, particularly along the coast. New oilfields located at Ranger, Desdemona, and Breckinridge in West-Central Texas brought boomtown conditions to those areas and added to the supply of petroleum necessary for the armies and the civilian population. Unemployment declined to almost nothing.

Jane McCallum and Austin Women Registering Women to Vote. In 1918 the
Texas legislature took the first step toward women's suffrage by allowing women
to vote in primary elections. In response to that law these women gathered on
the steps of the Travis County Courthouse in 1918 with suffrage leader Jane
McCallum to register to vote in the July 1918 primary elections. (Texas State
Library and Archives Commission)

The war effected a number of other significant changes. Inflation
brought a soaring cost of living not always matched by a comparable increase
in income, though farm prices generally advanced. The cost of state government more than doubled between 1913 and 1919, a permanent change. Still
another change was in the role of women, who provided a major part of the
additional labor force needed for the war effort. Often they worked in voluntary agencies, but some took jobs formerly reserved for men, such as in law
enforcement, real estate sales, and labor union management.

Wartime also saw the triumph of the women's suffrage movement.
Organized in 1903, the Texas Woman Suffrage Association had been relatively inactive for some time when it met again in a convention in 1913.
Eleanor Brackenridge and Annette Finnegan, former leaders who had
returned to the state, directed the renewal of the organization, which by
1915 claimed twenty-one local societies and 2,500 members. That year the
members elected Minnie Fisher Cunningham president and in the next they
changed the name of their organization to the Texas Equal Suffrage Associ-

Minnie Fisher Cunningham. Educated at home, she became first a teacher and then the recipient of the first degree in pharmacy awarded by the University of Texas to a woman. A leader in the women's suffrage movement in Texas, she was chairman of the state's Liberty Loan Campaign in World War I and later held several positions in state and national government agencies. Involved in politics throughout much of her life, she was one of the founders of the National League of Women Voters and was a candidate for U. S. Senator in 1928 and for governor in 1944. (Archives Division—Texas State Library)

ation. By 1918, there were ninety-eight local societies. African American women in Texas, such as Christie Adair, participated in the suffrage campaign even though they were not allowed to join the Texas Equal Suffrage Association, and they would be excluded from voting in the Democratic primary.

Meanwhile, the momentum for suffrage was growing. In 1915, the Texas Federation of Women's Clubs endorsed women's suffrage, and suffragists narrowly missed securing legislative approval of a constitutional amendment granting women the right to vote. The suffragists resumed their battle in the legislature in 1917, only to see the impeachment of the governor intervene. But in a special session in 1918, the legislature adopted a law granting partial suffrage by permitting women to vote in all primary elections. That same year several women were elected to posts in local governments, and Annie Webb Blanton won the race for the state superintendent of education. Voters in 1919 turned down a state constitutional amendment granting women's suffrage, but the cause was triumphant anyway, since the decision would be made at the national level. Another special session of the legislature in June 1919 ratified the Nineteenth Amendment to the Constitution of the United States; Texas was the ninth state in the union and the first in the South to give its approval.

Racial tensions grew during the period, though black Texans gave their support to the war effort. Ironically, as women were gaining the right to vote, at least in part because of their contribution to the war effort,

African Americans were losing it and were increasingly victimized by discrimination and violence. Blacks in large numbers served in the armed forces, and others took part in Liberty Loan drives, supported the Red Cross, and otherwise demonstrated their patriotism. But a mob lynched a black man at Huntsville who was accused of evading the draft, and before the turmoil was ended, six members of his family were also dead. Furthermore, the presence of black troops in Texas led to racial tension and violence, first in Waco in July 1917, and then in Houston on the night of August 23, 1917. In the Houston incident black troops stationed at Camp Logan west of the city mutinied in protest of segregation and police brutality. Armed, they marched on the city shooting white civilians—especially police officers. Seventeen people were killed, and as a result of the courts-martial that followed, nineteen black soldiers were executed and ninety-one were sentenced to prison. These events occurred during a wave of racial violence that resulted in a major race riot in East St. Louis in 1917, dozens of other riots in 1919, and an untold number of violent incidents across the country during and just after the war.

Racial violence was not the only problem generated by the war. Predictable but regrettable was a spirit of fear, intolerance, and enforced conformity. Following the example set by the general government, the state legislature in a special session in 1918 enacted a drastic law to promote loyalty. To utter criticisms of the U.S. government, its flag, its officers, or its soldiers' uniforms, or to question the wisdom of the nation's entrance into or continuance in the war was an offense punishable by fine and imprisonment. The election law was changed to deny the ballot to foreign-born persons not naturalized. It was required that all classes in the public school—the study of foreign language excepted—be conducted in English, that all schools devote at least ten minutes each day to the teaching of patriotism, and that the U.S. flag be displayed from a flagpole in every school yard. The law of 1923 requiring that the Constitution of the United States and that of Texas be taught in all public schools and that all teachers be citizens of the United States was a belated product of the war mood.

Sometimes there were excesses of patriotism, which ranged from the absurd to the tragic. In keeping with the spirit of the times was a legislative investigating committee's recommendation that all recent books and periodicals in the state library extolling the greatness of Germany be immediately destroyed or securely boxed and put out of the way. Governor Hobby in 1919 vetoed the appropriation for the German department of the University of Texas, observing that elimination of such courses would promote purer Americanism. In some communities the obsession for conformity led to terror. "Influential and esteemed" citizens of a central Texas town, for example, flogged six of their neighbors who declined to join the American Red Cross. A newspaper editor in a nearby community endorsed the action, remarking that "whipping may convert some, while others are beyond conversion and should be shot." Texans found that crusading may beget intolerance.

THE POLITICS OF CONSERVATISM

"You are assembled here in a new era. You have problems to deal with that concern a new age." With these words Governor William P. Hobby, in a message to the legislature in 1919, evaluated the importance of that time and occasion. Two years later, in the midst of a brief financial depression, Governor Pat M. Neff expressed a similar feeling in language even more startling: "We are pioneering today," he said to the legislature, "amid the rocks and reefs and whirlpools of the most disturbed and uncertain financial ocean the world has ever known. These are testing times. The affairs of men are shifting. Things are abnormal. The world is at a turning point in civilization."

Indeed, the sense of change was very pronounced in the postwar years. Most Texans seemed to feel that with the defeat of Germany and the triumph of democracy, time had turned a page and begun a new chapter. In a sense this was true; it was the dawn of a great boom. After a sharp but brief postwar economic recession the economy soared, and Texas shared in the prosperity that followed. New plants were erected for the manufacturing and processing of goods, land values doubled, millions were invested in public utilities, and thousands of new oil wells belched forth black gold. Construction of the state highway system began to accommodate the ever-increasing number of automobiles. New colleges were built, and thousands of youths crowded into all the institutions of higher learning; the public school system grew larger and more creditable each year. Prices of farm commodities lagged behind those enjoyed by industry, but bountiful crops tended to offset the low prices. No one anticipated that the boom would end and an economic disaster would follow.

Economic growth and progress did not lead to progress in government or politics. Indeed, there was little to distinguish the politics of the 1920s from politics in the years that preceded it. A few new government agencies were added and some of the old ones were enlarged, but there was little suggestive of the "new era" that Governor Hobby predicted. In many respects the governors recognized the political demands of the emerging industrial and urban society. But a reluctant legislature and a complacent electorate refused to respond.

Complacency in politics was apparent even before the end of the war. In February 1918, a legislative investigating committee made a report suggesting various changes in the state government, but little came out of the report. After the war Governor Hobby advocated more aid for education, a civil service commission, judicial reform, and state aid for home buyers, but

only a few educational improvements were made. The question of a constitutional convention was submitted to the voters in 1919 and defeated as
voters rejected ten out of thirteen constitutional amendments. Caught by the
spell of the new era, the legislature might propose changes, but the people
disposed of them.

The administration of Pat M. Neff is a case in point. Neff entered the
governor's race in 1919 championing "a new democracy." He won the
Democratic primary, defeating former Senator Joseph Bailey in a runoff. Neff
was renominated and reelected in 1922. He understood Texas politics,
having served two terms as speaker of the house, but neither the people nor
the legislature responded to his call for political change. Governor Neff
advocated a number of reform measures and got practically nowhere. The
legislature rejected his efforts to reform the state administrative system, convene a constitutional convention, and enact laws to combat what Neff called
the worst "crime wave" in the history of Texas. Neff did keep prisoners in
the penitentiary and greatly reduced the number of pardons granted, but
overall his accomplishments were limited. He was an ardent champion of
good roads and deserves a share of credit for the expansion and improvement of the highway system. Similarly, he used his influence effectively to
promote the conservation of natural resources. The state park system had its
beginning in 1923. A harsh comment on the lack of foresight of those who
had gone before is the fact that the state of Texas, which once had owned millions of acres of land, was obliged to solicit donations of a few hundred acres
here and there so that its people might have access to recreational facilities.
In 1923 the legislature also passed a law specifically prohibiting blacks from
voting in the Democratic primary, thus completing the implementation of
efforts begun at the turn of the century to exclude African Americans from
the political process.

THE KLAN AND THE BONNET

In 1921, there appeared in Texas an organization with a name from the
past. Beginning near Atlanta, Georgia, in 1915, the Ku Klux Klan took the
name of the organization of Reconstruction days and made white supremacy
one of its slogans. It was, however, more akin to the various racist political
movements that arose in postwar Europe than it was to the original Ku Klux
Klan of Reconstruction. But, of course, the Klan was ardently and violently
antiblack, as well as anti-immigrant, anti-Catholic, and anti-Semitic. It also
represented an effort to impose social, racial, and moral conformity on a
society in rapid transition from the farm to the city. The Klan made little
headway until after World War I, when various conditions combined to promote its growth. The war had caused Americans to question the loyalty of

the foreign-born—especially those who were immigrants from the countries at war with the United States. During the war this nativism led to anti-German hysteria; after the war it resulted in racially based immigration restrictions and fueled the Klan's version of "Americanism." But the Klan also appealed to those who were not attracted by its racist or xenophobic message by declaring war on crime and corrupt officials. It supported Prohibition and opposed the "breakdown of morality" that characterized the "roaring twenties."

The Klan experienced its maximum growth in Texas during 1921 and 1922, at a time when Governor Neff (not in sympathy with the Klan) was writing and speaking against the "greatest crime wave" in Texas history and giving credence to the estimate that "not ten percent of those who violated the law were arrested, and not half of those who are arrested are convicted." The Klan went further, assuming for itself the responsibility of protecting "virtuous womanhood," "premarital chastity," "marital fidelity," "respect for parental authority," and "abstinence from alcoholic beverages."

Covertly, the Klan entered politics, and soon its power was felt in almost every community. In 1922, it gained control of many local offices and participated in the campaign for the U.S. Senate. The strongest contenders were Earle B. Mayfield, member of the Texas Railroad Commission, and former Governor James E. Ferguson. Mayfield admitted that he had belonged to the Klan, and it was generally understood that he was supported by it, whereas Ferguson vigorously denounced the organization. Mayfield received the nomination. Disgruntled Democrats united with Republicans to support Houston attorney George E. B. Peddy, but Mayfield easily won the general election. This was one of the Klan's most imposing political victories.

In the gubernatorial election of 1924 the Klan played an even more important role by supporting Judge Felix D. Robertson of Dallas. His opponent, James E. Ferguson, disqualified from holding the governorship by the terms of his impeachment in 1917, entered the race through his wife, Miriam A. Ferguson. Robertson and Miriam Ferguson survived the first primary, and the runoff campaign became an ill-tempered battle. The Klan was powerful but it had already lost ground. From many communities came reports of hooded men, working by night, serving as sheriff, judge, and jury, and flogging persons, driving them from their communities, or otherwise terrifying them. Yet many voters found supporting the Fergusons a difficult task. However, in the primary Miriam Ferguson defeated Robertson by nearly 100,000 votes. Some dissatisfied Democrats united with the Republicans in an effort to defeat Mrs. Ferguson in the general election. The coalition supported George C. Butte, dean of the University of Texas law school, but Miriam Ferguson defeated him by more than 100,000 votes to become the first woman governor of Texas.

Miriam Amanda Ferguson. In 1924 Miriam A. Ferguson became the first woman to be elected governor of Texas. Although she won election primarily by fronting for her husband, who had been disqualified from seeking state office by his 1917 impeachment, a number of feminists celebrated the election, and many argue that M.A. Ferguson was more than just a shill for her husband. Though she lost her bid for reelection in 1926, Mrs. Ferguson would return to the governor's mansion for a second term in 1933. (Texas State Library & Archives Commission)

Some saw it as a great irony that Fergusonism was the undoing of the Klan. There were of course other reasons for the Klan's decline in Texas, but Jim Ferguson's unrelenting attack on the hooded organization, first in his senatorial campaign and then in his wife's gubernatorial campaign, ended the power of the Klan in Texas. In these campaigns he both ridiculed the Klan, claiming it would set up an empire in Texas under the rule of an "imperial gizzard," and attacked it for defying the principles of American democracy. In his senatorial campaign he charged that the Klan wanted to drive Jews and Catholics out of the country, and in his wife's campaign he accused them of attempting to subvert constitutional government. In a statement to the press Miriam Ferguson attributed her victory to the people of Texas who had learned firsthand the "real purposes of the Klan and its secret desire to set up here a supergovernment," and then she repudiated this vision in "terms unmistakable." Whether or not the Fergusons deserve the credit, one fact is clear. After the election of 1924, the Klan was no longer a political force in Texas.

Besides contributing to the decline of the Klan, not much good came from this second era of Fergusonism (1925–27). To no one's surprise Jim Ferguson played a dominant role in his wife's administration and served unofficially as her chief adviser. Yet Miriam Ferguson was the governor and did not always heed her husband's advice. The Fergusons had promised a conservative administration and they delivered on that promise. Other than a promised antimask law (directed against the Klan, and overturned by the courts), no legislative proposals of significance came from the governor's

Parades of hooded Ku Klux Klansmen were common in the early 1920s.
This one in November 1922 in Beaumont was one of the larger
exhibitions and demonstrated the strength of the organization in
Southeast Texas. (Printed by permission, Tyrrell Historical Library,
Beaumont, Texas)

office, and no outstanding laws were enacted. Ferguson's liberal pardoning
policy—2,000 acts of executive clemency, counting furloughs and extensions,
during twenty months—evoked gossip and unfavorable comment, and
earned the governor's mansion the name "House of 1,000 Pardons." But
despite rumors, no hard evidence surfaced that pardons were bought;
indeed, many of the pardons went to poor, infirm, and minority prisoners, a
large number of whom had been imprisoned for minor violations of Prohibition laws.

The chief attack by the enemies of the administration was aimed at the
Highway Commission, a body composed completely of Ferguson
appointees and dominated by the former governor. Ferguson favoritism
determined who received contracts for the construction of roads. Several
contracts were canceled as the result of suits brought by Attorney General
Dan Moody, who became the chief antagonist of the Fergusons. Similar
charges, never proven, accused the Fergusons of profiting from the awarding of textbook contracts.

A crusader for reform, Dan Moody entered the campaign for governor
in 1926 against Miriam Ferguson. The Fergusons were confident, but the
attorney general won the Democratic primary by a substantial majority and
became the next governor of the state.

DAN MOODY, 1927–31

In Dan Moody the friends of reform had an able spokesman. Although he was the youngest governor who ever served Texas (elected at the age of thirty-three), he had been seasoned by experience as a local prosecutor and by two years as attorney general. As district attorney in Williamson County, Moody had attained a statewide reputation for his vigorous prosecution of Klan members guilty of hooded violence, a distinction that brought him the office of attorney general.

Moody entered the governor's mansion committed to a broad and ambitious program of reform. He proposed a progressive tax system, judicial reform, civil service reform, state assistance to farmers, administrative reform of state agencies, regulation of public utilities and motor transportation companies, and increased funding for education. He also proposed modernization of the prison system, coordinated management of the Texas system of higher education, improved planning and funding for the state highway system, and the development of Texas port facilities. Like Governor Neff before him, Moody found it easier to propose reforms than to enact them. The legislature, conservative by nature and containing a hard-core band of Ferguson supporters, resisted change. His efforts at constitutional revision of the tax system and judiciary failed when voters rejected the proposed amendments. Moody achieved minor victories in prison reform and used his administrative authority to bring efficiency and honesty to state agencies—especially the highway department. He also reversed the liberal pardon policies of his predecessors.

Moody's problem was that he was out of step with most Texans. His vision was toward the modern, urban, industrial state that Texas was becoming, while legislative power was still concentrated in conservative, rural districts. Furthermore, his efforts at constitutional and administrative reform would have resulted in strengthening the power of the governor, a prospect resisted by both the legislature and the public.

In the election of 1928, the presidential contest in Texas attracted more interest than the state and local races. Governor Moody easily won renomination, defeating the Ferguson candidate, Louis J. Wardlaw. However, the presidential candidacy of Governor Alfred E. Smith of New York, an Irish-Catholic and an outspoken opponent of Prohibition, threatened the unity of Texas Democrats. The "Harmony Democrats" rallied behind Governor Moody at the state convention and prevailed against the "Constitutional Democrats" led by Thomas Love, who sought to block the nomination of Smith. After Smith was nominated at the national Democratic convention in Houston, the anti-Smith forces split with the regular Democrats. Most of the party leaders stayed with the regular organization, but they labored in vain. Herbert Hoover, the Republican presidential candidate, defeated Smith in Texas by 26,000 votes; he was the first Republican presidential candidate to carry Texas. Given the prosperity of the 1920s and the high esteem in which many held Hoover, any Democratic candidate would have faced problems. The fact that Smith was a Catholic, the son of Irish immigrants, and an opponent of Prohibition made his task all the more difficult. Still, this election should not be interpreted as a resurgence of the Klan as a political force in Texas, for Tom Connally unseated Klan-candidate Earle B. Mayfield in the U.S. Senate race.

Moody's first term coincided with the most prosperous period the state had ever known, but during the last year of his second administration the state began to feel the pinch of the Great Depression that had begun in 1929 with the collapse of the stock market. The brunt of the hard times, however, was born by Moody' s successors Ross Sterling and Miriam Ferguson.

THE ROARING TWENTIES–ECONOMIC GROWTH AND PROSPERITY

The 1920s brought great changes to many aspects of Texan life, especially in the areas of technology. In urban areas conveniences such as electrical appliances and lights, radios, and plumbing facilities became commonplace. In rural areas the lack of electricity prevented the spread of electrical appliances, and indoor plumbing remained the exception rather than the rule. However, the number of farm tractors tripled, signaling the acceleration of the mechanical revolution in agriculture.

Both farm and city shared in the growth of the automobile industry. The number of automobiles in Texas rose more than 500 percent during the decade, to the point at which by 1929 there was an automobile for every 4.3 Texans. The economic impact of the automobile was apparent everywhere, as were the many social consequences. By the end of the decade, many smaller towns were losing population, and some of the churches and businesses within them were disappearing as the automobile made long-distance travel practical. Another consequence, somewhat less tangible, was the belief of some that the freedom and mobility brought by the automobile undermined the morality of the people.

The decade of the 1920s was a period of rapid population growth and demographic change. With an increase in population from 4,663,228 to 5,824,715, Texas enjoyed one of the most rapid growth rates in the union. This growth had a particular impact on urban areas. Rural Texas gained only 9 percent in population, whereas urban Texas increased 58 percent. Between 1920 and 1930, the farm portion of the population declined from about 48 percent to 40 percent. All cities of more than 25,000—and there were 16 of them—grew at an average rate of 61 percent. In 1930, Texas's largest cities, Houston, Dallas, and San Antonio, each contained over

200,000 residents, and together they comprised more than 13 percent of the state's population.

Petroleum and transportation accounted for much of the urban growth after the turn of the century, especially during the 1920s. Railroads, largely in place by the beginning of the twentieth century, continued to influence the development of certain inland cities. Along the coast, the development of a system of deepwater ports combined with comprehensive rail systems to spur the growth of other cities. The natural ports of Texas, even in the days of light sailing craft and small steamers, had never been adequate. As early as 1883 a project was begun to deepen the channel of Galveston Port. By the early twentieth century a 25–foot channel had been provided, and by 1927 it had been increased to 35 feet. For many years, Galveston ranked second only to New York in exports and was the greatest cotton-shipping port in the world. By 1910, the Sabine and Neches system and the ports of Freeport, Port Aransas, and Houston had been improved. The development of the Houston Ship Channel, linking the city with the Gulf of Mexico, began in 1899, and by 1914 more than $14 million had been spent to develop the 55–mile thirty-foot deep channel. By1925 the ship channel had transformed Houston into a center for oceangoing traffic, and within a short period of time Houston supplanted Galveston as the leading port in Texas.

Oil similarly brought spectacular growth. Port Arthur expanded from fewer than 1,000 in 1900 to 50,000 in 1930, and oil, refineries, and related industries made Houston the state's largest city by 1930. In West Texas oil discoveries during the 1920s actually built towns such as Pampa, Borger, McCamey, and Wink, and substantially added to the populations of Amarillo, Abilene, and San Angelo.

While growing, Texas cities often acquired a distinct character and identity. San Antonio, perpetuating its early pattern of expansion, retained its military installations and historic sites and sustained a steady growth rate but a somewhat leisurely atmosphere. Dallas became a financial and mercantile center, widely known for its cultural achievements and aspirations. Fort Worth, generally regarded as a city of the west, developed an extensive livestock market and packing facilities, as well as the sobriquet "Cowtown." Houston, perhaps because of its more varied economy and sprawling explosive growth, could not be given only one label. In all these cities and in a host of smaller ones could be found substantial evidence of the ubiquitous oil industry.

During the 1920s, oilmen made significant oil discoveries at various places over the state. Geologists believed that a geological fault line extending from Corsicana and Mexia on the north to a point south of Luling contained oil. Their theory was confirmed with the discovery of the Mexia field in 1921 and the Luling field a short time thereafter. By 1922, oil fields were producing in South Texas, and other lands rich in oil came under production. One of the most important was in the Permian Basin of West Texas. Commercial production was opened near Colorado City in 1920, but the boom period began with the discovery of Santa Rita Number 1 near Big Lake in 1923. This discovery, soon followed by many others over the basin, brought wealth not only to the oilmen who opened the fields but also to the University of Texas and Texas A&M University, which owned significant amounts of this oil through the lands that had been set aside in the nineteenth century to fund the universities.

Supplementing oil was natural gas. In the Panhandle gas production was opened in 1918, and in 1926, the first Panhandle boom began with the discovery of a 10,000–barrel-per day well near the small community of Borger.

Oil refining and chemical manufacturing utilizing petroleum products likewise expanded rapidly during the 1920s. Large refineries and chemical plants, usually located in coastal areas where port facilities were available, took advantage of the ever-increasing volume of petroleum production to produce refined oil products and chemicals that were shipped to points all around the nation—indeed, around the world. However, though oil was rapidly becoming the dominant factor in the Texas industrial economy, the manufacturing and processing of agricultural products continued to be important. The value of agricultural goods, as late as 1929, exceeded the value of refined petroleum goods produced in Texas refineries.

Although industrial production increased in the 1920s, organized labor, ordinarily associated with the development of industrialization, did not fare particularly well. In fact, labor unions were more influential at the beginning of the century than they were at the end of the 1920s. From about 1890 to about 1915, a strong, militant labor organization, the United Mine Workers (UMW), organized in the coal mines of Erath and Palo Pinto counties and had some success improving the poor pay and pitiful working conditions that prevailed. At its peak, soon after 1900, 4,000 miners belonged to the union, but membership declined thereafter and almost disappeared during the 1920s. Oil workers in the Gulf Coast oil fields were organized by the American Federation of Labor (AFL) in 1905. For a time in the first two decades of the new century, the Texas State Federation of Labor grew in size and influence, attaining 783 organizations with 50,000 members by 1920, but thereafter it also declined. To some extent, the decline was caused by the open-shop campaign pursued by business interests and chambers of commerce and by the antilabor open-port law of 1920, enforced vigorously by state officials. Bad union management, including ill-advised strikes, also contributed to the decline, as did the general antiunion attitude that characterized the United States in the 1920s. By 1927, membership in the state federation had declined to 25,000.

Efforts of farmers to organize to protect their interests similarly enjoyed only limited success. In 1902, ten Rains County farmers laid the foundation of the Farmers' Educational and Cooperative Union of America.

Better known as the Farmers' Union, the organization exercised some influence for a time but declined on the eve of World War I. Two farm groups were formed in the 1920s. The Farm-Labor Union, which limited its membership to "dirt farmers," grew rapidly for a time but declined after 1925. The Farm Bureau Federation, however, fared better. It grew out of a national base, and though it experienced some difficult years in the late 1920s, it survived to become an influential, if somewhat conservative, voice of Texas agriculture.

LIFE IN THE ROARING TWENTIES

The 1920s are often remembered as a flamboyant age, replete with "flappers," raccoon coats, speakeasies, real estate promotions, bathtub gin and bootleggers, gangsters, and the Charleston. The image is probably greatly exaggerated for the nation as a whole; certainly it is exaggerated for Texas. But there were social changes evident in the life of the people, some that were viewed as wholesome and desirable, but others that many considered evidence of decadence and immorality.

Whether or not immorality increased during the decade is debatable, but certainly there was a great deal of concern about the matter. Parents, preachers, school authorities, social workers, editors, and others condemned the behavior of society. Concern was frequently expressed over immodest dress, modern dances, jazz and other forms of modern music, smoking, drinking, lewd movies, midnight joy riding, the rising crime rate, and an increasing traffic in narcotics. In addition to the automobile, the movies were often held accountable for the altered pattern of behavior. Surely, the movies were an important part of life at that time. By 1920, Texans were spending more than $24 million a year for movie tickets, an average per capita attendance of more than twenty movies per year.

Efforts to regulate morality took many forms. In some instances the violent and lawless methods of the Ku Klux Klan were used to punish suspected evildoers, but more lawful and less violent methods generally prevailed. A number of cities established movie censor boards; other cities passed ordinances prohibiting questionable behavior. One ordinance seems to have banned flirting; there were laws regulating the type and extent of clothing worn by bathers and prohibiting the showing of movies on Sunday. A law was even proposed, though never passed, to limit the height of a woman's shoe heel to one inch. Toward the end of the decade such efforts to regulate behavior tended to diminish.

The changing character of society was reflected in the status of the family. Texans married at a rate generally higher than the national average, but by 1929 the divorce rate in Texas was one of the highest in the nation and had more than doubled since 1916. At the same time, the size of the average family grew smaller, declining from 4.6 in 1920 to 3.5 in 1930; urban families were even smaller. On a more positive note, the employment of children declined rapidly. Whereas in 1910 more than 40 percent of the boys in Texas were employed, only slightly more than 7 percent of all children were employed in 1930. Compulsory school attendance laws, child labor regulations, and a growing urban population accounted for the decline.

Conditions for women also changed significantly during the decade. More and more women engaged in political activity, and by 1929 three women held seats in the state legislature. One of the more influential pressure groups in politics was the Women's Joint Legislative Council, better known as the Petticoat Lobby. It worked for laws that regulated child labor, provided care for expectant mothers and infants, and improved education, and other worthwhile causes.

The total percentage of women who worked outside the home rose only slightly, but the nature of their employment changed a great deal, as farm employment declined and more found urban jobs. During the 1920s the number of married women who worked increased almost two-thirds throughout the state, and even more in larger cities. But the quest for gender equality still had a distance to go. Wages for women were generally one-half as much or even less than those paid to men. Efforts to secure legal equality for women, particularly with respect to laws regarding property management and marriage rights, accomplished little or nothing.

Although the decade opened with a considerable amount of violence and oppression, conditions for black people improved in some respects in subsequent years. The number of African Americans in the population increased, though slightly more blacks left the state than moved into it. Similarly, there was a movement of black people from rural to urban areas. This demographic shift was the Texas aspect of the Black Migration, which saw hundreds of thousands of African Americans relocate from the rural south to industrial cities in the north. Some Texas blacks moved north, but blacks who left Texas were more likely to move to California than to Harlem.

The explosion of African American cultural and literary creativity that characterized the jazz age and the Harlem Renaissance also had an impact on Texas. Black writers and musicians toured the state, and their works stimulated creativity in Texas. Jazz clubs and speakeasies in Houston's Fourth Ward and in Dallas's black ghetto attracted racially mixed audiences looking for an evening of good music, dancing, drinking, and the excitement of crossing (though briefly) the racial barriers. Black poets, like Langston Hughes, held readings and sold their books on Texas's black campuses, and Melvin B. Tolson, a professor at Wiley College in Marshall, achieved a national reputation as Texas's Harlem Renaissance poet.

The racial violence of earlier years, which had often ended in lynching, diminished, though it did not disappear. Segregation remained as rigid as ever, and African Americans continued to have little or no voice in politics. When the legislature in 1923 prohibited black participation in the Democratic primary, Dr. Lawrence Nixon, with the support of the NAACP, challenged the law. The battle for black suffrage appeared to be won in 1927 when the U.S. Supreme Court ruled in *Nixon v. Herndon* that the legislature could not, by state law, establish a white primary. The legislature, however, quickly adopted legislation permitting, rather than requiring, parties to maintain white primaries, and most areas of the state continued the practice. Meanwhile, in the Republican Party, the long-standing quarrel between white leaders and black voters likewise continued to exclude blacks from any effective political voice.

A rapid increase in numbers characterized the Mexican-American people of Texas. Demographers have estimated that immigrants from Mexico numbered nearly 175,000 between 1910 and 1919, primarily because of the violence of the Mexican Revolution of 1910, and almost 500,000 during the next decade, with most lured north by the hope of high-paying jobs and a better life. Such estimates may be too high, and some immigrants returned to their native land, but the population of Mexican people in Texas certainly increased considerably. Most settled at first near the border in South Texas, but the movement of Mexican Americans eastward and northward and from the land to the cities greatly accelerated during the decade.

Regardless of where they lived, Mexican Americans still faced discrimination and prejudice as in earlier years, but several organizations were formed in the 1920s to work for equal rights. *La Orden Hijos de America* (The Order of the Sons of America) was formed in San Antonio in 1921 and soon spread into other South Texas cities. Later, a group composed primarily of Mexican-American war veterans formed the Knights of America, and in 1929 the League of United Latin American Citizens (LULAC) was founded in Corpus Christi.

Even against the obstacle of political complacency, education made substantial progress in Texas during these years. To be sure, Texas continued to lag behind the national norms. But through constitutional reforms, added local responsibility, expanded resources, and consolidation, public education came nearer to meeting the needs of a modern society. The creation of new institutions of higher learning and the dramatic growth of older ones were additional evidence of a maturing educational structure.

On the eve of the 1920s the legislature took several steps toward providing educational opportunities. In 1915, the legislature approved a special appropriation for rural schools, provided that the rural district itself maintained a specified level of taxation. This measure stimulated the levying of local school taxes in rural districts where they were most needed. Legislatures continued this practice until 1949, when more fundamental reforms were made. Ferguson's administration also gave the state a compulsory school attendance law, which went into effect in the fall of 1916. In

Formed in 1929 when several organizations joined together, the League of
United Latin American Citizens is one of the oldest organizations working
in support of political, social, and economic equality and opportunity in the
state. Active throughout the Depression, World War II, and the post World
War II years, LULAC continued its efforts as the century neared its end.
(Courtesy of The Southwest Collection, Lubbock, Texas)

1918, a constitutional amendment authorizing free textbooks was adopted.
At the same time the constitutional limit for the state school tax was raised,
and in 1920, the voters entirely abolished the limit on the tax rate that communities might levy for school purposes. Yet these measures, and even
more generous expenditures in the early 1920s, did not lift the Texas school
system from its low rank when compared with the systems of other states.
A 1923 survey of the schools revealed deficiencies and elicited a number of
recommendations, most of which the legislators and voters refused to
adopt.

Consolidation of small rural school systems was one of the most significant reforms that did take place. The building of the state highway
system and the improvements of other roads during this period made it possible for communities to take advantage of a 1914 law that permitted the consolidation of schools whenever a majority of the voters of two or more
districts favored it. A 1925 law permitted trustees to make consolidations
under certain conditions. With the decision to provide transportation at
public expense for students who lived at a distance, the beginning of the end
of the "one-room school" was at hand. By 1930, some 1,530 consolidations
had been made.

Annie Webb Blanton. A leader in Texas education, she was the first woman to be elected president of the Texas State Teachers Association. In 1918 she was elected state superintendent of public education, the first woman to hold a state-wide public office in Texas. (Archives Division—Texas State Library)

A second trend noticeable in the public schools involved curriculum changes. Especially in the urban areas, "progressive" educators insisted that schools must go beyond traditional teaching and prepare the students for "real" life. This involved changes in teaching methodology, school health programs, comprehensive student testing programs, and an expansion of vocation training, especially in courses related to business. Another curriculum issue focused on an ongoing effort to prohibit by law the teaching of evolution. Between 1923 and 1929, critics of Darwinian evolution fought the battle regularly in each session of the legislature, but no law was ever passed.

With the pattern of segregation as rigid as ever, black schools, already far behind those for white students, failed to share equally in the educational gains. Average salaries for white teachers increased from about $600 per year in 1920 to slightly over $900 per year in 1929 (still only about two-thirds of the national average). However, funds allocated for black teachers scarcely increased at all. Blacks constituted approximately one-third of the scholastic population of East Texas, but more than 97 percent of the high schools there were for whites only. Nevertheless, progress was made. By 1930, the illiteracy rate for African Americans had declined to 13.4 percent.

During these years the junior college movement, associated with Texas since its infancy, expanded rapidly. In 1897, the Baptist state convention established a coordinated system of higher educational institutions, with Baylor University and Mary Hardin-Baylor College as senior schools and Howard Payne College, Rusk College, and Decatur Baptist College as two-year institutions. Other denominations entered the field, establishing by 1920 a number of church-controlled junior colleges. About the same time the state created junior colleges in Stephenville and Arlington, and with the founding of El Paso Junior College in 1920, Texas cities had begun to provide junior colleges. One of the most successful of these urban junior colleges was established in Houston. In 1927 Houston school superintendent, E. E. Oberholtzer, established two junior colleges, Houston Junior College and Houston Colored Junior College, which were administered by the Houston Independent School District. At the time of its founding, Houston Colored Junior College was the only public junior college for blacks in the country. In the mid-1930s both institutions would be upgraded to municipal four-year colleges and would ultimately evolve into two state universities, the University of Houston and Texas Southern University.

Four-year colleges and universities also grew in number and size during the first three decades of the twentieth century. During the early years of the century, the state expanded the normal school system and acquired, founded, or authorized normal schools in Canyon, Commerce, Kingsville, and Alpine. In 1923, the state normal schools were reconfigured as teachers' colleges. The same legislature authorized the establishment of Texas Technological College in Lubbock.

The 1920s saw the most rapid growth the state colleges had known. Each year brought additional thousands of students to tax the facilities of the already overcrowded institutions. In fact, student enrollment grew about 150 percent during the decade. To solve the space problem temporarily, the University of Texas erected flimsy wooden structures dubbed "shacks" by the students. In a sense, the shacks symbolized the position of education in Texas at this point. Progress had been made, and the need for improvement had been recognized, but there remained much to do.

BIBLIOGRAPHY

General studies are Ralph Steen in F. C. Adams (ed.), *Texas Democracy* (four vols., Austin, 1937), and S. S. McKay, *Texas Politics, 1906–1944*. See also S. Acheson, *35,000 Days in Texas*, and *Joe Bailey: The Last Democrat*; Ralph Steen, *Twentieth Century Texas; An Economic and Social History* (Austin, 1942); and Seth S. McKay and O. B. Faulk, *Texas after Spindletop* (Austin, 1965). Of particular value is Lewis L. Gould, *Progressives and Prohibitionists: Texas Democrats in the Wilson Era* (Austin, 1973; rev. 1994); Lewis L. Gould, "Progressives and Prohibitionists: Texas Democratic Politics, 1911–1921," *Southwestern Historical Quarterly*, LXXV, 5–18; and Norman D. Brown, *Hood, Bonnet, and Little Brown Jug: Texas Politics, 1921–1928* (College Station, 1984). Robert A. Calvert and Arnoldo De León, *The History of Texas* (Arlington Heights, Ill., 1996), contains a comprehensive and balanced section on twentieth-century Texas history that offers much information on this period.

For special studies on the Fergusons, see Lewis J. Gould, "The University Becomes Politicized: The War With Jim Ferguson, 1915–1918," *Southwestern Historical*

Quarterly, LXXXVI, 255–276; R. Steen, "The Ferguson War on the University of Texas," *Southwestern Social Science Quarterly*, XXXV, 356–362; Shelley Sallee, "'The Woman of It': Governor Miriam Ferguson's 1924 Election," *Southwestern Historical Quarterly*, C, 1-18; W. F. McCaleb, "The Impeachment of a Governor," *American Political Science Review*, XII, 111–115; and Octavia F. Rogan, "Texas Legislation, 1925," *Southwestern Political and Social Science Quarterly*, VI, 167–168.

Activities of two other governors are described in James Clark, *The Tactful Texan: Governor W. P. Hobby* (New York, 1958), and in Emma M. Shirley, *The Administration of Pat M. Neff, Governor of Texas, 1921–1925* (Waco, 1938). Also see S. A. MacCorkle, "The Pardoning Power in Texas," *Southwestern Social Science Quarterly*, XV, 218–228; O. D. Weeks, "The Election of 1928," ibid., IX, 337–348; Paul M. Lucko, "A Missed Opportunity: Texas Prison Reform During the Dan Moody Administration, 1927–1931," *Southwestern Historical Quarterly*, XCVI, 27–52; and Dennis K. McDaniel, "The First Congressman Martin Dies of Texas," *Southwestern Historical Quarterly*, CII, 131-161.

Texas's place on the national scene is touched upon in Arthur Link, "The Wilson Movement in Texas, 1910–1912," *Southwestern Historical Quarterly*, XLVIII, 169–185; Lewis L. Gould, "Theodore Roosevelt, William Howard Taft, and the Disputed Delegates in 1912; Texas as a Test Case," ibid., LXXXV, 33–56; Dewey Grantham, "Texas Congressional Leaders and the New Freedom, 1913–1917," ibid., LIII, 35–48; R. N. Richardson, *Colonel Edward M. House: The Texas Years, 1858–1912*; W. P. Webb and Terrell Webb (eds.), *Washington Wife: Journal of Ellen Maury Slayden from 1897–1919* (New York, 1962); Lee N. Allen, "The Democratic Presidential Primary Election of 1924 in Texas," *Southwestern Historical Quarterly*, LXI, 474–493; Tom Connally and Alfred Steinberg, *My Name is Tom Connally* (New York, 1954); and Bascom M. Timmons, *Garner of Texas; A Personal History* (New York, 1948). Kenneth Hendrickson, Jr. and Michael L. Collins, (eds.), *Profiles in Power: Twentieth Century Texans in Washington* (Arlington Heights, Ill., 1995), contains biographical essays on the influence of Edward M. House and Morris Shepard on national politics.

Much writing has been done on border troubles of this period. See Don M. Coerver and Linda B. Hall, *Texas and the Mexican Revolution: A Study in State and National Border Policy, 1910–1920* (San Antonio, 1985); Clifford Alan Perkins, *Border Patrol: With the U. S. Immigration Service on the Mexican Boundary, 1910–1954* (El Paso, 1978); Frank N. Samponaro and Paul J. Vanderwood, *War Scare on the Rio Grande: Robert Runyon's Photographs of the Border Conflict, 1913–1916* (Austin, 1990); Manuel A. Machado, Jr., *Centaur of the North: Francisco Villa, the Mexican Revolution, and Northern Mexico* (Austin, 1988); C. C. Cumberland, "Border Raids in the Lower Rio Grande Valley, 1915," *Southwestern Historical Quarterly*, LVII, 285–311; Charles H. Harris III, and Louis R. Sadler, "The 1911 Reyes Conspiracy: The Texas Side," ibid., LXXXIII, 325–348; Charles H. Harris III, and Louis R. Sadler, "The Plan of San Diego and the Mexican-United States War Crisis of 1916: A Reexamination," *Hispanic-American Historical Review*, LVIII, 381–408; Frederick Katz, "Pancho Villa and the Attack on Columbus, New Mexico," *The American Historical Review*, LXXXIII, 101–130; Craig Smyser, "The Columbus Raid," *Southwest Review*, LXVIII, 78–84; Rodolfo Rocha, "The Influence of the Mexican Revolution on the Mexico-Texas Border, 1910–1916" (unpublished dissertation, Texas Tech University, Lubbock, 1981); and Walter Prescott Webb, *The Texas Rangers* (Austin, 1965). A different viewpoint of the Rangers is found in Julian Samora et al., *Gunpowder Justice: A Reassessment of the Texas Rangers* (Notre Dame, 1979), previously cited.

Texas's part in the First World War is treated, inadequately, in Army and Navy History Company, *History of Texas World War Heroes* (Dallas, 1919). Racial conflict during the war is thoroughly addressed in Robert V. Haynes, *A Night of Violence: The*

Houston Riot of 1917 (Baton Rouge, 1976), and in Garna L. Christian, *Black Soldiers in Jim Crow Texas, 1899–1917* (College Station, 1995), a fine study that covers this period and earlier episodes of racial discrimination and the military in Texas. Carole E. Christian, " 'Joining the American Mainstream': Texas Mexican Americans during World War I," *Southwestern Historical Quarterly*, XCII, 559–595; William E. Nicholas, "World War I and Academic Dissent in Texas," *Arizona and the West*, XIV, 215–230, cover other aspects of the impact of the war on Texas and Texans.

For additional reading on other crusades, see H. A. Ivey's biased but valuable study, *Rum on the Run in Texas* (Dallas, 1910); Elizabeth A. Taylor, "The Woman Suffrage Movement in Texas," *Journal of Southern History*, XVIII, 194–215; Ruthe Winegarten and Judith McArthur (eds.), *Citizens at Last: The Woman Suffrage Movement in Texas* (Austin, 1987); Janet G. Humphrey, *A Texas Suffragist: Diaries and Writings of Jane Y. McCallum* (Austin, 1988); John Carroll Eudy, "The Vote and Lone Star Women: Minnie Fisher Cunningham and the Texas Equal Suffrage Association," *East Texas Historical Journal*, XIV, 52–57; Jacquelyn Masur McElhaney, *Pauline Periwinkle and Progressive Reform in Dallas* (College Station, 1998); Emma Jackson, "Petticoat Politics: Political Activism among Texas Women in the 1920s" (unpublished dissertation, University of Texas, Austin, 1980); Nancy Baker Jones and Ruthe Winegarten, *Capitol Women: Texas Female Legislators, 1923-1999* (Austin, 2000). Debbie Mauldin Cottrell, *Pioneer Woman Educator: Annie Webb Blanton* (College Station, 1993); Fane Downs and Nancy Baker Jones (eds.), *Women and Texas History: Selected Essays* (Austin, 1992), a broad study that includes works on women active in this era. For information on the Klan in Texas see Charles C. Alexander, *Crusade for Conformity: The Ku Klux Klan in Texas, 1920–1930* (Houston, 1962); Kathleen Blee, *Women of the Klan: Racism and Gender in the 1920s* (Berkeley and Los Angeles, 1991), a general study that includes material on Texas; and Shawn Lay, "Imperial Outpost on the Border: El Paso's Klan No. 100" in *The Invisible Empire in the West: Toward a New Appraisal of the Ku Klux Klan in the 1920s*, ed. Shawn Lay (Urbana, Ill.,1992).

Social, cultural, and ethnic affairs in the 1920s are studied in Lynn Ray Musslewhite, "Texas in the 1920's: A History of Social Change," a manuscript in the Texas Tech University Library. See also Alwyn Barr, *Black Texans* 2nd ed. (Norman, 1996) Benjamin Marques, *LULAC: The Evolution of a Mexican-American Political Organization* (Austin, 1993); Mary Beth Rogers et al., *We Can Fly: Stories of Katherine Stinson and Other Gutsy Women* (Austin, 1983); Arnoldo De León, *San Angelenos: Mexican-Americans in San Angelo, Texas* (San Angelo, 1985); James J. Thompson, Jr., *Tried as by Fire: Southern Baptists and the Religious Controversies of the 1920's* (Macon, Ga., 1982); John W. Storey, *Texas Baptist Leadership and Social Christianity, 1900–1980* (College Station, 1986); John Davies, "Science and the Sacred: The Evolution Controversy at Baylor, 1920–1930," *East Texas Historical Journal*, XXIX, 41–53; and Charles R. Wilson, "Morons, Monkeys, and Morality: Reactions to the Scopes Trial in Texas," *East Texas Historical Journal*, XII, 51–63.

For oil and industrialization, see C. C. Rister's *Oil! Titan of the Southwest* and a list of more than sixty titles found in Walter Rundell, Jr., "Texas Petroleum History: A Selective Annotated Bibliography," *Southwestern Historical Quarterly*, LXVII, 267–278. See also David F. Prindle, "Oil and the Permanent University Fund: The Early Years," ibid., LXXXVI, 277–298; Nicholas George Malavis, *Bless the Pure and Humble: Texas Lawyers and Oil Regulation, 1919–1936* (College Station, 1996); and Ray Miles, *King of the Wildcatters: The Life and Times of Tom Slick, 1883-1930* (College Station, 1996). Kenneth Ragsdale, *Quicksilver: Terlingua and the Chisos Mining Company* (College Station, 1976), tells the story of a unique Texas industry; and Walter L. Buenger, " 'This Wonder Age,': The Economic Transformation of Northeast Texas, 1900–1930," *Southwestern Historical Quarterly*, XCVIII, 519–549, presents a broader study of a productive region. George T. Morgan's "The Gospel of Wealth Goes South: John Henry Kirby and Labor's Struggle for Self-Determination, 1901–1916," *Southwestern Historical Quarterly*, LXXV, 186–197, explains well the problems of unions in twentieth-century Texas, while Emilio Zamora, *The World of the Mexican Worker in Texas* (College Station, 1993), and Ernest Obadele-Starks, *Black Unionism in the Industrial South* (College Station, 2000) provide insight into the issues of race, ethnicity, and labor.

17

The Great Depression 1930–1941

In the early autumn of 1929, after a long period of soaring prices, the New York stock market turned downward. In October a sharp drop precipitated much selling, and on October 29 panic seized the exchanges of the nation as the stock market crashed. Although Texans suffered their share of losses in the stock market crash, their immediate injuries were not as great as those that followed later. Prices fell, business volume declined, unemployment rose, the number of bankruptcies increased, and with the closing of all banks in March 1933, the Great Depression reached every city, town, farm, and hamlet in the land.

Prosperity is "just around the corner" came to be a trite, sorry joke. President Herbert Hoover thought for a time that local relief agencies could supply those in need, but toward the end of his term, he advocated stronger measures. In 1933, newly inaugurated President Franklin D. Roosevelt announced his "New Deal." His positive actions restored a measure of confidence but did not bring the nation out of the financial doldrums. Meanwhile, state and local governments tried to survive and to offer a degree of assistance in troubled times.

Progress toward recovery was uneven until midsummer 1935; henceforth improvement was rapid until the autumn of 1937, when a recession wiped out a considerable part of the gain. Not until the gigantic defense program of 1940–41 stimulated demands for labor and goods did the economy attain "recovery," and even then many thousands of workers continued to be unemployed.

The times were difficult, but the decade was not without positive achievements. Conservation and environmental concerns received more attention than ever before, and cultural achievements were rich and varied.

HARD TIMES IN TEXAS

The Depression brought worry and concern to most Texans, and to others it brought suffering, even desperation. An unemployment census taken in 1933 showed that 105,045 families, representing 7.1 percent of the population, were on relief. The next year there were 246,819 relief cases, representing 1 million people, or about 13 percent of the population. Almost every sector of the economy was affected. Building construction came almost to a standstill. Cotton, which had sold for 18 cents a pound in 1928, dropped to 5 cents in 1932. East Texas oil, which was selling for 60 cents a barrel in 1930, fell to 5 cents a barrel; steak sold for 18 cents per pound; milk sometimes cost as little as 4 or 5 cents a quart; and hamburgers went for a nickel.

These statistics tell only part of the story, for even though the prices were low, many could not afford them. In one West Texas town a citizens' relief association killed, dressed, and stored wild rabbits to be distributed to those in need. The demand soon exceeded the supply. Aransas Pass businessmen donated tons of fish to feed the poor and hungry people of Dallas. Soup kitchens and bread lines appeared in most towns. Many farm laborers and tenants, dispirited and broken, gathered in towns and cities, hoping either to share in direct relief or to draw small wages on public works projects. Merchants, manufacturers, and shop owners laid off workers, adding to the ranks of the unemployed.

In many cases relatives and friends helped for a while and local charity organizations did the best they could, but all such efforts proved inadequate. Thousands of individuals and not a few families took to the highways, hitchhiking from place to place. Many were without funds, and persons living near the roads were often compelled either to give them food or to turn them away hungry. Swarms of unfortunate people sought shelter in abandoned buildings, caves, dugouts, and shanties made of discarded boxes.

Some groups suffered more than others in the Depression. The unemployment rate for African Americans was approximately twice that for the white population, and sometimes relief agencies refused to aid blacks or otherwise discriminated against them. In 1933 the percentage of Mexican Americans receiving aid in San Antonio exceeded that of all other groups. Some returned to Mexico, either by choice or because of governmental forced repatriation programs.

Schools and local governments shared in the hard times. In Houston in 1932, one-half of the streetlights were disconnected because money to pay for the electricity was not available. Beaumont in 1934 reduced funds for the city library to almost nothing and for the city schools by almost one-half. Streetlights were turned off altogether. Women schoolteachers in San Antonio and a number of other cities whose husbands were employed were not rehired. The severity of the budget cuts varied from city to city and from school district to school district, but few, if any, escaped altogether. Even churches suffered from the Depression. Other factors were involved, but financial problems played a large role in the decline of the number of churches by almost 4,000 during the period between 1926 and 1936.

Texans' reactions to the Depression varied but were not greatly different from reactions elsewhere in the nation. At first, most seemed to believe that there was no cause for worry. By 1930, there was still a considerable amount of optimism, but some were beginning to question the future. From 1931 on, the existence of the crisis was generally accepted and the search for solutions intensified.

On the whole, most proposed solutions were moderate. There were "Buy Now" campaigns, "Give-a-Job" and "Share-the-Work" programs, and most widely discussed of all, a "Back-to-the-Farm" movement. Some Texans advocated socialism or communism, and many believed that capitalism was threatened, but there is no evidence to suggest that revolution or rebellion was a serious possibility. There were demonstrations by the unemployed such as those in Houston in 1930 and in Beaumont in 1931, but these were orderly and peaceful. Sheep shearers in San Angelo and pecan shellers in San Antonio, both desperately poor Mexican American groups, struck for higher wages. There was some violence, but not of the scale found in labor disputes elsewhere in the nation.

Violence of another kind, however, did afflict the countryside of Texas from time to time. Perhaps to some degree a holdover from the lawless side of prohibition, or perhaps a reflection of the unsettled conditions of the Depression, notorious and outrageous gangs of criminals occasionally killed and robbed on a grand scale, apparently relishing the publicity they received. Of these, none were more flagrant in their disregard for human life than Bonnie Parker and Clyde Barrow. This pair terrorized large areas of Texas from 1932 until they were finally shot to death in 1934 in an ambush in neighboring Louisiana.

DEPRESSION POLITICS–ROSS STERLING, 1931–33

In the gubernatorial campaign of 1930, twelve persons filed for the Democratic primary. Governor Moody supported Ross Sterling of Houston, who was completing his fourth year as chairman of the highway commis-

Texas Rangers of the 1930s relied on some of the more modern equipment of law enforcement, such as automobiles and radios, in their search for criminals of the Depression, but they still depended on some of the tools and techniques of an older day in certain areas of the state. (Courtesy of the Texas Ranger Museum, Waco, Texas. Photo by Tom Burks)

sion. Another prominent candidate was Miriam Ferguson, who led in votes in the first primary, with Sterling running second. After a bitter contest Sterling won the runoff race by a majority of about 100,000 votes. His chief claim to the office was the promise of "a business administration to meet the demands of a growing State, by a successful business man." In the general election he easily defeated the Republican nominee.

During Sterling's administration, emergency followed emergency, and one crisis had not passed before another appeared. The Depression made taxes difficult to collect, and state income fell off sharply while expenditures remained nearly as high as ever. As the economic crises deepened, Sterling used his veto power often, and repeatedly called the legislature into special session in an effort to address the growing problems. For the most part these efforts were unsuccessful.

Two special problems added to the woes of the Sterling administration. The first was a crisis in the oil industry. In October 1930, wildcat oil prospector Columbus Marion "Dad" Joiner hit oil near Kilgore. The resulting East Texas oil field upset the industry in two ways. First, and most important, the incredible size of the discovery pushed oil prices down from about $1 a barrel in 1930 to about 8 cents a barrel in 1931. Second, the East Texas oil fields were controlled by small producers rather than the major oil companies. Joiner struck oil where the experts said it could not exist. Then, while other wildcatters rushed in and bought up oil leases, the majors stayed out, convinced that the early discoveries were just a fluke.

As oil prices plummeted, the major producers attempted to limit production from the East Texas fields. The Texas Railroad Commission had been granted authority to regulate oil production for conservation and environmental purposes in 1917. In April 1931 it attempted to raise oil prices by restricting production in the East Texas fields, although its authority over prices and marketing was questionable. Many small producers ignored the commission's orders. The major companies, which controlled the oil refineries, refused to buy East Texas crude; the independent producers responded by building their own refineries, and began to market "hot oil" (oil produced in violation of Railroad Commission restrictions) through independent truckers to independent service stations.

As the crisis continued, chaos threatened to envelope the East Texas oil fields. Threats to set oil fields on fire and dynamite pipe lines caused Governor Sterling (who was the former president of Humble Oil) in August 1931 to declare martial law and send in the National Guard to patrol the oil fields. Many citizens of East Texas, who were profiting from the oil boom, accused the governor of supporting the efforts of the major oil companies to drive the independents out of business. By early 1932 the situation was in shambles. Local hostility undermined the effectiveness of the guard, and in February 1932 the Texas Supreme Court ruled that Sterling's declaration of martial law was unconstitutional. The Railroad Commission's efforts to set production levels were also hampered by the courts and by widespread bribery of the commission's inspectors. Finally, in January 1933 the legislature clearly authorized the Railroad Commission to set production levels, and the Texas Rangers went to East Texas to stop the flow of hot oil. Also in 1933 the federal government placed oil production under the control of the National Recovery Administration, and in 1934 Congress made it illegal to transport hot oil across state lines.

The majors won the East Texas oil wars. Gradually the production and marketing of hot oil was suppressed, and by 1940 about 80 percent of East Texas oil was owned by the majors. Sterling, though, lost politically in this crisis. His actions were resented by East Texas voters, who saw him siding with the majors against the small producers.

The second problem Sterling confronted concerned the rapid decline in agricultural prices, especially cotton prices. Between the 1931 spring planting and the fall harvest, cotton prices dropped almost 50 percent, from about 10 cents to 5.3 cents per pound. As with oil, the solution to this problem focused on cutting production. Governor Moody resisted pressure from farmers to call a special session of the legislature for this purpose. Sterling responded to the crisis by convening a conference of the governors of other cotton producing states. Governor Huey P. Long of Louisiana proposed a radical "drop a crop" plan that would have required farmers to plant no cotton at all in 1932. With strong opposition to such a plan from the urban press and from shippers and the companies that marketed and processed cotton, no other state endorsed Long's proposal. As pressure from farmers mounted, Sterling called the legislature into special session in September 1931. The legislature passed a law restricting cotton acreage in 1932 to 30 percent of that planted in 1931. Enforcement was weak, however, and in February 1932 the Texas law was declared unconstitutional. A solution to the cotton crisis would have to wait until Congress enacted the Agricultural Adjustment Act in 1933. Under the terms of this legislation Texas farmers took almost 6,000,000 acres out of production in 1934 and 1935.

THE RETURN OF FERGUSIONISM—MIRIAM FERGUSON, 1933–35

The hard times bred discontent, and much of this discontent would be directed at Governor Sterling. In 1932 the voters were ready for a change. Always sensitive to political opportunity, the Fergusons again entered the contest. In supporting his wife's campaign, James Ferguson said to the voters: "Two years ago you got the best governor money could buy, this year you have an opportunity to get the best governor patriotism can give you." He added that when his wife was governor, he would "be on hand picking up chips and bring in water for mama." He charged that Sterling had wasted state highway funds; he attacked him for invoking martial law in the East Texas oil fields; and he proposed certain drastic changes in state taxes. Former Governor Moody and other prominent Texans worked diligently for Sterling, but in the runoff election Miriam Ferguson won by a few hundred votes out of a total of nearly a million.

The Forty-third Legislature, which convened in January 1933, found that the Depression was aggravating old problems and creating new ones. Governor Ferguson recommended a sales tax and an income tax, but the legislature refused to adopt either measure. To raise revenue they did impose a 2–cent-per barrel tax on oil and legalized pari-mutuel betting on horse races, but the administration found it difficult to make ends meet, and municipalities and school districts everywhere were impoverished. Texas joined in ratifying the Twenty-first Amendment to the Constitution of the United States, which ended national Prohibition on December 5, 1933. Then the Forty-fourth Legislature submitted an amendment repealing state prohibition, and the voters ratified it in August 1935.

It is difficult to evaluate objectively Miriam Ferguson's second administration. Relations between the legislature and the executive branch were not harmonious, as lawmakers distrusted the governor and her husband. The return of the Fergusons' policy of liberal pardons and paroles for state prisoners was attacked from various quarters. On the other hand, Ferguson supported many New Deal initiatives, including federal efforts to regulate oil production, and used "bread bonds" together with federal funds to provide relief for the destitute. Overall, this administration met with much greater public approval than did Miriam Ferguson's first term as governor.

In the election of 1934, Texas voters were not confronted directly by "Fergusonism" for the first time since 1914, as Governor Miriam Ferguson, honoring the two-term tradition, did not seek reelection. Nominated and elected was James V. Allred of Wichita Falls, who was completing his second term as attorney general. Although his platform was more conservative than those of his opponents, Allred was both responsible and sensitive to the needs of the people, particularly the elderly. All candidates favored, or at least refused to oppose, old-age pensions, an issue that would dominate Texas politics for the remainder of the decade.

By the beginning of Governor Allred's term, January 1935, the New Deal relief program was well under way and President Roosevelt's plans for national social security had been announced. The governor urged "planned recovery" for Texas, and to that end a Texas planning board was established for a period of four years. No fewer than a dozen boards and commissions were created by the legislature to aid in carrying out projects associated with the program of relief and security in its various forms.

RELIEF, RECOVERY, AND REFORM—THE NEW DEAL IN TEXAS

As the Great Depression deepened, it soon became evident that private relief organizations and antiquated public agencies, such as poor farms, could not care for the increasing number of persons who had no means of support. Governor Sterling in 1931 had suggested public works as a means of providing indirect relief, but of greater immediate value was his committee for the relief of unemployment.

Meanwhile, the federal government had attacked the problem in a program calling for billions of dollars for direct relief and work relief, much of which was to be spent through state and local agencies. There were two means of approach: the first by making grants to the states for general relief, and the second by carrying out a works program that would serve the double purpose of relieving unemployment and "priming the pumps" of business and industry. The first aid was extended late in 1932 under a law authorizing the Federal Reconstruction Finance Corporation (RFC) to lend funds to state and local bodies for relief activities. Through various state and local agencies, both public and private, these funds were used to provide work on different projects, supposedly of public value. The RFC insisted that the state should share with the federal government the burden of relief. The legislature accordingly submitted to the voters a constitutional amendment to authorize the issuance of bonds for the relief of the unemployed. Issued from time to time, the last of these "bread bonds" were sold during the Allred administration. The legislature also established a Texas relief commission as a coordinating and administrative organization through which the various agencies worked. County relief boards were set up to make plans for roads and other public improvements through which needy persons might be given employment.

The Federal Emergency Relief Administration, the first major New Deal relief agency, provided the states with funds for both direct relief and work relief. Through this agency and through the RFC, which continued to provide funds, Texas received approximately $50 million for the aid of its destitute in 1933 and 1934. Unfortunately, the number of persons requesting relief did not diminish.

While these agencies were meeting the pressing needs of the people who had neither property nor jobs, a broader program of government spending was launched to furnish employment and to revive business and industry. From 1933 through 1938, the Civilian Conservation Corps employed about 110,000 men. The National Youth Administration, directed for a time in Texas by Lyndon B. Johnson, was established in 1935 to administer a program of assistance to young people. The Federal Emergency Administration of Public Works (PWA) organized and coordinated a gigantic system of public building. The RFC lent funds both to private business establishments and to construction firms for the purpose of financing public and public-guaranteed projects. In May 1935, work relief was coordinated in a Works Progress Administration, which made possible construction and rehabilitation of all kinds of public property and provided hundreds of white-collar jobs. The various works program left some results of enduring value in Texas. For instance, in 1939 the PWA alone listed in its "physical accomplishments" 510 public buildings, 998.7 miles of new highway pavement, and improvements in 135 parks and playgrounds.

Between 1933 and 1936 the federal government, through various agencies, provided $351,023,546 for public works and relief programs in Texas. During the same period, state and local funds used for relief and work programs in Texas amounted to $80,268,595. Both state and federal expenditures continued without any substantial decrease through the end of the decade.

More permanent reform to cope with the problems of the needy came with the adoption of the National Social Security Act in August 1935. This law provided support for the elderly either through pensions supplied by state and federal taxes (old age pensions) or through funds provided jointly by employee and employer contributions (Social Security). The law, which also provided assistance to other groups in need, has been amended a number of times over the years.

INDUSTRY, TRANSPORTATION, AND LABOR

The Great Depression brought stagnation or even retrenchment to many areas of the state's emerging industrial economy. Spurred by business organizations, such as the Texas Manufacturing Association and regional chambers of commerce, manufacturing had expanded slowly and steadily in the early decades of the twentieth century. By 1929, industry in Texas employed more than 150,000 people and contributed almost a half billion dollars annually to the economy. The Depression hit Texas industry and industrial workers hard. By 1933 almost 30 percent of Texas factories shut down, leading to the loss of almost 40,000 jobs and more than $225 million of annual production. By 1932, some industries declined to about one-third of their normal level of activity. Not until 1939 would conditions in industry return to pre-Depression levels.

Chemicals, petrochemicals, and oil refining were the most prosperous of Texas industries during the Depression. A large paper mill that made paper out of yellow pine began production in a plant near Houston in 1937. The production of alkalies, used in the manufacture of a wide variety of items ranging from stockings to soap, began in a Corpus Christi plant in 1934. Oil refining, in particular, expanded. By 1939, more than 80 percent of the state's oil production was processed in Texas refineries, and volume had almost doubled during the Depression decade.

Oil, in fact, became more and more a mainstay of the state's economy in the 1930s. With Texas leading the petroleum-producing states of the nation after 1928, oil production generally edged upward until 1937. Production was increased greatly in the 1930s with the development of the East Texas field. Other discoveries after 1930, though not so sensational, added to the supply. A slowdown in pipeline construction during the Depression temporarily impeded the growth of the natural gas industry, but over the decade it, too, expanded.

Transportation suffered in some ways from the impact of the Depression. Railroad construction had continued at a slow pace in the early decades of the twentieth century. In 1932, however, railroad mileage in Texas reached its peak of 17,000 miles and began a slow decline. Electric railroads, which had come into use earlier in the twentieth century, similarly began to disappear in the 1930s.

Possibly the Great Depression slowed, but certainly it did not stop, the growing dependence of Texans on the automobile and the highway. Automobiles became commonplace in the 1920s and continued to grow in numbers in the 1930s in spite of the hard times. While the population increased about 10 percent, motor vehicle registration grew almost 25 percent between 1929 and 1939.

With the coming of the automobile came the demand for good roads, a demand that would not truly be answered until the 1930s. Until 1907, roads were built and maintained, or not maintained, by the counties, using the personal labor of local citizens who contributed their time. After 1907, counties could vote for bonds and build roads, but the state could not. In 1916, a limited amount of federal aid became available, and the next year the state set aside a small fund for roads under the supervision of a newly created state highway department. But as late as 1923 Governor Neff was quite correct in claiming that there were not a hundred miles of continuously good roads in the state. Texas had no highway system worthy of the name.

Reform and success came with the reorganization of the Texas Highway Commission through laws enacted in 1923 and 1925 and with energetic and efficient management during the Moody years. Under capable leadership and with sufficient funding from gasoline taxes and federal sources, the state by 1932 began to develop a highway system worthy of pride. In a decade not noted for tangible progress, the number of miles of paved roads in Texas more than tripled.

Although progress was slow and came mostly in the second half of the decade, labor unions grew in numbers and power during the Depression. During the 1920s, labor unions had declined somewhat, hampered by determined opposition from management, the competition of company unions, and governmental hostility. With the advent of the Depression, workers were more inclined to turn to unions in search of security, and the federal government lent a friendly hand. The organization of workers especially made headway among oil, chemical, and refinery workers after the Congress of Industrial Organizations (CIO) launched a campaign along the Gulf Coast. In addition to efforts directly affecting workers, unions regularly took stands on public issues. Organized labor aided in the repeal of Prohibition and secured favorable amendments to the Texas eight-hour law. It helped in delaying the adoption of a general sales tax and worked to secure a law prohibiting the sale of prison-made goods.

AGRICULTURE IN THE DEPRESSION

Despite disasters, such as floods and price fluctuations, the early years of the twentieth century were relatively prosperous ones for Texas farmers. Growing cities and the consequent enlargement of markets brought to them

The Dust Bowl in Texas. This 1937 photograph of a farm in Dallam County in the Texas Panhandle indicates the ravages of drought that added to the burdens Texas farmers faced during the Great Depression. Federal and state conservation efforts were put in place in an effort to halt the loss of topsoil that characterized the dust bowl. (Texas State Library and Archives Commission)

an affluence greater than they had ever known. Sharp price declines were temporary, and prices soon recovered. The value of Texas farms more than doubled between 1910 and 1920. The 1920s were more difficult. Mechanization aided production, but prices declined, and the value of Texas farms fell slightly. On the national level Congress passed several acts intended to assist the troubled farmer, but these had little effect.

The Depression brought hard times for the farmer. Of the many complex problems, the most obvious was the decline in agricultural prices. Following the failure of state programs to address this problem, the federal government stepped in. The Roosevelt administration made relief for agriculture a cornerstone for the entire New Deal structure. At the heart of the plan was a concept known as parity—that is, a fair price. Prices for farm products would provide farmers with the purchasing power they had in the years immediately preceding World War I.

To accomplish this goal, Congress passed the Agriculture Adjustment Act of 1933, which paid farmers to take land out of cultivation and produce smaller numbers of livestock. Texas growers received more than $44 million of desperately needed income under this program. The Agriculture Adjustment Act was declared unconstitutional in 1936, but other legislation was passed limiting acreage and providing payments to assure the farmer of at least a portion of parity. Other New Deal farm agencies extended credit to farmers, allowing them to avoid foreclosure and hold on to their farms.

The New Deal farm program was extremely popular with most Texas farmers. For many, only government payments enabled them to hold onto their lands. However, the New Deal programs did not solve the problems of Texas agriculture. The value of Texas farms declined 28 percent during the Depression decade. Texans talked a great deal about going "back to the farm," and there were a few experiments in rural resettlement. But the actual movement of the population was in the other direction. While the total population of the state increased, the number of Texans living on farms declined. Forty percent of the population lived on farms in 1930; only one-third of the population did so by 1940.

CONSERVATION AND ENVIRONMENTAL CONCERNS

One feature that characterized the Depression years was a growing concern for the protection of the environment. Conservation programs intended to preserve the state's natural resources made considerable headway. Soil, timber, water, and petroleum—all exhaustible resources—were affected by programs either begun or expanded during the Great Depression.

One area of environmental concern was soil conservation. A survey by the Soil Conservation Service of the U.S. Department of Agriculture reported that about three-fourths of the area of Texas suffered from soil erosion. Though some Texans had recognized the seriousness of this problem during the Progressive Era, little was accomplished until the United States Soil Conservation Service, created by the Department of Agriculture in 1935, began to apply its vast resources to the problem. To achieve the maximum benefit from the federal program, the legislature in 1939 passed a state soil conservation law under which landowners, by their own vote, could establish soil conservation districts. Today nearly all of the state has been organized into such districts.

Environmentalists also first became concerned about conserving the state's timber resources around the turn of the century. By the 1920s the spread of the lumber industry had reduced Texas virgin pine timber land from approximately 20 million acres to less than 1 million acres. As early as 1889 farsighted conservationists organized the Texas Arbor Day and Forestry Association to promote the "conservation, management, and renewal of forests," but little of substance was accomplished as long as the forests seemed inexhaustible. As increased lumber production began to noticeably deplete the woodlands, the Texas Department of Forestry was created in 1915. In the years that followed, the state acquired its first forest land and developed forest nurseries, research facilities, and demonstration plots. The major move to restore Texas forest lands came in the 1930s when the federal government, with the approval of the Texas legislature, began to purchase cut-over lands and established four national forests in East Texas. New Deal agencies such as the Civilian Conservation Corps participated in reforesting these lands. By 1999, East Texas contained 11.8 million acres of commercial timberland, approximately 735,000 acres of which were located in national or state forests.

Water is another resource of Texas that has long affected the movement of population and the comfort and prosperity of the people. Abundant surface water made the settlement of East Texas easy, while the lack of water in many parts of Central and West Texas retarded settlement. The High Plains were not settled until wells and windmills tapped the bountiful reservoirs of underground water. The scarcity of water in some places or times was balanced by periodic flooding. These problems—flood control and the equitable distribution of water for agriculture, urban growth, and industry—led to the enactment of numerous laws that attempted to regulate the surface waters of Texas. As the Depression began, the legislature created the first large Texas conservation district. The Brazos River Conservation and Recla-

Excessive production was a problem even earlier, but East Texas oil wells, such as these of Kilgore in the 1930s, led to determined efforts to establish production limits, sometimes called "proration." (Library of Congress)

mation District was provided with generous powers for conserving and exploiting the waters of the entire Brazos River watershed. A second large and powerful water district was the Lower Colorado River Authority (LCRA). In the Depression years LCRA began the construction of a series of dams along the Colorado River that formed the reservoirs now known as the Highland Lakes. Other river systems in the state were developed in a similar manner.

Conservation of oil and protection of the environment in which it is produced, which was the most hotly debated environmental issue of the 1930s, was also an old idea, dating back to the time of the Spanish. The first Texas law to regulate the production of oil and gas was enacted in 1899, just four years after the first commercial production of petroleum in Corsicana. It required that water be cased off from oil-bearing formations, that abandoned wells be plugged, and that gas not be permitted to escape. In 1917 the Railroad Commission was given authority to regulate oil and gas production, and in 1919 the oil and gas conservation law was enacted. Under its terms, the Railroad Commission issued regulations calculated to prevent waste in the production of oil and gas. The crisis in the East Texas oil fields in the early 1930s shifted attention from preventing waste and damage to oil reserves to regulating production to maintain prices. State laws were strengthened, the courts became more sympathetic to regulation, and the Railroad Commission's 1933 plan of proration, which set maximum production limits for oil wells, was finally upheld by the federal courts. Proration, strict limits of the production of individual wells, became a reality. The purpose of proration, claimed a senior member of the Railroad Commission, was to leave in the earth "the least possible amount of oil never to be recovered by man." Production limits, however, were generally restricted to the level that would supply the market demand but not result in an oversupply, which might depress prices unduly.

LITERATURE AND THE ARTS IN THE DEPRESSION

Although the times were hard, jobs were scarce, and life was often insecure, the age of the Great Depression in Texas brought forth a number of outstanding accomplishments in literature and the arts. The Texas Institute of Letters, organized in 1936, became an effective agency in encouraging writing and improving its quality. Perhaps J. Frank Dobie gave it its watchword when he wrote: "Great literature transcends its native land, but there is none that I know of that ignores its own soil. All great literature plumbs and soars to the elementals. Texas authors need not be antiquarians; in the rich soil of the novel there has not been even a furrow plowed."

Dobie was one of a trio long linked with the Texas Institute of Letters who constituted what is perhaps the nearest thing to a school of writers that Texas has known. The others were Roy Bedicheck, a naturalist, and Walter Prescott Webb, a historian. The range of Frank Dobie's writings was remarkably broad: cowboys and the cattle industry, folklore, and themes of nature. His publication of *A Vaquero of the Brush Country* in 1929 was soon followed by *Coronado's Children, Tales of Lost Mines, Buried Treasure in the Southwest, Tongues of Monte*, and others. Bedicheck twice won awards for his *Karankawa Country* and *Adventures with a Texas Naturalist*. Webb wrote convincingly on such diverse subjects as *The Great Plains* and *The Texas Rangers*, and later his *Divided We Stand* and *The Great Frontier* would receive national acclaim.

Folklore attracted the attention of a number of creative artists. J. Mason Brewer in prose and Hudie ("Leadbelly") Ledbetter in song captured many of the folk stories and songs of the black people of Texas. Another collector of folklore was John A. Lomax, who continued to collect ballads throughout the 1930s.

In fiction, Texas produced only one writer of note during this period, but she was outstanding. Katherine Anne Porter was born near San Antonio in 1890 and used Texas and Mexican settings in much of her literature. Her first volume of short stories, *Flowering Judas* (1930), and her two masterpieces, *Noon Wine* (1937) and *Pale Horse, Pale Rider* (1939), established her reputation as one of the finest twentieth-century short story writers. In 1966 she was awarded the Pulitzer prize. Her only novel, *Ship of Fools*, was made into a motion picture in 1965.

New types of media also offered opportunities for artistic creativity. Texas contributed a number of stars to the motion picture industry. Among the actors were Tom Mix, Joan Crawford, Ginger Rogers, Mary Martin, and Gene Autry; achieving fame as directors were King Vidor and Howard Hughes. Radio, which was little more than a curiosity in Texas during the 1920s, was of great value to the aspiring artists of the 1930s. During the Depression decade several network chains were organized, and by the end of the decade, Texas was well covered by radio stations. An important feature of radio programming was hillbilly music, later to achieve a kind of respectability as country music. Ernest Tubb and Bob Wills began their music careers in Texas, as did Leonard Slye, who became better known as Roy Rogers.

THE POLITICS OF RECOVERY—JAMES ALLRED, 1935–39

The Allred administration took office in 1935 during the middle of the Depression. One of the most complex and hotly debated issues confronting

Texas at this time was old-age pensions. The 1935 National Social Security Act required that states provide matching funds for assistance to the elderly, as well as to dependent children, the disabled, and the blind. In a special election held in August 1935 the voters of Texas approved a state constitutional amendment establishing a pension program for the elderly. The amendment, however, was vague, specifying neither the amounts to be paid nor the standards for determining who should receive them. Furthermore, the amendment made no provision for funding the pension program. The pension question occupied much of the work of the regular sessions of the legislature and led to the calling of several special sessions, but the problems persisted. Applications for aid quickly climbed to more than 80,000; the legislature voted more funds and made conditions for receiving pensions more difficult, but by June 1937 more than 125,000 aged Texans were receiving pensions. At that time the legislature conducted an investigation of the old-age assistance commission, and it was evident that the subject of pensions was a major political question.

Pensions and taxation, subjects necessarily linked, were the principal issues that confronted Allred when he sought reelection in 1936. Texans had heard a great deal of Huey Long's "share of the wealth" program in Louisiana; they were well acquainted with Dr. Francis E. Townsend's plan to pay a pension of $200 a month to most persons past 60 years of age; and they listened to Father Charles E. Coughlin's blend of anti-Semitism and social services on his national radio broadcasts. Most candidates endorsed a more generous pension policy but avoided specifics on how they would fund the program. Governor Allred took the middle ground, advocating pensions for the aged needy only. He easily won renomination and reelection.

The governor was obliged, nevertheless, to appeal to the Forty-fifth Legislature, which convened in January 1937, for additional revenue. Colleges, public schools, and almost all state institutions and agencies needed more money. The voters had, moreover, authorized workers' compensation for state employees and planned a teachers' retirement fund; the state also needed to provide funds for the care of the blind and for dependent children. Allred proposed to raise most of the additional revenue by an increase in all taxes on oil, gas, and sulfur. Despite the critical need, the legislature refused to raise taxes.

Some decisions made earlier in the decade brought more problems to the Allred years. An urgent need for revenue accounted in part for a measure, enacted in 1933, that made betting on horse racing legal. The act, denounced in the pulpits of the state and by many editors and businessmen, was repealed in 1937 by a special session of the legislature. Likewise, the end of Prohibition also brought problems. When voters in August 1935 repealed the state Prohibition amendment, they rejected a plan for state liquor sales. Shortly thereafter, the legislature provided for taxing and licensing dealers, prohibited the sale of hard liquor by the drink, authorized local option elections, and placed the administration of the sale and distribution of alcohol under a liquor control board. Soon there were complaints of violations by dealers, especially of the provision of selling liquor by the drink. Furthermore, the status of liquor in counties and cities that were dry at the time that state Prohibition was enacted in 1919 was not affected by the repeal of the amendment, and local option again became an issue in many communities. Complicating the issue was the fact that taxes on the sale of liquor provided much of the revenue for old-age pensions and other social service programs.

Pursuant to a mandate of the voters in a constitutional amendment in 1932, Texas celebrated in 1936 the hundreth anniversary of its independence. The state appropriated $3 million for the use of the centennial commission, and the U.S. government matched it with an equal amount. The WPA also made contributions. Public funds were divided between the main exposition at Dallas and various other historical and commemorative projects in different communities. A considerable part of the money was spent in erecting numerous monuments to historical personages and placing markers at historic sites. The most notable of these was the construction of the San Jacinto monument to commemorate the 1836 victory over Santa Anna.

When Governor Allred declined to run for another term in 1938, thirteen candidates entered the race for the Democratic gubernatorial nomination. What followed was a combination of politics and showmanship that characterized the emergence of another colorful phenomenon in Texas politics. W. Lee O'Daniel, a flour-milling company executive and salesman of Fort Worth, accounted for the theatrics. About a month before the election it became evident that he enjoyed the support of more Texans than all other candidates combined.

O'Daniel was a familiar name to most Texans. For several years he had conducted a noonday radio program, replete with a hillbilly band, humor, and homely advice. "Please pass the biscuits, Pappy," and "The Light Crust Dough Boys are 'On the Air' " were words heard by thousands each week. Many thought that O'Daniel's candidacy was only a device to sell more flour, and perhaps it was, at least at first, but he soon became a serious contender. He applied to the race the same tactics he had used in selling flour by radio: a bit of country music interspersed with comments and an occasional short, informal speech filled with blasts at "professional politicians." Whether it was the promise of a businesslike administration, the castigation of professional politicians, the music, the candidate's homely philosophy, or the promise of pensions that drew the votes has not been determined. Whatever the reason, O'Daniel's campaign was extremely successful. For the first time since the adoption of the Texas primary law, a gubernatorial candidate won without a runoff.

W. Lee O'Daniel, 1939-41 _____

From the beginning, O'Daniel was a controversial figure in politics. His admirers, as loyal as those of the Fergusons, accepted O'Daniel as the spokesman for the ordinary citizen who had long been victimized by the people in power. His critics were equally determined in their opposition. Many of them looked upon O'Daniel as someone who was more foolish and naive than he was wicked, an innocent who had strayed into politics. Actually, O'Daniel was neither a crusader for the ordinary people nor an innocent. He was a shrewd and tough businessman, a superb actor, and a successful salesman who was one of the first politicians in Texas to hire and rely upon a public relations firm. He had the ability to be inconsistent without alarming his supporters, but he did have some convictions that never wavered. For example, he was a dedicated enemy of organized labor.

O'Daniel's performance as a governor left much to be desired. His campaign promise to give a pension to every old person was pared down to a proposal to give only to needy persons past 65 years of age an amount sufficient to raise their income to $30 a month. Similarly, the governor soon abandoned the hope that new taxes would not be necessary. He proposed to fund his expanded pension program with a tax of 1.6 percent on all transactions. The lawmakers dubbed the proposal a sales tax (anathema in Texas at that time) and attacked it bitterly. The affair widened the breach already existing between the governor and the legislature. The legislature liberalized pensions but failed to provide additional revenue. As a result the state deficit continued to increase.

Six candidates challenged O'Daniel's bid for reelection in 1940. Although they attacked his record and his plan for raising revenue, his opponents did not directly attack his proposal for more liberal pensions. Texas had developed a "share-the-wealth" movement of its own, and the candidates did not dare to resist it. O'Daniel was renominated by an overwhelming vote and reelected in November 1940.

Like the lawmaking bodies that had preceded it for a decade, the Forty-seventh Legislature, which convened in January 1941, found that the problem of taxation was its chief worry. It could not, like its predecessor, take up the question, debate it, and drop it. The general fund, which supplied most of the agencies, showed a deficit of $25 million. There were predictions that Texas would be deprived of all federal Social Security money unless it raised more funds to meet the increasing demand of its own liberal pension laws. The teachers' retirement payments had not been matched by the state; the electorate demanded that it care for its destitute children and the blind. After extended debate the legislature approved an omnibus tax bill calculated to bring $22 million in additional revenue annually. Approximately one-half of the new revenue was to come from increased taxes on the production of oil and gas and the remainder from a variety of sources. This measure doubled the old-age pension income but did not quiet the agitation over pensions or solve the state's long-term revenue problems.

When the death of Morris Sheppard in 1941 opened a seat in the U.S. Senate, the governor appointed to the seat Andrew Jackson Houston, the 87–year-old son of the hero of the Battle of San Jacinto. Houston got to Washington but did not live to complete his short appointive term. Meanwhile, several candidates entered the senatorial race, including Governor O'Daniel. Although O'Daniel was elected to finish out Sheppard's term, his prestige was seriously impaired, for he barely defeated Congressman Lyndon B. Johnson, an "old friend" of President Roosevelt. In the Democratic primaries of 1942 O'Daniel faced a strong challenge from defeated ex-Governors Dan Moody and James V. Allred, who charged that O'Daniel had failed to adequately support President Roosevelt's defense and war policies. O'Daniel was reelected after a bitter campaign.

With the election of O'Daniel to the U.S. Senate, Lieutenant Governor Coke R. Stevenson, formerly a speaker of the state house of representatives, became governor in August 1941. Stevenson's term coincided with the years of World War II. Texas's preoccupation with the war, coupled with Steven-

John Nance Garner. He was first elected to the U. S. House of Representatives in 1903, and was a serious candidate for the Democratic party's nomination for president in 1932 but accepted the vice-presidential nomination and was subsequently elected twice to that post. Although he came to disapprove of many of President Roosevelt's policies and returned to Texas after two terms in that office, he remained a loyal Democrat, supporting the presidential candidacies of Harry Truman, Adlai Stevenson, John Kennedy, and Lyndon Johnson. (Archives Division—Texas State Archives)

son's strong conservative beliefs, meant that his years in the governorship would bring little change in state government, services, or programs.

During the 1930s, the influence of Texans in the national government became greater than ever before. John Nance Garner, who had served continuously in the House of Representatives since 1903, was elected House speaker in 1931. In 1932 he was elected vice president and was reelected in 1936. In presiding over the Senate, Garner used his legislative skills and personal influence to guide through Congress most of the measures that made up President Roosevelt's New Deal. A movement to nominate Garner for president in 1940 failed when Roosevelt decided to seek a third term.

Other influential Texans made their mark in Washington during the Roosevelt years. Jesse Jones of Houston was chairman of the RFC from 1933 to 1939. In 1939, he was appointed administrator of the powerful Federal Loan Agency and in 1940 became secretary of commerce. In 1933, Texans held the chairmanships of six major committees in the House of Representatives. Sam Rayburn of Bonham became Majority Leader and later Speaker of the House of Representatives. Morris Sheppard, mostly remembered for his work on behalf of national Prohibition, promoted President Roosevelt's New Deal in the Senate until his death in 1941. The other senator, Tom Connally, became chairman of the Committee on Foreign Relations and was a staunch spokesman for the administration in the enactment of the gigantic defense program and the war measures of the 1940s. He was also instrumental in the creation of the United Nations charter in 1945.

BIBLIOGRAPHY

General accounts of the Depression include the writings of S. S. Mckay and O. B. Faulk, *Texas after Spindletop*; Robert C. Cotner (ed.), *Texas Cities and the Great Depression* (Austin, 1973); and Donald Whisenhunt (ed.), *The Depression in the Southwest* (Port Washington, N.Y., 1980), and *The Depression in Texas: The Hoover Years* (New York, 1983). For political affairs toward the end of the decade, George Green, *The Establishment in Texas Politics, The Primitive Years, 1938–1957* (Westport, Conn., 1979), is invaluable, as is Mario T. Garcia's study of Mexican American politics,, *Mexican Americans: Leadership, Ideology, and Identity, 1930-1960* (New Haven, 1989).

Life in the Depression years has been studied from a number of different perspectives. Very useful is Maxine Holmes and Gerald Saxon, *The WPA Dallas Guide and History* (Dallas, 1992). John Neal Phillips, *Running with Bonnie and Clyde: The Ten Fast Years of Ralph Fultz* (Norman, Okla., 1996), provides insight into the lives of the era's most notorious criminals. Depression-era labor struggles are chronicled in Arnoldo De León, "*Las Tasinques* and the Sheep Shearers' Union of North America: A Strike in West Texas, 1934," *West Texas Historical Association Year Book*, LV, 3–16; Kenneth Walker, "The Pecan Shellers of San Antonio and Mechanization," *Southwestern Historical Quarterly*, LXIX, 44–58; and Ernest Obadele-Starks, "Black Labor, the Black Middle Class, and Organized Protest along the Upper Texas Gulf Coast, 1883-1945," *Southwestern Historical Quarterly*, CIII, 52-65. The following studies detail the impact of the Depression on African Americans and Mexican Americans: Richard García, *Rise of the Mexican American Middle Class: San Antonio, 1929–1941* (College Station,

1991); J. Gilberto Quezada, *Border Boss: Manuel B. Bravo and Zapata County* (College Station,, 1999); R. Reynolds McKay, "The Federal Deportation Campaign in Texas: Mexican Deportation from the Lower Rio Grande Valley during the Great Depression," *Borderlands Journal*, V, 95–120; Randy J. Sparks, " 'Heavenly Houston' or 'Hellish Houston'? Black Unemployment and Relief Efforts, 1929–1936," *Southern Studies*, XXV, 353–367; Christie L. Bourgeois, "Stepping Over Lines: Lyndon Johnson, Black Texans, and the National Youth Administration, 1935–1937," *Southwestern Historical Quarterly*, XCI, 149–172; and Eddie Simpson, Jr., *My Remembers: A Black Sharecropper's Recollections of the Depression* (Denton, 1995). See also Julia Blackwelder, *Women of the Depression: Caste and Culture in San Antonio, 1929–1939* (College Station, 1984); Thad Sitton and Dan Utley, *From Can See to Can't See: Texas Cotton Farmers on the Southern Prairies* (Austin, 1997); and Kenneth Ragsdale, *The Year America Discovered Texas: Centennial '36* (College Station, 1987). Robert L. Reid, *Picturing Texas: The FSA-OWL Photographers in Texas, 1935–1943* (Austin, 1992), offers reality that words cannot always convey.

The annual reports of the Texas Department of Human Resources give the most complete accounts of the aid given by the state to needy citizens. The *Annual Report* for 1949 is especially useful for the period preceding that date. On federal aid during the Depression years, see F. A. Williams, *Federal Aid for Relief* (New York, 1939). On Texas relief, see Carol A. Weisenberg, *Dollars and Dreams: The National Youth Administration in Texas* (New York, 1994); Booth Mooney, "925,000 Texans Getting Government Aid," *Texas Weekly*, November 11, 1939, 6–7. Also see William R. Johnson, "Rural Rehabilitation in the New Deal: The Ropesville Project," *Southwestern Historical Quarterly*, LXXIX, 279–295; Michael Barr, "A Comparative Examination of Federal Work Relief in Fredericksburg and Gillespie County," ibid., XCVI, 363–390; and Roger Biles, "The New Deal in Dallas," ibid., XCV, 1–19.

On national affairs, see Bascom Timmons, *Jesse H. Jones* (New York, 1956), and *Garner of Texas* (New York, 1948); Walter L. Buenger, "Between Community and Corporation: The Southern Roots of Jesse H. Jones and the Reconstruction Finance Corporation," *Journal of Southern History*, LVI, 481–510; James Olson, *Saving Capitalism: The Reconstruction Finance Corporation and the New Deal, 1933–1940* (Princeton, 1988); Jordan A. Schwarz, *The New Dealers: Power Politics in the Age of Roosevelt* (New York, 1993), which considers many Texans; C. D. Dorough, *Mr. Sam, A Biography of Samuel T. Rayburn* (New York, 1962); Lionel Patenaude, "Garner, Sumners, and Connally: The Defeat of the Roosevelt Court Bill in 1937," *Southwestern Historical Quarterly*, LXXIV, 136–151; "The Garner Vote Switch to Roosevelt: 1932 Democratic Convention," ibid., LXXIX, 189–204; and *Texans, Politics and the New Deal* (New York, 1980); and Richard B. Henderson, *Maury Maverick: A Political Biography* (Austin, 1970). Ken Hendrickson and Michael L. Collins's *Profiles in Power: Twentieth Century Texans in Washington* (Arlington Heights, Ill., 1995), contains essays on John Nance Garner, Jesse Jones, and Tom Connally.

The best general reference on industrial development is the *Texas Almanac*. The *Texas Business Review*, published monthly by the Bureau of Business Research, The University of Texas, Austin, is invaluable. Robert D. Maxwell and Robert D. Baker, *Sawdust Empire: The Texas Lumber Industry, 1830–1940* (College Station, 1983), is an excellent study. On the history of oil, good references are C. C. Rister, *Oil! Titan of the Southwest*, comprehensive and authoritative; W. Gard, *The First Hundred Years of Oil and Gas* (Dallas, 1966); Craig Thompson, *Since Spindletop* (Pittsburgh, 1951); Henrietta M. Larson, *History of Humble Oil and Refining Company* (New York, 1959); Alfred M. Leeston, John A. Chrichton, and John C. Jacobs, *The Dynamic Natural Gas Industry* (Norman, Okla., 1963); Jack Donahue, *Wildcatter: The Story of Michel T. Halbouty and the Search for Oil* (New York, 1979); Walter Rundell, Jr., *Oil in West Texas and New Mexico: A Pictorial History of the Permian Basin* (College Station, 1982); Gerald Lynch,

Roughnecks, Drillers, and Tool Pushers: Thirty-Three Years in the Oil Fields (Austin, 1987); Lawrence Goodwyn, *Texas Oil, American Dreams: A Study of the Texas Independent Producers and Royalty Owners Association* (Austin, 1996), and references cited in the previous chapter.

Texas Highways, official journal of the Texas Highway Department, Austin, and *Texas Parade*, published monthly in Austin with the endorsement of the Texas Good Roads Association, are rich sources of information on Texas roads. On railroads, see Everett L. DeGolyer, Jr., "The Railroads: The End of An Era," *Southwestern Historical Quarterly*, LXXIII, 356–364.

Considerable writing has been done on conservation efforts. The beginning of demonstration work in Texas is related in H. R. Southworth, "The Later Years of Seaman A. Knapp," *West Texas Historical Association Year Book*, X, 88–104. See also *Agricultural Research in Texas Since 1888* (College Station, 1956). For an account of soil conservation, the *Annual Reports* of the Agricultural Extension Service, Texas A & M University, are most useful. On water conservation, floods, and droughts, much has been written in recent years: for example, John A. Adams, Jr., *Damming the Colorado: The Rise of the Lower Colorado River Authority, 1933–1939* (College Station, 1990), and James H. Banks and John E. Babcock, *Corralling the Colorado: The First Fifty Years of the Lower Colorado River Authority* (Austin, 1988). See also W. P. Webb, *More Water for Texas* (Austin, 1954); and Robert Lee Lowry, *Surface Water Resources in Texas* (Austin, 1958). The long and involved history of the conservation of oil and gas in Texas is dealt with by Robert E. Hardwicke, *Legal History of the Conservation of Oil in Texas*, and Maurice Cheek, *Legal History of Conservation of Gas in Texas* (Mineral Law Section, American Bar Association, 1938); and David F. Prindle, *Petroleum Politics and the Texas Railroad Commission* (Austin, 1981). Brief studies are James P. Hart, "Oil, the Courts, and the Railroad Commission," *Southwestern Historical Quarterly*, XLIV, 303–320; and David F. Prindle, "The Texas Railroad Commission and the Elimination of the Flaring of Natural Gas, 1930–1949," ibid., LXXXIV, 293–308. Concerning the East Texas oil field, see Ruel McDaniel, *Some Ran Hot* (Dallas, 1939). The work of the Texas Railroad Commission is brought out in J. A. Clark's *Three Stars for the Colonel* [Ernest O. Thompson] (New York, 1957).

Texas writers are discussed in Mabel Major and Thomas M. Pearce, *Southwest Heritage: A Literary History*; J. Frank Dobie, *Life and Literature of the Southwest* (Albuquerque, 1972); Ronnie Dugger (ed.), *Three Men in Texas: Bedicheck, Webb, and Dobie* (Austin, 1967); and Lon Tinkle, *An American Original: The Life of J. Frank Dobie* (Boston, 1978). Also see the publications of the Texas Folklore Society. Texas music is featured in three studies: Bill C. Malone, *Country Music U.S.A.; A Fifty-Year History* (Austin, 1968); Dave Oliphant, *Texan Jazz* (Austin, 1996); and Charles R. Townsend, *San Antonio Rose: The Life and Music of Bob Wills* (Urbana, Ill., 1976). See Noland Porterfield, *Last Cavalier: The Life and Times of John A. Lomax, 1867-1948* (Urbana, Ill., 1996) for a study of the Texas folklorist and musicologist.

18

World War II and After 1941–1962

When the armed forces of Japan attacked Pearl Harbor on December 7, 1941, the nation entered World War II. A prompt declaration of war against Japan was followed by a German declaration of war on the United States. War in Europe had begun in September 1939 with the German invasion of Poland, an act of aggression that led to armed intervention by France and England. Until the attack on Pearl Harbor, the nation had avoided the conflict, but concern for the future of freedom had increased with each passing day.

The government and the people of Texas supported the war effort. The state's men and women responded to the call to arms. Its oil kept ships, trucks, tanks, and planes moving against the enemy, and its industries were strengthened and harnessed for the cause. Stimulated by the war, Texas industrial production soared to the highest level ever known. In spite of the many heartbreaking experiences, material prosperity generally prevailed, and after the victory was won, the problems of postwar readjustment were made easier by expanding industry, high prices for farm commodities, and a generous federal policy of providing schooling or on-the-job training for veterans. As in most of the rest of the nation, the Texas economy continued to expand; full employment, high wages, and high prices underscored the abundance of the period.

Prosperity did not bring tranquillity. Farmers protested that they were not sharing fairly in the general abundance and called for greater freedom in their farming practices or for more controls, as their interest and points of view varied. Labor unions chafed at restraints and penalties they considered unfair and grew stronger regardless of them. The public school system, growing costlier each year and declining in efficiency, was completely reorganized. There were pleas, fervent and often repeated, for better care of children; the advocates for the needy aged were not satisfied with the level of aid accorded them; and those with disabilities had their champions. During the war and the decade that followed, minority groups contrasted the freedom we were fighting for with the lack of freedom at home and intensified their struggle for equal treatment and opportunity.

THE POLITICS OF WARTIME

Public affairs in the state reflected the conditions of wartime. Although Governor Coke Stevenson was critical of the federal rationing program, he supported the war effort. He called for rigid economy in all agencies of government and entered into a no-strike covenant with organized labor that prevented work stoppages in Texas. Attorney General Gerald Mann announced that the strict Texas antitrust laws would not be enforced against industries directly involved in production of war materials. In its session of 1943, the legislature cut appropriations for most state agencies and colleges. Voters adopted a constitutional amendment, which went into effect in 1945, mandating that state spending could not exceed state income.

As the war proceeded, various federal agencies affected the lives of most Texans. The War Manpower Commission sought to see that all qualified people were employed and that those deferred from military service worked at essential jobs. The Office of Price Administration, in charge of rationing and price ceilings, used the staff and students of the public schools to implement sugar rationing. Later, rationing was extended to meats, fats, canned goods, coffee, shoes, tires, and gasoline. The Railroad Commission, in charge of the production of from 40 percent to 50 percent of the nation's gas and oil, supervised a careful increase in oil production.

For the most part, Texans at home accepted the problems of wartime with a minimum of complaints. In spite of the "freezing" of rents, salaries, and wages and the restraints on prices, the cost of living rose moderately during the war; but since almost every employable person was busy, family incomes increased significantly. The rank and file of people were in relatively good circumstances. They collected scrap iron and grew "victory gardens." They bought war bonds and gave to the Red Cross. They practiced blackout and air raid alerts and generally complied with the restrictions of rationing, although hoarding certainly was not an unknown practice.

It was during the war years that a political split between Texas conservative and liberal Democrats developed, with racial issues significantly contributing to that development. There were conservative opponents of

President Franklin Roosevelt and the New Deal, but they constituted a small minority in the party through the mid-1930s. The presidential candidacy of staunch Texas Democrat John Nance Garner held the factions together in 1940, but President Roosevelt's determination to seek a third and then a fourth term undermined that coalition. Adding to their objections, conservative Texas Democrats opposed the 1944 Supreme Court decision, *Smith* v. *Allwright*, that declared the white primary unconstitutional. When the conservatives tried to make opposition to the Supreme Court's decision a test of party loyalty, the 1944 state Democratic convention split, and the conservatives, organized as "Texas Regulars," made a futile effort to block the Franklin Roosevelt-Harry Truman presidential ticket. These factional contests had their repercussions in state Democratic politics, but Governor Coke Stevenson, a conservative Democrat, managed to stay aloof from them. He was easily reelected in 1944.

For the Forty-ninth Legislature, which assembled in January 1945, the problem of state finance was delightfully simple. Income had outrun expenditures so far that a $12 million deficit had been transformed into a surplus. Appropriations surpassed those of any preceding legislature in history; much of the surplus was distributed to the schools.

Before the legislature adjourned on June 5, 1945, it was evident that the war's end was near. Thousands of veterans had returned home and tens of thousands would follow them. Texas laws allowed them free voting privileges, the renewal of drivers' licenses without examination, and the privilege of attending state colleges without charge. Already the federal G.I. Bill of Rights was in effect, providing federal aid for schooling or training, health care, and low-interest home loans. These privileges were later extended to veterans of post-World War II service. Texas voters ratified an amendment to the state constitution authorizing the state to issue bonds to subsidize land sales to veterans.

The sense of change in the air that the end of the war created extended even to matters of fundamental law. For the new era that was opening, the old constitution seemed inadequate. Bales of proposed constitutional amendments were submitted to each legislature after World War II. In the Forty-ninth Legislature, eighty-four proposals were introduced and eight were submitted to the voters (not including one proposing a constitutional convention). The voters approved amendments extending benefits to veterans, raising to nine the number of Supreme Court justices, and raising the ceiling on social welfare payments. But there would not be a new constitution.

TEXAS AND TEXANS IN THE WAR

Long before the attack on Pearl Harbor, Texas was a huge training center for the armed forces. San Antonio during a considerable part of the war was the headquarters of the Third Army and the Fourth Army, while the Eighth Service Command had its headquarters in Dallas. For a period the

army had as many as fifteen training posts in Texas and twenty-one pris-
oner-of-war base camps and more than twenty branch locations. In addition
the Southern Defense Command, which was responsible for the defense of
the Gulf Coast and Mexican border areas, was headquartered at Fort Sam
Houston. Texas was also the most active aviation training region in the
nation. Randolph Field, Kelly Field, and Brooks Field, all near San Antonio,
were enlarged; Ellington Field near Houston was rebuilt; and additional air
fields were established in Wichita Falls, San Angelo, Lubbock, Midland, San
Marcos, Amarillo, and other cities.

It is estimated that 1.25 million men and women in all branches of the
service were trained in Texas, among them more than twenty combat army
divisions. Probably as many as .75 million Texans, including 12,000 women
and 80,000 African Americans, who were assigned to segregated units,
served in the armed forces. Secretary of the Navy Frank Knox stated in
December 1942 that Texas was contributing a larger percentage of men to the
fighting forces than any other state. Texas also contributed to military leadership. Oveta Culp Hobby was director of the Women's Army Corps. The
state could claim at least 12 admirals and 155 generals, among them Chester
W. Nimitz, commander in chief of the Pacific Fleet, and Dwight David Eisenhower, Supreme Allied Commander in Europe. Texans fought on every front
and paid their share of war's cruel toll. Their war dead for all branches of the
service amounted to 23,022. The seriously wounded and permanently
injured numbered many more.

Wherever they went, Texans seemed always to make their presence
known. The Thirty-sixth Division carried the Texas flag and often displayed
it. Where Texas troops were congregated, natives sometimes spoke of the
"Texas army." Many Texans were recognized for valor as well as for enthusiasm. Lieutenant Audie Murphy of Farmersville became the "most decorated" American soldier of World War II. The Congressional Medal of Honor
went to him and thirty-three other Texans. Another Texan was Commander
Samuel D. Dealey, killed in action, and known as the "most decorated man
in the Navy."

In addition to promoting patriotism, sacrifice, and prosperity, the war
also intensified racial and ethnic strife in Texas. Both African Americans and
Mexican Americans contributed to the war effort in every way that they
could. They worked in the fields and factories, and joined the armed forces,
and many died in the service of their country. Five Mexican-Americans won
the medal of honor; Doris Miller, a black high school football star from Central Texas, left his duties as a messman on a battleship, manned an antiair-
craft gun, and shot down four Japanese planes during the attack on Pearl
Harbor. Miller was awarded the Navy Cross for his heroism but then reas-
signed to kitchen duty—a position reserved for blacks in the U.S. Navy.
Miller was still serving in this position when he died in action in 1943. For
African Americans, Jim Crow segregation confronted them in every aspect

of their military service. Mexican Americans were generally integrated into regular military units, although some saw duty in Mexican American units such as Company C of the 141st Regiment, 36th Division.

The pride, self-confidence, and dignity that came from military service, together with the obvious contradictions of fighting and dying in defense of freedom while serving in a segregated military and facing discrimination, fueled the growing demands for equality among both African Americans and Mexican Americans. Segregation and hostility from white civilians and their fellow soldiers confronted black troops all across Texas. Protests from local whites forced the removal of black troops stationed at Camp Wallace near Galveston, and prevented the posting of some black troops at Fort Clark. At Fort Bliss in 1943 black soldiers attacked white soldiers in retaliation for the beatings suffered by black soldiers. Though it did not directly involve black troops, the June 1943 race riot in Beaumont, in which white mobs ravaged black neighborhoods for twenty hours in response to a rumor that a black man had assaulted a white woman, characterized the extent of racial division in wartime Texas. Only in Houston, where memories remained of the 1917 mutiny, did citizens organize to make sure that black troops were treated with hospitality. The true irony of a culture that treated German prisoners of war with more respect that it did its own soldiers was captured in this poem:

On a train in Texas German prisoners eat
With white American soldiers, seat by seat,
While black American soldiers sit apart,
The white men eating meat, the black men heart.

Mexican Americans also faced discrimination in wartime Texas. Though they were not subject to official segregation in the military and were less likely to face open hostility in the communities where they were stationed, there remained a definite prejudice against Mexicans and Mexican Americans throughout Texas. It was because of this pattern of discrimination and mistreatment that the Mexican government refused to allow workers to be sent to Texas under the 1942 bracero agreement. In an effort to respond to the Mexican government's criticism and provide a supply of Mexican labor for Texas agriculture and industry, the Texas legislature passed the Caucasian Race Resolution in 1943, assuring Mexicans and Mexican Americans equal rights in public places of business and amusement, and Governor Stevenson established the Good Neighbor Commission of Texas to combat discrimination. The Mexican government, dubious about the sincerity of these efforts, especially when the 1945 legislature failed to pass a bill prohibiting racial discrimination in restaurants, refused to allow Texas to participate in the bracero program until 1947.

Both Mexican Americans and African Americans organized for equality. In the 1930s and 1940s black Texans focused their first efforts on gaining political rights and providing equal funding for black schools and black teachers. Juanita Craft in Dallas and Lulu B. White in Houston took over leadership of their respective NAACP chapters and transformed these organizations into large and powerful organizations for equal rights. After achieving victory in the struggle for equal school funding, Lulu White spearheaded the effort to restore suffrage rights for Texas blacks. In 1942, with the backing of the Houston NAACP chapter and support from the national NAACP office and its attorney, Thurgood Marshall, Houston dentist and political activist Dr. Lonnie Smith filed suit when he was denied the right to vote in the Democratic primary. When in 1944 the Supreme Court ruled in his favor in *Smith v. Allwright* (1944), the quarter-century struggle against disfranchisement came to a successful conclusion. Even though there was vocal opposition to this ruling and efforts in Marshall and in Colorado County to keep African Americans from the polls, approximately 75,000 blacks voted in the 1946 primary, some cities appointed black poll tax deputies to register black voters, and Lonnie Smith was elected precinct judge. The Texas struggle for civil rights was well under way.

In the Mexican-American community LULAC had been the principal organization for equal rights since its founding in 1929. As World War II came to a close, LULAC focused its civil rights activity on school desegregation. The organization filed lawsuits in California in 1945 (*Méndez v. Westminster School District*) and in Texas in 1948 (*Delgado v. Bastrop Independent School District)* challenging the practice of providing segregated schools for Mexican Americans. Although the federal courts decided in LULAC's favor, ruling that school segregation violated the Fourteenth Amendment, most districts effectively avoided complying with the rulings until the 1960s. World War II contributed to the emergence of a new, more militant political organization in the Mexican American community. When the mortuary in Three Rivers refused to conduct reburial services for war hero Félix Longoria, outraged Tejanos organized under the leadership of Dr. Héctor Pérez to end discrimination. In a 1948 meeting in Corpus Christi they organized the American G. I. Forum in response to the Longoria case. The G.I. Forum initially focused on informing Mexican Americans about their rights under the G.I. Bill but quickly broadened its objectives to include political action. It conducted voter registration drives and filed lawsuits against school segregation and other forms of discrimination. It gave voice to the demands of the growing Tejano community for equality.

Perhaps the most extreme example of discrimination during the war was that experienced by Japanese Americans. Though the hostility toward Japanese residents of Texas never became as extreme as it was in California or other West Coast states, wartime laws calling for the internment of Japanese Americans were enforced by federal authorities in Texas. The census of 1940 identified 458 Japanese in Texas. During the war three internment camps, located at Kenedy, Seagoville, and Crystal City, housed a total of about 4,000 Japanese. Most of those interned were from other states, or from Peru, but all Japanese Texans, except for those who served in the armed forces, were interned for the duration of the war either in these camps or in relocation centers located in other states. Though some Texans rallied to the support of their neighbors when they were first questioned by authorities and then rounded up and transported to the camps, the hysteria of war combined with existing racial antagonisms prevented the vast majority of Texans from raising questions or voicing opposition regarding Japanese internment.

POSTWAR TEXAS—THE JESTER YEARS, 1947–49

As the gubernatorial campaign of 1946 began to take shape, Homer Price Rainey seemed to be the strongest of a long slate of candidates. Rainey was the former president of the University of Texas who had been dismissed from that post after a long, bitter controversy with the board of regents. He was supported by many liberals, and the newly enfranchised blacks organized and voted for him. But Railroad Commissioner Beauford Jester, somewhat more conservative, won the nomination in a runoff.

Like his predecessors in office, Governor Jester emphatically opposed any new taxes. Fortunately, an expanding economy and general prosperity allowed him to recommend substantial increases in appropriations without suggesting higher taxes. In his "Report to the People" in 1949, Jester could point to the doubling of appropriations for hospitals and orphanages and the opening of several other institutions that provided care for the unfortunate. However, proposed spending eventually exceeded expected income, and the comptroller refused to certify appropriations for a number of projects authorized near the end of the session.

Labor unions became the focus of attention in these years. In 1947, a veritable shower of laws regulating unions came to Governor Jester, some of which he had advocated. Most important was the "right to work" law, which made it unlawful to require union membership of any employee. Another law severely regulated picketing. Strikes by public employees were forbidden, and the picketing of utilities was prohibited. Even this was not the end. In 1951, a law was enacted that provided beyond the shadow of a doubt that there be no closed shops in Texas—no labor agreement could require that workers belong to a union.

On the national scene, many conservative Texas Democrats opposed President Harry Truman (who became president upon the death of Franklin

Roosevelt in April 1945), as they had opposed Roosevelt. They associated Truman with the Fair Employment Practice Committee, the CIO Political Action Committee, and other programs and groups that they had consistently opposed. Governor Jester worked for harmony, however, and Texas avoided the split in the Democratic Party that occurred in other southern states when the 1948 Democratic National Convention nominated Truman and approved his civil rights plank.

Jester was reelected governor without having to campaign, but the election for the U.S. Senate was a different matter. In a close and acrimonious contest for the seat vacated by O'Daniel, Congressman Lyndon B. Johnson opposed former Governor Coke R. Stevenson. For several days after the election, the final vote was uncertain. Eventually, Johnson was awarded a victory by eighty-seven votes and a federal court ordered his name placed on the ballot as the Democratic nominee. Stevenson's forces argued that fraud in several South Texas counties gave Johnson the victory, and there was some evidence of peculiar voting patterns, but Johnson received the nomination and won the election.

In the longest session the state had known, from January 11 to July 6, 1949, the Fifty-first Legislature enacted many laws, some of them of enduring value. In an effort to improve pitiable conditions in the institutions for the mentally ill, it created the Board for Texas State Hospitals and Special Schools and gave it supervision over state mental hospitals and state schools for handicapped children. A Youth Development Council was set up to take charge of schools for juvenile offenders. In an action long overdue, the legislators adopted an antilynching law.

During this session, state appropriations for the biennium, when supplemented by various federal grants, came to $1 billion, so the session was the first to be called a "billion-dollar legislature." Like its predecessors, the body refused to vote new taxes, and to keep expenditures within the limits of income, Governor Jester vetoed second-year appropriations for state hospitals and special schools. Two of its measures were far-reaching in effect: the modernization of the state prison system and the reorganization of the state public school system through the Gilmer-Aikin school laws.

Because of limitations brought about by the war and its aftermath, the Texas prison system, never particularly good, had deteriorated even further. The growth of the prison population—a gain of 1,000, or 29 percent, in 1946 over the preceding year—added greatly to the problems. The board secured O. B. Ellis, an experienced prison administrator, who drew a plan for rehabilitating the system. In 1949, the legislature appropriated $4.29 million for improvements; subsequent legislatures continued to improve the system.

Reorganization of the state public school system was the result of three far-reaching laws sponsored by Representative Claude Gilmer and Senator A. M. Aikin. By the end of World War II most school systems in the state had

Babe Dedrikson Zaharias. Born and reared in Texas, for more than two decades she was recognized as one of the outstanding athletes in American sports. After breaking four world records in track and field and winning acclaim in the 1932 Olympics, she went on to master a number of sports. She became a golf champion in the 1930s and continued to win tournaments in the post World War II years. Her achievements and recognition illustrate two major developments in post World War II Texas: the increasing importance of sports in the culture of the state and the increasing role of women in areas formerly considered to be for men only. (Courtesy of the Library, Lamar University)

added a twelfth year to their programs. Curriculum innovations, with increased emphasis on vocational subjects, music, and other fine arts, accelerated in the postwar years. The major problem facing public education was funding. Despite enormous increases in appropriations, Texas schools remained near the bottom of the list of state school systems.

The Gilmer-Aikin laws reorganized state school administration, established a system of minimum standards for programs, and altered the manner in which state funds for education were distributed. One law created an elective board of education with the power to appoint a commissioner and to supervise the Texas Education Agency. Another law required that all persons of school age be given a minimum of nine months of schooling each year, under teachers who met clearly defined teacher-training requirements, and in an environment conforming to specified standards. The third law established an intricate formula whereby schools were to be supported by state and local funds, with larger amounts of state aid given to poor districts.

The Gilmer-Aiken legislation had a positive effect on Texas education. It eliminated many hundreds of inoperative or "dormant" school districts, and it helped to improve school attendance. It stressed academic training for teachers, thereby encouraging thousands of teachers to enroll in college summer courses It enforced minimum salaries for teachers, and it removed much of the political pressure on the distribution of state education funds.

SHIVERS, POLITICS, AND TIDELANDS

When Governor Jester died of a heart attack on July 11, 1949, Lieutenant Governor Allan Shivers succeeded to the office. Shivers was just forty-one, but ten years in the state senate and two as lieutenant governor had seasoned him. The new governor called a special session of the legislature in 1950 to complete appropriations for the second year of the biennium.

Governor Shivers recommended additional taxes as the only way of meeting the demands for increased expenditures. "If we are going to appropriate in the spring," he said, "we must tax in the winter." Shivers pleaded for increased appropriations for hospitals to upgrade and expand facilities. Too many mentally ill people were in jails because of inadequate hospital space. The legislature responded with relatively generous appropriations for the operations of state hospitals and increased taxes slightly.

The Fifty-second Legislature, which met in 1951, discovered that additional taxes were needed. Two agencies worked on the budget for that year: the Board of Control, which had handled budget issues for years, and the newly created Legislative Budget Board. Both agreed that additional revenue must be found. Again the general tax rate was increased, and a tax on natural gas pipelines was added. However, the courts ruled that the transport of natural gas was interstate commerce and could not be taxed by the states.

The Fifty-Second Legislature also enacted the first law in thirty years that redrew the boundaries for legislative districts, shifting some political power from rural areas to the rapidly growing towns and cities. Another act, which aroused much criticism, required safety inspections for automobiles and required that drivers establish that they had sufficient resources to cover any damage they might do to others.

More and more, politics in Texas was dominated by national and international issues and by growing conflict between state and federal interests. Conservative Texas Democrats became increasingly critical of President Truman. Charges of corruption and the communist infiltration were hurled at his administration, and many second-guessed his policies in the Korean War. But it was Truman's tidelands policies that generated the most criticism among Texans.

The tidelands referred to the areas immediately off the coast of the states. The controversy involved the ownership of these undersea lands, which were believed to be rich in oil deposits. Initially almost everyone concurred that the states owned their tidelands, but in 1937 Secretary of the Interior Harold Ickes formally challenged the states' claims. In August 1947, the Supreme Court of the United States held that the state of California did not have the right to exploit its tidelands through oil leases and other means because the federal government had "paramount right and power" over this domain. In 1950, the Court by a vote of four to three (two not voting) handed down a similar decision against Texas. For Texas, the decision was a serious loss. Leasing of these lands for oil and gas development was under way, and already the state had collected nearly $10 million in lease bonuses. President Truman had vetoed acts of Congress in 1946 and 1952 that attempted to return control of the tidelands to the states.

For many Texans the subject of the tidelands became the paramount issue in the 1952 presidential election. The debate over the issue split the Democratic Party and delivered the state to the Republican presidential nominee. The split began when Adlai Stevenson, the Democratic nominee for president, refused to support state claims to the tidelands. Conservative Democrats led by Governor Shivers maintained control of the party organization and refused to support Stevenson in the election. Governor Shivers openly endorsed Eisenhower and turned over the machinery of the Democrats for the Republican presidential race in Texas. Liberal Democrats bolted the party and supported Stevenson. Two million Texans voted that November, the greatest turnout the state had known. Eisenhower carried the state by a majority of over 100,000, winning the second Republican victory in Texas within a quarter of a century. Governor Shivers was easily renominated that year over his chief opponent, the liberal judge Ralph Yarborough. Attorney General Price Daniel defeated Congressman Lindly Beckworth, a liberal Democrat, for the U.S. Senate seat held by the retiring Tom Connally. The divisive tidelands issue was finally resolved when in 1953 President Eisenhower signed a quitclaim bill restoring the tidelands to state ownership and extending ownership to "historic limits." For Texas and the west coast of Florida, where the rule of Spanish law still prevailed, "historic limits" meant three Spanish leagues or about ten and a half miles.

The 1952 elections reflected significant changes that were surfacing in Texas politics. The clash between liberal and conservative Democrats would continue over the next several decades, strengthened by the controversies surrounding civil rights and the emergence of African American and Mexican American political power. Eisenhower's victory in the presidential race was due in part to the personal popularity of the war hero, but it also signaled the growing strength of the Republican Party in Texas, at least in national elections. Hoover's success in the 1928 election was an early sign of this development, but its growth was forestalled by the Great Depression and the political success of Roosevelt and the New Deal. As the demographics of Texas changed, particularly through the in-migration of residents from the North and Midwest, as urbanization and suburbanization increased, and as racial and ethnic minorities asserted political power, old political coalitions would crumble, and the Republican Party would become increasingly competitive. One-party rule in Texas was slowly coming to an end.

SCANDALS AND REFORM:
POLITICS IN THE FIFTIES

In the turmoil of the 1960s and 1970s, some observers looked back to the 1950s with the nostalgic conviction that the decade was tranquil and complacent, with scarcely a dispute in sight to mar the peace of the day. Actually, the 1950s were neither tranquil nor complacent. A Communist "scare" began the decade, African Americans and Mexican Americans launched their struggle for equal rights, and in the second half of the decade, political scandal outraged voters and wrecked many political careers.

Tensions and frustrations in foreign affairs and fears of subversion at home resulted in a sensational and sometimes less than responsible search for Communists, socialists, and their sympathizers. Texas shared in this "Red Scare," often termed "McCarthyism" because its chief instigator was Wisconsin Senator Joseph McCarthy. McCarthy dominated the headlines by applying the label "Communist" to a wide variety of people. In Texas his supporters included right-wing extremists, who were prepared to believe almost anything about almost anybody and who made similar charges, and more moderate groups whose fear of subversion may or may not have been justified but certainly was real.

Except for the legislative requirement of loyalty oaths for public employees, Red Scare politics had little effect on state affairs, but in local politics there were often consequences. Agitated interests demanded that libraries be purged of books sympathetic to communism, that educators suspected of socialist tendencies be fired, and that speakers of dubious loyalty be silenced. Such groups were particularly active in larger cities such as Houston, San Antonio, and Dallas, but smaller communities also experienced their crusades. One Communist among the approximately 60,000 schoolteachers of Texas was discovered and discharged, but not much else was accomplished. By the mid-1950s most of the more extreme evidences of the fear had disappeared, though the ubiquitous loyalty oaths would linger in government agencies and public schools for many years to come.

In two areas, political rights and school desegregation, African Americans in the 1950s made significant progress toward the attainment of their civil rights. The expansion of African American political power came more easily than did the integration of the schools. Following the 1944 decision in *Smith* v. *Allwright*, political barriers fell fairly quickly. Some resistance by white citizens lingered, but black voters became numerous in the late 1940s. The first significant electoral victory came in 1956 when Hattie Mae White was elected to the Houston School Board. By 1958, more than one-third of the potential black voters of the state were registered; in comparison, almost one-half of the potential white voters were registered. In some areas of the state, however, as much as 70 percent of the eligible black population registered to vote.

Desegregation of the state's schools was another matter. Here progress was slow and often painful. Again, Houston's NAACP chapter teamed with Thurgood Marshall and the national NAACP to direct the attack. In 1947, in a carefully planned assault on segregation in higher education, Heman Sweatt applied for admission to the law school at the University of Texas. When his application was denied, the NAACP filed suit. The state of Texas attempted to undermine the suit by creating a black law school as part of the newly created Texas State College for Negroes (later renamed Texas Southern University) in Houston. This ploy failed, and in 1950 the Supreme Court ruled in *Sweatt v. Painter* that "separate but equal" was inherently unequal, at least in professional education, and it directed the University of Texas to admit Sweatt to its law school. Far more sweeping was the 1954 decision in *Brown v. Board of Education of Topeka*. Basing its opinion squarely on the Fourteenth Amendment, which guarantees to all persons the equal protection of the laws, the Court held that even if the schools that were maintained by the state for blacks were in every respect just as good as those for whites, segregation itself deprived the children of the minority group of equal educational opportunities. It concluded "that in the field of public education the doctrine of separate but equal has no place." Instead of ordering immediate desegregation, the court directed the lower federal courts to implement the ruling "with all deliberate speed." This process dragged on for decades.

Reaction to the *Brown* decision divided Texans along racial lines. Polls reflected four-to-one opposition in the white community and two-to-one support in the black community. Tensions began to build. Though Governor Shivers left little doubt of his opposition to the decision, his stand, on the whole, was not as adamant as that of some southern leaders. In his bid for an unprecedented third term, Shivers became involved in a bitter primary campaign against liberal Democrat Ralph Yarborough. The primary occurred in the immediate aftermath of the *Brown* decision, and race and segregation figured prominently. As the race tightened, Shivers used race-baiting tactics, accusing his opponent of advocating complete integration. Shivers was renominated and reelected. When voters went to the polls for the July 1956 Democratic primary, they also found three segregation issues on the ballot: a measure favoring stronger laws against racial intermarriage, a law exempting white students from attending integrated schools, and a law authorizing state action to block federally mandated desegregation of local schools. The voters approved all three measures. Here and there in the fall of 1956 there were threats of violence as the schools opened. In Mansfield near Fort Worth, attempts of black stu-

Texas Rangers at Mansfield High School. In the fall of 1956 Mansfield High School near Fort Worth became the first school in Texas to attempt to comply with the 1954 *Brown* decision. When segregationists threatened violence, Governor Allan Shivers sent in the Texas Rangers and prevented African American children from attending the school. The black figure hanging in effigy was placed above the school entrance on August 31 and remained there for several days. (Texas State Library & Archives Commission)

dents to attend the local school under a federal court order brought a threat of mob action, and Governor Shivers sent in Texas Rangers to restore order. No violence occurred, but the black students were not allowed to enroll. Integration proceeded peacefully in some other districts, with more than 120 carrying out at least some integration by the 1957 school term.

Integration of colleges generated less opposition. Del Mar Junior College in Corpus Christi desegregated in 1952, followed by the University of Texas and Southern Methodist University in 1955. A mob of outsiders sought to prevent blacks from entering Lamar State College of Technology in Beaumont in 1956, but without success, though a similar mob had succeeded in its efforts the previous year at Texarkana Junior College. By 1958, approximately two-thirds of the colleges and universities of Texas had integrated their classes. In 1964 and 1965 Rice University and the University of Texas integrated their faculty, and in 1965 the University of Texas desegregated its dorms and the Southwest Conference integrated its athletic competition.

Opposition to integration did not die easily. In response to the July 1956 referendum supporting segregation, in 1957 the legislature passed a law making mandatory the assent of the voters of any school district before the races could be mixed in the schools. The penalty provided was the withdrawal of all state aid for the district. In reaction to the desegregation crisis at Little Rock, the legislature approved another law, which closed any public school at which troops were stationed. But legislation against integration had little effect. Governor Price Daniel, elected in 1956, made no effort to interpose state authority against the federal agencies charged with carrying out the judicial decrees, and the legislative acts were quickly declared unconstitutional. Ultimately federal judges, by the authority of the Supreme Court of the United States, ordered each local school district to present plans for desegregation..

Mexican Americans also made progress in the 1950s in their struggle for civil rights. Although not subjected to the legal discrimination that confronted blacks, Tejanos nevertheless were denied equal rights and economic opportunities. Organized efforts to combat such discrimination began early in the century and picked up momentum after World War I. In the post-World War II period, the G. I. Forum and LULAC provided the leadership in expanding Mexican American political consciousness and political involvement. After their successful challenge of school segregation in Texas in 1948, LULAC won a 1951 decision that outlawed the exclusion of Mexican Americans from juries. In 1957 LULAC national president Félix Tijerina of Houston introduced his barrio preschool program, "The Little Schools of 400." This project was endorsed by the legislature in 1959 and became the model for President Johnson's Head Start program in the 1960s. The G.I. Forum's voter education and voter registration projects, begun in the late 1940s, began to bear fruit in the 1950s. In 1956 San Antonio voters elected Henry B. González to the state senate; in 1961 González would be the first of several Tejanos to win a seat in Congress.

Shivers's third term in office (1955–57) was his most troubled. He had weathered the civil rights storm and handled taxes fairly well, but corruption linked to the insurance industry would undermine his political reputation. Texas insurance laws were lax and long had left the door open for fly-by-night promoters and operators. Failures of insurance companies, never uncommon, became more frequent after World War II. In 1955, Lieutenant Governor Ben Ramsey reminded the lawmakers that during the previous ten years eighty-six Texas insurance companies had failed, largely because of an inadequate insurance code. In response, the legislature enacted twenty-two laws on the subject, providing for more effective regulation and placing the sale of insurance stock under the board of insurance commissioners.

Bankruptcies continued, however. The most significant was the collapse of the United Services Trust and Guaranty Company, a concern that controlled some seventy-four insurance and finance companies in twenty-two states and Alaska. Consequently, in 1957 the lawmakers complied with the governor's request that he be authorized to appoint an entirely new insurance commission, and they enacted additional insurance legislation. Meanwhile, Texas insurance companies were subjected to audit. As a result more than a hundred firms lost their permits to do business in the state. Among the irregularities uncovered was an unwholesome relationship between certain Texas lawmakers and some insurance companies. For example, nine members of the Texas Senate had received legal fees or other income from the United Services Trust and Guaranty Company.

In the midst of the unfolding insurance scandal, the conflict between the conservative and liberal wings of the Democratic Party intensified. The liberals, those loyal to the national Democratic organization, controlled the Democratic state presidential convention in 1956, but Governor Shivers again refused to support Adlai Stevenson, the Democratic nominee. Instead, he again campaigned for the reelection of President Eisenhower. Eisenhower carried the state by a majority almost double that of four years before. That same year Senator Price Daniel became a candidate for governor, running against Ralph Yarborough and a field of other candidates. Yarborough had the support of organized labor and a majority of the liberal Democrats. In the contest he charged Daniel, along with Shivers, with responsibility for irregularities and fraud in the work of the veterans' land board, of which Daniel and Shivers were ex-officio members. Reports of these brought investigations by grand juries and senate and house committees. Bascom Giles, commissioner of the General Land Office, who had just been elected to his ninth term, was sent to the penitentiary for six years on charges of misrepresentation and perjury. By a small margin, Daniel defeated Yarborough for governor in the runoff. Yarborough subsequently was elected to the U.S. Senate to take the seat Daniel had vacated to become governor.

The Fifty-fifth Legislature in 1957 worked under trying conditions. It was disclosed that many legislators were employed more or less regularly by corporations, some of which maintained very active lobbies in Austin. Charges of bribery were hurled freely, and one representative who resigned in the face of the charge was convicted in court. The legislature adopted annual budgets of well beyond $1 billion, and voters approved constitutional amendments liberalizing retirement benefits for state employees and increasing the state's share in pensions to the aged.

The final years of the 1950s offered hope to liberal Democrats and disappointment to aspiring Republicans. Encouraged by the election of Ralph Yarborough to the Senate, liberal Democrats under the leadership of. R. D. ("Frankie") Randolph of Houston, a Democratic national committeewoman, and Jerry Holleman, president of the Texas A.F.L.-C.I.O. organized the "Democrats of Texas" (DOT). Among the list of demands they made of the party were abolition of the poll tax, greater liberal representation in party affairs, and loyalty to the national Democratic Party. Joined by other liberals in 1958, the DOT gave Yarborough a decisive victory over his conservative oppo-

Lyndon Baines Johnson. The second United States President born in Texas (Dwight D. Eisenhower was the first), Lyndon Baines Johnson made his home state the base for a long and distinguished political career. Elected to Congress in 1937, to the Senate in 1948, to the vice-presidency in 1960, he became president when John F. Kennedy was assassinated and was elected for the next term in 1964. The University of Texas awarded him a degree as a distinguished American statesman as well as the state's most illustrious citizen of the day. After deciding not to seek reelection, Johnson returned to Texas in 1969 where he lived quietly until his death in 1973. (Library of Congress)

nent, William A. Blakley, in the Democratic senatorial primary. Yarborough was elected in November. In contrast, Governor Price Daniel, generally regarded as a moderate conservative, was continued in office by a generous margin, and he dominated the Democratic state convention. Republican hopes for electoral success following President Eisenhower's large margin in 1956 did not materialize. The party elected only one congressman in 1958, Bruce Alger of Dallas.

As the decade drew to a close, the outstanding feature in Democratic circles was the presidential candidacy of Lyndon Baines Johnson, the Texan who was serving as Majority Leader in the U.S. Senate. Johnson had the endorsement of most of the state's prominent Democrats, including Sam Rayburn, the powerful Speaker of the House of Representatives, and Governor Price Daniel. To promote Johnson's candidacy, the legislature moved the party primaries up to May and changed the convention system so that Senator Johnson's name could appear on the ballot as both the incumbent candidate for senator and as a candidate for president.

THE ELECTION OF 1960 AND THE EMERGING REPUBLICAN PARTY

Texas politics in 1960, rarely simple in the post-World War II years, was more complicated than usual. In his race for a third term as governor, Price Daniel easily defeated his more conservative Democratic opponent, Jack Cox, and was elected in November with little opposition. Liberal Democrats gained a few seats in the legislature. The complicating element in the election was the dual candidacy of Senator Lyndon B. Johnson. Johnson had hopes of securing the Democratic presidential nomination, but he had no intention of giving up his Senate seat should he fail in his presidential bid.

The Senate race was much closer than the contest over the governorship. Republican hopes rested on a young professor at Midwestern University, John Tower. Johnson's vote of 1,306,625 was sufficient to win reelection, but Tower's vote was surprisingly large. Resentment of Johnson's dual candidacy may have accounted in part for the vote, but Republican strength was also increasing.

Senator Johnson campaigned energetically for the Democratic presidential nomination. He relied heavily on the political strength and prestige of Texas Speaker of the House Sam Rayburn, and his supporters emphasized his experience in government, his leadership in the Senate, and the youth and inexperience of his leading opponent, Senator John F. Kennedy. But when the Democratic National Convention met in Los Angeles in 1960, the Johnson campaign for the presidency ended quickly. Johnson got only 409 delegate votes, mainly from the South, and Kennedy was nominated on the first ballot. Kennedy, very aware that the Republicans had carried Texas in the last two presidential elections, selected Johnson as his running mate.

Relative harmony prevailed among the Republicans. The state party organization centered its efforts on carrying Texas for Republican presidential candidate Richard M. Nixon. Republican efforts were supported by some conservative Democrats, such as former governor Allan Shivers, who campaigned for the Nixon ticket.

Texas was a pivotal state, with twenty-four electoral votes, and an electorate divided rather evenly. Both parties had strong organizations in the state, and neither candidate ignored Texas. Significantly, the campaign galvanized both the Mexican American and African American communities. "Viva Kennedy" clubs mobilized Tejano voters in the 1960 election, while the Democrat's strong civil rights platform and Kennedy's personal interest in the fate of the jailed Martin Luther King brought record numbers of blacks to the polls. There was a record turnout in November, with the Kennedy-Johnson ticket carrying Texas by only 24,019 votes—a margin of victory that clearly was the result of the black and Mexican American vote. The Democratic margin on the national level also was exceedingly close. By slightly more than 100,000 votes, Kennedy and Johnson were elected.

Despite their losses in the election of 1960, Texas Republicans were encouraged. Nixon and Lodge had polled the greatest Republican vote in Texas in history. Party workers set out immediately to increase their strength in the state legislature and in Congress. Perhaps the most significant political development to come out of the election was the 1961 election of Republican John Tower to the Senate seat vacated by Lyndon Johnson. Tower was the first Republican to win statewide election since Reconstruction. His victory was the first clear sign that the Republican Party was becoming a serious contender for political power in Texas. In 1962, the Republicans gained a second congressman and several house seats in the legislature, six of them from Dallas districts.

The gubernatorial election of 1962 offered additional evidence of a growing Republican Party. Within the Democratic camp there were a number of candidates seeking the nomination. Price Daniel sought a fourth term; Houston attorney Don Yarborough represented the liberal faction of the party; John B. Connally, who had close ties with Lyndon Johnson, claimed support from both conservatives and moderates; and there were others. Connally suffered to some extent from charges that he was running as the "Johnson candidate," but he won the Democratic nomination in a runoff with Yarborough, possibly because his promise to appoint blacks to state positions executives won him their votes. In the general election in the fall he defeated Jack Cox, a conservative Democrat turned Republican, but Cox polled almost 46 percent of the vote.

Cox's promising showing in the gubernatorial race and a few other victories raised hopes in Republican ranks, but internal dissension began to weaken the party in Texas. Many conservative Democrats switched to the Republican Party, which may help to explain a noticeable tendency toward the extreme right. Though an extremely conservative political philosophy appealed to some Republicans, other Republicans were uncomfortable with it. Moreover, some Democrats who were getting into the habit of voting for Republicans found right-wing extremism distasteful. In both parties, dissension and tension would increase as the 1960s unfolded.

BIBLIOGRAPHY

Literature on the involvement of Texas and Texans in World War II is relatively scarce, but a number of studies have been published in recent years. Dealing with the homefront, there are Louis Fairchild, *They Called It the War Effort: Oral Histories from WWII, Orange, Texas* (Austin, 1993); Joyce Gibson Roach, (ed.), *Collective Heart: Texans in World War II* (Austin, 1996); James Lee Wood et al., *Texas Goes to War* (Denton, 1991); Clarice F. Pollard, "WAACs in Texas During the Second World War," *Southwestern Historical Quarterly*, XCIII, 61–74; Arnold P. Kranamer, "When the Afrika Corps Came to Texas," *Southwestern Historical Quarterly*, XCIII, 61–74; L. Patrick Hughes, "To Meet Fire with Fire: Lyndon Johnson, Tom Miller, and Home-Front Politics," *Southwestern Historical Quarterly*, C, 453–476; and Melanie Wiggins, *Torpedoes in the Gulf: Galveston and the U-Boats* (College Station, 1995).

Racial issues dealing with the homefront are presented in Henry Bullock, "Some Readjustments of the Texas Negro Family to the Emergency of War," *Southwestern Social Science Quarterly*, XXV, 100–117; James Olson and Sharon Phair, "The Anatomy of a Race Riot: Beaumont, Texas, 1943," *Texana*, II, 64–72; and "Violence in an 'Arsenal of Democracy': The Beaumont Race Riot, 1943," *East Texas Historical Journal*, XIV, 39–51; and Emilio Zamora, "The Failed Promise of Wartime Opportunity for Mexicans in the Texas Oil Industry," ibid., XCV, 323–350.

The story of Texans on the battlefront is related in *The Infantry Journal*, March 1944, an account of the Thirty-Sixth Division (Paris, France, 1944); Lee Carraway

Smith, *A River Swift and Deadly: The 36th "Texas" Infantry Division at the Rapido River* (Austin, 1989); Major James E. Taylor, "The Thirty-Sixth Division at Salerno," *Southwestern Historical Quarterly*, XLVIII, 281–285; and Robert L. Wagner, *The Texas Army: A History of the Thirty-Sixth Division in the Italian Campaign* (Austin, 1972). Also see Robert L. Wagner, "The Odyssey of a Texas Citizen Soldier," *Southwestern Historical Quarterly*, LXXII, 40–87; Ronald E. Marcello, "Lone Star POWs: Texas National Guardsmen and the Building of the Burma-Thailand Railroad, 1942–1944," ibid., XCV, 292–321; and Philip Ardery, *Bomber Pilot: A Memoir of World War II* (Lexington, Ky., 1978).

Politics of the era are considered in George Norris Green, *The Establishment in Texas Politics*; James R. Soukup, Clifton McCleskey, and Harry Holloway, *Party and Factional Division in Texas* (Austin, 1964); Sam Kinch and Stuart Long, *Allan Shivers: The Pied Piper of Texas Politics* (Austin, 1974); Robert Dallek, *Lone Star Rising: Lyndon Johnson and His Times, 1908–1960* (New York, 1991); Anthony Champagne, *Congressman Sam Rayburn* (New Brunswick, 1984); and Irvin M. May, Jr., *Marvin Jones* (College Station, 1980). Kenneth Hendrickson, Jr. and Michael L. Collins's collection, *Profiles in Power: Twentieth Century Texans in Washington* (Arlington Heights, Ill., 1995),contains essays on Tom Connolly, Sam Rayburn, and Lyndon Baines Johnson.

For a discussion of the relationship between politics and business see Joseph A. Pratt and Christopher J. Castaneda, *Builders: Herman and George R. Brown* (College Station, 1999); and Don E. Carleton, *A Breed So Rare: The Life of J. R. Parten, Liberal Texas Oil Man, 1896–1992* (Austin, 1999); for accounts of the tidelands and the issues involved, see Ernest R. Bartley, *The Tidelands Oil Controversy* (Austin, 1953).

The post-World War II Red Scare is discussed by Don E. Carleton, *Red Scare! Right-Wing Hysteria, Fifties Fanticism, and Their Legacy in Texas* (Austin, 1985), and "McCarthyism in Houston: The George Ebey Affair," *Southwestern Historical Quarterly*, LXXX, 163–176. A political and economic issue of the time is discussed by Johnny M. McCain, "Texas and the Mexican Labor Question, 1942–1947," *Southwestern Historical Quarterly*, LXXXV, 45–64.

Some sources on education in Texas are C. E. Evans, *The Story of Texas Schools* (Austin, 1955); James T. Taylor, "Gilmer-Aikin Program and State Finances," *East Texas*, January 1950, 9; Kate S. Kirkland, "For All Houston's Children: Ima Hogg and the Board of Education, 1943–1949," *Southwestern Historical Quarterly*, CI, 461–495; Texas Research League, *Texas Public Schools under the Minimum Foundation Program, An Evaluation, 1949–1954*. Delightful reading is Joe B. Frantz, *The Forty-Acre Follies* (Austin, 1983).

In connection with scandals in insurance, see The Texas Legislative Council, "Insolvency in the Texas Insurance Industry; Insurance, Texas' Frauds and Failures," *Time*, May 31, 1954, 64; "Those Texas Scandals," *The Saturday Evening Post*, November 12, 1955, 19ff; D. B. Hardeman, "Shivers of Texas: A Tragedy in Three Acts," *Harper's*, November 1956, 50–56; and Ronnie Dugger, "What Corrupted Texas?" *Harper's*, March 1957, 58–78.

A number of studies focus on Mexican American issues in the post-World War II period. See David Montejano, *Anglos and Texans in the Making of Texas*; Carl Allsup, *The American G. I. Forum: Origins and Evolution* (Austin, 1982), and "Education Is Our Freedom: The American G. I. Forum and the Mexican-American School Segregation in Texas, 1948–1957," *Aztlán*, VIII, 27–50; and Guadalupe San Miguel, Jr., *"Let All of Them Take Heed": Mexican Americans and the Campaign for Educational Equality in Texas, 1910–1981* (Austin, 1987). See also Chandler Davidson, *Race and Class in Texas Politics* (Princeton, 1990).

On developments in African American history, Alwyn Barr, *Black Texans*, 2nd ed. (Norman, 1996), is very useful and reliable, but also see Norman V. Bartley, *The Rise of Massive Resistance: Race and Politics in the South During the 1950's* (Baton Rouge,

1969); William H. Wilson, "Desegregation of the Hamilton Park School, 1955–1970," *Southwestern Historical Quarterly*, XCV, 43–63; Darlene Clark Hine, "The Elusive Ballot: The Black Struggle against the Texas Democratic White Primary, 1932–1945," *Southwestern Historical Quarterly*, LXXXI, 371–392; "Blacks and the Destruction of the Democratic White Primary, 1935–1944," *Journal of Negro History*, LXII, 43–59; and *Black Victory: The Rise and Fall of the White Primary in Texas* (Millwood, N.Y., 1979); Michael Gillette, "The Rise of the NAACP in Texas," *Southwestern Historical Quarterly*, LXXXI, 393–416. Merline Pitre, *In Struggle against Jim Crow: Lulu B. White and the NAACP, 1900–1957* (College Station, 1999), examines women in the leadership of the early struggle for civil rights.

A number of studies have examined the desegregation of education in Texas during the 1940s and 1950s, including "Blacks Challenge the White University," *Southwestern Historical Quarterly*, LXXXVI, 321–344; Ronald E. Marcelo, "Reluctance versus Reality: The Desegregation of North Texas State College, 1954–1956," *Southwestern Historical Quarterly*, C, 153–185; Richard B. McCaslin, "Steadfast in His Intent: John W. Hargis and the Integration of the University of Texas at Austin," *Southwestern Historical Quarterly*, XCV, 32–41; Lewis L. Gould and Melissa R. Sneed, "Without Pride or Apology: The University of Texas at Austin, Racial Integration, and the Barbara Smith Case," *Southwestern Historical Quarterly*, CIII, 67–87; Robyn Duff Ladino, *Desegregating Texas Schools: Eisenhower, Shivers, and the Crisis at Mansfield High* (Austin, 1996); William Henry Keller, *Make Haste Slowly: Moderates, Conservatives, and School Desegregation in Houston* (College Station, 1999), and Glen Linden, *Desegregating Schools in Dallas* (Dallas, 1995).

19

Politics of an Urban Land 1962–2000

The final decades of the twentieth century saw significant changes in the public affairs of Texas. In many instances, public issues appeared similar to those of earlier times, but often there were fundamental differences. The existing "political" power structure was challenged by both new political coalitions and newly politicized groups. Women and minorities gained a greater political voice and increased their participation in the decision-making processes. Officials confronted an electorate that was at the very least more unpredictable than it had been in pre-World War II years. As the century came to a close, the monopoly that the Democrats had held in politics for over a century gave way to a competitive two-party system.

THE DYNAMICS OF POLITICAL CHANGE _____

A number of forces contributed to the changes in the political affairs of Texas in the final years of the century. One of the primary influences was the increased role that the federal government played in state and local affairs. The New Deal greatly expanded the role of the national government prior to World War II. More programs and more regulations were added after World War II, and the 1960s, 1970s, and 1980s saw even more. Most activities of the federal government involved either regulatory functions or financial support, or a combination of both.

A number of agencies carried on investigations to determine compliance with federal law and judicial decrees. Many of these stemmed from the civil rights legislation of the 1960s, with added emphasis in the 1980s and 1990s on protection of the disabled and the elderly, equal access to public services like education, and upgrading conditions in the state's prisons. Acting under the authority of the Voting Rights Act of 1965, as amended in 1975, the Civil Rights Division of the Justice Department supervised election practices and approved or disapproved any changes in voting procedures. A federal court in January 1992 declared an act of the Texas legislature's legislative redistricting plan to be unconstitutional and substituted a court redistricting plan. Federal court rulings concerning prison conditions and the funding of public education also required significant and costly changes in state programs and procedures.

Financial support was the other area in which the federal government loomed large in Texas. Although the level of support declined somewhat from that of the 1970s, federal funds in the early 1990s provided more than 20 percent of the monies spent by the state government. Welfare costs in 1990, administered primarily through the Texas Department of Human Resources, required more than 18 percent of the state's budget, but federal funds supplied about 70 percent of the need. More than 30 percent of the monies spent on highways and transportation came from federal sources. In addition, there were large sums parceled out through special grants to cities and other governmental units.

Ethnic and racial minorities assumed more and more active political roles after World War II. The increased political influence of minorities reflected both the changing political and social mores and changing demographics. The minority population of Texas—African Americans, Mexican Americans, and a growing Asian American community—comprised almost 45 percent of the population by 1998, and this "minority" was projected to make up a majority of the population by early in the next century. Supported by legislation and judicial rulings protecting their right to participate, Mexican American and African American Texans exercised considerable power in state and local politics by the 1980s. The election of African Americans, Mexican Americans, and more recently, Asian Americans to political office was only one indication of the growing influence of minorities; equally significant was the increasing recognition of their interests and potential power by both political parties.

Equally significant in the evolution of politics in Texas was the development of a viable Republican Party. The emergence of two-party politics, which began in the 1950s, grew steadily during the next three decades, and by the end of the 1990s not only was the two-party system a reality, but the Republicans controlled most of the power in the state government.

The transformation of Texas to an urbanized society effected all these changes. Although a majority of people lived in urban areas prior to World War II, the political and social impact of this change was not truly felt until later decades. Relatively few Texans in the 1990s had any experience with rural life or the problems associated with such an existence. Consequently, Texans at the end of the century were preoccupied with problems of urban life.

THE 1960S: THE JOHNSON AND CONNALLY YEARS

Tragedy in Texas on November 22, 1963, profoundly affected the course of public affairs in Texas—indeed, throughout the world. While the people of Dallas and of the state were receiving President John Kennedy with enthusiasm, a hidden assassin shot and killed him and seriously wounded Governor John Connally, who was riding with him. Within two hours after the death of President Kennedy, Lyndon Baines Johnson, a native Texan, took the oath of office and became the thirty-sixth president of the United States. As president, Johnson was able to control if not eliminate the

The Johnsons and the Kennedys. The Kennedys and Johnsons had dinner together in Fort Worth on November 21, 1963, the night before the assassination. Kennedy and Johnson had come to Texas to try to resolve the deepening conflict between liberal and conservative Democrats in the state. (Texas State Library and Archives Commission)

factionalism that threatened to split the Texas Democratic Party, but the relationship between Senator Ralph Yarborough, Texas's most prominent liberal Democrat, and Governor Connally remained cool. In the Democratic primaries of 1964, Connally was easily renominated for another term, and in the election he defeated his Republican opponent, George Bush. Connally's control of the Democratic state convention was complete, and the delegation was sent to the national convention in Atlantic City with instructions to "put forth every effort" to secure Johnson's nomination. Johnson was nominated with ease.

Although the Republican candidate, Barry Goldwater, visited Texas six times during the campaign, and Republicans worked hard otherwise, Johnson's strength proved invincible. Even former Governor Allan Shivers supported the Johnson ticket. Out of a record vote of over 2.5 million, the Republicans received less than 1 million votes.

Governor Connally was a determined leader in his first term, and his near martyrdom in the Kennedy assassination, his successful reelection, and his friendship with President Johnson strengthened his political authority in his second term. State finances, usually a major problem for both governor and legislature, were not as much of an issue during these years. After much wrangling between liberals who wanted additional taxes on business and conservatives who favored some form of a sales tax, the legislature in 1961 had adopted a sales tax. Governor Daniel, who opposed a sales tax, nevertheless allowed it to become law without his signature. The tax, with some additional levies adopted during Connally's first term, gave the state a firm financial base. When additional funds were needed, the sales tax was increased.

Two changes in the electoral process during these years had far-reaching implications. In compliance with the mandates of federal judicial decrees, the legislature redistricted the state, drawing new boundaries for the election of members of the state legislature and for the U.S. House of Representatives. Most agreed that redistricting would diminish the influence of rural areas in the government but disagreed about whether Republicans or liberal Democrats would benefit most from the changes. In another issue, federal courts ruled in 1966 that the poll tax was unconstitutional. The legislature quickly abolished the poll tax. While both of these actions had the potential to favor liberal candidates by increasing the political influence of minorities and the urban poor, their immediate impact on state politics is difficult to measure. In the election of 1966 Governor Connally, who had kept his promise to appoint blacks to positions in his administration, was elected overwhelmingly for a third term, and other conservative candidates fared well.

The outlook of Texas politics was changed greatly in 1968 when both Governor Connally and President Johnson announced that they would not seek reelection. Ten candidates sought the Democratic nomination for governor, and nearly 2 million voters took part in the primary. Lieutenant Governor Preston Smith, a conservative, and Don Yarborough, a well-known liberal, entered the runoff. Results were disappointing to the liberals. The "new voters" they had counted on either did not vote or split their vote. Smith won with 756,909 votes to Yarborough's 620,726. In November Smith defeated Paul Eggars, the Republican nominee, by a comfortable margin.

In national politics the Democratic convention in Chicago nominated Vice President Hubert Humphrey for president on the first ballot. Texas Republicans united in support of Richard Nixon. George C. Wallace, former governor of Alabama campaigning primarily on an anti-civil rights platform, ran as the candidate of the new American Party. The Democrats carried Texas by a close vote, and, by an even narrower margin, Nixon carried the nation. Wallace's vote in Texas was relatively small.

THE STRUGGLE FOR CIVIL RIGHTS

The civil rights movement, building upon the gains of the 1950s, added momentum in the 1960s. When the decade opened, the right to vote already was won and beginning to have an impact on Texas politics. In addition, the issue of school segregation was resolved, at least in the courts if not in the classroom. Discrimination and socioeconomic inequities persisted. Across the nation, the demands that the inequities of society be addressed became more militant, and by the mid-1960s national attention seemed focused on this issue. Texas, with one-third or more of its population either African American or Mexican American, was deeply affected by this struggle.

Although their interests and the problems that they faced were not dissimilar, there was rarely much cooperation between blacks and Mexican Americans. Blacks concentrated their activities in urban areas, particularly in Houston and Dallas; Mexican Americans, though increasingly urban, still focused much of their attention on the plight of agricultural workers and Tejano communities in south Texas. Long-established organizations like the NAACP, LULAC, and the GI Forum continued their campaign for equal rights, but much of the activity, especially the more dramatic and militant activity, was directed by new, often grassroots organizations. Among Mexican Americans, a wide variety of organizations, many of them formed in the 1960s and 1970s, reflected basic differences over the proper approach for solving the problems of discrimination and inequality. Some called themselves Chicanos, asserting the distinctiveness of their culture and rejecting that of the Anglos. Some Chicanos, though not all, were militant in their demands and in effect advocated a form of separatism. Other Mexican Americans rejected both the name Chicano and the idea of militancy, preferring to work "within the system."

In the early 1960s the civil rights movement in Texas focused on desegregating public facilities. Stimulated by the February 1960 student sit-ins in Greensboro, North Carolina, on March 4, 1960, Texas Southern University students launched their own sit-in movement in Houston, targeting the lunch counter at the Weingarten's supermarket near the campus. In the months that followed, nonviolent protests spread to other lunch counters, the city hall cafeteria, and the dining facilities at the railroad and bus stations; movie theaters, hotels, and restaurants were the next targets. The demonstrations in Houston remained peaceful. There were few incidents of white resistance. Instead, black community leaders and white business and political leaders moved to quietly dismantle segregation in public facilities. By the end of May 1963 the battle in Houston was won.

Barbara Jordan. Barbara Jordan became the first African American woman elected to the Texas Legislature. Her historic election to the Texas Senate in 1966 (along with the election of two black collegues to the state house of representatives) signaled the return of African Americans to positions in state government. In this photograph Senator Jordan, along with Senator Chet Brooks and Speaker Gus Mutscher, is greeting fellow Houstonian and Apollo astronaut Neil Armstrong as he is presented the Texas Medal of Valor on October 17, 1970.

In Dallas, Austin, San Antonio, Lubbock, Denton, and other Texas cities black and white students challenged the Jim Crow system with similar results. Though the movement was undoubtedly influenced by similar events occurring across the South, the leadership in Texas was local—students, black community leaders, and white business leaders guided events with little or no support from national civil rights organizations. By the time the 1964 Civil Rights Act passed Congress, public facilities in Houston and most other Texas cities already had been peacefully desegregated.

With the barriers to suffrage eliminated, both minorities launched campaigns to secure the election of their people to public offices, particularly to the legislature. In 1961 only two members of the state senate and five members of the house of representatives were Mexican Americans, and none were black. In 1966 Texas voters elected the first African Americans to the legislature since 1900. Houston voters elected Barbara Jordan to the state senate, while Curtis Graves of Houston and Joseph E. Lockridge of Dallas were elected to the house. Jordan served in the senate from 1967 to 1973; then in 1973 she became the first black ever to represent Texas in the U.S. Congress. She served in Congress until 1979 and won national acclaim for her role during the Nixon impeachment hearings. Meanwhile, with the support of a number of organizations on both the state and the local levels, minority candidates entered more contests, and the number of minority office holders in the legislature steadily increased. By 1999, the Texas House of Representatives included fourteen African Americans and twenty-eight Mexican Americans. Seven Mexican Americans and two African Americans served in the state senate. Two African Americans and six Mexican Americans held posts in the U.S. Congress.

Local politics also felt the impact of the civil rights movement. In a dramatic and hostile contest in South Texas in 1963, Mexican Americans won control of the Crystal City town government. The election focused on racial discrimination, and victory encouraged similar efforts elsewhere, especially in communities where the Mexican Americans were either a majority or a sizable minority. By the 1990s, more than 1,000 Mexican Americans held public offices in local government. Black politicians on the local level were somewhat less successful. However, by the end of the century Houston had a black mayor, and in most Texas cities blacks served on city councils and in county and local government.

Mexican American political activism led to the organization of a new political party, La Raza Unida, in the late 1960s. The party was an outgrowth of the Mexican American Youth Organization (MAYO), formed in 1967 with José Angel Gutiérrez as its leader. For a time the party appeared to have prospects of at least some success. La Raza Unida spearheaded electoral victories in the school board and city elections in Crystal City, and in the 1972 gubernatorial race, La Raza candidate Ramsey Muniz polled more than 200,000 votes. But the defection of liberal supporters and the organizational and legal problems, as well as the difficulties that typically faced a third party with a narrow political base, led to the decline of the organization.

In the late 1960s the nature of the civil rights struggle changed. "Black Power" replaced desegregation, and organizations like the Student Nonviolent Coordinating Committee (SNCC) and CORE, led by Texan James Farmer, abandoned biracial coalitions and occasionally embraced separatism. Nonviolence gave way as ghettos burned in Watts, Detroit, and a score of other northern cities. In 1968 Martin Luther King fell to an assassin's bullet, and the Black Panther Party with its advocacy of armed self-defense seemed to symbolize the new direction of the struggle for "black liberation."

Though Texas avoided ghetto riots, it did not escape racial violence. A major issue throughout the period was the strained and hostile relations between police and minority groups. African Americans and Mexican Americans had long claimed that they were often subjected to harassment and brutality at the hands of law-enforcement officers. The rise of civil rights activism, especially the militancy that appeared in the late 1960s, increased the potential for conflict, and a number of confrontations occurred. On the campus of Texas Southern University in May 1967, rumors of trouble and a gathering crowd of black students led to violence involving the students and the Houston police. Rocks and bottles were thrown, shots were fired, and a state of siege existed for several hours around one of the dormitories. Before order could be restored, a policeman was killed, apparently by a stray police bullet, and the police rampaged through the dorm, destroying student property but finding no weapons. Three years later, in the summer of 1970, a shootout between the Houston police and People's Party II, a militant black group affiliated with the Black Panthers, left the leader of that organization dead.

Violent incidents took place in Midland in 1968, in Lubbock in 1971, and in other cities. Frequently, African American community activists charged that the police resorted to undue force in making arrests and were too quick in the use of their guns. In an effort to add minorities to the police force and thereby lessen the tensions, Houston adopted a special recruiting program in 1971, and other cities followed with similar programs. Special police-community relations councils were established in a number of cities. Still, the problems and charges persisted. Between 1975 and 1978 there were more than thirty official charges of alleged police brutality, and in at least two Houston cases policemen were convicted on serious charges. Reports of such incidents across the state diminished in the 1980s and 1990s but did not disappear altogether.

Much of the enthusiasm and energy of the civil rights crusade of the 1960s and early 1970s centered on the student protest movement, which brought tensions and unrest to college campuses all across the nation. Underlying the movement was a broad reaction against the unpopular war in Vietnam, but civil rights was also an important goal. Texas students on a number of college campuses took part in these protests. In some instances these were the result of traveling student activist organizers, such as those associated with the Students for a Democratic Society (SDS). In other instances the demonstrations were altogether the product of local talent. Rarely did the protests assume threatening proportions, except for the tragic affair on the campus of Texas Southern University, but many college administrators had some anxious moments before the momentum of the movement waned in the early 1970s.

Women, another group subjected to discrimination and unequal treatment, joined the quest for equal rights. The National Organization for Women (NOW), which formed in 1966, quickly developed chapters in Texas. In 1971, women's rights workers met in Austin to organize the Texas Women's Political Caucus (TWPC), and launched a successful campaign to secure legislative ratification of the proposed Twenty-seventh Amendment to the U.S. Constitution, the Equal Rights Amendment. The TWPC promoted greater involvement of women in politics, urging more to seek public office and to take more active roles in party affairs. In 1972 voters approved an amendment to the Texas Constitution guaranteeing that "equality under the law" would not be denied on the basis of gender. Also in 1972, the cause of women in politics was advanced by the gubernatorial candidacy of Frances ("Sissy") Farenthold, who ran a strong, though unsuccessful, race.

Since the 1970s women have increased their influence in Texas politics, though progress has been slow. By the 1990s, more than 50 percent of the members of school boards were women, and women served as mayors of more than 100 Texas towns and cities, including Houston, Dallas, San Antonio, Austin, El Paso, Galveston, and Nacogdoches. At one point in the late 1980s Houston had a woman mayor, police chief, superintendent of its school district, and president of its chamber of commerce, and an African American woman as president of its largest university. In 1999 three members of the state senate were women, and twenty-nine women were members of the house of representatives. Voters elected Democrat Ann Richards to the office of governor in 1990 and Republican Kay Hutchison to the U.S. Senate in 1993. Women also have held influential positions in both Republican and Democratic Party organizations.

SMITH, SHARPSTOWN, AND BRISCOE

Though the struggle for civil rights provided some interest and excitement in the final years of the sixties, political affairs in Texas were generally less exciting. In style, appearance, and background, Governor Smith (1969–73) stood in sharp contrast to his predecessor, the colorful and aggressive John Connally. Although less than dynamic and not very articulate,

Smith was astute and experienced in the workings of Texas politics. He carefully cultivated his supporters and took advantage of the opportunities that came his way. Rural and small-town voters were his primary constituency. During his administration legislative leadership was strong but closely tied to business and financial interests and not particularly sympathetic to reform or change. Speaker Gus Mutscher ruled the house of representatives with a firm hand, and Lieutenant Governor Ben Barnes's rule over the senate was almost as complete. Barnes was an able, pragmatic leader, and many regarded him as the politician with the most promising future.

In the election of 1970, attention focused not on the governor's race but on the contest for the Senate seat held by liberal Ralph Yarborough. Yarborough, who had first been elected in a special election but had won reelection to two regular terms, faced a difficult task. Conservative business and financial leaders in the Democratic Party generally supported Lloyd Bentsen of Houston. The primary campaign, which was vigorous and somewhat bitter, ended in victory for Bentsen, who then defeated Republican George H. Bush in the general election. In the gubernatorial race Smith defeated Paul Eggars, his Republican opponent of the previous election, but his margin of victory narrowed.

Scandal and charges of corruption in the so-called Sharpstown affair dominated state affairs during Smith's second term. The details were complicated, but Sharpstown centered on the allegation that high-ranking officials had profited in stock transactions in which prices were illegally manipulated to assure profits. Frank Sharp, a prominent Houston banker, allegedly organized the scheme to ensure the enactment of special legislation that would shield his troubled banking empire from the supervision and regulation of the Federal Deposit Insurance Corporation. The politicians who profited in the stock transactions were expected to see that this legislation became law.

Several state officers did speculate in the stock, using funds lent to them by Sharp's bank. Governor Smith, Speaker of the House Gus Mutscher and two of his aides, and two other representatives quickly amassed profits of more than $300,000. The legislation was introduced in a special legislative session in August 1969, and with the strong support of Mutscher it passed both houses of the legislature. But Governor Smith, who had allowed the measure to be considered in the special session, vetoed it.

The consequences of the Sharpstown scandal were many. In the Texas House of Representatives a strange collection of liberals, conservatives, mavericks, and members otherwise unclassified, all known collectively as the "Dirty Thirty," led a fight not only to oust the embattled speaker but also to change the rules so that no future speaker could exercise so much power. The call for reform was strong and not entirely unanswered. The next legislature after Sharpstown adopted seven reform measures, including new rules for regulating lobbying, stricter financial reporting from officeholders, rules for opening public meetings and records, and tightened regulations on campaign financing. There was also support for a comprehensive revision of the constitution. In the legal fallout from the scandal Speaker of the House Mutscher and his two associates were convicted in March 1972 on charges of conspiracy and bribery.

The immediate political impact of the scandal was felt in the elections of 1972. It was not a good year for incumbents. Less than half the members of the house of representatives and the senate returned to take their seats in the next legislature. Among the losers was Gus Mutscher, who sought reelection despite his conviction. Members of the "Dirty Thirty" who had challenged the power of the speaker fared somewhat better, especially those who sought reelection rather than new offices. Several candidates entered the race for governor. Smith, who had profited from the stock deals but who had not been charged with a crime, campaigned for a third term. Other major candidates for the Democratic nomination included Lieutenant Governor Ben Barnes, Representative Frances Farenthold, who was one of the "Dirty Thirty," and Dolph Briscoe, a wealthy South Texas landowner. Smith ran a distant fourth and Barnes fared little better. Sharpstown clearly had an impact, though there was little or nothing to connect Barnes with the affair. Briscoe, who enjoyed the support of business and financial interests, defeated the liberal Farenthold in the runoff.

Briscoe won the general election, but the vote was close. He outpolled his Republican opponent, Henry Grover, by only 100,000 votes and won with only 47 percent of the vote. The La Raza Unida candidate, Ramsey Muniz, received 6 percent of the vote, and had he received more, the election might well have fallen to the Republicans. On the national level Republicans did well in Texas. President Richard Nixon, in his contest with Democrat George McGovern, received 65 percent of the vote and carried 246 counties. Republican Senator John Tower also won reelection.

In the long run the Sharpstown scandal contributed to the growth of the Republican Party in Texas. The scandal decimated the ranks of Democratic Party leaders in the state. Even those not directly implicated in the scandal, such as Ben Barnes, had their careers ended. The strength that Republicans showed in the 1972 gubernatorial, senate, and presidential races anticipated the political changes that were forthcoming.

The election of Briscoe brought little change to Texas politics. Briscoe, who had little active experience in political office, was less than aggressive in his new post. Indeed, he seemed to enjoy being governor but to care little about performing the functions of the office. And yet the governor had effective political skills. While maintaining a conservative reputation and the support of business and financial interests, he also maintained good relations with organized labor and much of the Mexican American electorate. The one political idea that seemed to dominate Briscoe's six years as governor was his promise of "no new taxes." It was a promise he kept, though not through frugal public spending. The state budget almost doubled during the

Briscoe years, but the state's economic growth provided enough additional revenue from existing taxes to more than keep pace with the increases in spending.

Constitutional Revision

Partially in reaction to the Sharpstown scandal, and partially in response to an atmosphere sympathetic to reform, voters in 1972 approved an amendment to the constitution authorizing the legislature to meet in a convention in January 1974. In the interim, a thirty-seven-member constitutional revision committee prepared recommendations calling for a new, shorter, and more general constitution. The committee suggested annual legislative sessions, more power for the governor, reorganization of the judicial system, and other significant changes.

With Speaker of the House Price Daniel, Jr. as its presiding officer, the legislative constitutional convention met as planned in January 1974. After much debate and compromise, the convention completed an eleven-article constitution in July. Though government reforms were not as extensive as those proposed by the commission, the document did provide for many changes. However, the convention refused, by a three-vote margin, to approve its own work, and the document was not presented to the voters. The controversy over a "right-to-work" provision, the dissatisfaction of some members who wanted more drastic reforms, the opposition of others who wanted fewer reforms, and still others who wanted no new constitution at all accounted for the defeat.

The following legislature, which met in 1975, revived the constitutional revision issue. Eight proposed amendments were drafted, which, in effect, amounted to a new constitution similar to the one prepared the previous year. The legislature adopted the amendments and presented them to the voters in the November elections. But with interest in reform waning, well-organized opposition from a number of interest groups, and the last-minute opposition of Governor Briscoe, the voters rejected constitutional revision by a margin of three to one. The only substantive change in the structure of state government that came out of almost three years of constitution writing was an amendment approved by the voters in 1973 that extended the term of the governor, lieutenant governor, attorney general, and other executive officers to four years.

The Republican Challenge

The 1978 elections in Texas provided more than the usual number of political surprises. Governor Briscoe announced for a third term, not an unusual move except that his reelection would mean he would be serving ten years in office because the governorship had been extended to a four-year term in 1973. His opponent for the nomination was John Hill, the moderately liberal attorney general. Hill, who made education the key to his campaign, received the enthusiastic support of the state's teachers and defeated Briscoe in the Democratic primary.

In the Republican Party the contest for the nomination was between Ray Hutchinson, a highly respected and able long-time party leader, and William Clements, a wealthy and outspoken Dallas oilman. Relying on an effective, well-financed media campaign, Clements won the nomination.

To the surprise of most, Clements also won the general election. By a very narrow margin and with less than 50 percent of the vote, Clements defeated Hill to become the first Republican governor elected in Texas since the end of Reconstruction more than a century before. Political observers offered many explanations for the victory. Voter turnout was light, many conservative Democrats voted Republican, Hill supporters were overconfident, and Clements's campaign, which spent more than $7 million on the primary and general elections, was better financed than Hill's. To these may be added the fact that Clements's campaign not only was well financed but also was shrewdly effective in its appeal to the conservatively inclined Texas electorate. Republican strength in the legislature increased slightly, to twenty-three members in the house of representatives and four in the senate.

Governor Clements's first term of office contrasted sharply with that of his predecessor. Energetic and aggressive, the new governor had an opinion on nearly all issues and a willingness to express it. His major objective was the reduction of state expenditures. During the campaign he had frequently complained about the excessive expenses of state government, particularly about unnecessary state employees, and had promised to reduce the number of state workers by thousands and to cut the cost of government by millions. In pursuit of that objective, the governor's office required state agencies to prepare elaborate reports explaining the work of the agency and defending their workforce needs. The reports were filed, but there was little decrease in the number of state workers, and salary costs increased considerably. However, the campaign was not altogether a failure. The population of Texas increased more than 10 percent during the governor's term, but the number of state employees remained relatively stable. Moreover, though salaries of state workers increased, inflation more than offset the increase.

As the elections of 1982 approached, many observers expected Governor Clements's reelection, confirming the establishment of two-party politics in Texas. For the most part, the state was exceptionally prosperous, enjoying the benefits of an oil boom of unprecedented proportions, and early polls showed the governor with a comfortable lead. Although the accomplishments of his administration were not especially notable, particularly with respect to legislation, the governor and his office were singularly free of any hint of scandal. Republican Ronald Reagan in his campaign for president in

1980 had won the vote of Texas by a large margin, and Clements's campaign fund seemed insurmountable. In spite of these advantages, the Democratic candidate, Attorney General Mark White, won with 53 percent of the vote.

Several factors seemed to account for the outcome of the election. In some instances, voters may have been alienated by the governor's abrasive manner. Public school teachers, in particular, believed that Clements's administration had done little for them or for education. Mexican Americans voted in large numbers, and most of them for White; rural Texans, who tended to support the Democratic cause, turned out in greater numbers, as did black voters. Overall, the vote was substantially larger in 1982 than in 1978.

The election of Mark White in 1982 brought into office a seasoned veteran of Texas politics. White had been a political associate of former governor Dolph Briscoe and had established a broad base of support among the party faithful across the state. His principles and goals, however, were not clearly known. Many liberals regarded him as a conservative tool of business interests, while many conservatives considered him a liberal masquerading as an advocate of conservative government. Others expected him to perform in much the same manner as his Democratic predecessors, enjoying the fruits of office but accomplishing little.

As an indication of his political skills, White managed to respond to many different interest groups in the state. In keeping with the practices of all Texas governors since John Connally, he frequently repeated the pledge of "no new taxes" (even though at the time, Texas ranked forty-first in the nation in the level of state and local taxation). Although he ordinarily rewarded party loyalists in matters of appointments to boards and agencies, he also took care to see that minorities and women were given some of the appointments. Fulfilling a campaign promise, he appointed a consumer representative to the Public Utility Commission. Consequently, utility rate increase requests received closer and less sympathetic scrutiny than under previous administrations.

It was, however, education and budgets that occupied most of the administration's attention. In the campaign of 1982, White had sought the support of the state's public school teachers, promising to improve the quality of education and raise teacher salaries. The necessity for both was evident in a contemporary report published by the U.S. Secretary of Education, which observed that Texas ranked forty-second among all states in the percentage of students who graduated from high school, next to last in per capita income spent on public education, and below national averages in standardized test scores, teacher-pupil ratios, and teacher salaries. White reacted to the report by appointing a select committee on public education headed by Dallas millionaire and industrialist, H. Ross Perot. After many months of hearings, the committee recommended a comprehensive list of reforms, which the governor submitted to a special session of the legislature in June 1984.

The Educational Reform Act was passed by the legislature and signed into law on July 2, 1984. Among its provisions were the reorganization of the state board of education, a broad and significant salary increase for teachers, and an arrangement for merit pay. Its most significant and controversial measures involved revamping the teacher education program, establishing mandatory competency testing of pupils, teachers, and administrators, and imposing a "no pass, no play" provision that required all students to be passing all subjects to participate in extracurricular activities.

While educational reform was being debated, the state became mired in budgetary crisis. In 1983 the oil boom that had fueled the Texas economy came to an end. Oil prices, which had risen to more than $35 per barrel, began to decline, oil companies reduced their expenditures, and unemployment increased steadily. Agricultural income fell, and economic chaos in Mexico generated hard times along the Texas border. Meanwhile, education reforms required more funds, court orders demanded substantial and costly expansion of the state prison system, and the highly prized highway system of the state was rapidly deteriorating.

The 1984 special session of the legislature, which enacted the education reform bill, also attempted to address the budget problem, but with little success. Then, beginning in the spring of 1986, oil prices declined precipitously, eventually falling below $10 per barrel. The result was disaster for the already badly damaged oil industry, overextended financial institutions, and thousands of Texas workers. But it was also a disaster for state government. In the late spring, the comptroller forecast a budget deficit of several billion dollars. After considerable delay, perhaps because it was an election year, Governor White called a special session of the legislature. Divided and unhappy, the legislature debated for weeks before finally agreeing upon a compromise. Legislation was passed that postponed obligations, increased taxes temporarily, moved funds from special accounts to the general revenue fund, revoked employee salary increases, and reduced expenditures wherever possible. The measure did little more than allow the state to limp along until the regular session met in January 1987 after the elections.

In the midst of the budget crisis, the 1986 elections were held and Governor Mark White and ex-Governor William Clements renewed their contest for the governor's office. The campaign was spirited and ill-tempered, with each candidate spending millions on television and other media. The election in 1984 of Republican Phil Gramm to replace John Tower as a U.S. senator had boosted the confidence of Republican Party leaders, and their confidence was justified. From the early stages of the campaign, polls showed Clements with a comfortable lead, and although the margin declined somewhat, the polls were accurate. Clements, who lost by 230,000 votes in 1982, won in 1986 by almost the same number. For the second time since Reconstruction, Texans elected a Republican governor.

Reasons for the Clements victory were many, albeit sometimes contradictory. To some degree, the education reforms of 1984 were responsible. Teachers, who had worked diligently for White in 1982, resented the competency exams that they were required to take and in many instances turned against him. "No pass, no play" was also controversial, especially among voters who considered victory at the Friday night football games more important than education. Others resented the modest tax increases necessary to fund the reforms. Undoubtedly the economic crisis was another factor. Many Texans were unemployed, others feared that they would soon lose their jobs, and many businesses struggled daily just to keep their doors open. Governor White, after some delay, had spoken out in favor of tax increases to meet the budget deficit. Increased taxes, never welcome in Texas, were even more unpopular in hard times. Although Clements never defined his strategy for dealing with the crisis, most voters seemed to believe that he was better equipped to find a solution. Finally, White simply failed to get Democratic voters to the polls. In most areas where Democratic voters dominated, the turnout dropped, but in Republican areas, voters went to the polls in numbers larger than in 1982. White simply failed to generate voter enthusiasm, even in his own party.

CLEMENTS, RICHARDS, AND TWO-PARTY POLITICS

Clements's second term as governor was in many respects very different from his first. The governor was less abrasive in his public pronouncements; in fact, he spoke out much less frequently on state and national issues. Budgetary problems carried over from the previous administration began Clements's second term on a difficult note. His campaign promises of "no new taxes" proved to be ephemeral, and while the added taxes offered little evidence of responsible long-term planning, more revenue was gained. Midway in the governor's term, another Texan, George H. Bush, was elected president of the United States. Though this brought prominent Texans into the national administration, increased the influence of Texans in the national Republican Party, and certainly bolstered the confidence and influence of local Republicans, there was little direct impact on state politics.

To a considerable extent, the problems Clements faced in his second term were beyond his control. The economic problems of the oil industry continued as the 1980s drew near an end. Oil taxes, once amounting to 20 percent of the state tax revenue, declined to as little as 8 percent. A series of federal court rulings concerning prison conditions provoked a crisis in the penal system, requiring significantly expanded and improved facilities. A

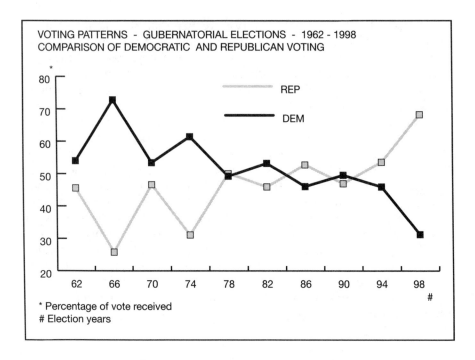

VOTING PATTERNS - GUBERNATORIAL ELECTIONS - 1962 - 1998
COMPARISON OF DEMOCRATIC AND REPUBLICAN VOTING

REP
DEM

* Percentage of vote received
# Election years

state court ruling concerning equity in the support of public schools suggested that more taxes would be needed to support the state school system.

As 1990 approached, the governor announced his decision to return to private life, and a number of candidates in both parties began their campaigns for the nominations. In the Republican Party, Clayton Williams, an outspoken West Texas businessman armed with a considerable amount of money and some unusual ideas about modern times, won the nomination. After a nasty battle with State Attorney General Jim Mattox, Ann Richards, the state treasurer, won the Democratic nomination. The contest that followed between Williams and Richards was equally nasty and ill-tempered. Initially, polls showed Williams in a comfortable lead, but he continually embarrassed himself with a series of ill-conceived and intemperate public statements, and his lead evaporated. Texas voters elected their second woman governor, awarding her about 51 percent of the vote.

In many respects, Richards's election marked a return to traditional Texas politics, particularly with respect to appointments that rewarded "courthouse crowd" Democrats in each county. There was, however, some evidence of concern for other interests. In her first two years, Governor Richards appointed a number of women and minorities to public boards and offices, survived a number of challenges, and on occasion demonstrated a certain amount of flexibility lacking in some of her predecessors. However, her administration was unable to develop long-term solutions to the prob

Ann Richards. Ann Richards was the second woman elected governor of Texas. The colorful, photogenic governor was more popular with the people and press outside the state than she was with Texas voters. (Texas State Library & Archives Commission)

lems of the state, particularly with respect to budgets and education. Though the legislature certainly shared responsibility for this, Governor Richards clearly failed to provide effective leadership. This was especially true in dealing with court-ordered demands to equalize funding for all the state's school districts. When one special session of the legislature after another failed to resolve this problem in a manner satisfactory to the federal courts, the governor seemed to withdraw from the process and leave it to the legislature to devise a solution.

Governor Richards also experienced failure as a party leader. When Democratic Senator Lloyd Bentson resigned his seat in 1993 to become Secretary of the Treasury, Richards's indecisiveness in naming a temporary successor created needless party divisions, and her eventual appointee, Robert Krueger, proved unelectable. The result was that in 1993 the Democrats lost Texas's second U.S. Senate seat to Republican Kay Bailey Hutchison.

In spite of these failures Richards remained a fairly popular leader within the Democratic Party, with the public, and especially with the national media. This personal popularity did not guarantee her reelection. Richards did easily win renomination, but after a lackluster campaign she lost the general election to a political newcomer, George W. Bush, son of the recent president of the United States. Not only did Bush win the election by a comfortable margin, but in the legislature, Republicans made substantial gains, although they did not achieve majorities in either house.

Political analysts offered many explanations for the Bush victory. Traditional Democratic strongholds either voted in smaller numbers or in some instances turned to the Republican candidate. Some believed that Governor Richard's veto of a law legalizing the possession of concealed weapons alienated a significant number of voters. Others argued that Bush's campaign was more positive and better organized than his opponent's. But the most frequently proposed explanation was the recognition that the election of 1994 reflected a major increase in Republican strength across the nation, with many veteran Democrats failing to win reelection.

GEORGE W. BUSH—BUILDING THE REPUBLICAN MAJORITY

Although Republicans did not control the legislature in 1995, Governor Bush proved especially adept at working with the Democratic leadership to get his programs through the legislature. As a result the session featured much less controversy than usual and, in comparison with legislative sessions of recent years, was more productive. Certainly, a considerable number of laws were adopted. Among them were tort reform measures limiting lawsuit abuse, and a number of changes in the state's welfare programs. Several laws concerned the control of crime, including one that permitted the carrying of concealed weapons and another directed at reducing the amount of juvenile crime in the state. Extensive revamping of educational programs increased local control of public education and somewhat weakened the "no pass, no play" provision adopted in the 1984. One success of Bush's administration was that in the elections of 1996 voters increased the number of Republicans in the state house of representatives, and gave the party a narrow majority in the senate.

The gubernatorial election of 1998 demonstrated the degree to which the Republicans had assumed control of Texas politics. Governor Bush was renominated without significant opposition, effectively silencing the extreme conservative wing of his party. The Democrats' hopes were dashed early when Attorney General Dan Morales announced that he was retiring from politics. Land Commissioner Garry Mauro won the Democratic nomination, but he was unable to mount a strong campaign in the general election. George W. Bush won reelection in a landslide, outpolling his opponent by a two-to-one margin. In addition Republicans swept all of the statewide elections, including lieutenant governor, attorney general, and three other executive posts, three seats on the Railroad Commission, and eighteen positions on the state's highest courts. The election of Rick Perry as the first Republican lieutenant governor since Reconstruction, together with a slim majority in the state senate, gave the party control over the upper house. The only bright spot for the Democrats was that they retained a four-seat majority in the house.

As the century came to an end, Texas was not only a two-party state but a state clearly dominated by the Republican Party. Furthermore, demographic and political trends suggested that the Republican majority would increase following the 2000 census. Demographically, political power was shifting from the cities, where Democrats held the advantage, to the largely Republican suburbs. With Republicans firmly in control of the machinery for redistricting, many political analysts expected the next census to bring Republicans a majority in the state house of representatives and perhaps give them a majority in the Texas congressional delegation. Of course, predicting political trends is always dangerous. If his presidential aspirations remove the popular Governor Bush from Texas politics, or if the potential divisions between conservative and moderate Republicans damage party unity, or if the Democrats attract new, dynamic candidates, then the Republican majority may be short-lived.

BIBLIOGRAPHY

George Green, *The Establishment in Texas Politics* (Westport, CT, 1969), surveys briefly the politics of the 1960s and 1970s. Robert Olien, *From Token to Triumph: The Texas Republicans since 1920* (Dallas, 1982), is also useful as a discussion of general political affairs after World War II. Kenneth Hendrickson, Jr. and Michael L. Collins's collection of political biographies, *Profiles in Power: Twentieth Century Texans in Washington*, (Arlington Heights, Ill., 1995), includes essays on Lyndon Baines Johnson, Ralph Yarborough, Barbara Jordan, John Tower, Jim Wright, Lloyd Bentsen, and George Bush.

With respect to more specific topics, one aspect has been thoroughly studied: for information on the bank bill scandals, consult Sam Kinch, Jr., and Ben Proctor, *Texas under a Cloud* (Austin, 1972); Charles Deaton, *The Year They Threw the Rascals Out* (Austin, 1973); Jimmy Banks, *Money, Marbles, and Chalk: The Wondrous World of Texas Politics* (Austin, 1971); and Harvey Katz, *Shadow on the Alamo: New Heroes Fight Old Corruption in Texas Politics* (Garden City, N.Y., 1972). A more recent and readable summary of the scandal is Mickey Herskowitz, *Sharpstown Revisited: Frank Sharp and a Tale of Dirty Politics in Texas* (Austin, 1994); for an analysis of the political upheaval the scandal generated, see Robert Heard, *The Miracle of the Killer Bees: 12 Senators Who Changed Texas Politics* (Austin, 1981). Frank R. Kemerer, *William Wayne Justice: A Judicial Biography* (Austin, 1991), describes the role of a judicial figure whose decisions have generated political issues and significantly altered education and penal practices in Texas.

For biographies of political figures, see Paul Conkin, *Big Daddy from the Pedernales: Lyndon Baines Johnson* (Boston, 1986); James Reston, *The Lone Star: The Life of John Connally* (New York, 1990); and Ann Fears Crawford and Jack Keever, *John B. Connally: A Portrait in Power* (Austin, 1973), which focus on the prominent figures of the period. John Barry, *The Ambition and the Power* (New York, 1989), is the story of Jim

Wright. See also E. V. Nemeyer, Jr., "Personal Diplomacy: Lyndon B. Johnson and Mexico 1963–1968," *Southwestern Historical Quarterly*, XC, 159-186. Barbara Jordan and Shelby Hearon present the story of one of the more extraordinary leaders of the era in *Barbara Jordan: A Self-Portrait* (Garden City, N.J., 1979); while Carolyn Barta, *Bill Clements: Texian to His Toenails* (Austin, 1996), discusses the first Republican governor since Reconstruction..

For interesting and not always predictable articles on Texas politics, read those found in the *Texas Monthly*. Also useful, but predictable, are those of the *Texas Observer*, especially those that analyze each statewide election. The lobby, often charged with exercising undue influence in Texas politics, is described and discussed in Lee Clark, "May the Lobby Hold You in the Palm of Its Hand," *Texas Observer*, May 24, 1968, 1-3; and in several studies in the *Texas Monthly*, July 1973.

Literature on African Americans, Mexican Americans, and women and their politics has increased in both quantity and quality in recent years. Chandler Davidson and Bernard Grofman (eds.), *Quiet Revolution in the South* (Princeton, 1994), deals with the effects of the 1964 Civil Rights Act, and Chandler Davidson, *Race and Class in Texas Politics*, is an excellent study that offers information beyond issues of race and class. For material on African Americans see Alwyn Barr, *Black Texans*, 2nd ed. (Norman, 1996), and Ruthe Winegarten, *Black Texas Women: 150 Years of Trial and Triumph* (Austin, 1995).

For information on Mexican Americans see Arnold de León, "Estudios Tejanos: A List of Historical Literature on Mexican Americans in Texas," *Southwestern Historical Quarterly*, XCVIII, 457-470. Of great value is David Montejano, *Anglos and Mexicans In The Making of Texas*. Julie Leininger Pycior, *LBJ and Mexican Americans: The Paradox of Power* (Austin, 1997); Douglas E. Foley, *From Peons to Politicos: Class and Ethnicity in a South Texas Town, 1900-1987* (Austin, 1988); and Mario García, *Mexican Americans: Leadership, Ideology, and Identity* (New Haven, 1989).

The struggle of African Americans for racial equality is discussed in Robert W. Talbert, "Poll Tax Repeal in Texas: A Three Year Individual Performance Evaluation," *Journal of Politics*, XXXVI, 1050-1056; Martin Kuhlman, "Direct Action at the University of Texas During the Civil Rights Movement, 1960-1965," *Southwestern Historical Quarterly*, XCVIII, 551-566; Ernest M. G. Obadele-Starks, "Ralph Yarborough of Texas and the Road to Civil Rights," *East Texas Historical Journal*, XXXII, 39-48. Michael Botson examines racism in the labor movement in "No Gold Watch for Jim Crow's Retirement: The Abolition of Segregated Unionism at Houston's Hughes Tool Company," *Southwestern Historical Quarterly*, CI, 496-52; while Thomas R. Cole uncovers the Houston sit-in movement in, *No Color Is My Kind: The Life of Eldrewey Stearns and the Integration of Houston* (Austin, 1997).

For material on the Mexican American struggle for equality see Armando Navarro, *Mexican American Youth Organization: Avant-Garde of the Chicano Movement in Texas* (Austin, 1995); John Shockley, *Chicano Revolt in a Texas Town* (Notre Dame, Ind., 1974); and Ignacio García, *United We Win: The Rise and Fall of La Raza Unida Party* (Tucson, 1989).

The women's rights movement is discussed in David W. Brady and Kent L. Tedin, "Religion and Political Ideology in the Anti-ERA Movement," *Social Science Quarterly*, LVI, 464-475; and "Ladies in Pink: Religion and Ideology in the Anti-ERA Movement," *Social Science Quarterly*, LVI, 564-575; and Jan Meadows, "Woman against Herself," *Texas Parade*, March 1975, 29-33. Nancy Beck Young and Lewis L. Gould, *Texas, Her Texas: The Life and Times of Frances Goff* (Austin, 1997), presents the life of an unusual late-twentieth-century Texas woman.

20

At the End of the Century

Change, dramatized by the development of computer technology, human flight in space, and atomic power, characterized the economic, scientific, and social development of the United States in the years after World War II. Economic, social, and cultural change in Texas during these years depended only to some extent on computers and space and even less on atomic power, but, nonetheless, these were years of change in which Texas experienced an economic and social transformation of almost revolutionary proportions.

Industrialization and urbanization, trends long apparent in Texas, accelerated in the years following World War II. In the 1990s, less than 2 percent of the population depended on farms and ranches directly for their income; eight out of ten Texans lived in urban areas; and about one-half of the people were concentrated in the Dallas-Fort Worth, Houston, and San Antonio-Austin areas. For most, Texas was no longer a country of wide-open spaces and the smell of the earth; instead it was a land of housing developments, freeways, and shopping centers.

These were the most obvious changes, but there were many others. Although it employed a much smaller portion of the workforce, agriculture was still important in the state. Social and cultural institutions grew in number and scope and contributed to the quality of life in postwar Texas, as did many Texas artists and writers. The population grew, in large part because of the appeal of the "sunbelt" and the emergence of Texas as a destination for immigrants. The role of women and minorities in Texas changed radically in the postwar years.

Until the early 1980s, Texans prospered, some at unprecedented levels, but a decline in oil prices and disasters in real estate and banking sectors combined to bring a major economic recession to the state. For the first time since the Great Depression, Texans questioned their future and that of their state. By 1991, recovery had improved economic conditions somewhat, and in the last half of the decade economic growth and prosperity returned to the state.

An Economy in Transition

Although the role of agriculture declined in the years after World War II, farming and ranching remained an important part of the postwar economy. Agricultural production, in terms of monetary value, increased seven-fold between 1958 and 1997, with livestock providing about 61 percent and field crops 39 percent of the income. Cotton continued to be the most valuable field crop, but cattle was the most valuable single agricultural product. With only a small portion of the population living on farms, the influence of agriculture declined significantly over the years, but the voice of agriculture in the state remained substantially stronger than the number of farmers would suggest.

Production levels fluctuate year to year, as does average income per farm. In the mid-1980s high interest rates and fuel costs and declining commodity prices brought many farmers to the point of bankruptcy and forced others to sell their lands. The number of farms has decreased from 418,000 in 1940 to 226,000 in 1998. For the most part this represents a continuation of the practice of consolidation that characterized Texas agriculture in the early twentieth century.

By any measure, industry grew vigorously in the years after World War II. Employment in manufacturing more than tripled between 1947 and 1999, rising to over 1 million workers, and the increased value added to goods by manufacturing was even more impressive. Oil refining, chemicals, and petrochemicals, all important in the 1930s, continued to dominate in the 1980s, but electronics, aerospace components, and other high-technology items were also important. Oil and chemical refining concentrated in locations along the coast, with many plants being established in the Beaumont-Port Arthur and the Houston-Baytown-Texas City area. The manufacture of oil-field equipment became a major industry in Houston. The aircraft industry, located in the Dallas-Fort Worth area during World War II, continued production following the war; electronics plants were built nearby in later years. Beginning in the late 1970s a number of plants manufacturing com-

The South Texas Project Electric Generation Station, located about 90 miles southwest of Houston, was the first nuclear power plant to be completed in Texas. Construction began in 1975 and the first unit began commercial operation in August 1988. Using nuclear fuel that costs only about ¹/₄ as much as conventional fuels, the power generated is more than enough to provide for a city the size of San Antonio. (Courtesy of the Houston Lighting and Power Company)

puter and related items as well as software development companies located in the "silicon hills" in and around Austin, while Dallas and Houston also became home to major computer companies, and Houston emerged as a major medical research and treatment center.

Oil production rose more or less steadily after World War II, reaching a peak of slightly more than 1.3 billion barrels in 1972. That year the Railroad Commission abandoned its practice, in effect since 1933, of restricting production. Nevertheless, declining reserves and weakening wells brought lowered production, and in 1988 slightly more than 700 million barrels were pumped. In the years that followed production continued to decline, dropping to less than 465 million barrels in 1997. Prices, however, remained high until 1983, and the oil industry prospered and contributed significantly to the prosperity of the state. In 1983, the petroleum industry employed 350,553 people; at the same time, oil and gas production provided slightly more than 20 percent of the tax revenue for the state government.

Beginning in 1983 the collapse in oil prices demonstrated the downside of an economy dependent on the oil industry. Overproduction and conservation efforts caused a steady decline in oil prices from 1983 to 1986. Then the collapse of the OPEC cartel in 1986 accelerated the decline in oil prices. Overall prices dropped from about $30 per barrel to less than $10.

The 1986 collapse only added to the troubles of Texas oilmen. Drilling activities had been declining steadily since 1983, while refinery production and the manufacture of oil-field equipment suffered similar reductions. All these developments affected employment. Analysts reported early in 1987 that more than 100,000 jobs in the Texas oil industry had disappeared in the previous five years. Thousands of highly trained geologists and technicians were unemployed, while factories that once produced oil-field equipment stood empty and refineries operated at minimum levels or closed their gates. Toward the end of the decade, prices improved slightly but not enough to encourage a significant increase in drilling and exploration. In the early 1990s, conditions in the oil industry were relatively stable; by the mid-1990s prices were up and the industry experienced modest growth.

Although affected somewhat by the recession of the 1980s, transportation in the postwar years reflected the growth of the population and the economy. Motor vehicle registration rose from 2,192,654 in 1947 to 16,150,654 in 1998, a rate of growth approximately five times greater than the rise in population. Only California had more automobiles on the highways. Commercial air passenger service began in the state in 1928, with schedules connecting Dallas with San Antonio and Fort Worth with Galveston. Growth was modest during the years of the Depression, but military aviation in World War II built interest and support. Air travel rapidly expanded in postwar years, and between 1957 and 1997 the number of people traveling by air increased almost 2,000 percent. At the same time rail travel dwindled to almost nothing, and miles of railroad track continued their decline, falling to approximately 10,000 miles in 1998. However, railroad freight tonnage increased over 78 percent between 1950 and 1998, and railroading in Texas continued to be profitable in most years.

Organized labor shared in the economic growth of the early postwar years, for, despite a barrage of laws regulating unions passed in the late 1940s and early 1950s, labor gained strength and membership. Unification of the American Federation of Labor (AFL) and the Congress of Industrial Organizations (CIO) in 1957 brought a larger role in politics. Labor's voice in state politics was heard more often, and in local politics of certain areas it was a voice that could not be ignored. Oil refining and chemical industries were, in most instances, unionized, as were most of the construction trades. In the 1970s there were a number of instances in which public employees formed unions or similar organizations. However, in the 1980s and 1990s union membership declined, both in Texas and nationwide. Among the reasons for the decline were the loss of manufacturing jobs, especially in the oil and chemical industries, the emergence of the postindustrial economy, and the general political and cultural antipathy toward organized labor.

Religion, Education, and Social Organizations

The growth of Texas churches has generally kept pace with the population. In 1890, church members represented 30.3 percent of the population, and by 1916 they had increased to 40 percent. A 1980 survey reported almost 8 million churchgoers, but the number was probably higher, since not all churches reported their members and some counts were incomplete. In this survey Baptists were the largest denomination, with more than 3 million members; Roman Catholics numbered more than 2 million; and United Methodists counted almost a million. The Church of Christ, Disciples of Christ, Presbyterians, Protestant, Episcopal, and Lutheran denominations were represented by large numbers, and there were many others. By 1990, largely as a result of the influx of Hispanic and Asian immigrants, Roman Catholics had become the largest denomination, surpassing the Baptists. The demographic changes associated with immigration also brought a number of non-Christian religions to the state. In addition to Jews, who had been in Texas from the early nineteenth century, Hindus, Moslems, and Buddhists could be found in all large Texas cities and even in many smaller communities. Religious bodies, whether Christian or non-Christian, served as community centers that provided its members educational and social services as well as spiritual sustenance.

Public education in Texas benefited significantly from the adoption of the Gilmer-Aikin Bill shortly after the end of World War II. The Soviet success in launching Sputnik in 1957 resulted in increased demand for more study and more effective teaching in the schools, especially in math and science.

In the aftermath of the civil rights movement there was pressure to increase educational programs for students deemed to be at high risk or whose educational needs had been neglected in the past. These initiatives focused on the needs of disabled students, as well as those from families affected by poverty or other social problems. In the 1970s bilingual education received special attention as the non-English-speaking population of Texas schools soared. Toward the end of that decade, declining scores on verbal and mathematical achievement tests generated widespread concern and gave rise to a "back-to-basics" movement.

The educational reforms of the 1980s were in fact the consequence of such concerns. The reforms encompassed in House Bill 72 that were passed by a special session of the legislature in 1984 included an emphasis on competency testing, increased salaries for educators, and expanded resources. At the heart of the program was a commitment to the idea that quality education was fundamentally necessary to the success and happiness of individuals and society. But the reforms were expensive and controversial and often conflicted with long-standing, almost sacred, institutions such as athletics. Increasing criticism and questioning of both policies and results led to a "back-to-local control" movement in the 1990s. Also in the early 1990s court orders required Texas to equalize funding between low-income and upper-income school districts, and at the end of the decade Mexican American groups challenged statewide competency testing as culturally biased and discriminatory. As the century came to an end, the demands placed on public education seemed difficult to resolve. There was a consensus that a well-educated workforce was essential for the continued growth and prosperity of the state. There was a concern that the quality of education was declining, and there were questions about the quality and competency of the educators. On the other hand, efforts to impose competency testing on students (or teachers) aroused strong opposition from various interest groups, while efforts to attract better-trained teachers always led to the question of the cost of raising teacher salaries.

In the early 1990s public education in Texas faced a special challenge. Beginning in the early twentieth century, the bulk of funding for public education came from local taxes imposed by local school districts. In the 1980s some school districts, especially those economically disadvantaged areas, argued that the system of providing money for the support of public schools was unfair because local school taxes were based on the value of the property in the district. Some school districts contained very valuable property, while others were poor. In one school district, the taxable property per student was $5,900. Nearby, a wealthy school district contained taxable property valued at $49,000 per student. Even if the poorer district taxed its population at a higher rate, it would not have the resources of the wealthier district.

After failing in 1973 to convince the Supreme Court of the legitimacy of their cause, critics of inequity in school funding raised the issue again in the state courts in the 1980s. In 1987 a state court ruled the state school finance system unconstitutional; two years later the Texas Supreme Court upheld the ruling and ordered the legislature to reorganize the system of school funding. Beginning in January 1991, the legislature debated a series of school funding plans, but no plan appealed to a majority of the legislators. Almost any program that would make school financing equitable across the state would reduce funds available to some schools, raise local taxes, or require higher state taxes. The first effort of the legislature was rejected by the courts. Finally, in a special session a compromise was reached that equalized funding by shifting some support of education from the local tax sources to the state. The new program would require more state spending, and some districts would not receive as much money from the state as they had received previously. Although the measure was adopted, and the courts upheld the program, the funding of public education remained one of the primary problems of state government throughout the 1990s.

In higher education the years after World War II have been a period of steady growth. The growth rate was especially high in the 1970s, when student enrollment almost doubled and 36 new units of higher education were created. By 1990, more than 150 institutions in the state provided opportunities for those seeking education beyond high school. In 1998 there were a total of 939,634 students enrolled in the state's public and private colleges and universities. Community colleges, the fastest-growing providers of higher education, enrolled 44 percent of the postsecondary students.

In 1990 there were forty-two private institutions of higher education, most with religious affiliations. Rice University, a nonsectarian institution, was noted for its educational excellence. Largest of a number of Baptist institutions was Baylor University, and Southern Methodist University, established in 1915, was the largest of nine Methodist schools. The Presbyterians had Austin College and Trinity University; the Church of Christ had Abilene Christian College and several smaller schools; the Disciples of Christ maintained Texas Christian University; and Saint Mary's University was the largest Catholic school. Even though their proportion of the enrollment had declined in recent years, the private and denominational schools were still important to Texas higher education and provided education for approximately one out of every nine students in 1998. In addition to their emphasis on religious training, several of these schools provided outstanding work in music, drama, and the other fine arts.

Lodges, clubs, and societies, some with roots that extended far back into pioneer times, continued to form an important sector of Texas's social and cultural institutions after World War II. Service clubs assumed a more important role over the years, and veterans' organizations exercised considerable influence in the state. The Texas Federation of Women's Clubs did much to promote adult education and other reforms. In earlier years the organization played a major role in the establishment of public libraries across the state. In addition to its library work, the federation promoted legislation in the interest of rural education, compulsory school laws, the protection of women and children in industry, and Texas heritage.

Indeed, Texans are confirmed "joiners." Apparently everyone belongs to at least one organization, and the average for adults of middle and higher incomes is surely three or more. There are hundreds and hundreds of organizations in the state. There is the Texas State Teachers' Association, a powerful group that has long wielded great influence in legislation. Similar organizations of strength are the state bar and the state medical association. There are also learned societies, such as the Texas Academy of Science and the Texas Philosophical Society, which was founded during the republic and revived in 1936. There are three geological societies and six organizations of engineers, one statewide historical association, and half a dozen regional ones. There are organizations as unrelated as barbers and cattle raisers, Indians and skeet shooters, veterans and Zionists. These provide outlets for the innumerable interests and emotions of the people and are channels of communication and cooperation. More perhaps than any other source, they reveal the nature of our civilization. They are the institutions of a free people and could not thrive except in an atmosphere of freedom.

LITERATURE AND THE ARTS

Since World War II the literature of Texas has grown in volume, quality, and diversity. The traditional topics of earlier years have continued to attract the interest of both writers and readers. Ernest Wallace and E. Adamson Hoebel dealt with both history and ethnology in *The Comanches, Lords of the South Plains*; Mildred P. Mayhall published a historical study of the Kiowas; Charles L. Sonnichsen wrote on the Mescalero Apaches; and W. W. Newcomb surveyed the entire subject in *The Indians of Texas*. In Ernest Wallace's *Ranald S. Mackenzie*, the story of Texas's last great Indian war is well told. J. Evetts Haley, W. C. Holden, J. W. Williams, Tom Lea, Wayne Gard, and others have added to the literature on the cattle industry.

A number of biographies have appeared. Llerena Friend published the authoritative *Sam Houston, The Great Designer*, in 1954, and three more biographies of Houston appeared in 1993. In 1999 Greg Cantrell published *Stephen F. Austin: Empresario of Texas*, the first major study of the "Father of Texas" since Eugene Barker's classic biography of 1926. Ernest Wallace's *Charles DeMorse, Pioneer Editor and Statesman*, Joe B. Frantz's *Gail Borden, Dairyman to a Nation*, Alvy King's *Louis T. Wigfall*, and Robert C. Cotner's *James Stephen Hogg* deal with other prominent nineteenth-century figures. The lives of more recent Texans are portrayed in R. N. Richardson's *Colonel House: The Texas Years*, John O. King's *Joseph Stephen Cullen: A Study in Leadership in the Texas Petroleum Industry, 1897–1937*, T. Dwight Donough's *Mr. Sam* (about Sam Rayburn), and Ann Fears Crawford and Jack Keever's, *John B. Connally: Portrait in Power*. A number of studies of Lyndon Johnson have appeared, several of which have stimulated considerable debate among historians.

Interpretative writing on Texas and Texans has increased greatly during the last quarter-century. Some books are autobiographical and at times sympathetic but more often they are critical. William A. Owens has produced several works, among them *This Stubborn Soil*. Edward Everett Dale's *The Cross Timbers*, Bertha McKee Dobie's *Growing Up in Texas*, and C. C. White's *No Quittin' Sense* emphasize the rural heritage of the state. Somewhat more critical are Willie Morris's *North Toward Home* and David Nevin's *The Texans: What They Are—and Why*. In his *Big Country, Texas*, Donald Day has sought to explain the country and its institutions through history, politics, and folklore. Joseph Leach in *The Typical Texan: Biography of an American Myth* has sought to find in history, novels, and biography a true account of Texan character. Frank Goodwyn's *Lone Star Land: Twentieth Century in Perspective* deals with the social changes Texas has known in the light of its culture, geography, and history. T. R. Fehrenbach's *Lone Star* offers some interesting insights into the forces that have molded the state. The cowboy, a type inseparably linked with Texas, is appraised by Joe B. Frantz and Julian Earnest Choate in *The American Cowboy: The Myth and the Reality*. James A. Michener, on the other hand, relied on fiction to interpret the nature of the Texas experience. His *Texas*, a novel that covers the history of Texas from the time of the arrival of the Spanish, tells its story in a way that is both sympathetic and critical.

The most significant development in historical writing in recent years has been the publication of studies on ethnic groups and women in Texas history. In the past two decades scholars have published more than 125 books and more than 200 articles that concern African Americans, Mexican Americans, or women. David Montejano, Arnoldo de León, David Weber, Jesús F. de la Teja, and others have written extensively about Mexican Americans. Montejano's *Anglos and Mexicans in the Making of Texas, 1836–1986* is a prize-winning book, and there are a number of other studies of great merit. Randolph B. Campbell's *An Empire for Slavery: The Peculiar Institution in Texas, 1821–1865* is a comprehensive and thoughtful study of the institution that molded Texas society before the Civil War. Alwyn Barr's *Black Texans* is a valuable general study of African Americans in Texas, and there are a number of specialized works such as Lawrence Rice's *The Negro in Texas, 1874–1900*, Darlene Clark Hines's *Black Victory: The Rise and Fall of the White Primary in Texas*, Garner Christian's *Black Soldiers in Jim Crow Texas, 1899–1917*, and Ruthe Winegarten's *Black Texas Women: 150 Years of Trial and Triumph*. Two recent works, Merline Pitre's *In Struggle against Jim Crow: Lulu B. White and the N.A.A.C.P., 1900-1957*, and Thomas R. Cole's *No Color Is My Kind*, examine the previously neglected history of the civil rights movement in Texas.

The publication of books concerning women in Texas has increased substantially in recent years, especially since 1980. Sandra Myers, Fane Downs, Ann Patton Malone, Ann Fears Crawford, and many others have written in this area, with new publications appearing each year.

In fiction during the middle decades of the twentieth century, Texas novelists were writing on an increasingly varied list of subjects. In *Wetback*, Claud Garner attacked the injustice often done to Mexican immigrants who crossed the Rio Grande unlawfully. William A. Owen's *Walking on Borrowed Land* is a plea for better understanding between the races, David Westheimer, in *Summer on the War*, deals with the humor and tragedy of a family in a summer colony near Houston. Madison Cooper's *Sironia, Texas* discusses the intimate affairs of the people of a town. In the *Brave Bulls*, Tom Lea treats the interplay of courage and fear in the mind of a matador hero. Larry McMurtry, perhaps the most prolific and successful Texas novelist of the late twentieth century, has explored almost every facet of Texas life. His *Lonesome Dove* is a powerful account of personal relationships on a cattle drive; *The Last Picture Show*, set in a fictional northwest Texas oil field and ranching community, critically portrays personalities limited by a provincial environment, and *Terms of Endearment* and the other two novels in his Houston trilogy capture life in urban Texas. In the 1990s the three critically acclaimed novels in Cormac McCarthy's *Border Trilogy* vividly depicted life in the Texas borderlands.

The expansion of Texas writing has led to the development of writers and artist colonies, especially in Austin and the Hill Country but also in Houston and Dallas. The creative writing program at the University of Houston is one of the most successful programs in the country for developing writers, and Austin has become renowned for nurturing filmmakers. Arte Público Press, established at the University of Houston in 1979, has become the nation's largest nonprofit publisher of literature and its largest Hispanic press. In the twenty years since its founding it has published about 400 works of Hispanic literature.

In folklore, the pioneering works of John Lomax, John Mason Brewer, and J. Frank Dobie have endured and been joined by others. *Adventures of a Ballad Hunter* by Lomax won a Texas Institute of Letters Award in 1947. J. Mason Brewer's collections of folklore dealing with the lives of black people, recorded in *The Word on the Brazos, Aunt Dicey*, and others, continue to be read. One of the first Mexican American folklorists to be published was Jovita Gonzales, and adding to her contributions have been the works of Américo Paredes. His study of the *corrido* (Mexican American folk ballad) is particularly noteworthy. "With His Pistol in His Hand," a study of Gregorio Cortez, is probably his most popular work. Moody Boatwright and William Owens have collected many tales that offer much about the culture of the state.

Societies and journals have done much to preserve the literature of Texas. Vital to the preservation of folklore is the work of the Texas Folklore Society, which over the years has published a large number of volumes. Of the two outstanding literary magazines in the state, the oldest is the *Southwest Review*, founded in Austin in 1915 and later moved to Dallas, where it is

Gregorio Cortez. Gregorio Cortez was the Mexican American landowner turned outlaw and folk hero who was celebrated in Américo Paredes's 1958 folklore classic, "With His Pistol in His Hand." Cortez symbolized the violence between Anglos and Mexican-Americans in the Texas-Mexican borderlands at the turn of the century. Paredes was noted for mining indigenous folk ballads for their literary and historic content. (Texas State Library and Archives Commission)

sponsored by Southern Methodist University. The quality of its articles is high, and it is a worthy exponent of the life and literature of the state. In 1958, the *Texas Quarterly* was established by members of the faculty of the University of Texas. It carries a wide range of narratives, biographies, poems, and art and provides an outlet for a number of talented writers. Through the pages of these journals, much of the poetry of recent times has been preserved and made available to readers.

Interest in the theater dates at least back to the days of the Texas Republic and has grown in the twentieth century. In 1909, the Curtain Club was organized at the University of Texas, and after the First World War the little theater became a community project in most towns and cities. Of such organizations, the oldest and best known in Texas is one in Dallas, founded in 1921. Professional drama presented in the Alley Theater in Houston and in the Dallas Theater Center has won national recognition since World War II. In 1998 Houston's Alley Theater won the Tony Award as the best regional theater company in the United States. By the end of the century, Texas theater companies were producing more and more plays by Texas playwrights. Horton Foote and Celeste Colson-Walker are Texans whose plays have received national recognition.

Texas has made some substantial contributions to twentieth-century music. Dallas, Houston, and San Antonio have major symphony orchestras, and interest in ballet has increased significantly in recent years. Beaumont, Dallas, Fort Worth, Houston, and San Antonio maintain opera groups. Since World War II there has been an unprecedented development of music education through the Interscholastic League. The University of North Texas, the University of Texas, Rice University, and the University of Houston are known nationally for their excellent music programs.

Affecting a larger proportion of the population was the growth of popular music, especially country and western and rock and roll. Drawing on the foundations made popular in the 1930s by musicians such as Bob Wills and Ernest Tubb, music once termed "hillbilly" by some evolved into western and then into country music. The change was more than a matter of names. Lyrics, emphasis, and instrumentations were altered, although many of the basic themes remained the same. In the 1960s, 1970s, and 1980s, elements of rock were added to produce a combination termed by some "progressive country."

Austin became a prominent center for country and western musicians. Willie Nelson, a Texan who abandoned Nashville to return to his home state, perhaps won the most acclaim, but there were many others. On occasion large festivals or "picnics" were held where literally tens of thousands gathered for all-day concerts.

Rock music also attracted a large following in the postwar years. An early pioneer in the development of rock and roll was a Texan, Buddy Holly, whose promising career was cut short in a plane crash. Janis Joplin of Port Arthur, in a brief but hectic career, won national fame for her versions of rock and roll. Touring rock groups regularly attracted large audiences, mostly youth, and in every city and hamlet, rock groups of widely varying abilities were formed. For a time, especially in the late 1960s, rock was often viewed as a part of the social protest movement, attractive to those who questioned the values of contemporary society, but thereafter, more seemed to be attracted to rock because they enjoyed it.

Widespread interest in art in Texas may be measured from the organization in 1911 of the Texas Fine Arts Association. During recent years this interest has grown. Most large Texas cities and many smaller ones have art museums. The colleges have art departments, and art is an increasingly popular subject in the public schools. Over the years the state has produced many fine artists, and some have gained national acclaim. Porfirio Salinas is known for his paintings of the Texas hill country, particularly for scenes featuring bluebonnets. Another artist, José Cisneros, is noted for his pen-and-ink illustrations. John Biggers has received national attention for his use of African imagery in depicting African American themes in his fine murals and paintings, and sculptor Luis Jimenez has received similar acclaim for use of folk icons in depicting the clash of Anglo and Hispanic cultures in the Southwest.

Thus, in many ways, the cultural progress of Texas in modern times has kept pace with the economic growth of the state. In literature, drama, music, and the arts, Texans have brought enrichment to their lives and to the nation.

A POPULATION IN TRANSITION

In the 1980s, Texans celebrated the tricentennial of the state's settlement by peoples other than native Americans (and also the sesquicentennial of the Texas Revolution). It was in 1682 that the Spanish friars established their first settlement in Texas, the mission of Corpus Christi de la Ysleta, located a few miles east of the modern city of El Paso. Three centuries have brought great changes in the land, as well as changes—perhaps even more dramatic—in the people who inhabit the land.

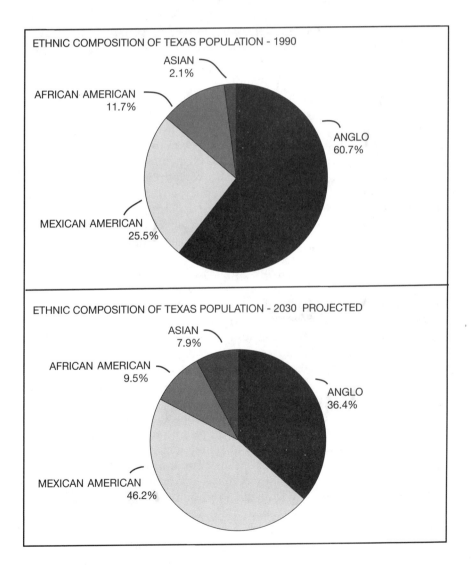

ETHNIC COMPOSITION OF TEXAS POPULATION - 1990

ASIAN
2.1%

AFRICAN AMERICAN
11.7%

ANGLO
60.7%

MEXICAN AMERICAN
25.5%

ETHNIC COMPOSITION OF TEXAS POPULATION - 2030 PROJECTED

ASIAN
7.9%

AFRICAN AMERICAN
9.5%

ANGLO
36.4%

MEXICAN AMERICAN
46.2%

The U.S. Census Bureau estimated the Texas population in 1998 as 19,759,614, second highest in the nation. It further estimated that the population would reach 20 million before the new millennium and double to 40 million by the year 2030. The bulk of the Texas population lives in the twenty-eight Metropolitan Statistical Areas (MSAs) and Primary Metropolitan Statistical Areas (PMSAs). In the 1990s the fastest-growing areas were the suburbs of the major cities, the Rio Grande communities in South Texas, and the Austin area. Because of a declining birthrate, Texas was increasingly dependent upon migration for its population growth. Among the many ethnic groups that made up the population in 1990, Anglos represented 61 percent; blacks, 12 percent; people who spoke Spanish as a native language or who had a Spanish surname, 25.5 percent; and 2 percent other nonwhites. By 2000 the Anglo population is projected to shrink to 54.5 percent while Hispanics increase to 31 percent. By 2010 Texas is projected to have a "minority, majority population" with Hispanic, blacks, and "other" (predominately Asians) comprising almost 52 percent of the population. The distribution of ethnic minorities within the population has also changed in the past twenty-five years. While Mexican-Americans remained the dominant ethnic group in South Texas, by 1980 they resided in every county and in large numbers in Dallas, Fort Worth, and Houston. By 2030 Hispanics are projected to be the largest group in the population. In 1990 two counties, Dallas and Harris, contained about 45 percent of the black population. Overall the black population is expected to decline slightly from 11.7 percent of the population in 1990 to 9.5 percent in 2030. The fastest-growing ethnic component of the population are Asians, who are expected to increase from 2.1 percent in 1990 to 7.9 percent in 2030.

In addition to their growing numbers, the most striking change of recent decades has been the increased role of ethnic minorities (and women) within the society. In the aftermath of the civil rights revolution, new opportunities for women and minorities have opened in social, political, and economic areas. African Americans and Mexican Americans, once almost automatically relegated to low-paying, common-labor jobs, today hold responsible and influential posts in industry, business, the professions, and government. Sports and cultural areas have been similarly strengthened by the contributions of the minorities.

Women have assumed a more visible role. Politically, they have become much more involved. In addition to holding elected offices, Texas women have served in the federal and state judiciary; a Texas woman was appointed as the U.S. ambassador to Great Britain; and others have served as the presidents of the University of Texas at Austin, Texas Southern University, and the University of Houston. More and more, women have sought employment outside the home, and in the 1990s women made up approximately one-third of the workforce. In a variety of ways, the women of Texas struggled for equality and the expansion of opportunities. Regularly, women's groups appeared at state public-school textbook hearings to ensure that a fair image of women and their role was presented to the schoolchildren of the state. With the support of grants from a variety of sources, the Texas Foundation for Women's Resources has conducted extensive research and compiled publications and films to present more accurately the role of Texas women in history. Toward the end of the 1970s, the National Organization of Women held its national convention in Houston, attended by thousands. Noticeable at the convention was some disagreement over both methods and goals, and this has been apparent in other ways. A group of Texas women, sometimes called the "Pink Ladies," campaigned tirelessly to secure the repeal of the legislature's ratification of the ERA amendment to the Constitution. But older organizations, such as the League of Women Voters (with more than forty chapters), the Texas Women's Political Caucus, and the Texas chapter of NOW, were joined by new organizations—Texas Women for the Eighties and the Governor's Commission on Women—to work on causes of particular concern to women.

As the century comes to an end, equality for ethnic minorities and women remains a goal, not a reality. The proportion of Mexican Americans, blacks, and women who hold low-paying, lower-status jobs continues to be much higher than that of Anglo males. In addition, challenges to methods of increasing minority opportunity, such as affirmative action, have been successfully waged in the courts. As a result, there is increasing concern within the minority communities about whether the gains made during the last quarter century will endure and be expanded upon, or whether a new era of discrimination will arise. Most Texans are committed to social equality, but continued progress in this area will be a challenge.

Texas began the last quarter-century on a high note. The 1970s was a decade of optimism, prosperity, pride, almost unlimited faith in the future. In some ways it was an occasion for pride that was not always justified. In 1970, Texans could claim that its people had completed an average of 11.7 years of school. But this was slightly less than the national average. Approximately 30 percent had not gone beyond the eighth grade, and 3 percent had not completed the first grade. On the other hand, more than 22 percent had attended college. There was the stereotype of the fabulously wealthy Texan who flaunted his or her money, and there always seemed to be enough of that sort around to perpetuate the image. Indeed, one of the most popular television programs aired in the late 1970s (and in the 1980s) was a fictional account of a rich Texas family whose outrageous wealth was exceeded only by its outrageous behavior. Certainly, there was much wealth in the state, but for the population as a whole, in 1977 per capita income was only $6,827, slightly below the national average. Disparities in the distribution of wealth in the state were also striking. In some communities in the Rio Grande Valley, income was only a little more than one-third of what it was in the city of Midland located in the West Texas oil fields. In providing for the needy and the unfortunate, Texas regularly fell into the bottom 10 percent of the states in terms of money spent for the disabled and the poor. Nevertheless, justified or not, the image of prosperity, success, and optimism persisted as the 1970s turned into the 1980s.

Unfortunately, much of that optimism and confidence quickly dissipated in the new decade. The economic recession, precipitated by many factors but particularly by hard times in the oil industry, left at times more than 10 percent of the workforce unemployed, the state budget with a shortfall in the billions, and the owners of businesses wondering whether there was any hope of continued operations. For the first time in many decades, perhaps since the Great Depression, Texans in the 1980s were questioning the future. Few expected the oil industry to return to its former status, and there was little agreement on what might replace it. Some economic experts talked knowledgeably about diversification, others advocated the advantages of high tech, and all seemed to agree that education was a part of the solution.

Begun in the early 1960s, the Manned Spacecraft Center near Houston, now named the Lyndon B. Johnson Space Center, has provided employment for thousands of Texans. The center houses the Mission Control Center, which monitors and processes information during space flights, provides training facilities, and develops new technology for the age of space. Shown here is the Mission Operations Control Room in the Mission Control Center during the lunar surface activity of Apollo 11 Astronauts Neil Armstrong and Edwin Aldrin, Jr. (NASA)

Prophets of gloom were few, but the confidence of the past was notably absent.

In the 1990s, however, Texans seemed more comfortable with both present and future. Influenced by a continual barrage of live media and the realities of life in an urban setting, Texans were less inclined to think of their state as a unique and different place and more inclined to recognize that life in their communities was similar in both opportunities and challenges to that of any urbanized city in the nation.

As the people of Texas prepared to enter their fourth century of modern civilization, many of the problems that had prevailed throughout the previous three were no more. Indian wars, starvation, and back-breaking physical labor were no longer a part of the daily struggle for survival. For most, but not all, the standard of living was at least comfortable, though certainly much higher for some than for others.

The challenges of the future, however, were obvious. City life had brought new comforts and conveniences, but posed problems in the form of poverty, congestion, cultural conflicts, transportation, and pollution. Though urbanization was not solely responsible for the creation of these social problems, living conditions in crowded urban places at the very least made the problems more visible. But as Texans entered the final decade of the century, spending for various social services remained almost as low as in the 1970s, per capita spending ranging generally in the bottom 20 percent when com-

Tu Do at Hàm Nghi, Houston. The transposition of Vietnamese street signs with historic Texas street names in Houston's midtown illustrates the demographic changes that Texas has experienced in the late twentieth century. Asians, the fastest growing component of the Texas population, along with Hispanics and African Americans will make Texas a "majority minority" state early in the twenty-first century. (Photograph by Cary D. Wintz.)

pared with that of other states. Per capita income, less than the national average in 1976, remained less than the national average in 1997. Texans continued to talk about the vital role of education, but there were few signs of action to match the talk. Environmental concerns received much publicity, with local governments particularly becoming aware of the problems of waste disposal, a federal report of 1991 claimed that Texas suffered more than any other state from industrial pollution and in 1999 Houston had the worst air pollution in the nation. Sometimes ignored, but a most serious problem for a large part of the state, was the declining supply of water reserves.

In one way or another, Texas resolved its problems of an earlier day. A free and contented life depends on its ability to solve those of the present and of the future. Ultimately, the outcome depends on the people.

BIBLIOGRAPHY

For information on contemporary industry and business in Texas, *The Texas Almanac* is indispensable, and the *Texas Business Review* is quite valuable. Robert Calvert and Arnoldo de León, *The History of Texas*, (Wheeling, IL, 1996) contains a good description of social and economic conditions in recent Texas history. M. Ray Perryman, *Survive and Conquer, Texas in the 80's-Money-Power-Tragedy... Hope!* (Dallas, 1990), is a narrative and analysis of the economic problems of Texas in the 1980s. Useful is Mary Ann Norman, *The Texas Economy Since World War II* (Boston, 1983). Char Miller and Heywood T. Sanders (eds.), *Urban Texas: Politics and Development* (College Station, 1990) emphasize the long-term development of urbanization but present materials on recent years. See also Christopher S. Davies, "Life at the Edge: Urban and Industrial Evolution of Texas, Frontier Wilderness—Frontier Space, 1836–1986," *Southwestern Historical Quarterly*, LXXXIX, 443–554. J'Nell L. Pate, *Livestock Legacy: The Fort Worth Stockyards, 1887–1987* (College Station, 1991), includes material on the years after World War II, and Jeffrey Share, *The Oilmakers* (Houston, 1995), describes development of the 1980s and 1990s in the oil industry. Looking at economic affairs in a somewhat different way, see Paul F. Lambert and Kenny A. Franks (eds.), *Voices from the Oil Fields* (Norman, 1984); Roger M. Olien and Diana David Olien, *Oil Booms: Social Changes in Five Texas Towns* (Lincoln, 1982); Janet M. Neugebauer, *Plains Farmer: William G. DeLoach, 1914–1964* (College Station, 1991); and Mamie Sypert Burns, *This I Can Leave You: A Woman's Days on the Pitchfork Ranch* (College Station, 1986). Mark Friedberger, "'Mink and Manure,: Rural Gentrification and Cattle Raising in Southeast Texas, 1945-1992," *Southwestern Historical Quarterly*, CII, 268-293, examines the new problems confronting the ranching industry in the late twentieth century. Studies of railroads that include the postwar period are Charles Zlatkovich, *Texas Railroads: A Record of Construction and Abandonment* (Austin, 1981); and Don L. Hofsommer, *The Southern Pacific, 1901–1985* (College Station, 1986). Jerry Thompson, *A Wild and Vivid Land: An Illustrated History of the South Texas Border* (Austin, 1997) examines an often neglected region of the state.

References on minorities may be found in the bibliography of the previous chapter. For an overview of the period, see Terry Jordan, "A Century and a Half of Ethnic Change in Texas, 1836–1986," *Southwestern Historical Quarterly*, LXXXIX, 385–422. Life for black Texans in the state's largest city is pictured in Howard Beeth and Cary D. Wintz, (eds.), *Black Dixie: Afro-Texan History and Culture in Houston* (College Station, 1992), and Robert D. Bullard, *Invisible Houston: The Black Experience in Boom and Bust* (College Station, 1987).

For works on Mexican Americans, see Vernon M. Briggs, Jr. et al., *The Chicano Worker* (Austin, 1977); Manuel A. Machado, Jr., *Listen Chicano! An Informal History of the Mexican-American* (Chicago, 1979); Arnoldo de León, *Ethnicity in the Sunbelt: A History of Mexican Americans in Houston* (Houston, 1989); Shirley Achor, *Mexican-Americans in a Dallas Barrio* (Tucson, 1979); Salavado Guerrero, *Memorias: A West Texas Life*, ed. Arnold de León (Lubbock, 1991), an account of life in the Depression, World War II, and after; Peter Skerry, *Mexican Americans: The Ambivalent Minority* (New York, 1993), contains considerable information on Mexican American activities in San Antonio; see also F. Arturo Rosales, "Mexicans in Houston: The Struggle to Survive, 1908–1975," *The Houston Review* III, 224–248.

Art is discussed in Al Lowman, *Painting Arts in Texas* (Austin, 1975). Harold V. Ratliff surveys Texas sports in "A History of Sports in Texas with a Unique Philosophy," *Proceedings of the Philosophical Society of Texas* (1968). John W. Storey writes on religion in "Texan Baptist Leadership, the Social Gospel and Race, 1954–1968," *Southwestern Historical Quarterly*, LXXXIII, 29–46, and *Texas Baptist Leadership and Social Christianity, 1900–1980*. Texas writers are receiving more attention in recent years. See James T. F. Tanner, *The Texas Legacy of Katherine Anne Porter* (Denton, 1990), and Clay Reynolds (ed.), *Taking Stock: A Larry McMurtry Casebook* (Dallas, 1989). William T. Pilkington surveys Texas writing in *Imaging Texas: The Literature of the Lone Star State* (Boston, 1981); but also see Lon Tinkle, *An American Original: The Life of J. Frank Dobie* (Boston, 1978). For a look at art, politics, and the media, see Ben Sargent, *Texas Statehouse Blues: The Editorial Cartoons of Ben Sargent* (Austin, 1980). Country music is discussed in *The Texas Monthly* and in a number of other contemporary publications, sometimes in depth. Hubert Rouseel has written *The Houston Symphony Orchestra, 1913–1971* (Austin, 1972).

Appendix

Governors of Texas[1]

1691–1692	Domingo Terán de los Ríos
1693–1716	Texas unoccupied but included in Coahuila
1716–1719	Martín de Alarcón appointed governor of Texas on December 7, 1716. (On August 5, 1716, he had been appointed governor of Coahuila.)
1719–1722	The Marqués de San Miguél de Aguayo, governor of Coahuila and Texas
1722–1726	Fernando Pérez de Almazan
1727–1730	Melchor de Media Villa y Ascona
1730–	Juan Antonio Bustillos y Cevallos
1734–	Manuel de Sandoval
1736–1737	Carlos Benites Franquis de Lugo
1737–	Fernández de Jáuregui y Urrutia, governor of Nuevo León, governor extraordinary and *visitador*
1737–1740	Prudencio de Orobio y Basterra (*governor ad interim*)
1741–1743	Tomás Felipe Wintuisen
1743–1744	Justo Boneo y Morales
1744–1748	Francisco García Larios (*governor ad interim*)
1748–1750	Pedro del Barrio Junco y Espriella
1751–1759	Jacinto de Barrios y Jauregui. Barrios was appointed governor of Coahuila in 1757, but was retained in Texas until 1759 to complete a task.
1759–1766	Angel Martos y Navarrete
1767–1770	Hugo Oconór (*governor ad interim*)
1770–1778	Baron de Ripperdá
1778–1786	Domingo Cabello

[1]The list of governors holding office before the Texan Revolution is based on Herbert E. Bolton. *Guide to Materials for the History of the United States in the Principal Archives of Mexico* (Washington D.C., 1913) pp. 478, 479. Bolton makes the statement that "there are some imperfections in the results, in spite of care, for the materials for compiling a correct list are still mainly unprinted." In a few instances information made available subsequent to the publication of Bolton's study has removed doubt as to the terms of governors.

1786	Bernardo Bonavia was appointed July 8, but apparently did not serve.
1787–1790	Rafael Martínez Pachecho appointed February 27; his removal was approved October 18, 1790.
1788	The office of governor was ordered suppressed and the province put under a presidial captain.
1790–1799?	Manuel Muñoz
1798(?)	José Irigoyen, apparently appointed but did not serve.
1800(?)–1805	Juan Bautista de Elguezábal
1805–1810	Antonio Cordero y Bustamante
1810–1813	Manuel Maria de Salcedo
1811(Jan. 22– March 2)	Juan Bautista Casas (revolutionary governor)
1814–1818	Christóbal Domínguez
1817–	Ignacio Pérez and Manuel Pardo (*governors ad interim*)
1817–1822	Antonio Martínez
1822–1823	José Felix Trespalacios
1823(?)–1824	Luciano García

Governors of Coahuila and Texas

1824–1826	Rafael Gonzáles
1826–1827	Victor Blanco
1827–1831	José María Viesca
1831–1832	José María Letona
1832–1833	Juan Martín de Beramendi
1834–1835	Juan José Elguezábal
1835–	Agustín Viesca
1835–	Ramón Eca y Músquiz

Provisional Governors During the Texan Revolution[2]

| Nov. 14, 1835–March 1, 1836 | Henry Smith |
| Jan. 11, 1836–March 1, 1836 | James W. Robinson[3] |

Presidents of the Republic of Texas

March 17, 1836–Oct. 22, 1836	David G. Burnet
Oct. 22, 1836–Dec. 10, 1838	Sam Houston
Dec. 10, 1838–Dec. 13, 1841	Mirabeau B. Lamar

[2]This list of Texas chief executives is taken in part from the *Texas Almanac*, 2000–2001, p. 461–62

[3]Robinson was elected by the council after Smith had been deposed and the office of governor declared vacant by the council. Thereafter both men claimed the right to exercise the executive authority.

Dec. 13, 1841–Dec. 9, 1844	Sam Houston
Dec. 9, 1844–Feb. 19, 1846	Anson Jones

Governors After Annexation

Feb. 19, 1846–Dec. 21, 1847	J. Pinckney Henderson
May 19, 1846–Nov. –, 1846	Albert C. Horton[4]
Dec. 21, 1847–Dec. 21, 1849	George T. Wood
Dec. 21, 1849–Nov. 23, 1853	Peter Hansborough Bell
Nov. 23, 1853–Dec. 21, 1853	J. W. Henderson[5]
Dec. 21, 1853–Dec. 21, 1857	Elisha M. Pease
Dec. 21, 1857–Dec. 21, 1859	Hardin R. Runnels
Dec. 21, 1859–March 16, 1861	Sam Houston[6]
March 16, 1861–Nov. 7, 1861	Edward Clark
Nov. 7, 1861–Nov. 5, 1863	Francis R. Lubbock
Nov. 5, 1863–June 17, 1865	Pendleton Murrah[7]
July 21, 1865–Aug. 9, 1866	Andrew J. Hamilton (provisional)
Aug. 9, 1866–Aug. 8, 1867	James W. Throckmorton[8]
Aug. 8, 1867–Sept. 30, 1869	Elisha M. Pease
Jan. 8, 1870–Jan. 15, 1874	Edmund J. Davis[9]
Jan. 15, 1874–Dec. 1, 1876	Richard Coke[10]
Dec. 1, 1876–Jan. 21, 1879	Richard B. Hubbard
Jan. 21, 1879–Jan. 16, 1883	Oran M. Roberts
Jan. 16, 1883–Jan. 18, 1887	John Ireland
Jan. 18, 1887–Jan. 20, 1891	Lawrence Sullivan Ross
Jan. 20, 1891–Jan. 15, 1895	James S. Hogg
Jan. 15, 1895–Jan. 17, 1899	Charles A. Culberson
Jan. 17, 1899–Jan. 20, 1903	Joseph D. Sayers
Jan. 20, 1903–Jan. 15, 1907	S.W.T. Lanham
Jan. 15, 1907–Jan. 19, 1911	Thomas M. Campbell
Jan. 19, 1911–Jan. 19, 1915	Oscar Branch Colquitt
Jan. 19, 1915–Aug. 25, 1917	James E. Ferguson (impeached)
Aug. 25, 1917–Jan. 18, 1921	William P. Hobby

[4]Lieutenant Governor Horton served as governor while Governor Henderson was away commanding troops in the war with Mexico.

[5]Lieutenant Governor Henderson became governor when Governor Bell resigned to take his seat in Congress, to which he had been elected.

[6]Houston refused to take the oath of allegiance to the Confederacy and was deposed. He was succeeded by Lieutenant Governor Edward Clark.

[7]Murrah's administration was terminated by the fall of the Confederacy. Murrah retired to Mexico, and for a period, May–June, 1865, Lieutenant Governor Fletcher S. Stockdale was acting governor.

[8]Throckmorton was removed by the military. Pease, the provisional governor who succeeded him, resigned September 30, 1869.

[9]Davis was appointed provisional governor after he had been elected governor.

[10]Coke resigned to enter the U.S. Senate and was succeeded by Lieutenant Governor Hubbard.

Jan. 18, 1921–Jan. 20, 1925	Pat M. Neff
Jan. 20, 1925–Jan. 17, 1927	Miriam A. Ferguson
Jan. 17, 1927–Jan. 20, 1931	Dan Moody
Jan. 20, 1931–Jan. 17, 1933	Ross S. Sterling
Jan. 17, 1933–Jan. 15, 1935	Miriam A. Ferguson
Jan. 15, 1935–Jan. 17, 1939	James V. Allred
Jan. 17, 1939–Aug. 4, 1941	W. Lee O'Daniel (resigned to enter U.S. Senate)
Aug. 4, 1941–Jan. 21, 1947	Coke R. Stevenson
Jan. 21, 1947–July 11, 1949	Beauford H. Jester (died)
July 11, 1949–Jan. 15, 1957	Allan Shivers
Jan. 15, 1957–Jan. 15, 1963	Price Daniel
Jan. 15, 1963–Jan. 21, 1969	John Connally
Jan. 21, 1969–Jan. 16, 1973	Preston Smith
Jan. 16, 1973–Jan. 16, 1979	Dolph Briscoe
Jan. 16, 1979–Jan. 18, 1983	William Clements
Jan. 18, 1983–Jan. 20, 1987	Mark White
Jan. 20, 1987–Jan. 15, 1991	William Clements
Jan. 15, 1991–Jan. 17, 1995	Ann Richards
Jan. 17, 1995–	George W. Bush

United States Senators

Houston Succession

Feb. 21, 1846–March 4, 1859	Sam Houston
March 4, 1859–July 11, 1861	John Hemphill[11]
Feb. 22, 1870–March 3, 1877	Morgan C. Hamilton
March 3, 1877–March 3, 1895	Richard Coke
March 3, 1895–March 3, 1901	Horace Chilton
March 3, 1901–Jan. 8, 1913	Joseph W. Bailey (resigned)
Jan. 8, 1913–Feb. 3, 1913	Rienzi Melville Johnson (filled vacancy on appointment)
Feb. 13, 1913–April 9, 1941	Morris Sheppard (died)
April 21, 1941–June 26, 1941	Andrew Jackson Houston (died)
Aug. 4, 1941–Jan. 3, 1949	W. Lee O'Daniel
Jan. 3, 1949–Jan. 20, 1961	Lyndon B. Johnson
Jan. 20, 1961–June 15, 1961	William A. Blakley
June 15, 1961–Jan. 21, 1985	John G. Tower
Jan. 21, 1985–	Phil Gramm

[11]Succession was broken by the secession of Texas. Louis T. Wigfall and W. S. Oldham represented Texas in the Confederate Senate. On August 21, 1866, the Texas legislature elected David G. Burnet and Oran M. Roberts to the U.S. Senate, but they were not allowed to take their seats.

Rusk Succession

Feb. 21, 1846–July 29, 1857	Thomas J. Rusk (died)
Nov. 9, 1857–June 4, 1858	J. Pinckney Henderson (died)
Sept. 29, 1858–Dec. 5, 1859	Matthias Ward (filled vacancy on appointment)
1859–1861	Louis T. Wigfall
Feb. 22, 1870–March 3, 1875	James W. Flanagan
March 3, 1875–March 3, 1887	Samuel B. Maxey
March 3, 1887–June 10, 1891	John H. Reagan (resigned)
Dec. 7, 1891–March 30, 1892	Horace Chilton (filled vacancy on appointment)
March 30, 1892–March 3, 1899	Roger Q. Mills
March 3, 1899–March 4, 1923	Charles A. Culberson
March 4, 1923–March 4, 1929	Earle B. Mayfield
March 4, 1929–Jan. 3, 1953	Tom Connally
Jan. 3, 1953–Jan. 15, 1957	Price Daniel (resigned to become governor)
Jan. 15, 1957–April 27, 1957	William A. Blakley
April 27, 1957–Jan. 12, 1971	Ralph W. Yarborough
Jan. 12, 1971–Jan. 20, 1993	Lloyd Bentsen
Jan. 20, 1993–June 14, 1993	Robert Krueger (filled vacancy on appointment)
June 14, 1993–	Kay Bailey Hutchison

Index